# Sweden

# Sweden

## The

# Nation's History

Franklin D. Scott

With an epilogue by
Steven Koblik

## Enlarged Edition

Southern Illinois University Press
Carbondale and Edwardsville

10  09  08  07      11  10  9  8

Library of Congress Cataloging-in-Publication Data

Scott, Franklin Daniel, 1901-
    Sweden, the nation's history / by Franklin D. Scott ; with an
epilogue by Steven Koblik. —Enl. ed.
        p.   cm.
    Bibliography: p.
    Includes index.
    1. Sweden—History. I. Title.
DL648.S36 1988
948.5—dc19                                          88-6931
ISBN 0-8093-1513-0                                   CIP
ISBN 0-8093-1489-4 (pbk.)

*To Helen and Karin*

# PREFACE

Sweden's Present Prosperity and prominence may seem to be unlikely consequences of a painfully slow historical development. For many centuries comparatively poor and backward, the Swedes were famed more for the violence with which the Vikings and Karl XII and Gustav Adolf impinged upon continental Europe than for their achievements in peaceful pursuits. Their nation has emerged in the twentieth century as a major exemplar of peaceful neutrality, of the "Middle Way" and the welfare state, as a disburser of the Nobel Prizes, the homeland of world-renowned scientists, writers, actors, and artists, with a technological culture second to none.

How has this come about? One thing at least is clear: it is a national accomplishment, the result of individual interaction and concerted effort on the part of the nation as a whole. Fratricidal strife there was in the past, and bitter differences of opinion still surface from time to time. But the people have learned to yield to necessity, to compromise and adjust — usually. Competition is channeled toward positive goals instead of conflict and disruption. The members of this small and rather homogeneous society realize that they are all "in it together." A striving for excellence is a national trait. But the record must speak for itself and that is what this book is all about — not in a spirit of praise or blame or justification but as an attempt to delineate the course of a unique national history.

Puzzling and controversial problems in Swedish history are many; this narrative recognizes interpretational disputes but does not concentrate on them. The attempt here is to give a cohesive explanation of national development, put in a chronological-topical framework, weaving together as many as possible of the multitudinous historical strands. This history of one nation is frankly based on the concept that the nation as a community of people has

vii

forged the most constructive bonds of large-scale cooperation among men. Groupings smaller than the nation have seldom if ever proved viable and groupings transcending the nation have, so far, struggled in vain to inspire deep loyalty and purpose.

The value of this survey of Swedish history has been enhanced by the epilogue contributed for this fifth printing by Steven Koblik. His concise interpretation of trends and events that occurred in the decade since first publication of *Sweden: The Nation's History* analyzes some of the basic continuities in Swedish history and describes significant new departures.

Sheer chance started my research on Bernadotte. But that research and the acquaintance with Sweden and the North to which it has led have held my attention. I have been privileged to travel and live in Sweden for many periods varying from a month to a year and a half, beginning in 1930 and continuing to 1976. Although remaining an outsider I have been able to experience some of the phenomenal changes that have transformed Sweden in the twentieth century. Happily my trips to Sweden have been complemented by visits of many Swedish and Nordic friends to the United States. My own detailed research has dealt only with certain segments of Swedish history, particularly Bernadotte, the union with Norway, emigration, and the relations of the Scandinavian countries with each other and with the United States. A work of this scope has necessarily required a great deal of dependence on the writings of others, and the Swedes are indefatigable and careful scholars.

One of the fortunate by-products of the acquaintanceships made through the years is the graciousness and the frankness with which Swedish historians have responded to my requests for critical reading of the manuscript for this work. Without their cooperation errors would have been more numerous. For their critiques both positive and negative I am deeply thankful to Birger Beckman, Sten Carlsson, Lars Kritz, Folke Lindberg, Sture Lindmark, Lars Ljungmark, Jane Lundblad, Nils Runeby, and Jörgen Weibull. Several American scholars have also given their knowledge and their time, especially H. Arnold Barton, Ernst Ekman, Frank Fetter, Erik Friis, and Steven Koblik. On certain sections I have called upon the expertise of Gösta Adelswärd, Carl-Henrik Brodin, Lars Gurmund, Bengt Rundblad, and Håkon Sterky. To each of this long list I owe a debt difficult to repay.

Others who through the years have helped in innumerable ways to make my studies of Sweden pleasant and fruitful I dare not begin to name except for three now gone, but the memories of whom remain warm: Herman Brulin, Sven Tunberg, and Charles Kingsley Webster. The staffs of the Swedish Institute and the Royal Library in Stockholm, the University Library in Uppsala, the Northwestern University Library where I worked for many years, and recently the Honnold Library in Claremont have been most helpful. Penelope Garris has been of immeasurable assistance in the compilation of the bibliography, and Jeffrey Broude has prepared the maps. For the exhausting task of indexing I bow in thanks to my sister Lavinia and my wife Helen.

I am grateful that time has been allowed me to complete a project conceived some forty years ago. Grants for other projects have contributed both to the delay of this study and to its ultimate character, and I appreciate the assistance given me by the American-Scandinavian Foundation, the Social Science Research Council, the American Philosophical Society, the Viking Fund, Northwestern University, and the Westergaard Program of Pomona College.

To Helen I add an inadequate word of thanks for the years of sharing with me in the learning process, all the way from *Bernadotte* to the writing of *Sweden: The Nation's History.*

Franklin D. Scott

# A NOTE ON SPELLING
# AND SWEDISH WORDS

THE SWEDES use three extra letters which they place at the end of the alphabet: *å*, *ä*, and *ö*. This book retains these letters but indexes them as if they were simple *a* and *o* (library practice commonly treats them as *aa*, *ae*, and *oe*). Pronunciation equivalents would be approximately: *å* = *o* in *for*; *ä* = *ai* in *fair*; and *ö* = the *eu* in *milieu* or the *e* in *her*.

Swedes of today are more particular about the spelling of their names than were their ancestors, who often showed a cavalier disregard of whether it should be Eric or Erik, Carl or Karl, Gustaf or Gustav. Current Swedish telephone directories put in one list all the variations of, for example, Gustafson, Gustavson, Gustaveson, Gustafsson, Gustavsson. In this volume, insofar as possible, the usage preferred by the individual is followed, thus it is double *s* for the inventor John Ericsson but single *s* for his brother Nils Ericson. For the names of kings it seems best to impose an artificial consistency: hence it will be uniformly Karl even for the king who is usually known in English as Charles XII; always Gustav, although the present king spells his name Carl Gustaf. For these and other Swedish names I have used as a guide the spellings in *Den svenska historien*. Swedish royal numerals, incidentally, apply to the first name only: it is Gustav II Adolf, Karl XIV Johan.

The national origin principle is followed, so that names of Swedish kings are spelled in the Swedish way, Danish in Danish, as for example, Fredrik for the Swedish, Frederik for the Danish. City names are given in their native form except in a few cases where spelling and pronunciation are particularly difficult and an English form has become well established, as with Gothenburg (Göteborg) and Copenhagen (København). The Norwegian city will be referred to as Oslo before 1624 and after 1925; during the intervening 300 years it was Kristiania.

A minimum of Swedish words are used in the text: *riksdag* (parliament); *härad* (hundred, district); *frälse* (the tax-privileged class). Occasionally Swedish words are given the plural *s* instead of the proper Swedish endings *er* or *ar*. Some words are capitalized to distinguish their specialized use from the more common English meaning, for example, Estates for the four houses or Estates of the riksdag before 1866; Thing for the medieval court gatherings. The word *bonde* (plural *bönder*) is unsatisfactorily translated as farmer, simply because there is no better alternative.

In the text all translations from Swedish, unless otherwise noted, are the author's.

Terms like social democratic and nazi are capitalized only when they refer specifically to the party organization.

# TABLE OF CONTENTS

Illustrations follow pages 46, 302, 526.

# MAPS

Sweden: The Nation's History

# I

# THE BEGINNINGS
# OF LAND AND PEOPLE

BACK BEYOND the horizon of time a massive sheet of ice covered Sweden and much of the northern hemisphere. The glacier crept south to the Alps in Europe, while its western arm moved halfway across North America. This cap of ice on top of the earth, waxing and waning through millennia, was only the latest in a series of glacial growths and recessions. Everything that existed before was ground into oblivion, and northern Europe was suffocated under billions of tons of ice and stone. Animals were obliterated, flowers and trees were frozen to death. Then the ice sheet slowly melted away under the power of the sun and the warming breezes from the western ocean.

By the thirteenth millennium B.C. central Europe had been freed of its cold burden, and the Scandinavian North (present-day Sweden, Norway, Denmark, and Finland) slowly began to be uncovered. By 8000 B.C. a wide peninsula of land appeared, extending northward from the continent. The overpowering forces of nature were creating a new earth. The newborn land and the waters from the melting glacier pushed each other back and forth in rivalry for space. The genius and the painstaking measurements of Professor Gerard de Geer have established the geologic timetable of the birth of the Scandinavian land.[1]

For some centuries the peninsula extended northward to a stream or sound, located approximately where the central lakes of Sweden now lie. Beyond the sound the ice sheet still covered the northern stretches of Fenno-Scandia. Then came a counteraction. The landmass of south central Sweden, freed from its glacial burden, rose and closed the sound that had drained off the melting glacier to the sea (c. 7000 B.C.). The waters of the sound, fed by

3

12,000 B.C.
ICE
LAND
WATER

# THE RETREAT
# OF THE GREAT
# ICE SHEET

continued melting, soon formed the Ancylus Sea, an extensive inland body of water which spread over the land to the east and rose until at last it burst its bounds. It found its outlet not where the sound had been but farther south at the base of the wide peninsula reaching up from Europe. The rising waters drowned many of the earliest settlements of men and carved sluice gates through the land. This gigantic cataclysm of about 5000 B.C. formed Öresund, which now separates Sweden from Denmark, the Great Belt, the Little Belt, and the islands of Denmark.

The period of warmth melted more and more of the ice, and the land continued to rise in relation to the water. The rate of uplift was much higher in the north than in the south. The shoreline of c. 5000 B.C. today lies about 20 feet above sea level in Skåne (in the south), about 200 feet above sea level in Uppland (in central Sweden), and as much as 600 feet above sea level in Medelpad (to the north). In 4000 B.C. large parts of Uppland were still under water, and Södermanland, south of Stockholm, was then 180 feet lower than now. Today many coastal areas around the Gulf of Bothnia are still rising at a rate of some 3 feet per hundred years, a phenomenon which has had profound

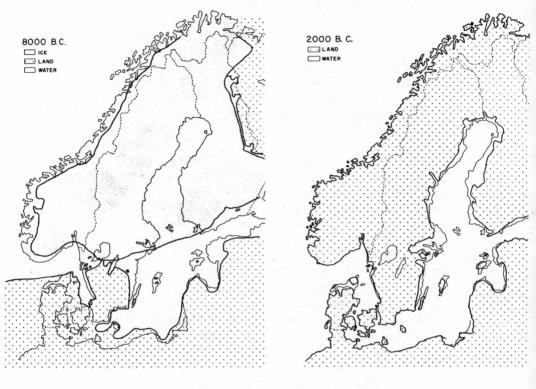

8000 B.C.
☐ ICE
☐ LAND
☐ WATER

2000 B. C.
☐ LAND
☐ WATER

effects on the life and death of cities and on the availability of tillable soil.

With the bursting forth of the Ancylus Sea new connections were established with the ocean, and the waters of the inland sea became mildly salty. On land birches, and oaks, and even pines were spreading northward in the Ancylus period. Then came lindens, beeches, and primitive grains. Reindeer, bears, wolves, and seals followed in the wake of the retreating glacier and attracted hunters from the south. Elk, beavers, urox, and a kind of deer migrated into the area before 7000 B.C.; then wild swine and dogs arrived. Not until the late Stone Age did man domesticate cows, sheep, pigs, and at last horses. Chickens and cats were domesticated next, in the Bronze Age.

The prolonged period of climatic moderation ended abruptly about 500 B.C., and the glaciers formed again. Plants that had prospered ceased to grow, and the settlements of men, judging by the archaeological remains for this four-century cold spell, diminished sharply. After some four centuries conditions improved once more. The pine spread farther north, while beech and spruce displaced it in the south, establishing vegetational boundaries which have been maintained to the present. Since about 100 B.C. the variations in climate have been brief and far less disturbing. In this period only the rising of land in the north, with the resultant extension of the coastline and the subsequent expansion of agriculture, has changed the natural face of Scandinavia.

The early human inhabitants of Scandinavia were hunters and gatherers who roamed widely and traded and fought with one another. The whole of Scandinavia was their realm. Here on nature's northern frontier they left as evidence of their presence implements of reindeer horn, but they may have been only summer visitors with no fixed abode. The oldest verifiable living places date to the period 7000–5000 B.C. in the south and west coastal areas. These Stone Age peoples apparently came north by way of the Danish islands. Their crudely chipped flint implements began to show traces of a style which was probably related to the tool-making style of the Fosna culture of Norway.

The variations in tool-making style in the area north of the central sound has led to the speculation that other groups had migrated into the area from the northeast, perhaps from Russia — as well as from the east and the south. At about the same time a "circumpolar" culture composed of interrelated groups was developing throughout northern Scandinavia, Finland, Siberia, Japan, North America, and Greenland. A characteristic implement of the circumpolar culture was the North Bothnian hatchet, a rough and heavy weapon found in diminishing numbers as far south as southern Sweden. To this culture in Sweden and Norway belonged the carvings of elk and other animals on steep cliffs in the mountain area. Flint from Siberia first and later from Skåne indicates the probability of trading for furs in the far north, and buried stocks of arrowheads and axes were clearly the storage deposits of traders.

For many centuries tools, weapons, and ceramic sherds are the chief evidences we have of many early cultures in the North. Articles of wood burned or rotted away, and clothing or bones survived only under exceptional conditions, though articles of bone and wood were undoubtedly more numerous than the stone implements that have survived. A few human skeletons from ancient times have been found preserved in water heavy with lime. Among the most interesting and revealing of all types of remains, however, are the seeds of plants and their imprints in clay. Through new techniques of identifying seeds in ceramics they supply one of the most useful means of dating the distant past.

As early as the Stone Age (before 1500 B.C.) many primitive grains were cultivated in the North. Researchers in the field of botanical archaeology have recently discovered in late Stone Age ceramics six different kinds of grain, though only two of them, barley and wheat, are related to modern grains. Predominant was the single-grain wheat, still found as a weed in Asia Minor. The fact that it is found with much greater frequency in Sweden than in Denmark (and with only one example from England) suggests that this form of wheat came to Sweden from the east. The species declined during the Bronze Age (1500–500 B.C.), giving way to barley and two-grain wheat (emmer). But even a more developed wheat was known in the Stone Age, though rare, and only in Skåne; *råglosta* (*Bromus secalinus*) was more common. Peas were cultivated, perhaps for use in a meal mixed with pine bark which was known later in the Viking period (c. 600–1100 A.D.), and pigweed seems to have been cultivated. Millet also was raised in the Stone Age. By the Bronze Age broad beans were used, and recent research has shown that oats were employed at least one thousand years earlier than was previously believed. In the early Iron Age (after 100 B.C.) appeared rye (at about the same time as in Germany) and mustard. Flax came late in the Iron Age.

The disappearance of several of the early varieties of grain can probably be attributed to the long epoch of cold and humid weather (500–100 B.C.). The facts that stand out are that, before the vanishing of warm weather, the cultivation of grain indicated many populations were doing something more than hunting seals and elk, and the varieties of grain used prove that these peoples had far-reaching connections, probably east to Asia as well as south to the continent and west to the British Isles.

The breakthrough of the Ancylus Sea, disastrous though it was for the inhabitants of the inundated settlements, probably had little effect on human intercommunication in the North. The people were already fishers and seafarers, and the waterways were their safest highways. Up the rivers and through the complex lake systems several groups of people from the south, largely of Germanic stock, worked their way farther and farther toward the north. Their weapons and tools grew steadily more refined — axes for weapons and chopping trees, knives for all kinds of cutting, scrapers for skins, harpoons for hunting seals. Flint, the hardest and best stone for weapons and tools, was carried hundreds of miles from its sources. Some of the flint axes were very well made. In a modern experiment a man was able to use one to cut down a large tree in little more than the time required to do it with a steel ax. Pottery, often with a few seeds imbedded in it, and the foundations of four-sided houses with packed clay floors suggest that some populations formed more or less permanent settlements. By about 2500 B.C. agriculture was established in the central area of Sweden around Lake Mälar, and thirty-odd dwelling sites dating from about this time have been discovered.

During the period the Danish custom of erecting dolmens, or great stone monuments to the dead, was adopted in western Sweden. Slightly before 2000 B.C. the megalithic monuments were superseded by passage graves, a style of burial borrowed not only from Denmark but also from western Europe. In these powerfully constructed vaults many bodies were buried, one after another — sometimes on shelves, sometimes on top of one another — each supplied with food and implements for the future life. This was the period of the lake-dwelling group at Alvastra, where evidence was also found of sheep, goats, and pigs. Seal were evidently plentiful, and well-designed harpoons show that they were avidly hunted.

Single burials began to appear in about 1800 B.C., used simultaneously with the passage graves. The most distinctive new feature was the presence of a different kind of battle-ax, carefully shaped like a boat. The discovery of the "boat-ax" culture, which eventually spread far and wide, raised innumerable questions: did a new people immigrate from the east or south, or did the culture originate in the north? Where in Sweden did the culture first appear? Were the culture bearers nomads? The evidence is slight and confusing. The culture may have included many different groups — some fishermen, some hunters, some agriculturists — living in proximity. In any case a degree of uniformity in the forms of graves and artifacts had evidently been achieved by about 1500 B.C.

Shortly after 1500 B.C. a more visible revolution occurred as the use of bronze was introduced in Scandinavia. The Greeks, who had learned to process this alloy of copper and tin, found that bronze was stronger than copper alone and could take a sharper edge. The Danubian peoples borrowed the technique from the Greeks in about 1600 B.C. When the traders from the North extended their routes to the Danube basin soon after this, they acquired drums, swords, ornaments, and also the raw materials for bronze. Sweden lacked tin, and its copper deposits had not yet been discovered. Western Sweden did have soapstone, however, which makes excellent molds for use in casting bronze, and this area became a center of manufacture and export. For hundreds of years the new metal remained a luxury, and everyday implements were still fashioned of stone; nevertheless, an improvement had been achieved, and bronze gradually came into use for both ceremonial objects and some implements.

Changes in the burial customs were also taking place. As we have noted inhumation was the standard practice during the Stone Age, and much of our knowledge of these early cultures is derived from the weapons and food left in the graves for the future life of the departed. Early in the Bronze Age crema-tion — sometimes in the graves, sometimes elsewhere (even in boats) — began to be used. The burning was not always complete, and the death-gifts that have survived show the gradual displacement of flint daggers with bronze weapons. Another new practice was the construction of mound graves. The mounds were pretentious displays by the wealthy overclass, and undoubtedly they helped to preserve evidences of the mighty ones far out of proportion to their numbers. Occasionally the same mound was used for successive burials through hundreds of years. In the farther north the increase of finds for the later

Stone Age suggests expansion of settlement, but the reduction of size of monuments in the Bronze Age, when they were often only simple piles of stones, implies an era of hardship.

The Bronze Age was the epoch of the puzzling rock pictures (the *hällristningar*). Hundreds of these etchings in stone survive in Bohuslän and Skåne and east central Sweden. The pictures, more numerous than the carvings of animals on lakeside cliffs in the north, are found on smoothly sloping rocks facing toward meadows or fields. Arranged neatly in rows or jumbled and overlying one another, the figures portray the sun disk, men with plows, oxen, and boats — everywhere boats. Although the etchings were shallowly incised, they remain remarkably clear even after some three thousand years.

Why did men painstakingly chip out hard granite to create these simple but vivid figures? Were the figures related to sun worship or to rituals appealing for the fertility of mankind and the land? What kind of pageantry was involved? Again we are mystified. All we know is that the rock pictures were created by an agricultural people, whereas the cliff carvings of the farther North were made by a hunting people. Though the rock pictures cannot vie with the colorful beauty of the cave paintings at Lascaux in France, these northern legacies of the Bronze Age compare well with primitive art from other parts of the world.

The character and extent of trade in the Bronze Age is only partly clear. Bronze itself has been found chiefly in the south and west of Sweden (in Gotland, Skåne, Blekinge, Halland, and Bohuslän), but even in this restricted area it occurs less abundantly than in Denmark and northern Germany. Most of the metals and also salt had to be imported. How were they paid for? Probably with furs, skins, and amber (from the Baltic), partly with slaves who for centuries were commercially important. Another export was the Mälar ax of bronze, a special type of ax common in central Sweden but found also in Norway and as far east as the great bend of the Volga. But Sweden's finest weapons were imported from the south; twelve Hallstatt swords have come to light in Sweden, mostly in the central region. The commerce of the Swedish traders was certainly far-reaching, and the boats, like those pictured on the rocks, were probably used in trade as well as in fishing and warfare.

The Bronze Age, with its vitality and extensive intercommunication, apparently came to a disastrous end. Archaeological finds cease abruptly with about the year 500 B.C., and for four hundred years there is silence from the graves. Only on Gotland and the nearby coast can we be certain that human habitation continued. The old trade routes may have been disrupted by the wave of Celtic invasions moving westward across central Europe, but this seems insufficient explanation for the lack of artifacts in this period. Perhaps human life and culture were frozen — literally and figuratively — by the great cold spell which we know snapped the continuity of plant life. And perhaps it was the deterioration of the climate which caused the migration of the Cimbri from Denmark and their invasion of the Roman Empire in the second century B.C. In any case there is no bridge between the archaeological finds for the period before 500 B.C. and those after 100 B.C. and no positive evidence that one population group departed and another had come to take its place. There is simply a void until the advent of the Iron Age in Sweden.

About one hundred years before the birth of Christ the climate of Scandinavia began to improve, and people reestablished contact with the outer world. Expanding Roman power reached into Gaul and Britain and was checked with difficulty by the Germans along the line of the Rhine and the Danube. Soon Germanic soldiers took service with the Roman legions, and brought north fresh ideas and money. But while the Roman Republic flourished, and as the Republic was transformed into the Empire, the North lagged far behind in the arts of civilization.

Iron was more easily worked than bronze and was more versatile in its uses; furthermore, iron ore deposits were more common than copper and tin (needed for bronze). The processing of iron was probably discovered in the Black Sea region about 1500 B.C., but the technique did not reach mid-Europe until after 1000 B.C. The domestic processing of iron ore in Scandinavia was easy, for both bog ore and sea ore were close at hand, and wood was plentiful as the smelting fuel. The best weapons, however, were still imported from Italy and the Germanic lands (especially Pomerania), along with rings and kettles. The steadily mounting number of finds indicate a reviving trade, and probably also an immigration of people. For example, ceramics of the Vandal type found in west Sweden probably came from Jutland.

The peoples of the North, though on the outer margins of the Roman world, were not entirely unknown to the main culture bearers of the age. Back at the end of the fourth century B.C. the Greek Pytheas traveled from Massilia to the Rhine and possibly to Jutland. In about 98 A.D. the Roman Tacitus wrote the famous *Germania*, idealizing the warrior-democracy of the Germanic peoples.

By the second century A.D. Sweden was using such gadgets as locks and scissors, which were Roman or copied from Roman prototypes. Bronze statuettes were popular, and coins came in increasing numbers. About 5500 of the 7500 Roman silver coins (dinarii) found in Sweden have been discovered in Gotland and Öland, off the southeastern coast; western Sweden was evidently not on the main route of trade in the early Iron Age.

Variations in the different regions of the country and the presence or absence of coins and artifacts lead to diverse speculations as scholars try to unravel the mysteries of the past. For example, in the first century A.D. the number of graves in central Sweden (Östergötland and Västergötland) seems to have declined sharply. This could be the result of a change in burial practices, but it could also indicate a major emigration (some scholars have speculated that the Goths then left the North).

Only meager evidence ties the Goths of the Ukraine (the Visigoths and Ostrogoths of Roman history) to the Goths of Gotland (or Gothland) in the Baltic, or to the Götar of central Sweden. As to the latter the names Goth and Göt are not identical. Nevertheless there is a tantalizing similarity of names, especially between Goths and Gotland. The evidence suggests that once the Goths were established on the Black Sea their commercial and artistic connections with the North were strong.

One is tempted to hypothesize a still more direct connection. Indeed, Jordanes wrote in the sixth century that the Goths did come from Scandinavia. But this account is not supported by other references. When the Swedish Bishop Ragvaldi made his claims of Gothic-Scandinavian relationship at the Council of Basel in 1432, he fashioned them not from proofs but from tradition and fantasy (Spanish as well as Swedish), and he advanced them for purposes of pride and politics.

Curt Weibull has argued that the Gothic myth is wholly fantasy. On the other hand J. Svennung has argued effectively, on linguistic and other grounds, that the Goths did originate in what is now Västergötland in Sweden and that the narrative of their wanderings is a genuine folk legend and therefore worthy of credence. But there is no fully satisfactory written record. Archaeologists have found no linking artifacts, and linguists have drawn no indisputable language parallels. Neither is there evidence that the Goths originated in any other place. At the present we must agree with Carl-Axel Moberg when he says that the only sure place of the Goths in Swedish history lies in the ideological conviction that they indeed had a role in it.[2]

Another puzzle involving migration has to do with the Herules who, according to tradition, originated in Scandinavia and then established themselves on the Danube. At one time they are supposed to have asked their relatives in the north to send them a king. Evidently they remained unsophisticated, even going into battle barefooted. When at last they were disastrously defeated and divided, one group, according to Procopius, returned to Scandinavia early in the sixth century. This is the only specific historical mention of early immigration to the North, and it is exasperatingly vague and unconfirmed.[3]

Nevertheless, we know that the North had lively contacts with the continent as far south as Rome. The routes of commerce shifted from time to time; in the second century goods came from Gaul by way of the Rhine mouth, but by the end of the ͺentury new trade routes were in operation along the Vistula and the Oder. Roman and Gothic influences competed for a time, then tended to coalesce, at least in native art. Gold rings, bracteates, and animal figurines of Danubian and Gothic patterns appeared frequently among artifacts in Sweden. Further evidence of early contacts with Europe is seen in the five hundred gold Roman coins from as late as the sixth century that have been found in Sweden. In the fifth century the lightweight gold *solidus*, which had at least partially replaced the silver dinar, was made for circulation outside the empire (in connection with the slave trade, for example). The *solidus* became the standard coin throughout southern Scandinavia.[4] And the *solidus* gave its name to the *soldat* (soldier) who received it.

The time of the great Teutonic migrations in the fourth and fifth centuries A.D. was a period of confusion throughout Europe. Germanic tribes invaded Gaul and the Roman Empire, and the Angles, Saxons and Jutes colonized parts of England. In Scandinavia itself widespread disturbance was indicated by the burial of treasure, burned homes, and Swedish migrations to the islands along the eastern shore of the Baltic. Signs of adversity were numerous on the islands of Gotland and Öland, to some extent also on the Swedish mainland. Can one deduce from the buried caches of gold bars, coins, and ornaments that people were wealthy, or merely that they were endangered? Or were the stores of treasure the caches of raiders? Or were they sacrifices? We cannot be sure, but clearly these peoples did not live an isolated existence.

A combination of evidence enables us to bring into historic focus the Sweden of the sixth century, at least that part of it known as Uppland. Archaeological finds from Uppland indicate a long-established connection with Gotland (since c. 300), which had been wealthy and active in trade. The whole region had access to excellent transportation throughout the year over the waterways, which froze in winter to provide equally smooth and easy highways. The land between the water and the rocks was richly fertile. Bog iron was available, and possibly ore from mines, though there is no positive proof that the latter *bergmalm* was used before the Middle Ages. The existence of an organized society is shown by the impressive grave mounds at Old Uppsala, which was an ancient political center and later a cult center. The first excavations of these enormous mounds, made in 1846 on the initiative of Crown Prince Karl (later Karl XV), revealed the burned bones of man and animals, gold filigree work, game pieces, and bronze objects, but no weapons; in 1874 another mound yielded similar results. Three large mounds of this type have been definitely assigned to the sixth century.[5]

An aid in mound identification was the literary evidence from *Ynglingatal* a tenth-century Norse poem about the family that ruled in Uppsala in the fifth and sixth centuries. According to the poem, three members of the family were buried in state in Uppsala. Four kings — Aun, Egils, Ottar, and Adils — are mentioned in the poem, which records the fact that Ottar was killed at Vendel. Some twenty miles north of Uppsala stands a mound known for at least three centuries as Ottar's Mound; evidence from Sune Lindquist's excavations in 1914–16 confirmed that the mound indeed belonged to the early years of the sixth century. (Incidentally, the Icelandic historian-skald Snorri Sturluson was wrong in identifying the Vendel of the saga with Vendsyssel in Jutland. The Uppland Vendel was certainly meant in both Snorri and *Beowulf*.) In this instance literary and archaeological evidence combined to provide a small cluster of guideposts for historians.

If only the epic of *Beowulf* (c. 700 A.D.) had been written as history — but it wasn't! Here once more is a tantalizing thing, packed with history but spiced with fantasy, and it is impossible now to separate the ingredients. Read as historical fiction, the epic does at least give an impression of the life and thought of Scandinavian peoples in the migration period. The compiler who finally pieced together the tale in England had an inadequate background in Scandinavian history, but unquestionably the setting is historical. The wars of the story were paralleled in reality, and several of the kings (such as Ottar and Adils) can be identified as historical figures. Frankish sources confirm that Hygelac's campaign against the Frisians occurred in 516. Historians have long been bothered by the literary treatment of the Geats. Were they the Göts or the Jutes? One possible explanation is that two traditions became blended in the *Beowulf* epic, and that the tale involved one people at one point, and then another.[6] If this theory is correct many of the inconsistencies of the story vanish.

After the tiny shafts of light thrown by *Ynglingatal* and *Beowulf* the literary sources are of no help to historians for another two centuries. Archaeology has filled in the gap only partially. Most colorful were the evidences of the rich culture of Vendel in Uppland, which has given its name to the whole period 550–800 A.D. Around Vendel, then connected with the Baltic Sea, burials in boats were especially magnificent. Men were laid to rest with full armor, including shields, helmets, swords, knives, spears, arrows, and undoubtedly bows (which have not survived) and with gifts and possessions such as glass bowls from western Europe, hunting dogs and falcons; cattle or cuts of steak, sheep, hams. The boats were rowboats, approximately thirty feet in length. In this region there was no cremation and the same burial pattern continued until the coming of Christianity in about 1000 A.D. Prosperity and an unusually high degree of artistic skill were obvious.[7]

The animal motifs in decorative art came into the Mälar area and to Gotland probably from southern Germany, and in the eighth century strong impulses were felt from France, England, and Ireland. But although foreign influences predominated at first, Scandinavia developed indigenous art between about 500 and 1100 A.D. and in turn influenced artistic traditions in the Rhine Valley and in England. The common characteristic of this art was "the animal ornamentation, a barbaric style, vigorous and wild-growing, filling all the decorated panels with bewildering crowds of animals, men, and birds, animating the free margins with animal figures in open work, and marking each projecting corner with masks and heads of fantastic forms."[8] The inspiration for this forceful, stylized primitive art was rooted in a complex interaction dating back to the third and fourth centuries and involving the adaptation of Oriental and Hellenistic forms by the Goths and Scythians. But by the sixth century, a Scandinavian barbaric art of independent character had developed. The original concepts of what later became the Vendel style may have come to Scandinavia by means of a Germanic invasion, but they were further developed and adapted locally with inventiveness and skill.

A recent find close to Stockholm is gradually adding another dimension to our knowledge of the so-called Vendel period. At Lillön (little island), formerly known as Helgön (Holy Island), in Lake Mälar the discovery of a peculiar dipper in 1952 started a systematic excavation of the site, which consists of a grave field, a dwelling site, and a work place. It may have been an iron foundry, and possibly a trading center or customs-house, which was occupied from c. 200 A.D. to about 1000 A.D. Among the artifacts from this site are beautifully decorated bits of glass, numerous tiny figures of enchanting loving-couple design in pressed gold, and a rare small Buddha. At the same site in 1961 a cottage builder and his son dug up a gold ring and a nest of Byzantine coins from the sixth century. The Helgön site is especially important because the artifacts include quantities of the everyday objects of life and work — evidences of an active community — as well as carefully-chosen ceremonial and burial objects.[9]

The archaeological finds on Helgön and in many other areas continue to bring to light new sites and artifacts of early history and to give us new insight into the past. But, as we have seen, the literary sources of early Scandinavian history are meager, mostly external to Scandinavia, and a confusing blend of transferred legends, myth, and historical fact. To recreate any part of the structure of Scandinavian antiquity one must winnow fragments of truth from the conglomerate of words and things and interpret the story from disconnected details. Out of this process only the broad outlines become clear.

The foundations of Swedish history were laid by the eighth century A.D. The Swedish landscape had been created as it was to endure, though the eastern coastline would slowly be extended and fertile fields would continue to rise above the water. The climate had become stabilized and trees and plants had formed permanent vegetational zones. The peoples and cultures of

Sweden represented a blending of traits from many migrations and infiltrations. The common Norse speech reached throughout Scandinavia. There were probably many small chieftaincies which are not named in any record, along with strong kingdoms, such as that centered in Old Uppsala, which were doubtless both rare and short-lived. A well-established social order with fixed patterns of custom and belief obviously existed. Extensive communication networks linked Sweden with the outside world, including not only western Europe and the British Isles but also Russia, Greece, and distant India. It is at the same time noteworthy that although cultural borrowing was extensive in this period, the native people of Sweden added original touches to borrowed ideas, sometimes creating new variations suited to their particular circumstances. This young society in the rugged North was in its achievements far behind the greatness of Greece and Rome, both of which had already passed their prime, but the vigor and the adaptive capacity of the Northerners promised something for the future.

# II

# THE FAR-RANGING VIKINGS

THE NORTHERNERS, long receiving and absorbing from the south, for centuries a part of a wider human society, at last burst boldly onto the stage of world history. The records of western Europe began to preserve accounts of their activities: the raid led by Hygelac the Geat against Frisia in 516, the attack by Danes and Saxons together near the Zuider Zee in 565 — both unsuccessful; and the notorious plundering of Lindisfarne in 793 — the prelude to over two centuries of incursions along the coasts of the British Isles, France, and the Low Countries, and the driving onward to Portugal and Spain and into the Mediterranean. Other warrior-traders were pushing their way down the Volga and the Dnieper to the Caspian Sea and to Constantinople. Simultaneously Iceland was settled, colonies were planted in Greenland, and the wave of discovery and colonization reached to the shores of North America. Dramatic, temporarily devastating, and ultimately constructive, the grandiose raiding of the Norsemen is the stuff of both saga and history.

"Free us, O Lord, from the frenzy of the Norsemen," was reported to be the prayer of the Franks, and the Anglo-Saxons added complaints of the "all-devouring fury." Those who suffered wrote the record, and it was a damning one. The best they could say was often ungenerous; when a group of Danish Vikings attacked some Norse settlements in Ireland in 852 they appealed to St. Patrick and gave alms, so the chronicler noted that the Danes showed a kind of piety and that they could for a time refrain from meat and women. Although the despairing wails of the victims have come down to us in written records, we have from the Norsemen only silence or the terseness of the memorial runestones: "Knut, son of Ole, died in Serkland" or "Sigurd, collected Danegeld in England." (Additional inscriptions are mentioned toward the end of this chapter.) But we do know that plundering and destruction in one generation was often succeeded by colonization and constructive achievement in the next.

Who were the Vikings? The word itself antedates the movement and probably stems from *vik*, the word meaning inlet or fjord in all Nordic languages. Vikings, then, were men of the fjords. Some were pirates, some were as much traders as raiders, probably most were an adventurous and opportunistic blend of the two. One of the simplest and briefest definitions is Holger Arbman's: "The viking was a combination of robber and merchant in nordic ships along foreign coasts." [1] The Vikings were the aggressors, and they were brutal in an age of brutality. Yet they lacked the fanaticism of nationalistic hatred or ideological zealotry. Even their brutality could not exceed that of their captors when the tables were turned: it was the English, one must remember, who threw Ragnar Lodbrok into a pit of adders.

The Viking movement was a Pan-Scandinavian phenomenon. Vikings came from all round the Scandinavian lands and seas, and they sailed anywhere accessible by ships. Though rough in manners, they, like the more cultivated Arabs, were the cosmopolitans of their day. Their fleets were often composed of men from diverse localities, for courage and strength were the only qualifications that mattered. It may be that the larger and more distant fleets were augmented by non-Scandinavian recruits, Irish, Finns, or Slavs. But it was the Norsemen who led the way, whose technical and nautical skill dominated the seas. It was the Nordic vikings who gave the Franks a navy and their seafaring vocabulary, including their terms for the rigging, the parts of the ship, and seamanship. [2]

Viking activity dates back at least to the sixth century and probably much earlier, and it continued into the twelfth and thirteenth centuries. Its heyday was the period of some three centuries from about 800 to about 1100 A.D. It was braked and finally halted not by the victimized peoples overseas but by the increasing pressures from government and business enterprise within the North itself. We can envision the entire movement to have encompassed three broad thrusts: to the south along the coasts of France and the Iberian Peninsula and swinging around into the Mediterranean as far as Sicily and southern Italy; to the west into the British Isles and beyond to Iceland, Greenland, and Vinland; to the east across the Baltic Sea and on to the Black, Caspian, and Aegean Seas. The southward and westward thrusts were the work of men from the areas we know today as Norway and Denmark, with a few from the western coast of Sweden. The presence of Swedes in many of the western campaigns is clearly recorded and is evidenced likewise by the booty buried in Swedish soil, such as some thirty thousand Anglo-Saxon coins. Yet the raids on France and Britain are so much more a part of Norwegian and Danish history that the details will not be recounted here. The eastward thrust, on the other hand, was largely the work of men from the Swedish lands and is a vital part of Swedish history. The outward thrusts in all three directions exploded almost simultaneously.

The eastward surge of the Vikings may have been more planned and purposeful than historians have generally assumed. Basic organization was highly developed, and this may have sprung from defensive need. Territorially the base of operations was Uppland (then Sve-Tjud or Svitiod), the cradle of the Swedes, or Svear, centered in Old Uppsala (north of Lake Mälar). By the opening of the Viking era the Svear had extended their authority to the south and west of Lake Mälar into Södermanland and Västmanland. Perhaps it was during the Viking era itself that the Götar of Västergötland and of Östergötland were drawn into union with the Svear. By about 850 the Baltic island of Gotland had come under the dominion of the Swedish kings. The dynamic Swedes of Uppland were expanding. As we have seen, even their homeland, patches of fertile land interlaced with water passages and outcroppings of rock, was still rising out of the sea, making available additional tillable soil that did not have to be won by force of arms. The network of water channels plus the far-reaching drainage complex of Lake Mälar provided ideal routes for traders and also for pirates and organized invaders who could stab quickly into the heart of settlements.

This area between land and sea, lifting its rugged countenance out of the water by as much as three feet per hundred years, became the natural defense belt of the Swedes. It was called Roden (and later Ro[d]slagen),[3] land of the rowers, and the settlers here were given special responsibilities in the manning of the fleet — the lid or ledung. In a law that may date as far back as the first century A.D. it was proclaimed that the king had the "right to call out lid and ledung, rod and red," the alliterative phrase for fleet and rowers.[4]

The systematic political organization of the Swedes was related primarily to sea power. In the German lands, in England, and even in France the general obligation of military service was recognized, but in each country the system had to be adapted to individual needs. In Sweden the organization was unusually detailed. The main Uppland regions were divided into ship districts called hundreds. Each hundred was obligated to provide two ships, each with its complement of men, for the warfleet. In Roslagen each hundred provided one ship. Farther north the sparse and scattered people were not required to send ships, for they were left with the responsibility of maintaining their own defense as best they could. For Uppland and its subordinate Roslagen the records suggest that in early times the fleet went out each spring — for conquest, for maintenance of colonial settlements, or with the idea that attack was the best defense. The commander of this ever-ready navy was the jarl, an officer second only to the king in power. This system of organization spread southward along the coasts of Sweden and to Gotland. The Norwegians apparently thought the system good and installed their *leidanger* on the same pattern; there came to be sixteen ship districts in the then Norwegian province of Viken (the area around Oslofjord), whence it may be that the first major Viking enterprises originated. Denmark also took over this type of organization and called it *leding*.

Strict naval laws governed the men of the fleet; punishments for crimes were two to four times as severe on board ship as on land. A close-knit system of beacons was established along the eastern shores and on the coast of Finland, and strict military law governed the behavior of the guards. The foundation of the system had been developed in the first to third centuries A.D., and the highest level of refinement was reached in the early Middle Ages. Then gradually the military obligations were commuted into a system of taxation.[5] Effective organization was supported by technical advances, most important of which were the sleek longboats rowed by standing oarsmen. These highly maneuverable boats could be used for attack from either end. Slaves served as caretakers for the arms, leaving the warriors free for fighting. Yet the custom was for the boats to be used mainly for transport, and the Vikings made their terrifying inland raids on foot or horseback, saving their ships for quick retreat. Occasionally, though, bloody naval battles were fought between opposing fleets, as at the famous battle of Svolder described in the *Heimskringla* (1000 A.D.).[6] These swift ships were refinements of the two-keeled skin boats used a few centuries earlier. They were clinker-built, usually of oak, and were trimmed down by hand with amazing skill. By the fifth century oarlocks were known, and their use spread as the ships grew larger and more sleekly streamlined. Sails, though long used in the Mediterranean, were surprisingly slow to appear in the North. Picture-stones such as those found in Gotland, attest that sails were known by the sixth century, and it may be that the idea was indigenous. The art of tacking against the wind was discovered only centuries later, but by the ninth century the Vikings had large and gaily-colored square sails which could be used with favorable winds. In the Viking period twelve to twenty oarsmen were pictured on each side of a longboat, and "forty oarers" came to be the standard. Many of the boats carried a hundred men all told. Fleets varied in size from small raiding parties to scores of ships. Year after year the warriors harried coasts both east and west; many "fed the eagles" with their blood in far-off lands, and many stayed abroad to found settlements for trade and defense.

When Roslagen and its fleet were at the peak of their activity, in the seventh to ninth centuries, the records were disappointingly meager — perhaps exactly because this was a period of violence, of defense against pirate raids, and of aggressive action overseas. Accounts in the sagas of mighty clashes between Danes and Swedes (as at Bråvallaslätten near Norrköping in the eleventh century), and of the far-ranging expeditions by Ivar Vidfamne of Denmark and by Yngvar of Sweden and his son Anund have been viewed with skepticism. Yet in recent years archaeological discoveries have produced evidence confirming at least the broad outlines of the saga record and the accounts given in Rimbert's *Life of St. Ansgar* and in the account given by Adam of Bremen. Recent excavations have exposed the foundations of extensive fortresses of the Viking epoch on the Swedish island of Öland and Danish Zealand. At Grobin (Seeburg) near Libau on the coast of Courland (Kurland) remains have been uncovered of a large fort and town from the period c. 600–800, definitely built by Uppland Swedes and Gotlanders. Similar finds at Elbing in Poland and north of Kaliningrad (Königsberg), together with individual graves and the evidence of Swedish runestones, indicate a lively connection between the east side of the Baltic and Sweden. About 885 King Olof of Sweden briefly reconquered Seeburg and the neighboring area, according to the account of Rimbert. Much earlier the Swedes had made contact with the coast of Finland, and during the Viking period settlements of Finns moved south toward the shore to take advantage of the Varangian,[7] or Rus, trade routes developing to the East.

It was easy for sailors to take their ships into the head of the Gulf of Finland, and from there it was also easy to navigate the Neva, from the site of present Leningrad up into Lake Ladoga. From Ladoga by the connecting Svir they could move on to Lake Onega, and from either of these lakes they could penetrate southward by river. Hence it was that they moved up the Volkhov a few miles south of Ladoga and at a strategic location founded or conquered Aldeigjuborg (Staroja Ladoga), where Russian archaeologists later dug up remains of a fortified town containing many objects of Swedish origin. The earliest houses were of the large community type, the later ones single dwellings. A little farther to the south lay Novgorod, which became the center of Varangian power in the tenth century (under Svyatoslav). Eastward from Ladoga and Onega the Varangians or Rus reached the headwaters of the Volga. With slaves, furs, swords, and forest products they floated to Itil at the mouth of the Volga, sailed across the Caspian, and went on as far as Baghdad.

The pioneers were explorers and traders. Then, according to Arab sources, toward the end of the ninth century and on several occasions in the tenth, large fleets of Rus conducted raids on cities around the Caspian Sea, even in the Baku region. Once, after several months of plundering, the Rus were cut to pieces by a Moslem army, and the Arabs wrote that they left thirty thousand dead on the shores of the Caspian. This statistic, plus the mention of five hundred ships, however wild an exaggeration, indicates an impressive force. In the year 943 an expedition laid waste the city of Berda'a. In one or both of these operations the Rus may have been allied with the Khazar states. Their ships may have traveled from Kiev, across the Black Sea and up the Don, then through a drag or canal between the Don and the Volga, and so down the Volga to the Caspian Sea. (The Khazar fortress of Sarkel stood somewhere on the Don, perhaps where it is closest to the Volga.)

On the Volga the trading activities of the Rus were overshadowed by these destructive raids, but along the Dnieper the story is somewhat less grim and more constructive. The *Russian Primary Chronicle*, originating in a Kiev cloister in the twelfth century, is the classic, capsule account, some excerpts of which will give the flavor:

> In the year 6360 (852) . . . the land of Rus' was first named. . . . In the reign of this emperor [Michael] Russes attacked Tsar'grad [Constantinople], as is written in the Greek Chronicle.
>
> 6367 (859). The Varangians from beyond the sea imposed tribute upon the Chuds, the Slavs, the Merians, the Ves', and the Krivichians.
>
> 6368–6370 (860–862). The tributaries of the Varangians drove them back beyond the sea and, refusing them further tribute, set out to govern themselves. There was no law among them, but tribe rose against tribe. Discord thus ensued among them, and they began to war one against another. They said to themselves, "Let us seek a prince who may rule over us and judge us according to the Law." They accordingly went overseas to the Varangian Russes: these particular Varangians were known as Russes, just as some are called Swedes, and others Normans, English, and Gotlanders, for they were thus named. The Chuds, the Slavs, the Krivichians, and the Ves' then said to the people of Rus', "Our land is great and rich, but there is no order in it. Come to rule and reign over us." They thus selected three brothers, with their kinsfolk, who took with them all the Russes and migrated. The oldest, Rurik, located himself in Novgorod; the second, Sineus, at Beloozero; and the third, Truvor, in Izborsk. On account of these Varangians, the district of Novgorod became known as the land of Rus'.
>
> 6371–6374 (863–866). Askold and Dir attacked the Greeks during the fourteenth year of the reign of Emperor Michael. . . . a storm of wind came up, and when great waves straightway rose, confusing the boats of the godless Russes, it threw them upon the shore and broke them up, so that few escaped such destruction and returned to their native land.
>
> 6378–6387 (870–879). On his deathbed, Rurik bequeathed his realm to Oleg, who belonged to his kin, and entrusted to Oleg's hands his son Igor', for he was very young.
>
> 6388–6390 (880–882). . . . Oleg set himself up as prince in Kiev, and

declared that it should be the mother of Russian cities. The Varangians, Slavs, and others who accompanied him, were called Russes. Oleg began to build stockaded towns, and imposed tribute.[8]

This narrative, coming to us in a version of some 350 years after the events it recorded, simplified both events and chronology. The Varangians were in the Volga and Dnieper regions earlier than 852, and the "call" in 862 to return was doubtless a much more complicated matter than is implied here. We can only surmise the process by which the name *Rus* was gradually extended from the aristocratic Scandinavian overlords to include the Slavic people who formed the bulk of the population, and with whom the Rus rapidly amalgamated. Probably in only a few towns such as Novgorod were the Scandinavian people significant in number.[9]

Greek sources confirm the still more distant impact of the eastern Vikings. For example, in 866 two "Princes" of Kiev, Askold and Dir, attacked Constantinople but a terrific storm forced them to withdraw. Trading by small groups became a regular thing, the longboats following a route across the Baltic, up the Dvina, over to the upper reaches of the Dnieper, and down to Kiev. After a winter of trading and "tax-collecting" (the euphemism for tribute-taking) around Kiev, the boats reloaded and moved down river and across the Black Sea to the Byzantine capital, a city of luxury in brilliant contrast to the harsh conditions of life in the North. Yet the Byzantines learned geography from the Northerners, and knew many of the rapids in the Dnieper by Swedish names — Holmfors, Barufors, and so on. The Byzantines wanted the furs, wax, honey, slaves, and other products that the Rus brought with them, and they had fine silks and jewelry, glass and ceramics, arms and money to give in return. But their fear of the rugged Northerners, as of other "barbarians," prompted them to impose special regulations.

After an attack by the Varangians the Byzantines made a treaty with them in 911 A.D. which set up housing regulations for an area up the Golden Horn outside Constantinople and granted permission for not more than fifty men to enter the city at one time. A generation later some misunderstanding led to another massive threat against the city, but attack was averted by diplomacy, and a new treaty was made in 945 reaffirming the privileges and the restrictions of 911. Byzantine appreciation of the military prowess of the Rus was indicated by the establishment of the Varangian Guard of the emperor — an elite corps which for years gave employment and discipline to later generations, including most notably Harald Hårdråde. It may have been soldiers of the Varangian Guard who carved memorial runes to the memory of a comrade on the flanks of the handsome Piraeus lion (now in Venice). Whether as traders, raiders, or mercenaries of the Empire, these blond Northerners reached into the far corners of the European-Mediterranean world, and they took home with them coins, jewelry, and other products of the wealthier cultures.

By the mid-tenth century Kiev was a power to be reckoned with, and in 955 (or 957) Olga, ruling for her infant son Svyatoslav, was received in high state and baptised by Emperor Constantine Porphyrogennetos. Svyatoslav later rejected Christianity, but his son Vladimir (a name the equivalent to Waldemar in Danish and Swedish) became Christian in 988 and proceeded to convert the Russian people to the eastern form of Christianity. In the next generation Yaroslav fought his way to the succession; he maintained connections with Sweden by marrying Ingegerd, daughter of Olof Skötkonung, and also by recruiting Varangian reinforcements from Sweden. Yaroslav's daughter Elizabeth married at Novgorod Harald Hårdråde, "that prototype of all the Vikings, who fell at last at Stamford Bridge."[10] But in the eleventh century Russia was standing on its own feet. If one attempts to assess the long-range impact of the Rus on the people who took their name, he would have to emphasize most strongly not the direct influence of the Swedes but the part they played in introducing Byzantine Christianity and culture among the Slavs.

Did the Uppsala kings attempt to build an empire in Russia? Hardly. On the other hand, they did operate purposefully far afield. Their fleets swept the Baltic Sea, and royal authority undoubtedly stood behind the establishment of forts and settlements along the eastern shores of the Baltic. But these were difficult to hold, and Finland, which became Sweden's eastward arm, was not effectively brought under control until the twelfth or thirteenth century. The forays into Russia, down the Volga and the Dnieper, and on to Constantinople were the business primarily of bands of armed merchants and adventurous young warriors. The political power attained by the Varangians was probably but a by-product of their commercial enterprise in a region of internal chaos. There was no evidence that any political authority over the "Russians" was exercised from Uppsala. Nevertheless there was a similarity here with the contemporary establishment of Viking power in Normandy and Sicily, even if not with the more systematic empire-building of the Danish king Canute in his conquest of England in the early eleventh century, or the Norse colonization in Iceland.

The conjecture that some sort of grand planning lay behind Viking activities is strengthened by a glance in other directions. Northward to the White Sea Ohtere (or Ottar of Hålogaland) led an exploring expedition in c. 890, and Erik Haraldsson (Bloodaxe) led another in c. 930. New lands, new routes, new wealth — all were constantly sought, and the importance of the North-

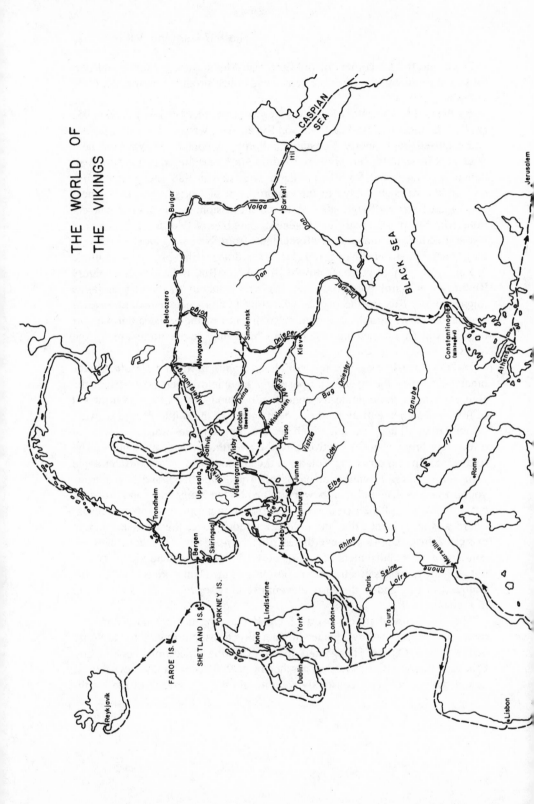

THE WORLD OF
THE VIKINGS

land and its furs was emphasized by the campaign undertaken by Erik Haraldsson in 918 against the Biarma men of the northerly region.

Central direction and clear economic purpose were also indicated by the Swedish conquest of Hedeby in the years around 900. Hedeby, near the present-day city of Schleswig at the narrow base of the Jutland peninsula, guarded the trade route from western Europe to the Baltic. Excavations from the 1880s to the 1930s showed that it was an important industrial and commercial community. Hedeby was a vital point in the days when ships would not sail round Skagen, at the northern tip of Denmark, because of the treacherous sandbars. Rule over the city in the tenth century shifted from the Swedes to the Germans to the Danes. The evidence of place-names indicates Uppland-Swedish colonization took place in a considerable area adjoining Hedeby, north of the Danevirke (an earthen wall across southern Slesvig, built in the ninth century) and on some of the neighboring islands. Perhaps it was as late as 995 that the conquering Dane Sweyn Forkbeard finally drove out the Swedes and destroyed Hedeby. Soon thereafter Canute went on to establish an empire based in Denmark that included Norway and England and the claim to rule over part of Sweden. He at least was a purposive empire builder.

Except where Swedish history thus impinged on neighboring lands, it is difficult to discover even the names of the kings during the Viking epoch. The little we know about the rulers during this period is summarized in the accompanying list.

### Early Medieval Kings

SIXTH CENTURY TRADITIONAL SEQUENCE:
Aun
Egils
Ottar
Adils

[then a blank until the travels of Ansgar the missionary, recorded by Rimbert.]

| c. 830 | Björn, king in the Mälar district |
| c. 855 | Olof |
| c. 890 | Ohtere, who campaigned in the North |
| c. 900–934 | Olof and son Gnupa, conquered and ruled in Hedeby |
| ? | Björn, Anund, Erik |
| c. 930 | Ring, king in Uppsala |
| c. 983 | Erik the Victorious, conquered Skåne Vikings |
| c. 994–1022 | Olof Skötkonung, first king known surely to rule over both the Svear and Götar; exiled by the Svear |
| c. 1000 | Battle of Öresund (Svolder) where Olof Skötkonung |

and Sweyn Forkbeard defeated Olav* Tryggvason
of Norway

1013–1042    Danish rule over England, Norway, and part of Sweden
(King Canute to 1035)

c. 1022    Anund Jakob, first Christian name among the rulers
of the Swedes

*Olof is the usual Swedish spelling; Olav or Olaf is the usual Norwegian.

These kings are but shadowy figures to us. In some ways we feel more secure in our knowledge of the Vikings abroad than of those at home, yet the records of raids in foreign parts are but fragmentary bits from which to construct the history of a people. From laws obviously well developed, though not given written form until later centuries, from runestones and place-names and caches of coins and jewelry, from the accumulating evidence of archaeological discoveries, from their own sagas and the chronicles of outsiders, we can piece together a hazy image.

One tangible collection of evidence is the ruins of Birka, commercial center of Sweden during the ninth and tenth centuries. Birka, situated on an island in Lake Mälar some twenty miles west of present-day Stockholm, lay on the main route for ships that came in through the Södertälje passage. The town occupied a semiprotected position near the entrance to Lake Mälar, with easy access to the hinterland by means of the many branches of Mälar. In winter transportation over the ice was even easier and a great annual "ice-market" was held in Birka. The city apparently enjoyed only a short life, but it was a prosperous one for about two centuries after 800 A.D. The finds at Birka in the "black earth" (the top soil in which cultural relics are found) and the extensive burial grounds at Birka show an active trade was conducted with both West and East. Many Frisian merchants visited or perhaps lived there, and control of the Hedeby route was of special significance for their trade. A rocky height near the town provided a good location for a fort and refuge. On a nearby island were the terraces of Helgön (see chapter I), and round about were other settlements which have vanished in the intervening centuries.

Birka's day of glory was cut short. It is possible that the city was destroyed in connection with a Danish campaign against the Swedish king at the end of the tenth century. At about the same time Hedeby was taken from the Swedes and trade with western Europe was disrupted. At the beginning of the eleventh century Sigtuna, lying on a northern arm of Lake Mälar on the mainland near Uppsala, emerged as the chief trading center, and it was here that Christianity made its breakthrough. Probably the merchants of Birka transferred their activities to Sigtuna, which enjoyed a more protected position and briefly became the political capital of Sweden. Here too power was short-lived, and Sigtuna was dealt a deathblow in 1187 when Finnish or Estonian raiders sacked and burned the city. Again, as at Birka, the commercial importance of the city was never reestablished, though the community of Sigtuna remained and in the twentieth century rose to prominence as a cultural center.

The steady rising of the land changed the position of Lake Mälar in relation to the Baltic and destroyed the advantages of location previously enjoyed by Birka and Sigtuna. The southern opening at Södertälje became shallow, and simultaneously what had been a rough and difficult passage to the east became narrower and more controllable. The many different outlets to the sea were reduced for practical purposes to one, and here a control point could be established for both commerce and defense. Thus, sometime about the middle of the thirteenth century Stockholm came into being, perhaps through the influence of Birger Jarl. The kings had transferred the political and religious centers from Sigtuna to Uppsala, and there the religious seat was to remain. Gradually Stockholm became the main seat of political authority and by the fifteenth century was called the "head" city. Nature had dictated that the center of defense and of commerce must lie there where the waters narrowed. The new city was protected by miles of rugged skerries, yet faced eastward to the Baltic; on the west it opened on Mälar's many-pronged passages reaching more than sixty miles into the populous interior. To the north and the south land routes ran into well-populated and fertile agricultural areas. The location of Sweden's chief city was fixed when man adjusted himself to the decisions of geography.

Relatively little of our knowledge of these Viking centuries in the homelands comes from the written accounts of men such as Rimbert or Adam of Bremen. The clearest records are geologic, archaeologic, and linguistic. Caches of coins, personal ornaments, and art objects, which continue to be unearthed even in the late twentieth century, attest eloquently to the wealth of the age and to the cosmopolitan culture of the far-ranging Vikings. Forty thousand Arabic coins, thirty thousand Anglo-Saxon, and forty-eight thousand German have been found in Sweden, and their locations clearly mark the trade routes that crossed Sweden between Asia and western Europe. Many of the finds are from Gotland, where a cache of gold discovered in 1774 weighed fifteen pounds and a silver-find of 1967 weighed over twenty pounds. The burials of treasure reveal the economically significant fact that wealth was hoarded rather than invested and also imply that the Swedes at home were not secure from raids. Valuables were safe only in the ground and not safe even there from the death or forgetfulness of the owner. Art objects, often exquisite in design and dazzlingly beautiful in pure gold, plus bars and rings of gold ready to be worked, display native craftsmanship of a high order. Sword-hilts, armbands, and pendants tell of the tastes and the skills of the Swedes themselves and the maintenance of the Vendel tradition. To all this must be added imported glass bowls from western Europe, ceramics from the south, figurines from Asia — some the products of trade, some the booty from Viking forays.

Scandinavian place-names such as those for the falls of the Dnieper suggest that it was the Varangians who first made known these rapids, if indeed they were not the first to conquer their rough waters and rocks. Communities named after pagan gods (e.g. Torsvik = Thor's bay) or with endings such as -by or -tofte, when found in Sweden showed the direction of expansion within the home country. When situated abroad, as in hundreds of locations in England and Russia, they left clear evidence of the presence and power of the Vikings. In England alone are found over seven hundred place-names ending in -by, e.g., Derby, Grimsby, Maltby. The numbers are augmented by hundreds more in -tofte, -thorpe, -beck, -holm. Sometimes the names are more obscure, as with Swansea in Wales (Svens ö = Sven's island) or Yvetot in Normandy (corresponding to Ivetofte in Skåne). Scores of personal names and loanwords unnumbered add to the evidence: Thor, Freya, hug, fog, brink, both, bleak, knife, law . . . [11] These linguistic evidences indicate that the Vikings were not just hit-and-run raiders, but also colonists, builders.

The records deliberately left for posterity by the Vikings consist almost solely of the runestones. These monuments erected to the memory of brother, father, or leader have been found far down on the Volga River and scattered thinly throughout northern Europe. But the vast majority, some three thousand, have been found in Sweden itself. Each told its terse story, for example:

> The brothers were among the best of the men in the land and out in ledung.
> They took good care of their men. In battle he fell, out East in Gardarike
> [Russia].

Another with poetic power read:

> They journeyed hard and far after gold
> And eastward gave food to the eagles;
> They died in the south, in Serkland [land of the Saracens].

And a longer one ended with three lines of verse:

> He was drowned in the Holm's sea,
> His ship sank bodily,
> Those who lived were only three.

But for the most part the runic inscriptions were laconic, simpler records, such as:

Tumme raised this stone in memory of Assur,
his brother, who was King Harold's seaman.[12]

The runic characters formed an alphabet of twenty-four letters in the ancient system, sixteen in the later, and their sharp angles were easily carved in either wood or stone. Their origin is shrouded in mystery, but it is obvious that the form preserved in the runestones was derived largely from Greek and Roman letters and possibly some Etruscan letters. The mystic, symbolic power of the runes was viewed with awe long before they were used for the stone memorial inscriptions. That they never established themselves for longer passages of writing was attributable to the introduction of Christianity. The widest use of runic inscriptions was in the eleventh century, and it was just then that the church brought in the more universal Roman alphabet. The runes, associated as they were with paganism and superstition, gradually fell into disuse, though they were used in farmers' calendars as late as the eighteenth century.

ᚠᚢᚦᚨᚱᚲᚷᚹ ᚺᚾᛁᛄᛇᛈᛉᛊ ᛏᛒᛗᛘᛚᛜᛝᛟ.

ᚠᚢᚦᚨᚱᚲ:ᚺᚾᛁᛏᛋ:ᛏᛒᛦᛚᛙ

The older 24-letter runic alphabet (above)
and the newer 16-letter alphabet

So too the dynamic epoch of the Vikings faded and Swedish history turned for a time inward. What had caused the great surge of expansive energy? Necessarily the identification of the manifold causes must be rather speculative, as we look back from a twentieth-century perspective. The disruption of southern trade routes by Arab conquest was doubtless a factor in the development of northern routes. Another factor was the expansion of the Frankish empire, which instilled in the peoples beyond its borders the need to defend and counterattack. In the sixth and seventh centuries the Swedes had already developed the Vendel culture of Uppland, rich in barbaric splendor, thus proving the presence of wealth and of delicate artistic skill. Yet perhaps this culture had attained as much as it could by itself. With the increase of contacts with central and southern Europe the Scandinavians developed a taste for sunnier climes and finer things. As they probed southward they discovered not only the refinement but also the weakness of their neighbors. The Franks after the fall of Charlemagne were divided and feeble; the Britons could not resist the attacks of the Danes and the Norsemen; the Slavs were in chaos and may indeed have welcomed the strong organizing hand of Rurik and his men; Byzantium was plagued with feeble rulers and perpetual rebellion in a far-flung empire; even Islamic areas were vulnerable. Such situations were irresistibly tempting to people whose culture glorified the rights of power.

Furthermore, polygamy was widespread throughout Scandinavia and the birth rate was high. We know from place-name evidence that new settlements were being established within Sweden as well as beyond. Though we have only presumptive evidence and no dependable population figures, it seems clear that a population explosion preceded or accompanied the phenomenal expansion of Viking activity.

What kind of men were these Vikings who terrorized the West, organized government in Russia, and opened their northern lands to new cultural currents from the south? Certainly many were young men going "a-viking" as their equivalent of tournaments, Olympic games, and even the Grand Tour. After a year or a few years of sailing, fighting, and trading they could come home to marry and settle down to work on the farm or the manor. For some, "viking" may have become a lifelong career — as long as such a life could last. As we know, some died abroad, remained as settlers in Russia, Normandy, or Ireland, or carried on as merchants in a widespread trade. They were restless, seeking men, daring their lives for adventure and gain. Yet the Vikings represented but a small segment of the total population, for most people stayed at home to fish, till the fields, and tend the livestock.

From Ibn Fadhlan and other Arab observers we get descriptions of Viking traders as uncouth and dirty people with unusual strength and stamina and with pious respect for the dead — whether they cremated a chieftain on a great pyre for the soul's swift flight or buried a warrior-merchant with armor and food for a slow journey to Valhalla. John of Wallingford left another picture of Vikings in the British Isles (from around 1100, some two centuries later than Ibn Fadhlan's account): "They were wont, after the fashion of their country, to comb their hair every day, bathe every Saturday [lördag = washday] change their garments often, and set off their persons by many frivolous devices . . . and were thereby enabled to lay siege the virtue of women."[13]

The code of life of the Vikings was different from that of either the Byzantines or the west Europeans, far different from the Christian ethic. But it was a code based on a well-thought-out rationale, and it fitted the conditions of the times. This code emphasized the rights and responsibilities of the individual and his dignity as a person. In the Elder Norse Edda is a key passage:

> Cattle die,
> Kinsmen die,
> You too must die,
> One thing I know that shall ever live:
> The Fair-Name of each one dead.[14]

It was a heroic code: one must live out the destiny decreed for him, and the thing that counted was not just the ultimate result but how a man "played the game." Hardship and pain should be endured, not for the sake of others, not for a principle, but simply for the fulfillment of fate, the realization of the foreordained purpose of a man's life. Violence and cruelty were common, they did not have to be excused — were these not also fate?

Perhaps, as Eric Linklater says, there was even a conscious sense of artistry in the code by which the Vikings lived:

> They were unabashed by social obligation, undeterred by moral prohibition, and they could be quite contemptuous of economic advantage and the safety of their skins. But they saw clearly the difference between right and wrong, and the difference was aesthetic. If what they did became a story that would please the ear, then it was right and beautiful.[15]

Here was rugged individualism without apology and without constraint. Perhaps it was just because this code was completely asocial and irreconcilable with the needs of a civilized community that the Scandinavians developed especially elaborate legal codes regulating interpersonal relationships.

This individualistic philosophy encouraged adventure by unfettered men. And it placed women in positions of honor. Not only could Olga rule in Russia as regent for her son Svyatoslav, but other proud women held the keys of the farmsteads and controlled the households. This kind of social situation, portrayed vividly in Sigrid Undset's *Kristin Lavransdatter*, was common throughout most of the North. In eastern Iceland the high position of women was especially marked. There they exercized rights of land ownership and frequently both farms and children were named after women, who even in pre-Christian times held considerable spiritual authority. The special emphasis on women's rights may have originated, as Barthi Gudmundsson insists, among the Herules who had returned to Denmark, Norway, and Sweden only a few generations before the emigration to Iceland.[16] The sagas reveal a society in which women occupied a position as near to equality with men as most societies have attained only in the twentieth century.

It was an era of rough cosmopolitanism in which the Vikings from all of Scandinavia considered as their universe the vast sector of earth and water from Iceland and Greenland in the west through Britain, France, and central Europe on into Russia and southeast to Constantinople, the Mediterranean, and the Caspian Sea; in Grettir's Saga we find a quarrel beginning in Iceland which ends with death in the Varangian Guard in Constantinople. It was a time of mobility and vigor rarely paralleled in the annals of man.

# III

# THE COMING OF CHRISTIANITY

ODIN, FREY, AND THOR are enshrined in mythology and confusion. Basically Germanic (or Gothonic may be better), they also assumed special Nordic characteristics. Like all gods they were worshiped differently by different groups and differently in successive periods — sometimes with solid faith, sometimes with faith tinged with skepticism. In the tolerant, all-embracing world of paganism the chief gods shared the altar with rivals and lesser deities. The pantheon of the Vikings and their religious ideas and customs are especially difficult to know. Despite its persistent struggle against the advance of Christianity, paganism left no written defense. The groves that were its temples, the trees on which were hung its sacrifices, the springs and stones that were its altars — none spoke a message to the uninitiated. Vague memories and superstitions survived, lurking longest in the rural districts and the distant mountain valleys, slowly being modified and absorbed into the idea-world and ceremonial practices of Christianity. For what the new faith could not blot out it shaped to its own ends or attempted to ignore.

Knowledge of the old beliefs and customs comes primarily from the sagas and the Eddas, a rich and fascinating body of literature, although neither scientific nor contemporary. Snorri Sturluson, the great Icelandic scholar, did magnificent work in preserving what was still remembered in his day, from oral tradition, of ancient Scandinavian tales of the gods. But Snorri wrote in the thirteenth century, and despite his travels in Norway and Sweden he was distant in both time and place from the Vikings and the activities of the foreign missionaries in the ten hundreds. Before its downfall, paganism had already been colored by Christianity, and its true nature was altered even more in the next one to two hundred years. It never possessed a clear-cut doctrine nor a fixed hierarchy, although this Nordic mythology was an outgrowth of an ancient Indo-European outlook on life.[1]

Odin, god of wisdom, Frey (Frö), god of fertility, and Thor, god of strength were the dominant deities of the immediate pre-Christian epoch. Their roles were not sharply distinguished, however, for Frey sometimes carried a sword, and for many people Thor threatened to supplant the wise All-Father, Odin. Thor was the congenial god of the bold and aristocratic Vikings, personifying strength and action. Already relegated to shadowy status were the once all-powerful Ull and the earth-god Njord (the Nerthus mentioned by Tacitus). Christianity did not stamp out memories of the gods and sacred places, as attested by continuing place-names — Odinslund, Ultuna, Torsvik, and scores of others.

The bloody sacrifices to Thor and phallic obeisance to Frey were celebrated in local ceremonies and at the major political center of Uppsala. At nine year intervals, according to Adam of Bremen, great sacrifices were made at Uppsala with as many as seventy bodies of men, horses, and dogs swinging from the trees in the sacred grove, and the blood sprinkled over worshipers and temple. Odin had set an example of self-sacrifice by hanging himself in the "world-tree" and is therefore sometimes referred to as "Hangatyr." In early times a king who failed in his duty to provide good weather and good crops was sacrificed to propitiate the gods, but by the time the Christian missionaries arrived the kings who did not wish to die had begun to delegate this function, doubtless usually to convicted criminals. It was the king who had to officiate at these ceremonies of all the people, whereas the clan chiefs and family heads served as the presiding priests at local ceremonies. The purpose of religion was to protect the group, small or large, and help it prosper. Hence the head of each group was its natural priest, and the chief's high-seat (the clan's equivalent of a throne), which was also his sleeping place with wives and concubines, was a sacred place given extra protection of the law.

Ritual was of profound importance, and the timing of religious ceremonies like the mid-winter Jol (Jul, Yule) was carefully arranged. Customs surviving even in the twentieth century, such as building bonfires on hilltops on Walpurgis Night, hark back to a time beyond the pale of human memory. Neither Christian faith nor scientific reason has been wholly able to eradicate the age-old folk beliefs in trolls and elves. For the Swedes of the Middle Ages special fertility rites were long practiced, some within families, others in clan or village communities. In the Disa cult, which was perhaps the most important of this latter group, the central figures were the *diser*, demigoddesses associated at first with Frey but later with Odin. The tenacity of these folk beliefs and ceremonies, continuing without benefit of priesthood or organization or temples, was attacked with slow success by the denunciations of Christian missionaries.

The paganism of the North was adapted to the needs of the people and the times. It had gone through repeated changes since the sun worship of the Bronze Age yet had retained many characteristics of more ancient beliefs, such as the return of the dead to plague the living. It syncretized animistic and polytheistic concepts from many sources — with trolls and giants, and myths of the family of gods in Valhalla reminiscent of Greek beliefs, and acknowledged the majestic power of Odin as well as the sly trickery of Loki. Balder the beautiful, beloved by all but martyred, reminds us of Jesus. The persons and the names of the gods changed, but their basic functions, protection and fertility, remained. The gods were called upon to help, but only in a general rather than a personal way. Belief in man's own powers was emphasized; strength and success were glorified. Along with the desire for immortality in Valhalla was a yearning for fame on earth. The runestones of both heathen and Christian times testify to this earthly yearning, which occasionally manifested itself in direct expression:

> This [stone] shall stand in memory of the men as long as menfolk live.[2]

This heathen society of the North, at least its warrior-merchant aristocracy, had been in contact with the more Christian European continent and with Christian Ireland and Britain for almost five hundred years before it yielded at last to the formal acceptance of Christianity. The first missionaries to Sweden were forgotten long before their faith finally triumphed some two hundred fifty years later.

At the beginning of the ninth century the visit of the missionary Villibrord to Denmark had been fruitless, and Charlemagne then refused to permit a mission by Liudger. But the North came out to meet the South. Vikings in their longboats first raided isolated villages and monasteries, then commercial centers, for example, the attacks on Frisia in 810 and 813. Violent assaults on Flanders and along the Seine in 820 inspired new mission attempts. In Jutland King Harald, who needed imperial support, accepted Christianity in 826 but was driven from his kingdom in 827.

Most notable of the early missionaries to the North was Ansgar (801–65), an outstanding personality and a successful clerical politician. Ansgar, himself a West Frank or Saxon, first tried to reach Denmark, then was sent by Louis the Pious and the Archbishop of Rheims far north to Lake Mälar's thriving island port of Birka. There he could rely upon the interest of Frisian merchants based in the town, and he also met some Christian slaves. The "mayor" or administrator, Hergeir, was sympathetic, took baptism, and built a church. But it is obvious that in the brief time Ansgar stayed in Birka — from about 829 to 831 — he failed to nurture deep roots for Christianity. There is no indication that he moved beyond the city itself. Yet Ansgar was an ambitious priest; he reported success to the emperor and won appointment as bishop of Hamburg. Others tried to carry on the work in Birka, but Gautbert, Ansgar's successor, had to leave the town in 839 after the outbreak of an anti-Christian riot in which his house was demolished and his nephew Nithard was killed. The vigor of Viking attacks increased, and even in Hamburg Ansgar temporarily lost his see when the city was destroyed by raiders in 845. The division of the Frankish empire in 843 had signaled the end of Frankish expansion. Ansgar and two companions returned to the North for a brief visit in about 855. They banqueted Olof, the king of the Swedes, and gave him presents; in return they were allowed to build a church. Ansgar's companion Rimbert was left to nurse the feeble flame of Christianity, but the whole endeavor soon collapsed. Rimbert's lasting contribution was the pious *Life of St. Ansgar* which provides us with fascinating details of the Birka community.[3]

The Vikings were enjoying their heyday in both West and East, and for them Thor's hammer was a more fitting symbol than the cross of Christ. According to Rimbert, it was just at the time of Ansgar's second visit to Birka that the Danes were defeated in a major attack on Kurland. Olof then led a force across the Baltic Sea against Seeburg and Apulia (in present day Latvia). Following the advice of Christian merchants, Rimbert records, Olof and his men had trusted in Christ and thus won an alliance and great booty; in gratitude they fasted for forty days on their return. However, this incident — if true — was but an isolated example. The Christian king Harik the Younger of Denmark was forced in the 850s by the clan chiefs to close the church that his father had let Ansgar build in Hedeby, and pagan-Christian conflict continued. The men who were conquering the Danelaw in England and those who were setting up the state of the "Rus" in Novgorod and Kiev were unreconstructed pagans. The North still belonged to Thor and Odin.

Ansgar's energy and persuasive skill won converts and the approval of king and Thing (court of the freemen). But when Ansgar departed the progress of Christianization ceased. After his trip in the 850s he returned to administer his vast bishopric of Bremen and died in 865. For seventy years after that the record is silent. When Bishop Unni of Hamburg went north to "recall" the Swedes to Christianity he survived only a few months. Unni died in Birka on September 17, 936, the first precise date we know for domestic Swedish history. Meanwhile, in 934, the probably Swedish King Gnupa down in Hedeby had been defeated and forcibly baptized by the German emperor Henry I.

The second chapter of the record comes to us from Adam of Bremen, a scholarly cleric who in about 1070 wrote a history of the archbishops of Hamburg-Bremen and so included north Germany and all of Scandinavia. For his knowledge of Sweden Adam relied upon the records of the see and the testimony of his own contemporaries, especially King Sweyn Estridson of Denmark, who in his youth had fought for twelve years in Sweden. Adam included much sound history, blended with fantastic tales and spiced with special pleading against the English and the Byzantines. He hated the Anglo-Saxon missionaries because they did not acknowledge the Hamburg-Bremen authority, and he hated the Byzantines because of their "false" doctrine.[4]

We do not have any dependable information about these two non-Germanic mission groups, because neither a Rimbert nor an Adam wrote their stories. Yet through the fog of Adam's bias we can see that both groups were present in Sweden. Folk legends confirm the activities of the English Sigfrid, martyred somewhere in Sweden. Vague memories survived of a David and a Botvid and a Staffan in the far north. Adam's bitter complaints prove the presence of the English Osmund, who had attended mission school in Germany, then had accepted Orthodox Christianity, and finally had made a place for himself as a bishop in Sweden — a thorough rascal as pictured by Adam. At least two Swedish kings, influenced by intimate connections with Constantinople, were baptized into the Byzantine church, but one of them (Olof Skötkonung) was either religious enough or diplomatic enough to be friendly with the British and Hamburg-Bremen archbishoprics at the same time.

The Britons left their record not only in legend but in stone. The first Christian churches, however, were not constructed of stone, but in upright timber (*stavkyrka*) style like the churches of Norway. Most of these, incidentally, have either disintegrated or burned; the torches necessary in their dark interiors must have been highly destructive. (The best Swedish example surviving is the little church of Hedared, near Borås.) In the early thirteenth century about five hundred such churches served the worshipers of Västergötland, where the pattern was to have one church for each village, usually erected by the manorial lord. But English builders taught Swedes the use of stone, and the magnificent ruins of the eleventh-century churches of Sigtuna are monuments to their influence.[5] Often these churches had private balconies where the lord of the manor and his family could sit in dignity and oversee both the priest in front and the common people below. English also were the mint-masters, perhaps themselves missionaries, who helped Olof Skötkonung produce his "Sidei" coins in the early eleventh century (Si-dei for Sigtuna Dei).

Modern scholars have developed challenging theories about the sources of Swedish Christianity from the words brought into Christian usage. Place-names were often left untouched, even though they retained references to pagan gods and their worship. But new names appeared, too; the place formerly called Tuna now became Eskilstuna, thus perpetuating the memory of

Eskil, another martyred English priest. Basic words like *gud* (God), *jul* (Yule, Christmas), *häl* (helvete, hell) were retained in their pagan forms. Others such as *fader* (father), *son* (son), were taken from Swedish nonreligious terms. But for Christianity's new ritual and new concepts many words had to be borrowed from abroad. Latin terms were used, and a number of words came from an indeterminable western Germanic root that was English or German — for example, *Kristin* (Christian), *ängil* (ängel, angel), *apostel* (apostle). It is striking, however, that many other words were obviously of English origin (out of Latin or Greek): *kappa* or *prästkappa* (cape), *skript* (scripture), *penkost* (*pingst*, like the German Pfingsten, Pentecost), *rit* (rite, ritual), and others. The word *sal* (själ, soul), a word of English origin, has been found already in the runic inscriptions. Such words also give significant clews to the area and the time of specific mission activity, and because they appeared more often and earlier in Västergötland than elsewhere, we have confirmation that this was a region of special English influence.

In the glossary of church terminology there were also a number of German words: *kapitel* (chapter), *vighsl* (*vigsel*, marriage), *förbanna* (damn), *skapare* (creator). The German terms were introduced later than the English terms and were concerned with theological refinements, ritual developments, and church and clerical organization, rather than with the fundamentals of faith. It was therefore reasoned that the English made the first *lasting* impact on belief (in Västergötland), whereas the Germans made their influence felt a bit later in the elaboration of ritual and the establishment of organized churches and bishoprics.

The French were active as well. Ansgar, whose influence was but fleeting, came originally from Rheims. In the late eleventh century, at the critical period of the final conversion to Christianity, a Frankish mission was sent to Sweden, and in 1080 Pope Gregory VII (Hildebrand) wrote a letter directly to King Inge the Elder. From Charlemagne's Latin name Carolus Magnus came the personal name Magnus which became popular in Norway and Sweden for both princes and commoners. But other Frankish influence was slight in the Christianizing epoch.

The part played by the Greek Orthodox or Russian Christianity is a puzzling question. A few Russian-style crosses, in wood or on runestones, are of only minor significance. Quite possibly Gotland was converted from the East, but we cannot be certain. The first Christian king of the Swedes, Olof Skötkonung, as mentioned above, had several connections with the Orthodox church — his mother was of Slavic birth, his wife was a member of the Obotritisk tribe, and his daughter Ingegerd married the Christian Yaroslav at Novgorod. Bishop Osmund at the court of Emund the Old was consecrated in the Byzantine Church. Most important of all, Swedish merchants, who played a significant role in the process of conversion, had lively connections with both Russia and Byzantium. Missionaries from Russia were briefly active in Sweden and still more so in the regions on the east side of the Baltic, but they were a little late and still had work to do at home. In the rivalry between Rome and Constantinople, as played out in the northern outposts, Rome won not only Scandinavia proper but also Finland, the Baltic states, and Poland. The Orthodox Church from Constantinople won Russia and Karelia and the lands and peoples to the east. There through the long marsh and forest belt east of the Finns and the Baltic peoples ran the line of demarcation between Eastern and Western culture — for Christianity in the North, as elsewhere, led culture by the hand.

We find evidence of the broad impact of Christian culture in the form of secular loanwords. The Swedish words *bok* (book) and *rita* (originally meaning write) came from English whereas *läsa* (read) came from German. Such words merely emphasize that the whole world of books and writing was brought to Sweden from outside, along with Christianity. Indeed we can ask, was it because of piety that merchants and princes were first interested in the Christian missionaries who became their friends, or was it because these traveled and knowledgeable missionaries could read and write and could teach men of affairs how to keep records and send messages?

Christianity in Scandinavia came not by way of the masses, as it had come into the Roman Empire, but through the upper ranks of society. Viking raiders and traders observed Christianity in various forms among the Britons, Franks, Germans, and Byzantines. They saw it was always associated with cultures more advanced than their own, with wealth greater than their own. For the weaknesses of Christendom the Vikings could have only contempt, and they must have been shocked by such ideals as "turning the other cheek." But there was much in Christianity that inspired their respect, and the first Christians we know of among the Scandinavians were just those Viking traders who had contact with it abroad. Curiously they seldom went home as missionaries of the newfound faith, but rather only as individual believers. Christ and the Christian God did not at once displace Thor and Odin in their minds, but instead were added, tentatively, to the pagan pantheon. Some warriors perhaps accepted Christ as a god of war who gave them victory, as at Seeburg and Apulia (c. 855), and when they were later defeated they abandoned the new god in disillusionment. But we get only tantalizing glimpses of the early course of events — as at Birka, where Hergeir built a church, and where a few years later the mob rioted against the Christian disturbers of old forms. We hear of chieftains and kings who became Christian and then were driven out by their people. In Denmark King Gorm and his son Harald were strong enough to weather the storm and bring conversion to the Danes in the tenth century. In Norway St. Olaf's martyrdom kindled a rapid general acceptance of Christianity in the early eleventh century, after a long period of Christian activity.

In Sweden conversion was longer delayed. The successors of King Olof Skötkonung, who was baptised in about the year 1000, had also converted to Christianity, but they could not bring the Swedes over to the new faith. Instead they had to end their reigns as rulers only over Västergötland. In that province the combination of royal leadership, early English missionary work, and persistent organizational activity of the Germans from Hamburg-Bremen, brought about a voluntary conversion. Uppland or Svitiod remained stubbornly heathen. Neither Anund-Jakob, who followed Olof Skötkonung, nor Stenkil, in the middle of the century, could bring others to their own Christian beliefs. Legend has it that as late as 1080 King Inge the Elder was driven from Uppsala because of his refusal to conduct the great sacrifice that was the traditional duty of the priest-king. According to the legend, a pretender, Blot-Sven (Sacrifice Sven), Inge's half-brother, then made the sacrifices and took power, but Christianity had made progress by that time, and Inge was strong enough that in three years' time he reestablished himself as king. He continued to rule into the 1100s; his reign marked the period when paganism lost its grip and Christianity emerged victorious.

But why was Sweden slower to adopt the new faith than Denmark, Norway, Poland, and Bohemia? Our answers can only be reasoned surmises rather than absolutes. In the first place the kings in those other countries had greater authority and, with the possible exception of Norway, they had better success in unifying their states, thus providing a more favorable basis for conversion. In Sweden the magnates and local chieftains held great power in the Things and long retained the right of electing the king. Unanimity among these chieftains in favor of a new belief was hard to attain.

Heathen beliefs were held with such extraordinary tenacity among the Swedes that even when Christianity was outwardly accepted people often held reservations about it. An English cleric wrote of this transition period:

> The Swedes and Goths seem certainly, as long as everything goes well for them, in name to hold the Christian faith in honor. But when the storms of misfortune come over them, if the earth denies them her crops or heaven her rain, storms rage or fire destroys, then they condemn the worship which in name they seem to honor. This happens not only in words but in actions, through pursuit of believing Christians whom they seek to drive from the country.[6]

It also appears that the leaders of the old faith learned enough of the techniques of Christianity to use them to solidify their own position. Amulets in the design of Thor's hammer, for instance, are found in graves, and they are all of later date than the first Christian crucifixes, leading to the supposition that the custom of wearing the hammer came as a direct response to the Christian custom of wearing the cross. Similarly, it is probable that no heathen temple was built at Uppsala until the pagans had seen the function of Christian churches. The way in which Odin took on some of the attributes of the paternal Christian God further confirms the idea that paganism made an attempt to save itself from extinction by adapting from Christianity. Meanwhile, the Christians also borrowed from the pagans. For example, the pagans bore through the fields idols and symbols of Frey and other gods to guarantee fertility; hence the Christian converts painted banners with pictures of Christ and the saints and bore these in prayerful processions at planting time, a custom surviving in some districts for many centuries.

A third factor among those that delayed the transition from paganism was the personal deficiencies of the missionaries, mentioned several times by Adam of Bremen. In one place, after discussing the Swedes' appetite for sex and their generous hospitality to travelers, he continued:

> They also cherish with great affection preachers of the truth, if they are chaste and prudent and capable, so much so that they do not deny bishops attendance at the common assembly of the people that they call the *Warh*. There they often hear, not unwillingly, about Christ and the Christian religion. And perhaps they might readily be persuaded of our faith by preaching but for bad teachers who, in "seeking their own; not the things that are Jesus Christ's," give scandal to those whom they could save.[7]

Adalward the Elder was "truly a praiseworthy man," and a highly successful bishop, but

> after him the archbishop consecrated . . .  Acilin, a man in no respect worthy of bearing the episcopal title unless it was for his portly figure. He indeed loved carnal ease. In vain did the Goths send a delegation, for until his death he stayed with his pleasures in Cologne.[8]

After Adalward the Younger had converted Sigtuna and the region roundabout, a new setback came, says Adam, with the appointment of Tadico, "who out of love for his belly preferred even to starve at home rather than be an apostle abroad."[9]

Adam may well have been wholly correct in his diatribes against individuals, yet the personal animosities that were thus evidenced must have created their own weakening tensions. The missionary rivalry between the English and the Germans was un-Christian and weakening to the cause, although it was neither unnatural nor unparalleled in other times and places. Events in England in 1066 may also have had telling effects abroad. This was the crucial period in Sweden for the final grapple between Christianity and heathenism. Undoubtedly the lack of assistance from England at this moment prolonged the struggle.

The tenacity of paganism is impossible to understand on the basis of religious belief alone, for religion and its customs are inextricably interrelated with the secular culture. The strength of the old order lay precisely in this mutual reinforcement of the religious and secular culture. For the law-minded Swedes it was hard to abandon the formalities anchored in the institutions and legal procedures of the pagan faith. Conversion to Christianity vitiated the validity of an oath in the Thing court and excluded a person from the ceremonies of the community. Because it was the chieftains, the presiding officials, who first were inclined to become Christians, their nonparticipation in pagan oaths and customs was particularly disruptive and was therefore bitterly opposed. At the level of the kingship it was this problem that explained the repeated unseatings of kings in the eleventh century when they refused to perform the sacrificial rites at Uppsala.

Hence for Sweden individual conversion was especially awkward. The established sociopolitical structure required that the Things must decide by vote on a change in religion (as Iceland had become Christianized). Conversion of the Swedes to Christianity was therefore a slow process. Not until the last years of the eleventh century did Christianity definitely gain the advantage. This was the time when Christian Europe was sending forth its peasants and knights on the First Crusade to the Holy Land (in 1096). But opposition persisted and we hear of a campaign of the 1120s, called a crusade and led by the Norwegian king Sigurd the Jerusalem-traveler, against the pagan Smålanders of southern Sweden.

The process of Christianization was not mass conversion either by persuasian or by the sword, nor was it a formal act decreed by a sovereign. Rather, it was the accumulation of individual conversions within a social order that resisted to the bitter end. Sympathy grew slowly, but when the Christianization of the community came at last it came by the formal determination of the entire society through its constituted authorities. The members of the Things voted for abandonment of the old gods and established laws requiring belief in Christ, as Uppland's law code states:

> In Christ shall all Christians believe,
> That He is God
> And there are no several other gods
> Than He alone

No one shall sacrifice to idols
And no one shall in groves or stones believe
All shall respect the church.
There shall all go,
Both living and dead
They who come into the world
And they who depart.[10]

Because of such laws passed when the time was fully ripe, the social structure was disturbed only slightly, and old districts of pagan worship even retained their pagan names.

Change was evolutionary rather than revolutionary and involved the reconciliation of old and new. Christ was portrayed as fighting a duel with Odin, Christian churches were built on the foundations of wrecked heathen temples as at Uppsala, runestones were erected along the road to fallen heroes whose bodies were laid to rest in the churchyard, and babies were baptized with names such as Thor. Paganism did not completely disappear, and it might be better to speak not of conversion but of symbiosis.

A great many runestones were erected in the middle quarters of the eleventh century, coinciding with the time of decision for Christianity, and the association may have been more than coincidental. Runic memorials had long been purely pagan, but in the mid-eleventh century Swedes began to assert in everlasting granite the Christian character of their deceased relatives. One runestone in Vallentuna read:

Holmhög and Holmfrid raised these stones for Faste and Sigfast, their sons.
They died in white clothes.[11]

In other words the boys died in their baptismal clothes, having accepted Christianity on their deathbeds. Another runic inscription ended:

God and God's Mother help his spirit and soul, grant him light and paradise.[12]

Crosses in various forms were carved in many of the stones. We cannot know whether such inscriptions were simply examples of normal Christian piety or protests against prevailing heathenism. Or was the runestone merely a second line of protection in an age of mixed faith? Christian burial *plus* a heathen or neutral memorial showing respect to family continuity? Some of the stones, like one in Östra Ryd, fitted this category exactly:

Gunne and Åsa raised this stone and vault for One, their son. He died on Ekerö. He is buried in the churchyard. Fastulv inscribed the runes. Gunne raised the stonepile.[13]

Or do the many eleventh-century stones reflect the conversion of members of the upper class, who as a group had the earliest association with Christianity and who individually had the money to pay for the making of runes and to send sons and brothers off on expeditions abroad? Or, again, were some of the rune-masters themselves missionaries, either foreign or native? We do not know the answers; we only know that the runestones flourished in the eleventh century, especially in Uppland, and that with the fall of the heathen temple at Uppsala and the victory of Christianity the making of runic monuments practically ceased.

Slowly the bloody worship of Thor and the phallic worship of Frey gave way before a new faith that offered hope instead of grim fate and encouraged men to work for the improvement of their society. The fact that the acceptance of Christianity was authorized politically by the Things emphasized a relationship between state and religion which has remained deeply embedded all the way from the pre-Christian centuries to the age of social democracy. The universal character of Christian belief as well as the organization of the church promoted the centralization of political authority in Sweden as it did in many countries in Europe. The new religion was a force that could be used by a striving ruler as an excuse for his campaigns, an inspiration to his followers, and a weapon against his enemies. Christianity brought with it an international language and literature and trained priests who could read and write. Education of Swedish boys for the priesthood made them also available for clerkships with the kings and the merchants. These innovations facilitated increased relationships with the European continent, relationships that could be more peaceful and constructive than those of the Viking epoch.

No aspect of Swedish society was unaffected by the religious revolution. Change was multi-faceted and fundamental, ranging all the way from the new ideals of brotherhood to techniques of architecture and improvements in agriculture introduced by the monks in their cloister farms and the priests in their gardens. Art became more kindly and music more refined. The church's insistence on monogamy undoubtedly reduced the population pressure and enabled internal migration instead of foreign ventures to satisfy the need for expansion. The Christian parish assumed the duties of charitable assistance. We can only wonder to what extent the emphasis on love for one's fellowman may have blunted the thrust of the Viking sword, but raiding declined — diverted to some extent toward crusading in Finland.[14]

Certain of the economic aspects of Christianization were probably less revolutionary in Sweden than in most countries owing to Sweden's lack of resources. For instance, Sweden did not have the silver with which to continue to issue the Si-Dei coinage of Olof Skötkonung. Absence of coinage was so serious that Peter's Pence could not be collected on a household basis, according to the principle of the tax, but had to be paid in districts in lump sums (regular Swedish coinage dated only from the middle of the twelfth century).

But steadily, irresistibly, Christianity took hold. Early in the twelfth century Scandinavia succeeded in breaking away from the domination of the Hamburg-Bremen see when Lund in Skåne was made the seat of an archbishopric for the North (Denmark, Norway and Sweden). Lund retained a vague preeminence even after Norway gained its archbishopric in Nidaros (later known as Trondheim) in 1152 and Sweden attained its archbishopric in Uppsala in 1164.

This phase of Christian progress in Sweden was riddled with problems of dynastic succession and with instability and strife which plagued both state and church. As we will see in the next chapter, politics did not ease the process by which Christian influences were slowly absorbed.

# IV

## MEDIEVAL SWEDEN
## c. 1100–1500

THE HIGH MIDDLE AGES in Sweden was a valley of depression, a low point in the historical profile. Sweden ceased to act on others and allowed itself to be acted upon. Bloody strife between kings and great noble families characterized the anguished progress toward centralization. Towns developed slowly, dominated politically and economically by German merchants and German craftsmen; German artists decorated the churches. The Black Death decimated the population. The old social order of simple rural equality gave way to a society of status. In political and social development Sweden lagged behind continental Europe and its neighbors Denmark and Norway. The direction of events was determined less by design than by the uncertainties of birth and death, by foreign interference, and by the decisions of war, treachery, and accident. As the *Vadstena Chronicle* recorded in 1363, "This was a time when birds of prey roosted on every mountain top.":

During this epoch of stormy chaos the Swedes did little to keep records or write history. Even the runestones ceased to tell their tale of travel and death, and the sagas were recorded not by the Swedes but by the Norwegians and Icelanders. Fortunately these sagas often referred to Swedish persons and events, so that through them, and through the historically unconscious evidence of laws, social customs, church regulations, treaties, architectural remains, and the like, we can reconstruct the main events and characteristics of the period. One valuable literary-historical work of the early fourteenth century, the *Rhymed Chronicle* or *Erik's Chronicle*, left a record of the confusion.[1]

As the intervals of calm gradually grew longer, the constructive efforts of

45

rulers were more successful, and life became more secure. The unification and codification of law was especially important in laying the foundations for a more orderly future.

## The Early Middle Ages

Only toward the east, through its tenuous hold on the Finns, did Sweden in the Middle Ages reach beyond its twentieth-century borders. The southern tip of the Swedish peninsula with its fertile fields was held (most of the time) by Denmark. The north was a vast expanse of forest and fell traversed by the Lapps, their reindeer, and a few trading *birkarlar* who acknowledged the suzerainty of the Swedish king. In the northwest the forest provinces of Jämtland and Härjedalen leaned geographically to Sweden, economically and politically to Norway. In the southwest Sweden reached to the sea only in a tiny outlet at the mouth of the Göta River (Lödöse). In the Baltic, off the southeast coast, Öland and Gotland were inhabited by people of Swedish stock and so were the Åland Islands east of Stockholm. The medieval Swedish heartland comprised the area around Lakes Mälar, Vänern, and Vättern: Svitiod, the original home of the Swedes or Svear, in the north; Götaland (Västergötland and Östergötland), stretching from west to east across the peninsula, just to the south; and Småland, sparsely populated, forested, and rocky, serving as a southern barrier against the Danish provinces of Skåne, Halland, and Blekinge.

From a visit in about 1220, the Icelander Snorri Sturluson left a clear description of Svitiod, the political center of the kingdom:

> In Svitiod itself is a division that is called Södermanland; it is a bishopric. So one part is called Västmanland or Fourhundredland; it is a bishopric. The third part of Svitiod is Tenhundredland, the fourth is called Eighthundred-land, and fifth Sealand (Roslagen) and that which belongs to it eastward along the sea. Tenhundredland is the foremost and the best region in Svitiod. Under it lies the whole kingdom; there is the king's palace and the archbishop's seat, and after it the Uppsala *öd* [estate] is named; Uppsala *öd* the Swedes call the land holdings of the king.[2]

We cannot fully know how Tenhundredland (Uppland) and the larger Svitiod became preeminent.

Doubtless earlier political organizations had existed in many clans or petty kingdoms — Procopius mentions thirteen in the sixth century. During the chaotic early Middle Ages the Götar had consolidated some of these clans and the Svear others. Then, still in the dimness of unrecorded history, the Götar of Östergötland and Västergötland became associated with the Svear of Svitiod,

Ship-setting at Gnisvärd, Gotland, c. 1000 B.C. Courtesy of the Swedish Institute, Stockholm. Photo: Bror Karlsson.

Elk head from Alunda, Uppland, c. 2000 B.C. Courtesy of the Historical Museum, Stockholm. Photo: Sören Hallgren.

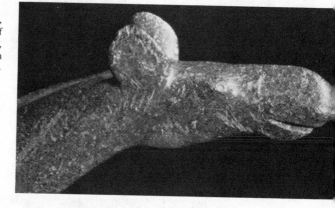

Rock carving in Tanum, Aspeberget, Bronze Age. Courtesy of the Historical Museum, Stockholm. Photo: Claes Claesson.

Gilded weathervane from the eleventh century, probably used originally as a chieftain's pennant, with metallic disks dangling from the small holes. Found in Söderala, Hälsingland. Photo: Sören Hallgren.

Crucifixes, Thor's hammers, figures of Odin and Frey, 800–1050 A.D. Photo: Sören Hallgren.

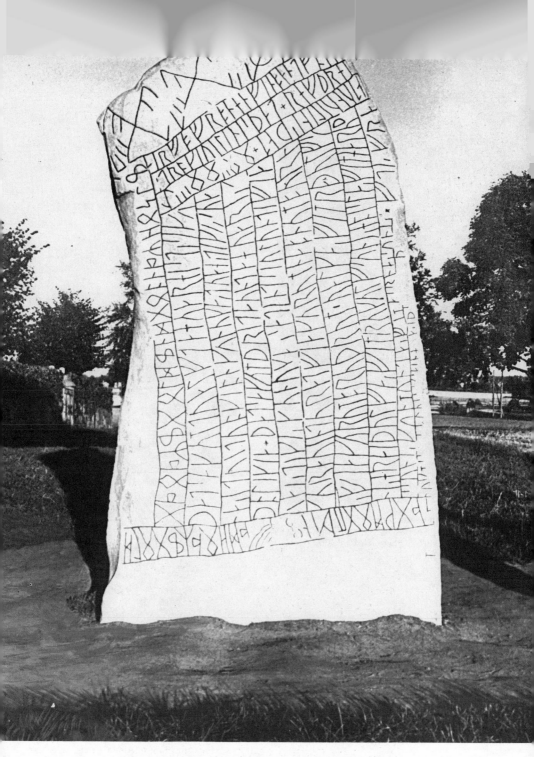

The Rök stone of the ninth century, Östergötland. Eight feet high, covered on all sides with the longest known runic inscription; inclusion of ciphers makes interpretation difficult. Courtesy of the Swedish Institute, Stockholm. Photo: S. Larsson.

The Sparlösa runestone, Västergötland, eighth century. Courtesy of the Swedish Institute, Stockholm. Photo: H. Faith Ell, ATA.

Baptismal font in Alnö Church, Medelpad, c. 1200. Courtesy of the Historical Museum, Stockholm. Photo: ATA.

Husaby church, Västergötland, twelfth century. Tradition has it that on this site in the eleventh century Sweden's first bishopric was established and its first Christian king was baptized. Courtesy of the Swedish Institute, Stockholm. Photo: Calergi.

Document concerning ownership of the Falun copper mines, Dalarna, 1288. Photo: Gruvmuseet, Falun.

Hedared, Västergötland. Sweden's only surviving stave church using upright timbers. Probably late thirteenth century. Photo: J. Hyltskog.

Vadstena convent church, Östergötland, fourteenth century. Photo: Calergi.

Courtesy of the
Swedish Institute, Stockholm.

St. Birgitta, statue in
Vadstena convent church.
Photo: G. Heurlin.

Church in Rättvik, Dalarna, fifteenth century, showing sheds
for parishioners and their horses. Photo: A. Hedling.

The Anders Zorn home in Mora, Dalarna, built in the nineteenth to twentieth
centuries according to ancient traditions. Photo: Kamera-Reportage.

Gustav Vasa, statue by Anders Zorn in Mora, Dalarna, 1903. Courtes
the Swedish Institute, Stockholm. Photo: S. Walt

Magnus's Carta Marina, 1539 A.D. From one of the two surviving copies, Uppsala University Library, Uppsala.

Portaging

Making fur coats

Crafts and manufacturing

Military stratagems:
fire-birds used against a fort

Lapp hunters on skis

From Olaus Magnus,
*Historia de gentibus
septentrionalibus*
(Rome, 1555).

## RULERS OF MEDIEVAL SWEDEN
(with approximate dates)

?–1050       Anund Jakob (died c. 1050)⎫ joint rulers
1050–1060    Emund the Old            ⎭

1060–1066    Stenkil

1066–1080    Inge the Elder Stenkilsson                        ⎫ joint rulers
             with Halsten Stenkilsson (died c. 1070)⎭

1080–?       Blot-Sven

1083(?)–?    Inge the Elder

?–1130(?)    Inge the Younger Halstensson                 ⎫ joint rulers
             with Filip Halstensson (died c. 1110)⎭

1130–1156    Sverker the Elder

1150–1160    Erik Jedvarsson (St. Erik)

1161–1167    Karl Sverkersson

1167–1196    Knut Eriksson

1196–1208    Sverker the Younger, Karlsson

1208–1216    Erik Knutsson

1216–1222    Johan Sverkersson (died at age 21)

1222–1229    Erik Eriksson (assumed throne at age 6)

1229–1234    Knut Holmgersson

1234–1249    Erik Eriksson (returned after death of Knut)

1250–1275    Valdemar Birgersson (but Birger Jarl his
             father ruled until death in 1266)

1275–1290    Magnus (Ladulås) Birgersson

1290–1318    Birger Magnusson (under regency 1290–1298)

1319–1364    Magnus Eriksson, king of Sweden and Norway,
except:      1355–1380 Håkon Magnusson, king of Norway
             1357–1359 Erik Magnusson, king of Sweden (and
             Skåne)

1364–1389    Albrekt of Mecklenburg

1388–1410    Margareta, ruler in Norway, since 1387 regent in
             Denmark

1389         Margareta, ruler in Sweden

1397         Union of Kalmar unites Sweden, Norway,
             and Denmark

very likely by defeat in war, as indicated in *Beowulf*. It was the Svear who were left with the right to choose the common king. At Mora Meadow near Uppsala in Uppland the leading Svear met and "took" their king, sat him on the Mora stone, and thus "doomed" him to the rights and the duties of office. If he proved unsatisfactory, a similar assemblage could literally overthrow him by upsetting him from the Mora stone and then could choose another king in his place (a system like the West African custom of destooling unpopular rulers). Selection was not completely free, for the king had to be in the vigor of manhood, and he was normally chosen from the available members of one or two "royal" families. Once chosen, the king was given his royal name and charged by the lawman of Uppland "to govern the land and guide the kingdom, to uphold the law and maintain peace," and he was endowed with the Uppsala *öd*.[3]

After his election the king went on the *Eriksgata*, a carefully prescribed tour of the realm in which the Svear-chosen king showed himself to his other peoples and received their allegiance. He then returned, guarded all the way by shifting groups of hostages. From Uppsala the king rode south through Strängnäs and Svintuna. Hence he traveled with the men of Östergötland through their land and into the forest Holaveden, where the Smålanders took charge and followed him to Junabäck at Lake Vättern. There the men of Västergötland met him with a safe-conduct and hostages and took him to the border of Närke; thence he rode to the Arboga River and through Västmanland back to the boundary of Uppland, where the Upplanders received him again. When Christianity was accepted, a final ceremony was added, coronation by the archbishop in the cathedral of Uppsala. "Then he has full right to be king and to bear the crown . . . then can he give fiefs to those who serve him. If he becomes a good king, then may God let him live long."[4]

The new Christian kings, lacking religious leadership in their own right, did everything in their power to retain the support of the church. Nevertheless, the sanction of Christian coronation was doubtless not as impressive to the people as had been the pagan kings' service as high priests.

The powers and functions of kingship varied with individuals and circumstances, as did the titles and functions of subordinate officials. Traditionally the king was the leader in all matters of common concern but held absolute power only while commanding the army (including his own special guard, the *hird*) or fleet in war. Parallel powers were exercised by the *jarl*, who was a kind of "mayor of the palace" and the chief military officer of the kingdom; it was usually the jarl who led expeditions to Finland. The position became almost a family fief, and by the middle of the thirteenth century the great jarl Birger (Birger Jarl) took over the royal functions when his infant son Valdemar was chosen king. Other officials such as the *drots* (actually a vice-king) and the *kansler* (chancellor) gradually came to overshadow and displace the jarl. Though their duties were not clearly defined, these men made up the core of the council (*Råd*).

The king had numerous local strongholds with storehouses, managed by stewards (*bryte*), where he and his entourage lived or visited. Because of problems of supply and communication, he could not enjoy a really permanent seat of government but had to use in succession the various estates belonging to his family and those of the Uppsala *öd*. Among these royal manors were numerous places called *Husaby*, which became centers also of tax collections "in kind" and probably served in other capacities for local administration and defense. Originally the provinces or hundreds may have been subkingdoms governed by *Hundekonger*.[5] Certain chief residences were maintained early in the Middle Ages at Visingsö, an island in Lake Vättern, later at Nyköping, and eventually at Stockholm — but these were only the places where the king resided most frequently. He and his court were highly mobile, and they literally ate off the land.

Centralization was more an ideal than a reality, though kings strove mightily to attain it. The political divisions mentioned by Snorri had ancient traditions and retained much power, thus delaying the real unification of Sweden until long after unity had been attained in both Denmark and Norway.

## A Medieval Commercial and Social Revolution

When the rough and tumble Viking era calmed to a close Christianity had been accepted if not fully absorbed. Hard on the heels of political and religious change came a sweeping economic and social transformation. The Scandinavians, instead of continuing to take trade and sword to foreign peoples, were themselves subjected to a second overpowering external force. This time the prime movers were the German merchants, who redirected trade, stimulated the growth of cities, introduced new techniques and institutions, and forced new political alignments.

The immediate background to this long and complex process was the expansion of the Teutonic peoples into the north German plains. Near the mouth of the Trave, for example, an old Viking town had disappeared and a Slav town grew there instead. It in turn was conquered and burned by Adolf of Holstein, who in 1143 founded there the new German city of Lübeck. The site of the new city was well protected from pirates and lay only forty miles from the westward-linked port of Hamburg. But Lübeck opened on the Baltic Sea and within half a century became the vital link between the fields and shops of western Germany and the wide trading area to the north and east. The north Germans swept eastward by land, overwhelmed the sparse Slavic settlements,

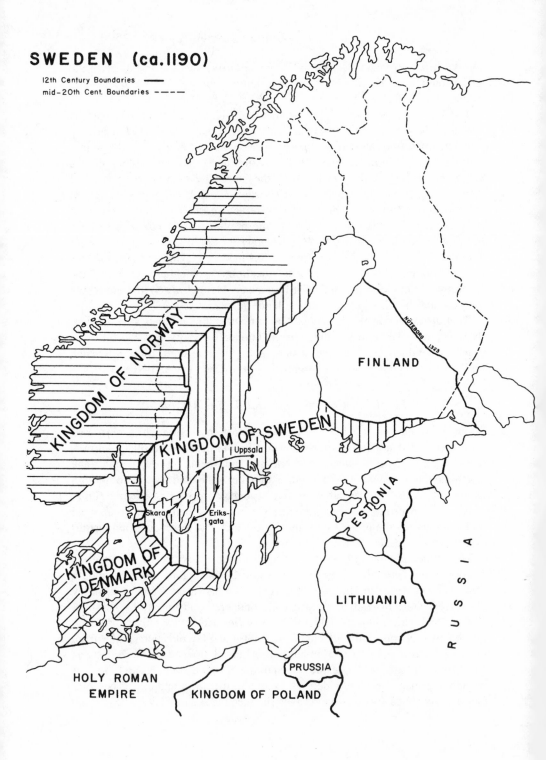

# SWEDEN (ca.1190)

12th Century Boundaries ———
mid-20th Cent. Boundaries – – – –

KINGDOM OF NORWAY

KINGDOM OF SWEDEN

FINLAND

NÖTEBORG 1323

Uppsala

Skara

Eriks-
gata

ESTONIA

KINGDOM OF
DENMARK

R U S S I A

LITHUANIA

PRUSSIA

HOLY ROMAN
EMPIRE

KINGDOM OF POLAND

founded new cities (e.g., Wismar, Rostock, Elbing), and revitalized old ones. Farther afield the energetic merchants established themselves in Visby on the island of Gotland and soon outdid the casual local traders who for generations had mixed commerce with fishing and agriculture. The Lübeckers sailed on to Finland and to Novgorod, where they displaced the long-established Swedes; they also sailed to Bergen in Norway. During the thirteenth century the Lübeckers, along with other Germans, became the dominant economic group in both city and country. The German Hanseats sent merchants to Kalmar and Söderköping in Sweden and established merchant colonies in all the cities of the North, including Åbo and Viborg in Finland, and they helped build Riga and Reval. Along the coast of Skåne they gained control of the rich fisheries, the chief prize from their bitter struggle with Denmark.

This Germanic thrust, backed by a population outburst, involved far more than Lübeck and its satellites. In the course of the thirteenth and fourteenth centuries the scattered cities of northern Germany, led by Lübeck, Hamburg, and Bremen, created the Hanseatic League. Visby, on the island of Gotland, became one of its leading members, and the sea codes of Visby and Lübeck became the common law of the northern seas. The Hansa was a thoroughly German organization, for even in an outside city like Visby it was only the resident *German* merchant company that was part of the league. Outposts such as Bergen, Novgorod, and London were not members but external branches — *Kontors* — where journeyman-merchants from German cities managed the local affairs of their home firms and gained experience for bigger things. The Hansa generated cooperation among its members (varying from year to year between seventy and one hundred cities), promoted trade between distant points, and kept control of that trade in German hands. But it was a loose-knit organization based on changing annual membership and lacking in firm loyalties and real cohesiveness.

How was it possible for the Germans, with this feeble structure, to build their network of economic empire across northern Europe, to oust the Swedish merchants from their centers abroad, and to take over the development of cities within Sweden itself?

One of the reasons for Hanseatic success was the very looseness of the organization, which permitted flexibility of method. In Norway, for instance, the means of operation became direct control. But in Visby the method was a slow process by which merchants from Lübeck settled in the town and by helping one another gradually gained preeminence. Thus Visby became a Germanic city on foreign soil and an important member of the Hanseatic League. The merchants tended to become residents and identify themselves with their new home while they continued to cooperate closely with Lübeck and the other member cities. In other Swedish cities like Kalmar, Söderköping, and the west coast port of Lödöse the Germans created active communities, but they remained special groups within the larger Swedish society. In the course of time they were absorbed. Although all these "cities" were small towns by modern standards, from one to seven or eight thousand people, they were important centers for the distribution of goods.

Stockholm provided a unique case for both Sweden and the Hansa. Where many-fingered Lake Mälar narrowed and joined the Baltic, in through the skerries at least a five-hour sail from the open sea, there appeared with the rising land a remarkable location for a city. Here Lake Mälar flowed through two main channels past rocky islands and poured its fresh water into the Baltic. A defense post may have existed there in the early thirteenth century, but under Birger Jarl the Swedes, in about 1250, began to construct on the central island a major fort, whose foundation stones still support the royal castle. Simultaneously Birger Jarl and the German merchants saw the possibilities of building a city on the islands between the streams. About 1252 the jarl signed a peace treaty with the Lübeckers who had aided his domestic opponents but had been defeated. In this first treaty of his rule Birger Jarl granted to Lübeck freedom from customs dues and taxes and allowed its traveling merchants to use their own law. But he also stipulated that if these merchants should settle in the city they must be subject to Swedish law and be called Swedes. Half of the members of the city council were to be German. The agreement was meant to be advantageous to both parties, and it was perhaps the vital founding document of the city.

Lübeckers flocked to Stockholm and soon made this new port the chief commercial and industrial city of the Swedish realm. German immigrant merchants tended to dominate the economic life of the city, and often they had more than their legal 50 percent membership on the council. The German church was and has remained one of the imposing buildings of the city. One estimate for the mid-fifteenth century reckons that 35 percent of the city's burgher class and 40 percent of the homeowners were German and that Germans paid over 50 percent of the taxes. Yet Stockholm did not become a regular member of the Hansa (it was represented only once, in 1366, at a *Hansetag* in Lübeck). What the Germans wanted was economic advantage, and they got it; what the Swedes demanded was political control, and at least in a legal sense they held it. But the adaptability of the Germans to differing local situations was only one factor in their success.

At the beginning of their spectacular advance in northern commerce the Germans had a style of ship new to the Baltic, the "cog." It was stubby and top-heavy — not graceful and swift like the Viking longboat, but its large hull could carry a great cargo, and it could bear the weight of many sails instead of the longboat's one. It was a ship for merchants rather than for warriors and better suited the conditions of the times. The Northerners had no shipyards in which to build such elaborate vessels nor the necessary capital; in addition they lacked the inclination to discard their beloved longboats. The Germans had no drag of tradition to hold them back, and they did have the capital to get what they needed. The cogs could not sail up rivers, but now towns were being built to serve as relay stations between sea and hinterland. So it was that technological development, capital resources, and the birth of cities all coincided with the appearance on the scene of the aggressive German entrepreneurs. The result was a revolution in both shipping and merchandising.

With the new ships and new people came new business methods. In Viking trade the owner of the ship was usually the captain, and the crewmen participated in the profits of the journey in exchange for their labor. With larger ships and cargo this simple democratic organization became impractical. On the Hansa ship the captain was a professional sailor, and his crewmen were hired hands. Their employers were businessmen and financiers who owned ships and merchandise — landlubbers, organized in companies, who arranged enterprises and took the financial risks and profits. The age of corporate activity, already established in Venice and throughout the south, came north with the Germans, who long held for themselves its attendant advantages for large-scale operations.

Under the new Hanseatic trade Sweden's imports consisted of about two-thirds textiles and one-third salt, though definite figures are preserved only for scattered years (especially the Lübeck records for 1368–69 and 1492–96), and precise totals are therefore unknown. Imported cloth from the Low Countries and England was used to make clothing for the well-to-do and as a means of exchange among the farmers. Salt was vital for the preservation of both meat and fish in the domestic market, and it grew in importance. In the export of fish one barrel of salt was needed for every three to four barrels of fish, and the import demand grew to as much as eighty-four thousand barrels of salt per year. The dependence of the Swedish market on foreign salt gave to the Lübeckers, and later to the Dutch, an unfortunate power over the Swedish economy and led to fundamental changes in the type of products traded. In return for textiles and salt Sweden's exports to the west came to be quite different from the furs and forest products taken by the Varangians to Miklagård (Constantinople) and the Muslims.

In the thirteenth and fourteenth centuries export of copper increased considerably, and iron remained an important export item. Sweden along with Hungary provided Europe's copper. The great mine at Falun, "Stora Kopparberget," was operating on a corporate-share basis at least by 1288 and the company was given a charter by King Magnus Eriksson in 1347. This mine became Sweden's greatest economic asset, and the company continued to function into the twentieth century, though by that time its copper was exhausted. Spain and other places competed in the production of iron, but Sweden's *osmund* was especially prized, selling at a 50 percent premium in Germany and enjoying the same price as steel in England. Made for centuries by slow smelting from bog ore, the osmund pellets were particularly pure and malleable. That of the later Middle Ages was made by faster smelting of rock ore from Utö ("out-island," a southerly island of the Stockholm archipelago) and Västmanland and was really pig iron. Another important item of trade was butter, and leather goods ranked fourth in export. This new pattern of exchange remained fundamentally the same into the seventeenth century. It indicated the lessening role of the forest, the growing place of mining, and the commercialization of fishing and farming. Timber, it should be noted, had not become an important Swedish export. Britain had obtained some of its forest products from Norway, but during the Middle Ages used the east Baltic region heavily.

As Eli F. Heckscher has pointed out, commerce was characterized by an oddly passive attitude on the part of the Swedes who, contrary to their active role in commerce in the Viking period, now allowed the bulk of their trade to be carried on by foreigners in foreign ships.[6] A certain differentiation seems to have developed in which native Swedes carried on most of the trade with Danzig and the eastern shores of the Baltic, whereas the Germans predominated in control of the trade with Lübeck and the West. Gradually other nationalities competed for Sweden's foreign trade, and increasing numbers of Dutch, Danes, and Scots settled in Stockholm. The Germans remained, nevertheless, the largest group of foreigners in the Swedish cities, and they came to include not only merchants but artisans.

Carpentry, shoemaking, and other crafts continued to be practiced in Sweden as by-products of general farm work. But the emergence of cities created the need for specialization, and skilled German workers were brought in to meet the demand. One result was that the Swedish names for these crafts were often taken directly from Middle Low German, as indicated in the accompanying list suggested by Ernst Ekman.

| Middle Low German | Modern Swedish | Modern English |
| --- | --- | --- |
| schomacher | skomakare | shoemaker |
| schrader | skräddare | tailor |
| borgemester | borgmästare | mayor |
| maler | målare | painter |
| hantwerker | hantverkare | craftsman |
| timmerman | timmerman | carpenter |
| garver | garvare | tanner |
| slachter | slaktare | butcher |

Only in Stockholm were the German merchants numerous enough to maintain their own language over a long period, but everywhere German words crept into the Swedish language.

Obstinate argument continues concerning the place of the German immigrants in the iron and copper mining industry in Sweden. It is certain that German miners went to Sweden in considerable numbers, and it is also known that the mines had been worked by Swedes before the Germans came. Apparently the Germans aided in the organization of the mining industry and helped to finance its expansion. They introduced refinements in techniques of mining and processing, although the basic methods of mining the copper at Stora Kopparberg remained the traditional Swedish methods that were adapted to local circumstances. The immigrant miners stayed, intermarried, and helped to found what became in time a special and very independent-minded class in Swedish society, ranking somewhere between the land-owning peasants and the city merchants.

Agricultural methods remained static throughout the Middle Ages, though a variety of social changes affected the rural population profoundly. In the eleventh century Sweden was a nonspecialized farmer or *bonde* society, with few distinctions except those between slave and free. The creation of cities with well-defined groups of merchants and artisans, along with the development in certain areas of the mining class, inevitably robbed the farmers (*bönder*) of their position as the universal class, and their status degenerated both relatively and absolutely. For instance, traditionally fairs had been held in the rural districts where peddlers and other merchants brought their wares. With the growth of cities the settled merchants felt they should have exclusive rights to the farmers' business and persuaded the king to decree that fairs could be held only in the cities, only at certain times, and that the farmers might not buy or sell except in the cities. Jönköping, for example, in the 1280s, was allowed to have two fairs a year and a monopoly on trade in its district. Local authorities were set up to regulate the needs of travelers as well as residents and to protect them from each other and from unreasonable distant officials.

As for slavery, the combined influences of Christianity, the increasing difficulty of getting slaves from the lands east of the Baltic, and the development of cities, gradually drove it out of existence. The former slaves or thralls tended to be absorbed into the peasant population, though some doubtless became laborers in the towns. The 1335 decree of Magnus Eriksson abolishing slavery in two provinces was, like many laws, not so much a bold move toward change as it was a recognition of a *fait accompli*.

Internal trade was extensive, but throughout the Middle Ages it continued to be largely a barter, with only minimal use of money. The farmers of

Dalsland, for example, took their butter to the mining districts, exchanged it for iron, took the iron down to the coast, and there got the fish they needed for food while the iron was shipped abroad. Taxes were paid largely in kind which meant that, to reduce long distance transport of bulky produce, royal officials and soldiery were scattered throughout the country; bailiffs and their storehouses were widely dispersed. Nevertheless it was far easier to carry goods over long distances in Sweden than might be expected. Transportation could go by waterways in summer, by smooth sledding over frozen lakes and fields in winter. The resultant wide-open routes of travel created few bottlenecks where avaricious lords could set up tollhouses. Geographic conditions helped Sweden escape both the economic and the political burdens of feudalism. Many of the coastal ports, most notably Stockholm, were entered through such a maze of passages among the skerries that here again feudal barons were discouraged. Conditions of travel by road were often difficult and in the sparsely settled country towns were far apart and inns were rare. Therefore ancient regulations required peasants along the routes of travel to provide hospitality and aid to wayfarers. Thus all forms of transportation avoided local control and emphasized the values of central direction.

Such factors made possible an extraordinary scattering of the landholding of kings and nobles. Large, contiguous estates were rare. Rather the great landholders, like Bo Jonsson Grip in the fourteenth century, sometimes held thousands of *gårds* (farms) dotted all over Sweden and Finland, both individually operated farms and tiny farm villages. The scattering was produced partly by the method of settlement, whereby freed slaves and the younger or less fortunate sons of free farmers pushed out into the common lands of the villages (the *allmänning*) or into clearings in the forests. Because such people often lacked capital for seed or livestock the tendency was for land ownership to fall into the hands of the lords or "great farmers" (*storbönder*), who provided the necessities and collected rent on the basis of one half of the assessed land value. The expansion of settlement into the forest borderlands was clearly marked by place-names ending in -*torp* (new settlement), and -*ryd* (forest clearing): Perstorp, Danderyd, and so on. Despite fratricidal wars among the royal families the movement went on:

> The mighty lords with shrieks and with thunder
> Throw lands and kingdoms in turmoil;
> Quietly build the farmer and his son
> Where they sow in blood-drenched earth.[7]

Only after the disastrous visitation of the Black Death in the mid-fourteenth century did the outward push of settlement cease for awhile. In that awful time, in Sweden and throughout Europe, villages were decimated or even annihilated, and some reverted to forest. The plague had reached first Denmark in 1349, then Norway, and within the same year invaded Sweden by way of Skåne and the Norwegian border. Terror accompanied disease. In Visby, for example, people frightened by the death-dealing mystery burned nine "poisoners" at the stake. One "confessed" that he had poisoned wells in several cities and that "Jews and evil-doers" had infected all Christendom. Wild exaggerations put the death toll in Uppland at five-sixths of the people. The devastation was indeed great, perhaps taking as many as a third of the people. The terror and the spread of the plague were increased because the people had no means of dealing with them. Some factual indication of the impact is given by the decline of Peter's Pence to 40 percent of previous collections. Perhaps the one beneficent effect of the plague was that it wiped out the final vestiges of slavery (already made illegal).[8]

Two other classes were now gradually being differentiated — the clergy and the nobles. At first the clergy married, clerical positions tended to pass to their children, and Rome found it most difficult to introduce celibacy. But after celibacy was slowly and partially accepted, the clerics had no problem recruiting from all classes and instilling in the chosen priesthood a sense of professional solidarity.

The development of a separate noble class was one of the most fateful changes of the Middle Ages. Distinctions of status had existed earlier, but they were vague. No differences between freemen were recognized before the law. In the course of the thirteenth century, however, the *ledung* became obsolete and need arose to provide a mounted armed force on land. Individual knights appeared in the mid-thirteenth century, and even a lone knight on horseback and in armor made footsoldiers seem exposed. The kings could not afford to outfit armies of knights, but they could encourage their officials and the greater landowners to equip themselves. Hence King Magnus Ladulås, who had married a German princess and had come into contact with continental feudalism, issued a statute at Alsnö in 1279 by which he gave exemption from taxation to men who would supply themselves with horses and armor:

> Because it is proper that those who support us with advice and help should
> have more honor we give to our men and those of our brother Bengt, and all
> their stewards and peasants and all on their estates, freedom from royal
> taxes (and penalties), so also all the archibshop's men and all the bishop's
> men. It is our will also that all the men who serve with war-horses, that they
> have the same privileges, whomever they serve.[9]

Thus King Magnus got an army and also created a lay upper class, the *frälse*, distinguished by its tax-free privileges and its social status. Although Magnus won a reputation for protecting the persons and goods of the common man, and thus was nicknamed Magnus Ladulås (Magnus Barn-lock), the social change he introduced was aristocratic in its essence. From an egalitarian peasant society with distinctions only between slave and free, Sweden became, with this new institution of knights and *frälse*, a status society with sharp gradations between ranks.

The social effects of the Alsnö statute emphasized that "unto him who hath shall be given." As the lands of the newborn *frälse* became tax-free the lands of the ordinary free farmers had to bear an increased load. As the privileged *frälse* discovered how advantageous it could be to own land with no responsibility other than maintenance of a few knights, they bought up additional farms and took them off the tax rolls, thus increasing further the burden on the small landholders. The state found it harder and harder to collect taxes. Tax-free privileges were extended by successive kings to the clergy as well as to the nobility, and as lands were bought by the church or bequeathed to it the number of taxpayers diminished further. The *frälse* (both lay and clerical) served as functionaries of the state. They enjoyed mobility, contacts with foreign countries, and educational opportunities for their children; they wore fine clothes and built fine houses.

This changing Swedish society was nevertheless resistant to feudalism. Feudalism of the continental variety never became rooted in Sweden, primarily because, no matter how sharp the distinction between *frälse* and *bonde* (the freehold farmer), privileged status did not become hereditary. Also, the poverty of the country, and perhaps even the climate, made the refinements of courtly life difficult to maintain. The farmer never lost his legal position of free equality, even when his social and economic position had sunk to its lowest level. A few of the great landlords reduced their peasants to serfdom, but the system did not become widespread, and in 1335 serfdom as well as slavery was abolished by law. It should be noted that in Skåne, which during the Middle Ages was under Danish rule, the Danish feudal order did become entrenched.

Closely interrelated with the revolutionary changes taking place in the economic and social structure of Sweden in the thirteenth and fourteenth centuries were changes involving the legal and political structure of the society which were influenced by both indigenous and foreign factors.

### *"On Law Shall the Land Be Built"* [10]

In the medieval laws of the North we hear the call, the demand of the deep-felt ideal: "On law shall the land be built." This was a demand that grew out of the needs of men as the earliest groups formed political communities. Yet in different communities the kinds of law differed widely, and the attitude toward law differed too. Among the Swedes and other peoples of the North law came to have such a central significance that we can call it the cultural focus of their society. The story is often told of the lawman of medieval Sweden who had memorized the law of his land, as was his duty, and recited it all in one long day at the Thing. At nightfall he collapsed and fell dead. These lawmen were held in high honor — second only to the king — for they represented law and order in society.

It was a society of violence, yet the rules of law confined violence more or less within the channels of custom. The lawman and the Thing decreed fines or exile, and a murderer — such as Eric the Red from Iceland who sailed off to settle Greenland — had to go into banishment; a homeburner had to take ship to exhaust his unruly energy on foreign shores. Voluntarily accepted law was probably the only way to restrain the wild violence of the Vikings. Within their own community it worked, because following the rules of the game was part of their way of life. Violation of the rules subjected a man not only to out-lawry and the application of the code of vengeance, but to self-condemnation, to disgrace in his own eyes.

The demands of law and orderly procedure were enforced against the king as well as others. Snorri Sturluson tells, for example, of how the Swedish king Olof denounced a certain Jarl Ragnvald at the Thing for wanting to make a peaceful settlement with King Olaf of Norway. Then one of the leaders of the freemen, Torgny, stood up in support of Ragnvald's policy:

> And when he arose so stood all the bönder up, who had been sitting, and
> those who had been elsewhere crowded forward to hear what Torgny said.
> At first there was great commotion of the many people and arms, but
> when it grew quiet Torgny said:

> "Otherwise is now the king's attitude from what it used to be. But now we
> bönder wish that you, King Olof, make peace with Olaf Digre, Norway's
> king, and give him your daughter Ingegärd to marry. But if you want to win
> back the kingdom in the east that your forefathers have owned, then we will
> all follow you. If you do not wish to do as we say, so will we go against
> you and kill you. So have our ancestors before us done. They threw five
> kings in a well at Mora Thing, when they were full of presumptuousness as
> you are now toward us. Say quickly, which you will choose."[11]

Then there was a great clatter of arms in agreement . . . and the king had to bow.

Although the historicity of the incident has been questioned, it does prop-erly illustrate the relationship between king and commoner. Such incidents went down in the record, and illustrated the law. However, individual cases did not actually make law for the future; the ancient Swedes did not follow the principle of fixed legal precedents. Rather, they recognized differences in individual cases and attempted to apply the basic principles of law to each case.

It was the attitude of seeking justice in each instance that made the position of lawman so important, for the lawman was not simply the recorder and repeater of the law — he was its interpreter. Before the time of the unified state each province or land had its own law — Östergötland, Västergötland, Uppland, Småland, Skåne, and the others — and each its own lawman. Yet the laws all stemmed from the oldest traditions of the Nordic peoples and retained basic similarities. They possessed a common trunk, though they developed separate branches and further growth in response to new circumstances and new interpretations of the old laws by different lawmen and Things. In the older laws only a description of a particular situation was given, such as someone stealing another's animals and having a slaughter pen in the woods. Alliteration and poetic style aided the memory while the laws were passed on orally, as in the marriage laws in which a wife was taken "to honor and housewife, to locks and keys." During the Middle Ages the kings began to assume responsibility for appointing commissions to draw up the laws of the different provinces and then to approve the whole body of law. In this process the laws advanced from the description of individual cases to statements involving general principles.

The oldest of Swedish written laws was that of Västergötland, which may have been revised and written down in the 1220s, about the time of Snorri's historical writing. The oldest existing copy of the law of Västergötland was made in about 1280 and became Sweden's first book. With this law was preserved an account of the succession of seventeen lawmen. The first was Lumber, "who thought out and composed a great part of our law. . . . He lies buried in a mound for he was a heathen." The seventeenth was Eskil Magnusson — oldest brother of Birger Jarl, the strong man of the thirteenth century. Eskil was described as a careful researcher into the traditional law who also used his own reason to make revisions.

> He had that gift of God, that he had a keen understanding. He had also a worthy learning, equal to that of good clerics. And in all respects he supported the West Goths and their leading men. . . . He was an outstanding man to give advice in all matters and to give right advice, so that he stood out among all the kingdom's great men. . . . He was also an able man in bearing a sword and also in strife. . . . Rarely is born such a man.[12]

Presumably it was Eskil who was responsible for the writing of the laws and for their division into sections and paragraphs, but he had as prototypes the written laws of the Danes in Skåne and several Norwegian laws. In the law of

Västergötland the section on kingship detailed the method of selection, the provisions for the *Eriksgata* (the king's inaugural tour of his domains), and the duties of the king. Sections on murder, mayhem, theft, building, legal procedure, inheritance, marriage, landholding, the church — *Västgötalag* contained fifteen in all. Some samples may give the flavor of thirteenth century attitudes: If a murderer did not himself come to the Thing he could be accused by the victim's heir, following the taking of oaths; if convicted the murderer was declared outlaw and the heir could either take revenge or accept a fine. If a woman committed murder her husband had to pay the fine or flee as an outlaw. On marriage a bride immediately owned one-third of the property. But if a man died leaving both a son and a daughter the son inherited all. (This law was changed in the fourteenth century, evidently under German influence, to allow the daughter to inherit one-third.) If a cow or horse was killed in another village and the killer could not be found, the entire village had to pay compensation. Three kinds of thief should all suffer the same hard punishment: he who stole and took, he who helped a thief, and he who received stolen goods in his house. These written laws conserved age-old custom and principles of justice and ancient expressions; certain phrases dating from the period of the folk-wandering remained in the law until the major codification of 1734.[13]

The older law of Sweden was similar in its principles to that among other northern and Teutonic peoples and was made familiar through the Icelandic sagas. One of its characteristics was the family or clan responsibility for crimes of a member. Vengeance was the responsibility of the group, and vengeance often seemed more important than punishment. (Under such a system of private sanctions feuds were inevitable and persisted for generations.) Justice was likewise different for different social classes; he who wounded or killed a freeman (*bonde*) was punished more severely than he who killed a thrall. And the king and king's agents, including tax gatherers, were protected by specific and very high fines imposed on any who threatened or wounded them. On the other hand, he who was thus protected was also obligated to pay a correspondingly high penalty if he became an offender. It was not considered much of a crime to kill an Englishman or a German, but if a man killed a Dane or a Norwegian he had to pay a higher fine and to kill a Swede cost still more (an early example of Scandinavian preference).[14]

In the facsimile series in which the older laws of the Swedes are being republished a recent addition is *Dalalagen*. This law from the interior forest province of Dalarna is illustrative of the society in which, until the late Middle Ages, the clan shared the guilt of the individual and which still retained the rule that the brother but not the sister could inherit. One provision reads: "For the fields the fence is wall, and heaven the ceiling . . . and he who steals out in the fields shall redeem himself with [a fine of] 40 marks or be stoned and banished.'' *Dalalagen* made explicit that a man who had inherited land could sell it only because of necessity and that he had to offer it first to relatives of the mother or the father from whom he had inherited.[15] One of the appendices of *Dalalagen* contains a warning for the judge to give the oath taker, one that calls upon the sanctions not of God but of the devil: ''He who swears falsely on the book, he stigmatizes himself; when he signs, he signs with the devil's hand.''[16] This charge, which dates from deep in the heathen past, remained in practice in the Middle Ages; crude as it is, it nevertheless illustrates the moral compulsion implicit in Scandinavian law, both old and new.

The laws that were written down showed, however, a different emphasis from the law of the early Vikings. The barbarous ordeal by iron was abandoned during the thirteenth century (partly because of Christian persuasion), and the use of juries sitting beside the judge became more extensive. Slavery disappeared, and every man already equal before God now tended to find legal equality with his fellow man as well. Women were granted rights of assent to marriage and improved rights of inheritance. The laws were put into writing at a time of powerful church influence, asserting itself through the clerics who kept the records and the judges who were susceptible to imported ideas. Hence the principles of Christianity and canon law and the regulations of a Christian state were blended in the newly written law with the age-old oral tradition. Gradually new ideals were established of equality before the law, security for the individual, and reconciliation in place of revenge. Furthermore, because of the expanding influence of the church and the authority of Birger Jarl, the founder of Stockholm and the greatest ruler of medieval Sweden, these security laws also inaugurated the first truly national legal system.

During the thirteenth century a strong push was made to put all the *land* (provincial) laws into writing. Archbishop Andreas Sunesen of Lund urged the Gotlanders to write down their laws to avoid the variations and quarrels that arose from forgetting and from the tendency to adopt ''different opinions according to one's pleasure.'' Hence the law of Södermanland was written in about 1325 and that of Hälsingland at about mid-century. The various laws were commonly stated as illustrative examples. For instance, one clause in the Hälsingland law read: ''If a farmer drives away his legal wife and takes another to bed and gives her locks and keys — this is called bridalseat infringement — he pays a fine of 40 marks divided in three lots, if 12 men sentence him.''[17] Among the best of the law codes were those of Östergötland and Uppland. These formed the basis for Magnus Eriksson's codification (the MELL), which he tried to make valid for the entire kingdom in about 1350.[18] Although it lacked a church code, this law was revised in 1442 and was generally accepted as the law of the country by 1500. Thus the codification and the writing of uniform law became one of the several forces working toward centralization of power, diminishing the importance of the *land* and its lawman.

Special laws for cities developed independently of the *land* laws, necessitated by the special and more recent problems of trading centers. Among the most difficult of these problems were the relationships between the foreign merchants and the natives and the threat that the Germans doing business in the towns would take over their administration. Hence the rulers, beginning again with Birger Jarl, placed restrictions on the German merchants to check the development of a colonial situation like the situation created by the foreign traders in Bergen, Norway, and other cities. The oldest city law in the North, adopted by Stockholm and other cities after about 1254, was known as Bjärköarätten or the Birka Law, and the degree to which the name and the content of the law stem from Birka, the town, is a puzzling question. For the odd fact is that *björk* meant birch and *bjärk* meant commerce and that each could be Latinized to *birk* (cf. *birkarlar*, the earliest traders to the far north).[19] In any case this Birka Code contained much maritime law and was mostly indigenous Swedish law, dealing with salt, meat, and herring, with Scandinavian ports and the rights of kings. Quite unlike the Birka Statute was the Sea Code of Visby, copied after German and French prototypes, which was useful for the far-trading merchants of that Baltic port and which significantly illustrated the penchant of the Swedes for adapting to their own uses the institutions — even the laws — of other peoples. Borrowing was greater in laws regarding commerce and property, much less in fields such as family and criminal law. The kings, as early as Birger Jarl, eagerly applied the sanctions of Roman law when seeking justification for executing and dispossessing traitors.[20]

Olaus Petri, the reformer, during the sixteenth century nation-building under Gustav Vasa introduced no new legal philosophy in his rules for judges (*Domareregler*), as Professor Ernst Ekman has pointed out, nor did he apply Roman and other foreign concepts to an incompatible situation. The Swedish legal tradition had long breathed the same spirit as Roman law, and Olaus merely expressed and fortified this and injected a strongly Christian moral tone. His rules for judges, still reprinted in each annual edition of *Sveriges Rikes Lag*, combine the best of several traditions and provide a foundation of principle for the work of the courts. The rules begin: "A judge shall first consider that he is the agent of God and the office which he holds belongs to God and not to him personally." There are quotations from the Swedish provincial laws, such as that "The advice of honorable men shall be heard," and from the Jutland law that "On law shall the land be built." Cicero is quoted repeatedly, or paraphrased, as in the dictum that "the good of the common man is the supreme law." Olaus went to Roman law for the idea that "the intent of all punishment ought to be improvement," a thought which he stressed again and again. He approved the practice of fixing fines in terms of ordinary property ownership or daily income — "he who lacks a sow pays with a cow" and, as is obvious, he loved alliteration and the poetic phrase, as he found them in the oral tradition. An important point was that the decisions should not be handed down for the sake of revenue from fines — "all law is established for justice and cause and not for the sake of money." [21]

The total body of law and the system through which it was developed and applied represent one of the great achievements of the older Scandinavian society. The German legal historian, K. von Amira, has said of the Swedish provincial codes: "They mark the high point of a development where such a balance was reached between juridical knowledge on the one side and popular concept of justice on the other, such a complete agreement between the two, that its like is not to be found in the whole world's history of justice." [22]

The organization of the courts probably changed but slightly under the impact of Christianity. *Fjärding Things* (one fourth of a härad) handled petty matters, but the most important lower court was the weekly härad's *Thing* presided over by the *häradshövding* (chief) who was assisted by two judges and "the twelve," a kind of jury who decided matters of fact and declared guilt or innocence. The twelve, called the *nämnd*, became a permanent part of the court and thus somewhat different from the Anglo-Saxon jury. Appeals could be taken to the *landsthing*, which was made up of magnates and men from the *härad(s)* and served as both court and legislative body. It met probably once a year to make new laws as well as to interpret and apply the old. Here at the level of the *land* was the vital point in the legal structure, though appeals might be carried to the king. The lawman of the *land* collected fines, determined the need for extra sessions — all this as well as being responsible for remembering the law.

Districts smaller than the *land* had not enjoyed autonomous existence for many centuries, but their organization showed a carefully arranged hierarchy of authority and responsibility related directly to the needs of the Viking fleet. Next below the *land* was the *härad* (called "hundred" in Uppland, but *härad* is the Gothic term which has survived). The *härad* or hundred was the unit that provided one ship (later two ships) for the *ledung*; when the fleet ceased to sail each year the obligation was transformed into taxes, first in kind and then in money. In time each *härad* was divided into halves, fourths, eighths, twelfths and *hamnor*. The *hamna* (literally "port") was the ultimate subdistrict responsible for equipping one man for the fleet. The smallest district significant for other purposes was the *tolfte* (twelfth), composed of a few *hamnor* and consisting ideally (perhaps at one period actually) of ten free farmers (*bönder*) together with their families and slaves. A *härad* or hundred made up of twelve *tolfte* could be reckoned as having 120 farmers, and Uppland with its twenty-two hundreds thus should have 2,640 farmers.[23] (This cannot tell us much about the total population, for it gives no clue to the number of thralls and other members of each household, and of course changes occurred as the population increased and pushed into the new coastal areas and the cleared forest land). In pagan times the *tolfte* was a cult district that was larger than the family, and it ordinarily became the parish when Christianity was introduced. This systematic organization of the smallest units of society, pyramided in hierarchical fashion up to the state level, joins with the emphasis on law as another facet of the people's penchant for order.

It would be difficult to overestimate the importance of the traditional law and the judicial and administrative organization; these provided stable institutions in a chaotic period. Sometimes a king such as Gustav Vasa would later take a high-handed attitude. Once he said frankly: "Need modifies law, not only men's law, but occasionally God's law."[24] But the noteworthy thing is that such attitudes were rarely expressed, for most kings of the Middle Ages lacked the strength to oppose the peoples' conservatism and sense of right. Change had first to be sanctified by legislative agreement, and it was not forgotten that kings might be thrown into the well.

New constitutions were formulated for changing times, as the pendulum of power swung from aristocracy to king, back again to aristocracy, and at last to an elected kingship that came under increasing constitutional controls. The laws of everyday life, distinct from the framework of government, maintained more permanent forms. The code of 1734 retained much that was centuries old, and some of the code is retained in the law of the twentieth century.

A deep respect for law-ordered living has long pervaded Swedish society. The law book and the Bible are the two books commonly found in a Swedish home, and often the law book gathers less dust than the Bible. It is noteworthy that respect is for principle rather than for specific laws. Laws are recognized as living, flexible things that must be modified to meet changing conditions.

We might sum up this tenacious tradition of a society based on law in a few brief statements:

It is pragmatic, within a framework of ideology.

It is secular, though imbued with moral compulsions and affected by Christian law and practice.

It recognizes the necessity for flexibility and change and is based on reason rather than on precedent. (There is no principle of *stare decisis*). Change was determined in the Middle Ages not so much by kings as by lawmen and magnates; in recent times it is determined by legal experts and democratic representatives.

It emphasizes the legal basis of interpersonal relationships and the necessity for law-bound order in the society as a whole.

The ancient emphasis on justice for the individual persists, along with the attempt to reconcile the interests of the person and the community.

## Kingly Chaos

The sequential story of Sweden's medieval kings is confusing and scarcely edifying. In the dreary record of the kings in the first period, from the mid-eleventh century to 1397, many suffered exile for at least a portion of their reigns, several obtained the title before reaching six years of age, others died of illness or by the axe before attaining an age beyond thirty, and at least fifteen kings or hopeful heirs were murdered or died battling for office. The two leading families of the twelfth and thirteenth centuries, the Sverkers and the Eriks, died out by 1250; four members of the two families alternated in brief and troubled reigns. (See list of rulers at the beginning of this chapter.) Twice or thrice two pairs of brothers were set up as joint kings. Sons were either too few, making succession dubious, or too many, threatening the kingdom with division. The marvel is that the state proved viable.

The meagerness of surviving records makes it possible to explain only tentatively the dynastic strife of the twelfth through thirteenth centuries. The continued trouble was occasioned partly by the dying out (by 1066) of the long-respected Yngling line of kings and partly by the tensions over the acceptance of Christianity. Regional rivalries doubtless added their own complications, as did the personal ambitions of men. The dual nature of the kingdom no longer mattered but was perpetuated in the title "Rex Sveorum et Gothorum" (given to Karl Sverkersson in a letter from the pope in 1161 and used in its Swedish form by Magnus Ladulås in 1275 when he styled himself "Sveriges och Götes Konung").

By the early thirteenth century some of the forces behind conflict began to be understandable, at least if we accept the well-reasoned conjectures of Erik Lönnroth.[25] The weakness of the kings and the rapidity of their succession made it possible for a party of Uppland nobles to dominate the kingdom. These aristocratic chieftains called themselves Christians, but their loyalties and their interests were with the ways of the "Old Svitiod." They insisted on the right of the "folk" through the Things to elect the king and to depose him; they wrote into law the right of popular election of bishops, to be followed with investiture by the king. The papacy and its local representatives in Sweden denounced both these demands, supported claimants to the throne on the basis of inheritance only, and of course refused to accept either popular choice of bishops or their royal investiture (although this system had been sanctioned in the law of Västergötland). The nobles also clashed with the church authorities concerning conquest across the Baltic; the church tried to channel conquest into religious crusading, which remained nevertheless primarily military and economic. The opposition to royal power was strong, as was the resistance to foreign interference. The real power in Sweden in the early thirteenth century was obviously held by the warrior upper class representing the old traditions and led by the great lawman Eskil. The position of the Uppland magnates was strengthened because their interest in foreign campaigning and trade also attracted the support of the commonalty. On the eastern shores of the Baltic lay booty and profit for many; there the Uppland Swedes could fight for their outposts in rivalry with the Gotlanders and the Germans; there the Swedes could carry on the Viking tradition under the banner of Christianity. The merchants of Sigtuna, the land-owning sailors, the young adventurers — all had a stake in maintaining the old customs of raiding and plunder.

Yet the forces of change were persistent. The will of the church might be thwarted again and again but the church remained and continued to exert pressures. The establishment of its influence in Denmark, Norway, and Germany made the continuance of the old order in Sweden increasingly difficult. The church was always there to lend a helping hand to any ally against its opponents. Hence, during the 1230s and the 1240s the balance of power shifted, and by about 1250 a kind of amalgamation of forces occurred. The process was aided, as is so often the case, by a man of extraordinary ability and adaptability, the great jarl, Birger.

Birger Jarl, though he never held the title of king, was the most constructive ruler of this three-century period. He was the last in a succession of able "mayors of the palace," and he was perhaps both last and first of the Folkungs,[26] founder of a new dynasty. Birger became jarl in the late 1240s and carried out part of the duties of his office by leading a crusade to Finland. While he was there King Erik Eriksson (the Lisper and Lame), the last of his line, died. But Birger had married Erik's sister, and their infant son Valdemar was chosen as king. Since Birger was himself descended from the Sverkers, little Valdemar was heir to both lines. (The situation was similar to that in England after the Wars of the Roses, when York and Lancaster were replaced with Tudor.)

Hence Birger Jarl came home from Finland to find himself regent and king *de facto*. He quickly defeated and slaughtered other contenders for the throne (at Herrevads Bridge in 1251), and for sixteen years he ruled Sweden with firmness. To his neighbors he held out a friendly hand. He entered into concert with Norway and arranged for his daughter Rikissa to marry the Norwegian heir Håkon Håkonsson. He met his neighbor kings in three-way negotiations (in 1254 and in 1257) and got his son Valdemar married to the Danish princess Sofia (in 1260). In 1261 he topped the family alliance structure by appearing in Danish waters with his fleet and by wedding Mechtild, widow of the Danish king Abel. This was all a farsighted program designed to forge bonds of unity that would strengthen the north against the threat from the south. Out of necessity but with caution Birger had made a treaty with Lübeck and later with Hamburg, but nevertheless he feared the Germans. He tried unsuccessfully to bolster his position vis-à-vis the aggressive southerners by a commercial agreement with Henry III of England. It was Birger who saw the strategic and economic potential of the Stockholm site. He took advantage of the upsurgence of the land that narrowed the water passages, and there at the meeting of Lake Mälar's waters with the Baltic he built both port and city. For Birger Jarl the city served as a useful base of power against the restless, frequently rebellious inland.

In his domestic policy Birger Jarl worked steadily to centralize power. When he settled with the defeated rebels at the beginning of his rule, he forced on them the permanent commutation of the old ship's service into taxes. He worked in cooperation with the church. He enhanced both defense and internal order by his "King's oath" laws which doubled penalties for crimes against women, the church, the Thing, and the home, and he discouraged the practice of personal revenge. He proclaimed the end of ordeal by iron and liberalized the laws of inheritance for women in line with Danish custom: one-third for women, two-thirds for men; an exception was the equal distribution agreement for the cities, by treaty and according to German law. On one important matter Birger Jarl may have been over influenced by foreign example: he attempted to provide for all his four sons by making three of them dukes over different parts of the kingdom, answerable in a vaguely feudal manner to the oldest son, who served as king. Had firstborn Valdemar been strong, a useful precedent might thus have been established. But Valdemar was too weak to maintain the preeminence of his birthright, and the nature of the monarchy was beclouded and would be argued in blood throughout the Folkung period (1250–1387) and on to the time of Gustav Vasa. In the meantime no clear feudal relationships were created, and the old indecision remained concerning the extent to which the kingship was hereditary or elective.

When Valdemar assumed full responsibility on his father's death in 1266, he was married, but still a boy, and obviously lacked both interest and skill in politics. He achieved nothing constructive and did not keep his agreement with his brothers. His first big mistake was an extramarital affair in which he had a child by his frivolous queen's even more frivolous sister, a postulant nun who had left her Danish convent to visit her sister at the Swedish court.

To win forgiveness Valdemar made a pilgrimage to Rome where he allowed the Pope to inveigle him into making disastrous concessions: he declared he had no lord but the Pope, that Peter's Pence was like a feudal contribution, and that Sweden was responsible for the tax to Rome. This gave his three brothers the excuse to rebel, and they got aid from the Danish king. By 1275 Magnus, the next in line, had made himself king. Brother Erik soon died, and brother Bengt became duke of Finland. Valdemar was defeated in battle and fled to Norway, then returned and continued to intrigue, encouraged by Norwegian and Danish support. But Magnus had the strength and the shrewdness to hang on.

Magnus was endowed with something of the ambition and the ability of his father Birger Jarl. He won the support of the church and made new treaties with Riga and Lübeck. Although he strengthened the privileges of German and Swedish merchants in Visby, he blocked that city's attempt to control the whole island of Gotland. He extended the tax immunities granted for church lands and skillfully used the church, which had become the prop of royal power, as a balance against the nobility. He succeeded in reestablishing good relations with Denmark and won King Erik Glipping's daughter for his son Birger. He later arranged also for the marriage of his daughter Ingeborg to King Erik Menved of Denmark. Magnus himself married the daughter of Count Gerhard of Holstein. He had a goodly stock of female relatives, and he used this advantage shrewdly; he married them into the families of the internal opposition. But there were not quite enough brides to go around, and he had to execute three rebels.

Magnus did imposing work in internal administration, using patterns from abroad — especially the German city-state pattern — to update the Swedish system. The institution of the council came to have great importance for both the cities and the state. In the 1280s a council of twelve, plus a royal observer, was created for Jönköping. Magnus emphasized royal justice as paramount, and he also went along with the church in urging codification of the various *land* laws. While he systematized practices and extended royal authority, he used the representative institutions of council and *landsting* to approve changes. As an example, he got first the royal council (in 1281) and then the Skänninge meeting of magnates (in 1284) to promise to accept his son Birger as king and Erik as duke upon his own death. The council was largely composed of high prelates and lawmen, and significantly it included three foreigners: two Germans and one Dane. Although the title of jarl had disappeared, that of *hertig* (duke) took its place, and new royal offices were created: *drots*,[27] *kansler* (chancellor), and *marsk* (marshal). It was in Magnus's reign that knighthood and the privileged *frälse* came into being (see p. 57), making Sweden a status society with sharp gradations between ranks.

In his fifteen years at the helm of the ship of state Magnus Ladulås set his sails purposefully to catch the winds of influence from the south. He ran a trim ship and tried to set a well-charted course for the future. But after he died in 1290, the ship foundered for a generation in stormy seas.

The new king, Birger (1280–1321), was only ten years old when he succeeded to the throne; he had two younger brothers, Erik and Valdemar. Regent was the marshal Torgils Knutsson, who was both able and respected and who carried on successful campaigning in Finland. In 1293 Torgils built there the key fortress of Viborg, which would long stand as the guardian of the boundary against Russia and the mistress of the trade routes from the west. On a later expedition he built a fort still farther east on Lake Ladoga, but this outpost was too distant and was razed by the Russians only a year after its completion. Torgils's activities laid the foundations for the Peace of Nöteborg (1323) by which Russia agreed to a favorable but vague and long-disputed boundary (see map). At home the only significant change was a stricter policy toward the church, including the futile attempt to require military service of the tax-exempt clergy.

The story of the first two decades of the fourteenth century is illuminating only because it evidenced in microcosm the perennial problems of medieval Sweden and its northern neighbors. Birger married the Danish princess Märta (Margareta). When Birger was crowned in 1302 Erik was named Duke of Sweden and Valdemar Duke of Finland, an arrangement which encouraged rivalries and threatened a split in the kingdom. In the triangular jostling for position among the Scandinavian states, Birger sided first with Norway, then swung back to his wife's country, Denmark. Erik was the shrewdest if not the most unscrupulous of the brothers, and apparently his influence over Valdemar was complete.

The two dukes repeatedly rebelled against their brother, then combined with him to get rid of Torgils Knutsson, who stood for stability. Valdemar married and then divorced Torgils's daughter, and the three brothers together had Torgils executed in 1306. Then the dukes could deal with Birger, whom they promptly imprisoned with his queen. Erik Menved of Denmark tried to help Birger, and Håkon of Norway helped the dukes, as did Erik Menved's rebellious brother Kristofer. When Håkon wavered in his support, Erik retaliated by canceling his engagement with the Norwegian princess Ingeborg. At length the dukes released Birger, who at once started a new campaign with Danish aid. Then came truce for a year, after which both Norway and Denmark aided Birger against the dukes. Duke Erik invaded Norway, but by 1310 changed his tactics, promised to give Håkon North Halland and Kungahälla, and thus rewon alliance with Norway and a new promise of the hand of

Ingeborg. In this complex game the princes were playing with lands and peoples the next move was a general agreement among Norway, Sweden, and Denmark, splitting the Swedish kingdom among the three brothers. With the special consent of the pope, Erik at last married the Norwegian princess Ingeborg in 1312, while Valdemar married Ingeborg Eriksdotter in a double wedding in Oslo. Then the tangle grew more complicated.

In 1316 Duke Erik and Ingeborg had a son, Magnus, and in the same year Valdemar and his Ingeborg had a son Erik. These two babies made Birger fear for the continuation in power of his line. So a new plot was hatched. Birger and Margareta enticed the two dukes to Nyköping, feasted them royally, and then imprisoned them (the Nyköping Banquet, December 10–11, 1317). This treacherous coup lost Birger the last shreds of his popularity; the people rose to support the dukes, and a national meeting in Skara in the summer of 1318 chose Mats Kettilmundsson as drots and "foreman." Mats, with the help of King Håkon of Norway, retook land and forts and drove Birger to desperation. The story has it that in anguished vengeance Birger threw the key to the princes' prison into the lake as he fought his last-ditch defense. When the popular forces recaptured the city, it was too late — the two dukes had starved to death.

Warfare, treachery, and political chaos were accentuated by crop failures, famine, and disease. Even the papal taxation was increased in these troublous years. At last things got so bad that the commoners and the aristocracy got together to restore order. Birger was forced to flee to Denmark and died there in 1321. His brothers, the dukes Erik and Valdemar, were dead because of his treachery. His son Magnus (Birgersson) was executed in 1320. All that remained of the line were the two infant sons of the dukes and their scheming, widowed mothers.

When the Norwegian King Håkon died in 1319, three-year-old Magnus Eriksson became, by inheritance, king of Norway. In July of the same year he was elected king of Sweden at Mora Meadow, where commons and magnates were all represented. When the regent Mats Kettilmundsson lifted little Magnus in his arms and presented him to the assemblage of nobles and freemen, hopes were reborn. At that same meeting a charter was granted assuring the nobility recognition of their rights and promising the commoners that any new taxes would be determined by the council, in consultation with representatives of the people in various parts of the kingdom, and administered by a commission for each bishopric. Careful arrangements were also entered into with Norway providing that during the king's minority he should spend alternate years in each of his two kingdoms. Another tragic epoch had ended with a fair promise of better things to come.

## Magnus Eriksson (1316–74; king, 1319–64)

The early years of Magnus Eriksson's reign seemed to fulfill the happy promise of peace and prosperity in both realms. The intrigues of the boy-king's mother and her favorite Knut Porse created only minor problems and were ended by 1330. Only a generation later was it realized how fateful was her arrangement of marriage for her daughter Eufemia, young Magnus's sister, to Albrekt of Mecklenburg. One of the few documents surviving from this hopeful period is a book of instructions on how to be a king, compiled for Magnus probably by Bishop Filip of Linköping, who had been influenced by his studies in Paris.[28] More original was the *Rhymed Chronicle*, or *Erik's Chronicle*, a long and artistically composed historical poem which remains the chief source of knowledge about state affairs from Birger Jarl's time to Magnus Eriksson's. This dramatic saga-poem was well designed to inspire a young ruler to emulate the idealized characters of Birger Jarl, Magnus Ladulås, Mats Kettilmundsson, and especially Duke Erik.[29]

Opportunity for adventure offered itself easily, for Denmark was suffering a period of disintegration following the death of Erik Menved in 1320. Weak Kristofer of Denmark had to divide and mortgage his lands, including Denmark's eastern provinces of Skåne and Blekinge. The administrator in Skåne and Blekinge, Johan of Holstein, was harsh and unpopular, and the local nobility begged Magnus to take over the rule. Sweden thereupon agreed to buy out Johan for 34,000 marks. For this productive region with some 350,000 inhabitants the price may have been fair enough — but how could Sweden raise it? It was useless to try to obtain funds from the poorer northern region, and to increase the tax levies on the fisheries in Öresund or the prosperous international fairs would be dangerous both politically and economically, arousing antagonism in the Hanseatic cities. Already the Germans were worried because Magnus and his mother had gotten control of Copenhagen and thus put Sweden astride the Sound. In time all might have been worked out, but there was no time, for Denmark would not stay down.

By 1340 Denmark had a new and unusually able king, Valdemar, who was to be nicknamed Atterdag (Day-again) for his genius in restoring the state. Valdemar recovered Copenhagen after a brief struggle but felt it necessary to recognize Magnus Eriksson's possession of all the former Danish lands east of the Sound — Skåne, Halland, and Blekinge — by the treaty of Varberg (1343). These southern provinces were constant objects of contention, but for the moment everything looked so peaceful that the king of Sweden-Norway, inspired by family considerations rather than by empire building, arranged to divide the kingdoms he ruled jointly. Magnus Eriksson had married Blanche of Namur, and they had two infant sons with the well-known names of Erik and Håkon. The younger, Håkon, was made king of Norway; he would take over the rule when he came of age in 1355. Erik was named king of Sweden and Skåne; he would take over only on the death of his father (the Varberg agreement of 1343). Such agreements raise questions: Was it necessary or wise to divide the kingdoms while the princes were minors? Was it impossible at that time to build a united kingdom of Sweden and Norway? And if Sweden and Norway were considered to be divided by geography and culture, what about Sweden and Skåne, which were supposed to remain united?

Certainly Sweden could use the fertile lands of Skåne and Blekinge and the close ties of this region with the continent. Yet there were complications in this new relationship. For one thing, the densely wooded borderland between Skåne and Småland was a natural as well as a historical barrier. For another, the archbishop of Lund and the great landholders of Skåne, for all their onetime eagerness to escape from Denmark's anarchy into the arms of Sweden, still held estates and other interests across the Sound in the Danish islands and in Copenhagen. Lund in Skåne was the great city of the whole area and the ecclesiastical headquarters for all Denmark. Skåne's ties of culture and trade were to the Danish west and not to the Swedish north. This seedbed of trouble was cultivated by Valdemar Atterdag.

Adventure beckoned also in the East. The Swedish merchants and magnates could not remain satisfied with the Peace of Nöteborg, and in the 1340s they demanded protection of their trade route through the Gulf of Finland and a new crusading expedition to eastern Finland. Magnus Eriksson himself went to Estonia, and the Swedes proclaimed a blockade on trade with Novgorod. This activity plus the Swedish control of Skåne irritated the Hanseats. However, Swedish expansion was checked by a combination of factors: the severe financial difficulties involved mortgaging of lands, customs duties, and a tax burden so heavy that the king had to issue a public letter of apology. The devastation of the Black Death in the late 1340s reduced the Swedish population by about one-third and sapped the energy of the people. The situation brought to a head the conflict between the king and the aristocracy and between the principles of monarchic power and government by the nobility.

Magnus Eriksson's difficulties accumulated with the years. Birgitta (of whom more later) was in this period at the height of her influence. She had been for a time chief lady at the court of the young Magnus and his bride Blanche and had denounced the king for his immoral life as well as for his policies. Royal financial policy created the sharpest discontent. The burden of the Skåne purchase was augmented by the practice among the *frälse* (the privileged nobility) of bringing taxable lands under their tax-free umbrella. The king tried to check this erosion of the finances by limiting the tax exemptions to those who bore arms, according to the original intent. But the *frälse* took their privileges for granted and forgot their obligations. The church, too, resented the governmental hand interfering with its tax-free privileges. Even Magnus's son Erik grew restless. Both Erik and the aristocratic landholding class had ample reason to detest and fear the growing power of the court favorite, Bengt Algotsson ("the devil's servant," according to Birgitta), who was made duke of Finland and Halland in 1343 as well as viceroy in Skåne. It was natural that all these discontents should find each other and ally, and the combination spelled trouble for Magnus. Especially so because off in the wings, alert to every nuance of the play, the Hansa cities watched with eager eyes, and Valdemar of Denmark awaited his cue to enter.

The breaking point came in 1356. Magnus had turned over Norway to his son Håkon. The other son, Erik, decided he could not wait for his inheritance and joined the rebellious magnates against his father and the hated duke Bengt Algotsson. Erik died in 1359, but in the meantime Magnus had made an alliance with Valdemar of Denmark. When Magnus was then reconciled with the magnates, they forced him to renounce his alliance with the Danish king. Valdemar thereupon invaded Skåne and pounced upon Gotland in 1361, an attack that inaugurated three centuries of turmoil.

Gotland was an idyllic island in the midst of the Baltic Sea, lying athwart natural trade routes between east and west. Its farmers were also fishermen and traders moving freely around the Baltic. The treasure they accumulated is evidenced by the modern discoveries of buried caches all around the island: thousands of coins from Byzantium, the Arab lands, England — more than have been found in all the rest of the North. From the early Viking period on through the twelfth and thirteenth centuries, Gotland's age of glory, trade was conducted out of many small ports, for many were deep enough to handle the shallow-draft open boats of the day which were only forty-three to sixty-two feet in length. Gradually Västergarn and Visby, and especially Visby with its larger and deeper harbor, attained preeminence. Visby became one of the chief cities of the Hanseatic League and a distributing point for goods all the way from Bruges to Novgorod, where Gotland had its own factory. Visby attracted large numbers of foreign merchants, especially Germans; some settled permanently, and some were only temporary residents. Each group was so large that it had its own merchant guild. As both city and island prospered, more than ninety churches were built, and because of Gotland's quantity of limestone the churches were built of stone while those of the mainland were still built mostly in wood.

To protect its well-stocked warehouses from the constant threat of plunderers Visby constructed a great wall in the thirteenth century, about a mile long on the side of the sea and a mile and a half long on the land side. It was completed about 1288 and was added to from time to time thereafter. It still stands (though lacking a few of its fifty-five towers), a lasting monument to its masons, to the power and wealth of the city, and to the merchant sailors of Sweden and the Hansa who braved the Baltic for goods and gain. It is rivaled in Europe only by the city wall of Carcassone in France.

At the time of Valdemar's invasion in 1361, the wall discouraged attack against the city itself, and the citizens were able to buy their safety by paying a huge ransom. Outside the walls the Danish army literally slaughtered the islanders' last peasant army, eighteen hundred of whom were buried in their makeshift armor in mass graves where they fell. The city's soldiery looked on from their battlements, because city and countryside had long been at odds. For Valdemar the victory was important, but most of the loot he took from the city was lost when his fleet was destroyed in a storm on the voyage home.

Visby and Gotland lived on, but their days of glory were gone. Overlord-ship of Gotland, whose symbol was the lamb, was hotly disputed between Danes and Swedes, and actual power shifted from one ruthless adventurer to another — the Victual Brothers, Erik of Pomerania in his exile, Ivar Axelsson, Sören Norby. During the prolonged period of strife over the union early in the fifteenth century Erik of Pomerania built the fortress of Visborg in the southwest corner of the city wall, and it proved to be impregnable to military attack. Repeatedly it served as a base for pirates who ravaged the Baltic trade routes. The chaos of northern political strife was epitomized and exaggerated in this once idyllic island. At last the Lübeckers could no longer tolerate the harassment of their commerce and in 1525 they attacked Visby, plundered it, and burned a portion. They could not take the castle of Visborg, but they did succeed in reestablishing the legitimate authority of the king of Denmark. Hence it was that the Danes remained until the peace of Brömsebro in 1645 forced them to yield Gotland to Sweden. In the war of 1675–79 they retook control but had to depart in 1679. As they did so they blew up Vis-borg.[30] But this digression to Gotland has carried us away from the main story.

In the rough and tumble of the fourteenth century nothing was stable. Magnus Eriksson was seemingly a man of good intent, as his codification of the laws for the entire country would imply. But he could not control the ambitious magnates or hold his own sons in line. After Erik's death in 1359 the other son, Håkon of Norway, joined the magnates against his father, but these allies abandoned him when he married the daughter of Valdemar Atter-dag. The next move of the rebels was to offer the crown in 1363 to Magnus's nephew, Albrekt of Mecklenburg, the son of Magnus's sister Eufemia. Here was a great opportunity for the Germans. Not only the twenty-year-old Al-brekt, but also his father Duke Albrekt, came to Sweden with alacrity, bring-ing the Mecklenburg fleet and a host of German retainers, soldiers, and adventurers.

The Germans seized in their harsh grip not only the kingship but also estates and provinces throughout the kingdom. The Swedish nobility fought for the Mecklenburgers against the stubborn resistance of Magnus and Håkon (now reconciled with his father), and only gradually did they come to understand the disaster they had invited in with the foreign rulers. In 1366 Albrekt even made a secret treaty with Valdemar of Denmark promising him Gotland and parts of Småland and Västergötland.

The Mecklenburgers were not the only Germans rampaging through the North. The Hanseatic cities had been severely stung by Valdemar's conquest of Visby and the Skåne fisheries, and in 1367 they combined to destroy him. In two years of war the Hansa fleet forced Copenhagen to capitulate, and Valdemar had to accept a humiliating peace at Stralsund in 1370, the highwater mark of Hanseatic power. Though Albrekt tried to gain control of Skåne, the Hanseats prevented this and obtained for themselves the rights (for fifteen years) to the forts of the western coast and the tax collections there. Hansa aid in supplying the Mecklenburgers had been essential for the Albrekts in gaining the kingship, but the merchant cities were then careful to try to hold their own gains.

Hatred against Albrekt's rule increased, especially among the common people but also among the nobility. Håkon came in from Norway, gained support along the way, and with a large force reached the gates of Stockholm. However, still many of the magnates would not have the Folkungs back, and instead of completely overthrowing Albrekt, a compromise was reached in 1371. One of the most powerful nobles in the kingdom, Bo Jonsson Grip, took the lead. Albrekt kept the kingship, but he admitted that his rule had been disastrous for Sweden, gave up to the council all the forts and districts held by him and his father, which in the future should be assigned only to native Swedish men, and he promised to accept the advice of the council on all important matters. The men of the council included the archbishop and bishops and twelve temporal magnates.

Magnus Eriksson, a prisoner of the Mecklenburgers since 1365, was released from custody and given three provinces (Dalsland, Värmland, Västergötland) to administer. Three years later (1374) he died in a ship wreck. His son Håkon died in 1380 and his grandson Olav in 1387. With Olav died not only the Folkungs in Sweden but also the long line of Norwegian kings from Harald Fairhair.

The magnates of Sweden now held power, though they did not know how to govern. They were held together only by their opposition to Albrekt's feeble struggling and his attempts to curtail their tax privileges. Bo Jonsson Grip was shrewdest and strongest among them. During this epoch of dissolution he acquired the title of drots, and he accumulated vast holdings, much of them on borrowed capital. Part of his acquisitions were personal, part were for the common account of the council of the realm. He was lawman in Finland and Östergötland, *härad*'s chief (sheriff) in several *härads*; he held some ten forts and administered Finland, Södermanland, Dalarna, and eastern Götaland; he bought up the mortgages held by the king's father, and by an irresistible variety of methods got possession of several thousand farms scattered throughout the kingdom. He died in 1386, to Albrekt's relief. But even in death the farsighted drots thwarted the king. He left his properties under the control of ten executors, all of whom were Swedish born and had to choose Swedish successors. Much of his estate went to repay loans, but he left the beginnings of a notable monument in what was to become the great castle of Gripsholm, named for the *grip* (griffin) in the family coat of arms. To get control over the recalcitrant executors, Albrekt sought to redeem some of the properties that had become tax-free. Again he only united the *frälse* more determinedly against him. They at last swallowed their pride and their doubts and sought an agreement with Margareta, widow of Håkon, and her seventeen-year-old son Olav.

The century and a half from Birger Jarl to Margareta was an era of increasing pressure from Germany and from Denmark, within a pattern of crisscross strife between church and state, nobles versus kings, and royal brothers against one another. Magnus Eriksson's rule over both Norway and Sweden offered prospects of a united North with economic and political opportunity. But Magnus Eriksson was neither wise enough nor strong enough to retain his vast domains in the face of expansionist Germans and Danes, ambitious sons, and squabbling nobles. While the farmers sought to tend their fields, the nobles and the kings quarreled for power, and the Germans, both princes and merchants, only enhanced the chaos. Underlying the chaos and the clash of personalities lay a fundamental constitutional conflict between the principles of monarchy and the principles of aristocracy or oligarchy. Two extraordinary women, one a pious advocate of aristocracy, the other a shrewd and strong ruler of people, tried to point the way back to order.

### The Holy Birgitta [31]

The crises of the fourteenth century revealed that many men were not equal to the tasks confronting them; the same events gave opportunity to two women: the Holy Birgitta and Queen Margareta. Oddly enough it was not only in the North that women came to the fore, but also in other parts of Europe: Catherine of Siena, queens Johanna I and Johanna II of Naples, Maria of Hungary, Jadviga of Poland, and, a little later, Joan of Arc.

Birgitta was born in 1303 at Finsta in Uppland, seat of one of the great families of Sweden. Her father was a lawman or judge, as was her brother, and her mother belonged to the family of the Folkungs. Yet life was simple and hard even in such a household. Finsta was a collection of wooden buildings, with one large house where the family gathered around a flaming fire in the evenings for sewing and talking politics and listening to a sermon by the house chaplain. Then they retired to their sleeping chambers, cold and empty rooms furnished only with beds, wooden chairs, and a praying desk. In such an environment Birgitta's youthful fantasy and religious passion developed. At the age of seven she had the first of her revelations — visions of the Virgin Mary and of Christ, soon also flashes of insight on problems of the day. But she was not left free to become a mystic.

At the age of thirteen Birgitta was married against her will to an eighteen-year-old nobleman, Ulf Gudmarsson, and moved to his manor. He became a knight and soon a judge in Närke, while she led the life of a wife and mother of the aristocracy. For a time she was at Magnus Eriksson's court as mistress of the robes for the queen, Blanche of Namur. The pious young matron was shocked by the life she saw around her, and her visions began to relate to politics and the royal family. Legend has it that she did not hesitate to tell King Magnus Eriksson that if he did not lead a better life he would not remain a king, not live long on this earth, and not bear any sons.[32]

Sometime during the 1330s Birgitta and her husband made a pilgrimage to Nidaros in Norway. Although Ulf was not a pious man, he was affected by his wife's fervor, and in 1341 he was converted. Then the couple made a pilgrimage to Santiago di Compostella in Spain, and Birgitta had a chance to learn something of the Continent, of a poverty there that was worse than the simplicity of Sweden, and of the shameful state of the church, with the pope living in Avignon in subservience to the French king instead of in Rome as vicar of Christ. On the journey Ulf took ill, and in 1344 he died. Birgitta's six children had begun to grow up, she herself was just over forty years old, and the possibilities of a new life opened before her.

Birgitta threw away Ulf's ring, freed herself of the cares of this life, and decided to devote her energy and her spiritual and literary powers to following the injunctions given her from above. No longer was her reforming zeal confined to her home and the court of Sweden, but it grew into an enthusiasm for the whole world, for the church as an institution standing for world unity, for the Kingdom of God. To lift herself above her own will, to live only for God, she sought guidance in her revelations. These revelations came to deal with a great variety of personal affairs, but especially with the political and religious issues of the day; some were expressed in beautifully poetic style. Written in Latin and known as *Revelationes celestes*, they were widely circulated at the time, and as edited by her confessor they comprised eight volumes. Guided by her own revelations Birgitta journeyed to Rome in 1349 and lived there until her death in 1373, gathering about her a devoted circle, including her daughter Katarina.

She worked persistently for the establishment of her order and for the return of the pope to Rome, which he did in 1367 (for three years). While in Rome Pope Urban V approved the foundation of the Bridgittine Order (within the Augustinian Order). One of the special features of the order was the cooperation in one establishment of monks and nuns, both using a common church and helping one another in their work. Each community was to consist of sixty nuns, thirteen priests, four deacons, and eight lay brothers. In worldly matters the abbess was to be supreme authority, and this female superiority was to cause controversy and eventually rejection of the system. The order grew rapidly for a few decades, spreading over most of western Europe and numbering over eighty convents; the few that remain in the twentieth century are for nuns only. The chief center of the order was created in Vadstena where Magnus Eriksson had donated a royal manor and where cloister construction had begun in 1369, along with a church ordered by Birgitta to be "plain, humble, and strong." Birgitta was canonized in 1391. She was by far the most widely known and the most cosmopolitan Swede up to her time.

Saint Birgitta was a rare combination of humility and will to power, of mysticism and sense of reality, of contemplation and activism, of piety and worldliness. Her monument is the order she created, but her literary production was also significant. The effect she had on the social attitude toward women and on women's attitude toward themselves was profound, yet impossible to measure. She was one of the exceptional figures of her day. Even so, it may be that her greatest practical importance was indirect, through the influence of her daughter Maereta on Queen Margareta, second of these outstanding Scandinavian women.[33]

## Margareta and the Union of Kalmar

Margareta was born in 1353 while her father Valdemar Atterdag was fighting to rebuild the kingdom of Denmark. He was a shrewd, far-sighted ruler, who had spent part of his exiled youth at the court of the Wittelsbachs in Germany and thus gained something of a European view. Valdemar was concerned with the expansion of his own power, traditional boundaries meant little to him, and he might have been puzzled by the suggestion of "national feeling." Margareta learned her first politics from him, and soon she began to learn more. She had been pledged in marriage to Håkon of Norway by treaty between Valdemar and Håkon's father Magnus Eriksson; then in the whirl of the wheel of politics she was cast off. It so happened, however, that Valdemar then captured the countess who was on her way to displace Margareta as Håkon's bride, and by this high-handed means he was able to force Magnus and Håkon to honor the original contract. Since waiting was clearly unwise, the wedding took place at once, although Margareta was but ten years old.

The child-queen was sent to Norway, but for six years she lived not with her husband but in the home of Maereta, daughter of Ulf and Birgitta who was married now to a Norwegian magnate. In this Swedish-Norwegian home the Danish princess rounded out her education in an atmosphere of piety, discipline, and genuine Scandinavian outlook. The thoughts and activities of Birgitta, then in Rome, like the struggles of Margareta's father, King Valdemar, in Denmark against the Hansa and the Swedes must have been regular household fare. One of Maereta's brothers, Birger Ulfsson, was a leader among the magnates who in Sweden had renounced Magnus Eriksson and gone over to Albrekt (and who twenty years later was to renounce Albrekt in favor of Margareta). Maereta, an excellent mother-substitute, thus presided over an inter-Scandinavian household, detached but not indifferent, the center for the comings and goings of couriers and statesmen from all the North. Margareta had a superb opportunity to observe and to think, and she made the most of it. Unfortunately for the historian, the record of her thoughts and plans was not written down — at this time, or ever. Her personality and her mind must be read from her actions. There the record is imposing.

When Margareta was sixteen she and King Håkon set up their own home, and in 1370 the future brightened with the birth of a boy who was named Olav. But Håkon was often absent, the royal money-chest empty, and Margareta had to care for both domestic and state affairs. The Hansa, at the apex of its power, had just brought her father to his knees and held the entire North in economic shackles. Her husband and his father shifted in and out of alliance or war with each other and with her father. Beyond the borders of Scandinavia things were no calmer. The papacy, after 1378 locked in the Great Schism, yet challenged the growing assertion of monarchic control over the clergy. The lust for power was everywhere, and denunciations of the "evil lords" by Catherine of Siena and Birgitta of Sweden did little to change things.

In the fall of 1375 Valdemar Atterdag died, and Margareta had to go to Denmark. There she was able to win over the key Danish leaders and to outmaneuver the Mecklenburgers who thought they had guarantees that the Danish throne would go to a young Albrekt (grandson of both Valdemar and Duke Albrekt). Instead the indefatigable Margareta got her own young son Olav approved as the future king of Denmark. She made some shrewd deals with Danish nobles, and of course she had to give assurances to the Hansa. In the spring of 1376 when Håkon came to Denmark they both confirmed the Denmark-Hansa treaty of 1370 (the Treaty of Stralsund) — except for the clause giving the Hansa a veto on choice of successor to the throne. Then in 1380, when Olav was but ten years of age, King Håkon died, and the rule of Norway was endangered. Margareta hurried north and managed to guide events there, and by 1385, when Olav was fourteen, he was recognized as king of both Norway and Denmark.

Olav had clear title, although the direction of both kingdoms was in the now experienced hands of Margareta. Her main task was to hold off the Hansa. She could cooperate with these merchants in attempts to curb piracy and robbery, and in 1385, using the threat of Albrekt against both herself and the Hansa, she got the Hansa to yield the castles they still held in Skåne. Her other job was to thwart Albrekt in Skåne and in Sweden. Taking advantage of the increasing discontent against Albrekt among the Swedish magnates who had so long suffered him, she put forth Olav as contender for the Swedish crown. Then, on August 3, 1387, after a sudden illness, seventeen-year-old King Olav died. There was no king of Denmark or Norway, there was no direct heir, there was only Margareta.

Margareta had no claim to the throne in either Denmark or Norway, and she wisely made no claim. No woman had ever held such office in a Scandinavian country and law as well as custom was against it. For the Norwegians the proper legal heir to the throne was bungling Albrekt or, if he was passed over (and he was never seriously considered), then his nephew, another Albrekt of Mecklenburg. This was the boy who had also as good a claim as any on the Danish throne and had been promised it by Valdemar. But the Mecklenburgers were not popular in either kingdom, and Margareta had shown extraordinary ability. Perhaps it was a time to violate tradition, at least temporarily. Margareta let no time be wasted; she was already in Skåne, and one week after Olav's death the notables of Denmark met in Lund and declared her regent of Denmark. The Danes chose her as "all-powerful lady and mistress and the whole Danish Kingdom's regent." Norway was more legal about it, but the result was the same. Without the title of king, she ruled as king and won the right to name her successor. This successor, it soon became apparent, could be only her niece's son, Erik of Pomerania (born in 1381 or 1382), then about seven years old.

Swedish decisions, however, would not wait on settlements in Denmark and Norway. The death of the powerful Swedish lord Bo Jonsson Grip had precipitated new conflict between Albrekt and the nobles, for the king developed the illusion that with the strong man gone he might now really be king. He tried to take over castles and fiefs and cancel grants made to his opponents. Bo Jonsson's will had offended his German-born widow who was deprived of influence and also some of the magnates who were not chosen as executors. Further, the clergy seemed to be on King Albrekt's side. While the two groups were jockeying for position and bidding for support in the summer of 1387, both Margareta and Olav were in Skåne, and it appears they were preparing to negotiate with one or both parties of Swedes. Olav's death added a new complication. Nevertheless, by winter the executors' party among the Swedes, led by Birgitta's son and Maereta's brother Birger, was ready unreservedly to accept Margareta's leadership.

On January 5, 1388 two castles in Västergötland were placed at Margareta's disposal, and in March a series of documents was drawn up at Dalaborg in Dalsland. Margareta was hailed as "all-powerful lady and rightful mistress" [34] of the Swedish kingdom in a formula parallel to that used by the Danes and the Norwegians, and the Swedes also agreed to accept Margareta's choice as future king. Clearly Margareta was dictating the terms. Several provinces, other half-provinces, and practically all of the royal castles and forts were turned over to Margareta, and restoration was guaranteed of the expropriated holdings in Sweden of Danish and Norwegian men. On her part Margareta pledged to maintain "all the rights, freedoms and privileges" of Swedes "before King Albrekt came to Sweden," to proceed in accordance with Swedish law, to assist against all common enemies and especially King Albrekt, to guarantee to her supporters that they would regain any properties lost in Denmark or Norway and would retain their rights to their estates and mortgages, and last but not least that she would work to restore Sweden's former boundaries. [35]

The challenge rang clear, and civil war spread through Sweden. As the *Rhymed Chronicle* puts it:

> Ill stood the realm without reason:
> One brother slew another
> And sons moved against father.
> No one asked after law or right,
> For some they held to the king
> And some the queen would follow. [36]

The main armies were gathered from outside — Albrekt's from Mecklenburg and Margareta's from Denmark and Norway, with a Danish knight and a Mecklenburger (Henrik Parow) as commanders. Early in 1389 Albrekt's force landed (probably) at Kalmar and moved rapidly to relieve the besieged fortress of Axvall. The queen's forces moved in from the west but were not fast enough to cut off Albrekt's army. When he learned that they were on his heels, however, he turned to give battle and the decisive engagement was fought at Åsle (or Falan) in the flat land east of Falköping on February 24, 1389. It was a tense battle and Margareta's General Parow was killed. He had nevertheless won the victory. Both Albrekt and his son Erik were taken captive, and the Mecklenburg rule in Sweden was ended. Diehard elements held out, and not until nine years later did Margareta get possession of Stockholm. But the opposition had no effective leadership, no free claimant to the throne, and its tactics degenerated into piracy rather than war. The so-called Victual Brothers, using Stockholm and Gotland as bases, ravaged the seas and raided and burned Bergen and Malmö and other cities. But such methods were almost as hateful to the Hansa as to the queen.

With the single exception of Stockholm, castles and cities of Sweden quickly and peacefully accepted Margareta's authority. In October of 1389 at a riksdag in Söderköping she formally took over the rule of Sweden and was granted in gratitude for her help in the "great war" a one-time tax of one mark per person, in money or in kind, from bishops and knights and churches as well as from farmers and merchants. A combination of circumstances had brought the direction of affairs in all the North into the hands of one person. Law was not a factor, for both law and precedent were against it. Accidents of birth and death, the self-defeating rivalries of the aristocracy, the brutality and foreignness of Albrekt's rule in Sweden, the pressures and threats from external powers such as the Hansa — all these played their parts. But the determining positive factor in the chain of events was the patience and shrewdness of Margareta, combined with her personal magnetism, self-confidence, deep religious faith, and an aura of integrity that drew people to her and gave them assurance. A Danish chronicler expressed the feelings of many when he wrote, "God be praised to all eternity that he laid the unexpected victory in the hands of a woman, put shackles on the feet of kings and handcuffs on their nobles."[37]

Margareta overcame the political handicaps of womanhood, but she was realistic. She knew that a woman's rule could not be secure or permanent, hence she made Erik of Pomerania her successor. Already in 1389 Erik was proclaimed king in Norway. In 1390 he was recognized as the rightful heir to Sweden. Thus the combined kingdoms could continue to show a solid front against the Hansa and other external enemies. Each kingdom would continue to be governed by its own laws, as Margareta explicitly promised. Each retained its separate council, and no union institutions were established. The nobility, the clergy, and the monarchy all had inter-Scandinavian ties and interests, but no one thought of a fusing of peoples or institutions. The concept was rather of a league of common interests to preserve the local customs and authority by a pooling of resources and leadership vis-à-vis encroachments from beyond. The immediate threats were the German Hansa and the German princes backed by the Hansa. At other times there might be other threats — the papacy or Russia. Together the Scandinavian kingdoms could protect themselves, separately they not only could not defend themselves from foreign threats, but they were repeatedly enticed by foreign intrigues into warring with one another. How could their beneficial and formidable union be preserved?

One of the first evidences of cooperative action was the meeting of the councils of the three kingdoms at Lindholm in Skåne in 1395, where the treaty with the Mecklenburgers was finally agreed upon. Albrekt was to be released on a pledge that within three years he would return to prison or pay a ransom of sixty thousand silver marks; otherwise Margareta would get possession of Stockholm, which the Hansa held in trust in the meantime. Since Albrekt could not raise the ransom, in 1398 Stockholm was handed over. The victory was an all-Scandinavian one. Margareta did not push matters too fast — in fact, she may have dragged her feet just a little. But when Erik was fourteen years old, he was formally made king in Denmark in January 1396, and in Sweden he was raised on the Mora stone in July 1396. The following year on Trinity Sunday, June 17, 1397, an unprecedented conclave of the North was organized at Kalmar on Sweden's east coast: two archbishops, ten bishops, four churchmen, and some fifty nobles. Norway was sparsely represented and Finland not at all, probably because of the Victual Brothers' renewed harrying by sea, and the hardships of long land travel by horseback. However, this was the greatest Scandinavian assemblage yet held. Men were gathered to participate in the coronation of the first king of all three kingdoms of the North. And more than that, to come to agreement on the future relations between these three. For four weeks or more they negotiated, for the two documents they produced were dated July 13.

There is no record known to historians of what the discussions concerned — only the letter announcing the coronation and the union document. And the latter was not drawn on parchment and hung with seventeen seals, as the text says; it was written on paper, with corrections written over, and with ten seals not hung, but stamped on. Why only ten, and why stamped on paper instead of hung attached? Debate will doubtless continue on these questions as long as there are historians. Obviously the representatives of the three kingdoms had difficulty in attaining a common draft. The document attested by the ten seals provided that the three kingdoms "should eternally have one king and not several so that the realms will never again be divided, if God wills." If a king should die leaving sons, one of them shall be elected, but in any case the three councils must unite on that king who suits them best. Between the three realms peace shall reign and in case of attack from outside they shall help each other. In each realm the king shall govern according to law therein, and no law shall be taken from one country and applied in another. In negotiating with foreign states the king may make decisions together with the council (of whichever kingdom) he has with him. Queen Margareta shall rule over the territories she holds in each kingdom in full royal authority as long as she may live.[38]

What was it in this document that caused doubt and controversy? Was it a basic disagreement on the form of union? The paper document was sent to Oslo, and there it remained until it was taken to Copenhagen in 1425. Halvdan Koht has theorized that since only a few Norwegians were present at Kalmar, the agreement was taken to Norway to get additional signatures, and that the Norwegians then hesitated to sign it.[39] Were they averse to union, did they fear for Norwegian autonomy? Was it a point of law because the Norwegians had already arranged for a different succession in the event Erik had no offspring? Or was the sticking point not on law or union, but on the character of the kingship? "The argument at Kalmar," says Erik Lönnroth, "was between hereditary monarchy and elective, absolute against limited — not between union and national separatism."[40]

Whatever was the problem at Kalmar (and there may have been several), it is probable that neither the nature of the union nor the principles of monarchic rule were there determined in legal form. What we know is that Margareta, superb realist that she was, led the clerics and the magnates as far as she could and then, without forcing issues to a breach, calmly proceeded to function, along with Erik as co-ruler, as head of a union-in-fact. Still it had no name. Only later did historians label it, for the sake of convenience, The Union of Kalmar, and they could not agree on whether it was formed in 1389 or in 1397.

Nationalism, be it noted, played no part either positively or negatively. Nowhere in the world had the particularism of princes and provinces ripened yet into national sentiment. Opposition, such as it was, to Margareta's union, stemmed from the ambitions of the local nobility and from those who hoped to prey on weakness, not from romantic ideas of blood or linguistic brotherhood. Support for the union came from those who prized order in the community, peace, and trade. Individual kingships had failed owing to internal dissensions, external interference, and accidental deaths. Traditional customs and institutions in each country were strong and had to be preserved. These were guaranteed, and there was nothing else "national" that aroused emotional loyalty, just as the union itself attracted no emotional loyalty. It was Margareta's pragmatic solution to a practical necessity. Problems were indeed left for the future, but they were problems that could not be resolved at that time. For the moment royal authority was in the ascendant — the councils pledged fealty to King Erik and agreed to accept his decisions in assignment of fiefs and castles; the king pledged nothing. And union was a reality.

Only slowly did Erik take an important part in government; as long as Margareta lived she dominated. She traveled much between Denmark, Norway, and Sweden, always keeping her hand on the pulse of events. She taxed ruthlessly, and she regained many of the alienated crown lands from both church and nobility. She got Albrekt out of his last stronghold on Gotland, and he retired to Mecklenburg; at last, with a money payment, she even persuaded him to abdicate the Swedish throne and to apologize to the Swedish people. She won title to Gotland by a payment to the Grand Master of the Teutonic Order (1407). It was the queen who conducted the negotiations which won for Erik the hand of Philippa (1405), the daughter of Henry IV of England. She was active also in arranging marriages among the nobility of the different Scandinavian countries, so as to cement union ties. Her interest in Birgitta and her work was evidenced in donations to Vadstena and her founding of Maribo convent in Denmark, as well as in widespread charitable gifts. When Margareta died in 1412 she left the legacy of a firmly established union, of just rule, and of royal power enhanced.

For at least a moment in time the entire North acknowledged one suzerainty, all the way from Lake Ladoga in the east to Greenland in the west, from the North Cape to the Eider River. Was it a fault or only a misfortune that Margareta could not pass on her capacities to her successors?

# V

# THE FIFTEENTH CENTURY:
# THE UNION THAT FAILED

THE FIFTEENTH CENTURY (meaning here c. 1412–1520) was an era of strenuous uncertainty in the North. As in the Hundred Years War between the English and French the shape and character of the state was the crucial issue, and, as in that great conflict to the south, incipient nationalism was struggling to life. Hence one of the issues in Scandinavia was union or separatism, a separatism based on the differences in languages and institutions that had accumulated through recent centuries as the Danes, Norwegians, and Swedes had gone their individual ways. Another vital issue was: where should sovereignty lie? The Danes leaned to the idea of monarchic sovereignty, while the Swedes clung to an aristocratic constitutionalism and an elective kingship. Different principles of landholding confused relationships when lords held lands in two or three countries, with Denmark operating under a feudal system and Sweden avoiding it. Economic interests, and especially relations with the Hansa cities, continued to divide people. The personal element was prominent, too, as ambitious men strove for leadership. The rivalries between church and lay authorities became extremely bitter. This complicated interplay is the framework within which the North moved from union back to separatism.

## The Union of Mutual Frustration

Long before Margareta's death in 1412, Erik of Pomerania was king in name of all three countries (1396, 1397); hence there was no dispute over succession. Much of his policy was a continuation of Margareta's, but Erik lacked

Margareta's tact, her keen sense of the possible, and her prestige. However, to mend his political fences he went immediately to Sweden and took an elongated *Eriksgata*, traveling even as far as Viborg in Finland. He was vigorously purposeful in his attempt to hold the union together, but he provoked a strong Swedish opposition.

By 1412 the church leaders of Sweden had come into open opposition to Margareta. She had antagonized them by refusing to approve some cathedral elections of bishops; she had instead made nominations of her own and had gone to the pope to force them through. Erik and the clergy reached an agreement that the chapters would draw up lists of three nominees from which the king would then choose. This reasonable procedure soon broke down, and Erik reverted to Margareta's practice of making royal appointments and then getting papal sanction. He insisted that since the archbishop of Uppsala was a chief adviser of the king, that official must be a person on whom the king could depend — but when, for instance, this policy resulted in the appointment of the royal treasurer to the highest church office, the local clergy became wrathful.

A similar problem arose in the naming of the castellans and bailiffs for the royal strongholds. According to Swedish law these men had to be native-born, and Erik had agreed to govern by Swedish law. Margareta had put some men from the border provinces and some Danes into vital posts; Erik named some Danes, an increasing number of Germans, and even one Italian. He thus deprived the native aristocracy of jobs and power in an effort to create a clientele that was dependent on him. The only major military district still ruled by a native Swede was the one farthest east, Viborg in Finland. At the same time that Erik used foreigners increasingly as bailiffs and officials, he brought in men who had a contemptuous, continental-bred attitude toward the peasantry and who were more interested in the collection of taxes than in the long-term welfare of the people and land.

Furthermore, Erik continued the policy already begun of "reducing" to the crown those lands alienated during the time of Albrekt (see p. 216 below). Some of these properties were regained from the church, but about three-quarters of them were taken from the aristocracy. The more opposition developed to his policies of appointments and reduction, the more necessary he felt it was to enlarge the same practices. Hence bad became worse, especially after the death of his queen Filippa in 1430.

Gradually another policy became linked with the introduction of foreigners into Swedish fiefs. Erik's marriage remained childless, but he wanted to control the succession. Instead of accepting as heir apparent a child of his sister Katarina (who had married Duke Johan of Bavaria), Erik chose his cousin Bogislav IX of Pomerania and made the receivers of fiefs promise to put them at the disposition of Bogislav on Erik's death. This requirement applied, for instance, to the extensive assignments in central Sweden made to Queen Filippa (the daughter of Henry IV of England), who was popular in the North. The Bogislav succession was consonant with the Norwegian stipulations of monarchic descent made in 1389 but violated both the union agreement of Kalmar (which required three-state consultation) and the elective practices of Sweden and Denmark. The king's high-handed attitude antagonized the Swedes who had so recently fought free of Albrekt and his German cohorts. The choice of Bogislav emphasized Erik's Pomeranian-German orientation and the principle of royal authority.

Erik's Baltic ambitions brought further antagonism. He already held most of the Baltic coast — Danish, Swedish, Finnish, and Pomeranian areas. Why, he thought, should he not have all of it? In the earlier centuries the Danes and Swedes had vied for cities and islands along the east Baltic littoral; hence such ambitions were not unprecedented. But their wisdom was another matter. The Teutonic Knights were weakening, as witnessed by their defeat at Tannenberg in 1410. Yet Erik's own position was, to put it mildly, not well consolidated. He tried to gain possession of Slesvig, but there he met the undying opposition of the counts of Holstein. The extent of his present holdings also aroused the concern of the Hansa, still the major sea power in the Baltic. Erik tried to counter this power by the reintroduction of the old *ledung* system. He tried further to check the Hansa by imposing restrictions on the Skåne markets, constructing forts at the northern narrows of Öresund (Krogen and Kärnan), and collecting tolls on all non-Scandinavian ships passing through. Lübeck and other cities of the Hansa retaliated against Erik at various times (first in 1422) by imposing a blockade of Scandinavian ports. This hit Sweden particularly hard because of its dependence on Lübeck for salt and for most of its export shipping. English and Dutch trade was beginning to be important, but goods could reach Sweden only through its western port of Lödöse (upriver from present-day Gothenburg).

Erik's almost continuous warfare with Holstein and the Hansa necessitated heavy tax demands which were the more onerous because they were extracted in coin rather than in kind. The resulting shortage of money led to the minting of copper and the debasement of the coinage, thus making the situation worse. Discontent simmered among broad classes of the Swedish population. Finally it found a focus and a scapegoat in the commandant at Västerås (responsible for Dalarna, Jämtland, and Västmanland), Jösse Eriksson. Jösse, of Danish origin, had long been a king's official in Sweden and complaints against him had accumulated. He was harsh but scarcely the devil incarnate portrayed in the "Karl's Chronicle" (a contemporary popular poetic record); for instance, he probably did not hang up the peasants in smoke. Shortly after 1430 the pent-up hatred found a leader in Engelbrekt Engelbrektsson, a Dalecarlian of the lower nobility who represented the mining interests.

Engelbrekt twice carried the protests of his compatriots to King Erik in Denmark but could get no real satisfaction; he promised to come again. Although the Swedish council dismissed Jösse, this was not enough. In June of 1434 the rugged men of Dalarna gathered for action. They burned the castle of Borganäs and captured Västerås. In Uppsala Engelbrekt won the support of the lawman of Uppland, and the elected archbishop came back, replacing the king's appointee. The army proceeded to the gates of Stockholm. There Hans Kröpelin, the German-born commander, entered into a truce with the army until November. Engelbrekt swept through Norrköping to Vadstena where the council of the kingdom was in session. Legend has it that here Engelbrekt argued with the councillors and finally took a bishop by the collar, led him to a window, and threatened to throw him down to the peasant army with their crossbows of horn, their pikes, pitchforks, and axes. Impressed and frightened, the members of the council — three bishops and sixteen laymen — agreed to support the rebels' complaints and renounced their allegiance to King Erik. The spirit of revolt spread through the country faster than Engelbrekt's men could march. By September the brush fire started in Dalarna had set Sweden ablaze. There were then three rebel armies and among the commanders were men of the great families: Bo Stensson Natt och Dag, Karl Knutsson Bonde, and others. Strongholds like Stegeborg and Kalmar held out, but a number of smaller castles were burned. Engelbrekt moved into Halland (then Danish) where he made a separate peace with a force sent against him from Skåne.

Erik sailed with a strong fleet to Stockholm; Engelbrekt and a newly recruited army from central Sweden met him there in November. Again there was an agreement instead of a battle. Its terms were that there should be arbitration by a court of twelve, composed of four councillors from each country. But military movements continued. In January 1435 a meeting, commonly known as Sweden's first riksdag (parliament), assembled in Arboga. Here gathered representatives not only of the clergy and nobility but also of the townsmen (burghers). (At this time or soon after rural freeholders [bönder] were also called to such meetings.) The council too was there in enlarged form — at least thirty-six councillors were present. Engelbrekt was officially named "Commander in Sweden," and several nobles were designated as assistant commanders.

In the spring, instead of the arbitration court, a joint commission of Danes and Swedes met in Halmstad. Compromise was arranged on May 3 by which the Swedes would again recognize Erik as king but requiring that he meet with the council in Stockholm and repledge to act according to Swedish law and

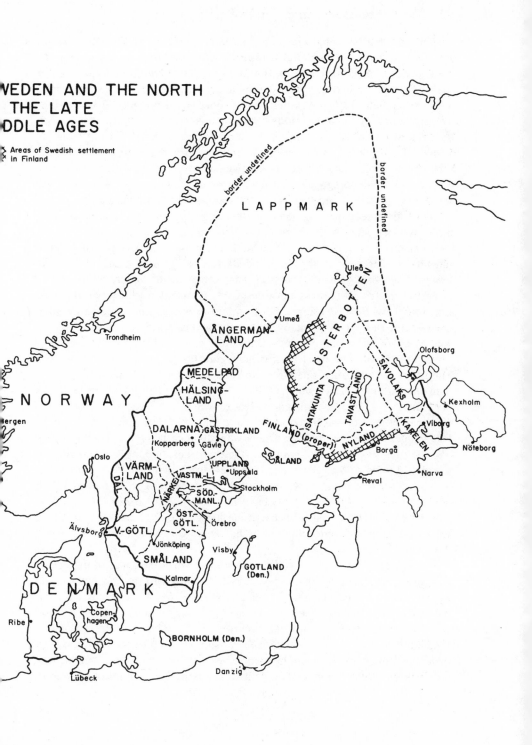

SWEDEN AND THE NORTH
IN THE LATE
MIDDLE AGES

Areas of Swedish settlement
in Finland

LAPPMARK

border undefined

border undefined

NORWAY

Trondheim

Bergen

Oslo

ÄNGERMAN-
LAND

Umeå

Uleå

ÖSTERBOTTEN

MEDELPAD

HÄLSING-
LAND

SATAKUNTA

TAVASTLAND

SAVOLAKS

Olofsborg

DALARNA

GÄSTRIKLAND

Kopparberg

Gävle

FINLAND (proper)

NYLAND

KARELEN

Kexholm

Viborg

VÄRM-
LAND

DAL

UPPLAND

Uppsala

VASTM.-L.

NÄRKE

SÖD.-
MANL.

ÅLAND

Borgå

Stockholm

Nöteborg

Narva

Reval

Älvsborg

ÖST-
GÖTL.

Örebro

V.-GÖTL.

Jönköping

Visby

SMÅLAND

GOTLAND
(Den.)

Kalmar

DENMARK

Copen-
hagen

Ribe

BORNHOLM (Den.)

Lübeck

Danzig

custom and that he bring with him the Union Letter of 1397, which would serve as the basis for future government. King Erik, his back to the wall, made peace with Lübeck and its Hansa allies, promising to continue the old trade privileges he had struggled so long to abolish. He thus averted Hanseatic aid to the rebels. In October the Swedes once more accepted Erik as king. The office of drots (at this period practically a viceroy) was reestablished with the appointment of Krister Nilsson Vasa of Viborg, and the office of marshal, with Karl Knutsson. Less favorable to the Swedes were the provisions that the king might name either Danes or Norwegians to commands at Stockholm, Kalmar, and Nyköping, and that even at other posts he need only hear the views of the council and then he could appoint whom he wished.

Once this agreement was achieved the king, with no conciliatory caution, put subservient men in the posts at his disposal and levied new taxes. Disorders began anew and at a meeting in January 1436 at Arboga the council renounced allegiance to the king and its forces again took Stockholm and besieged the castle. Karl Knutsson was elected commander, but vigorous protests won for Engelbrekt the title of co-commander. Not long afterward Engelbrekt, while answering a call to return to Stockholm, camped near the manor of an old personal enemy, and there he was murdered by the enemy's son, Magnus Bengtsson Natt och Dag, on May 4, 1436.

Engelbrekt was the most fascinating figure of this period of turmoil. His family origins probably dated back to immigrant German miners. He was a man of standing, a squire who had lived "in the houses of great men" but was not fully noble. He was a magnetic leader who could give expression to the emotions of the masses, a man with sound military sense who knew where to lead his peasant hordes and who knew when to negotiate rather than fight. He was the man who set aflame not only the castles of the king's agents but the hearts and wills of Swedish men. However, the leadership of the movement he had started was being contested by men of higher rank when he was struck down. His career blazed furiously but briefly. He lived on in popular memory, and it was inevitable that he became the hero of ballads and the symbol of what people of later times thought he had stood for, or wanted to *make* him stand for.

Engelbrekt was a popular leader at a moment when the cause of the people and the cause of the magnates coincided. But although the magnates could accept and build on the initiative of Engelbrekt, they had a natural fear of popular armies and a distaste for leadership from the lower ranks. A clash with Karl Knutsson had already occurred, and further trouble lay ahead. Engelbrekt's death made it easy for the aristocracy to take the lead into their own hands and to contend among themselves for power. Yet the bitter strife of the fifteenth century cannot be explained merely by the rivalries of obstreperous nobles or by their antagonism to royal authority. Such factors were present, but the deep understructure was composed of broader issues.

Among these fundamental bases of conflict were the structural differences between the Danish and the Swedish political systems. Denmark had a strong tradition of royal authority, whereas in Sweden the king's power was customarily limited by the council of the higher aristocracy. In spite of some scholarly debate on the precise origin of the council, it was clearly an ancient institution which was thoroughly established in law and practice by the end of the thirteenth century. According to Magnus Eriksson's *landslag* of 1350, the king had power to appoint the members of the council, but in 1371 Albrekt agreed that the council should consist of the archbishop, the bishops, and twelve lay magnates who could elect their own successors. Later councils varied in number from six to thirty-six, but the basic pattern remained the same. Members included the chancellor (who at first was usually a bishop), the drots, the marshal, and other high-placed officials and men of wealth and power. The council was representative of the upper echelons of church and aristocracy, and its members considered themselves obligated to maintain the interests of their corporations in government. The changing titles of the council reflected its changing powers which were dependent on the shifting personnel of councillors and kings. Originally the name was the king's council (*kungens råd*), then it became the national council (*riksråd*), and under Gustav Vasa it was to become briefly the government council (*regementsråd*). Always it represented at least a potential check on royal power.[1]

This system of limited monarchy was later to become known in Sweden as constitutionalism; it continued as an ideal and a goal for centuries, and it kept the Swedish nobility violently opposed to autocracy. An important factor in the long-continuing controversy was, in the fourteenth century, that the king of the union was Danish and therefore enjoyed the additional element of strength in his home base; but this weakened his support in Sweden, where the yearning for national independence was already obvious — and was used with telling effect by Karl Knutsson. It was primarily for this reason that the "union" had to guarantee that each of the three peoples would be governed according to its own laws and customs — the reason, in short, why the union remained a loose federation and did not become a centrally governed state. But other factors pushed and pulled the Scandinavian peoples toward closer cooperation. One of these was German expansion. Another was the system of interlocking family relationships and landholdings. The Danish aristocracy intermarried with the Swedish and the Norwegian, and by the fifteenth century many Danes held land in Sweden, and many Swedes held lands in Denmark and Norway. These inter-Nordic nobles were naturally interested in maintenance of the union and peace as well as in their personal ambitions.

Engelbrekt's rebellion spotlighted the weakness of King Erik, who had real friends nowhere. Revolt also broke out in Norway, and at last the Hansa tried to arrange a conciliation. In meetings at Kalmar in July 1436 the delegates from the Danish council, supposed to represent the interests of King Erik, soon took the side of the Swedes. The Danish leaders were doubtless influenced by their desire to preserve the union, even with another king, and by the Swedish agreement to recognize actual land *ownership* by the Danish magnates in Sweden, in contrast to the fief relationship offered by the Danish king. The result was humiliating to Erik, who had to promise once more to govern Sweden according to its own laws and to accept the advice of the Swedish council; he had to give up his claim to appoint a Pomeranian or any other heir. In Sweden castles were taken from the royal appointees and turned over to men of the Swedish aristocracy — the Stockholm castle was given jointly to the two commanders of the realm, Krister Nilsson and Karl Knutsson, the Kalmar and Stegeborg castles were given to the Natt och Dag family. Karl Knutsson soon pushed himself forward as the unscrupulous strong man. Two of Engelbrekt's chief lieutenants (Erik Puke and Broder Svensson) were executed; even the high-ranking Krister Nilsson was forced to return to distant Viborg; and the Natt och Dags were removed from their two forts (but not until 1440). Then Karl Knutsson got himself elected regent (*Riksföreståndare*).

Karl Knutsson was more than a brutal strong man. He realized that he lacked the authority that comes with inherited dignity, and that he had to find other bases of support. Since his chief opponent was a Dane, and since the bailiffs hated by the farming class were Danes and Germans, it was quite natural for him to emphasize the homegrown aspect of his authority. Engelbrekt had fought for the common man, and there is no evidence that he had thought in nationalistic terms. But Karl Knutsson capitalized on the hero worship of Engelbrekt and gave it a new significance. In a poem that he ordered to be written and circulated in 1439 it was emphasized that Engelbrekt was born in Sweden but that foreigners ruled the country; Swedes had to have interpreters in their own land. Bishop Tomas of Strängnäs may have written that poem, for a little later he wrote a famous poem on liberty. Both poems were imbued with emotion against the foreign tyrant, who was compared with Nebuchadnezzar, and with rallying cries to the noble Swedes, who, in freedom's name, should gather as one people around the banner of the noble Karl, God's tool. It was strong nationalistic propaganda, and it took root.

In the meantime Erik attempted to solidify his position in Denmark but succeeded only in rousing firmer antagonism. The Danish council, maintaining contact with the Swedish council, approached Kristofer of Bavaria, the nephew of Erik, asking if he would be willing to accept the throne. In the summer of 1439 the Danish council renounced the now despised Erik, and Kristofer took over the government; soon the Danish council elected him king, and the Swedish council followed suit. The council of Norway, meeting in Lödöse, chose Kristofer king in 1442. It was not an election-in-common according to the Kalmar prescription, but at least Denmark, Norway, and Sweden each selected the same king. Karl Knutsson stepped down as regent, became drots, and received most of Finland to administer.

Kristofer's rule showed promise. In the first place the union was preserved. Kristofer's pledges and a revised general law code of 1442 reaffirmed the elective character of the Swedish monarchy and left much authority in the hands of the nobility; even the disposition of castles was to be determined by a six-man commission of archbishop and magnates. Although Erik still occupied Gotland, the new king promised to regain this island for Sweden. Suddenly all the fine plans collapsed when, on his way to Sweden early in 1448, King Kristofer died.

With Kristofer's death the entire North entered a renewed era of confusion. Quickly Karl Knutsson, with his keen eye for the possible and a complete disregard for union procedures, appeared in Stockholm with an armed force, got himself elected king of the Swedes, and was hailed at Mora Meadow according to ancient practice. However, he wanted to be not only Sweden's king but also Norway's and Denmark's. Norway accepted him, but Denmark, having failed in a bid for a joint election, proceeded to choose Kristian of Oldenburg, who became Kristian I of Denmark. The new Danish ruler then snatched Gotland away from the Swedes and Erik persuaded Norway to renounce Karl Knutsson. Thus the union was split, though a meeting of Danish and Swedish leaders tried to salvage it for the future by solemnly agreeing that *next time*, on the deaths of the two kings, a common choice would be made and the union reestablished.

The inevitable war between Karl and Kristian soon complicated matters further. For war — even the intermittent warfare of the fifteenth century — cost money and necessitated heavy tax demands. Karl Knutsson tried to bolster his finances by reclaiming alienated crown lands and aroused the ire of the threatened landholders. A hot dispute also arose over the Swedish lands that had been included in the morning-gift of Queen Dorothea, who when widowed by the death of King Kristofer soon married King Kristian. These problems were exacerbated by the decline, owing to the war, in exports from the mines and by the pervasive feelings of dislike and jealousy toward Karl Knutsson on the part of many of the nobles and the clergy. The result was a rebellion led by the archbishop himself — Jöns Bengtsson (of the Oxenstierna family). After defeat in a passage at arms Karl yielded power and fled to Danzig. The aristocracy had succeeded again as it had twenty years earlier. The plan now was to reestablish the union under Kristian as king but severely to limit his power. In 1457 the nobles and the Hansa cooperated to force Kristian to accept the limitations on his royal prerogative. The 1397 union agreement of Kalmar was reaffirmed, but guarantees of the nobility's privileges were lacking, and a renewed struggle was foreshadowed.

Now it was Kristian's turn to tax and antagonize. His inheritance of Slesvig-Holstein in 1459 strained his finances because he had to buy off his brothers; hence he laid special taxes, including a ship tax in Sweden. His Oxenstierna-Vasa supporters in Sweden who had complained of Karl's illegal taxes began to be restless about Kristian's. They got control of a number of castles, and in January 1464 Kettil Karlsson (Vasa), the bishop of Linköping, began openly to oppose the king. The commonalty of Dalarna sided with the rebels, as usual, and by April they had defeated the royal troops at Haraker. Karl Knutsson was brought back from Danzig by the same groups that had exiled him. However, he could not establish his authority, and in January 1465 he once more relinquished the office and withdrew to Finland, although he retained the title of king and the estates he had owned before his first period as ruler. Jöns Bengtsson, an Oxenstierna, and Kettil Karlsson, a Vasa, the one an archbishop and the other a bishop, became the administrators of the realm.

It appeared that the Oxenstierna-Vasa faction had achieved its goal. However, there burst upon the scene a new family constellation, the nine Axelsson brothers. They descended from the Danish Thott family, one of the border families with estates in both Denmark and Sweden who had shrewdly gained control of places along the trade routes between the two countries. In 1464 Åke Axelsson was the commander of Varberg castle and controlled most of Halland. His brother Ivar had large holdings in Skåne and Blekinge along the routes to Småland. In 1466 at Nyköping Ivar married a daughter of Karl Knutsson. By an earlier marriage Ivar had a daughter who now, in a double ceremony at Nyköping, married the Småland magnate Arvid Trolle. Another daughter of Ivar Axelsson was engaged to marry Sten Sture, the nephew of Karl Knutsson, and after this girl died Sten married Ingeborg, the daughter of Åke Axelsson. Another Axelsson, Erik, had been long established in Finland and had risen to be one of the administrators of 1457. Here was an interrelated power group that rivaled the Oxenstierna-Vasas.

After the Nyköping weddings a group of the council magnates went to Stockholm, ousted Jöns Bengtsson (who had become the sole administrator after Bishop Kettil's death), and replaced him with Erik Axelsson. Warfare was going on between the Oxenstiernas in Västerås and a besieging force of Dalsmen (men of Dalarna) under Nils Sture, the leader of the Swedish nationalistic movement. It was under such circumstances that Archbishop Jöns Bengtsson, just before he died, seemingly tried to make contact with

King Kristian. The Axelssons, whom Kristian had deprived of their Danish fiefs, and the members of the Swedish nationalistic movement found themselves thrown together. They issued an invitation to Karl Knutsson to come back, and before the end of 1467 he was hailed as king for the third time! Until he died in 1470 he was, nevertheless, only a shadow-king, with Ivar Axelsson as the wielder of power who was pledged to become the administrator on the death of Karl.

Whatever the advance arrangements may have been, it was Sten Sture who was on the spot in Stockholm when Karl Knutsson died. Sten was Karl Knutsson's personal executor and the guardian of his little son. He was a man of substance and full of drive who had inherited many estates in Sweden's south central provinces and had married Åke Axelsson's daughter, thus allying himself with the powerful Danish-Swedish Thott family. He had gained business experience exporting the products of his farms — butter, hides, grain, iron. He personally represented the powers then dominant: his uncle Karl Knutsson, the national movement that Karl had aroused, and the Axelsson group of magnates. These were the bases from which he vaulted to power.[2]

King Kristian was of course determined to use the death of Karl Knutsson as the occasion for the reassertion of his authority in Sweden and the reestablishment of the union. With astute judgment of the situation he was promising the Swedish leaders a reformed union at the same time that he was assembling military might and consummating a deal with the Hansa for a blockade of Sweden. In September 1471 he sailed with his fleet to Stockholm for further negotiations. The Swedish parties were divided. The Oxenstierna faction, supported by the landed gentry and farmers in Uppland, favored the union cause. They continued to negotiate with Kristian, but Sten Sture, as leader of the irreconcilables, left to gather his cohorts: those members of the aristocracy who stood with the Axelssons, the mountain and mining men of Dalarna, the farmers he could gather from central Sweden, and the burghers of Stockholm.

Interests and emotions clashed too sharply to be appeased by talk, and one of the bloodiest battles in Swedish history resulted. On October 10, 1471 the opposing armies met on the sharp declivity of Brunkeberg (now in the heart of modern Stockholm, where the hill has been leveled to make way first for homes and finally for skyscrapers). The Dano-Swedish, unionist forces of Kristian held the heights; the Swedish army of Sten Sture repeatedly stormed the stronghold, and Nils Sture attacked the enemy's rear guard. The hill was strewn with corpses until at length the Sture forces won the day. Kristian retired to the narrow peninsula of Blasieholm, sustaining heavy losses in the flight, and then had to withdraw entirely with his fleet.

The Sture victory at Brunkeberg gave a tremendous impetus to Swedish nationalism. Sten Sture had himself portrayed as St. George in Bernt Notke's handsome wood-sculpture group in Stockholm's Great Church, in commemoration of the battle (the dragon was obviously Denmark). National self-assertion was responsible for the repeal of the long-standing rule that half the city councillors be German; a foreigner could no longer hold an official position in any Swedish city. As a further assertion of the maturity of the national spirit the University of Uppsala was founded in 1477.

Sten Sture became a hero of Swedish nationalistic history, although this reputation was based more on his own eager propaganda than on his deeds. He opposed King Kristian and King Hans, Kristian's son, and any outside pressures, but he also opposed the Swedish council and any individual who threatened his position. His motivation was more personal than national as he thwarted every attempt to reestablish the union. His concern at first was to maintain the solid support of the mountain men of Dalarna, and hence when Nils Sture grew too old to take vigorous leadership in his fief of Västerås, Sten simply transferred him to Stegeborg on the east coast. As he got a firmer grip on power Sten pushed his earlier allies, the Axelssons, out of their influential position. In 1483 Ivar Axelsson attempted to oust Sten and replace him with Arvid Trolle. However, the majority of the council feared the Axelssons more than they feared Sten Sture. When the coup failed Ivar retreated to Gotland, soon turned over the island to the Danish king, and became a Danish nobleman. "Herr Sten" had outmaneuvered his own family rivals and ended the Axelsson era in Swedish history, though Gotland was lost in the process.

The perennial question of the union became acute again in 1481 on the death of Kristian and the accession of his son Hans in Denmark. Hans had once been recognized as heir to the Swedish throne, and he pressed his claims. The negotiations of the three Scandinavian councils produced in 1483 the Kalmar Recess, a notable constitutional document asserting in extreme form the supremacy of the high nobility. According to this agreement: the king should be guided by the council in distributing fiefs and levying taxes; a commission of two spiritual and two lay councillors would control the treasury and the castle pledges would revert to them on the death of the king; the clergy and the nobility were guaranteed their privileges; the church was assured its canonical rights; and the king agreed not to appeal to the pope in church appointments. The Kalmar Recess remained important as a future item of reference, but Sten was able to avoid its application and to retain his power against both king and council.

Foreign complications revivified the Kalmar Recess in 1494. In the 1470s the expanding Swedes had built Nyslott in eastern Finland. The Russians claimed it was beyond the border agreed upon at Nöteborg in 1323. But they were expanding too and soon conquered Novgorod, built Ivangorod fort at Narva, and pressed the Swedes all along their eastern frontier. The most ominous development was the Russian alliance with Denmark in 1493 — an activation of the principle that a country should be a friend of its neighbor's neighbor and a threat that would plague Sweden for centuries. Under these circumstances the council forced Sten Sture to declare that Hans was king of Sweden. However, Sten got the backing of a meeting of popular representatives at Linköping and proceeded on his independent course. In 1495 the Swedes repulsed the Russians from the strong fort of Viborg and the next year destroyed Ivangorod. Tsar Ivan III agreed in March 1497 to a six-year truce.

In that same month, however, several years of tension between the administrator and the council in Sweden came to a head. The council dismissed Sten and deprived him of his fiefs. He reminded the commonalty of his sacrifices for the good of the land, of the peace and prosperity he had brought, and of the "wickedness" of the men who opposed him. Dalarna and Stockholm remained loyal, and if Sten could have combined force with his usual diplomatic skill, he might have won. But King Hans decided this was a good time to intervene. Danish armies moved up from the south and the west, took one castle after another, and a Danish fleet sailed into the harbor of Stockholm. Sten's Dalsmen were defeated in an engagement at Rotebro, outside Stockholm. Shrewdly assessing the situation, "Herr Sten" decided to make terms with Hans; he became the king's man and was enfeoffed with Finland, Nyköping, and some lesser lands. Hans was at last crowned king on November 26, 1497, and the union was reasserted.

The three kingdoms of the North were presided over again by the same king, but this did not mean togetherness. In Sweden the council dictated policy and ruled during Hans's absence. The executive committee was composed of four men in accordance with the Kalmar Recess: Archbishop Jacob Ulfsson, Bishop Henrik of Linköping, Svante Nilsson, and Sten Sture — the latter two recently reconciled after years of bitter rivalry. All must have felt that their cooperation was sham and hypocrisy.

The balance of power shifted when, in the winter of 1500, Hans suffered a humiliating defeat on the southern border of Denmark, in Ditmarschen. A year later (August 1501) Sten Sture was ready to rise again. He spread revolt through central Sweden, Hans retaliated by harrying the east coast, and by November the Swedish lords were sufficiently angered to renounce the king and raise Sten anew to his old post of national administrator (*riksföreståndare*).

Sten Sture was one of the men without whom history would have been different. Without benefit of royal lineage or royal title he held the reins of power in Sweden for almost three decades. He kept Sweden from becoming reabsorbed into a northern union while the country's economic strength was developing and thus laid the groundwork for the sixteenth-century assertion of full independence. His trading, fighting, and negotiating, his incessant travels within Sweden and to Finland (for warfare on the Russian border) — all gave evidence of an amazing physique and nervous energy. The idealized countenance of calm portrayed in the St. George figure was obviously not the real man, and no other portrait, painted or written, has survived. From the diatribes of his enemies, from his letters, but mostly from his deeds, Sven Ulric Palme has compiled a picture: Sten Sture was a man of infinite patience who could burn with wrath yet could wait for the moment of advantage. He was flexible and independent of mind and will. Atypical of his time, he was free from doctrine, whereas opponents like Archbishop Ulfsson and Svante Nilsson believed in the principles of constitutional government. In both political and economic affairs he was unscrupulous. He had no respect for truth and honor. No fraud was too extreme, no deceit too evil. He worked not for family or class or country but for himself, yet he was not above appealing for support on the basis of popular gratitude for his services and sacrifices. He was a plunderer of church property and was twice excommunicated, yet he bore St. Erik's banner against the Russians, he built churches and gave large donations to cloisters, and he appreciated good preaching. He had no hesitations about using force and was a highly skillful commander of troops. The battle of Brunkeberg was a noteworthy achievement. But it was not the commanding general Sten Sture who won political power and held it for nearly three decades. It was the political intriguer.[3]

It was under the government of Sten Sture, the practical, amoral man who had no more conscience than the contemporary condottieri in Italy, that the Swedish economy prospered and the administration of the state was centralized to some degree. Despite the tension between Sten and his council and the brief war with Russia along the Finnish frontier, his era was far less destructive than the previous epoch. Over the door of the sacristy in Kalmar the famous artist Albertus Pictor could inscribe:

> Peace blooms in Sweden
> For Herr Sten rules.

Nevertheless, the last two years of Sten's life, while he was regaining his position from King Hans, were strife-torn. Hans's queen Kristina had stayed in Stockholm castle and was taken prisoner in May 1502. Åbo and Viborg were captured late in 1502, Älvsborg changed hands twice, and Norway was invaded by Svante Nilsson. Toward the end of 1503, with the national-Sture cause in the ascendant, and just as the peace discussions were begun, the skillful leader died at Jönköping. The situation was so delicate that news of

Sten's death was suppressed by Hemming Gadh (then bishop of Linköping), while a squire, dressed as Sten, hurried to Stockholm so that friends could arrange Svante Nilsson's take-over before the opposition could organize. The plans succeeded and at the beginning of the new year (1504) Svante Nilsson of the Sture family and the Natt och Dag clan was duly elected.

The ensuing eight years of Svante Nilsson (Sture)'s period were characterized by alternating war and truce with King Hans and by increasing difficulties between Svante and the council. An interesting aspect of the latter conflict is that Svante, despite his principles of constitutional rule and his former opposition to Sten Sture's policies, found himself following precisely those policies: attempting to name fief holders without the consent of the council, opposing the union interests of the council and the claims of Hans, appealing to the men of Dalarna for support, and trying to ally with Lübeck.

In 1505 Danish and Norwegian councillors meeting in Kalmar adjudged the crown to Hans and condemned the leaders of the 1501 rising. The Holy Roman Empire was brought into the game and ordered the Hanseatic cities to stop trade with Sweden. The embargo hurt the Swedes, though some trade continued. After long, drawn-out negotiations an agreement was reached in the Peace of Copenhagen in 1509 whereby Sweden would pay King Hans an annual tribute of 12,000 marks. However, the agreement did not go into operation. Swedish recalcitrance was facilitated by a breach between Denmark and Lübeck in 1510 which gave Sweden the opportunity to capture Kalmar and Borgholm and to enter into a new alliance with Lübeck. Hemming Gadh remained one of the chief figures of the regime, commanding the siege of Kalmar and conducting the negotiations with Lübeck, but at last he lost his bishopric in 1512. The disagreements between Svante and the council were to be discussed at a meeting in Arboga in January 1512, but on the second of January Svante died.

Svante's twenty-year-old son, known as Sten Sture the Younger, showed much of the daring and skill of the first Sten. Although the council at once elected Erik Trolle as administrator, Sten the Younger was able to get the election shelved while talks were held with Denmark. In the summer a new agreement was reached whereby Sweden would accept Hans or his son Kristian as king or would pay 12,000 marks as an annual tribute. Then, under threat of force, Sten got the council to make him administrator in exchange for his promise to rule according to the council's will.

Hans died in 1513, but Sten succeeded in delaying action on the acceptance of Kristian. The council favored submission, but the young heir of the Sture tradition roused the people to protest. He made himself spokesman for the personal independence of the Swedish farmers, their ideological inheritance from the old Germanic concept of the relationship between individual and community. In negotiations with Kristian II held at Copenhagen in 1515, the Swedish representatives replied to the king's demands for recognition or tribute that Sweden was a free realm where nothing could be done without the knowledge and consent of the common man; Sweden had a law book, statutes, and other writings which the people had sworn to respect and place above any agreements made here. How could agreement be reached? Decision was delayed until 1517. The conciliar aristocracy fought back against Sten Sture and what he stood for: a more popular power base. To provide more vigorous leadership against Sten the eighty-year-old archbishop Jacob Ulfsson in 1515 gave up his post in favor of Gustav Trolle, the son of the Erik Trolle v;ho had been maneuvered out of the office of administrator. Gustav Trolle was thereupon invested by the pope in Rome and obtained special rights: most importantly, to maintain an army of four hundred men to safeguard and regain church property and to issue an interdict if necessary.

The struggle between state and church was thus coming to a head in Sweden as it was in other countries of Europe during the same period, and it intermeshed with a struggle between the council and the commonalty. In the face of a divided council, and certain of the archbishop's support of Kristian, Sten Sture stood his ground firmly with the commonalty. Gustav Trolle avoided contact with the administrators and refused to attend a meeting to which he was called. He was accused by Sten of conspiracy to give the crown to Kristian, and Sten's propaganda aroused the people and persuaded some to withhold their tithes. The issue with the archbishop centered on the question of the estate Stäket. The successive archbishops claimed that both that castle and its district north of Stockholm belonged to the church. Sten claimed that the district was at the disposal of the crown (i.e., the council) and that in other hands the fortress castle was a threat to the realm. In 1516 he besieged it. In 1517 King Kristian invaded Sweden, backed by a new alliance with Russia. However, after a skirmish at Vädla, just north of Stockholm, the Danish fleet departed from Swedish waters.

"What concerns all should be agreed by all," argued Sten Sture, and in accord with this principle he called a general meeting in November 1517 of council, *frälse*, copper and silver miners, Dalsmen, mayors, and the Stockholm city council. This broadly representative group declared against the archbishop and ordered the demolition of Stäket. The members also formed a confederation, anticipating a papal ban, to protect themselves against expected papal retaliation. The castle was then taken and destroyed and Archbishop Gustav Trolle was imprisoned and forced to renounce his office. Sten then had difficulty in getting any man to accept the archbishopric and finally assigned it on a temporary basis to Arcimboldi, the papal legate.

Again, in 1518, the Danish fleet under Kristian's command made a sortie, again the accompanying troops were defeated, and again the fleet retired. But this time there was a difference. To guarantee future discussions Kristian took with him six hostages, among whom were Hemming Gadh and Gustav Eriksson (Vasa). There were indications that the long period of postponement and maneuvering was past when the Danes rebuilt the fort of Älvsborg and captured Borgholm and the island of Öland. The hardening of attitude was further illustrated when a papal court in Lund excommunicated Sten Sture and placed Sweden under interdict.

Kristian was thus strengthened in his position as he was given the task of executing the church judgment. On New Year's Day of 1520 Otto Krumpen led an army of mercenaries into Västergötland on behalf of the king. On the ice at Åsunden (Ulricehamn), when the armies met, Sten Sture was severely wounded, and the Swedes were defeated and scattered. Sten died on February 3, and the Danes overran the country. The castle strongholds were still in the hands of Sture supporters and were taken only gradually. The two most powerful, Stockholm and Kalmar, were held by women; Anna Bielke commanded Kalmar and Kristina Gyllenstierna maintained her position in Stockholm until September. The common folk heeded Kristina's summons in the spring and at first had some success. They captured Västerås and drove the Danes back to Uppsala, but they lacked skilled leadership and were soon overwhelmed. Guerrilla warfare continued but accomplished nothing.

In May the two chief actors in the forthcoming drama landed on the Swedish stage. While King Kristian came boldly north for the mopping-up operations with his army, on the southeast coast near Kalmar, quietly dropped off by a Lübeck merchant ship, an escaped hostage named Gustav Eriksson (Vasa) returned to his native soil. Kristian laid Stockholm under siege and at last Kristina Gyllenstierna, after four discouraging months, was forced to surrender on September 5. Kristian II made the old promises to rule according to Swedish law and custom, agreed to forgive the past, and pledged a general amnesty, and Kristina Gyllenstierna and other Swedish leaders were to receive good fiefs. The terms looked generous. But disillusionment followed.

On October 30 a Danish bishop presided at a meeting of the magnates at the Franciscan cloister in Stockholm where Kristian was proclaimed king not by election but by inheritance. Basic Swedish law and a long series of agreements were thus summarily annulled. A few days later the king returned from a brief trip to Copenhagen. On November 4 he was crowned, and three days of feasting ensued. The merrymaking ended abruptly on November 7 when Archbishop Gustav Trolle came forth with charges of heresy against the leaders of the Sture regime. Kristina Gyllenstierna vainly reminded the court of the riksdag resolution of 1517 regarding the archbishop's unseating and that a few could not rightfully be punished for a decision of the entire community through its legal representatives. But Gustav Trolle seemed to be concerned with vengeance. By bringing charges of heresy (for acts of violence against the archbishop and the church), he made all the guarantees and promises of the king invalid, for no promise to a heretic need be fulfilled. A decision was quickly reached. The king was obligated to carry out the sentence, which he apparently did with a right good will. The Bloodbath of Stockholm came on November 8 when the executioners beheaded eighty-two men in the Great Square near the castle. Hatred was so intense that the body of Sten Sture was taken from its grave and burned with the others in a heretics' pyre. Orders were sent to Finland for the execution of Hemming Gadh and still more beheadings bloodied the homeward journey of Kristian as he traveled south through Jönköping and Nydala — the victims even included monks and children. Kristina and Anna Bielke were taken as prisoners to Denmark. Perhaps Kristian and Gustav Trolle thought that now, with all leadership eliminated, the separatists (or nationalists) in Sweden could make no trouble. But frightfulness seldom subdues opposition. Retribution was at hand.[4]

## Socioeconomic Stagnation

In this "lost century" of the 1400s peoples who were once vigorous allowed themselves to stagnate, their strength dissipated in internecine strife, their leaders absorbed in the struggle for power and the disintegrating contest over the union. Sweden made progress slowly for reasons that must be sought in a complex of factors, partly internal and partly external. Political strife was the most important factor. Also, the debilitating impact of the plague was felt for several generations and caused further deterioration of an already backward situation. Did the combination of disease and warfare happen to strike in unusually catastrophic fashion in Sweden? We cannot know. But life was hard in all the countries of the North. Man could conquer harsh nature but to make the meager resources support a viable society required strenuous labor and wise leadership, and there was never enough of either.

Although the Scandinavia of the union period was one of the largest states of Europe territorially, it was meager in population and wealth. As of 1400, Denmark had some 750,000 people, Sweden (including of course the eastern province of Finland) had about 500,000, and Norway had about 250,000. Except for Denmark this population was spread thinly over vast expanses of land, with towns separated by forests and mountains. The largest city of Sweden in the fifteenth century was Stockholm with 4,000 to 5,000 inhabitants. By the year 1500, Sweden may have had as many as 750,000 people.

The homes of the common folk, although almost none of them have survived and we can know them only through scattered bits of descriptions and drawings, were plain wooden structures. Styles ranged from the four-square, center-courtyard layout of the farmsteads in the south to the straight long buildings in the north. The buildings for animals and for storage were usually separate. The simpler houses had an open hearth in the center of the single room with a smoke hole through the roof. If there were windows they were small, covered perhaps with the stomach-skin of a pig to let in a little light. Beds and benches were built against the walls. Utensils like bowls and spoons and mugs were made largely of wood, there were a few pieces of pottery, and metal was used only when it was essential, for such items as cooking pots and knives. An occasional broad-bowled decorative silver spoon might be a prized possession and perhaps also a weaving to hang over the sooty walls on festive days.

The homes of the merchants in the towns and of the squires and great landholders in the countryside were larger and more comfortable, but usually even the manor houses were starkly simple. Here would be the newer masonry fireplace in the corner of the room, possibly with a chimney, and with heat canals in the walls. A few of the houses were built of stone, usually in a severely plain style, but in the towns they were occasionally erected with the decorative stucco and timber construction known in Germany. The wealthier people had more ceramic and metal wares, the best of these imported from Germany, some made to order in Lübeck. The patrons of luxury items even supported eighty-five goldsmiths in Stockholm in the period from 1420 to 1530. Many of these craftsmen came from Germany.

The food of the late Middle Ages left much to be desired. Not only was variety limited, but the food had to be preserved, often for a full year. With oats for porridge, and with wheat or barley, preservation was not too difficult, and breadstuffs were therefore all too common in the diet. But fish had to be cured, salted, smoked or dried, milk had to be processed into butter or cheese or sour-milk products, and meat had to be heavily salted (which frequently failed to preserve satisfactorily). The result was both unpalatability and thirst, a thirst that could be satisfied only with quantities of beer. The ordinary Swedish beer was weak and easily soured, and only the wealthy could afford the German import. Eggs could usually be fresh, and they could at least be cooked in a variety of ways. One of the reasons feast days were important was that then fresh food might be eaten, even freshly slaughtered animals.

The churches like the manor houses of the aristocracy were often austere, evidently from taste as well as need. Birgitta specifically ordered that the cloister at Vadstena be kept plain, but it was beautiful, too, in warm pink granite. Many churches were built during the fifteenth century; they were small but strong stone structures that replaced the wooden ones which burned down too frequently. Often they had thick towers for defense, after the petty

local forts of Albrekt's time were razed. Even Sten Sture was an eager support-
er of church building. Some fifteenth-century interiors were delightfully
painted with designs and biblical scenes; they were whitewashed during the
Reformation, then restored in later times. Albertus Pictor, a German, was one
of the most famous of the artists, but many native Swedes painted their local
churches. There were stories and sermons on the walls for any who got bored
with the sermons — a practical, realistic art *par excellence*. Since the costumes of the Hebrews in the pictures were carefully kept up-to-date with
Swedish fashion these became excellent sources for the study of clothing and
the mode.

How deep was the actual religious feeling of the era? How can such a
question be fathomed for any age? Lip service was ample, and the building
and decoration of churches might indicate devotion. But in the affairs of state.
business, and farm one looks in vain for much influence of religion or of basic
moral principle. The piety of Birgitta and the religious concern of Margareta's
activities were not evident. History recorded instead the rivalries of archbishops and regents, the military activities of bishops, climaxed by the bloody
revenge against the Stures required by Archbishop Trolle. And if the situation
of Christianity in Sweden was tragic it was not led into happier paths by the
quarreling of Avignon and Rome and the corruption in both religious and
political life in southern Europe. The restoration of religious faith as a factor
in human affairs would require strong measures.

Some sixty schools throughout the country attempted to teach the fundamentals. Most were connected with cathedrals or churches, and some like
those at Skara and Uppsala had good academic standing. About ten lay
schools operated in the larger towns. The times were hard, however, and the
three colleges for Scandinavians that had flourished in Paris were reduced to
one, and it was rather feeble. Those who wanted foreign study could go to
German universities which had begun to displace the Paris colleges. To help
the situation, however, and as a gesture of national pride, the University
of Uppsala was founded in 1477. (Copenhagen established its university in
1479.)

German printers came to Stockholm in the 1480s, and presses were operating in Vadstena and two or three other places in the 1490s. Their work was
almost entirely religious publication. In fact, there was little else to print.
Other Germans (merchants, artisans, and miners) introduced new business
methods as well as new techniques in mining and crafts and broadened business contacts. Yet purposeful innovation was rare, the relations with the
continent were meager, and the pace of change was slow.

Sweden was never subordinated, either politically or economically, to the
rigidities of the feudal system, although Denmark did accept it, and Denmark

then included the province of Skåne and the neighboring regions. The reasons for Sweden's difference are obscure. The sparsity of population may have played a role. One important factor was the scattered pattern of landholding, with the great landholders having farms and villages in different parts of the country and in Denmark and Finland; lacking was the concentration of settlement necessary for the close supervision of serfs and villeins. The scattering of landholding was maintained through the centuries because Swedish law never established rights of inheritance in fiefs, and hence lands were frequently redistributed. Bo Jonsson Grip, who in the fourteenth century acquired vast holdings in Finland and throughout Sweden, is a good example. On his death these extensive possessions were parcelled out among heirs and creditors. The Axelssons in the fifteenth century built up a great network of holdings, but these were also widely scattered. And the Axelssons, like Bo Jonsson Grip, were interested in the acquisition of power in the kingdom and the union, not in the circumscribed affairs of a potential duchy or county. Perhaps it was significant also that these men were concerned with trade rather than with tournaments and the courtly arts.

Some Swedish scholars, among them Folke Lindberg, suggest that the real protection against feudalization was the poverty of the Swedish soil: the country could not, under medieval agricultural conditions, produce enough grain to comprise a significant export for the hungry continental markets, and therefore the demand was lacking for large-scale operations involving the subjection of labor. Some might argue that the independent spirit of the Swedish peasant reacted against the subservience innate in the feudal system. Certainly the wide distribution of land ownership enhanced the spirit of individualism. The shareholding system established in the mining operations in Dalarna encouraged initiative. The farmers and miners, who had won at least a degree of success in the Engelbrekt rebellion, and who had been called into consultation in riksdags like that of Arboga in 1435, were not likely to submit easily to the hierarchical controls of feudalism. Their representation in the political deliberations of the state gave both dignity and power to the peasant proprietors. At critical points (especially in the seventeenth century), the kings supported the independent farmers, for the kings were usually eager to keep the nobles from gaining overweening power. Hence, despite the statute of Alsnö which inaugurated knighthood, despite pressures similar to those on the continent, counterpressures in Sweden were strong enough to prevent the decentralization and the personal subjection inherent in feudalism.

The ideal of personal and national freedom expressed itself in a variety of ways, usually immediate and practical, sometimes philosophic and poetic. One who gave it voice was Bishop Tomas of Strängnäs, who was strongly opposed to the Union of Kalmar and the Danish overlordship in Sweden. In ringing tones he called for freedom of the individual and the people in one of the most notable literary works of the Middle Ages. Because both rhythm and power are lost in translation, two brief samples from his famous "Song of Liberty" are worth quoting in Swedish:

> Frihet är det bästa ting
> som sökas kan all världen kring,
> den som frihet kan bära.
> Vill du vara dig själva huld
> du älska frihet mer än guld,
> ty frihet följer ära. . . .

> Gud haver givit dig sinne och själ,
> var hellre fri än annans träl,
> så länge du kan dig röra!

> (Freedom is the finest thing
> that can be sought around this earth,
> among men who can handle freedom.
> If you will be true to yourself
> you will prize freedom more than gold,
> for freedom and honor go hand in hand. . . .

> God has given you mind and soul,
> be rather free than anyone's thrall
> as long as you can move.) [5]

The historical chronicles such as *Erikskrönikan* and *Karlskrönikan* breathed much the same spirit.

The tradition of freedom and the working of economic interests combined to build effective barriers to any form of subjection. In this rural and isolated society there was naturally a high degree of self-sufficiency. Each manor had to produce its own carpenters and cabinet makers, its masons, its smiths — the farmer had to be versatile in his skills. The women not only did the cooking and cared for the cattle and other animals, but they also wove garments for the family and helped in the fields. The men were foresters as well as farmers, sometimes miners. Farming was an undifferentiated family enterprise which nurtured individual skills but demanded the cooperation of everyone. The families lived in their small cottages on the manor or along the village street, their plots of arable scattered beyond the community of homes and church. The village elder or perhaps the parish council determined when to sow and when to reap.

A moderately complicated system of barter characterized internal trade in Sweden, and in the fifteenth century this system began to increase in complexity and outreach. This was partly brought about by the influence of Hanseatic merchants who wanted to export butter, hides, fish, and iron and exchange these items for foreign products like cloth, salt, and luxury goods. Sweden stood in dire need of some of these products. The country had no salt, yet salt was essential for the preservation of butter and fish as well as meat. Food was rarely eaten fresh. Slaughtering was done in the fall, for it was difficult to feed animals over the winter, and the meat had to last for many months. Internally Sweden was on a storage economy.

As the Germans stimulated Sweden into more participation in foreign trade, they also made the country more dependent on their supply of the prerequisites, such as salt for the packing of fish. Thus a Hanseatic blockade arranged for by the king of Denmark was a potent military threat against Sweden. Since the Hansa cities not only supplied the goods Sweden needed and bought the items Sweden exported but even provided the shipping in which these goods were carried in and out of Sweden, they had a stranglehold on the external trade relations of the country. Toward the end of the fifteenth century this hold was loosened by the declining political power of the Hansa and by the competition being offered by the Dutch. Swedish rulers could not break the Hansa grip but repeatedly had to renew the trading privileges of the German cities. Small gains were sometimes made for the safeguarding of Swedish interests, however, as when in 1505 Svante Nilsson Sture prescribed that Lübeck traders could not import goods to Sweden unless they agreed to use their ships to carry Swedish as well as German goods.[6] Lübeck was the most important commercial partner and dominated the trade with Stockholm, as it had done for several generations. Among the Swedish cities Stockholm had become by far the most important, but Visby was an active point of exchange, and on the west coast Lödöse traded with Rostock and the Dutch towns. A number of other Swedish towns had city privileges but were really little more than market towns: e.g., Linköping, Uppsala, Norrköping, and broken Sigtuna. Others were basically agricultural villages with very modest commercial activity. One city, Borås, was specially designated as the hometown of the peddlers who distributed goods through the countryside.

The dependence of Sweden on foreign ships for its carrying trade is illustrated by figures for two years — not necessarily typical, but the only ones surviving — showing passages through Öresund. (See the accompanying tabulation.[7])

One of the most important exports was still the osmund iron which was unusually pure and malleable. In the middle of the fifteenth century a type of blast furnace was introduced, operating at higher temperatures and producing a less malleable pig iron. This iron was superior, and it was exported from Småland and Västmanland, from Visby, and from the rich mines of Utö (Out

| | Ships Passing through Öresund | |
| --- | --- | --- |
| | *1497* | *1503* |
| English | 0 | 21 |
| Dutch | 567 | 856 |
| French | 0 | 2 |
| SWEDISH | 0 | 0 |
| Norwegian | 0 | 0 |
| Danish | 5 | 5 |
| Wendish towns | 61 | 123 |
| Danzig | 113 | 120 |
| Scottish | 21 | 43 |
| Pomeranian | 21 | 48 |
| Other Baltic towns | 0 | 4 |
| | 795 | 1222 |

Island) to the southeast of Stockholm. Copper was mined after the 1280s but had not in the fifteenth century reached great prominence. Only a small amount of silver was produced. Insofar as the output of the mines found its way into foreign trade it was in the form of a semi-processed raw product such as pig iron. Although the Swedes made their own implements, they did not develop industrial exports.

The miners themselves were interested in foreign trade, along with the farmers both great and small who were eager to export their butter and hides, and the fishermen their fish. (The richest northern herring fisheries, however, were located along the Sound on the shores of Skåne, which was then Danish.) The rulers, too, were often trade-minded. Erik of Pomerania wanted to build a Baltic commercial empire. Sten Sture the Elder, before his period as regent, was interested in Livonia as an outlet for the grain, butter, hides, and metals produced on his lands in Östergötland. And the members of the nobility were transformed from military aristocrats to rural entrepreneurs and landowning functionaries of the state. All groups were influenced by the theory prevailing in the latter fifteenth century: buy from abroad as little as possible but sell and bring into the country as much bullion as possible. Trade restrictions as well as taxation affected all these groups, and they reacted in common against the attempts of the Danish-union kings to pay for their wars by levies on Swedish farms and business; they were especially antagonized by the Danish alliances with the Hansa that used blockades to enforce the royal will. Much of the rebellious discontent of the fifteenth century stemmed from the disappointments of the farmers who had begun to expand their individual holdings and then got caught by the taxes or the devastation of war and lost their gains. Occasionally local associations of peasants would combine to withdraw themselves from warfare by instituting the *bondefriden* or farmers' peace.

The clash of contending political forces in the fifteenth century hampered cultural and economic progress and delayed constructive achievement in every aspect of life.

## *The Beginnings of the Riksdag*

During the fifteenth century the riksdag became a political power, one of the few constructive accomplishments of the period. The roots of popular political participation reached back to the provincial Things and magnates' meetings (*herredagar*) and to the electoral assemblies at Mora Meadow. In 1319, at a time of decision, men from far and near gathered to hail the boy-king Magnus Eriksson. Late in his reign, plagued by troubles, the same king, in 1359, called a meeting of clergy and magnates, representatives of the landholding farmers (*bönder*) from every province, and merchants from every city. (Although the call was made, it is not certain that the meeting took place.) When the kings were weak the council usually became prominent, but this body represented only the higher clergy and nobility, with occasional expansion in periods of crisis. However, as society grew more complex, as towns grew and the interests of their citizens became more diversified, as mining expanded, and as farmers and great landholders became involved in international trade — as these new relationships developed, it was necessary to find a broader means of political representation. The formula was worked out during the fifteenth century.

During the Engelbrekt rebellion a meeting was called at Arboga in January 1435, and there gathered (according to the *Rhymed Chronicle*) "bishops, prelates, knights and squires, merchants and common people of the realm."[8] Some scholars object to calling the 1435 session in Arboga Sweden's first riksdag, although traditionally and officially it is so recognized. It was a representative gathering including men from all ranks of society, though we do not know how the meeting was organized nor how it reached decisions. It was more than a mere electoral assembly, for it not only approved Engelbrekt as commander (or captain-general) of the country; it also made other men responsible for specific provinces, and it considered and accepted the proposal of Hans Kröpelin, king's commander in Stockholm, for negotiations between himself and a mediator from the Teutonic Order. In June another general meeting took place in Uppsala, and in January 1436 there was still another at Arboga. Although these were both fairly central locations, the representation at the different meetings was undoubtedly more numerous from the surrounding area than from the more distant districts. These gatherings were of course used by Engelbrekt to enlist support, but divergent opinions could find expression. In line with Swedish practice and contemporary European political theory the body politic as a whole thus took part in major decision making, though the institutions were crudely organized. In the struggles with the kings the council remained the center of continuing power.

Gradually both the forms of procedure and the records became clearer. In the 1460s, as Karl Knutsson was being successively abandoned and reelected, several assemblies made political decisions. Sometimes these gatherings were armies, frequently the clergy were not mentioned, but the assembled men were spoken of as representatives of social groups (Estates) and provinces. In a number of the late fifteenth-century assemblies the dominating elements were the miners, the Dalsmen, and the burghers of Stockholm, but representation was never closed to special groups alone. During the same period somewhat similar concepts of an Estate society were developing in Norway, and in 1468 the Danes called together their first Estates-riksdag.

These national gatherings, at first called *riksmöte* (kingdom meetings), came to be called riksdag about the middle of the sixteenth century. The direct initiator was usually the council or sometimes a warlike bishop like Kettil Karlsson (Vasa), after his victory over Kristian I at Haraker in 1464, or a popular leader such as Engelbrekt, back in 1435. In this latter case popular pressures impelled the council to action, in other cases the council at least appeared to hold the initiative. With increasing regularity riksdag meetings were held, and increasingly they were depended upon to make the decisions by which the Swedish community expressed its policy regarding its ruler and therefore regarding the union. Seldom were men present from all the provinces, but always there were men of different Estates. For example, in 1504 a national meeting in Stockholm was composed of the council, the nobility of Uppland and Södermanland, representatives of the copper and silver miners of Dalarna and Bergslagen, and forty-eight commoners from Stockholm plus the magistrate of that city. Usually there was a wide geographical representation. The nobility, the clergy, and the burghers (in that order) were the influential elements, but a full riksdag also had to have representation from the commonalty. Thus the fundamental issues of the separatist-unionist conflict created the need for a representative assembly and brought the riksdag into being, whereas the social character of the time determined the division into Estates. The clergy at first sat with the nobility but was thought of as a distinct Estate. This was not yet democracy, but it was a step in the slow progress toward democracy.

### Unionism, Nationalism, and Constitutionalism: An Interpretive Summary

The significant practical effect of the Union of Kalmar was accomplished early, and the bickerings and bloodshed of the succeeding century only prolonged an institution that had served its purpose and no longer had a *raison d'être*. Yet the union remained throughout the fifteenth century the overarching political institution in relation to which all issues had to be resolved.

In the fourteenth century the German Hanseats had made the ports of Norway colonial economic outposts, they had acquired all but monopolistic position in Swedish foreign trade and strong influence in its domestic crafts and businesses; in Denmark they had obtained castles and extensive trade privileges and the right to veto the choice of a Danish king. The Mecklenburg princes had captured the throne itself in Sweden. Not one of the Scandinavian states was strong enough alone to stand against this powerful infiltration. But the opportunity for opposition fell into the lap of Margareta. She was farsighted enough and ruthless enough to seize the opportunity, and using the united power of the three Scandinavian peoples she drove Albrekt out of Sweden, recovered the Danish castles and the right of Denmark to choose its own ruler, and broke down the power of the Hansa. But after Margareta's time the outside pressures were not strong enough to hold the three countries together, and the centrifugal forces reasserted themselves.

Did the development of the riksdag, the repeated clashes of arms with the Danish-union kings, the elections of Karl Knutsson as king of Sweden and of the Stures as regents — did these things signify the growth of nationalism in Sweden in the fifteenth century? At the opening of the century there was nothing that could be labeled nationalism. Each of the Scandinavian countries was a kingdom, each had a slightly different language and different though compatible traditions in law and social customs. Each had its separate archbishop, though the Danish archbishop in Lund claimed preeminence. Many of the nobility owned fiefs or other grants in two or three of the Scandinavian countries. No serious obstacle of economic or emotional or cultural content blocked the formation of Margareta's union.

Yet union never became fusion. The three peoples chafed under the frictions of enforced cooperation. The kingship was the only unifying institution, and the ruler guaranteed repeatedly through the years that he would rule each kingdom according to its own laws and customs. The union developed neither common institutions nor sentimental support, and it never had a name — a most revealing lack. To this day it is called the Union of Kalmar simply because Kalmar was the place where the agreement was made. Erik Gustaf

Geijer was more poetic than precise when he said that the union was an incident that looked like an idea. Indeed, the union's only real claim on men's loyalty was that it could extrude the Germans and check intra-Scandinavian war, and it accomplished the latter only to the end of Margareta's reign.

As the fifteenth century progressed a cleft widened between king and people. Erik's wars of expansion made tax demands grow heavy, and the presence in Sweden of Danish and German bailiffs emphasized the fact that these expensive wars were for territories in Slesvig or across the Baltic Sea and that they were conducted by a union king who was Danish, nay, not even that, but really Pomeranian. How easy for a Swede to rationalize that he should not pay taxes for the Germanic aggrandizement of a king of Denmark! When the Hanseatic blockade assisted in the enforcement, foreign oppression became more of an irritant. Separatist feeling intensified against the harshness of foreign tax collectors who disregarded the local law they were pledged to obey.

Strong forces did of course continue to work for the union. The kings favored it if for no other reason than that it widened their realm of authority. For Queen Dorothea only the existence of the union could assure her enjoyment of her extensive fiefs in Sweden.[9] For the archbishop in Lund union meant the possibility of enlarged ecclesiastical influence. For the rich province of Skåne, which alternated between Swedish and Danish suzerainty and had trade relations in all directions, union offered the best possibilities for peace and prosperity. Skåne, Halland, and Blekinge, as crossroads and granaries, were inevitable battlegrounds in inter-Scandinavian feuds. Individual nobles who owned estates in two or more of the countries were usually inclined toward union. Others favored it because it gave them the opportunity to play on a larger stage or simply because they thought it would promote peace. Hence efforts were maintained to preserve the union. Early in Kristofer's reign (c. 1442) a new union act was apparently drawn in Stockholm, and kings continued to pledge allegiance to the agreements of 1397. After the separate elections of 1448 representatives of the three Scandinavian councils got together and pledged that on the death of the existing kings a common election would be held.

But all of these unionist tendencies were weakened not only by the overambitious aims of Erik but most of all by an improbable series of negating accidents: Margareta left no direct heir, Erik had no children, Kristofer died early and without heir. Succession rights were attenuated and too often had to be found in Germany. Only Margareta had a thoroughly Scandinavian background and a thoroughly Scandinavian policy. The kings, though they wanted to rule the three kingdoms, tended to be primarily Danish. The councils of the three kingdoms were often divided in opinion, tending to be unionist in the first part of the period and increasingly separatist toward the end. The Norwegians were dissatisfied but not strong enough to oppose the monarch. The Swedes, after a century of struggle, were able to break loose. What were the elements of Swedish strength?

The political resilience and persistence of the Swedes in the fifteenth century were impressive testimonials to growing strength. Despite doubts and differences and occasional detours the Swedes maintained a rather steady and ultimately successful opposition to outside control. As long as the union functioned on a basis of equality the three states stayed with it. But they were sensitive to violations of their rights. The council aristocracy objected to the autocratic procedures of the king and wanted to share power. The landholders and the miners objected to burdensome taxation and to authority that they could not influence. The first major protest, the Engelbrekt uprising of 1434, was a popular movement that could be supported by the aristocracy. It was not aimed against the union as such but against the king and his agents. At least a part of the nationalistic tone attributed to the uprising was a later interpretive emphasis. The revolt was couched at the time in terms of the demand for justice, for fair treatment. The charges were that King Erik had violated his royal oath, installed unworthy bishops, imposed unfair tolls on cities, impoverished the knighthood by long wars, and treated the commonalty as thralls.

There was also a note of incipient nationalism, as indicated in the report of a German merchant from Stockholm to the council in Danzig in the summer of 1434:

> The Dalsmen ask and intend that they have a king in Sweden, and they want to drive the king of Denmark from the three kingdoms and have their own rulers. This they do with the aim of reestablishing here in Sweden the conditions that existed before in the days of King Erik [St. Erik] — who is very holy and much worshipped in this country — when there were no tolls, taxes, or imposts on the peasants. They want thus to have back their old laws as in years gone by.[10]

It was a simple and primitive nationalism that protested foreign rule and demanded a return to the old Swedish system of electoral kingship. It was a spirit and a policy comparable to that of Joan of Arc who in that same decade raised the banner of Orleans against the English "goddams." And it was in that same year, 1434, that the Swedish bishop Nicolas Ragvaldi at the Council of Basel proudly identified the Swedes with the achievements of the ancient Goths. A national spirit was clearly at work.

After the Engelbrekt rebellion Erik of Pomerania was ousted by Danish as well as Swedish action. Under Kristofer the union was preserved but it had been challenged and weakened. Kristofer's untimely death then made it possible for Karl Knutsson to assert his claim: union, too, if possible, but at least Sweden must be his. The fact that Karl was in and out of the kingship three times indicated the transitional nature of his position. That he was consciously nationalistic was illustrated by the chronicle he ordered composed to glorify his reign. According to the chronicle, Kristian of Denmark sent him a message:

> You must at once from Gotland withdraw
> For the island to Denmark's kingdom belongs.
> But Karl regarded the demands as invalid
> And asked, why Denmark became so covetous
> After a part of the Swedish kingdom.[11]

Karl portrayed himself throughout, and in effective propaganda, as the protector of things Swedish.

The real breakthrough of Swedish nationalism came with Sten Sture. At the battle of Brunkeberg in 1471 the Swedes were divided, some still fighting with the Danes and for the union. But Sture and his purely Swedish host won the day. Herr Sten made the most of the victory and its Swedish character. National pride and self-consciousness were enhanced. Bernt Notke's magnificent wood-carved group — St. George and the dragon — in Stockholm's Great Church, commissioned to celebrate Brunkeberg and depicting Sten Sture as St. George and Denmark as the dragon, remains as a symbol of the exuberant national spirit. The Stures made Swedish nationalism stronger than unionism and laid the foundation for the independent nation state under Gustav Vasa.

However, although nationalism was a lusty infant it did not yet dominate the scene. It was but barely conscious of itself. The struggle that overshadowed nationalism was that between absolutism and constitutionalism or between royal authority and rule by council, to put the conflict in its fifteenth century terms. The king might be unionist, like Erik, Kristofer, or Kristian, or he might be nationalistic, like Karl Knutsson or the Sture regents; the council might be (and often was) unionist at the beginning of a king's reign but separatist later (or vice versa). For there was a tendency on the part of all the rulers to assert power increasingly, and as they did so the councils demanded legal limitations. If all the rulers had been kings of the union it might appear that council opposition was chiefly nationalistic. But often the council was unionist, favoring a king who was far enough removed that the council could exercise its authority. It seldom worked out that way for long, and the Swedish council found it had to oppose the union monarchs Erik and Kristian as well as its own Karl Knutsson and Sten Sture. The urge to enhance power by more power gripped each man who held the reins (only Kristofer did not live long enough for the disease to take hold), and the urge to restrain the expansion of royal power impelled the councils.

The result was a seesaw conflict repeated again and again. The councils insisted on the principle of elective monarchy, the recognition of traditional Swedish law, and the rights of Swedes to enjoy the major fiefs in lands and offices within their own country. The kings in both Denmark and Sweden sought to curb these magnates and to force the great inter-Scandinavian families to choose and become either Danish or Swedish. (The Axelsson-Thotts were a notable example.) Once their position was weakened it became possible for a regent such as Sten Sture to appeal to the commonalty to rise against them in the name of nationalism. Thus were the aristocracy and their instrument the council gradually subordinated as a power factor by the strong man they had, with great hopes, lifted into authority. The council ideal of a government constitutionally limited through a king or regent who was the tool of the council struggled but failed. The long fight by the council against unionist autocracy was a decisive factor in the defeat of the union, and therefore, ironically, a factor in the establishment of strong *national* monarchy.

At the time of Stockholm's Bloodbath none of the crucial issues was resolved, but all were brought vividly to a head. Although it was a violent and bloodthirsty age, in "advanced" Italy as well as in "backward" Scandinavia, a dramatic peak was attained in the combined treachery and horror of the executions of 1520. This act proved to be the catalyst that brought a new leader to the fore and gave new vitality to the national spirit.

# VI

## THE SIXTEENTH CENTURY:
## FOUNDING THE NATIONAL STATE

THE STOCKHOLM BLOODBATH of 1520 was the act of desperation of an obsolete institution. The union of the three Northern countries, produced by a set of adventitious circumstances at the end of the fourteenth century, had assisted the loosely organized peoples of Scandinavia to maintain their independence vis-à-vis the encroaching Germans. A union leadership wise enough to emphasize cooperation, shrewd enough to share power, farsighted enough to encourage a sense of group loyalty — such a leadership might have been able to create a viable Scandinavian state. But when Margareta died her successors became nation-bound. As the kings of the union came to regard their Danish interests as primary, they more deeply antagonized the Swedes. That anyone could believe large-scale executions to be necessary illustrated the cleavage, and the Bloodbath deepened that cleavage beyond the possibility of bridging.

### Gustav Vasa and the Birth of Modern Sweden

WINNING INDEPENDENCE

Gustav Eriksson Vasa was the only one of the six hostages taken to Denmark in 1518 who was not won over by the arguments and the charms of the Danes. Shrewd old Hemming Gadh himself became an adviser to King Kristian. But Gustav resisted both blandishment and brainwashing and escaped from his mild imprisonment in September 1519. He made his way to Lübeck, where he got the city fathers to protect him and help him get back to Sweden.

He arrived in May 1520, while Kristian's army was fighting its way north-ward. Anna Bielke after her husband's death still held Kalmar and not until September did Sten Sture's widow, Kristina Gyllenstierna, negotiate the sur-render of Stockholm. In the meantime Gustav tried to attract support in Småland but found men too cautious. He moved northward until he reached some of his father's estates in Södermanland. Even here he could not arouse people. Kristian was winning, and he appeared for the moment to be able and reasonable. Gustav pondered reconciliation with the king, and his friends urged it upon him. After Kristina gave up Stockholm what hope was left? Yet Gustav so distrusted the Danes that he hesitated.

When word reached him of the November executions in Stockholm — his father, two uncles, and a brother-in-law were killed and his mother, grandmother, three sisters, and his aunt Kristina were imprisoned — his decision was made for him. Hunted by the king's men, the young nobleman slowly made his way to Dalarna, the backbone province of the Stures and of national resistance. Yet, whether it was old friends from Uppsala or the com-monalty that he addressed from the church wall in Mora, everywhere he met doubt and rejection. Legend has embellished the tales of his narrow escapes, one of them thanks to the wife of a "friend" who was out rounding up a posse for his capture. On he fled toward the Norwegian border. According to the story, some young men there caught up with him on their skis and told him that the Dalsmen had changed their minds and that he should return. The tales of Kristian's bloody *Eriksgata* as he continued executions during his return trip southward to Copenhagen and the news of fines and heavy taxes had swung the balance toward revolt. In January 1521 Gustav Vasa was hailed in Mora as captain of Dalarna, and the war of liberation began.

Gustav Eriksson Vasa, age twenty-four, had excellent qualifications for the job ahead. Behind him, through his father and his mother, were generations of nobility who had been on both sides in the separatist-unionist controversies. He was related to Karl Knutsson and the Stures; Kristina Gyllenstierna (Sture) was his aunt, a half-sister of his mother. Before he was taken as a hostage to Denmark he had lived for a time at the Sture court and had learned something of Machiavellian statecraft from Hemming Gadh. He had already fought in two battles against the Danes. On his father's estate at Rydboholm in Uppland and on others of his widely scattered possessions he had learned agriculture and management. His schooling had not been thorough, but he had been sent as a young boy to elementary school in Uppsala and for a brief time to the university. His early education was terminated when his Danish teacher, Master Ivar, struck him, and Gustav left in flaming anger. But he did learn Latin, passable German, and he became a master of his Swedish mother tongue. With the older generation of leadership chopped and burned to death, and with only two little boys left in the Sture family, this high-spirited, uncompromising youth was the natural leader of the national cause.

Once accepted as leader Gustav lost no time, and in early February 1521 he and a small band struck Stora Kopparberg, acquiring supplies and money and winning a bit of fame. He captured the Dalarna seal (an ax and a bow) and could thus issue "official" proclamations. In the meantime Gustav Trolle, who had resumed his position as archbishop, was named general of the king's troops; but Gustav Vasa's volunteers defeated him and the archbishop resigned his military role. Men flocked to the Vasa banner. At the end of April Gustav defeated a royal army at Västerås where the Danish defenders burned the city but held the fort.

Local revolts, some taking place earlier than the Dalarna outbreak, had sprung up in various parts of Götaland (central and southern Sweden), and the participants accepted the Vasa generalship. A trusted lieutenant was sent to Finland and soon that entire region was in his hands. Like a prairie fire revolt raced through countryside and city. People were only awaiting leadership. On August 23, 1521, a national meeting in Vadstena named Gustav Vasa regent.

Yet it was not all that easy. The enthusiasm of the masses was shared by some but not all of the privileged classes. The outstanding leaders of the skeptics were Ture Jönsson (Tre Rosor), the great man of Västergötland, who was hesitant, and Bishop Brask of Linköping, who was strong-willed. Gustav Vasa had to conciliate them in the summer of 1521 by promises that he would consult them on appointments and negotiations and guarantee church properties and privileges. Gustav's original commoner supporters distrusted these cautious men who played both sides but whose support was nevertheless necessary.

From a military point of view the rebels' position was weak. Smaller forts fell into their hands, but Stockholm, Kalmar, Viborg, and other major strongholds were still in the possession of the union-Danish government. The yeoman army that had been good for swift raids lacked power for extended campaigning; the men wanted to go home for the harvest and to take care of their families and in any case were neither trained nor equipped for action against fortified places. Yet the buildup continued, and Kristian II himself was forced to go off to the Netherlands to raise military and diplomatic support. The Swedish resisters needed money and armament and some trained mercenaries. Their natural source of aid was Lübeck.

Lübeck was interested in trade privileges, and its favored position in the North was now flouted by the Danes. Kristian II was tied to Lübeck's rivals, the Dutch, in a variety of ways. His Queen Isabella was the sister of Emperor Charles V, whose other sister, Maria, was the ruler in the Netherlands.

Kristian tried to get the emperor to place Lübeck under his sovereignty, but this maneuver succeeded only briefly. The most direct shock to the Hansa city came when Kristian, confident of control of Sweden in the fall of 1520, opened Swedish trade to the Dutch. After this threat the Lübeck city council smiled on the appeal of the new Swedish regent and hoped that his personal sense of gratitude would combine with economic and military dependence to make him a longtime ally. Gustav promised Lübeck far-reaching privileges and dispatched a shipload of silver. In return Lübeck lent him a small fleet (which did some highly profitable trading) in June 1522 and then rented him further major naval and military support in the fall of the year. Gustav Vasa wanted to use the fleet to capture Stockholm, but Lübeck insisted that it attack Copenhagen. Because the Danzig fleet delayed the operation was largely futile, and the clever Danish admiral Sören Norby slipped by them both. With Lübeck's aid, however, the Swedish pressure on the forts increased, and Gustav's army could push into the Danish provinces. He made a Lübecker, Berend von Melen, his general in the invasion of Skåne (and von Melen married Gustav's cousin).

Kristian's harsh policies brought him into conflict with his uncle, Frederik of Holstein, and at last with the emperor. At this point the Danes themselves turned against Kristian, and in April 1523 he fled with his family to the Netherlands. His uncle Frederik had already been chosen to succeed him. Oddly enough this shift of kings in Denmark changed the whole situation and threatened the success of the Swedish rebellion. For as king of Denmark Frederik had to pay for the assistance he had received from Lübeck, and he did so with grants of trade privileges in Denmark, Norway, and Sweden. Frederik the king had different interests than had Frederik the contender for the throne. He now had claims on the kingship in all three countries and thus was no longer a natural ally of the Swedish nationalists but their opponent. His position was what Kristian II's had been. Lübeck for its part was playing all the angles, though the city doubtless preferred that the North be divided rather than united and must have found Gustav Vasa's promises and prospects eminently satisfactory. Frederik, moreover, did not press his claims to Sweden when he found that the kingship question there was settled, probably feeling that he had enough problems in Denmark.

The Swedish council had acted in time to thwart complications. At Strängnäs on the sixth of June 1523 Gustav Vasa was elected king by a full council of five clerics and twenty-five laymen (including the Lübecker von Melen). The demands of Lübeck for payments and privileges were approved four days later, after all Swedish pleas for relaxation were rejected. On June 24 Stockholm surrendered, and King Gustav rode into the city. It was a time of triumph and of complications, well illustrated in a letter from Gustav's good friend in Lübeck, the merchant Herman Iserhel: "Praise be to Almighty God and Mary, queen of heaven, that it has now gone so far with Your Grace. Now I can die happy." But that was only the gracious preamble; the real purpose of the letter became apparent as the merchant continued: "I sit here in great sorrow. My creditors press me hard. Send at once as much wares as you can — salmon, lard, oil, furs, silver, copper, iron."[1] And the same Henrik Möller who had taken Gustav to Sweden in 1520 had ships ready to take the goods to Germany. For Gustav had won his crown on credit, and he was not allowed to forget this; the unrelenting pressure by Lübeck would continue for years.

The privileges required by Lübeck (and Danzig), and to be extended to other Hansa towns at Lübeck's pleasure, specified that their citizens would be the only foreign traders in Sweden, that they would be free from customs duties and taxes for all time, and that the Swedes would not ship or trade outside the Baltic Sea. Lübeck was to hold a tight monopoly on Sweden's export to the West and on its imports of salt and cloth. Only Danzig and the eastern shores of the Baltic were open to Swedish merchants and ships. However, few treaties are held for eternity, despite their solemn phrases.

Although Frederik I quickly recognized Gustav, others were in no hurry. Sören Norby, the Danish admiral and agile condottiere of the sea, had been ousted from Finland and Kalmar but established himself on Gotland and made the island the base once more for piracy in the Baltic and for raids on the Swedish mainland. He was a threat to both Sweden and the Lübeck trade, and Lübeck therefore persuaded Gustav to accept a new loan and prepare a campaign against Gotland. Von Melen was given the command, and all went well except at the solid fortifications of Visby. The wily Norby escaped his proper chastisement by shifting allegiance from Kristian II to Frederik I and thus forced the Swedes to wage war on Denmark rather than on the leftover admiral of an exiled king. Lübeck was caught in the middle and hastily got Gustav to negotiate with Frederik at Malmö. By the Malmö Recess of September 1, 1524 Sweden, for all practical purposes, surrendered its rights in both Gotland and Blekinge to Denmark and got in return only temporary possession of Bohuslän (the western province then known as Viken). Lübeck got paid for its mediation when King Frederik granted new Danish trade privileges to the Hanseatic city. For Gustav the defeat in Gotland and at the peace table, compounded by the new friendship between Lübeck and Denmark, made him feel tricked and discarded. Bitterness began to replace gratitude in his attitude toward Lübeck, and problems at home loomed larger and larger.

PROBLEMS OF THE YOUNG STATE

Since the success of the war of liberation was assured and a king was chosen, people within Sweden slipped back into their old ways of thinking. The peasants balked at paying the taxes for war and wondered how they were better off. The men of Dalarna thought it was they who had put Gustav on the throne, and so they wanted more voice in political affairs. The church people were distressed about the financial demands placed upon them and disturbed by the religious revolution that was spreading rapidly beyond Germany. Neither merchants nor farmers liked the rising prices for salt nor the bad coinage. The gentry resented the appointments to office of Germans and former supporters of Kristian. Several among the nobles questioned why the king should be Gustav Eriksson Vasa instead of some other among them.

The most immediate problem was the war debt, amounting to 114,500 marks. Gustav put this in terms that could be understood by the peasants: the fleet had cost 10 barrels full of money, foreign knights 6 barrels per month, the Swedish soldiery 8 barrels per year. (He boasted that never before had wages been paid to Sweden's own warriors.) All told the debt was 8 wagonloads of money. By 1525 Sweden had paid about one-third of the amount, largely through a special silver collection from the churches. Then the king began to think he should build reserves for an emergency. Well he might, for opposition grew.

The discontented were numerous, and they were attracted to the Sture circle. When Sten Sture's widow Kristina was released by the Danes in 1524 she returned to Kalmar. Rumors spread that she and the commander Berend von Melen engaged in political intrigue and that she was going to marry Sören Norby to use the aid of this condottiere of the sea to gain the throne for her son Nils. One by one these early threats to the Vasa regime were overcome. Von Melen was developing illusions of independence and had to be thrown out of Kalmar by force; but he retired to Germany whence he fomented trouble for years. Eventually Kristina was reconciled with Gustav and married one of his loyal supporters. Sören Norby shortly became intolerable to his Hanseatic protectors, who drove him out; four years later he was killed in battle in Italy, a soldier of fortune to the last. Peter Sunnanväder, a high Swedish official who had escaped the Bloodbath because he was on a mission to Danzig at the time, returned to expect an influential position at court. Instead, his pride was hurt by insufficient appreciation and he shifted into opposition and intrigue. He was captured, and before he was executed, in a crude and bitter joke, he was forced to ride into Stockholm sitting backward on a decrepit horse with a straw crown on his head and a wooden sword in his hand.

The Sture name was potent in Dalarna, and there a full-fledged but brief revolt was waged in an attempt to put on the throne the so-called Daljunker, who claimed to be the boy Nils Sture. The real Sture had spent some time at the court but hated Gustav. Had he actually died and was this merely an imposter who happened to serve the purpose of the disgruntled Dalsmen? Probably, but in any case Gustav's luck and leadership proved superior, the movement was snuffed out, the Daljunker fled and at last was executed in Rostock. The firm hand that crushed one revolt was perhaps just what stimulated another, in 1529, among the restless nobility of Småland and Västergötland. Gustav's quick call for troops from Finland and his ringing appeals to the farmers left the aristocratic conspirators without followers, and this threat from the south was averted. The leaders Ture Jönsson and the bishop of Skara (Magnus Haraldsson) fled into exile, a few conspirators were executed, and the crown took many estates by confiscation. Until his death about thirty years later Bishop Magnus remained an active rebel in exile. These were not the last uprisings, but Gustav was learning how to be ruthless and how to make adversity work for his aggrandizement. Other problems could not be handled with such brusque finality.

### BEGINNINGS OF THE SWEDISH REFORMATION

It was accidental that the national revolt in Sweden coincided with the Lutheran revolt in Germany, but it was not an accident that the Swedish king took advantage of the situation. The religious ferment added complexities but also provided opportunities.

The Protestant Reformation was an individual and national phenomenon that displayed different characteristics in each country affected. In Sweden, Denmark, and England it developed at about the same time, and it succeeded in each of these countries, but at a different pace and with different effects. In all three countries the leadership from the top was vital, but in Denmark and England there was also vigorous participation by the people themselves, and especially in England the Reformation was characterized by thorough theological debate. In Sweden, on the other hand, the leaders were few, the people were long antagonistic to change, and there was a minimum of theological discussion. The revolution began with changes in ritual and custom, accompanied by a fundamental change in power. It emanated from the king and was kept under the king's control. And although it moved at a slow pace, in the long run it proved to be exceptional in its universality and the strength of its hold on the nation. These characteristics were the product of time and circumstance and especially of the king himself.

Gustav Vasa's uprising was in the first instance as much against Archbishop Gustav Trolle as against King Kristian II, two enemies in close alliance. In the fifteenth century the church in Sweden had opposed the trend toward national political power, and by the early sixteenth the rivalry of archbishop and regent had become intensely personal. Early in the national uprising Trolle led troops against the forces of Gustav, and when he was defeated he fled into exile and long continued to plot against the new government. Gustav was no religious revolutionary and he moved warily into the Reformation. His goal was the establishment of royal supremacy, not the conversion of a nation to a new faith. He was conscious of the importance of the church as a social institution and as an instrument for maintaining order and good principles. He wanted preachers to preach and enjoined them strictly to do so. By no means did he wish to destroy the church, but he also did not wish the church to weaken or dominate the state. On this score he was to be as adamant against the Lutheran reformers as against their Roman predecessors.

However, Gustav came to power at a time when the winds of Protestantism were blowing strongly from out of Germany, and they blew northward as well as westward. They were felt all the more keenly because the old political institutions had collapsed and the new ones were too frail to provide windbreaks. The king, as he reshaped the structure of the state, was sensitive to the new ideas wafted in from abroad. Lutheranism gave sanction to the denial of political authority of the archbishop and his foreign superior the pope, to the establishment of royal supremacy over all subjects of the crown, and to the policy of tapping the economic resources of the church. Gustav's responses to these forces — to these temptations, if you will — shaped the course of the Reformation in Sweden.

Events moved slowly and erratically, characterized by extemporizing rather than by farsighted planning. There was no program of reform. With Archbishop Trolle discredited and in exile the country had to get along without an archbishop for years, because Gustav could not persuade the pope to consecrate a new one. With the leading bishops the king soon came into conflict. The presumptuous and oppositional spirit of men like Bishop Brask of Linköping and Bishop Magnus of Skara made the king feel increasingly the need to subordinate the church to the state. The king needed money, and when Bishop Brask objected to the illegal royal demand for the church silver Gustav replied curtly, "Need modifies law, not only men's law, but occasionally God's law."[2] He thought in terms of the nation as a whole, and he demanded service from both the spiritual and the lay *frälse* for the common good; he tried, for example, to get monks to go as teachers up into the northern frontier. "In need all must work for the common good and protect the community from its enemies, be they churches, cloisters, monks or priests."[3]

The king's concept of the oneness of the nation in need was doubtless as sincere as it was firm. Pressed hard by Lübeck's demands and his own defense needs, Gustav required from every church its largest (or next largest) bell or the equivalent in other metal. Why not, when the whole country was in such desperate straits? Didn't the wealth of the church really belong to the people? And the church then owned one-fifth of the land, the nobility another fifth, the taxpaying farmers half, and the crown less than one-sixteenth. (The situation was different in Finland, where 96 percent of the land was taxable.) The church also held extensive mortgages and accumulated treasure. By demanding contributions the king could both diminish the material strength of an institution that rivaled the state and simultaneously strengthen the state itself. Furthermore, by recovering estates that had been given to the church in earlier generations he could accomplish the additional objective of gaining the gratitude and support of the nobility. Hence when he repossessed Gripsholm convent, on the excuse that the elder Sture had forced his father to donate it to the church, he set a pattern of recovery for the nobility as a whole; since he acted in this case not as a king but as an individual, the example was particularly tempting.

Step by step Gustav moved to assert the supremacy of the state and to deprive the church of property and power. By tentative advances, cautious retreats, and skillful maneuvers he guided the transition of the church from a Rome-dominated to an exclusively Swedish institution.

One of the early measures was the levy of financial exactions on the bishops-elect which made it impossible for them to pay their annates to Rome; thus they could not be fully sanctioned by the pope and were kept dependent on the king. On the question of the translation of the Bible and the use of the Swedish language in church services the king came out clearly: Why not Swedish, which the people can understand, instead of Latin, which they do not understand? The inclinations of the head of state were apparent, and he was denounced as a Lutheran. Except for the church in Stockholm, small groups influenced by German merchants, and young priests just returned from German study, the Swedish people were still loyal to the old church and especially to the old faith. Gustav Vasa had to reaffirm repeatedly his own loyalty to the established Christian beliefs. He nevertheless acted decisively in matters of church government.

The first broadside attack came at the riksdag of Västerås in 1527. Here the representative body of the nation, stirred by the financial plight of the country, by Gustav's flattery and his threat to resign if he was not supported, and by subtle references to the wealth of the church, decreed a revolutionary program: the bishops' castles and forts should go to the crown as well as all "superfluous" property of cathedrals and canons; the mendicant orders would be put under lay control; the nobles were authorized to reclaim properties lost to the church since 1454; the king would regulate the number of the bishops' soldiery (and he decided they needed none at all); almost all the duties of the church courts (and the fines) would be transferred to the state courts. In brief, by the decisions of Västerås the church was deprived of its secular power, although it is noteworthy that doctrine was not mentioned.

The vast majority of the clergy could accept this much reform, even if they did not like it. For some it was already too much. Bishop Brask, a strong man of the church, left for Germany where he joined Trolle and von Melen in exiled opposition. In 1524 the king had already nominated as archbishop the promising young Johannes Magnus, who was, however, recognized by the pope only as administrator of the see. The challenge of Västerås came at a moment when Henry VIII was asking for a divorce, and when the emperor's soldiers were running wild in Rome. Gustav's bold yet carefully prepared and limited step was well timed. And it was probably necessary if the kingdom was to meet the insistent demands of Lübeck and prevent this voracious ally from inciting Denmark into hostility.

The religious aspects of the Swedish Reformation moved forward at an irregular and slow pace. The king was sympathetic only to some of the new ideas and was most concerned with the political and economic advantages that Protestantism could give him and the state. With his desire to de-emphasize the formalities of worship and with his positive concern for preaching his advisers were wholly in agreement. For the king the real job of the church was teaching morality and good citizenship; he showed not the slightest interest in theology and the dogmatic differences between Catholicism and Lutheranism — unlike, for instance, Henry VIII. Under these circumstances it was natural that the ideological leadership should be assumed by clerics who were close to the king and that there would be strong differences of opinion.

Laurentius Andreae, an experienced churchman who had studied in Germany before Luther's time and had journeyed three times to Rome, in 1523 became King Gustav's secretary-chancellor. He had become acquainted with Lutheran doctrines through Olaus Petri, and to the end of the 1520s he helped shape the king's policy, teaching the king that "the church's wealth was the people's wealth." His too vigorous measures in promoting the national church at last antagonized both people and king, and he was dismissed in 1531.

Olaus Petri succeeded to the chancellorship, but this was not his type of job, and when he was fired in 1533 the king said that he was as fit to be chancellor as a Frisian cow was to spin silk or an ass to play the lute.[4] His talents were better suited for preaching and for writing, and he more than any other shaped the religious (in contrast to the legal and political) phase of the Reformation in Sweden.

The son of a smith in Örebro, Olaus went to Germany in 1516, probably when he was in his early twenties. He studied first in Leipzig and then in Wittenberg shortly before Luther nailed his theses to the church door. In 1518 he became a magister in Wittenberg. We do not know how direct was his contact with Luther, but he was deeply influenced by the reformist teachings and by the wave of German humanism. On return to Sweden in 1519 his first position was as a teacher in the famous cathedral school in Strängnäs. He also became a deacon and did considerable preaching, although he did not administer the sacraments, and he hesitated for years before being ordained a priest in 1539. His talents were brought to the attention of the king through Laurentius Andreae, and in 1524 Gustav appointed Olaus, Master Olof, secretary to the city council of Stockholm.

Olaus's minutes of the council and city affairs in the *Tänkebok* are masterpieces of the secretarial art, concise and colorful. He also wrote statutes for the city, some of which were imbued with a sense of social responsibility that went well beyond the royal taste. He composed rules for judges that were clear in statement, humane in spirit. But Master Olof was inspired by a still higher purpose, and he enthused those about him with the new religious doctrines. He wrote profusely and with a remarkable persuasiveness; he had a knack for establishing intimate contact with his reader. For ten years he enjoyed almost a monopoly of the printing press that had been introduced in Stockholm in 1526, and he produced a flood of translations and pamphlets.

In his reforming zeal Master Olof wanted to arouse debate on the whole question of church reform, but the powerful Bishop Brask refused. Nevertheless the eager young man found occasion to answer in print various objections of those who clung to Roman doctrines and practices. And he took the initiative with "A Useful Information," "A Little Book on the Sacraments," "Answers to Twelve Questions," a psalm book, and many other writings. He had a hand in the translation of the New Testament into Swedish although its magnificent prose was probably more the work of Laurentius Andreae. The project was begun in 1525 and was completed in print by August of 1526. Obviously enjoying the approval of the king, Olaus boldly took a wife in 1525, some weeks before Martin Luther did the same, and he wrote a pamphlet on marriage and another on the cloister life. Marriage brings complications and responsibilities, he admitted, but it is a holy state sanctioned by God, and it can be good for a man to have a wife and children, as illustrated by Abraham, Isaac, and Jacob. "So I conclude that celibacy is no better in God's sight than marriage." [5] He wrote on subjects that concerned people: the relations of church and state and of king and people, the need for salvation, and the deeper meaning of man's existence.

Olaus's frankness and sense of mission as the voice of God are well illustrated in a sermon he preached in the Uppsala cathedral on the occasion of King Gustav's coronation on January 12, 1528. His tone and content reflected his theocratic philosophy: "Kingship is ordained and established by God for the welfare of man, that peace and happiness may exist in city and countryside, so that no man does violence to another; because of this it is a Christian office useful and good when used in a Christian manner. . . . The king is not installed so that he may seek his own good . . . but that he may promote the welfare of the common man. . . . God said that the Israelites should take as king him whom his brothers had chosen . . . not from among foreign peoples, but from among their own brothers. . . . He shall not collect many horses, or gold or silver [for himself]. . . . But kingly power gives opportunity to fall from God's advice out of power and arrogance."[6] Olaus goes on to spell out the duties of the king to the people and vice versa, for all is properly ordained — that the king will hold the government, that the bishops and priests will preach God's word, and so on.

Olaus still enjoyed royal favor when Gustav appointed him chancellor in 1531, but it is understandable that the fervor and firm reforming purpose of Master Olof would run counter to the political opportunism of Gustav. The wonder is that cooperation lasted so long; it did so only because each could use the other to help fulfill his own purposes, though temperaments and ideals were at opposite poles. Shortly after Olaus's bitter dismissal a conspiracy against the king was reported to Olaus in the confessional. The sanctity of the confessional prevented him from telling anyone except Laurentius Andreae, although he did help to avert the deed. Gustav learned of the incident but did nothing until, in a fit of depression a few years later, he charged Olaus with treason and had him condemned to death (along with Laurentius). Gustav pardoned them immediately but imposed a heavy fine, which was paid by the city of Stockholm. It may appear odd that after such events the king in 1543 appointed Olaus school inspector for Stockholm and preacher in the Great Church. Nevertheless, Olaus thereafter felt constrained and devoted himself increasingly to writing — much of it not published until after his death.

His most noteworthy later work was his Swedish Chronicle (*En swensk cröneka*), a history of Sweden to 1520 characterized not only by a superb literary style but by a critical method far surpassing that of any previous chronicler. The history was dominated, naturally enough, by a moralizing purpose and the doctrine of God's will and power. It also reflected Olaus's opposition to Gustav's policies without mentioning Gustav. The comments on Magnus Ladulås's heavy tax policy and his dependence on German advisers were obviously as applicable to Gustav as to Magnus. No wonder Olaus steadfastly refused when the king urged him to write the history of Gustav's own regime.

As "one of God's commonalty" Olaus wrote for his fellows in a picturesque style, e.g., "it does not help to tell us how old the pope's authority is: the devil is old but he is none the better for that." In his use of the Swedish language Olaus was a renewer and purifier; in this and in his nationalistic inspiration he was comparable to Luther. He stood at the forefront of the challenge to the old regime and the old ways of thinking. He preached with authority and eloquence and did not hesitate to point the true way for both king and people. He was the heroic figure of the Reformation in Sweden — a humanist, creative spirit, and man of piety and principle. Primarily to him is due the credit for making the Swedish Reformation a product of education and therefore firmly rooted. Especially after the secular changes of Västerås, individual churches and church councils made changes in worship, Olaus's handbook gained acceptance, the use of the Swedish mass spread, clerical marriage was permitted, and Catholic practices such as the use of incense declined.[7]

Laurentius Petri, the younger brother of Olaus, played a different but also significant role. He was a more submissive personality — or at least he could adapt to circumstances and await his opportunity. When Johannes Magnus could no longer stomach the trend in church affairs and left for Rome, Laurentius Petri was elected by the clergy as archbishop in 1531. Because he was consecrated by Bishop Petrus Magni, who had been ordained in canonical fashion in 1524, he preserved the apostolic succession in the Swedish church. He was a dedicated reformer, and he was willing to follow the royal commands, even voting for his brother's death sentence in 1540. He allowed himself to accept the king's plan for organizing the church under superintendents instead of bishops, and as archbishop he took second place behind Georg Norman, who was the top superintendent. (This demeaning and secularizing policy was unacceptable to Olaus.) Throughout Gustav's reign Laurentius and his office were repeatedly disregarded and degraded. But Laurentius was granted a long life and under Erik XIV and Johan III he saw his plans for church government enacted into law.

The reformers led a reluctant people and a hesitant king. Progress was retarded by royal compromises and clashes of temperament as well as by popular uprisings against both taxation policy and liturgical reforms. The country eventually and with unanimity swung into the Protestant camp; there were no martyrs to stain the record (assuming that we do not count the numerous exiles or the political executions). Not until 1593 was the Lutheran creed officially agreed upon for the nation. It had been a slow process.

## THREATS AND ALARUMS

By the later 1520s Gustav Vasa sat firmly in the saddle, but Sweden was still a balky horse, and many were the hands from outside eager to grasp the bridle. For a decade the external threat to the Vasa rule came from the machinations of the exiled but stubborn and resilient Dane Kristian II. The emperor Charles V retained a modicum of interest in his brother-in-law, not for his own sake but for his two daughters and grandson. And the daughters' husbands had claims for themselves. Intrigues of international scope were constantly in the air. Their most substantial support came in the end from the Netherlands, a country as eager to dethrone Lübeck from its trade monopoly in the North as Kristian was hopeful to unseat Gustav.

After years of frustration Kristian II and a small force landed in Norway in November 1531. The Norwegians swung to his support and with an increasing force he marched south into Bohuslän on his way to the granary of Skåne. Frederik I and Gustav now became natural allies in the common cause of defense, though each wanted the other to do the fighting. Gustav ordered caution and delay, and his commander was able to capture or destroy enough supply lines so that it was impossible for Kristian to march through. Without a battle the invader had to return to Norway. He lost all hope of settling by force and sailed to Denmark to appeal to Frederik. There he was forthwith imprisoned and spent the rest of his life in jail. Both Sweden and Denmark were saved from becoming the northern flank of the Hapsburg empire. The Dutch, too, gave up on Kristian II in July 1532 and concentrated on achieving success in their commercial rivalry.

The threat from Kristian was removed for the moment. Could Sweden now escape the tutelage of Lübeck and win a degree of economic freedom? Perhaps Gustav could take advantage of the rivalry between Lübeck and the Dutch. Events in the Hanseatic center seemed to offer hope. In Lübeck a young and vigorous Protestant group, headed by Jürgen Wullenwever, overthrew the conservative council that had aided Sweden and soon found itself at war with the Netherlands. Lübeck asked for aid from Sweden, its pledged ally. Gustav had been angered by Lübeck's overbearing attitude and particularly by an undervaluation of the wares that Sweden had sent as payment on its war debt. He grasped this as an excuse for refusing aid, claiming that Sweden's debt was paid, and used the opportunity to denounce the city's privileges in Sweden and to tax its merchants. The provocations he had suffered were undoubtedly great, but his renunciation of his obligations was too extreme for his councillors, who said the debt should be paid in proper fashion. Johan av Hoya, Gustav's brother-in-law and the viceroy in Finland, had pledged his person to Lübeck that the loan would be repaid; he was so shocked at the king's attitude that he left the country and returned to Germany to join the Swedish exiles. Lübeck was of course enraged.

Denmark debated how it should treat similar demands from Lübeck, and its situation was confused further by the death of Frederik I. For successor the nobility favored Frederik's son (who became Kristian III and reigned from 1534 to 1559), though the Danish towns opposed him. In the meantime the council controlled the country, and in February 1534 it made an alliance with Sweden against Lübeck. Faced with almost certain defeat the Lübeckers made a sudden about-face, signed an armistice with the Dutch, and proceeded to invade Holstein, Skåne, and the Danish islands. They righteously condemned the "unchristian rogues and robbers of the Danish Council and Norway and the tyrant and bloodhound king of Sweden."[8] Furthermore the Lübeckers promised to free Kristian II and restore him. This was perhaps their fatal blunder, for even the hint of Kristian's restoration was enough to enable Gustav to get the Swedes solidly behind him. Gustav lent money to Kristian III and supported him and the Danish nobles in their internal struggle for the Danish throne. After initial Lübeck victories in 1534 this "Count's Feud" or *Grevefejden* (named for Lübeck's commander, Count Kristofer of Oldenburg) changed character. While the Danes drove the Lübeckers out of Holstein the Swedes took Halland and broke into Skåne, their combined fleets defeated the Hanseatic navy, and in a battle on Fyn in June 1535 the Hansa army was beaten and the careers of Gustav's enemies Johan av Hoya and Gustav Trolle were abruptly ended.

The Count's Feud ended only in a truce for five years, but the essential objective was accomplished. Materially and psychologically the Swedish debt to Lübeck was wiped out. New privileges were issued to Lübeck traders but these were granted on Swedish terms, not extorted by Lübeck's power. Now Sweden could impose taxes, could permit other foreign traders to enter Sweden, and its own traders could move freely beyond the Baltic. Hanseatic hegemony was destroyed, and Sweden was economically emancipated.

With Denmark relations continued to be cordial but cautious. Kristian III had Swedish cooperation to thank for his throne and he honored his obligation. He swung Denmark into the Protestant camp and tried to get Gustav admitted with him into the Schmalkald League of Protestant princes and imperial cities. The league, however, embarrassed the Swedish king by rejecting him. Perhaps it was for the best; Gustav had much to do at home.

The strain of constant strife, suspicion, and fear took its toll even of the strong man Gustav Vasa. He was subject to periods of depression, and the late 1530s were especially difficult years for the king personally. It was during this period that he lashed out at the Lübeck emissaries in an almost Hitlerian invective. On another occasion he chased one of his own state councillors through the courtyard with a drawn dagger. He was being attacked by his onetime favorite Olaus Petri and was beside himself when he discovered that Olaus knew of a plot against him but would not report it because he had learned it through the confessional. Hence the treason charge against Olaus and Laurentius Andreae and their sentence to death followed by immediate pardon. Gustav was neither so sure of himself nor so brutal that such things could leave his spirit unscathed.

Fortunately the 1540s opened auspiciously in the realm of foreign affairs. Gustav's German adviser, Conrad von Pyhy, instigated negotiations with a variety of governments, both Catholic and Protestant, but gradually Sweden swung into the Protestant camp. In the spring of 1541 Gustav met with representatives of the Hansa and must have enjoyed playing Lübeck off against the others, for he now held the upper hand. Thereafter ensued a cordial conference with the Danes at Brömsebro, on the border just south of Kalmar, probably masterminded by Pyhy. Gustav and Kristian III got along famously, submerging their suspicions, and on September 15, 1541 signed the Treaty of Brömsebro, which provided for friendship and alliance. Denmark paid off its debt to Sweden for the loan incurred during the Count's Feud, and the epoch of happy cooperation continued. Kristian III again tried to draw Gustav into the Protestant prince's club, but certain complications now made the Swedish king less eager to join.

During 1541 both Denmark and Sweden were negotiating with France for economic and political agreements. In November Kristian III concluded a treaty with King Francis I of France, and in the summer of 1542 Gustav sent to France a mission headed by Pyhy. Gustav directed caution and restraint, but the brocaded throne of Francis I, the Gobelin tapestries, and the Renaissance splendor of the entertainment, plus the flattering attentions of cardinals and courtiers, went to Pyhy's head. He promised that Sweden would send twenty-five thousand men and fifty ships to France for its war with the empire. He spent lavish sums on gifts, and in Germany on his way back to Sweden he contracted for still greater outlays and hired a number of German knights to come to Sweden to aid in suppressing the new uprising in Småland. When the men began to arrive and the accounts piled up Gustav was first worried, then angered, and he learned also that Pyhy was charged with bigamy. Soon after the envoy returned, after a year and a half abroad, he was dismissed and imprisoned for life.

The Germans hired by Pyhy were supposedly needed to suppress the largest revolt of Gustav's reign. Although Dalarna had learned its lesson through the suppression of the Daljunker and other rebellious outbursts, Småland was the area that was seething with discontent in 1542. The people complained about the fines imposed for their 1537 revolt, the weight of taxes, and most bitterly about the removal from the churches of the bridal crowns and "monstrances and other ornaments, and all that our fathers and ancestors have given in honor of God, so that soon it will be as pleasant to walk in a desolate forest as in church." [9] The royal protection of deer and trees harmed the fields under culture. Most obnoxious was the royal interference with traditional trade activity. Down the rivers and along the forest roads of Småland and Halland the farmers took various products — cattle and sheep, skins and hides, wood, kegs of butter and tallow, and barrels of tar and osmund iron — to the markets not of the Swedes but of the Danish merchants in the towns of Blekinge and in western ports like Varberg, Halmstad, Hälsingborg. Gustav forbade this export activity, partly to check the expenditure of valuable goods for the hops, beer, and fish the farmers brought back, partly to redirect the trade and the profits to the Swedish port of Kalmar. The farmers were annoyed and demanded a return to the "good old times."

Nils Dacke spearheaded the protest. Nils and a Jon Andersson had killed a hated bailiff in 1536 and fled for a time to the woods of Blekinge. Nils's prosperous family had paid his fine and he had returned to a border farm at Flaka. It was possibly after another brush with the law that he decided in 1542 to instigate a general uprising. He had political sense and organizing ability, and the people scarcely needed persuasion. By some historians he has been labeled a Småland-Engelbrekt. He mounted a formidable revolt before the king realized its seriousness. With the peasant force vastly outnumbering the government contingent there was at last nothing for the king to do but make an armistice. Nils Dacke established himself at Kronoberg, returned the churches to Catholicism, and attracted support from the Kristian II-Hapsburg circles and from Gustav's other enemies. Maybe he thought he could hold Småland as a fief. The rebels offered the crown to Svante Sture (son of Sten Sture the Younger), who refused it, though Lübeck pressed him hard. Kristian II's two sons-in-law vied eagerly for the prize, but their rivalry weakened the power of both.

Gustav, with Pyhy gone, had to handle everything himself. While he was gathering strength to take decisive action he drew up a typical piece of Vasa propaganda to the people who were demanding back "the good old times":

You want it like old times, do you? What were the old times? With 400–600 soldiers when the land lay open to invaders, merchants were robbed of ships and goods, people thrown overboard and drowned like dogs, fishing stopped, cattle taken, houses burned? Is it such old customs? Now we have 4000–6000 soldiers, with deadly guns and swords, harness and horses, good ships and sailors. And no one has lost even a chicken. We hope people are not ungrateful for these new customs.

In Finland the old ways as you know meant murder and burning. And also in Västergötland under King Hans and Kristian. And there was Åsunden for Herr Sten, and the bath house in Tiveden — that was a hot fire! And Good Friday in Uppsala where many poor men lay for the dogs and never got to a churchyard. [These were reminders of civil wars and encounters with the Danes.] Such was part of the burden and hardship the common people had to bear with the old customs, with wives and children sitting at home in hunger and sorrow, fields and meadows in ruin — but the taxes had still to be paid. So our understanding Swedish man can weigh whether these old customs were so good for the fatherland.

And think of the might of the bishops and prelates. Think of Archbishop Gustav [Trolle] and how he sanctified the salt for the Swedish men at Uppsala and poured hot water on them at Stäket and burned incense so that our noses smarted. No, Sweden is a kingdom and not the realm of priests and bishops.

But it's complaints everywhere. Gladly does a man have a warm cottage, but he doesn't want to split firewood. Everything is dearer, yes [and details are given]. . . . But we have to have soldiers, and they have to be paid, and out of the king's treasury, that is, out of taxes and income. How will all this go if the peasants ask for everything as it was?

We hope all you dear yeomen will consider all the great burden and unpleasantness we have had, gaining peace on all sides, and freedom to move by land and water, and friendship with cities and princes, and purchases of hops and salt and all needs, unlike the old customs.[10]

Such a speech was for Småland's consumption. In other parts of the country the artful propagandist started a whispering campaign that Småland had not done its part in the war of liberation and that the Smålanders were making a lot of money in their commerce with the Danes and were responsible for the high prices everywhere.

Gustav had a healthy respect of the military skills of the forest rebels, perhaps especially for their proficiency in building the abatis (bråte) to trap the unwary on sharp tree branches, or to smash them under trees that were almost cut through and ready to be pulled down over horses and men. And he learned to feel contempt for the German mercenaries he had hired who could not cope with woodland warfare. Here was something that had to be handled by Swedish men and methods. The Dacke uprising was not merely an intrigue by an ambitious power-seeker; it was a real civil war resulting from perceived abuses and backed by an aroused peasantry throughout a large area of Småland. It was a fundamental economic, social, and religious protest. But Gustav Vasa was by this time well entrenched on the throne and he was able to muster the overwhelming strength needed to crush this most serious internal rebellion in Swedish history. In the spring of 1543, at last aware of the threatening situation, he launched an irresistible force against the rebels. Nils

Dacke was killed on the border of Blekinge, several hundred of the rebels were shipped to Finland, and heavy fines were levied against the others. The kingdom was restored to peace and submission.[11] Gustav had reason to be thankful for the recent Brömsebro accord with Kristian III and for the Danish king's faithfulness to his pledge of noninterference. One small compensation that came out of the trouble was that it gave Gustav an excuse for withdrawing from the dangerous commitments that Pyhy had made with the French. Now Gustav could turn his full attention to internal organization and development.

With the strengthening of the monarchy and the passage of time the dynastic claims of the heirs of Kristian II became less and less significant, but they were a source of possible trouble as long as the emperor Charles V remained interested. In 1550–51 Sweden agreed at last to the terms of the Danish-Hapsburg treaty of 1544 (the Treaty of Speier), which provided for the renunciation of the claims of Charles V's granddaughters in return for the bridal payment. The thirty-year-old shadow of Kristian II was obliterated, but Gustav never made the agreed bridal payment. By the late 1540s Gustav had lost interest in the Schmalkald League and hence avoided involvement in its defeat. The intimate alliance with Denmark faded into forgetfulness, but at least did not, during Gustav's time, end in bloodshed. The controversy over the use of the three crowns in the Danish coat of arms had just begun. The most serious of the foreign complications of the next decade was with Russia.

Treaties between Sweden and Russia habitually solved nothing and had to be renegotiated upon the death of the sovereign of either country. Despite the sixty-year truce made at Novgorod in 1537 the Russians attacked in Finland in 1555 to try to halt the Finnish-Swedish expansion of settlement in Karelia and the recurrent murders and clashes in the wilderness. Gustav himself went to Finland and the Russians were repulsed at Viborg and Nyslott, but military events were inconclusive. In 1557, nevertheless, Sweden had to be satisfied with a rather humiliating peace "by the grace of the Tsar" (signed incidentally for the first time in Moscow rather than in Novgorod). Gustav had a hard time holding a peaceful line thereafter, for his sons Erik and Johan were enticed into commitments in the Baltic lands to the south and Russia struck there in 1558. For the moment the king's authority prevailed, but he knew that his time was drawing to a close.

## CONSTRUCTIVE STATE BUILDING

Suppression of rebellion at home and maneuvering for peace abroad represented the negative aspects of government. On the positive and creative side Gustav's tremendous energy enabled him to contribute much, and there were manifold state problems needing solution. One of the obvious problems was that of maintaining a dynasty.

Gustav had had little time to consider matrimony, but as he got the country somewhat under control he began to think of a wife and an heir. His emissaries looked for a bride who would bring prestige and maybe a useful alliance such as Kristian II's alliance with the Hapsburg family through marriage. To his chagrin Gustav discovered that the parents of princesses were not eager to see their daughters move north where frequent revolts still challenged the new monarch. An interesting aspect of the search is that the religious question hardly entered the king's thinking. It only happened that the agreement finally reached was for the hand of the daughter of the Protestant duke of Sachsen-Lauenburg. The Västergötland rebellion of 1529 and arguments about financial security caused hesitation, but Lübeck's diplomacy helped to arrange the match. On September 24, 1531 in the Great Church of Stockholm, on her eighteenth birthday, Katarina married the thirty-five-year-old king of Sweden. It was a brilliant affair, solemnized by Laurentius Andreae who had become archbishop only a month earlier. (Johannes Magnus had gone into exile.) A son Erik was the only issue of the union and the queen died in 1535. The marriage did not result in important diplomatic alliances, but the queen's parents remained friendly with Gustav after her death, and the later marriage of Katarina's sister to Kristian III of Denmark may have been a help in the personal relations between the two Scandinavian kings.

For his second marriage the king could afford to stay closer to home, and he took as queen a Swedish noblewoman, Margareta Leijonhufvud. With her he had ten children, of whom three sons (Johan, Magnus, and Karl) and five daughters outlived the parents. Upon Margareta's death Gustav married her niece, Katarina Stenbock. There were no more offspring, but the dynasty was already insured. In Uppsala cathedral the body of King Gustav lies between those of his first two wives.

One of the great lacks in Gustav's own state building had become glaringly evident — trained manpower. The king was that type of dominating, efficient administrator whose memory and capacity for detail were phenomenal and who could do all tasks better than any subordinate. Yet time did not permit him to do everything. He discouraged and antagonized his assistants so that few stayed with him long. And he had no reserve of trained human talent. Since his own brief student days the University of Uppsala had scarcely functioned, and early in the 1530s it closed its doors. The church, without lands and extra income, found it hard to support its schools. The king who had taken the lands did amazingly little for education. He did grant scholarships to bright young men to study abroad, e.g., Olaus Petri's younger brother Laurentius and Olov Larsson, who was sent abroad as a trainee in mining. But such grants were meager and few. When qualified Swedes were not available for government jobs — accountants, secretaries, diplomats — the king had to look to foreigners. To find such men who were not simply adventurers but were able and loyal was difficult; Gustav had to take whomever came along, and his luck was not good.

The time around 1540 was known as the "German period" because then Germans dominated the king's councils. Men from Brandenburg and Mecklenburg and Stralsund were given court posts. Most important and most disappointing was Dr. Conrad von Pyhy, a German-born diplomatic adventurer with experience at several continental courts, including that of the emperor. He was a clever administrator, and the government was weakened when he had to be dismissed. Another aide was Georg Norman, a more solid sort, who started as a tutor and became a church administrator; he was used for confidential missions, was loyal, and stayed for a long time, the happy exception. These men and others brought to Sweden the German ideas of Church-state relations, the German administrative and military systems, and the German concepts of strong monarchy. It was Pyhy who, during Gustav's illness, read off the new church regulations. With him a new tone crept into proclamations which seemed to transform the simple folk-king of earlier days into a lordly prince. The change was formalized in 1540 when the monarchy was made hereditary. Torture was introduced into judicial procedure, the military organization was put on a more regular basis, and state finances were carefully systematized with detailed accounting required from the bailiffs. The fief system of compensation and appointments was retained but tightened, for Gustav kept close track of his men and shifted them about so that they would not become too secure. For the more important administrative posts he used nobles and especially his own family, all of whom served at his pleasure. One of his most trusted men for special missions was Svante Sture, the second son of Sten Sture the Younger, and this appointment represented a reconciliation with a jealous branch of his family.

In 1544 the first full riksdag in fourteen years was called at Västerås, not to assist in crisis as before but to plan in peace for the future. It was notable in the first place because now for the first time the clergy assembled as an Estate separate from the nobility. In a far-reaching political action the riksdag revised the principle of monarchic succession to inaugurate the German and continental model by order of birth rather than according to the looser hereditary-elective system of Swedish tradition; younger sons would be granted duchies and accorded a high degree of independence in the government thereof (preparing trouble for the future). This riksdag also reorganized the defense system in response to the king's desire to have local troops ready to cope with rebellion. Soldiers would be recruited by districts; the nobility would constitute the mounted force and the soldiers would be bowmen with imported steel weapons (although on the continent most soldiers were by then pikemen). Universal service would be the rule for wartime, but in times of peace only one man in five or six would be called. Mercenaries would also be used, but as much as possible these too were to be Swedish not foreign; the guard in Stockholm that was 64 percent German in 1545 dropped to 10 percent German in 1553. Thus Sweden became the first country of modern Europe to combine both universal service and a native standing army even in peacetime.

Gustav Vasa pounded the refractory people of Sweden into submission to the crown and into unity as a nation. He was both a harsh taskmaster and a superb demagogue. Even though he denounced their weaknesses the people demanded to hear him speak, because he was a master of imagery and invective and cajolery. He was a lover of music and an artist with the lute, and he was an infectiously gay and charming host. As statesman it was Gustav who carried the policies of the Stures and of Karl Knutsson to fulfillment. He brought the medieval natural economy to its culmination, collected taxes in kind (and also in money), and made the crown a major commercial company — selling the hides and butter collected in taxes for cloth and gold. He destroyed the church as an economic institution and augmented fivefold the share of the crown in the economy. He built great treasure rooms in Stockholm and Gripsholm where he kept gold and ornaments from the churches. Gustav made himself the richest man in Sweden, but he could hardly draw a line between his personal holdings and those of the crown — "God, we, and Sweden's crown" were all one concept; together he and the crown owned by the end of his reign almost nineteen thousand *hemman* (homesteads), more than one quarter of the lands and farms of the country. "As his land up against the midnight sun and the Lapps has no end, so also with his income," wrote Sebastian Münster.[12] The lands of the church had been reduced drastically, and of the nobles somewhat, so that the nobility and church together now held only about one-fifth; almost half was owned by the independent tax-paying farmers. Forty years had brought a minor revolution in land ownership.

The founder of the Vasa line managed his kingdom like a vast estate. It was all his, and the people were his children and his workers. He applied to Sweden the attitudes and methods he had learned as a boy at Rydboholm. He gave advice and orders on how to fish, how to build a barge, how and when to harvest — hay had to be in by St. Olof's day (July 29), grain by St. Bartholomew's day (August 24), and unnecessary social and church affairs had to be cancelled when people had to tend their fields. The royal farms were models for others to copy. If a man let his buildings fall apart and left his fields uncared for they reverted to the crown, being then the proper demesne of the king like the fish in the streams and the iron in the mines. No wonder that two-thirds of the land came to lie under bailiffs' direction and that products were gathered into great central warehouses for distribution.

Stubborn and ruthless though Gustav was in quelling rebellion he was also a leader who could wait. When he sensed that opposition to new Lutheran beliefs was strong, he slowed the process of the Reformation. Although he crushed the Nils Dacke uprising he also learned from the complaints of the rebels that the burdens of taxes and restrictions were intolerable, and he lightened them; he then went further and abandoned Pyhy and his adventurous foreign policy which had created the burdens. In the economic sphere, where he was shrewd if not imaginative, he began with the idea that it was best for Sweden to trade abroad through Lübeck and let the Germans take the risks. Perhaps he feared that Swedish traders, if they traveled abroad, would be too inclined to import useless luxuries; repeatedly he railed at them for being stupid. But gradually he came to realize that by allowing Lübeck to conduct its foreign trade Sweden lost control and lost profits. Hence by guile and by force he broke Lübeck's stranglehold on the Swedish economy. Then he drew up a plan for a Swedish Trading Company. It would be based on voluntary principles, he said, but it would use appointed ports (Stockholm, Lödöse, Söderköping, Kalmar, and Åbo) and ship abroad only through Stockholm. No one outside the company would be permitted to handle the goods in which it dealt. Craftsmen would be employed by the company in Sweden to concentrate on the making of a few items — like hats and bonnets of felt. Foreigners would be attracted to Sweden, and an able foreigner would head the company. Losses abroad would be made up by increasing prices in Sweden. Though this grand plan was stillborn, it showed Gustav's capacity for rethinking his problems.

The king developed a navy and a well-trained army. But he avoided war. Although he was attracted by dreams of continental diplomacy and military activity, he drew back before the point of final commitment. The defense of Sweden was his consistent aim, and he did his best when Russia attacked. Then he made peace quickly and he refused to involve Sweden in the defense of the Baltic lands south of Finland.

This volatile, pragmatic, paternalistic, and nationalistic nobleman prepared Sweden for the modern world. He was deceitful, unscrupulous, violent. He was also single minded in his will to establish his own power and to make Sweden strong, and he was granted a life-span in which he could accomplish his work. Out of chaos and strife and poverty he started Sweden on the road to national self-realization, order, and strength. His restless energy, his versatile interests, and his care for detail were what the country needed. He was a man of stature and character comparable to great contemporaries like Henry VIII of England, Francis I of France, Charles V of the Holy Roman Empire, and

Suleiman the Magnificent of the Ottoman Empire. In forty years, Gustav Vasa built a strong and respected state. In June 1560 at his last riksdag, in Stockholm, Gustav produced his testament. The crown would go to his firstborn, Erik; Finland to Johan as duke and other provinces to the younger sons; 100,000 daler to each daughter for dowry; and all the younger siblings were ordered to be subject to the king. The will was an appeal to his children and to the Estates to cooperate in a constructive peace.[13]

## Consolidation under the Vasa Sons

| | |
|---|---|
| Erik XIV | 1560–1568 |
| Johan III | 1568–1592 |
| Sigismund | 1592–1599 |
| Karl IX | 1599–1611 |

The half century after Gustav I was both confusing and constructive. The new state still had to find its place in the power structure of northern Europe. Kings other than the dominating innovator had to test the relationship of monarchy to aristocracy and to the rest of society. The process was complicated because the Vasa sons divided among them, rather than combined, the talents of their father. The Protestant religious settlement had to go through a period of trial. Economic rivalries both within and without had to be adjusted. The jostling and strife were bitter and dangerous, and it was only good luck that they proved in the long run to be strengthening rather than disruptive in their effects.

PROBLEMS OF SUCCESSION AND FAMILY CONTROVERSIES

Since the monarchy had been made hereditary Erik, the son by Gustav's marriage with Katarina of Sachsen-Lauenburg, succeeded without question, and his romantic sense of history led him to append the numeral XIV. His half brothers, the sons of Gustav and his second wife, Margareta Leijonhufvud, were next in line: Johan (1537–92), Magnus (1542–95), and Karl (1550–1611). There were five daughters too, who needed husbands and dowries. The father of the kingdom also wanted to be a good father to his children, and he arranged that each son should have a separate duchy. It was a dangerous piece of generosity that might easily have destroyed the centralization that he had achieved. Johan had taken over Finland as early as 1557, and for the moment only he created problems. Magnus was mentally ill, and Karl was but ten years old.

Erik XIV had been trained for the kingship, and in personality he seemed at first to fit his career and his era. Tall, graceful, versatile — in appearance and manner he was a prince of the Renaissance. In the years before he became king he developed his own court at Kalmar, where he decorated the castle in the brilliant style of the day, and to which he invited foreign painters and musicians. For a decade he had assisted his father in affairs of state, and in 1555–57, when Gustav was off fighting the Russians, Erik supervised the government at home. Romantic and ambitious, imbued with visionary dreams of Sweden's greatness, it is no wonder that he sought the hand of one fair princess after another. But always in vain. The prestige of the Swedish monarchy was not yet established. Most eagerly of all he sought marriage and political alliance with Elizabeth of England, and he was on his way to sue in person when in the late summer of 1560 he was recalled to Sweden by the death of his father.

Relations between Erik and Johan had been good and the brothers had already shown a mutual interest in Swedish expansion. But Erik had reason to suspect that Johan might act independently from his Finnish base. To assure his own authority and to maintain the unity of the kingdom, he called a riksdag to Arboga in 1561 and pushed through new regulations (the Arboga Articles) that established royal oversight of the duchies and forbade the dukes to engage in foreign diplomacy except in matrimonial matters. But Duke Johan refused to be checked by his brother's assertion of authority. He directly challenged the king by his marriage in 1562 with Katarina Jagellonica, sister of the king of Poland, and by his projects for independent expansion in Livonia. From his stronghold in Åbo castle he tried to organize opposition. Erik, however, struck quickly and clapped Johan and his wife in prison.

Erik's suspicious nature and sharp retaliation only engendered more antagonism. The king tried to ingratiate himself with the nobility by creating the new titles of count and baron and by honoring several of Johan's relatives, for it was Johan and not Erik who was interrelated (through his mother) with the Swedish nobility. Nevertheless, for his close advisers Erik used commoners, especially the legal-trained Jöran Persson. Among the nobility he did not win love (which Machiavelli said was best) and had to fall back on fear (which was second best). Some three hundred death sentences were used more to frighten than to kill, but soon the most frightened man in the kingdom was the king. His astrological studies boded ill for the spring of 1567, his pride was hurt by the failure of his matrimonial proposals, and his mind was strained by the pressures of war and political decisions. In May the riksdag in Uppsala, at the king's urging, condemned four of the mistrusted Sture clan along with a number of others. Emotions were tense all around, within the king especially. Just before the legal process was complete Erik, in a sudden consuming rage, rushed in and struck his dagger into Nils Svantesson Sture, then ordered the guards to kill all except two of the other condemned men. Whether he was insane before the killings is a moot point. Immediately afterwards he rushed into the woods and for the rest of the year was incapacited for the work of government. The council took over direction of the state. It released Johan and Katarina and held the detested Jöran Persson accountable for the crown's malicious treatment of the nobility. Persson was vulnerable, for he was the head of Erik's espionage organization as well as the chief prosecutor. Now he was sentenced to death, though execution was delayed.

By January 1568 Erik had recovered his health and now not only resumed control of the government and reinstated Secretary Persson but also led the Swedish army successfully against the Danes. The king's illness and even his violence might be accepted as being in the nature of things, but old conflicts were still not resolved. Furthermore, at the end of his period of insanity Erik had married his beautiful young mistress, Karin Månsdotter, who in January 1568 bore him a son. The marriage was a new affront to the aristocracy, and the son was a threat to Johan's hopes for succession.

In the summer of 1568 Johan raised the standard of revolt, with the support of his eighteen-year-old brother Karl and steadily increasing numbers of the nobility. Erik found himself more and more alone. He had to turn Jöran Persson over to the rebels, who promptly executed him. His ablest loyal general, the Frenchman Charles de Mornay, was in Danish captivity. Johan issued persuasive propaganda portraying Erik as a tyrant and soon completely controlled public opinion and assumed military control of Stockholm. In January 1569 the riksdag recognized the fait accompli, deposed Erik, and raised Johan III to the throne. Erik was taken from one castle prison to another, first with his family and then alone, occasionally sane, sometimes lapsing into insanity. In 1577 he died, and soon rumor said it was because of arsenic in his pea soup. In 1958 a reexamination of the body did indeed indicate the presence of an unusual amount of arsenic as well as a laming blow from a guard's sword. Whether Johan was responsible or only relieved we cannot say.

Johan III was a less dramatic figure — suspicious like Erik XIV and many of the Vasas, shrewd, vacillating but stubborn, interested in religious theory, and with grand ideas of Swedish power. He had aesthetic concern and taste and remodeled several important castles — Kalmar, Gripsholm, Åbo, and others, giving a Swedish touch to an imported Renaissance style. He lacked the practical turn of mind and the strong economic interest of his father yet he wrestled bravely with the wrecked finances left by Erik. When he came to the throne he granted to his brother Karl, the duke in central Sweden, those royal privileges that Gustav had granted to his sons and that Erik had taken away. Perhaps these concessions only whetted Karl's ambition, and conflict was exacerbated by differences in religious outlook and the issues of foreign policy. Not that there was any threat to Johan's kingship, for he held an impregnable legal position. He further strengthened his ties with the native nobility when, after Katarina's death in 1583, he married Gunilla Bielke in 1585. However, when he allowed his son Sigismund to be elected to the throne of Poland in 1587, tensions increased all around.

Sigismund, more vacillating and probably less able than the older Vasas, had a complex role to play. Born in 1566 while his parents were imprisoned, raised as a Roman Catholic according to his mother's faith and by foreign tutors, transferred to Poland as king at age 21, he had little chance to become familiar with things Swedish. When his father died it was only with difficulty that he got permission from the Polish diet to return to Sweden, where he was crowned king of Sweden in 1594. Since his primary seat was in Poland, he had to delegate authority in Sweden. His appointees in key fortress-castles found it difficult to compete with the influence of the council and of Duke Karl, who forcefully took over as regent already in 1594. Sigismund's attempts to introduce Catholicism antagonized both clergy and people, for the Protestantism that Gustav Vasa found difficult to establish had now become deeply rooted. In Poland Sigismund was unpopular, and in Sweden his position was so undermined that in 1598 he had to invade his own country. He won Kalmar in a quick stroke, and probably most Swedes at this point supported him as their legitimate sovereign. But he was no match for the wiles and the ruthlessness of his uncle Karl. Sigismund was outmaneuvered in an engagement at Stångebro, was placed in a desperate military situation, and was forced to agree to the humiliating treaty of Linköping on September 28, 1598. Yet all was not yet lost, and to this day we can't explain why he withdrew to Kalmar instead of to Stockholm and then sailed off to Poland. He did not resign his claims to the throne but by retreat he sacrificed the councillors he left in Karl's hands and lost the respect of thousands of his loyal subjects. Stångebro marked the turning point. Alienation led to his deposition in 1599, and although he struggled for years through arms and intrigue to reassert his rights, he became more of a nuisance than a threat. He never saw Sweden again.

Duke Karl, youngest of the sons of Gustav Vasa, knew early the reality of power in his duchy (Värmland, Närke, Södermanland and a few parishes in Västmanland and Västergötland), and in the kingdom he experienced both its reality and its uncertainty. After maneuvering the overthrow of Sigismund, Karl knew himself to be a usurper, and he hesitated to assume the actual title of king. He did so in 1604 only after Johan III's younger son Johan, the half brother of Sigismund, had renounced his claim; at last Karl allowed himself to be crowned in 1607 as Karl IX. Though Karl lacked the aesthetic inclinations of his brothers, he had the practical administrative and economic talents of their father. In his vast central principality he founded cities (e.g., Karlstad and Mariestad), regulated the guilds closely, made himself the biggest merchant, promoted agriculture and mining, and ruled with a firm hand. As regent and as king he pursued similar policies, but he became increasingly involved in foreign affairs and campaigns in Livonia. His assertion of authority made for strained relations with the aristocracy, though he was flexible enough and strong enough to retain the upper hand. In his rivalry with Sigismund he used effectively a talent for talking to the people at markets and at musterings of troops; he displayed a demagogic genius reminiscent of his father. And when the nobles or the council were recalcitrant he could take harsh vengeance. As for the leaders who sided with Sigismund to the end, Karl used both threats and bribes to get the court of the Estates to decree death sentences against Erik Sparre, Ture Bielke, and two of the Banérs. (The sentences were carried out in what was later to be known as the Linköping Bloodbath of 1600.) He executed the cultured but rebellious Hogenskild Bielke in 1605. Karl's roughshod methods angered the nobility but silenced them, and he kept the kingdom unified. Royal authority was savagely asserted.

Karl's two marriages with German princesses provided for the succession, both immediate and distant: by Maria of the Palatinate a daughter Katarina (whose son became Karl X a half-century later); by Kristina of Holstein-Gottorp two sons, Gustav Adolf and Karl Filip, and a daughter, Maria Elisabet. Politically Karl may not have helped himself with his independent and almost Calvinistic religious views, but he could and did subordinate his own preferences in order to use Protestant nationalism against Catholic and Polish influences.[14]

Before passing into the new epoch that opened with Karl's death in 1611, we should examine the main trends present as Sweden moved into the seventeenth century.

KINGS, NOBLES, AND POLITICAL STRUCTURE

Gustav Vasa had established the independence of Sweden and the central authority of the monarch. He had used the riksdag to tighten the bond between king and people and to subordinate the nobility. He had created new administrative organs and he had filled the state treasury with silver. To a large extent, however, he had ruled and managed through the power of his own personality. He ruled a patriarchal state. Under new leaders the kingdom would need institutions and regulations that were more carefully defined.

It was natural enough that Gustav Vasa, in his planning for the future, should take the autonomous German states as patterns. Yet this boded ill for the continued unity of the state, as German history would amply illustrate. It was never clearly established whether the heirs of Gustav were in the first instance hereditary princes with equal status and almost equal power or ducal vassals of the king that were subject to feudal law. Their own changing power positions only confused the matter more. The involved history of the coinage privilege exemplifies the problem. Gustav originally planned to give each of the princes the independent right of minting money, as was the practice in the German states. Because of a controversy with Johan, he subsequently deleted that clause from his will. Erik, when he became king, provided in the Arboga Articles that the princes might mint if they would put the symbol of the king on one side of each coin. When Johan became king he refused Duke Karl the privilege of coinage. In spite of this, Karl soon began to issue coins which bore an image of Jehovah instead of the king. In the early 1590s he began to think increasingly of his potential position as regent and therefore changed his attitude. As king, when he had to decide on the privileges to pass on to the young dukes, he returned to the principle of the Arboga Articles and required that the king's prerogative be indicated on all coins; the dukes might enjoy only the economic advantages of independent coinage. The problem of semi-independent duchies was not decisively settled, but the dangers were recognized, and fortunately later sovereigns did not have as many children to provide for as did Gustav I.[15]

The relations of king and nobility were also continually in flux. Under Gustav Vasa the nobles had to accept a humble position. Erik had to upgrade their status to assure their support against Johan. His first gesture was to create the new ranks of count and baron to give added prestige to a few of the great families. He also augmented the honors with grants of land, meager in his reign but increasing under the generosity of Johan. At first most of the "fiefs" were granted in return for services, and none were to last beyond the life of the king. Gradually the practices of renewal and heritable donations alienated more and more land from the crown, a process that became extensive and dangerous in the seventeenth century. The whole system represented a continuation of the medieval method of recompensing officers of the state. Administrators, advisers, both local and national officials, and military men collected their compensation in produce, as fees from the tenants on their farms. Even the king still received his income in the form of some two hundred seventy commodities recognized for payment. As late as the sixteenth century the Hansa actually forbade payments in money in Scandinavia — merchants wanted goods to use in trade.

One of the side effects of this system of honors and payments was to nurture a spirit of independency in the men who had to administer estates to be paid for government work. Many felt themselves more tied to their properties than to their jobs, and the lesser nobility especially were obliged to spend most of their time on their estates and in rural villages, directing agriculture or mining, the disposal of crops and the exchange of crops for supplies. To help in this work a large class of stewards or farm managers developed, serving especially the higher nobility and the king.

Because of the paucity of the nobility and their interests in the land, as well as because of their independent spirit, the kings had to call on *ofrälse* (non-nobles or the unprivileged) for assistance in government. Often the sons of merchants or the clergy were trained in law and were most valuable in clerkships or high positions in government (for example, Erik's secretary Jöran Persson). For the highest positions, especially in the army, the king often had to use foreigners like the Frenchman Charles de Mornay or the Belgian Pont s de la Gardie of whom more will be heard. Problems arose because of the dual loyalties of such officials. And naturally the old landed aristocracy resented such rivals for favor and power. These commoners and foreigners were dependent solely on the king, who liked to use them because they were easily disposed of if they proved unsatisfactory; they did not have clans of influential relatives who could cause trouble. Erik particularly suspected the loyalty of the leaders of the great native families that were related to Johan. When Johan came to power he enhanced the dignity and power of these magnates, and he used them against Karl, who insisted on his independence. The general tendency of the period was to improve the status and hopes of the nobility, who asserted themselves in favor of feudal relationships and increasing limitations on royal authority. How best to use the nobility in the service of the state remained an unanswered question.

The outstanding innovation in the administrative structure in the half-century of the Vasa sons was Erik's high court, an institution that might well have grown into a permanent strong arm of government. But the nobles whom Erik appointed to the court soon disappeared from the scene, and he had to man it with commoners. Worse, he misused it by demanding those death verdicts which he used to hold both bumblers and opponents in line. As a result the court gained such a bad reputation that Johan allowed it to perish.

The traditional council (*råd*) remained, though for most of this epoch it was but a tool of the king. It played an independent role in only two periods: in 1567 during the incapacity of Erik XIV and in 1592–99 during the absentee reign of Sigismund. Because the kings of the time were self-assertive and European opinion was veering toward the acceptance of royal absolutism as emanating from God, even powerful nobles hesitated to demand power. England was wrestling with the problems of royal authority throughout the reign of Elizabeth (1558–1603), and James I strongly asserted his God-given rights. Jean Bodin was painstakingly thinking through the question on philosophical grounds.

In Sweden the issues of monarchic power and the place of the aristocracy in government were particularly acute because of the newness of the state structure and the traditions of aristocratic participation. Gustav Vasa's solutions had been clear and simple. He rode roughshod over opposition from the commonalty, and he enjoyed cooperation from the nobility, for they feared outside rule more than they feared their own king (they had been given a bloody lesson in 1520). However, the proud old families such as the Stures, the Bielkes, the Brahes, the Oxenstiernas, the Sparres, and the Trolles had not lost their spunk. In times of trouble the nobility had to direct affairs. They felt responsibility when the king dragged the country into foreign conflict or failed to maintain domestic prosperity. Careful appraisals of the nature of the monarchy and the state were forced on them by complications such as the dual role of Sigismund as king of both Sweden and Poland, the divisive religious question, and the claims of Duke Karl. Sweden did not produce a Jean Bodin or a James Madison, but it had Erik Sparre (1550–1600).

Erik Sparre's father had been Gustav Vasa's top general, and his mother was Brita Trolle. Sparre himself, after studies in Padua and perhaps Frankfurt, returned to Sweden in 1574, married Ebba Brahe, the daughter of Per Brahe who was the most highly placed noble at the court, and attained high posts in government. He was a noble but a believer in monarchy — under controls. In response to the problem of division of authority between Johan III and Duke Karl, he wrote, in the 1580s, "Pro lege, rege, et grege" (for law, king, and people), arguing the "constitutional" principle that hereditary monarchy could be accepted but that the ruler should be bound by law as interpreted by the conciliar nobility. His theories were further developed in his "Postulata nobilium" of 1594, supported by ideas borrowed to some extent from the French monarchomachs. Sparre's relations with Duke Karl, after the death of Johan III, were at first good, and he even stood as godfather to Gustav Adolf in 1594. But like Hogenskild Bielke and many more of the wealthy and interrelated aristocracy he felt that Sigismund was the rightful king. Sparre was therefore one of those who, as Karl pushed more vigorously for power, fled to Poland and returned with Sigismund's invading army in 1597. After the defeat of Stångebro he was among those yielded to Karl by Sigismund and was executed in 1600. His ideas of conciliar preeminence lived on, however, and were influential in 1611 and on into the Age of Freedom more than a century later.[16]

The riksdag was used little by Johan, more frequently by Erik, and most often by Karl, who needed popular as well as divine support, and who could there use his talent for meeting with people and discussing the problems of farmers and merchants. Membership in these riksdags was not regular. Representatives of different groups were invited to meet in one or another of the market towns in local assemblies as the king moved about the country investigating and overseeing. Attendance was regarded more as a burden than a privilege. Since 1544 when the clergy appeared as a separate Estate, there were customarily four Estates, each, at least theoretically, casting one vote on propositions. It was not yet an initiating body, and its functions and procedures changed character with the policies and powers of succeeding monarchs. Nevertheless, its increasing importance was something of a gauge of the increasing participation of people in government.

AGGRESSIVE FOREIGN POLICY: EXPANSION ABROAD

The expansionist urge infected all the younger Vasas. Erik was at first concerned primarily with Denmark and with the desire to gain a larger foothold on the Kattegat. He soon came to share Johan's eagerness for conquest on the eastern side of the Baltic, but he wanted to be sure Johan did not act alone. Commercial interests were a powerful factor not only for Sweden but for its rivals, each of whom wanted to control the Russian trade that passed through the Gulf of Finland. Viborg had been the Swedish base for this trade and Reval the Hanseatic center.

Power and strategic interests played a vital role. Sweden was vulnerably weak, with long open frontiers. It was poorer in manpower and resources than the kingdom of Denmark-Norway, which bordered it on the south and west, controlling all but a small window on the Kattegat at Älvsborg, which the Danes captured repeatedly during wartime. Sweden could not compare in population with Poland, which was jealous and aggressive, and backed by European Catholicism and the might of the Holy Roman Empire. And off to the east lay vast Russia, a disorganized giant at the opening of the seventeenth century, yet casting a shadow that darkened the future. Even to the north in barren Lappland, Denmark-Norway and Russia disputed with Sweden the right to tax the Lapps and their reindeer and to have access to the icy sea. A little Sweden was at the mercy of its neighbors; a fighting Sweden might win elbow room if not security.

In the mid-sixteenth century the Baltic littoral was ripe for the plucking. The Hanseatic cities had been outdistanced by the developing monarchic states. The Teutonic Order that had Christianized and long dominated the eastern shores of the Baltic had been weakened by the rise of Polish power and by the spread of Protestantism. The leading commercial city, Reval, had been dealt a heavy blow by the recent Russian capture of Narva and by the attempt of Tsar Ivan IV to make Narva the entrepôt of the Russian trade. Russian attacks in the last two years of King Gustav's reign worried Duke Johan, but the patriarch forbade adventure. However, in this disintegrating situation both the Grand Master of the Teutonic Order and the city of Reval appealed widely for aid. Obviously the status quo could not be maintained. Denmark, which already held the gates of the Baltic and the island of Gotland, wanted to control the inner routes of trade as well; it took the first step by buying the island of Ösel off the coast of Estonia. Poland, backed in its expansive ambitions by the Catholic powers, was eager to take the lands of the Teutonic Order under its protection. And Lübeck, weakened but seeking to salvage whatever possible, appealed to both Denmark and Sweden for joint action. Territorial aggrandizement and Russian trade were the prizes to be taken by the quick and the strong. When Erik came to the throne in September 1560 decisions had to be made.

Erik's choice was to act, and to act independently. He answered Reval's appeal for assistance by offering to incorporate the city in Swedish territory, along with three castle-fiefs of the Teutonic Order. Reval had to accept the offer, and Sweden was thus embarked on a century of empire building. This meant a direct challenge to Poland and to Denmark, an indirect challenge to Russia. It meant also a test of strength between Erik and Johan, for Johan proceeded with his Polish marriage plans on his own, and in return for a loan to the king of Poland Johan got as security a small principality in Livonia; this independent action led Erik to imprison both Johan and his bride Katarina Jagellonica.

Erik thus staked out the Swedish position astride the Gulf of Finland and by his restrictive trade edicts roused the antagonism of his Baltic neighbors. Denmark, Poland, and Lübeck entered into an alliance against him and in 1563 declared war. To avoid war with Russia, too, Erik felt he had to bow to Russian demands, including the barbaric one that Johan's Polish princess Katarina be turned over to Ivan IV (the Terrible). The Swedes procrastinated for months and finally avoided making delivery using the excuse of Erik's insanity (which may well have been hastened by the emotional tensions of the situation).

This Seven Years War of the North was not notable for great actions. Early in the war, in 1564, the Swedes invaded central Norway and captured Trondheim, but later in the same year the Danes reconquered the province. Repeatedly the Swedes sent raiding parties into Norway, Skåne, Halland, and Blekinge and burned Ronneby and other towns. The able, ruthless general Daniel Rantzau and his Danish forces raided Västergötland and Östergötland. The Danes took the vital port of Älvsborg, and the Swedes could not retake it. On the positive side Erik XIV trained a national army so that he did not have to depend on mercenary troops from abroad. Just before he was deposed Erik won a strategic victory over Rantzau. On the sea success and failure alternated, with Sweden gaining somewhat the advantage. Denmark and Lübeck nevertheless blocked the Sound, which stopped international trade and the tolls therefrom. When Johan III came to the throne in 1568, his Polish brother-in-law kindly withdrew from the war, and in 1570 peace negotiations could finally succeed in Stettin.

The so-called peace for eternity in the main merely restored the status quo ante bellum. It settled one important question — the reconstruction of the Union of Kalmar for which the Danes were so eager. Sweden had established itself as an independent power to be reckoned with. It renounced its claims to Skåne, Halland, and Blekinge, while Denmark in turn abandoned its claims against Sweden. One costly item for the Swedes was the heavy ransom required to redeem Älvsborg. Here at the mouth of the Göta River was the only Swedish outlet to the western seas, and it was essential for the farmers of the interior and for the traders who handled their butter, meat, and skins. The fortresses built there from time to time, and repeatedly destroyed, were as important as Kalmar and Borgholm. The Danes wanted to destroy both fort and port, but the Swedes *had* to have them both.

The Swedish drive eastward into the Baltic and the Russian push westward were bound to clash, and the Swedes could be thankful that this was held off until 1570 and that by an odd twist of fate they had acquired by then a good general. Pontus de la Gardie, a career soldier from France, had been captured from the Danes when the Swedes took Varberg; with the simple ease of moving from one job to another he entered Swedish service and founded one of the great Swedish families. He commanded a mercenary army of Germans, English, Scots, and Swedes which captured Narva in 1581. With the three chief ports of the Gulf of Finland (Narva, Reval, Viborg) in their hands the Swedes had attained their goal of controlling trade through the Gulf. But they had captured an empty sack. There was little trade left to control. Unhappily for the Swedes, at just this juncture in time the English had found the northern route to Russia by way of the White Sea, and the other Russian trade to the West sought passage overland through the Baltic territories to Riga or Pernau.

King Johan III therefore widened his sights and at one time demanded from Russia the territory as far east as Novgorod and north to Archangel, which was founded in 1584; he also had hopes of joining with Poland to gain mutual control of the Livonian routes. Internal unrest in Russia and then the election of Johan's son Sigismund to the Polish throne in 1587 might have made such dreams seem reasonable — yet they never approached realization. In his longer reach, such as the attempt to gain cooperation from the Tartars against Russia, Johan had little success. Duke Karl achieved some military success in his eastern campaigns, but after Johan's death it seemed necessary to make peace. In the peace of Teusina in 1595 the Swedes agreed to withdraw from Kexholm, whereas the Russians renounced Estonia (including Narva) and promised to send their commerce through Viborg, Reval, and Narva. However, they did not keep this promise, and Russian trade continued to bypass its natural outlet; the Russians simply would not pay the high Swedish tolls. For Sweden it was nevertheless significant that the Russians were blocked off from the Gulf of Finland and from the Gulf of Bothnia and that they withdrew from the three-way rivalry in the western Lapp area.

In the background at various times were rumblings from other quarters, including a Spanish threat to take Älvsborg. A great Catholic naval power established on Sweden's west coast, and cooperating with Poland, might have proved disastrous. In addition, the Poles were still eager for northern territories, and in 1593 they had forced Sigismund, then the king of both Sweden and Poland, to promise to cede Estonia to Poland. Six years earlier he had promised the Swedes he would never do so. The Swedes held their ground, both figuratively and literally. Vaster conquests became necessary to protect and make worthwhile the positions already won. This led to further involvement in the confused situation in Russia and, along with the dynastic question, to the long-continuing war with Poland, fought for the most part in Livonia.

Russia's Time of Troubles in the early years of the seventeenth century encouraged foreign interference. Poland and Sweden could not calmly watch while the tsar's crown was picked up by a prince or adventurer favorable to one country or the other. Each supported a rival candidate, and then Sigismund pushed the choice of his son, although he wanted the prize for himself. Karl put forth for consideration his sons, the young princes Gustav Adolf and Karl Filip. During this strife Jakob De la Gardie, the son of Pontus, led a Swedish army into Moscow and later captured Novgorod. In spite of his defeat at Klušino in 1610, he built up a strong party for Karl Filip. But Stockholm hesitated, and the game was lost. In 1613 the Russians chose Michael Romanov from among the native boyars and slowly achieved stabilization and a strength that Sweden would feel a century later.

Relations with Denmark were strained during the entire period, for the Danes thought they were the proper heirs of the fallen Hanseatic dominance in the Baltic, and they viewed Sweden as their chief rival. When the peace of Stettin of 1570 only postponed decision, and when negotiations produced no result, renewed war was all but inevitable. Tension tightened after Sweden, through the treaty of Teusina with Russia, gained hopes for control of Lappland and the extreme northern coasts. Denmark regarded this cold open region as Norway's sphere, and Kristian IV, the king of Denmark-Norway, was all too eager to subdue Sweden on the battlefield and rebuild the Scandinavian union. Karl IX, king in fact after 1599, insecure and lacking allies, evaded action. Again and again conferences were agreed to, but the Swedish delegates were either late in arriving or made demands to which the Danes would not accede. Many of the controversial subjects were petty matters (at least in the eyes of later generations), for example, the possession of a castle on Ösel, the prohibition of trade through Narva, and the Swedish blockade of Riga. Pettiest and most emotional was the question of the use of the three crowns in the coats of arms of the king. Two hundred years earlier Albrekt of Mecklenburg used a coat of arms with three crowns. Possibly these three crowns were intended to represent the three wise men of Christian legend, but during the Union of Kalmar they were assumed to symbolize the three kingdoms of the North. Karl Knutsson quartered them in his shield in 1448, and the Danish Frederik III used them along with other symbols in his royal escutcheon. In one treaty negotiation after another the Swedes tried to force the Danes to cease using the symbol, for they believed it signified Sweden and only Sweden, although it had been used rather widely on the continent in the Middle Ages. Sweden alone has clung to it.[17]

On all these matters each king was adamant, and each gave ample provocation to the other. Karl steadily strengthened his position at home, though his efforts to win friends among the Protestant powers of Europe were always thwarted. At length, in this perennial conflict of dynastic ambitions, Kristian IV persuaded his peace-minded Danish council that war was the only means of resolving the problems. On April 4, 1611 a declaration of war was issued from Copenhagen. The next month the Danes took Kalmar, and when Karl IX died in the autumn Sweden was pressed hard by both Denmark-Norway and Poland. The Swedish expansionist program looked sick indeed.[18]

## PROTESTANTISM QUESTIONED AND CONFIRMED

The coincidence and interplay of religious reform and national self-assertion gave character to the sixteenth-century conflict that pervaded western Europe. Often it was hard to tell to what extent sovereigns were leading and to what extent they were being led. Strong currents of social and religious change swirled throughout the continent. Near parallels to Swedish developments appeared elsewhere: for example, the clash of ideas among the people and the succession of rulers in Sweden, with their varying attitudes on religion, may be compared with the shifts of personnel and policy in England through the succession of Henry VIII, Edward VI, Mary, and Elizabeth.

Gustav I was much less of a theologian than was Henry VIII, but like the Tudor monarch he used Protestantism as a weapon in the fight for national unity and royal power. Despite strong opposition he and his religious advisers fixed the new philosophy and the new forms in a congenial environment. When Erik came to the throne Lutheran continuity was provided by the continuance in office of Archbishop Laurentius Petri. In fact Laurentius breathed more freely under Erik, issuing new church ordinances in 1562, a psalmbook and a catechism in 1567. He lived on into the reign of Johan III and formulated also the Ordinance of 1571 that codified past developments and laid down the rules for continuing Protestant organization.

Although King Johan approved the Ordinance of 1571 he soon attempted to modify it. His *Red Book* of 1576, a new liturgy, got reluctant clerical sanction, but Duke Karl refused to accept it for his duchy, and many of the clergy rejected it. Johan had been influenced by his own religious studies and by the continental ideas of George Cassander and others for a *via media* between Catholicism and Protestantism. Queen Katarina may not have influenced him strongly, but her Catholic advisers worked strenuously to convert him. Johan's sincere religious concern, and his marriage, made him a good target. Laurentius Nicolai Norvegus, one of the agents used in this effort, was a young, learned, exceptionally clever and personable Jesuit. He came to Sweden from the continent in the guise of a scholar and was accepted as a Lutheran. Because of his Norwegian origin his speech could be understood by all. When he established a school he won the respect of a large number of boys (and the nickname Klosterlasse) and succeeded in converting dozens of them and sending them to central Europe for further training. He was in close contact with the king and thought that he had almost won over Johan to Rome. For two years, indeed, the king refused to take the Lutheran sacrament.[19]

At this point the shrewd and persuasive Antonio Possevino arrived in Sweden as an imperial emissary. He was another Jesuit who had come direct from the Roman curia, and his real mission was to win Johan to the church. The personal part of his task he accomplished, for in May 1578 the king accepted the Roman Catholic faith. However, his taking of the mass was secret, and he evidently counted on the quid pro quo of a series of papal dispensations. He wanted Rome to agree to the trial of bishops before Swedish courts, the retention by present owners of property confiscated during the Reformation, and other items up to a total of twelve demands. On three matters he obdurately insisted the pope had to concede: communion in both kinds to the laity, mass in the vernacular, and marriage of the clergy. He was disconcerted to discover that the papal curia, in the aftermath of the Council of Trent, was not in a mood for compromise, though Possevino and others repeatedly presented his appeals. Without the three primary concessions Johan knew that an attempt to take the Swedish people into the church of Rome would produce insurrection. In brief, he knew that his country was protestantized. His wife's faith, the difficult negotiations over her inheritance in Italy from Bona Sforza, the political situation in Europe, and above all his own religious inclination, drew Johan to Rome. On the other hand his political responsibilities tied him to Sweden. He had reason to be reminded of this in 1579 when his brother Karl was in Germany getting married to Maria, the daughter and granddaughter of leading Protestant princes of Hesse and the Palatinate. Disillusioned by the stubborn refusal of Rome to make allowances for the difficulties of his situation in Sweden, Johan in July of 1579 publicly returned to the Lutheran communion table, but this reaffirmation only slightly mollified feelings.

Johan's liturgy remained, and since it was neither Lutheran nor Roman it was referred to as the king's religion. For a decade tensions mounted, and the small coterie of foreign and domestic Catholics could still maintain hope. Sigismund was heir to the throne, and he was a thorough Roman Catholic, eager to bring Sweden back into the Roman fold, with none of his father's reservations. The churchmen of Sweden had ample time to contemplate their problem and make decisions, while Sigismund off in Poland was like a man with one hand tied behind his back. When Johan died and Sigismund succeeded to the throne the jealous Poles would not let him go to Sweden for fear he would not return. (Indeed he was trying to transfer the Polish throne to a Hapsburg.) In Sweden the forceful but widely hated uncle, Duke Karl, was able to manipulate events. In 1593 he called a general church council to meet in Uppsala. The steward of the realm reminded this body of the need for national unity and then withdrew to let the clerics work independently. By that time it was clear that Lutheranism would be accepted as the national religion. It did not take long for the delegates to consider the Augsburg Confession point by point, to accept it as their basic expression of faith, and to ratify the church ordinances of 1571 and Olaus Petri's handbook of 1529. The president of this Uppsala Meeting could declare that Sweden had become one with one Lord and God. The protocol of the meeting was sent around the country and was signed by some two thousand persons and civic groups. It became both a statement of faith and a declaration of national unity. At the same time the requirement that Sigismund accept this statement of faith challenged his claim as hereditary monarch and made the religious issue also a constitutional one.

Sigismund found his attempts to gain a foothold for Catholicism thwarted at every turn, and his position as monarch highly unstable. Duke Karl knew how to use the forces of nationalism and religion to make the king's situation untenable. Though Karl was Calvinistically inclined he worked with the decisions of the Uppsala Meeting and the staunch Lutheranism in Sweden. Oddly, Archbishop Abraham, who had been chosen by the Uppsala Meeting of 1593, turned against Karl and supported Sigismund in 1598, but he was imprisoned and had no further influence on events. Although not a single Swedish king in the sixteenth century was a theologically concerned Lutheran the Swedish people became slowly but thoroughly united in this faith; it was a unity attained through clerical leadership and popular inclination. This faith and unity had been tested and tightened by the external threat from Poland and Rome, and it would strengthen the country in the trials to come.

The religious history of the century illustrates both the importance and the limitations of leadership. Each of the five kings had a different religious outlook, and each contributed to the ultimate national consensus. Yet the Swedish people did not move quickly to do the bidding of Gustav or of his sons. The very differences among their leaders forced the people to think for themselves. They long resisted the shift to Lutheranism, and in the end conversion required not the fiat of a king but the self-persuasion of the people; slowly they came to realize that Protestantism fitted their urge for national independence and religious individualism and that Lutheranism gave them the anchor they needed in fixed doctrine. It was the reaction against Sigismund and the threat of re-Catholicization that produced the agreed national creed of the Uppsala Meeting and the decision that all future kings must be Lutheran. And, once the decision was made, it was unanimous and firmly anchored.

## SLOWLY CHANGING ECONOMY AND SOCIETY

Eli F. Heckscher, a leading economic historian, said the Sweden of the sixteenth century was still essentially medieval and even compared it with the France of the Carolingian period. In many ways Swedish society was more isolated from continental everyday life and currents of thought than it had been a century earlier, for Protestantism had prevented intercourse with Rome. Germans continued to dominate external trade, and Swedes maintained vigorous association only with the lands to the east — Finland, Estonia, Livonia, and Russia. The break with Rome and the simultaneous severance of ties with Denmark had dealt a heavy blow to learning, and the young University of Uppsala had faded out of existence. Much as the kings needed educated advisers, clerks, and diplomatic agents, their own country could not produce them, and they had to depend much on foreigners.

Overwhelmingly Sweden was a rural society. As of 1570 about 5 percent of the people lived in towns, and the total population was about 750,000. The population density was less than two per square mile. (In Germany the density was about twelve per square mile, and 25 percent of the population lived in towns.) Stockholm was the largest city, but its population was under 9,000. Like smaller towns, even the capital city smelled somewhat rural, with more than two hundred pigs inside the city proper, plus sheep, goats, and other animals.

Agriculture, the basic sector of the economy, had changed hardly at all from the previous century. In much of the country the farmers lived in small villages, in clusters of cottages in the midst of their strips of tilled land. The whole village had to decide on the days of sowing and of harvest, and in some cases the crop was shared among all, although the individual retained at least the semblance of ownership of his land. It was a kind of communism without common direction. Occasionally half the land would lie fallow, to be cultivated only in alternate years; in other places the three-crop system had spread from Skåne, using one-third fallow, one-third in spring planting, and one-third in fall planting. The livestock was small sized, grazed on the common during the summer, and fed on whatever might be available when brought in for the winter. Frequently the animals died in the long and stringent winters or were so weak by spring that they had to be carried to the field. Many were slaughtered in the autumn, but preservation of the meat was difficult. The grain produced was about half barley, one-third rye, and small but increasing amounts of wheat and oats.

It is obvious from the records of mines, garrisons, and courts that food supplies were usually ample. Large amounts of butter, meat, and fish were consumed; in fact, the use of fish was many times greater than it would become in later times. But there were bad years, like 1601–3, when the farmers had to eat their seed and then replace it with seed bought abroad. To buy seed many a household parted with its treasured silver spoons, only to find that the seed sometimes did not grow well in Swedish soil. Even in the best of years people had to eat stale meat and wash it down with oceans of beer — three quarts per day was reckoned as normal for a grown man or woman, and soldiers and aristocrats got more. Gradually the diet of cereals, fish, meat, and beer was expanded to include vegetables, dairy products, and sugar, but in the sixteenth century such luxuries were mostly for the aristocracy.

The interrelationships of the prices of butter, grain, and meat were surprisingly balanced from the sixteenth century to the turn of the nineteenth. However, monetary prices meant little in what remained essentially a natural economy. Butter was traded for iron and iron was traded for fish. Taxes and rents were paid in kind or by the end of the sixteenth century partly in kind and partly in cash. And the taxes collected in various districts reflected the economy: from Norrland taxes in 1530–31 were 40 percent in skins and furs, 60 percent in fish. For the kingdom as a whole in the same period the taxes paid in kind were over 7 percent fish (16 percent for Finland), two-thirds of which was salmon. The *birkarlar*, a guild of northern merchants, still handled the fish and skins of the northland.

Mining was of growing importance, and was promoted strongly by Gustav Vasa and by Karl IX. The well-known pellets of osmund iron were produced in steady quantity to the end of the century, but the manufacture of bar iron and even small amounts of steel were increasing. Gustav I introduced the new hammering process, and Karl IX built a number of new forges in Värmland in the 1580s. Though total iron production is not known, export figures showed a doubling in value between 1560 and 1600, half of this from the export of bar iron. The total quantity, nevertheless, was only 2 percent of the 1913 figures.

Silver was of some importance during the sixteenth century, when the mine at Salberget employed one hundred to two hundred men. The production of copper was encouraged, but the yield was still very small. Altogether about 4 percent of the people were engaged in mining, and the governmental eagerness to promote it was indicated by the fact that asylum was granted to prisoners when they agreed to work in the mines. Agents went abroad to Danzig, Passau, Nuremberg, Austria, and the Netherlands to obtain miners. The kings had large interests in the mines, especially the copper mines — in 1554, 65 percent of the production at Stora Kopparberg in Dalarna was from the smelting houses owned by Gustav Vasa.

Manufacturing was small in scale but included a large variety of tools, anchors, horseshoes, spikes, armor, and weapons. The cannon and munitions industry was stimulated by warfare. For this and other crafts Gustav and later kings loaned money to craftsmen for the purchase of materials and for labor and thus enabled ironworks and other factories to increase.

The deep forests covering much of the land from Småland to Norrland and from the Stockholm skerries to the mountain border with Norway provided resources of inestimable value. They furnished lumber for buildings, furniture, and boats as well as fuel for the cottage fireplaces. Out of timber came charcoal for smelting ore; material for bowls, spoons, spades, and other implements (except for the cutting edge), and for toy horses and blocks for whittling character-sculpture; and saplings for picturesque slanting fences. From the trees of the forest came tar and pitch and turpentine. Although the Swedes probably used more iron than most of their contemporaries it was the bounteous and self-renewing forests that supplied most of their needs. The dense dark woodlands along the borders provided defense against neighboring Danes and Norwegians, refuge for social outcasts, and a realm for fantasy that housed all manner of goblins. The forest was the home of the deer, the bear, the squirrel, the fox, and the marten — the animals that man took for meat and fur and hides. The cold forest streams were spawning grounds for trout and pike and salmon-trout. Up in rocky clearings people of the villages built their *fäbod*, a summer retreat for women, children, cows, goats, and pigs. Each villager was a farmer in summer and a woodsman in winter. The forests provided the means for and a way of life.

As vital as this versatile and rich resource was for Swedish life, the forest was almost untapped for export purposes in the sixteenth century, although Norway had already begun to realize its forest wealth. This was largely because the continental countries, though lacking the vast reserves of Sweden, had enough forest resources for their populations and their perceived needs at that time; the demand for imports was small, and Norway was closer to the markets.

The citizenry who functioned in this economy and this society were freemen, not serfs. They paid fees or taxes to a lord or to the crown and tithes to the church. Some worked for others in the towns or the mines or on the large estates. But the overwhelming majority were farmers living in village communities, tilling their own plots of ground. In the winter they timbered or hunted or perhaps cultivated handicrafts, and some were part-time miners or laborers in the scattered *bruk* (rural mills or works). Although legally free, those who owned less than three marks' worth of property were subject to laws requiring them to take whatever employment was offered. And occasionally, in sixteenth-century attempts to rationalize production, peasant smiths would be forced to move into towns. More often the workers in the *bruk* could not relocate because they were in debt to the works owner. Essentially, however, it was a free society.

The concepts of land ownership were a bit vague. It was Gustav Vasa's idea that all uncultivated land belonged to "us and Sweden's crown," and he insisted that cultivated land that was badly managed or delinquent in taxes should revert to the crown. His patriarchal policies gave way under his successors to more legalistic distinctions between the peasants who owned property and paid taxes and those who were not landowners but nevertheless paid similar amounts in kind or labor. The holdings of the great families increased, beginning especially with Erik and his grants to the new counts and barons. Eight of these clans came to own about 5 percent of all the land and about that percentage of the national wealth. The clans and the king had profited not only from grants but from the *reduktion* during the Reformation of properties that had passed into the possession of the church.

Towns and trade were little more significant than they were some centuries earlier, partly because of the long trade dominance by the Hansa and the Danes, partly because of the policy of the kings and the long-standing habits of the people. Destructive fires were common, destroying the close-built wood houses. Frequently city taxes were remitted after fires, and people were encouraged to rebuild in stone. The value of cities was gradually recognized and government authorities granted them trade monopolies and tax privileges. From Gustav I Vasa to Karl IX the kings tried various regulations to force all buying and selling into the cities. Karl encouraged infant industries by forbidding imports of goods that were also made by the Swedish guilds and by restricting trade to the staple cities. As for foreign commerce, Gustav Vasa, despite his demand for political independence, felt that Swedish merchants were too stupid to handle foreign trade with discretion, and for years he seemed content to let the Germans continue to dominate; after the Germans it was others. Even at the end of the sixteenth century foreigners and Swedes of foreign ancestry controlled one-half of Swedish exports. Second to the Germans were the Scots, several of whom had settled in Stockholm and won enviable shares of the export business. The Dutch were beginning to be important, and there were a few Frenchmen; both these groups were closely involved with the vital import of salt from the Bay of Biscay region. Swedes were very slowly entering foreign trade, at least the illusion was dispelled that it was advantageous for Sweden to let others handle its economic interests. Gustav's sons broke away from the idea of passive trade, and Karl dreamed of a canal across Sweden that would enable the country both to export its products and to transport Russian goods all the way from the Gulf of Finland to Älvsborg.

Perhaps it was natural that in this first century of national self-realization effort should be concentrated on internal development, at least in the economic realm. It was for reasons partly economic and partly political that Gustav and Johan sought to colonize in Norrland and on toward the Arctic Ocean, but Denmark-Norway regained possession of that distant territory in spite of the Swedish settlers. In the central part of the country, in Värmland and Västmanland, new farmsteads were being started, and growth was at the rate of about 1 percent per year at the end of the century. Roads and canals interested Karl IX especially, and he also planned to build a series of taverns along the main highways, but a multitude of pressing political concerns diverted his attention from this project.

Unfortunately autarchy was the rule not only in economic affairs but also in broadly cultural matters. Erik XIV yearned for broader contacts, but his reign was brief and troubled. Johan III was involved to the east rather than to the south. Sigismund's influence was meager. Karl IX realized that the country needed educated civil servants and pointed to the duty of the nobility to be trained; he also aided in restoring the University of Uppsala. But the chief contacts with continental learning came through men like Laurentius Norvegus; as a result of the conversions he made to the Roman faith able young men went off to the continent and never returned. If sixteenth-century Sweden was an underdeveloped land in industry and trade, it was far more so in things of the mind. The national breakaway from Denmark and the union and the Protestant revolution from Rome were jointly responsible for severing the cords of cultural communication. Rigid and parochial orthodoxy ruled the land. Only toward the end of the century did some relaxation appear, when we even hear of Elizabethan players acting in Nyköping. Church art was of course discouraged, and the charming fifteenth-century mural paintings in the churches were whitewashed.

It is ironic that the most significant historical writing was done in exile. Olaus Magnus fled Sweden in 1530 because of his religious differences with King Gustav, and in succeeding years abroad he wrote his famous descriptions of the North — the *Carta Marina* (or *Carta Gothica*) and *History of the Northern Peoples*. His brother Johannes, the last Catholic archbishop of Sweden, wrote his romantic *History of the Goths* and a more reliable *History of the Archbishopric of Uppsala* after he had left Sweden. These writings blended fantasy and history, glorified the ancient Goths and related them to modern Swedes, and condemned the Danes; they did much to shape the sixteenth- and seventeenth-century Swedish concepts of their national character and their past. These "histories" were doubtless all the more influential because of Sweden's cultural isolation. More valuable as history and literature were Olaus Petri's *Swedish Chronicle* and his other writings.

Perhaps the most typical and most lasting artistic innovation of the century was the architecture of the Vasa castle, with its heavy round towers, its isolating moat, its great stones taken from demolished churches. Here the solidity and the austerity of the nation were symbolized. Gripsholm and Kalmar, Åbo and Viborg — these stand to this day as monuments of the will and the crude strength of a nation newly asserting itself.

Sweden did not leap but crawled from the Middle Ages to modern times. The sixteenth century was a slow transition. In many ways Gustav I Vasa invigorated the old more than he introduced the new. Revolution characterized only the political break from Denmark and the religious break from Rome, both of which were long-term phenomena — the political revolution occupying the century from Engelbrekt to Gustav Vasa and the religious revolution requiring the reigns of five kings for its consummation. Administrative machinery changed slowly, and in the realms of economic affairs and social organization change was even slower paced. Barter and payments-in-kind were intermingled with a developing money economy into the seventeenth century, and the handling of shipping and foreign trade only gradually passed into the hands of the Swedes. The ways of life of the peasantry retained the old characteristics of immobility and rurality. At the end of the sixteenth century the nobility were partly employed in public office, partly occupied as rural managers of their enfeoffed farms. Increasing wealth and commercial activity are indicated by the fact that the number of ships trading annually through Stockholm doubled from about seventy-five in Gustav Vasa's period to about one hundred fifty by the end of the century. Everything was still small-scale and narrowly national. And yet the sixteenth century produced one fundamental achievement: national unity under monarchic leadership. This laid the foundation for the outburst of vigor in the seventeenth century.[20]

# VII

## SWEDEN'S AGE OF GREATNESS:
## I. THE STRUGGLE FOR EMPIRE
## AND DOMESTIC REFORM, 1611–54

GUSTAV I had created the modern Swedish state and his sons had threshed out some of its problems in a half-century of constructive strife. Gustav II Adolf harnessed the raw vigor of the new state and expanded it into an empire. His successors were bequeathed the enjoyments of eminence and wealth and the responsibility of preserving what had been won. The task was beyond their strength, and with Karl XII the edifice of empire collapsed. Like the inexorable workings of fate in the Icelandic sagas, this rise to power and decline to impotence is one of the most fascinating chapters in Nordic history.

### Gustav II Adolf: The Man and His Background

He who was to become the "Lion of the North" was born on December 9, 1594 in the castle of Stockholm, although this was not the primary seat of his father, Duke Karl. Sigismund his cousin was king and several others stood between Gustav and the throne. It was a complex series of events that brought him there.

King Sigismund, son of Johan III and grandson of Gustav I, was also king of Poland, although there was no other bond between the two kingdoms. He had been raised a Roman Catholic and he regarded Poland as his first responsibility. He therefore remained in Poland and left his uncle Karl, the youngest of Gustav I's sons, as regent in Sweden. Karl was in his own right duke of a large area of central Sweden, and he was accustomed to rule. Now he had an unusual family as well as political responsibility. For Sigismund also left with Uncle Karl his (Sigismund's) half-brother Johan, five years older than Gustav Adolf, son of Johan III by his second wife, Gunilla Bielke. The boy Johan had as much of the Vasa blood in his veins as Gustav but he had a completely different temperament: passive, slow, seemingly indifferent to power. According to the rules of royal succession Johan outranked Gustav and even Karl, his uncle, but in 1604 when he was fifteen he renounced his rights to the crown in favor of his then ten-year-old cousin. In the meantime, of course, much had happened, but we need not retell that story. The important factor was Gustav Adolf.

Gustav Adolf was exceptionally bright, imperious in disposition and from infancy began to get the training and experience to rule. At the age of five he went with his parents to Reval, close to the theater of war across the Baltic. On the return trip more than a year later, after a narrow escape from shipwreck and a few months in Finland, the party returned by land over the top of the Gulf of Bothnia. This was the first voyage in what would be a life of almost incessant travel.

The prince grew up bilingual, fluent in Swedish and German, for his mother was Kristina of Holstein-Gottorp, and his squire and nurse were both German. His father chose for chief tutor Johan Schroderus (later known as Johan Skytte), who had just returned from nine years in the great universities of the continent. For the next nine years this dynamic pedagogue had a task comparable to that of Aristotle with the young Alexander. Skytte (along with Johan Bure [Bureus]) introduced the prince to Livy and Polybius, Cicero and Seneca, and Gustav Adolf quoted them all years later in his speeches to German dignitaries. The renowned general Maurice of Nassau and mercenary soldiers from all parts of Europe gave the eager boy pointers on the military craft. Others opened to him the world of music and other arts. Unlike his father and uncles who had divided among them the talents of their father Gustav I, Gustav Adolf combined the positive facets of the Vasa genius and enhanced them. He played the lute and wrote poetry. He became a persuasive and brilliant speaker and was adept in many languages; one contemporary report made the claim (perhaps an exaggeration) that in addition to his Swedish and German he knew Latin, Italian, French, and Dutch by age twelve and that he later acquired some acquaintance with English, Scottish, Spanish, Russian, Polish, and finally Greek. Another influence was equally important; he was imbued by his Calvinist-inclined father with the Protestant moral code and a sense of thrift. With all this mass of absorptive learning he still retained an eager lust for living and an unusual creative genius.

No wonder that this extraordinary youth somewhat overawed his mild cousin Johan and that he was declared king before the legal age. At fifteen he began to administer his duchy of Västmanland; during his father's last illness he was his mother's partner in conducting government affairs; and he directed one of the armies in the campaign against the Danish invaders. Though he was but sixteen when Karl IX died on October 30, 1611, his seventeenth birthday would come in six weeks (on December 9). The legal arrangements provided that he would come into half-rule at age eighteen, full kingship at twenty-four. But this was no time to quibble over legalities. The dynastic issue was delicate, the nobles were eager to reassert themselves, and no real decision had been reached in the power struggle with Sweden's voracious neighbors. The religious question was resolved but not validated in practice. Given a boy of Gustav Adolf's unusual capacities, the sensible procedure was to give him full authority as quickly as possible. In a brief interregnum his mother Kristina and Prince Johan served as regents. Again, Johan might have had the throne, but he did not take advantage of the opportunity.

The man who maneuvered the shift of power was twenty-eight-year-old Axel Oxenstierna, scion of one of the great families of Uppland and related to several others. Oxenstierna had been studying on the continent during the bitterest years of conflict between king and council. At age twenty-two, more or less a hostage for the loyal behavior of his family, he was taken into the royal service and rose steadily in rank until he became a member of the council at twenty-six. His mind and his heart were with his fellow nobles but also with his country. He was calmly determined to do away with the injustices of Karl's absolutism. The council stood with him, and when Kristina and Johan, soon after the riksdag met on December 6, 1611, each rejected further service as regent, Oxenstierna had a plan ready. The Estates of the riksdag formulated their grievances and so did the council itself. In a month of negotiations these demands were drawn up into a charter of guarantees, and Gustav Adolf was asked to pledge to uphold these in return for being immediately accepted as king. The thirteen articles of the charter represented return to the old system of rule by council.

Gustav Adolf signed the charter of guarantees, and on January 4, 1612 the council pledged allegiance to him. The young king thus renounced many of the prerogatives exercised by his father. But what he yielded in law he regained in practice. Because of his ability and personality and because of the extraordinary partnership that developed between the monarch and his chancellor — none other than Oxenstierna himself — Gustav Adolf in actuality came to wield greater power than the autocratic Karl.

The promise of his youth was more than fulfilled by his reign of twenty-one years. He grew tall and strikingly handsome despite the corpulence of his later years. He was as blond as those ancient Gothic ancestors of whom he was overfond and had large round eyes set in a long face. His hair was white and his "pointed beard of an almost golden hue"; the Italians called him "il re d'oro." His nose was long, slightly hooked, and his shoulders were broad. Gustav Adolf needed no decorations to appear regal, and his usual dress was starkly simple. His disposition was sanguine, positive, aggressive. He was gracious, bold, sagacious, lovable, abounding in infectious energy. As Nils Ahnlund put it, "Enthusiasm was with him a normal condition. . . . He had the art of lightening labor with a jest [and] the knack of getting on well with high or low, cleric or layman." He loved to dance; his daughter Kristina had no criticism of him except that he was perhaps "too fond of the ladies." He was a man of action, though "he took unusual care to choose the precise moment to act." "As a negotiator he seldom lost the spirit of attack. . . . He could command either bitter irony or dignified appeal. . . . His orders were peremptory." As a warrior he characteristically thought in terms of the offensive.[1]

His volatile and uninhibited temperament was legendary. His anger was terrifying. Words could pour forth in picturesque torrents of condemnation, as in his indictment of the German officers at Nürnberg in June 1632:

You — princes, counts, gentlemen, nobles! It is you who have been guilty of infidelity and impiety towards your fatherland — that fatherland which you yourselves are despoiling, harrying, reducing to a desert. You — captains, officers — high and low alike — it is precisely *you* who steal and plunder, without a single exception. . . . God my Creator is my witness that my blood turns to gall within me when I set eyes on one of you. . . . It enrages me that I must have dealings with so perverted a people.[2]

After the outburst against the officers he saw two stolen cows outside a corporal's tent, took the corporal by the ear, and dragged him off to the executioner. On another occasion the king, angered at the apparent insolence of one of his Swedish officers, struck him so hard over the head with the flat of his sword that he broke it. Yet he attracted into his service most of the nobles who had fled to Poland and made devoted followers out of several sons of men executed by his father. More successfully than Napoleon, Gustav Adolf absorbed potential opposition. His outbursts of temper were often justified and, if not, he could apologize as graciously as he could denounce viciously.

It is the combination of qualities that is decisive. The contradictory tendencies of his nature . . . are really a fundamental and indivisible feature of it. Side by side with his calculating caution there lay within him a *penchant*, profound and unmistakable, for the bold stroke; side by side with his methodical circumspection, an urge to rush in and stir things up by his own personal exertions. . . . The discords inherent in his temperament were never fully resolved, but the spiritual riches they brought him were of a fortunate quality that transcended the common measure of humanity.[3]

Courage went hand in hand with piety. The king seemed to court danger and he had no difficulty finding it. Cannon balls ripped through his tent or hit where he had stood a moment before; he carried a musket ball in his neck; two horses went through the ice under him, another was shot as he was riding. He attributed his escapes to divine providence and said he would die when God willed it, though he realized, too, that God helps only those who help themselves. The Lutheran faith in which he had been grounded as a boy grew deeper with the years. He held prayers regularly for his army in the field and punished absentees. He feared nothing but God.

Next to his belief in God was his belief in the greatness of Sweden's past and the glories of its future. At his coronation tournament in 1617 he dressed as the legendary Gothic king Berik. He was proud to dilate upon the beauties of the Swedish landscape and the richness of its resources. He helped by both word and example to stimulate that Gothic patriotism that characterized the later seventeenth century. It was Olof Rudbeck, son of Gustav Adolf's chaplain Rudbeckius, who wrote of Sweden in his great work *Atlantica*:

> One may travel night and day over land, lakes and streams, whereas in other countries, such as Germany, France, Italy, Spain, etc. one must travel in greatest darkness . . . in fog and evil odor . . . When winter is here it is clear, healthy, and wholesome and fresh; when summer comes it is so marvelous both day and night that no place in the south is comparable.

Even the birds, he went on, come to Sweden to have their young; children grow larger, and women are more fertile. "There is something special in the northern places."[4]

Sweden, beginning in Gustav Adolf's day to take pride in accomplishment and to bask in prestige, could also be thankful for the king's versatile creativity. He was curious about everything and could do everything — as the following pages will testify. He was a youthful leader — seventeen as king, not yet thirty-eight when cut down at Lützen — who brought a new generation of youth into power with him.

### The War of Kalmar and the Peace of Knäred (1613)

> First, it is generally known that all our neighbors are our enemies, the Poles, the Russians, and the Danes, so that no place in Sweden, Finland, and Livonia can say that it is safe from the enemy. Second, we have simply no friends who take our difficulties to heart. Third, there are none of our enemies who are not, or do not at least think themselves to be, greater and stronger when we.[5]

So spoke the chancellor to the council in 1612. When Gustav Adolf became king there was no absence of challenge.

All along Sweden's southern and western borders lay the kingdom of Denmark-Norway, able to shift forces from one point to another and to apply pressure at will; moreover, its king was eager to rebuild the union once ruled by Margareta. In the far north, where the curtain of cold might give an illusion of security, the long arm of King Kristian IV reached out for territory. The small opening to the western seas at Gothenburg, guarded by Älvsborg, was vulnerable to Danish attack, and the Danish fleet could block Swedish access to German markets and supplies. Even the southern river outlets of Swedish Småland ran to Danish ports. In the south and east Poland was presided over by a king who had been ousted from Sweden and who fought for years to regain his lost heritage. East and northeast stretched the vastness of Russia, crudely strong and restlessly expansive.

The most immediate threat in 1612 was the War of Kalmar with Denmark, and the young Swedish king left for the front immediately after signing the royal charter. King Kristian of Denmark-Norway was making a new bid to annihilate the Vasas. The Danes remained masters of the sea, and the Swedish squadrons had either to run for cover or be scuttled as at Kalmar and Älvsborg when the Danes captured these two key forts. Only the deep forests of central Sweden and the vicious defensive traps (the *bråte*) restrained the Danish advance. Disease and starvation assisted the defense. But the Danes and their German mercenaries pushed almost to Jönköping and took Öland and much of eastern Småland. It was a war of bitter cruelty all around the borderlands. The devastation of the scorched earth methods made it terrible for civilians as well as for soldiers.

Gustav Adolf's harrying raids in Skåne had no decisive effect, and on his return he was almost captured and his horse went through the thin ice of Vittsjö. In August 1612 Kristian IV brought his fleet of thirty-four sail into the Baltic and tried a bold stroke against Vaxholm, Stockholm's defensive outpost. Gustav Adolf was called from his sickbed, but probably the saviors of the day for Sweden were some twelve hundred fresh Flemish mercenaries who had marched across from Trondheim fjord in Norway — the Danish hold on Sweden's west coast prevented them from landing where planned. Vaxholm's resistance was so determined that by early September Kristian, realizing that he could not succeed before the northern winter set in, withdrew his fleet and became discouraged enough to parley.

The new king of Sweden was eager to get one enemy off his back, and he had a helpful intermediary in the person of James (Jacob) Spens, a Scottish recruiter empowered by James I to mediate. Through Spens and Robert Anstruther, another Britisher sent to Copenhagen, negotiations on the border led to the Peace of Knäred on January 20, 1613. Denmark restored some of the conquered territory, reestablished free trade between Sweden and Denmark, and reaffirmed Sweden's freedom from the Sound Dues demanded of ships passing through Öresund. Sweden had to agree that each king might use the three-crown emblem, but without any implication of territorial claims. And Sweden made more concessions: it gave up Jämtland and northern Finnmark and compromised its claims to levy tolls at Riga; most vital, it agreed that Denmark might hold Älvsborg and Gothenburg until Sweden paid a ransom of 1 million riksdalers. For six years Denmark would hold Sweden's entrepôt for western trade, and Kristian hoped the ransom could never be paid. For the second time (the first was in 1570) Sweden had to buy back its port and fort, and the financial strain was almost strangling. Payment was accomplished only by imposing extraordinary taxation on the whole country and by obtaining loans from the Dutch. For the Dutch, like the English and the Germans, did not want to see Denmark dominate the entire North. Otherwise the only silver lining in the heavy cloud of Knäred was that Sweden still lived — Kristian had failed to reimpose the union.[6]

### Russian Involvement and the Peace of Stolbova (1617)

Simultaneously with the Danish invasion of the homeland Sweden was deeply involved in the Russian chaos known as the Time of Troubles. The issues concerned the choice of a new tsar, boundary disputes among Russia, Poland, and Sweden (with Finland), and control of Russian trade. Poland was interested in territory but especially in the Russian throne, which Sigismund hoped to gain for his son Vladislav, if not for himself. Both Denmark and Britain were interested in trade privileges. For Sweden all these problems were bound up in one package.

Although Sweden was not in a position to send troops eastward, it had been conducting the war largely with mercenary forces, whose leader, fortunately for Sweden, was Jakob De la Gardie, a brilliant soldier and shrewd diplomat. He later married Ebba Brahe, Gustav Adolf's youthful love. Like his father Pontus before him, Jakob De la Gardie spent much of his life in the wars with Russia and Poland, and he learned soldiering not only in that theater of war but on the continent under Maurice of Nassau (c. 1606–9). He was in 1611–13 largely on his own, and in the absence of money from Sweden he sometimes even had to pay troops out of his own funds (wealth he had acquired by extracurricular trading in Russian sables). He was rather flexible in his support of parties in Russia but for the most part worked with the nationalists. They, for their part, to overcome anarchy and avoid submission to the Poles, in 1611 offered the crown to one of the sons of Karl IX. Gustav Adolf evidently toyed with the idea of accepting it for himself, but after he became king the only possible candidate was his younger brother Karl Filip. Because of opposition from the queen mother and hesitation all along the line the opportunity was lost, and the Russians selected Michael Romanov, one of their own boyars, in 1613. Meanwhile, De la Gardie had obtained control of a large section of northwest Russia and had taken Novgorod by storm. If a Swedish prince did not become tsar, then, as second best, a buffer state might be established that would block off the Russian expansionists from Finland.

In 1613 the Russians, however, pressed hard against the Swedish outposts and recaptured Gdov on Lake Peipus. The next spring Gustav Adolf brought 2,000 reinforcements, but after two seasons of battles and the futile siege of Pskov the situation changed little. Exhaustion finally brought both sides to the council table, again under British mediators (especially Sir John Merrick). In the midst of ravaged land and bitter cold the stubborn negotiators haggled over titles and precedence and tried through the winter of 1615–16 to hammer out an agreement. On through the summer months and through the fall they argued, and not until February 27, 1617 was the Treaty of Stolbova actually signed. Here at last was a Swedish victory, though hard-won.

Sweden renounced all claims to the Russian throne and to Novgorod and agreed to restore three other towns against an indemnity of 20,000 rubles; it would hold Gdov as a pledge until the new boundaries were delimited. Russia renounced Ivangorod, Jama, Kopore, and Nöteborg and abandoned claim to Livonia (which was still largely Polish); it confirmed the treaties of Teusina and Viborg and the cession to Sweden of Kexholm (which had been reconquered by the Swedes in 1611); and it agreed not to aid the Poles against Sweden.[7]

The Gulf of Finland was now all Swedish, along with a wide, marshy borderland to the east. A strategic victory had been won over Poland. Most important, the creeping advance of Russia was contained for a century. Questions of trade had receded into the background, while the issue of security had become paramount. And in this Sweden had achieved success on its eastern frontier.

### The Polish Serial, to the Truce of Altmark (1629)

Once Sweden's conflicts with Denmark and Russia were temporarily resolved the government could turn its attention to the underlying dynastic and religious dispute with Poland. This dispute was in turn inextricably interrelated with European questions that reached to Rome, Madrid, London, even to Constantinople — the whole continent was an interconnected web of religious rivalries, national struggles for territory and power, economic competition, dynastic quarrels, and political adventurism. Gustav Adolf and Oxenstierna learned earlier than most statesmen to realize the repercussions that an incident in Livonia might have in the Netherlands or at the Vatican. The English were interested in anything that affected Russian trade, as of course were the Danes, the Dutch, and the German Hansa. The Spaniards' long struggle with the Dutch triggered Spanish attempts to ally with Denmark in its competition with the Dutch and to use Spanish naval power in the Skagerrak and the Baltic. At Cecora in the southeast corner of Europe, a Turkish victory over the Poles in October 1620 encouraged the Swedes to invade Poland from the north. And when Gustav Adolf married the Hohenzollern princess Maria Eleanora he soon found himself in contact with Bethlen Gabor (briefly king of Hungary), who married Maria Eleanora's sister. These are but samples of the confusing interplay of forces that exploded intricate patterns of fireworks and diplomacy even before the Thirty Years War came to confuse matters more.

Because Sigismund III insisted upon his right to try to regain the Swedish throne by any means (and wanted such a stipulation inserted in a treaty), it became Gustav Adolf's task to prevent him. First he attacked the northern borders of Poland and was victorious in a six-week siege of Riga in the summer of 1621. Success against this key port gave Sweden control of several river mouths and power to collect tolls that helped the exchequer. It spotlighted for Europe the naval building and military reforms that had enhanced the strength of Sweden. But continued campaigning accomplished little more in Kurland and did not weaken Sigismund's will.

An alternating pattern of war and truce continued for years. Neither side could inflict mortal damage on the other, so each sought allies to strengthen its attack. Poland made an alliance with the emperor Matthias in 1613, and the Hapsburgs later proclaimed their ambitions by naming Wallenstein admiral of the Baltic and the Ocean Seas. When the Thirty Years War broke out in 1618 the rivalries in northern Europe became intermeshed with the continental conflicts of Protestants versus Catholics and Bourbons versus Hapsburgs. In 1623 the Poles hatched a plan for the invasion of Sweden with the help of the Spanish fleet and British mercenaries. At the same time Gustav Adolf was actively seeking the support of the German cities or the Dutch for a diversionary invasion of Poland. He also tried on his own, but unsuccessfully, to frighten Sigismund by an incursion into the harbor of Danzig with a fleet of twenty-one sail.

By 1624 England was trying to arrange an alliance of Protestant powers, and Brandenburg changed its stance and also sought such a grouping to be headed by Gustav Adolf. Gustav Adolf would have nothing to do with the alliance unless he had complete control over the direction of the operation and had in advance two ports on the German coast, an army of 50,000 (two-thirds of it provided by the allies), and a fleet in the North Sea and another in the

Baltic. He felt the need of protection against a possible Danish attack, and he distrusted the stability of alliances. The potential allies were not yet ready to commit themselves to such demeaning terms, and they agreed instead to support Kristian of Denmark. In doing so they made the mistake that Gustav Adolf feared: by their lack of support and cooperation they permitted the defeat of Kristian and the invasion of Denmark by the imperial armies. Kristian had bid for the Protestant leadership of Europe and had ended on his knees.

Gustav Adolf meanwhile turned once more to the Livonian theater and enjoyed a remarkably successful 1625 summer campaign, capturing Dorpat and Mitau and completing the conquest north of the Dvina and east to the Russian border. It appeared to the king and his chief minister, as they surveyed the situation in the spring of 1626, that a Polish campaign might force Sigismund to accept a peace or at least a long-term armistice. And a threat to Silesia might be a diversion useful for the main theater if Denmark could hold the imperial forces in Germany. Both the Catholic and the Protestant groupings were having organizational troubles, with some of the German states shifting sides or trying to stay neutral, Cardinal Richelieu of France playing an ambiguous role, and Charles I of England lacking funds and willpower. George William, elector of Brandenburg, had dreamed of an evangelical league, but now, in fear and trembling before the might of the imperial forces under generals Tilly and Wallenstein, he wanted anything that would keep Gustav Adolf away from Prussia. He sent an emissary to Sweden to plead for a thrust up the Elbe or the Oder. Gustav Adolf was deaf to these entreaties, and when he saw that the elector would not support him in Prussia and that other possible allies would not accept the terms necessary for success, he determined to act alone. He got the approval of the Swedish council and in utmost secrecy prepared to sail with 125 vessels and 14,000 men.

At the end of June 1626 the Swedish fleet anchored off Pillau, and the weak defenses of Prussia began to fall. Soldiers transferred to shallow draft boats prepared for the Vistula Lagoon (Frisches Haf), quickly took Braunsberg and then Elbing, and soon Gustav Adolf controlled the rich trading area of the lower Vistula. He failed to gain the cooperation of Königsberg or Danzig, and his independent action antagonized his friends to the west. The Danish disaster at Lutter in mid-August deepened their despair. They could take little satisfaction from the fact that in September Gustav Adolf won a victory over Sigismund's more numerous forces at Mewe. They could not see the significance for the future of that success which was the result of "the intimate combination of musketeers, pikemen, and gunners, . . . the spirit of initiative shown by individual units and their commanders, and . . . the superior morale of the Swedish forces."[8]

During the winter of 1626–27 Gustav Adolf was back in Sweden, while Oxenstierna sat out an unhappy time as governor of the conquered territories, subjected to constant harassment by the Poles under Koniecpolski. The negotiations for a truce were fruitless, for the Poles did not want a thirty-year truce and the Swedes had no interest in a mere fifteen-month respite. Nor could the kings of Sweden and Denmark agree on cooperative action. For 1627, therefore, each went his separate way. Gustav Adolf's leather-wrapped guns worked effectively, and the battles of Dirschau showed that the Swedes had finally learned the lesson of their humiliating defeat at Kirkholm in 1605; now their cavalry thoroughly bested the Polish — reputedly the best in Europe. However, the outcome of the 1627 season still failed to convince the Poles they were beaten; and they took heart from the prospect of imperial support.

The Protestant cause as a whole had suffered near-collapse; Tilly had penetrated far north into Jutland, and Mecklenburg and Pomerania were taken. Spain was making proposals to the Hansa cities and threatening to move into the Baltic with a fleet of twenty-four ships. The Empire had the audacity to offer to Sweden an alliance against the Dutch and to tempt Kristian IV with the position of imperial admiral. The Scandinavian rulers not only turned down the proposals but began to see that they had a mutual interest in holding the Hapsburgs away from the Baltic. The depth of Gustav Adolf's concern and the shift of his focus of attention was indicated by his request to the riksdag to appoint a Secret Committee on foreign affairs, which would later become an important institution. The committee, wholly persuaded by the king's views, recognized that Swedish rule in the Baltic must be preserved, that the emperor was a threat to Sweden, that Sweden should aid Denmark, and that the best policy was to fight the enemy abroad rather than at home. No further consultation with the riksdag would be necessary. Reluctantly the defeated and embittered Kristian IV allowed himself to be drawn into a three-year alliance with Sweden on April 28, 1628.

Danish-Swedish cooperation was forced by Wallenstein's attack on Stralsund, for neither of the Scandinavian rivals could afford to see an imperial naval base on nearby shores. With aid from the new allies Stralsund was able to hold out until in July an army of 1,100 Scots turned the tide and made Wallenstein retire. Oxenstierna then forced Stralsund to accept an association with Sweden which was to last for almost two hundred years. Gustav Adolf sent troops and Stralsund became the secure base he had been looking for on German soil. However, he was not yet prepared for full participation in the main war.

The Polish war could not be allowed to go on interminably, yet it was hard to end it partly because of diversion of interest, partly because the campaign of 1628 bogged down in soggy weather. Victories and defeats tended to balance each other, though the Swedish position remained strong.

Diplomatic activity was more imaginative than military activity. Emissaries came and went; Gustav Adolf used his agents to try to build a Protestant front, while the French and English tried to persuade the Swedish hero to join the common cause. In January 1629 Gustav Adolf set up a ten-day conference with his council, which again favored action on the continent and a free hand for the king. On February 20 the king met for a day of heated debate with Kristian IV. Perhaps the fact of their meeting was what finally brought about, on May 27, 1629, the Peace of Lübeck, by which the imperialists made peace with Denmark on remarkably lenient terms. Three months later Gustav Adolf got an armistice with the Poles, assisted by diplomats from France, England, and Brandenburg. The Truce of Altmark was to extend for six years, and it (with subsidiary agreements) gave Sweden control of key ports on the Baltic and the right to collect tolls from Danzig north through Pillau, Libau, and Windau. It also meant that Sweden would continue to have access to the grain of the Baltic littoral. Sweden would be safe and well provided from the east while it turned to greater ventures in the south.

Why did Gustav Adolf turn his attention from profitable conquest in the east to dangerous invasion southward, even leaving the crucial dynastic question unresolved? The answer lies in the man's character as well as in the issues at stake. In 1630 Sweden was threatened more from the emperor and Wallenstein than from poor Sigismund and his son Vladislav. Religious liberty, that spiritual self-determination gained by the Reformation, was threatened throughout the North. Political goals were intertwined with religious. Other goals would develop later, for Gustav Adolf was also an opportunist who changed his strategy from day to day as he had to confront new situations. Military power was a means to an end — security. Economic advantages such as the tolls were in the same category. His debates with himself and others indicated he had a high intelligence and, as Michael Roberts put it, "too tender a conscience to be a wholly convincing Goth." [9]

Anguish and foreboding, as well as his deep concern for his people, came out in Gustav Adolf's farewell talk to the four Estates of the riksdag on May 19, 1630. First he thanked them for the understanding they had shown in agreeing to do what was necessary for the security of the kingdom. He sympathized with them for the burden of the recruitment but pointed out that the Swedish soldiers, with God's help, had won great cities and many provisions and, with the aid of foreign diplomats, had obtained a six-year armistice. He reminded his audience of the devastation of property and the daily peril to life in the neighboring countries where warfare was raging, thus reiterating the advantages of fighting an offensive war in other peoples' homelands rather than a defensive war in their own; even if the Swedes had to give soldiers and contributions they could sit securely in their cottages. In a typical (and, as it turned out, a prophetic) passage, he likened himself to the pitcher carried repeatedly to the well that must eventually break, and he spoke of his wounds from the Polish war. He asked God's blessing on his people and had paternal words of valediction for each of the Estates: "May the knighthood bring renewed luster to the Gothic fame of their forefathers and in the war for the fatherland win a deathless name and also manors and wealth." "May the priesthood, who have the power to turn and twist the minds of men, lead their people in unity and hope yet avoid the sin of pride." "May the burghers' small houses become stone mansions and their small boats be great ships." "May the commonalty's meadows be green and their fields bear a hundred-fold."[10]

The Swedish fleet sailed forth on June 17, 1630 and nine days later arrived in Pomerania at Peenemünde. Sweden was making its bid for greatness.

## Glory and Death in Germany, 1630–32

Diplomatically Europe was, in 1630, but little more ready for Gustav Adolf than it had been in 1624. Gustav Adolf, however, was much more prepared for Europe. His most dangerous rival, Kristian IV, was discredited and Gustav Adolf's prestige had grown. A few weeks after the Swedish landfall in Germany, Wallenstein, the ablest general of the imperialists, was ousted through the intrigues of his enemies, and the Empire was involved in Italy. Disunity among the opposition was at the moment more serious than the disintegrating fears and interests of "friends." Gustav Adolf had the firm support of his own country, which agreed with his policy that it was best to defend Sweden by fighting in Germany. (It reminds one of a parallel many years later in William Allen White's campaign to "defend America by aiding the Allies.") For a decade Gustav Adolf had had one eye fixed on this German venture while he was warring in Poland, he had trained his soldiers with this possibility in mind, and he had carefully built up a cadre of eager, loyal young officers. Both morale and organization were at a high point. Territorial conquests in the Baltic lands provided 1 million riksdaler in annual tolls, and the Truce of Altmark guaranteed six years of safety from Polish attack. Gustav Adolf had a good base in Stralsund under his control. Now was the time to strike in Germany to make Sweden secure from imperial expansion and to preserve Protestantism.

Sweden had mustered over 70,000 men, but almost 20,000 of these were fresh recruits, and much of this native Swedish force had to be kept at home to guard the country against its neighbor Denmark. When he landed in June,

Gustav Adolf brought about 13,000 men, of whom almost 3,000 were cavalry. From the garrison at Stralsund and from mercenaries and German recruits he had gathered an additional 26,000 men by September. He seldom had more men immediately available, for, although he could sometimes count 130,000 to 140,000 men under arms, the majority were scattered in garrisons and task forces and were dispersed more and more as his conquests spread. Usually his forces were roughly comparable in numbers with those of the imperialists, who faced much the same problems of recruitment, pay, and supply.

The landing place at Peenemünde was well chosen, halfway between Stralsund and weakly defended Stettin. This military foothold facilitated Gustav Adolf's first diplomatic success when he forced Pomerania into alliance. From that base Gustav Adolf labored unsuccessfully to get his brother-in-law, George William of Brandenburg, into the alliance. But George William was duke of Prussia, not yet freed from Polish suzerainty, as well as elector of Brandenburg, and he had reason to fear both Polish and imperial retaliation, while he was resentful of the presence in Germany of a Swedish army. John George of Saxony was the most powerful of those who refused to cooperate. In that early stage, the Swedish king dared not cross the territory of Brandenburg or Saxony without an agreement, and therefore he could not reach Magdeburg, which had declared itself an ally of Sweden.

In the meantime, however, Cardinal Richelieu of France, also fearing Hapsburg expansionism, had bowed to Gustav Adolf's demands and had signed a treaty of alliance at Bärwalde in January 1631, providing a subsidy to the Swedes of 400,000 riksdaler per year until 1636. Gustav Adolf had also formulated a pattern for treaties with German states, though none had yet affixed their signatures and seals. This plan provided that the king of Sweden would be not only the director of the common enterprise but also the protector of the allied principalities who would have the right to retain conquests. The purpose of the alliance was to win freedom of conscience, the liberties of Germany, and the safety and welfare of Sweden. On the rights of conquest Gustav Adolf was making good use of the new treatise on international law written by Hugo Grotius. Here the king found support for two of his principles: security for Sweden and compensation for its sacrifices in the German cause.

Gustav Adolf did not just bring another army to fight in the European fray. He brought new techniques and tactics and a new spirit. Gustav Adolf was an experimenter and an innovator. Although he had learned the best military techniques of the day from Maurice of Nassau and others, he always sought a better way. Livonia was his laboratory, Prussia his testing ground, and Germany his final field of action. By experience as well as by precept he early learned the importance of firepower; he knew that to bring firepower to bear at the right point at the right time required mobility and that mobility in battle required discipline.

The king took a personal interest in the improvement of guns, with greater use of the musket for the infantrymen and of lighter-weight artillery pieces. Under his encouragement the gunsmiths of Sweden tried various ideas, such as the famous leather-bound three-pounder that could be drawn by one horse. Before the assault on Germany this gun in turn had given way to the regiment-piece, which had a barrel of copper (c. twelve parts copper and one part tin) and weighed no more than the leather-bound gun. With eighty of these guns Gustav Adolf had the best artillery known in 1630–32. Not only were the guns made in Sweden, but the local smiths built an extensive export business in regiment-pieces — and also in muskets.

The chief suppliers and manufacturers of these modern munitions were two Netherlanders and the large aggregation of Walloon craftsmen whom they brought north. Willem de Besche began a cannon factory at Finspång in 1618, and as he expanded operations he gained financial assistance from his countryman Louis De Geer, who was an active financial agent for the Swedish crown. Swedish interests grew so large that a decade later De Geer migrated to Sweden. As demand for weapons increased and these products proved their excellence De Geer established a major factory at Norrköping, then another at Leufsta, and others. A general export business developed as De Geer made himself the Krupp of his day. He acquired extensive estates and was ennobled in 1641; he and his sixteen children provided the country with progeny who would be important in Swedish history for several centuries.

The king gave personal attention to recruitment and training of soldiers and cavalry. He became convinced of the superiority of the native soldier over the mercenary, but he could never supply his personnel needs from Sweden alone. The recruitment system grouped all eligible men in tens and took one man from each group, or rote. Those not taken were assessed for the outfitting of the inductee. Peddlers, the unemployed, and any who did not appear for the call were automatically drafted. Exemptions had to be allowed for family need and for miners and munition makers. In the years between 1626 and 1630 when there was a conscription each year the number taken averaged about ten thousand annually, reduced by a rather alarming number of desertions, especially in 1630. The nobility were expected, ever since the institution of the frälse in 1289, to furnish equipped cavalrymen, but gradually this requirement had been diluted until it had almost disappeared. In the early years of his reign Gustav Adolf tried to force the nobles to fulfill their obligations, but exceptions were common. Volunteers and mercenaries in large numbers had to supply the cavalry for the seventeenth-century wars. Professional soldiers drifted from country to country, from one war to another, sometimes attracted by a particular commander. Thus many Germans and Scots took service with Gustav Adolf because of his success and because of what he stood for.

The discipline and training of these heterogeneous forces was perhaps Gustav Adolf's most brilliant achievement. He had prayers twice a day and a sermon at least once a week; each company had its own chaplain. The king drew up carefully revised Articles of War and had them read to the troops once a month. Basic training was thorough, maneuvers were regular, repeated drill was given in loading muskets and handling pikes, and every man was taught his designated function in battle. For instance, the day before the battle of Breitenfeld the whole army was put through practice. Although none of these things was unique in itself and although the system produced neither a Sir Galahad nor a Hercules, the total combination was probably more thorough and more effective than in any army up to that time. The genius of Gustav Adolf lay in his judicious eclecticism, his refinements of the ideas of others, and his administrative skill in blending the whole. He attended to every detail and often risked his life in reconnaissance. Most important for his soldiers was his character as a leader, reinforced by his royal authority but innate in his personality. He exuded the dynamism of youth and an aura of idealism; he also had the practical intelligence and the concern for others that commanded respect and emotional response.

Gustav Adolf's tactical arrangements were carefully planned to take advantage of his strengths and the enemy's weaknesses, but especially to utilize mobility and enhance firepower. He rejected the Spanish system of massed *tercios* (50 men across and 30 deep) at Breitenfeld, for a linear formation only six-men deep (Maurice used 10), and he interspersed musketeers with cavalry. Thus he spread out his men, made it possible for them to fire more rapidly and more effectively, and enabled them to move more freely. He strengthened the front with the regiment-pieces. The effectiveness of the innovations convinced even Wallenstein, who at Lützen modified his own order of battle toward the Swedish system.

Gustav Adolf's navy won little glory. Yet Sweden became in his time *the* naval power of the Baltic. It had a skerries fleet of small and shallow-draft vessels to guard the coast and special squadrons of such boats on Lakes Ladoga, Peipus, and at Vistula Lagoon; it also had a high seas fleet to sail the Baltic, to transport troops and supplies, to guard the ports, to collect the tolls along the Baltic coast from Finland to Germany, and to stand watch against Denmark and Poland. Erik XIV had been interested in sea power and had had some success, but Johan III had allowed the fleet to decay and Karl IX had paid it no heed, concentrating on the conflict with Russia. The devastation of the War of Kalmar was the result. Gustav Adolf realized the vital importance of the fleet and once took direct command, amazing the sailors with his nautical knowledge.

But the real rebuilder of Swedish naval might in the seventeenth century was Klas Fleming. Despite the monotony and hardships of Baltic service and the fact that it did not have a good reputation the navy carried 14,000 soldiers safely to Riga in 1621 (with 106 transports and 52 warships), another 14,000 to Prussia in 1626 (with 81 transports escorted by 60 battleships and other vessels), and during the Thirty Years War not only took thousands of soldiers back and forth to Germany but maintained an unbroken lifeline of communication. The fact that it fought no major naval engagement is the best evidence of a superiority that discouraged challenge. Its greatest catastrophe came in 1625 when ten ships were driven aground by a storm on the Kurland coast; the members of the council at that time voluntarily contributed funds for rebuilding. About that time, too, the grand *Wasa* was commissioned as the flagship of the king's navy. Someone failed to give it sufficient ballast, and on its maiden voyage in 1628 it capsized in Stockholm harbor. Three hundred thirty-three years later it was raised and now stands in Stockholm in misty splendor as a museum. The practical result of the disaster was that the Dutch naval architects (who had built the *Wasa*) thereafter constructed advance models for testing.[11]

The military confrontation grew serious in the early months of 1631. Gustav Adolf captured Gratz and made a successful incursion into Mecklenburg, the duchy that had been won by Wallenstein. Now, with Wallenstein ousted, Tilly had been called back into service, and he and Gustav Adolf maneuvered and sparred with each other. In April the Swedish forces took Frankfurt-on-Oder in a brilliant strike, which, however, released Tilly for the horrible vengeance he wreaked on Magdeburg. Even the disciplined troops of the Swedish monarch had got out of hand at Frankfurt, and chaos was to follow on both sides. Gradually and grudgingly some of the princes of important states like Brandenburg and Saxony came over to the anti-imperialist side. Carefully watching these allies and his line of communications, Gustav Adolf pushed into central Germany and crossed the Elbe. At Werben, in an arc of the river, he constructed a defensive position so strong that generals Tilly and Pappenheim tried futile sorties against it and then withdrew.

At length the two main armies met on the plains north of Leipzig on September 7, 1631 in the battle at Breitenfeld. The day began with prayer and proceeded to five hours of bloody conflict. Gustav Adolf's Saxon allies were routed by the massive *tercios* of Tilly, but Pappenheim's cavalry charged and was thrown back, charged again, and was thrown back, and again, and again. He could neither break the Swedish lines nor outflank them; their maneuverability foiled his tactics. This first major battle of the German campaign

ended at dusk in a resounding victory for the Swedish and Finnish veterans of the Livonian and Polish campaigns, accomplished by the lighter weapons, greater mobility, and newer tactics of Gustav Adolf. The Swedish casualties numbered some 2,000, while the imperialists lost almost 20,000. Many of the captured joined Gustav Adolf's army, and the Swedes took all the enemy artillery and sent home 120 banners to Riddarholm church. Tilly was wounded. Throughout Europe Protestants rejoiced, Moscow rang its bells, and even in envious Denmark Kristian IV had bonfires lighted.[12]

The way to use success now became the problem. Tilly escaped and soon collected a new army. Johan Georg, in plans coordinated with Gustav Adolf, led his Saxon soldiers off toward Silesia. Gustav Adolf considered a drive to

Vienna but took instead the route to the Rhine. He marched through rich country and collected treasure, including libraries of books and manuscripts to send to Uppsala. His mobile court became a center of European diplomatic activity. He put himself forward as a candidate for the Polish throne, exchanged emissaries with Turkey, and agreed to recruit an army of mercenaries for Russia. He now became the dominant partner in the Swedish-French alliance, and he was both too clever and too strong to fall into the traps set for him by Richelieu. But the Swedish lines were far extended, and he got suggestions that Kristian IV had begun to intrigue with Wallenstein (as did Gustav Adolf himself in 1631) and with Maximillan of Bavaria. Along with military planning Gustav Adolf had to direct, with Oxenstierna's help, a Europe-wide diplomatic and intelligence service.

The Swedish king found himself drawn irresistibly into governing and planning the reorganization of Germany. He saw that temporary victory was not enough, that he had a long-term interest in the German settlement. Hence, in February 1632 he dictated a treaty of alliance that forced Mecklenburg to grant him military assistance, the right to collect toll, the directorate of the alliance, the cities of Wismar and Warnemünde for the duration of the war, and an agreement to accept and use Swedish copper coinage at face value. Of individual cities he required special tribute — Hamburg had to pay 150,000 riksdaler to be left in peace, Nürnberg 100,000, and Munich 300,000. In general he allowed Catholics the free exercise of their religion, but he made them pay tribute. Lands that had changed hands and had been restored to Catholicism by the Edict of Restitution were often given as donations to Germans or Swedes — it was the king's only way to reward good service. And he sincerely felt that "war should sustain war." Still justifiably fearful for his own and Sweden's security, seeing weakness and shifting allegiances all about him, and annoyed by the ingratitude of the Germans, he tended to become increasingly dictatorial. He also kept seeking a plan that would solidly unite all the Protestant states in a general league and was working on this in the last weeks before the battle at Lützen.

The long marches through western and southern Germany, the occasional armed clashes that produced both successes and failures, the state occasions, the constant negotiations — nothing led to a decision. The northern king grew worried at being so deep in south Germany. Oxenstierna, oddly enough, argued that the important thing was to stay in the area where men and resources were plentiful. But Gustav Adolf clung to his own feelings and plan and turned northward to support Johan Georg against Wallenstein. (Wallenstein had been reinstated in command and was now threatening Saxony.)

For a moment Gustav Adolf thought he could surprise the imperialists with their army divided, but an accident gave his opponents advance warning.

Even on the day of battle, November 6, a heavy mist caused further delay, enabling Pappenheim to appear with his feared cavalry before the day was won. Again the battle was in the Leipzig plain, now at the village of Lützen. Wallenstein had chosen an excellent position hinging on a group of windmills and awaited the Swedish attack. This day the Scots and other mercenaries were mostly absent on other duty, and the army was largely Swedes and Finns. After the mist cleared the elite right wing of Gustav Adolf's army was in the process of routing Wallenstein's left wing when Pappenheim appeared about noon. Then this able cavalry general was wounded and again chaos reigned. At that crucial moment in the turmoil of battle the mist once more obscured friend and foe. Gustav Adolf had decided to move over to assist the hard-pressed Swedish left. He was hit in the arm by a musket shot, then by a pistol shot in the back. He fell from the saddle and was shot through the head, face down in the mud. Out of the ensuing panic the Smålanders started to flee when the chaplain Fabricius, informed of what had happened, started to sing "Sustain us by Thy mighty word." The group around him grew and the song rang out. Morale was restored, and soon the Swedish army once more held its ground. Bernhard of Saxe-Weimar took command, and the inspiration of anguish and revenge overcame all other emotions. In the remaining hours of desperate fighting the Swedes took the windmills and then the imperial artillery; they drove both infantry and cavalry before them and won the day. Wallenstein fled to Leipzig and left the field to those Swedes who yet lived — but almost a third of the loyal and inspired army had perished.

The blood-stained field of Lützen was the homage paid to the memory of a great man by an army of subjects and mercenaries who loved and admired him. But gratifying as was the victory it could not decide the war.

Gustav Adolf the Great expanded Swedish territory in the east, gained an armistice with Poland, averted the threat of a Catholic-imperial conquest of the North, and drove deep wedges into Germany. He made the Baltic a Swedish sea and within less than twenty years reversed the power relationship between Sweden and Denmark. Together with his chancellor Axel Oxenstierna he surveyed the entire range of Swedish government and society, infused new purpose and cooperative accomplishment, created new institutions, and remodeled the old. He built upon the past but was never bound by the past. His reign was characterized by revolutionary improvements in military techniques, spectacular advances in the organization of industrial production, stringent but successful financial exactions. He enjoyed the unanimous loyalty of a population noted for obstreperousness and implanted a deep sense of spiritual unity and cultural pride.

A coincidence of circumstances in the breakdown of the European system of religion and politics created a vacuum into which Sweden could move.

Because of Gustav Adolf and Axel Oxenstierna Sweden was ready to take advantage of the situation. The national achievement of a marginal state was a great group enterprise, but it was inspired and directed by a man. At his death a shock ran through Europe, among friend and foe alike. "The evangelical Joshua," the "Lion of the North," was gone, his work in mid-career. The world would be different both because of what he had done and because he was no longer there to carry on. "Weep, ye priests and laymen, weep, young and old, rich and poor, great and small," cried a leaflet in Stockholm.[13] And Axel Oxenstierna, Gustav Adolf's closest collaborator, wrote to the council:

> In the world is now none that is his equal, nor has there been for centuries such a one; and indeed I doubt whether the future will produce his peer. Yea, truly we may call him King Gustav the wise and great, the father of the fatherland, whose like never yet reigned in Sweden, as is acknowledged not by us alone, but by men of all nations, whether friend or foe.[14]

## Systematizing the Governmental Structure, 1611–34

Gustav Adolf is known outside Sweden primarily for his military exploits. But it was in his regime that the administrative structure of the modern Swedish state was constructed, one of the most efficient and well-organized governments in Europe, and Sweden's progress was dependent on political organization as well as on military conquest.

Domestic reorganization began immediately on the accession of Gustav Adolf, at first largely through the thoughtful foresight of Axel Oxenstierna. After a solid education in Germany Oxenstierna had returned to Sweden and in 1603, at age twenty, had entered the service of Karl IX. Only three years later he was appointed to the king's council and was used in diplomatic assignments. When in 1610 King Karl IX suffered a stroke Oxenstierna joined with young Gustav Adolf to direct the government. When Karl died in 1611 Oxenstierna helped assure Gustav Adolf's selection as king. He was twenty-eight and Gustav Adolf was almost seventeen and these two men brought Sweden to greatness. The chancellor was a perfect partner and foil for the sanguine, impulsive king. Oxenstierna was the balance wheel, a cautious adviser on campaigns, a shrewd diplomat in dealing with the statesmen of Europe. In fact, some historians would name him the most influential statesman of the century. The power and the ability of his numerous clan made it plausible at one point (or more than one) that a "mayor of the palace" might repeat the feats of Charles Martel and Birger Jarl and boost his family to the throne. Oxenstierna seems to have hoped that his son would marry Gustav Adolf's daughter Kristina, but she was not so inclined. Hence at that moment and in other personal relationships through the century the lieutenants of the king remained just that, moving in orbit around the sovereign, operating within the limits of that relationship.

In the complex of domestic and foreign affairs during Gustav Adolf's reign it is usually impossible to separate the activities and the decisions of the king and his chancellor. They worked as a team and undoubtedly were in close agreement on most issues. In the early years they had to face not only the annoying claims of the duchies but various intrigues from Sigismund and his sympathizers, repeated threats of invasion from Poland, truly desperate financial difficulties before the ransom for Älvsborg was finally paid, continuing tension with Denmark, rebelliousness in Dalarna, and the vast network of problems connected with the wars across the Baltic, including recruitment, provisioning, and governing. At least two geniuses were needed to manipulate all these.

The basis for the cooperation between Gustav Adolf and Oxenstierna was laid in the charter of 1611 which Oxenstierna formulated to prevent the new king from becoming the tyrant his father had been. The charter embodied both old ideas and new but definitely redirected the constitutional structure. Alongside guarantees to preserve the Lutheran faith and the riksdag and promises to consult with Duke Johan, the council, and the Estates, it provided explicitly for the power of the nobility. The five highest officers of state (steward, marshal, chancellor, admiral, and treasurer) plus members of the national and exchequer councils, lawmen, and provincial governors all had to be Swedish-born nobles. Thus the annoying foreigners and secretaries would disappear from the Swedish government. Aristocratic monopoly of high office was fixed for a long time to come. The last of the ten clauses was a rudimental bill of rights: no man could be punished on the basis of charges alone but only after judgment in a court of law.

The system at least had the advantage of enhancing the nobles' sense of proprietorship and responsibility, and Gustav Adolf found that he could work satisfactorily within its bounds. The tendency of the document was to put authority in the hands of the king and the administrative bureaucracy. The riksdag was recognized as a vehicle of communication between king and people, but it did not have final taxing power, and the king promised to call the riksdag only after consultation with the council and not too frequently.

To be declared of age Gustav Adolf had to sign what the nobles prescribed, and what they wanted was a constitutional monarchy. The new king therefore agreed that the nobles would have the chief positions in the state and that he would govern with the advice of the council and riksdag. The aristocratic council, traditionally an elite group within the house of nobility of the riksdag, gradually became an administrative college residing in the capital and associated with the king rather than the riksdag. It was a system that could lead to faction and futility, as it was to do a century later. In the seventeenth century three factors prevented such frustration. One factor was the sense of responsibility on the part of the nobles, led by Oxenstierna, and inspired by the need of the time. The second was the leadership of Gustav Adolf. The king accepted the conciliar machinery and then used his own dynamic personality to guide the machine set up to control him. Instead of fighting with the man who devised the controls he asked Oxenstierna himself to become chancellor. He put into other key positions men with ability, and he animated in them a will to cooperate for the common good. He absorbed and used the potential opposition. A third important factor in holding the nobility in line was the wartime stringency, bringing with it demands from commoners as well as king that the aristocracy accept special financial levies and fulfill their military duties.

Around the five major administrative offices (steward, marshal, admiral, chancellor, and treasurer) grew within the next twenty years five well-organized colleges or administrative boards, each with carefully defined functions. Other administrators and advisers were added, and a group of the highest officials was recognized as the council (*Råd*). A supreme court (*Svea Hovrätt*) was inaugurated and the exchequer and chancery were reorganized. The government had by now settled in Stockholm, and its activities were becoming increasingly complex and wide-reaching. The chancery alone touched almost every aspect of the government, including commerce, education, hospitals, and of course all foreign affairs. With the king gone from the country almost half the time it was essential to have efficient authorities at home. The nobility, now given responsibility, proved their ability to carry on loyally as well as efficiently. The king asked for their advice and their help and made them co-responsible, although he never yielded his own final authority. Oxenstierna had worked out a system to prevent the king from exercising excessive power. Gustav Adolf directed that system to use the nobles and yet prevent them, too, from gaining excessive power. He made them junior partners in a common enterprise for the good of the nation. As Michael Roberts has said, it was for the seventeenth century "one of the best-developed, most efficient, and most modern administrations in Europe."[15]

The riksdag had not yet developed into a truly legislative body, and in the Oxenstierna-Gustav Adolf scheme of things its importance was de-emphasized. In the early years of the seventeenth century its meetings were still irregular and often inconclusive, and the members thought the meetings to be a burden. Although Karl IX had used these gatherings to bolster his absolutism they were frequently local rather than national in representation. Members continued to question whether or not they were empowered to legislate for their entire Estates. The representative principle was not yet established, hence, while sovereignty was considered to reside in the king and the Estates, this meant the entirety of each Estate, not just the members present at a riksdag. The ancient Teutonic principle of unanimity remained to inhibit action. After a few years of experience with this system Oxenstierna and Gustav Adolf presented to the Örebro riksdag of 1617 a Riksdag Ordinance (RO) to regularize proceedings.

The riksdag ordinance provided for six Estates: the hereditary princes, the nobles, the clergy, the burghers, the farmers, and the army officers. The deaths of Gustav Adolf's mother, brother, and half-brother quickly eliminated the Estate of the princes; the army officers never developed their position because many were already in the Estate of the nobles and many were abroad in service. Of the others the nobles were the most important in numbers and attendance, partly because many resided in Stockholm in government service. The clergy represented the top authority for the church, and they often spoke out for the commonalty. The burghers preferred to stay home and conduct business. And they were the smallest of the four remaining Estates. The farmers (*bönder*) represented the overwhelming mass of the population, and they were chosen at assemblies in the *härads*. Technically the bönder represented in the riksdag were only the landholding farmers, owners and renters, who comprised the majority but not the entirety of the agricultural population. The independence and the economic position of the farmers deteriorated during the seventeenth century. (See the later section of this chapter, "Reduction, and the accompanying social and economic revolution.") Their local meetings often drew up memorials of complaint. However, this Estate was not always called to riksdag meetings. Finland was a major province of the kingdom, with about one-third of the population, but because of distance and expense its representation in the riksdag was usually meager. Representatives of the four Estates would commonly meet, hear the propositions from the king, and then each would retire to its separate hall for consideration. Each Estate would draw up its responses in written form, and when the Estates met again a spokesman for each would elaborate orally on the written response. If all agreed there was no problem. If the Estates disagreed and could not be reconciled by discussion, the king was left to choose "whichever view is best." The arrangement suited Gustav Adolf perfectly, for he could always swing a riksdag to his will, and anyway he retained the power of decision.

However, Gustav Adolf wanted thoughtful agreement, and he went to great lengths to get riksdag and council to join with him, not only in the final action but in the decision-making process. Before the move into Germany the king held repeated discussions in the council, making sure that his own case was argued and that opposing views were well presented and that the decision was a joint responsibility. His thoughtful preparation and his extraordinary powers of persuasion assured that the ultimate unanimous decision was his own.

Most difficult for the king were relations with the nobility, for they yearned for power and were bitter against the autocracy of Karl IX. Under the leadership of the Gustav Adolf-Oxenstierna team the old enmity of crown and aristocracy was ameliorated (though not eliminated), submerged in grants, donations, and daily activities. Some nobles became wealthy and acted like petty monarchs: Per Brahe had 747 farms and a private guard in uniform plus 1,000 holdings in Finland; De la Gardie had 300 farms. Yet Gustav Adolf was king and allowed no one to forget it. Gradually the obsolete requirement that each noble provide mounted knights for the army was abandoned but in its place the nobles were expected to serve in governmental office. Only slowly were the new arrangements formalized. As of 1611, for instance, there were some four hundred noble families, with many of the family heads little more than rural squires. In 1626 differences in status were recognized in the *Riddarhus* (House of the Nobles) Ordinance. This picked 126 of the leading families to be represented in the noble Estate of the riksdag and divided this select group into three classes: counts and barons (12), council families (22), and regular nobility (92). Since voting was by class (one vote for each), the votes of two classes could determine the decision of the entire Estate.

In the years after 1626 the king began to ennoble commoners, starting with his old tutor Johan Skytte. Sixty-one men were designated as nobles before his death in 1632, and of these almost half were foreigners. This extension of privilege stirred antagonism within the ranks of the elite, but this was not yet a serious issue in Gustav Adolf's time.

Judicial procedure had become chaotic, with too much dependence on the king as a court of last appeal, and with a blending of the traditional law with the stern Mosaic or the Roman law. Frequently comparisons were made between Roman and native law. Karl IX had failed to obtain agreement on law revision and had compromised by printing Kristofer's law code. In 1616 Olaus Petri's Rules for Judges were printed, with such prescriptions as "a good judge is better than good laws" and "that which is not right and reasonable cannot be law." [16] And the fertile brain and untiring hand of Oxenstierna kept on composing ordinances. The Judicature Ordinance of 1614 established the Supreme Court (*Svea Hovrätt*), and high courts were established in Åbo (in 1623), Dorpat (in 1630), and Jönköping (in 1635). The Procedure Ordinance of 1615 relaxed the process of appeal somewhat by restoring the king's final authority and by leaving with him the responsibility to confirm death sentences. Many obsolete practices remained, but progress was indicated by the installation of a professorship in Swedish law. This innovation, the continuance of the *härad* jury, and the ingrained tradition that "On law shall the land be built," helped safeguard the inherited liberties of the individual.

Gustav Adolf inherited a system of local government that had grown antiquated and chaotic. Since in his time improved accounting methods became particularly important he and Oxenstierna made the local bailiffs of the crown responsible to an administrator (*ståthållare*). By the early 1630s they changed the title of *ståthållare* to *landshövding* (governor of the *län*) and divided all the Swedish possessions into twenty-three *län*, with eleven for Sweden proper. The governor (*landshövding*) became a viceroy for his province, and a neat hierarchical structure was established, confused a bit by the existence also of the counties and baronies. The smaller districts known as *härads* survived, each with its *häradsting* and *häradsnämnd* (jury or committee) overseeing purely local affairs. Alongside the *härad* was the parish and its democratic parish meeting, responsible for religious matters and the care of the poor.

Professor Sigurd Erixon thinks that the most significant innovation of Gustav Adolf's reign was the establishment of the land survey office, an institution designed to map the entire country. The approximately six hundred thousand maps eventually compiled provided the base for taxation and ownership, for redivision of land in the enclosure reforms of the eighteenth century, for everything that had to do with orderly management of landed property. The land survey office, founded in 1628, served as a model for similar bureaus later established in other European countries.

These wide-ranging reforms of administration, of which the foregoing are samples, gave Sweden a system advanced for its time, and much of it is still functioning in the twentieth century. It developed piecemeal but was guided by Oxenstierna's judicious planning. Gustav Adolf was deeply interested, but it is not known how thoroughly he approved of the codification in the Form of Government (*Regerings Form*) of 1634. This basic statute was sent to Stockholm by Oxenstierna from Germany only eight days after Gustav Adolf's death. Its sixty-five articles were almost all-inclusive. Here was a systematization of reforms already made and an explicit recognition of Lutheranism as the religion of the state, of the legislative powers of the riksdag, of the bureaucratization of administration, and of the primacy of the nobility. It recognized the monarchy and provided for the machinery by which the state could function during the minority or absence of a king. The apex of the pyramid of power under a regency was to be a five-man board of the conciliar aristocracy, presided over by the chancellor.[17] Oxenstierna thus assured continuance of his own power, but neither Queen Kristina nor later monarchs ever formally accepted the document.

It was difficult in the seventeenth century to limit the authority of a monarch. As we shall see, when Kristina became queen in her own right she overrode the will of the venerable chancellor, and both Karl X Gustav and Karl XI were able to exercise the full powers of sovereignty.

## Seventeenth-Century Socioeconomic Reconstruction

The whole seventeenth century was characterized by increased emphasis on centralized planning and direction. Initiative for change came from Stockholm, often inspired by foreign example and assisted by foreign personnel and foreign capital. Imported mercantilistic policies came as natural adaptations of the paternalism of Gustav Vasa, and the new emphasis on industry and commerce applied in this underdeveloped country transformed its society.

The new trends were early evident in copper mining and export. Gustav Adolf owned many of the mining huts on Falun's "Copper Mountain" until 1620, and after that date he continued operations through the newly founded Swedish Trading Company. It was largely through production and export of copper that he was able to pay off the Älvsborg ransom in 1619; later he tried to force the cities he conquered to use copper as coinage and to accept Swedish coinage at face value. He met resistance because of the inconvenience of the bulk and weight of copper, about one hundred times the weight of silver for equal value; the chief advantage was that this weight discouraged thievery. Demand for copper was chiefly from Spain and from the Far East, by way of Amsterdam and Hamburg. Serious problems arose when Spain ceased minting copper and the price fell 37.5 percent on the Amsterdam market between 1626 and 1631. The Swedish government attempted to manipulate prices by withholding copper from the market until a shortage raised prices, but it did not have a strong enough monopoly to make this policy succeed. Of some influence was the threat of Japanese copper coming on the European market, though European imports from Japan did not become extensive until the 1670s and 1680s. Despite the price decline Swedish copper export quintupled in 1631–35 over 1621–25 and iron export increased sevenfold. For a long time copper was Sweden's chief export; even as it declined it remained second in importance after iron through the seventeenth century. Production in the 1620s ran from 1,300 to 1,500 tons and in the 1640s and 1650s averaged 2,100 tons; not until 1715 did it sink below 1,200 tons. Silver mining was tried but never became important. More than any other item it was copper that paid for the wars that built the Swedish Baltic empire.

The mercantilistic policies displayed in the handling of copper were practiced throughout the economy. To encourage industry the traditional export of half-finished goods was prohibited; only finished products could be sold abroad. Strikes were regarded as mutinies and were usually squelched early. Iron manufacturing was particularly encouraged, and the government attempted to distribute it as widely as possible to prevent exhaustion of the forest in the mining regions, for smelting required vast quantities of timber. The central office of control was established in 1637 and was raised in status in 1649 as the Board of Mines (*Bergskollegium*).

Sweden needed the managerial skills of foreigners like Louis De Geer and the de Besche brothers and the processing techniques (such as the new blast furnaces) brought in by some three hundred Walloon and Dutch workers who came to mines and industries — especially to the rapidly developing arms industry discussed earlier. Sweden had the ores, both copper and iron, but it needed capital for the expansion of industry and this, too, came largely from the Dutch. De Geer invested his capital first and followed it in person some years later. Although he was unscrupulous he was an organizing genius who lifted arms manufacture out of the handicraft stage to a factory operation and a considerable export industry. In 1629–30, as director of the royal munitions works he provided 20,000 muskets, 13,670 pikes, and 4,700 suits of cavalry armor. Then he went into private business, and by 1644 he was sufficiently wealthy to supply Sweden from his own resources with a fleet of thirty warships. He was involved in salt peter, shipbuilding, sulphur, tin works, general stores, and in the lending of money to the nobility.

Other factories of importance were the textile mills that made uniforms and the mills just getting started that made paper from flax. Clothing was often homemade, but the finer garments of the nobility were imported. Utensils like bowls and spoons, plows and axes, were made of both wood and iron on the farms themselves and in small shops and then sold by traveling peddlers and at fairs.

Although much of the manufacturing was carried on in the rural *bruk* (works), towns became increasingly important for both crafts and commerce. Karl IX had been premature in his encouragement of cities, but Gustav Adolf supported them vigorously and more successfully. Riga was the most active port of the kingdom. Stockholm was the largest city in Sweden proper, with about ten thousand inhabitants in the year the *Mayflower* sailed to Plymouth. It was declared a staple city in an attempt to concentrate trade. The king promulgated a new city law in 1618 and a guild ordinance in 1621. In 1619 Gustav Adolf reestablished Gothenburg, which had withered while the Älvsborg ransom was being paid, and it grew slowly. It became the export mart for Swedish copper and iron and a city of much interest to the Dutch in their rivalry with the Danes. The layout was Dutch, with a rectangular street pattern and a canal reaching into the heart of the city. The city council too gave evidence of its foreign connections; its original membership included ten

Dutchmen, seven Swedes, and one Scot. The number of Germans in the city later increased, but Gothenburg never received as many Germans as did Stockholm. Norrköping was not a new city, but it grew with the industries of De Geer. Other cities were founded: Sundsvall, Luleå, and Umeå in the north, Borås in the southwest as a center for peddlers. Eighteen new towns were founded between 1611 and 1654, most of them destined to remain small. The wealth of merchants grew, and gradually their houses were built of stone instead of wood, which succumbed to many disastrous fires.

Workers were subject to a variety of regulations. The guild ordinance prescribed three to four years of apprenticeship, then two years as a journeyman before a craftsman could become a master. Rural smiths were frequently forced to move into cities to practice their trade, though the farmers still had to be versatile and skillful. A farmer had to be his own baker, brewer, shoemaker, carpenter and smith. Most of the workers in the *bruk* were either forbidden to move or were held to their places by debts to their employers. Emigration was really no problem in the middle and later part of the century, but a law of 1620 already forbade emigration. Immigration was encouraged by government agents going to Austria, Scotland, Germany, and the Low Countries to get workers, especially miners. Several thousand Finns were brought to the Umeå Lappmark, in the far north, in the years following 1673, to settle and hold it against the Danes and Norwegians, which led to complications with the Lapps and their reindeer culture.

Commerce and shipping were of course vital in the mercantilistic system, and here fundamental changes occurred. Lübeck, still handling about 75 percent of the Swedish trade in the 1620s, was finally edged out by Hamburg, Amsterdam, and the Swedish port of Stralsund. In the Dutch-English rivalry for the trade of the Baltic, the English gradually got the upper hand. They needed naval stores from Russia and Sweden, and they found a good market for their textiles. However, the Swedes were no longer content with the passive trade of Gustav Vasa's day. They built their own ships and sought their own markets, though they were seriously hampered by continued warfare. They exported iron, copper, hides, butter, timber, grain from the east Baltic, and manufactured goods such as guns. In 1655–62, for example, Sweden produced 11,000 cannons and exported 9,000 of them.[18] From 1690 Sweden maintained an export surplus, though it diminished after 1702 and especially after 1708. Trade was sufficiently important that in 1690 and 1693 Sweden allied with Denmark to enforce neutral rights on the seas.

No innovations in agricultural techniques were introduced. The Finnish settlers in northern and western Sweden continued to use the wasteful and primitive burn-beat system of cultivation — destroying the forest, providing a brief crop period, and then reverting to forest. For the rural population as a whole the system of storage economy still prevailed. Land was divided in the community strip system and was usually farmed on a three-field basis: one-third fallow, one-third spring planting, and one-third fall planting. Taxes might be paid in kind or in cash, and as much as possible was paid in cash because the inflation of the coinage made this far cheaper. Barley was still the chief crop, with rye second and oats and wheat slowly increasing in importance. At best the yield was three to six times the seed. Livestock consisted largely of cattle with a few sheep.

Recurrent crop failures produced misery and sometimes stark starvation. Among the worst years were 1691–93, 1695–97, 1708–9, and 1717–20. When bubonic plague was added to hunger, as in the period around 1710, desperation stalked the land and farms lay vacant. Nature had to take its course, for as one foreign observer put it, the country had "one king, one religion, one medico." [19]

The farmer's clothing was simple but warm and of good quality, and his food was usually adequate, even if it still had to be washed down with quantities of beer. Vegetables were rare; the first mention of them (green peas) in soldiers' rations was in 1676. [20]

The fees and other burdens of the peasants differed by district and by classification, though there was a trend toward standardization. The crown peasants paid fixed rents plus special fees like "salt-peter help," building help of eighteen loads of firewood, and days of work service. The nobles' peasants paid animal fees and fees for forwarding travelers, usually settled for two dalers and one and one-half dalers respectively. All paid tithes, of which the priest got one-third and the crown (or nobles) two-thirds. The great majority lived on only a subsistence level; when the infirmities of disease or old age struck, care was financed partly by donations, partly by governmental money coming from fines. [21]

One of the advances sought by the government in the early seventeenth century was the move from a natural economy to a money economy, and Gustav Adolf achieved a considerable changeover. He was prolific in formulating schemes for development and taxation. To pay the all-important ransom for Älvsborg a special tax was imposed on everyone — even the queen mother and the tax-free *frälse*. Levies included a tax on livestock and on fields of grain, a so-called Little Toll on all edibles brought to market, a mill toll on grain — later commuted to a charge per family — a ship tax, and a recruitment aid, and on and on. Unlike the taxes of previous centuries these new levies were usually demanded in cash; some of them survived into the twentieth century. Because of collection difficulties the government resorted to farming out the taxes to men like Willem de Besche and Jakob de la Gardie. Since there still wasn't enough revenue crown lands were sold, and grants (*förläningar*) were made to recompense state officials. The early wars across the Baltic were a heavy drain on national resources, as was the beginning of the war in Germany. Only the extraordinary success of Swedish arms reduced the burden and at least partly validated Gustav Adolf's policy that "war must sustain war."

Toward the end of the century Karl XI relaxed the efforts to maintain a money economy. Through establishments like the *indelningsverk*, the apportionment system for the army, he assigned much of the revenue of the state to specific and local uses, never gathering it into the central treasury. One result was the absence of a basis for credit which severely inhibited Karl XII when he needed to borrow extra funds. This in turn led to some of the extraordinary financial schemes of wily Baron Görtz, who in the pattern of John Law juggled coinage and state obligations to finance the king's last army. Even earlier, in 1661, the first modern bank notes had been issued by Stockholm Banco but had failed. Sweden long wrestled with the problems of the dual coinage of silver and copper and a serious lack of credit.

In this century of new beginnings Sweden was also reaching out overseas with colonization and trading. It organized several tar companies (1648 and later), an African or Guinea Company (1649–1717), a Tobacco Company (1651–53, 1664–c. 1690), a Sugar Company (1647–97), West India companies (c. 1640–1793), and a Levant Company (1646–1806). This does not include those founded in the eighteenth century. As early as the 1620s two sanguine dreamers had put their heads together when the Dutchman Willem Usselinx and Gustav Adolf met in Gothenburg. Gustav Adolf thought that the welfare of the nation depended on trade and navigation, and he had before him the example of the spectacular success of the English East India Company. It was not too difficult for Usselinx to persuade him to found the "General Company for Commerce and Navigation with the Lands of Africa, Asia, America, and Magellanica" in 1624; for short it was called the Southern Company. The king agreed to invest 400,000 daler in the enterprise, but he never paid it. After his death and while the armies were still marching in Germany, Oxenstierna found time to resume one of the old projects — an overseas colony.

Even while the Thirty Years War held top priority on the Swedish agenda Oxenstierna recognized the importance of commercial expansion. Markets were needed for copper, and no one knew what rich prospects might develop from trade with the New World. At hand was an experienced leader, Peter Minuit, who had bought Manhattan Island from the Indians and had been the governor of New Netherland from 1625 until his dismissal in 1632. He was put in charge of the expedition of 1637–38 that sailed with the *Kalmar Nyckel*

(Key of Kalmar) and the *Fogel Grip* (Griffin) to the Delaware to establish a trading post and settlement. Half the capital and about half the crews were Dutch, but it was a Swedish venture challenging the far-reaching claims of New Netherland. Unfortunately Minuit was lost at sea on his way back to report on progress, and the cargo of furs and tobacco was not sufficient to pay the costs of the expedition. However, a footing had been gained. A large area along the Delaware had been bought from five Indian chiefs; it eventually was expanded to include most of the present state of Delaware and sections of New Jersey and Pennsylvania. Fort Kristina, named for the young queen, had been built, and villages had been founded. In the years that followed more settlers came, usually in small groups of a dozen to fifty people, and villages of Finnish and Swedish farmers and woodsmen extended from the present site of Wilmington north to where Trenton now stands.

Although the trading potential was not enough to enthuse officials in Stockholm agriculture flourished and the colonists prospered. The Indians were mostly friendly, and they were much impressed by the governor who arrived in 1643 — Johan Printz, a huge man nicknamed Big Belly by the Indians. He was an able and enthusiastic administrator, but he grew discontented at the lack of support from home and returned to Sweden in 1653; later he became landshövding in Småland. The largest single contingent of new settlers, some 250 remaining after 100 had died on the harrowing voyage, arrived in 1654. Their vessel brought the new governor, Johan Rising, and a young fortification expert, Per Lindeström, who wrote a dramatic account of his experiences. These reinforcements were needed to bolster the defenses of the colony, but they were inadequate. The Dutch were just as eager as the Swedes to control the sparsely settled valley, and they were more numerous. Neither the new arrivals nor the little forts nor the two-story stone blockhouse built on Naaman's Creek could thwart the fleet of seven ships that the Dutch brought up the river in 1655. The forts had to be surrendered, and the Swedish flag no longer flew in the western hemisphere. The Dutch remained in control until 1664 when the English took over the entire region.

The Swedish administrators and some of the immigrants stayed but a short time in America, but enough remained to put the stamp of Swedish and Finnish culture on the lower Delaware valley. Names changed: Finland became Marcus Hook, Kristina became Wilmington, and Tranudden in translation became Crane Hook. Settlers continued to come even after political control was lost, including a group of 140 Finns in 1664. The language long lived on, with some 1,200 to 1,500 Swedish-speaking people at the end of the seventeenth century. Undoubtedly the tenacity of the language was closely associated with the strength of the Lutheran churches in every community, whose supply of ministers was replenished from Sweden until 1770. Gloria Dei church in Philadelphia and other Old Swede churches survived into the nineteenth and even the twentieth century.

One of the notable contributions of these Swedes and Finns was the log cabin, patterned directly after the construction methods of the old country and admirably suited to the conditions of the American frontier. It spread from the Delaware settlements through Pennsylvania and into the Ohio Valley and became the symbol of frontier politics. The descendants of the early immigrants blended gradually into the mixed American society; John Hanson became the first "President of the United States in Congress Assembled," and John Morton, a signer of the Declaration of Independence, was another American patriot of Swedish origin. The Delaware was an extension of empire much too distant for Sweden to maintain, but the impact of the Nordic settlers was long lasting.[22]

More ephemeral than the American project but another indication of the ambitious outreach of the seventeenth-century Swedes was the establishment of a post on the west coast of Africa. The Africa Company was founded on the initiative of Louis De Geer to deal in slaves, gold, and ivory. Again the operation was entrusted partly to foreigners, and again it was caught up in the rivalry of European states. Henrik Carloff (of Rostock) bought land from the king of Futu at Cabo Corso, once a Portuguese factory, later known as Cape Coast Castle in what is now Ghana. Carloff was angered when a new governor was named, defected to the Danes, returned in 1657 and captured the fort he had built in 1652 for the Swedes. Sweden should have got the fort back in 1660, but it had been sold to the Dutch by a subordinate of Carloff who then absconded. The natives then attacked the Dutch and restored the fort to the Swedes. However, the Dutch retook it and held it until the English ousted them in 1664. Such vicissitudes ruined the Africa Company.

Sweden was bidding for a place among the leading powers, dreaming of empire and commerce far beyond the Baltic, but this competition was even more costly and complicated than that of the battlefield.

### New Emphases on Religion and Education

"The Swedes, when they emerged upon the historic scene, appeared not only as a nation of resurgent Goths but as the godly heritors of Israel."[23]

From the priest-kings of Swedish paganism, through Gustav Vasa's political guidance of the Reformation, to the varied but sincerely Christian interests of the Vasa sons, religion and the state had grown inextricably intertwined. Gustav Adolf and Axel Oxenstierna shared with the clergy and people the intensity of orthodox Lutheranism, which, like nationalism, was a unifying and energizing force. Rulers and ruled alike agreed on the literal truth of the Uppsala declaration of 1593. The Bible followed the sword as Lutheran priests went into the Baltic lands in the wake of the armies to give the true word to the Greek Orthodox inhabitants. Yet Gustav Adolf was a philippist like his father; he hoped for reconciliation between Lutheranism and Calvinism, and he did not persecute Catholics even during his German campaigns. Within Sweden he permitted foreigners like De Geer and his brother-in-law Johan Casimir to practice their Calvinism freely, for he believed that "no sovereign has the power to rule and control a man's conscience."[24]

In the government itself membership on the council was limited to the nobility, hence no priest could serve. Yet the clergy as a class were the most universally educated members of Swedish society, and they exercised influence in many ways. In the first place they were mediators with God, interpreters of God's will for men. Through sermons and writings they were the chief instruments for spreading ideas and news in an age when newspapers were in their infancy. Chaplains at court and in the army spoke out on issues in magisterial tones, and the stentorian voice of Bishop Rudbeckius could be heard throughout the land.

The clergy carried out much administrative work, oversaw poor relief, kept records of births and deaths and marriages, and read royal manifestoes to their congregations. Gustav Adolf used the local ministers to aid in recruiting, in assessing contributions for the Älvsborg ransom, and in reporting on run-down farms. The parsons represented the government in exactly those areas where government impinged most directly on the individual, and in the riksdag it was often they who could best express the sentiments of the common man. The most active and democratic local governing bodies were the parish meetings and the elected six-man vestries and church wardens. It should be noted that women as well as men participated in the parish meetings.

Parson and parish were intimately related. It was the priest who knew the problems, heartaches, and petty weaknesses of the people. He was concerned about their welfare for their sakes and for his own, for the parson's livelihood and his family's were dependent on payments in kind from the produce of his parishioners. He could feel with his people, and sometimes he may have done a bit too much partying and drinking with them. He was aware that they needed his three sermons and more to overcome the still widespread belief in the trolls that lived in the forests and the whole gamut of folk superstititions. Even Karl IX had shot at a water sprite in the stream outside the castle, and a "witch" was burned for causing the illness of Duke Johan and the insanity of his wife. An undertow of darkness had not yet been completely conquered by Christianity, and education was in a parlous state. Yet progress was being made.

The religious bequest of Gustav Adolf was not only the preservation of Sweden from the externals of Catholic power but the establishment of church and state as working partners in the Swedish community.

Aside from the shock that rippled through Sweden when the people heard that their ex-queen Kristina had become a Roman Catholic, there was no unusual event in church history until the middle of Karl XI's reign. In 1686 Karl promulgated a new church ordinance that defined the true faith and placed the church definitely under the authority of the king; banishment was decreed for any Swede who departed from the official Lutheranism, and everyone had to take communion at least three times a year. The Holy Sacrament became a civic duty. Karl XI issued stern warnings against the pietists. At the end of the century a new hymnal appeared and a new translation of the Bible was begun.

Education was in desperate need of reform. Karl IX had reestablished the University of Uppsala at Gustav Adolf's birth. (It had expired under Gustav Vasa for lack of sustenance.) But by the time Gustav Adolf became king the seven professors had not accomplished much in the way of training either clerks or ambassadors for the service of the state. The whole educational system of the country was by and for the church. Gustav Adolf's practical concern and his deep national pride made him eager to raise the level of Swedish education, to make it more practical, and to reduce the governmental dependency on foreigners and continental universities.

Progress was slowed by the inadequacy of the School Ordinance of 1611 and the scandalous controversy at Uppsala between the two brilliant professors Johannes Messenius and Johannes Rudbeckius. Messenius had been deeply affected by his continental travel and Jesuit education abroad, although he had supposedly turned against the Jesuits. At Uppsala he established a Collegium Privatum which he promoted in spectacular ways. He wrote popular dramas and gained a large student following. The personal aspect of the conflict with Rudbeckius and Messenius has been paralleled many times in other universities: the man of sober correctness resentful of his colleague with flair. In this case the feelings were exacerbated by national religious and diplomatic strife. The controversy became so tense that both men had to leave the university. Rudbeckius became bishop of Västerås. Messenius took his following with him to Stockholm but was soon charged with treasonous correspondence with the Poles and spent the next twenty of his twenty-one remaining years of life in the far northern fortress-prison of Kajaneborg.

Incidentally, both his son and his grandson, also facile writers, were executed simultaneously in 1651 for a suspected plot against the monarchy.

In the 1620s Gustav Adolf turned his attention to the educational situation and things began to happen. He used some of the estates that had reverted to the crown from Johan and Karl Filip to endow the university with three hundred seventeen homesteads (*hemman*) together with other privileges. Professorships were increased and divided into faculties, and Johan Skytte, the king's wise tutor, was made chancellor. Theology and philosophy were the main subjects, but medicine, politics, and law were added, and the king hoped that sometime in the future Sweden could educate its own public servants. For the nobility a special school of statecraft established by the House of the Nobles helped a little. But Swedish education was meant not only for the nobility, and at least a few peasant lads rose through education to the ministry or to high office. The approved method of earning their way was the summer begging and singing tour (*sockengång*) which was doubtless something of an education in itself.

In his emphasis on the new and on higher education Gustav Adolf made the local communities responsible for elementary education. Beyond the *trivium* the educational system was inadequate to prepare the student for university work without the private instruction that Messenius, for example, offered in his Collegium Privatum. Hence a big forward step in secondary education was taken with the establishment and state support of the *gymnasia*. The first was founded in Västerås, at the urging of Bishop Rudbeckius, then others were set up in Strängnäs and Linköping, and across the Baltic in Åbo, Dorpat, Reval, and Riga. These preparatory schools bridged the gap between *trivial* school and university, offering work in Latin, Greek, Hebrew, and theology, but also in new subjects chosen at the local bishop's discretion, including science, ethics, mathematics, Swedish law and politics, history, geography, and even modern languages. The *lektors* (senior masters) were subject specialists rather than teachers of everything to a single year-group. Gustav Adolf was specially interested in reducing the prevailing emphasis on mere recitation, and instead in teaching children to read.

Religion permeated the entire educational system, and Latin was its language. The school day, in the early seventeenth century, lasted from 5:00 A.M. until 5:00 P.M., with a three-hour midday break. Within a 51-hour week 31 hours were devoted to Latin (grammar, vocabulary, drill), 31 hours to music, 7 to religion. In 1611 differentiation was made between the cathedral schools with 6 two-year classes and the provincial schools with 4 classes, and in the cathedral schools instruction was added in Greek, rhetoric, and logic. Students were usually from the middle and lower classes of society, while the nobles used private tutors. The catechism was the most essential item of learning. Practically all subjects were taught by rigid memoriter methods. There could be "no doubt, no variations, no opposition, but a stringent discipline, a domineering faith."[25]

Gustav Adolf's urgent plea for trained secretaries and officials and Johan Skytte's demand for practical education led to the establishment of a kind of internship system at the chief court. Auditors were trained through a two-year term of attendance at the court, unpaid, and the experience could lead to high office and even to ennoblement. The system provided a corps of technical, trained-on-the-job clerks, and also burgomasters, and it lasted into the twentieth century. But it did not supply administrators with the broad-based education needed as state functions expanded.[26]

The educational system was flexible enough to change with changing needs. In one case Gustav Adolf became dictatorial. Jönköping had failed to fulfill the condition of its charter that it establish a technical school. The king thereupon ordered that every boy in the city should be sent to school at seven years of age to learn a craft, or his father would be fined; if at age sixteen a boy had not shown satisfactory achievement the town was commanded to confiscate his inheritance. The king wanted the Swedish citizenry to have an education in Christianity, the three Rs, herbs and healing, geography, astronomy, law, and history.

Later in the century the educational system was significantly expanded. A medical school was inaugurated in 1663, and the first technical school (a mechanical laboratory) was founded in 1697 by Christopher Polhem, an engineer and inventor. Most important was the establishment in 1668 of Lund University for the new citizens of the south, making altogether four universities for the kingdom (Uppsala dated from 1477, Dorpat from 1632, and Åbo from 1640); in addition, Greifswald in Pomerania, founded in 1456, became a popular center for Swedish students.

## Diplomacy and War Go On and On

When Gustaf Adolf died in 1632 he left on the battlefield well-trained generals, in the chancellery his close partner Axel Oxenstierna, and in the royal palace only his six-year-old daughter. Yet both diplomacy and war had to go on.

During the minority of Kristina (1632–44) the Swedish position in Germany remained fluid but strong. Axel Oxenstierna as the survivor in the king-chancellor combination continued to give general direction both to the armies in the field and to the government in Stockholm. Yet despite Oxenstierna's outstanding abilities the death of Gustav Adolf required a reappraisal of the power position of Sweden. If there had been any thought or possibility of a Swedish-Protestant empire with a strong German base (and no one can know what may have been in Gustav Adolf's dreams), that resolution of the German political chaos had to be abandoned. Saxony was openly antagonistic, Brandenburg felt it must have Pomerania. No one of stature lower than genius could hope to thwart their power and ambitions. Poland was still unsatisfied, though the armistice that expired in 1635 was renewed. In the Baltic littoral Sweden controlled a valuable food-producing area and along the coasts held all the important ports and collected tolls from neutral shipping. Russia looked on this with envy, and though temporarily quiescent it would not remain so. France under Richelieu and Louis XIV was interested in using Sweden as an outer bastion of its own power and was therefore liberal with the subsidies and the diplomatic support that Sweden needed, but France did not want Sweden to build too mighty an empire. Dutch merchants now conducted the lion's share of trade in the Baltic (65 percent of the ships going through the Sound were Dutch at mid-century and 10 percent were Swedish), and their interest led them to play a game of balance so that neither Sweden nor Denmark could become strong enough to exclude them nor weak enough to cease to threaten the other. The English were also concerned with Baltic trade, but their internal disturbances in the seventeenth century took precedence over the interests of Englishmen in the northern seas. The state whose ambitions most worried the Swedes was Denmark-Norway, the immediate neighbor.

The glory and the high goals were gone, as was the genius-leader. But Sweden had injected its men and guns into a continental imbroglio. The armies could not be disentangled and had to fight to a decision of some sort. Oxenstierna pushed on with Gustav Adolf's project for a Protestant League. Many of the German states, though resentful of the Swedish presence in Germany, signed up and made the chancellor the director; the undependable Saxons rejected the invitation. In the first major engagement after Leipzig forces now under Bernhard of Weimar and Gustaf Horn (Gustav Adolf's right-hand man in the field) suffered a crushing defeat at Nördlingen on August 27, 1634, and Horn was captured. The league fell to pieces, Johan Georg of Saxony agreed to help the emperor drive the Swedes out of Germany, and soon others joined the pack. The religious tone and purpose was forgotten. The Swedes fought on for gain, and their French allies fought to humble the Hapsburgs. Oxenstierna in 1636 returned to Stockholm, and Johan Adler Salvius became the representative of Swedish authority in Germany.

The troops marched back and forth across a devastated land and the high spots of battle were few. The armies were small, but the generalship was excellent, for Gustav Adolf, unlike many of the strong men of history, had carefully trained a corps of young military and civilian officials to carry on.

The reconciliation of monarchy and aristocracy paid good dividends. And merit easily won promotion. The dashing Johan Banér won an important engagement at Wittstock in 1636 and died in Germany in 1641. Lennart Torstensson succeeded to the command, and in October 1642 he was victorious in a second battle of Breitenfeld and took Leipzig. In 1643 he led his forces off to Denmark (see below) and soon thereafter retired home. During the last two years of the exceedingly long war General Carl Gustaf Wrangel, in cooperation with the French under Turenne, ravaged Bavaria, and General Hans Christian von Königsmarck looted a section of Prague. Prince Karl Gustav, Gustav Adolph's nephew, became generallissimo at the end of the war.

Meanwhile negotiations for peace were dragging on in Münster and Osnabrück, complicated by the great numbers of states involved. The Swedish diplomats were Salvius and Oxenstierna's son Johan, who were relieved at last in the fall of 1648 when the emperor accepted terms. Sweden's long-sought satisfaction came in the acquisition of Pomerania with Stettin and the island of Wollin, Wismar, the bishoprics of Verden and Bremen (not the city), and some smaller districts in north Germany; 600,000 riksdaler from the emperor, plus 5 million from the German states (never fully paid). As duke of Pomerania the Swedish king had a seat in the German Diet. Sweden had won recognition as a great power, and had acquired significant holdings on the continent, although it lacked the foundation strength of population and resources to make full use of its position.

One of Sweden's most troublesome problems was that whenever it sent an army across the Baltic or into Germany it had to face the prospect of a two-front war. Denmark was always ready to take advantage of a moment of Swedish weakness. However, in the early 1640s the sword and the opportunity were in the other hand. After their defeat in the early stages of the Thirty Years War the Danes had not yet rebuilt their military strength. The Swedes, however, had successful and well-trained troops, and at the moment they were accomplishing little in central Germany. It seemed an ideal moment for a preventive war to push back the frontiers from which Denmark had so often attacked. In the fluctuating situation of the seventeenth century, in which all states were in and out of alliances and wars, it was not at all unnatural for Sweden to see and use its advantage. The fateful decision was made in Stockholm in 1643.

General Torstensson was ordered to break off his campaign in Germany and move north, with neither declaration nor warning. He quickly subdued Danish resistance in Jutland, and Gustaf Horn conquered most of Skåne and Blekinge, those Danish provinces east of the Sound. The Danes got naval aid from the Dutch, while De Geer hired other Dutch armed ships for Sweden. On the sea the Swedes were also victorious and dealt the Danes a catastrophic defeat in the Femern Belt in October 1644. The Danes had to yield and at Brömsebro, on the eastern border below Kalmar, six months of bitter negotiations between Axel Oxenstierna and Corfitz Ulfeldt led at last to peace on August 13, 1645. Denmark retained sovereignty in Öresund but extended the Swedish freedom from Sound dues to ships from its new Baltic provinces, gave Halland in pawn to Sweden for thirty years, and ceded outright the islands of Ösel and Gotland, while Norway parted with the vast northern provinces of Jämtland and Härjedalen.

Neither Denmark nor Sweden regarded the Brömsebro cessions as a final settlement between them, but neither started any further action during Kristina's reign. Caution and peace were her guideposts, and with the conclusion of the Peace of Westphalia in 1648 Sweden was to enjoy a brief breathing spell.

## Kristina, Unhappy Heiress to Glory

Two possible male successors to Gustav Adolf died early: his cousin Johan in 1618 and his younger brother Karl Filip in 1622, both without heirs. The duchies held by Johan and Karl Filip reverted at their deaths to the crown, and this gave Gustav Adolf the opportunity to correct a mistake made by Gustav Vasa in allowing large chunks of the kingdom to become semi-autonomous fiefdoms. Gustav Adolf pledged that he would never create new duchies, and thus the dangers of friction and decentralization were reduced. Gustav Adolf's own illegitimate son by the Dutch Margareta Slots of course did not count. As of 1622 the closest Protestant heir was Gustav Adolf's sister Katarina, and next was her son Karl Gustav. Reversion to Sigismund and his Catholic line was unthinkable; it would have caused religious strife and political chaos. Therefore Katarina, her husband Johan Casimir of the Palatinate, and young Karl Gustav were given Stegeborg castle and invited to come to Sweden. Fortunately for Sweden this Palatine family was available because of its tragic reverses in the early years of the Thirty Years War.

Clearly it would be best for Gustav Adolf to have an heir of his own, but his mother would not sanction marriage with his youthful romantic attachment, Ebba Brahe, the charming daughter of an important Swedish noble family. On a voyage of exploration to the continent he discovered a beautiful German princess, Maria Eleonora of Brandenburg. The elector approved, but this time the girl's mother was opposed — until she had reason to fear that the daughter would be pledged to Vladislav of Poland, and then she reconciled herself to the importunate Swede. For Gustav Adolf had stormed the princess' tower with the same vigor he attacked a fort. Diplomatically the match proved useless, and all too soon Gustav Adolf realized that Maria Eleonora was a weak woman. She was pathologically devoted to him, and he remained fond of her, but he would not trust her with any state business, nor even with the upbringing of their daughter. The first daughter, Kristina, died within a few months of her birth, and it was a second Kristina, born in 1626, who became sole heir. At least the succession was clear, and when the king was killed at Lützen the six-year-old daughter inherited.

Gustav Adolf did not admit disappointment that Kristina was not a boy, but he had her raised as if she were. After the tragedy of Lützen and because of her mother's incompetence, she was sent to Stegeborg, the seat of her Palatine relatives. There she grew up with her cousins, Karl Gustav, four years her senior, and Maria Eufrosyne. She developed a strong affection for the dashing Karl as they played together and studied languages and statecraft. In 1638 her aunt Katarina died, the family circle was broken, and Kristina moved back to Stockholm. From the death of her father in 1632 Kristina was under a regency directed by Chancellor Oxenstierna.

Her education continued under the thoughtful guidance of Johannes Matthiae. Her mind showed an unusual keenness and breadth of interest, and she early evidenced the independence of spirit that was to be expected of a Vasa. She was restless under the sober guardianship of Axel Oxenstierna, a most respected statesman but hardly a sympathetic mentor for a vivacious young girl. She loathed the multitudinous sermons of the Lutheran priests. In a later day the young Queen Victoria was to be more fortunate with her beloved Melbourne and especially with her understanding Prince Albert. It was early remarked by one foreign observer that Kristina had "nothing of a child but the age, and nothing of a woman but the sex."[27] She was as much an enigma as Mary Queen of Scots, and with almost as many interpreters. She was a woman in a man's world, destined for a man's job. She could neither be a man nor fully and naturally a woman. Frustrated and lonely, she never rightly found herself. Medical records attest that she was a woman, yet her voice was like a man's, her tastes and her habits were at least as much masculine as feminine. Her passions were not people but religious and philosophical discussion, literature, art. As a French woman wrote of her, "science is to her what needle and cotton are to other women."[28]

In 1644, on the eve of her eighteenth birthday, she became queen, though the luxurious pageantry of coronation waited until after the war, in 1650. She gathered youth and brains about her and introduced in court life both an unprecedented gaiety and an unusual cultural emphasis. On her twenty-fourth birthday Karl Gustav gave a party for her, with eating and dancing and three hours of fireworks; it lasted from six in the evening to eight in the morning. On friends of her generation she lavished gifts, especially on favorites such as

Magnus De la Gardie whom she made a member of the council, a general, governor of Livonia, marshal and treasurer of the kingdom, and whom she showered with scores of estates in Sweden and Finland. Older intellectuals from Sweden and abroad were invited to court and were treated handsomely. Georg Stiernhielm was a versatile Swedish genius who wrote poetry for the royal pageants and studied archeology, languages, and natural science. Descartes was the star of the imported talent, who for four months in 1649–50 gave the queen early morning instruction in his philosophical system; it was probably the climate and the dark early hours that caused his pneumonia and death.

As early as age sixteen Kristina had begun to sit in on meetings of the council. Both the theoretical background and the practical experience of government she got in ample measure. But it bored her. Tension grew between young queen and aging chancellor and came to open conflict in 1648 when Kristina forced the choice of Johan Adler Salvius to the council. As the powers of the old statesman declined it was the queen herself who took over. Kristina had strong ideas about the prerogatives of the monarch, and Oxenstierna had ideas just as strong on the powers and prestige of the nobility. Between the two there was nothing of the mutual respect that had made the cooperation of Oxenstierna and Gustav Adolf a constructive phenomenon. They agreed on the advisability of peace, and they agreed on the granting of royal lands as compensation to the aristocracy. Perhaps the lands would then be more productive, as Oxenstierna argued, and in any case they gave Kristina an opportunity to be generous — whatever trouble might be thus planted for the future. Under Kristina a kind of political standstill reigned. Initiative was lacking, while Oxenstierna marked time and Kristina pursued first the pleasures of gaiety and then the more consuming pleasures of philosophical speculations.

That Kristina was highly intelligent and sincerely interested in intellectual pursuits there can be no doubt. It is just as clear that she was not a profound or original thinker. Her written works consist chiefly of an autobiography and aphorisms, the latter representing a traditional talent in her family but also a degree of borrowing from Loisir and others. A few samples will show her turn of mind:

> One must know how to punish and how to forgive.
> All that is not genuine is ridiculous.
> Strength and courage never lie.
> Men would not be fruitless and deceiving
>     if they were not weak and stupid.
> One loves those for whom he has done good,
>     hates those whom he has treated ill.

> Those who do not please us seldom deceive us.
> It is as dangerous to be good to people
>     as it is to caress wild animals.
> Only kings should direct; all others should
>     obey and carry out their orders.
> Love beautifies the object loved, and
>     makes it all the more worthy of love.[29]

But aphorisms and philosophical discussions did not resolve affairs of state. Military and diplomatic problems were handled primarily by Oxenstierna and Salvius and the generals. One of the major domestic problems involved finance and taxation. The poverty of the state in contrast to the growing wealth of individuals was bothering many of the thoughtful burghers and farmers. They thought the trouble lay with the alienation of crown properties through gifts to the nobility. In the riksdag of 1650 the question became acute, and the three lower Estates attacked the nobility in a "Protestation" demanding reduction (return of fiefs to the crown) and reform. The alienation of crown lands and revenues to worthy servants of the king began to assume large proportions in Gustav Adolf's day, and it increased under the generosity of Kristina. It did not seem to worry the queen, but she saw how she could use the discontent of the lower Estates for her own purpose. Therefore she encouraged their agitation and then agreed to abandon them if the nobility would approve Karl Gustav as hereditary prince. To preserve their own estates the nobles agreed. Out of her perplexity and aloneness the shrewd queen had hit upon a clever bargain that would help her solve her personal problems. Reduction was forgotten in return for agreement on Karl Gustav.

Marriage, with heirs, was one of the responsibilities of monarchs, but Kristina came to abhor the thought. When rumors flew about linking her with Magnus De la Gardie, for whom she seemed to have a real fondness, she saw to it that he married Maria Eufrosyne. For diplomatic reasons there was talk of a marriage with Frederick William of Brandenburg, but it never became serious. Apparently her deepest romantic interest was the girlhood attraction to cousin Karl Gustav, but this died during his travels abroad. His playboy escapades and affairs with other women (with at least three acknowledged sons) may have dampened the young queen's ardor. Or was it something in her own nature? By 1649 she had determined not to marry, and when insistent Karl Gustav pushed his suit she would only assure him that she would marry no one else.

Kristina thought that Karl Gustav would make a good king, and she had him named heir apparent in 1649. But she wanted him to receive the more secure title of hereditary prince, and it was this to which the nobles objected. Hence the queen's clever and determined manipulations.

With Karl Gustav securely in line of succession Kristina could proceed with her next objective — abdication. The simplest explanation of her desire to quit her job was that she was miscast as a ruler and that she realized it. The national finances required attention and reform. The social crisis was acute. Demobilized officers, often recently ennobled, who were loaded with the loot of Germany and with a taste for luxurious living, their minds filled with new and un-Swedish ideas of the subservient position of the peasantry, created restlessness and tension. The times were rife with wars and rumors of wars. In all these troublesome and worldly matters the queen had little interest. A man was needed, or a woman like Queen Margareta. But Kristina did not want to take a husband. Her running feud with Oxenstierna probably did not count heavily, for she knew he would soon be gone. And how important was the religious aspect in her renunciation?

Kristina had been much attracted by the attitude toward life of Descartes and of the French ambassador Pierre Chanut. Others such as the Spanish ambassador Pimentel and his confessor and two Italian Jesuits had more purposefully worked upon the queen's interest in Catholicism. In spite of the authoritarian structure of the Roman church there was in its bosom more of the permissiveness that Kristina needed than she could find in the rigid orthodoxy of Swedish Lutheranism. To Bulstrode Whitelocke, representative of Cromwell who came to Stockholm to negotiate an alliance (1653–54), Kristina said she hoped England would grant toleration to Catholics, but though they discussed religion (as well as copper and naval vessels and much else) Kristina gave him no indication of her inner convictions. Nor did she for some months.[30] Both her abdication and her conversion came as shocks to her officials and her people. After she shed the symbols of power, her coronation robe, crown ( riksäpplet), and scepter, in the ceremony of June 6, 1654 in Uppsala, her flight took her to Antwerp, Brussels and slowly to Rome. At Innsbruck, just before entering Italy, she renounced the faith of her father and became a Roman Catholic.[31]

Her later life as a queen without a country was a difficult adjustment. She was treated as a monarch and her imperious ways indicated that she could not slough off the past. When the storm broke over her conversion she coolly commented, ''Men can never admire, never approve a deed which they themselves are incapable of performing.''[32] Although the pope made much of his convert no other princes followed Kristina's example. Inevitably, first the Spaniards and then the French attempted to use her as a political tool, and there was once a possibility she would become queen of Naples. Only twice did she return to Sweden, primarily to see to her economic interests, for she had been granted for life the revenues of Norrköping and a few other localities. She was received with coolness by her former loyal subjects who were horrified to realize that they had been governed for several years by a queen who was at heart already a Catholic. It was a strange epilogue for the daughter of the "Lion of Protestantism."

# VIII

## SWEDEN'S AGE OF GREATNESS:
## II. CONQUEST, AUTOCRACY,
## AND COLLAPSE, 1654–1718

SWEDEN'S POSITION OF POWER in the early 1650s was more apparent than real. Internally the unsolved problem of the alienated lands embittered relations between the nobles and the commoners and created serious deficiencies in the national budget, all accentuated by crop failures and hunger. The old generation of leadership, the group of bright talent that came in with Gustav Adolf, was rapidly passing from the scene. Axel Oxenstierna's last public service was the drafting of the royal assurance given by Karl Gustav at his installation. A new generation would now take over. Externally no chinks in the wall were visible, but Russia, Poland, Austria, Denmark, and Brandenburg were jealously watching and ready to strike whenever opportunity might arise. In the process of seeking alliances to strengthen his position Karl X found but one ally, tiny and Denmark-hating Holstein-Gottorp. The alliance brought with it the king's bride, Hedvig Eleonora, and she became the mother of the boy who was to carry on as Karl XI after Karl X's six year reign ended in 1660 (and it was she who built Drottningholm castle).

### Karl X Gustav and the Resumption of Conquest

On the same day as the abdication, and clothed in Kristina's robe, Karl X Gustav was crowned as king. He had as much of the Vasa blood in his veins as Kristina, but he is considered the monarch who started the new Palatine branch. Intrigues among the Oxenstiernas had built up some opposition to Karl's succession, and the chancellor devised a royal assurance for him to sign. He was nevertheless soon all-powerful. His respectable but impecunious family did not lend him high status, but this he would attain by his own efforts. He was neither pacifist nor philosopher but a man of action who yearned for glory and power. He came to the throne with a good general education and six years of military experience (from 1642 to 1648) which culminated in his position as generalissimo. He had also sowed a goodly crop of wild oats. Had war not occupied so much of his attention Karl Gustav might have been a leader in agricultural and other domestic reforms, for he showed real concern for conservation in his lands on Öland and Gotland and had ideas about quarrying and agricultural improvement. During his period as a squire on these southern manors he led a robust life; although he took only two meals a day they had twenty-four courses, and he and six companions washed down the food with ten quarts of beer and ten quarts of wine per meal. But life had to change with the serious business of kingship. The characteristics that predominated during his six years on the throne were his exuberant and aggressive nature and his belief that might makes right and solves problems.

When Karl X Gustav acceded to the throne in 1654 the eastern horizon looked ominous, and the new king was not a man to let trouble brew untended. The weakness of Poland enticed Russia to invade Lithuania, and in the south Johan II Kasimir, the king of Poland, faced a Cossack uprising. Karl Gustav prepared for war by getting from the riksdag and council the freedom to make his own decision. Although Magnus Gabriel De la Gardie and Gustav Bonde, with keener insight, saw Russia as the formidable enemy, Karl Gustav and most Swedes gave that honor to Poland. Hence his move was to converge on Poland with three armies, one from the west, one from the north, and one by sea under his own command. It was at first a triumphal march. Then the courageous resistance of the monks at Czestochowa against a small Swedish force showed that the Swedes were not invincible supermen, and Polish national feeling reasserted itself. Karl Gustav got temporary support from Brandenburg, but soon he found himself opposed by the forces of both Brandenburg and the Empire; Holland became antagonistic when the Dutch thought Sweden gained too much, and the Russians drove as far as Riga. All Karl's marching around Poland achieved no usable victory, for the Poles would not be trapped into a major battle. The Swedes were frustrated. When in the summer of 1657 Denmark attacked Bremen Karl was probably relieved and reacted instantaneously. He sped westward, as Carl Gustaf Wrangel retook Bremen and helped the king overrun Jutland with troops who "had learned to conquer and had forgotten how to be beaten."[1] This too might have been but a fruitless march if unusual weather had not opened new opportunity.

The winter of 1657–58 grew colder and colder. Approximately once in a hundred years the Great Belt and the Little Belt freeze over. Karl Gustav happened to be there when that happened. After careful reconnaissance and in full recognition of the danger, the army moved out on the ice of the Little Belt on January 30, 1658. Almost across, two squadrons of horses and riders broke through and were swallowed in the icy waters, but the king kept calm and restored confidence. An army of 3,500 foot and 1,500 cavalry reached the opposite shore and amazed the Danish defense forces on Fyn. The Swedes subdued the Danish detachments and overran the island, while they looked anxiously at the weather. Would the ice hold for a march on to Sjaelland? Warmer weather threatened to thaw it and winds to break it up. Eagerly Karl X sent out patrols to test the surface, and some were lost. Others returned and reported the ice was strong enough only for small detachments. Some, the engineer Erik Dahlbergh specifically, took five days to report back. Karl X remained hopeful. He was bolstered by Corfitz Ulfeldt, exiled steward of the Danish court, who was filled with hatred for Frederik III and undoubtedly willing to take risks for the sake of revenge. His encouraging words were what Karl wanted to hear, and Ulfeldt became the Swedish chief of staff.

If the direct route from Nyborg could not be used why not take the shorter jumps between a series of small islands and reach Sjaelland from the south? The weather stayed cold, and on February 6, a full week after crossing the Little Belt, Karl and some 2,000 men moved on to Langeland through slush deep over the ice, pushed on to make the nine-mile passage to Lolland, continued to Falster, and on the twelfth the Swedish army stood at Vordingborg on Sjaelland. Wrangel followed a few days after. Copenhagen, strongly fortified on its sea approaches, had perceived no need for land defenses, for who could imagine in his wildest nightmare that an army could march across the Great Belt? The capital and the kingdom now lay at the mercy of a small but daring and efficient army. Peace, therefore, came quickly.[2]

The treaty of Roskilde on February 26, 1658 marked a peak achievement for Sweden in its relations with its rival. Denmark signed over to Sweden the fertile Danish lands east of the Sound: the provinces of Skåne, Halland (now in perpetuity), Blekinge, Bohuslän; the island of Bornholm; plus Trondheim province in Norway. Sweden won partial control of the Sound and improved the position of its partner Holstein-Gottorp. As a bonus Denmark pledged to hold enemy fleets out of the Baltic (referring to Holland).

Sweden's successes and acquisitions were extensive but not as large as Karl Gustav's hopes. During the spring and summer of 1658 Swedish troops gathered at Kiel for an attack on Brandenburg, but as Karl could not draw the Danes into alliance with Sweden he changed his plans. He suspected that

KARL X GUSTAV'S CAMPAIGNS
IN POLAND AND DENMARK

Frederik III had hedged in the negotiations and that Holland was now urging the Danes to seek revenge. Fearing to get caught in the rear, he abandoned the attack on Brandenburg and astonished everyone as he swung his forces around against Copenhagen. He now planned to annihilate Denmark-Norway as a state and to govern it as Swedish provinces. The Danes moved quickly from confusion to anger. Copenhageners burned the suburbs and made the city impregnable. They withstood siege and storm, responding to disaster with the same kind of courage and sacrifice that were to save London in 1940. Finally a Dutch fleet fought its way through the naval blockade and brought the Danes food and relief. In the meantime an imperial army conquered most of Swedish Pomerania, another in collaboration with Brandenburg and Poland overran Jutland and besieged the Swedish garrison in Frederiksodde. The people rose against the Swedes in Trondheim, and on Bornholm a mob shot the Swedish governor in the street. In Skåne guerrilla bands from the border regions plagued the entire province. Within a year the whole complexion of events had changed. As the weight of misfortune increased Karl Gustav sickened with fever and catarrh and died on February 13, 1660. Yet for Sweden things turned out better than it had any right to expect.

France, England, and Holland had already agreed to force Denmark and Sweden to make a new peace along the same lines as that of Roskilde. France was also interested in peace between Poland and Sweden. And Russia was ready to quit. The total result was a series of treaties that cost Sweden portions of its most recent gains but left it stronger overall than ever before: At Oliva on April 23, 1660 Poland at long last abandoned claims to the Swedish throne and to Livonia, and Brandenburg and Austria agreed to evacuate Pomerania. In the treaty of Copenhagen on May 27, 1660 Sweden retroceded to Denmark Trondheim and Bornholm, and Denmark withdrew its pledge to keep enemy fleets out of the Baltic; otherwise the provisions of Roskilde were reaffirmed. At Kardis on June 21, 1661 the Russians, also under French pressure, returned to Sweden the areas they had conquered in the Baltic lands. Sweden was now alone, but questions were settled and it could remap its future. Planning for the future was nevertheless difficult because the heir to the throne was but a child and a regency could not count on solid support or on permanence in office.[3]

## The Establishment of Autocracy under Karl XI

Both domestic and foreign problems demanded immediate attention. During Karl X's war-filled reign a start, but only a start, had been made to recover the alienated crown lands. The noble recipients of these lands were worried, and with the shift in kingship they moved quickly to protect their interests. They

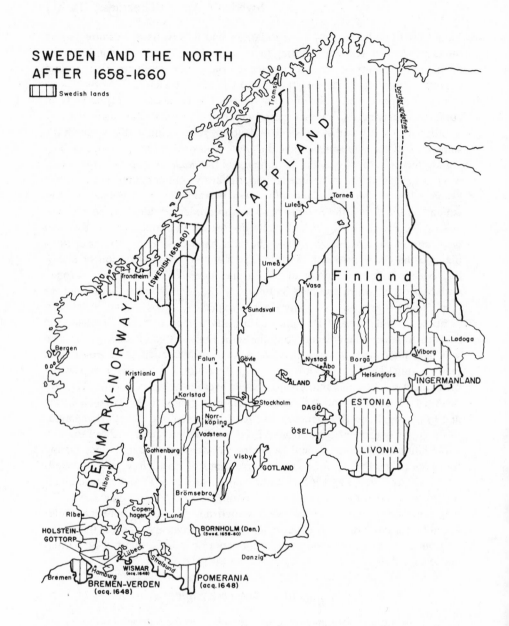

SWEDEN AND THE NORTH
AFTER 1658-1660

⊞ Swedish lands

LAPPLAND

Tromsö

border undefined

Luleå

Torneå

Trondheim

(SWEDISH 1658-60)

Umeå

Vasa

Finland

L. Ladoga

Bergen

Sundsvall

DENMARK-NORWAY

Kristiania

Falun

Gävle

Nystad

Åbo

Borgå

Viborg

Helsingfors

INGERMANLAND

Karlstad

ÅLAND

Norr-
köping

Stockholm

DAGÖ

ESTONIA

Vadstena

ÖSEL

Gothenburg

Ålborg

Visby

GOTLAND

LIVONIA

Ribe

Copen-
hagen

Brömsebro

Lund

BORNHOLM (Den.)
(Swed. 1658-60)

HOLSTEIN-
GOTTORP

Lübeck

Danzig

Hamburg

Stralsund

Bremen

WISMAR
(acq.1648)

POMERANIA
(acq. 1648)

BREMEN-VERDEN
(acq. 1648)

reconstituted the regency that Karl X had carefully planned for his four-year-old son, reacting strongly to the assumption that the kingdom belonged to the king and could be handed on at his pleasure. They demanded, among other things, a voice in the education of the heir to the throne.[4] They eliminated from the regency the dead king's brother Adolf Johan, and also Herman Fleming whom they hated for his reduction policies (see the next section on reduction). Magnus De la Gardie as chancellor, Per Brahe as attorney general (under the old title of drots), and Gustav Bonde as chief financial officer became the influential figures as council and riksdag attempted to sail the ship of state. The experiment was not too successful. The conflict between the higher and lower nobility grew increasingly bitter. The government maintained its military forces, but armed politics without the winnings of war was costly, and the financial difficulties of the government mounted until the army and navy could not be paid. Quarrels and inefficiency and ineffectiveness of the regency prepared the way for its antithesis — a government of strong authority.

The first indication of future foreign policy came in 1661 with the treaty of Fontainebleau wherein France granted subsidies to Sweden, and Sweden in turn agreed to support France in the matter of the Polish throne. France next allied with Denmark, hoping to keep both northern states on its side, a policy distinctly distasteful to Sweden. But Sweden's status as a great power was undermined by its basic weakness in population and economy and by its current lack of forceful and dependable leadership. The best that the regency could do was to maintain peace and try to develop trade. Magnus Gabriel De la Gardie, as chancellor, led Swedish foreign policy for a decade and a half after 1660, essentially pursuing a pro-French line. Insofar as there was any ideological base it was mercantilism, natural enough in the heyday of Colbert. Hence there were trade agreements — with England in 1661, with France in 1662, and with Holland in 1667 — incorporating for the first time the principle that "free ships make free goods."[5]

The rivalries of the continental powers at last caught Sweden in the undertow, and the "French connection" almost proved its undoing. In 1674 France, involved in new warfare, demanded the Swedish aid for which it had been paying subsidies. Sweden could not refuse, and De la Gardie's not-too-shrewd diplomatic structure had therefore brought not peace but war. After three months Sweden bought itself out of war with Holland by making large concessions to Dutch trade in the Baltic. A Swedish army supporting the French marched on Brandenburg and was trounced in the battle of Fehrbellin in June 1675.

Denmark was now in the war and Kristian V took Holstein-Gottorp. This led young Karl XI, in one of his first independent acts as king, to launch a futile naval attack on Denmark. Further disaster befell in Germany when the Germans again occupied large sections of Pomerania and the Danes took Wismar. On the first of June 1676 a Danish-Dutch fleet routed the Swedish off Öland. To deliver the coup de grace Kristian landed in Skåne and the Norwegians invaded Bohuslän and Västergötland. Freebooters from the northern border of Skåne wreaked havoc throughout the province.

Karl XI proved equal to the challenge, and as a courageous leader he won a bloody encounter at Lund on December 4, 1676; 5,000 Danes lay on the field with 3,000 Swedes. War continued into 1677 and 1678, with guerrilla depredations plus Dutch harrying of the eastern shores and sieges of forts. The defeated Swedes barely hung on, and suffered further humiliation at not being allowed a seat at the peace negotiations. However, their mighty French ally succeeded in dictating terms that were highly favorable to Sweden (at Nijmegen in 1678, at St. Germain-en-Láye in 1679, and with Denmark at Lund in 1679). Basically the status quo ante bellum was restored, and certainly Sweden could hope for no more.

The coming of war had discredited De la Gardie and had allowed the clever Johan Gyllenstierna to gain influence. The cornerstone of his policy was alliance with Denmark, and to the Danes he swore mighty oaths and pledged his potential position in paradise to guarantee his sincerity. The basis was to be a common independence of Holland. Gyllenstierna was made governor of Skåne in 1679. However simple were his personal tastes, he insisted on luxury and pomp in his governorship and for state occasions such as his fetching of Karl XI's Danish bride, Ulrika Eleonora. He burned out his tremendous energy too soon, and when he died in 1680 his northern policy died with him. Sweden's opportunistic foreign relations were then managed by the king and Bengt Oxenstierna, son of the great chancellor, and the whole system was reversed.

Bengt Oxenstierna was sixty years of age and amply experienced. It was reasonable for him to want a sea-power ally, which he found in the Netherlands (1681), and he added Austria (in 1682), and Brandenburg (in 1686). His position was strong enough that he could use the War of the Palatinate and William of Orange's accession to the throne of England to force Denmark (through the 1689 Treaty of Altona) to disgorge Slesvig, which it had annexed in 1684. A new problem was now presented to both Denmark and Sweden by Dutch-English highhandedness on the sea. In defense of neutral rights the two Scandinavian states in 1690 (and again in 1693) renewed and extended the alliance of 1679; it was the first armed neutrality agreement. But Denmark kept intriguing for control of Gottorp. In the midst of a new crisis Karl XI died on April 5, 1697, leaving a warning that Sweden should not involve itself in European problems with which it was not directly concerned. At the moment he died he was nevertheless scheduled to be a mediator in the general European conflict.

Karl XI had provided some great surprises. At first it looked doubtful that he could ever offer leadership. He was a feeble boy, and hence his political education was neglected in favor of emphasis on physical fitness. An Italian traveler described him as "ignorant in everything."[6] He was not lacking in basic intelligence nor in will. His desperate courage at the battle of Lund probably turned defeat into victory. Shortly after he became king in fact (in 1672) he took the reins of government firmly into his hands, got the riksdag to declare that he need ask the advice of the council only when he wished and that the ultimate decision was the king's. He demanded, somewhat belatedly, an investigation of the regency administration, and when this showed tragic mismanagement of affairs he required the resignations of all members of the council (fifteen), following which he reconstituted the weakened council as merely a royal advisory body. The collegial system so carefully built up through Gustav Adolf and Axel Oxenstierna he destroyed by his preference for secretaries rather than the aristocratic ministers who had made a shambles of government. At the king's suggestion the riksdag declared that the form of government of 1634 was not a binding constitution; through what may have been happenstance the national representative body also declared that the law-making power belonged to the king and that he was answerable only to God. As if to guide the hand of God, a new church ordinance of 1686 made the church subservient to the crown. Criticism of the king was called treasonous, and thus freedom of expression was suppressed.

In essence, power was congenial to the personality of Karl XI, whose mind and temperament were not equal to the tasks of discussion and persuasion. Absolutism was also congenial to the times — this was the age of Louis XIV. Karl was paternalistic enough that he liked to move about incognito among his people, clad only in a gray cape by which eventually he became known. He walked oddly, as if on glass, and looked the king only when mounted on horseback. He was crude and "folksy" and liked to correct injustices arbitrarily and on the spot. For example, he once found in his wanderings a priest who spent all his attention on the church to make it look fine and another who made his residence look beautiful but neglected the church; Karl simply had the two exchange parishes. For Sweden it was a retrogressive autocracy; Karl XI walked in the footsteps of Gustav Vasa rather than in those of Gustav Adolf. He "reduced" a large portion of the lands recently alienated from the crown, and he carried through a major reform of the system of military recruitment and maintenance, the so-called *indelningsverk* (see later section in this chapter), which involved a partial return to a natural economy. As to foreign affairs, the king suffered early humiliations both on the field of battle and at the council table — or, more exactly, by being excluded from the table — and he became a staunch champion of home defense and peace. Dull and unimaginative he may have been, but he was well suited to his time and his problems. His two most lasting achievements were the reduction and the *indelningsverk*.[7]

## Reduction and the Accompanying Social and Political Revolution

The background of Karl XI's land and income problems leads back to Gustav I's time and even to the Middle Ages. Before the realization of a money economy a ruler could reward his lieutenants only with grants of land or the produce of land, and such grants also became a means of distributing responsibility for management. On the continent the complex relationships of feudalism served a similar purpose. The dangers of any system of this type were exaggerated decentralization, strife among petty princes, and curtailment of the king's income.

Under a strong and nation-conscious king such as Gustav Vasa the tendency was for property to come to the crown by reversion and by expropriation of church and other lands. Gustav was able to get for king and crown a full 20 percent of the 103,500 *hemman* of the country. (A *hemman* was the homestead as a tax unit; by the seventeenth century most farms had been subdivided into fractions of the original *hemman* units.) But Gustav and his sons felt called upon to give away many of the royal estates in exchange for services or out of sheer generosity. Swedish law forbade a king to diminish the income of his successor or to give away part of the kingdom; as Birgitta had put it in the fourteenth century, "the king is not lord of the crown but its caretaker." Hence when he granted fiefs they were for fixed terms or for a period not to exceed the lifetime of the king. The usual grants were called fiefs (*förläningar*) and might be in the form of either temporary ownership of landed estates or income from certain farms or privileges; they might involve merely the release from taxes on lands already owned. Another class of gifts were the "donations" that, legally or illegally, were made inheritable. Gustav Vasa himself, influenced by German feudalism after 1542, made such grants, and for his sons he set up duchies that took 28 percent of the state property and 25 percent of its income. Sometimes the dukes in turn alienated their estates to their aids or favorites. Spasmodically the duchies and other grants reverted to the crown as a result of death or banishment; thus it happened that all the duchies had been reabsorbed by 1622, when Gustav Adolf promised he would create no new ones for any sons he might have.

Although most of the lands and privileges granted to the nobility were subject to tithes and a few special charges, they were free of ordinary taxes. (Thus *frälse*, "privileged," was a term that applied to both land and owner.) Originally the fiefholders were expected to provide a certain number of armed knights for the king's service, but this requirement was increasingly disregarded. Because of other supposed military obligations even the peasants on the lands of the noble *frälse* served in the regular army only half as often as the peasants on crown lands or the yeomen freeholders. Recipients of land did of course manage the property and thus served a socioeconomic function.

The direct interest of the *frälse* in the income from their estates probably led to more efficient management than the crown lands received under the royal bailiffs, and perhaps the system encouraged the expansion of the cultivated area of the kingdom. The dangers were that large grants could breed delusions of grandeur in princes or nobles and that conditional and time-bound grants might come to be regarded as absolute. Pressures mounted for the alienation of more and more land, which would result in the steady weakening of the economy of the state itself in favor of the enrichment of a few families. Another evil was that the nobles often demanded of their peasants services and payments beyond those permitted by law, thus engendering deep resentment.

Erik XIV created the first counts (*grevar*): Per Brahe at Visingsborg, Svante Sture at Västervik with estates in Småland and Östergötland, and Gustaf Johansson at Bogesund. Johan III expanded these and added another county for the Leijonhuvuds, and he originated the barons (*friherrar*) by providing estates for the families Stenbock, Gyllenstierna, Fleming, Bielke, and De la Gardie. These endowments were later extended, then began to die out, so that by 1644 there were but three counts and seven barons. Kristina, however, raised the number to twenty counts and thirty-four barons. In the twelve years of her minority the government made two and one-half times as many grants as Gustav Adolf had made in twenty-one years of kingship, and in the nine years of her reign Kristina multiplied grants eightfold over the regency record. Not only was the amount of alienation unprecedented, but it included lands that had been set aside to provision the fleet and to provide hay for the cavalry, and whose alienation was therefore prohibited by law.

During the Thirty Years War the government needed money so desperately that it sold crown lands to the privileged nobility, already becoming a wealthy class. Thus the state, for immediate advantage, parted with its endowment and could no longer collect taxes on the alienated property. In 1638 the council authorized land sales of 200,000 riksdaler; the amount increased in succeeding years. In defense of its policy the government replied to a protest of 1639: "If we will not let our state collapse, so must we sell estates of the crown, so that it won't all come tumbling down." [8] Oxenstierna favored both sales and grants and convinced Kristina, on the theory that individual nobles operating farms would produce more efficiently than could the ruler through bailiffs. Perhaps, but whence would the government get its income after it had dissipated its own endowment?

Regularization had been attempted several times, notably by Karl IX in the 1604 Norrköping Resolve, which relaxed some of the older rules but prescribed that: the recipient of a grant of land had to get reconfirmation at each change of king; inheritance ran only in the male line and when this ran out the land reverted to the king; before transfer by sale or mortgage the property had to be offered to the king. Violations of these Norrköping rules, irregularities by the nobles and extensions of various kinds, the kings' disregard for laws prohibiting certain grants, and most important the sheer exaggeration of royal benevolence had produced by the mid-seventeenth century an intolerable situation. The stifled protest of the riksdag of 1650 was the foreshadowing of an irresistible demand. There was such a general recognition of the need for reform that its beginnings were marked by moderation and acceptance.

The year after Karl X came to the throne the process got under way. A start was made in the riksdag of 1655 toward reduction[9] of "forbidden places" like forts and mines, and an investigation was ordered of all grants made since 1632 and of all donations made since 1604. Many of the nobles, particularly the newly created, realized that they faced embarrassment and therefore attempted to limit the process of reduction. Their privileges came into direct conflict with the financial necessities of the state. Nevertheless even the high nobility in the council agreed that estates granted since 1632 should be subject to the Norrköping Resolve (because some had been made illegally as allodial grants) and that all grants in forbidden districts should revert to the crown. The king's request for reduction of one-fourth was tentatively compromised into payments for three years of the income from one-fourth of each grant. For two years the reduction commission worked hard, and altogether the crown recovered about 78,000 dalers in annual income. But the absence of the king and the need for good will and calm during the war years brought a slowdown.

During the regency for Karl XI the process of reduction continued at a slow pace, up to 1673 adding about 34,000 dalers. Karl then infused vigor into the commission, and between 1673 and 1680 some 200,000 dalers were recovered. Meanwhile a few new donations had been made. In the riksdag of 1680 the simmering discontent of the nonprivileged classes demanded completion of the reform. In the House of the Nobles Hans Wachtmeister, undoubtedly as agent of the king, promised favored handling of the lesser beneficiaries. He thus brought to the boiling point the latent hostility of the lesser nobles against the greater, and during a scene of violent confusion an approving vote was recorded. The lands of counts and barons and others in both Sweden and the Baltic and German provinces, to the extent that they surpassed 600 dalers in income, were to be reduced to the crown; estates that had been mortgaged or sold were also included. A commission under the brilliant young Claes Fleming would administer the decision.

But the return was still not great enough to pay the state debt. In 1682 came the proposal to remove the 600-daler protective limit. The nobles protested to the king, who in a shrewd move requested clarification from the riksdag: was the king entitled under Swedish law to give and to take back grants with or without approval by the Estates? The Estates replied that he had sole right to do exactly that. As a result the king ordered thorough reports on all grants to be made by local investigating bodies and the national commission which now became a royal body; a whole battery of administrative groups worked on the involved problem. Claes Fleming died from the pressure of this and other duties. Others carried on. The job was essentially finished by 1700 when because of the war the remainder was dropped. For the whole period of reduction the accompanying estimates[10] indicate the annual rents recovered by the crown.

|  | *dalers* |
|---|---|
| Sweden-Finland | 700,000 |
| Skåne | 85,000 |
| Bremen-Verden | 200,000 |
| Pomerania | 66,500 |
| Ingermanland and Kexholm | 188,000 |
| Estonia | 155,000 |
| Livonia | 543,000 |
| Total | 1,937,500 |

This sweeping reform broke the political power of the greater nobles and curtailed their economic base. Many had to sell lands to get money, although only a few of the recently ennobled were stripped down to one manor each — the treatment of the De la Gardies and the widow of General Torstensson being notable examples of extreme severity. The older magnates fared better, and Karl XI himself created six hundred new nobles. He was therefore not wholly antinoble, but he wanted a dependent nobility that needed to serve in public office as well as to administer farms. By acquiring extensive lands which he could then redistribute, he could favor the lesser nobility and open the way for the farmer to buy his own land. This in turn helped to restore the dignity and independence of the farming population. Whereas in 1650 the nobility owned 72 percent of the land, while tax and crown peasants together held 28 percent, by 1700 the nobles owned but 33 percent, the free farmers 31.5 percent, and the crown 35.5 percent.[11] By the reform, also, special taxes disappeared, and only the land rents remained. In essence the reduction was a revolution — political, social, and economic.

The significance of the reduction reached far beyond the matter of money and land. Karl IX had, back in the sixteenth century, represented the idea of strong monarchy with a moral responsibility to God. The Royal Charter of 1611 and the long years of Axel Oxenstierna's direction of affairs, plus the wealth and prestige gained by the nobility during the Thirty Years War, swung the pendulum of power toward a mixed system, with the aristocracy almost in the ascendancy. The practice was justified by reference to French and German theory as well as the idea of aristocratic *ephors* and a *monarchia mixta*. But then, in the later seventeenth century, amid the controversy over reduction, the king won a new and absolute authority. An alliance of frustrated commoners and lesser nobility with a strong-willed king carried the day against the divided and indecisive higher nobility. The concentration of the Estates on the problem of privilege led them to resign their own position in law making into the hands of the king, and thus they created an absolutism. The nobles, seeing themselves deprived of their vast estates, wanted at least to retain their official positions and were afraid to antagonize the king; thus they fought the process of reduction with one hand tied behind their backs. The council was stripped of power; the riksdag surrendered it.

John Robinson, who went to Sweden in 1680 as chaplain in the English embassy and was later to become ambassador to Karl XII, wrote *An Account of Sweden* in 1694 in which his analysis was not far from the mark:

> So favourable was the Conjuncture for the Advancement of the King's Authority that he scarce needed to ask whatever he desired: each Body of the States [Estates] striving which should outbid the other in their Concessions. The Nobility and Gentry, who universally depend on the King, as not being able to subsist upon their own private Fortunes, without some Additional Office, were under a Necessity to comply with everything, rather than hazard their present Employments, or future Hopes of Advancement. . . . These Dispositions of the People . . . gave him an Opportunity to lay the Foundations of as Absolute a Sovereignty, as any Prince in Europe possesses.[12]

## Indelningsverk: *Military Reconstruction*

An important by-product of the reduction was the reconstituted military recruitment system, known as the *indelningsverk*. (Allotment or apportionment system might be acceptable translations but since these terms do not carry adequate connotations the Swedish term had best be used.) In some ways it was a throwback to the "Old *Indelningsverk*" that Gustav Adolf had used for cavalry recruitment, in some ways it reminded one of the *ledung* system of ancient times or the systems of compensation in land used in the Ottoman and Roman empires. But although the idea was old and widespread the application was new and carefully adapted to the Swedish situation. It was possible only because the reduction had made land available for redistribution in all districts of the country.

The knight's service once required of the nobility had slowly disappeared, and in his reconstruction of the armed forces Karl XI had to find a means to attract and pay native cavalrymen. Hence each cavalryman was to have as wage the income of one tax unit (*hemman*); therefore, either he was provided a *hemman* by the crown or he was given something less and was paid the balance by another who had been given a *hemman*.

For the infantry the arrangement was based on a contract between crown and province (except for Skåne, Halland, and Blekinge) by which each province provided a fixed number of soldiers. Under the old system Dalarna and part of Norrland had escaped the drafting of recruits by maintaining their own regiments, the only standing army. Now all the provinces supplied a regular force, one regiment to a province. Local commissions were set up, and all the *hemman* in the rural districts were registered. The norm was for two *hemman* to comprise a *rote* and for each *rote* to supply a soldier. Thus obligations were equalized, eliminating the favored status formerly allowed the nobles' peasants. Within a given district each 150 *rotar* comprised a company and the company was named after the tract from which it came. Eight neighboring companies made up a regiment of 1,200 men. Each man had his small cottage and piece of land, and each officer had a better cottage (designed by Erik Dahlbergh) with a larger amount of land and lived in the district from which his soldiers were recruited and supplied. Thus he could hold regular monthly exercises, and once a year the entire regiment got together in an encampment. The geographical organization of the forces eased problems of supply and transportation and created a local pride in the companies and regiments. In addition to the compensation provided by cottage and land only small additional payments in money were needed. And the army was a professional one in which men customarily served to age fifty-five.

Karl XI was deeply concerned with the navy also, and the coastal areas of the country were organized in an *indelning* system like the one for infantry and cavalry. At Trossö on the southern coast Hans Wachtmeister built the new central naval station of Karlskrona and by 1697 had a well-based fleet of fifty sail and 11,000 sailors.

The *indelningsverk* produced a regular army of 38,000–40,000 men, and the king hired an additional 25,000 mercenaries, chiefly to garrison the overseas provinces. The methodical structure looked good and worked well — in peacetime. It provided a good defensive army. But a system of payment in kind does not work for armies fighting abroad, as Gustav Adolf had discovered. Karl XI did not want foreign war and the system worked advantageously for his time, freeing Sweden from foreign subsidies and the resultant dependence on foreign powers. For the wars of Karl XII, when some entire regiments were killed or captured, it was inadequate. Recourse had to be made to doubling and even tripling the demands on each *rote*, and this placed a severe strain on the manpower of the country. Nevertheless, despite all its limitations, the *indelningsverk* was well enough suited to Sweden's needs that it continued with only slight modifications to the mid-nineteenth century and was finally abandoned only in 1901.[13]

## The Cultural Stimulus

In every varied facet of its cultural life seventeenth-century Sweden responded to the achievements of its soldiers and statesmen with an outburst of vitality and creativity. A psychological reaction asserted itself. No longer were the Swedes poor and untutored dwellers on the frozen frontier of Europe, plagued with frequent overturns of government, massacres, and executions. Self-assurance was restored and enhanced; the glorious deeds of Gustav Adolf made it possible to believe in those still more extraordinary accomplishments of the ancient Goths as told by Johannes Magnus. There seemed to be no limit to what the people could do. The national image had changed, and now a Swede could travel as student or as merchant and be met with respect. There need be no fear of receiving foreigners in Sweden and learning from them, for Swedes had their *own* contributions to put in the scale.

The reinvigorated intellectual climate evidenced itself first at court. Gustav Adolf, with his unfettered interests, wide acquaintance with languages and significant books, and his intellectual approach to problems, stimulated a like attitude among his entourage. He loved music, had boys taught singing in the schools, and imported from Germany an orchestra and a chorus for the court. He was himself the best literary stylist of his day, and some of his addresses were masterpieces. In succeeding years the court of Queen Kristina became a center of philosophical discussion and reading as well as of social display. Foreign scholars and diplomats graced state occasions and made Stockholm realize its position of cultural importance. Hedvig Eleonora and Karl XI did what they could to carry on the new trends but Karl X and Karl XII gave priority to other matters.

All the forms of contact with the continent were important for the nurture of the new values. Officers returning from the wars on the continent brought back new manners, new styles of dress, new attitudes toward the peasantry. They had learned languages such as French and German and they had become more tolerant in matters of religion. They could maintain relations with friends and business associates on the continent through an improved postal system with Swedish offices in Hamburg and Helsingör. Citizens could keep up-to-date on the news of the outside world through their first newspaper, the *Ordinari Post Tijdender*, which began in 1645 and continued under different names, since 1821 as the *Post-och Inrikes Tidningar*. Winds from the south blew strongly and were welcomed.

Architecture offered the best opportunity to display both wealth and aesthetic interests and to set off the heightened importance of the aristocracy. Great manor houses and châteaus appeared in the southern and central parts of the kingdom and houses of magnificence in the cities. For both burghers and nobles the prayers of Gustav Adolf were realized — their small houses had become stone mansions, and they had won wealth and deathless fame. One of the first to set the pace was Axel Oxenstierna, who built the handsome castle of Tidö near Västerås (1625–45) in late Renaissance style, with a touch of baroque. Jean de la Vallee was probably its first architect, and Nicodemus Tessin the Elder completed it.

Tessin was born in Stralsund and served as assistant to the Swedish military architects who rebuilt Stralsund's city wall. In the 1640s he not only worked for Oxenstierna but laid out city plans for Gävle, Hudiksvall, Härnösand, and others; in the 1650s he traveled to France, Holland, Germany, and Italy and gained new impulses for later buildings that were restrained adaptations of French, Dutch, and Italian classical styles. He built palaces for Carl Gustaf Wrangel and Seved Bååt, rebuilt Borgholm and others, and designed a number of churches in Kalmar, Stockholm, and other cities. One of his most notable structures was Drottningholm castle outside Stockholm, begun in 1662 for Queen Hedvig Eleonora. Nicodemus Tessin the Younger continued and improved upon his father's art. In three major trips abroad he became imbued with the ideas of Bernini and in his Swedish work solved remarkably the problem of adapting the magnificence of Roman facades to the northern spirit. Balanced and locale-oriented classicism was the essence of his genius. He more than any other embodied in stone the ideals of Sweden's Age of Greatness. He was responsible for much of the interior and furnishings of Drottningholm and built the small but notable Steninge in Uppland. He succeeded his father as architect of the royal castle, and when in 1697 that castle burned while Karl XI's body still lay within, he quickly produced plans for the monumental structure that took its place. In his later years Tessin gave up architecture for statecraft.

Another father and son pair, Simon de la Vallee and his son Jean, of French origin, were employed by the nobles of Sweden and began several of the castles that one or other of the Tessins finished. Notable among the works of the younger de la Vallee was the superbly proportioned and highly decorated House of the Nobles in Stockholm (*Riddarhuset*).

The unique palace of Skokloster in Uppland may serve as an example of the union of architectural ingenuity and aristocratic pomp. It was financed from the Thirty Years War "earnings" of Carl Gustaf Wrangel, who had the plans drawn by Jean de la Vallee and the building completed by Nicodemus Tessin the Elder. This massive square structure of four stories is guarded by towers of five stories topped with cupolas. Its large, high-ceilinged rooms house one of the world's great collections of arms. Many of the rooms were never finished; others were elaborately decorated with Gobelins, gorgeous chandeliers, paintings by Swedish artists, and other art brought home from the wars in Germany.

In 1661, in keeping with the self-consciousness of powerful Sweden and its sense of the past, Erik Dahlberg was commissioned by the regency to compile his invaluable *Suecia antiqua et hodierna*. This is a mine of 448 handsome engravings of cities and buildings depicting Sweden at the height of its glory.[14]

Pictorial records of persons are less complete and less satisfactory, although a number of foreign portraitists were attracted to Sweden in the seventeenth century. Paintings tended to be almost as stiff as the sculptured figures on grave monuments, though an occasional artist such as Sebastien Bourdon could capture the character of a man like Johannes Matthiae, Kristina's tutor. David Klöcker, ennobled and known as D. K. Ehrenstrahl, was another partial and happy exception. He preferred the conventional and the colossal, but within elaborate design he portrayed personalities. Furthermore, he painted a number of more casual pictures of soldiers, servants, jesters, and the varied personnel about the court; these are simple and charming.

A shipful of early seventeenth-century decorative sculpture has been amazingly preserved and recovered in the flagship *Wasa*, built for Gustav Adolf in 1628 and raised from the deep in 1961. Through this find we can also see ship construction as practiced by the Dutch builders as well as the tools, pots, pans, and even the clothing of the sailors of the day. In the first half of the century not only were the builders foreign, but the sculptors, too. When a sculptors' guild was organized in 1638 in Stockholm none of the seven members was Swedish born. When the Gustav Adolf Bible was printed in 1618 printers came from Germany to do the type work. But gradually such things changed, and Swedes began to make original contributions to peaceful pursuits.

The progressive tendencies of early- and mid-century slowed down toward the end under Karl XI's autocracy. Orthodoxy and intolerance showed themselves in academic life, but a wave of witch hunts was soon exposed as based on hearsay and superstition. The last two decades of the seventeenth century comprised a period of peace and stability before the reign of war in the first two decades of the eighteenth century.

## Karl XII

At the end of the seventeenth century the lines of interest in Swedish history converge on the person and the activities of Karl XII, dramatic boy-king and military wizard. He is still regarded by the national romanticists as Sweden's greatest king. He claims the appeal of boldness and of genius, and he is identified with national tragedy.

When Karl XI died at age forty-two on April 5, 1697, his fifteen-year-old son became king. After a regency of only a few months, in October of 1697 he came into the full powers of the autocracy created by his father. He had two sisters but of five boys he alone survived infancy. His mother lavished on him attention and affection, and both parents tried to prepare him for kingship. He was a wild youth, with overflowing energy, but he was bright and learned early to exercise authority. In less than three years after he became king he was at war with Denmark, directing the first campaign of the prolonged Great Northern War. When he left Stockholm for the Danish front in 1700 he started a series of campaigns that took him to the Baltic lands and Poland and Germany, then into Russia and five years in Turkey, across Europe on a spectacular horseback ride, and at last to the border of Norway and sudden death. Throughout those eighteen years he never returned to his capital.

Thrones were changing hands all round Europe, and uncertainty was in the air. William of Orange had assumed the English throne in 1689. In that same year Peter became sole tsar of Russia, and he took his trip to western Europe in 1696–97. The question of the Spanish succession complicated the diplomacy of all western Europe after 1697 and led to general war in 1701. Augustus II of Saxony became king of Poland in 1697, uniting under one leader two of Sweden's enemies. In the Swedish satellite of Holstein-Gottorp, Frederik succeeded his father as duke in 1694 and in 1698 married Hedvig Sofia, the sister of Karl XII. In Denmark, Kristian V died in 1699 and Frederik IV became king. All these persons and events interlocked with the concerns of Sweden, whose involvement in Europe is illustrated by the 1697 treaty of Ryswick, whereby Zweibrücken was restored to the king of Sweden in his capacity as count palatine of the Rhine.

What manner of man was this who blazed through Europe like a meteor? He was a fascinating enigma: as a soldier he was a genius in quick decision and unexpected action, as the director of the fate of a nation he brought disaster. He had more persistence than adaptability, more bravery than finesse, more military genius than political savoir faire. The Russian historian Eugene Tarle calls him an impetuous adventurer. He was strong in himself and he could not condone weakness in others, and he was authoritarian to his finger tips. He was both honorable and loyal — often loyal for too long and to the wrong people. Bitter experience taught him that he could trust no one, but finally, in desperation, he was willing to join in the conniving of Baron Georg Heinrich von Görtz, hoping that some of Görtz's fantastic schemes diplomatic and financial might work. Most of all he distrusted women, or he distrusted himself with women. He was a crude man of the barracks — or did he merely assume this pose for self-protection? He spoke little and he wrote little, hence he must be judged by actions rather than words.

Sweden was weak in everything except military leadership and organization. The country therefore needed allies, but Karl XII had only Holstein-Gottorp because he could not adapt his foreign policy sufficiently to create a community of interest between Sweden and any other state. At several different times he probably could have made an agreement with Prussia, but he would have had to have made concessions. This he refused to do. He might, after Augustus the Strong became disillusioned with Russia, have had an alliance with Saxony, but personal sentiments and his sense of obligation to Stanislas Leszczynski, whom he had made king of Poland, made this impossible. Görtz showed him the way to an accommodation with Russia, but he would not agree to it. If he felt, as some believe, that his mission was to suppress the threat to Europe from Russian barbarism, then certainly he should have accepted the cooperation of others. If he considered, as others believe, that his primary task was in the west, against Denmark, then how can one justify his long campaigning in the east and his five years of futility in Turkey?

The disadvantages of fighting long distances and long years away from home were many. Yet the devastation wrought by the Danes in a few months in 1709–10 in Skåne show what advantages there were, also, in living off the enemy's land. Probably the most deleterious effect of the Swedish campaigns abroad was the bifurcation of government and especially the king's loss of contact with his people. Among the definite advantages possessed by Karl XII were the unchallenged absolutism bequeathed him by his father and the regularized system of manpower supply and training that Karl XI had created through the *indelningsverk*. Grumbling and disagreement grew, but during Karl XII's life there was no serious challenge to his rule. Harsh as were the demands for men for the armies, those demands were met year after year and more men than ever (60,000) were under arms in 1718. Chaotic and unreasonable as were the finances of the state, the manipulations of Görtz maintained the tottering structure.

Surrounded by rapacious enemies Karl XII had no simple task. But his only solution was the sword. Could there have been another way? Could Sweden, by a diplomacy of delay, have solidified its imperial position? Karl did not try it until all was already lost. His appraisal of the situation was for years oversanguine, unrealistic. He was perfectly willing to have others cooperate with him — on his terms. He could not compromise. He could not accept the advice or the decisions of his government in Stockholm, and hence he and they frequently worked at cross-purposes. Could things have been done otherwise? The historian cannot be sure; he knows only that there were alternatives that might have been tried and that the methods used resulted in catastrophe on both foreign battlefields and the domestic hearth. The ultimate judgment must be that the king's self-righteous rigidity lost the two things he fought to retain: the empire of the Baltic and monarchic absolutism.

Behind the drama of blood and thunder rational forces were at work. Karl XII was more a product of his times than the creator of them, though what he did certainly helped to shape the future. In the perpetual process of decay of the old and the dynamism of the new that makes for change, the inescapable process that is history, some periods are more chaotic than others. The seventeenth century had been a time of turmoil, of violently clashing religious forces erupting in the Thirty Years War, the conquests of Louis XIV, and the Puritan rebellion in England, compounded by the vigorous expansion of Europe overseas and the struggle for trade and power on a world stage. Not only the great powers were involved in this compulsive activity but also smaller political entities that reached for grandeur. Among the latter were Holland, Brandenburg-Prussia, and Sweden.

In that tumultuous century Sweden had done more than its share to upset old relationships and to lend sanction to the rule of might. It had made enemies all around. The question was, did Sweden have the resources, national will, and the leadership skill to maintain or strengthen its position in cutthroat competition with its neighbors?

Sweden's only dependable ally was tiny Holstein-Gottorp, this because the duke was married to Karl XII's sister Hedvig Sofia, because the duchy was located on Denmark's "soft underside," plus the fact that the duke and the young king were kindred spirits, in love with bear hunting and other wild sports. By the geographic nature of things both Holstein-Gottorp and Sweden were enemies of Denmark, hence dependent on each other.

Denmark had suffered much from Sweden in the seventeenth century and could hardly be expected to forget that Sweden had displaced Denmark as the leading Scandinavian power. Denmark wanted desperately to regain the lost provinces across the Sound and to be assured of a position of strength in Baltic trade. Its last attempt to grab Holstein-Gottorp had been foiled by Karl XI's diplomatic pressure and Kristian V had ignominiously to withdraw (Treaty of Altona, 1689). When Denmark occasionally entered into alliance with Sweden as in 1679 and 1693 it was for the accomplishment of immediate goals in which both were concerned, for there were common interests at stake; Denmark's more natural and more frequent alliances were with Holland and England, and especially with Russia, for the sake of curbing Sweden. And when Sweden got into difficulty with Poland or Russia, or whomsoever, Denmark was always a potential threat to Sweden's flank. Chiefly on this account Sweden had always to maintain a considerable army on the home front, and the more it got into trouble and needed reinforcements abroad just that much more it needed them in Sweden.

Poland was a less serious problem, for the issue of the Vasa inheritance had been settled and the chaotic politics of the country canceled it as a factor to be reckoned with — until, in 1697, Augustus the Strong of Saxony was elected king of Poland. His ambition and his large unemployed army made the Polish-Saxon combination the chief stumbling block that delayed Karl XII in coming to grips with Russia.

Brandenburg was building closer and closer ties with Prussia, and in 1701 the emperor permitted the elector to crown himself king in Prussia. Like his predecessors he was eager to get control of all of Pomerania, which made him an opponent of the Swedish position in Germany and a ready ally of any combination that might bring him his desired territory. For Sweden Pomerania was important as an entrepôt for trade and for the grain it produced.

In the east the relentless enemy was Russia, weak in the early seventeenth century but growing strong and assertive. Even after the defeat at Narva Tsar Peter did not retire from the Gulf of Finland; instead he began in 1703 to build in the swamps the city of St. Petersburg, determined to have a port and his capital city on the Gulf of Finland. He and his successors, backed by the millions of Russians and their massive resource base, would press steadily on the borderlands lost at Stolbova in 1617, seeking outlets for trade and expansion of power.

Holland and England had no interest in a power position in the Baltic, but they were deeply interested in trade. Their commerce in the north was increasing rapidly in the late seventeenth century and early eighteenth, and England was becoming dependent on Russia for its naval stores — English trade with Russia increased threefold in the period 1700–15. The two sea powers were therefore interested in peace, and at almost any time after 1700 peace could be had only at the expense of Sweden.[15]

Among all the continental powers the interests of France most frequently coincided with those of Sweden, for Louis XIV wanted to keep things stirred up, especially to keep the German states and the sea powers occupied. His emissaries tried to persuade Karl XII to cooperate with France in Germany, and they worked with the Swedes in urging the Turks to harass Russia. Austria and Spain were involved in the whole constellation of power, but they were less connected with the north either geographically or politically. The Turks, the Tartars, the Transylvanians, and the Cossacks came into the play occasionally because of their enmity toward Russia or Poland.

The wide-stretching empire that Sweden had built by force lacked cohesive principle; even the southern and western provinces taken from Denmark had not yet been fully absorbed into the kingdom. The disintegrative forces grew chiefly in the neighboring lands, but they often had geography on their side, and they had allies in internal discontent. The man who stirred the witches' brew at the end of the seventeenth century was a product of such discontent.

Johan Reinhold Patkul was a Livonian noble who had led an aristocratic rebellion against Karl XI's reduction policies (see above) in his Baltic province. After he was driven into exile, he nursed his resentments and plotted revenge. In the years of shifting rulers at the end of the seventeenth century he found exactly the elements he wanted; all he had to do was bring them together. His embittered wanderings brought him in 1697 to the court of Augustus the Strong, and he became the intermediary in the negotiations among Saxony-Poland, Denmark, and Russia. In Copenhagen he sneaked in disguise from the court to one legation and then another and put together the alliance that was to tear apart the Swedish empire. He tried to add Prussia to the combination, but his intrigues and double-dealing in Livonia and Russia at last caused Augustus to arrest him.

Allied action began in the late winter of 1700 when Saxon troops invaded Livonia, attacked Riga, and succeeded in blocking it from the sea. Frederik IV of Denmark sent troops into Holstein and besieged the main fort of Tönningen. With Erik Dahlbergh on hand in Riga and Finnish troops ordered to the rescue, Karl XII turned his attention first to Denmark. He organized the troops in Skåne and prepared a fleet at Landskrona. With the assistance of an Anglo-Dutch squadron, come to help enforce the treaty of Altona, he landed his army on the coast of Sjaelland in July 1700. This brilliant military coup, backed by the diplomatic pressure of the great sea powers, led to peace even before Karl XII could attack Copenhagen. The treaty of Traventhal, signed on August 8, 1700, restored the status quo ante bellum and forced Denmark out of the alliance, although its fleet was still intact and therefore a constant threat to the Swedish rear.

Karl XII moved quickly to the eastern front. A Finnish army had already driven the Saxons from Livonia, so precipitately that they left their "wigs on the wall, food on the table, and steak on the stove." [16] Augustus retired to Poland to try to inveigle his second country into the war. Tsar Peter, meanwhile, had declared war on Sweden and besieged the stronghold at Narva. The

Swedes landed at Pernau and marched swiftly across Estonia to succor their friends. Peter departed while his army waited. On November 20, 1700 the Swedes came on with a driving snowstorm at their backs, punctured two holes in the entrenched Russian lines, wrought fear and confusion and chaotic defeat to the tsar's forces. The drilled soldiers of the *indelningsverk* proved once more the superiority of Swedish arms. It was a glorious victory, and it won the young king great prestige. Yet it was only a battle won; it decided nothing.

After building up military strength from his winter headquarters in Dorpat, Karl had choices to make. He was not yet strong enough to invade Russia, especially with the armies of Augustus in his rear. He moved south across the Dvina, defeated a Saxon force in Kurland, and demanded of the divided Poles (not yet at war) that they unseat Augustus as their king. Augustus tried the delaying tactics of diplomacy, even sending his beautiful mistress Aurora Königsmarck as an emissary to Karl — who would not receive her. Soon Poland was entrapped in the war, and Karl took one city after another, often without striking a single blow. Finally a Polish force joined the Saxons who met the Swedes at Klissow, where in a brilliant and bloody battle the Swedes destroyed them. Karl occupied Warsaw and Krakow, and to protect his communications he took Danzig and Thorn. All this required time, and gradually the combination of the humiliations and the exactions of war roused the Poles against both Augustus and Karl. At a diet in Warsaw early in 1704 the Swedish general Arvid Horn got the Poles to dethrone Augustus, but it took the threat of Karl's army to bring the assembly to a decision on a new king, Stanislas Leszczynski. It then required many months to overcome exasperating procrastination, to crown Stanislas king, and to sign Poland into an alliance with Sweden against Russia (in November 1705).

Meanwhile the armies were exercising themselves in pursuit and flight across the Polish plains, occasionally fighting meaningless engagements. The Saxons and the Russians were outmaneuvered by the Swedish generals — especially by Karl himself and Carl Gustaf Rehnskiöld (Horn too, until he was sent to Stockholm in 1706 to guide affairs of state). After Rehnskiöld destroyed the Saxon army at Fraustadt, Augustus found himself boxed in Kurland with the Russians under Menshikov. To bring things to a head Karl XII boldly turned toward Saxony itself, marched across Silesia to the anguish of the emperor, and made himself master of Leipzig and of all Augustus's ancestral lands. This forceful action brought negotiations at Altranstädt wherein Augustus abdicated the Polish throne and withdrew from the anti-Swedish alliance on September 14, 1706. Patkul the intriguer was handed over to the Swedes and executed for treason.

Now Karl could give himself wholly to what Otto Haintz insists he regarded

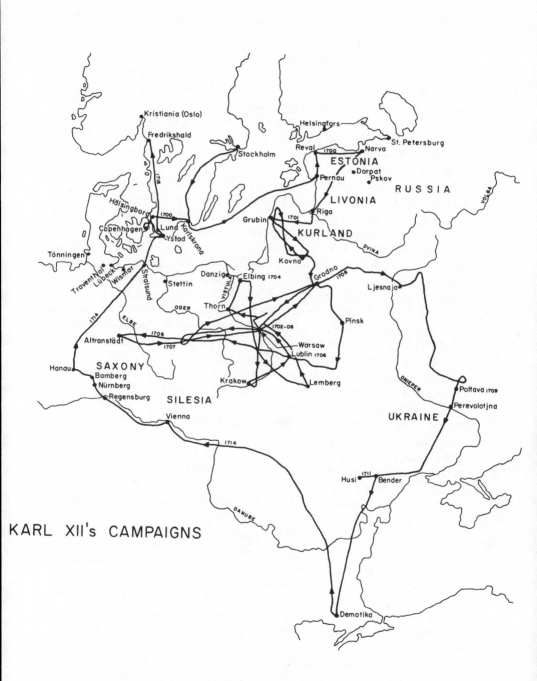

Kristiania (Oslo)

Fredrikshald

Stockholm

Helsingfors

St. Petersburg

Reval 1700 Narva

ESTONIA

Dorpat

Pskov

RUSSIA

VOLGA

Pernau

LIVONIA

Hälsingborg

1700

Grubin 1701 Riga

DVINA

Copenhagen Lund Karlskrona

Ystad

KURLAND

Tönningen

Kovno

Traventhal Lübeck Wismar Stralsund

Danzig Elbing 1704 Grodno 1708

Ljesnaja

Stettin

ODER

Thorn

VISTULA

Pinsk

1714

ELBE

Altranstädt 1706

1707

1702-06

Hanau

SAXONY

Bamberg

Nürnberg

Warsaw

Lublin 1706

Regensburg

SILESIA

Krakow

Lemberg

DNIEPER

Poltava 1709

Perevolotjna

Vienna

UKRAINE

1714

KARL XII's CAMPAIGNS

Husi 1711 Bender

DANUBE

Demotika

as his mission: the destruction of the Russian state and the salvation of the west from the ominous threat of Russian barbarism. Karl XII's own thoughts are hard to fathom, for he was one of the most closemouthed of statesmen. He even had two sets of foreign policies, one secret and one ostensible. He alone knew what he meant, and even he did not always know what was planned by officials in Stockholm, whose agreements he frequently canceled. Since dispatches from his headquarters to the government at home took circuitous routes and sometimes as long as a year in transit the total confusion is the only thing wholly understandable. Diplomatic activity was strenuous. During the year that Karl was in Saxony the French seemed to be gaining influence, and in fear of closer cooperation between French and Swedes the English sent the Duke of Marlborough to sound out the intentions of the new Lion of the North. Negotiations with the emperor succeeded in gaining religious toleration for the Protestants in Silesia. Conferences on a possible Swedish-Prussian alliance came to nought; the unwillingness of either to compromise on West Prussia kept them apart.

As Karl XII moved his armies eastward again across Poland for the final denouement with the Russians, the tsar and his generals tried to wear out the Swedes in small battles. The Cossacks were a constant harassment. The vastness of Mother Russia, as long as human will could utilize it, was well-nigh unconquerable. Peter could withdraw or even be defeated, yet fight another day. On the other hand Karl's army was numbered, and so was the manpower supply in Sweden. Nevertheless, the king of the Swedes adroitly evaded barriers, realizing that only a blow at the heart of the tsardom could have any permanent effect.

Karl XII's dispositions were careful. Georg Lybecker with 14,000 men in Finland was to hold off the Russian Fjodor Apraksin with 24,000. Adam Ludvig Lewenhaupt with 11,000 Swedish reinforcements would gather supplies and catch up with the main army enroute to Moscow; he was opposed by Rudolf Baur with 16,000 Russians. Ernst Krassow was to advance into the Ukraine with 8,000 Swedes and Saxon mercenaries, and assistance was hoped for from Stanislas and his 16,000 Poles. Recent negotiations had also brought an alliance with Ivan Mazeppa, ambitious and shrewd hetman in the Ukraine. Far though he was from home, tenuous as were his communications, Karl XII had reason to hope for continued success. Yet his position was precarious both militarily and diplomatically, dependent on the proper functioning of many interdependent factors. A few strokes of ill luck could bring his plans to nought.

The slowness of Lewenhaupt and some false intelligence to Karl enabled the Russians to cut off the reinforcing army and capture the supply train at Ljesnaya. Lybecker's blunders resulted in his defeat in the north, and made it possible for Apraksin to join Peter with some 10,000 men. Karl, looking for the local population to rise against the tsar, swung still farther south. But the people wanted to see first a solid Swedish victory. What they saw instead was the sudden annihilation of Mazeppa's stronghold by the Russians. Guerrilla attacks and scorched-earth techniques and the severe weather of 1708–9, plus insufficient reinforcements and supplies, weakened the exposed Swedish forces. Meantime Krassow and Stanislas were defeated in Poland. The Turks were afraid to join the Swedes. Yet a Carolinian victory was still possible.

To force Peter into a decisive battle Karl began the siege of the fort at Poltava. Peter accepted the challenge and battle was joined on June 28 (July 8, new-style calendar) 1709. The first tragedy for the Swedes came two days earlier in a skirmish when the king was wounded in the foot, so that he had to be carried into the Poltava battle on a litter swung between two horses; he could not see clearly the progress of events, and only Gustaf Henrik Siegroth and Rehnskiöld knew the battle plans. As a result there was wasted effort in taking some Russian redoubts, then confusion and a premature breaking off of pursuit of the Russian cavalry. Hence the Russians were not, according to plan, driven into the swamp at their rear but were allowed to reform their lines and turn the tide of battle. The sharp rapiers of the Swedes failed before the improved cannon of the Russians. Badly mauled, with 7,000 killed and 2,500 taken prisoner, yet with 15,000 veterans still together, the Swedes retreated to Perevolotjna. There the wounded Swedish king with a few hundred men was persuaded to cross the river into Turkey, leaving the main army under the command of Lewenhaupt. Rehnskiöld had been captured at Poltava. Exhausted and disheartened, reduced to a fraction of his former strength, Lewenhaupt the next day surrendered the entire army to Menshikov and a Russian force smaller than his own. Only a few Carolinians survived the next twelve years of imprisonment, to be exchanged at last and sent home as old men.

Poltava was one of the decisive battles of the century, for both Sweden and Europe. The Swedish lion was struck down, the Russian bear was rampant. Those who had been beaten rose again. Augustus gathered a fresh army and invaded Poland while the Russians came in from the east; Stanislas was overthrown and Augustus replaced on the throne. Danish troops moved once more on Skåne in November 1709. Russian forces conquered and devastated Kurland, and by the end of 1709 the Swedes held only Riga, Pernau, and Reval. In 1710 these capitulated, and the Russians took Karelia and the key fort of Viborg. Everything east of the Baltic lay open to the Russians. It had taken them ten years to reverse the humiliation of Narva. But now no state in eastern or central Europe stood as a barrier against the great Slavic power.

However, Karl would not yield. Even as in his days of power he rejected compromise solutions. From his "guest" quarters at Bender his fertile brain dreamed up one combination of powers after another. Four successive times he prevailed upon the Turks to go to war against Russia, but never did they fully carry through. Once they actually won a strategic victory in 1711 at the Prut River but signed it away in a quick peace. Karl XII was able, astonishingly enough, in 1710 to gather an army of about 10,000 men at Bender, including Swedes and Poles and Zaporozhian Cossacks and others. At home the *indelningsverk* squeezed out additional men from the file squads, and a new army of 16,000 was collected and trained. Under the leadership of Magnus Stenbock it saved Skåne by throwing the Danes back into the Sound at Hälsingborg and holding off the Norwegians in Bohuslän. Encouraged by such news Karl vetoed an agreement for the neutralization of the Swedish possessions in Germany and thus alienated the sea powers (Holland and England) who were eager for peace in the Baltic arena. He ordered Stenbock to take a Swedish army to Pomerania, and despite the destruction of his supply fleet by the Danes in September 1712 Stenbock eventually won a victory at Gadebusch in December 1712, aided by new quick-firing artillery. Nevertheless, he was strategically outmaneuvered, could not move eastward to Poland, and lacked the strength to maintain himself in Germany. He marched into Holstein, was soon confined at Tönningen, and there surrendered to the Danes in May 1713.

Stenbock's failure at length made untenable the position of the caged lion in Turkey. The humiliating result was the king's arrest in the Kalabalik (fracas) of Bender in February 1713. Still he stayed on, deceived by hopeless negotiations with the Saxons until at the end of October 1714 he knew that he was needed at home and began his famous horseback ride across half of Europe. In fifteen days he and two companions rode 1,350 miles incognito to Stralsund. Only Stralsund and Wismar remained as Swedish footholds on the continent, and the neighboring princes all banded together to pick up the pieces of the shattered Swedish empire.

Through the years in Poland and Turkey Karl XII hatched schemes and propaganda and there were always others ready to negotiate or mediate. In general the sea powers urged peace and inclined toward Russia, while France supported Sweden in trying to get Turkey to make war. Denmark and Prussia and Augustus of Saxony each plotted for individual advantage and allied with Russia against Sweden. Perhaps Karl could have made favorable arrangements with Prussia, as Otto Haintz insists, but he would never yield enough to suit anyone. His rigidity may have been honorable and heroic, but it was not constructive. After the Peace of Utrecht in 1713 the western powers were free to turn their attention to trade and their desire for peace in the north; Prussia was free to press its demands for territory. The Russians pushed on relentlessly in Finland, and Carl Gustaf Armfelt could no longer hold them back. Sweden was fighting a desperate rearguard action.

At Stralsund Karl and his cornered Swedes for a year fought off the ring of enemies in a masterful defense, but in December of 1715 he had to acknowledge another defeat and escaped to Trelleborg and Lund in Sweden — fifteen years after he had left the homeland. New projects emerged. He planned an attack on Copenhagen, but the breakup of the ice prevented it. He tried a diversion in Norway but had to withdraw. He hoped for the disintegration of the enemy alliance from its inner jealousies, but though increasingly ineffective it held together. At length, in 1718, with a large new army Karl tried an invasion of southern Norway while Armfelt came in from the north and attacked Trondheim. In the darkness of the evening on November 30, 1718, while besieging the border fort of Frederiksten, the king went out to inspect the ramparts; a bullet of unknown origin crashed through his skull and he died instantly. The dynamo, the perennial breeder of schemes, the military genius and inspirer of men was gone. The war was over and the book was closed on Sweden's century as a great power.

As the rivalries and special interests of the powers had held back Sweden in its days of rampaging conquest, so now they cushioned its fall. Had Sweden been pared down to the area in which its government then exercised authority it would have been virtually the Sweden of the twentieth century. Instead, in the treaties laboriously threshed out in the following three years, Sweden recovered Wismar and both Pomerania and Finland, though with boundaries somewhat crimped. The Holstein manipulator Görtz (Baron von Schlitz), who had joined Karl XII in Stralsund and had become his chief agent and confidant, had already been negotiating with the Russians, and with Karl's death others became interested. Sweden's problem was to choose whether it would yield territories in the east or in the west and then try to find an ally who would help preserve what was left. Görtz had been working in this vein at the Åland congress of 1718 and had obtained tentative agreement from the Russians that for cessions in the east Russia would support Sweden in demands for equivalents in the west, especially in Norway and against Denmark. Karl had rejected this plan, evidently thinking he could do as well on his own. With his death the whole scheme of trading east for west fell through.

England helped Sweden get peace in the west, bought with Sweden's territorial concessions. To George I's Hanover went Bremen and Verden, compensated by 1 million thalers; to expanding Prussia went Stettin and a large slice of Pomerania, against a payment of 2 million thalers; to Denmark Sweden paid 600,000 riksdalers for the return of conquests but allowed the Danes to annex Slesvig, including Karl Frederik's Gottorp, and Sweden relinquished its freedom from the Sound Dues. In the east England tried to mediate with Russia but was frozen out by the tsar; not even the fleet, sent twice to the Baltic, could bring any pressure to bear. Russia and England were important to each other in trade, but Russia, and Austria too, feared English influence in the Baltic. Most important, Russia now had no need to bargain with Sweden, hence the treaty of Nystad, reached only in August 1721 with the aid of French diplomats, was written at the tsar's dictation. Any possible Swedish opposition was discouraged by Russian naval raids on Baltic and Bothnian coastal towns in the summer of 1719 and again in 1721, as the peace was being negotiated. The Russians burned crops, mills, and over a thousand homes at Umeå. Russia gained all the Baltic lands taken by the Swedes from the tsars and the Teutonic Knights since the time of Erik XIV: Kexholm, Ingerman-land, Estonia, Livonia. Russia returned Finland, except for the famous border fort of Viborg and paid Sweden 2 million riksdalers. Finland's eastern boundary was approximately that of independent Finland after 1947. Russia's day was dawning as Sweden's set.[17]

# IX

# THE AGE OF FREEDOM
# 1718–71

THE DEATH OF KARL XII brought the collapse of the military and diplomatic supports of the Swedish state. Peacemaking had to be carried on from a position of unprecedented weakness: Tsar Peter shrewdly used as pressures not only the ravaging of the Bothnian and Baltic coasts but the threat to support Duke Karl Fredrik against the insecure Fredrik I. The threat was real because Fredrik I and Ulrika Eleonora (the younger) had no heirs and were fearful of the intrigues of the Holstein party in Sweden and abroad. Prussia became increasingly eager to acquire Swedish Pomerania. England gave a special personal subsidy to Fredrik to bolster his position, and Denmark wished to strengthen him if for no other reason than to prevent the duke of Holstein-Gottorp from coming to the Swedish throne.[1] These countries were all directly concerned with the Baltic and with Sweden; and the positions of England and Russia in the European power complex made Austria and France jealous of any advantages won by another state. It was a tangled mélange of commercial and political interests that, with the disintegration of the Swedish Baltic empire, was sucked into the vacuum of power in the North.

The discord and complexity of the Age of Freedom can be understood, perhaps, through an attempt to unravel three of the main historical strands. The first was the fear of one-man dominance, the reaction to the autocracy of Karl XI and Karl XII. The resultant drive for a broader base of political authority produced a constitution founded on aristo-democratic principles, creating a parliament with supreme power. If this body became infected with corruption and disintegrating factional strife it was at least a noble experiment. Its ultimate collapse led to the establishment in 1772 of an autocracy at least somewhat more enlightened than those of the seventeenth century.

The second strand, intermeshed with the riksdag's assertion of its supremacy over the king, was foreign interference. Sweden had had its day of intervening in the affairs of Germany, Poland, Denmark, and Russia. Now these states as well as the sea powers of western Europe wanted to guard against a reassertion of Swedish aggressiveness, and they wanted to gain whatever advantages they could from Sweden's weakness. By the Treaty of Nystad of 1721 the territorial losses thereof and the foreign intrigues over the succession to the throne made Sweden dependent on the rivalries of outside states. They subsidized Sweden to fight in one alliance or another or to stay out of the fighting, and they bribed individual politicians. From time to time Sweden strove to assert itself, but for decades to come both its successes and its failures in foreign affairs were attributable primarily to the actions of others; even domestic policies and personnel were strongly affected. Sweden's problem was to stay afloat in a period of shifting international alliances and keen competition for position. But the country had no pilot with sharp eye or firm hand. No wonder that Sweden's little ship of state bounced about in the wake of the bigger ships, especially since the sails were torn to shreds and the hull was battered after a century of bold sailing on its own.

A third theme pervading the political life of the era was the economic travail of the Swedish society. Poverty was the basis of Sweden's weakness and the reason that degrading subsidies were so important. Hence one of the chief tasks of the state became the upbuilding of the economy. Two views were held as to method, both of them mercantilist, but one more extreme than the other.

The interrelatedness and complexities of these strands will become evident first in a brief sketch of constitutional structure and practices.

## The Constitutional Experiment, 1718–72

With the death of Karl XII the pendulum of power was sharply reversed. During the period of glory, while the army's banners still waved in pride and the king was a powerful figure in Europe it was difficult to protest against absolutism. Voices of opposition, like Erik Sparre's, were easily silenced in the reign of Karl XI. The early years of Karl XII were more spectacular with military prowess, but the ultimate result was defeat, the loss of one-third of the population (from 3 million to 2 million), and long years of abject hardship. The objections to autocracy could not then be stifled. The result was a half-century of experimentation with aristocratic rule through semi-democratic processes. In Swedish history this is known as the Age of Freedom (*Frihetstiden*).

The change in the power structure was facilitated by the insecurity and vulnerability of the succession. Not only was there no son of the last king, there was no brother or uncle. There was, indeed, the sister Ulrika Eleonora, and female rights had been recognized by the Norrköping Agreement of 1604, but only for an unmarried woman. Ulrika Eleonora had not only married but she had married without consultation with the riksdag, and her spouse, Fredrik of Hesse, was a Calvinist. However, Fredrik was near the army when the fatal shot ended Karl XII's career and he acted quickly. He sent immediate word to Ulrika Eleonora in Stockholm and, in a lightning move, he had the hated Baron Görtz arrested. As a Holsteiner Görtz was the natural adviser, and a shrewd one, for the other claimant to the throne.

Karl Fredrik of Holstein-Gottorp was the son of a deceased sister of Karl XII. He was one step further removed as an heir, but he was a male. With Görtz as his manager and decisive action on his own part he might well have won the title. As it was, Ulrika Eleonora's head start gave her the advantage.

She was nevertheless disappointed, for she did not receive unquestioning recognition of her hereditary right nor acceptance of her husband as king. The council grasped its opportunity to achieve a "contract" between sovereign and people. This was a reassertion of the powers the council had exercised in the period of the union and in 1611 and 1660. The councillors had long acted as guardians of the political heritage. They had chafed under the restrictions imposed upon them during Karl XII's extended absence, while they had to direct domestic affairs. They were now ready to assert themselves. They agreed to receive Ulrika Eleonora as queen on conditions: she had to accept the constitution to be drawn up, rule according to the advice of the council, and approve all laws passed by the riksdag — the veto power was thus abolished. A few days later the army agreed to accept her but would take no oath until a new formula was drafted. When the Estates met they accepted what had been done and carried on. They too were prepared for self-assertion. The politicians were solving practical problems in a practical way, though observing certain principles. Theorizing about those principles began afterwards.

The first general principle was that the king was only one among several agencies of government. Neither inheritance nor divine right supported the monarchy any longer. Autocracy died with hardly a whimper but kingship survived, deeply rooted in tradition as it was. Power for the moment resided in the council, which was in turn responsible to the Estates. The king had to govern with the advice of the council and accept the will of the Estates. Erik Sparre was long gone but his ideas were remembered. This is called by Fredrik Lagerroth, an outstanding apologist and constitutional historian for the period, the *constitutional principle*. He defines several other guiding principles.[2]

The *parliamentary principle* regulated relations between Estates and council; the Estates in the riksdag nominated members for the council and the king appointed. The Estates gradually became in fact the supreme power and some of their enthusiastic apologists considered that they not only represented the Swedish people but that they *were* the people, that the state was personified in them. While the four Estates were in session, sometimes for as much as twenty-one months at a stretch, they exercised authority down to the smallest detail: they demanded to see the lecture notes of Anders Berch, the first professor of economics at Uppsala, to make sure he was teaching proper mercantilist principles; as a whole and through their numerous committees they investigated the most minute questions over and over and examined every appointment, promotion, and complaint about nonappointment; one committee debated how many lines there should be to a page in court decisions. The riksdag gave orders to the council about how to function during periods between sessions and, when it returned to work, went through the minutes of the council and of all the bureaus of administration. Its ambitions were immense, and unrealizable, and it "floundered in billowing tides of paper."[3] The parliamentary principle was elevated to such a pinnacle, because of fear of monarchical tyranny, that the riksdag became itself a tyrant — and an inefficient one. The "judicial murders" of Görtz, and later of Alexander Blackwell, and of Erik Brahe and seven colleagues were products of power gone wrong.

The parliamentary principle meant that power (executive, legislative, and judicial) lay in the riksdag. But the functioning of the system was not exactly what we understand today as parliamentary. Since decision making was the prerogative of the riksdag itself there was hardly occasion for dismissal of a ministry (the council), but individual ministers were dismissed (*licentierad*) — and sometimes executed. Not until 1769 and 1771 did entire councils fall.

The *democratic principle* regulated relations between people and riksdag; elections to the riksdag were conducted by the separate Estates instead of, as earlier, by parish or provincial councils. Exceptions were that bishops among the clergy and heads of families among the nobles would still be members automatically. One of the semi-democratic features of the system was that among both the burghers and the farmers certain "qualified" women could vote for delegates to the riksdag. Gradually there developed a corollary to the principle that the Estates really were the citizenry: the concept that a riksdagsman was chosen not merely to represent the will of his constituents but to exercise his own judgment.

Committees within the riksdag were elected by the Estates at the beginning of each session. The most powerful was the so-called Secret Committee, whose proceedings were shielded even from fellow members of the riksdag. It handled questions of foreign policy and finance and anything else of primary importance, and it was virtually a parliament within a parliament. The 100 members of the Secret Committee were composed of 50 nobles, 25 clergy, and 25 burghers. The farmers were excluded on the grounds that they could not keep secrets of foreign policy and could not understand national finance. If it seems a denial of democracy to exclude the representatives of 95 percent of the population from the most important committee, it should be realized that even with this limitation the peasants of Sweden occupied a unique position in the Europe of the eighteenth century: they met regularly, they had at least technical equality with the other Estates, and they had a voice in final decisions. They had proud traditions of independence and many of them had some education. Probably all farmers sent to the riksdag could read, though ability to write was less common. The educational level of the farmer delegates from Finland was probably higher than that of the Swedes from other provinces because special attention had to be paid to the Finns' knowledge of the Swedish language. In the decisions that had to be made by the Riksdag as a whole the farmers had real influence. The traditional decision-making principle was unanimity, and even after the requirement was abandoned every effort was made to bring all four Estates into agreement.

The *bureaucratic principle* recognized tenure, fixed salaries and standards of promotion for officials, and riksdag oversight of administrative bureaus. Each member of the council was at first the head of an administrative bureau but soon, because of antibureaucratic sentiment, these heads were forbidden to sit on the council, and councillors could not serve in the bureaus. The bureaucrats tended to be specialists — for law, navy, and other departments. Overlapping between officialdom and riksdag was extensive, for 80 percent of the nobles were officials, all the clergy were state appointees, and many burghers were urban magistrates; only among the farmers were there no officials. Quite naturally officialdom could expect sympathetic treatment in the legislative body. However, as Sten Carlsson has pointed out, the nobles were not only officeholders but also landowners and investors in mines and factories; the burghers were not only mayors or members of town councils but were primarily merchants and artisans. Hence there was often a strong antibureaucratic mood in the riksdag, especially among the burghers and farmers. And the clergy did not think of themselves as bureaucrats.[4] The farmers had obtained a constitutional provision in 1723 that no one who had been an officeholder or belonged to another Estate could be chosen for the farmers' Estate. In the council the king had two votes — both a recognition of his superior dignity and a subtle reminder that he was really just another member.

The *corporative principle* emphasized the separateness of the four Estates. The Swedish people were not represented as a whole, but as four interest groups. Under the new constitution any three of the Estates could decide an issue if unanimity was impossible. And the king was not included in the decision-making process. Incidentally, the three-class voting system among the nobles was abolished (to be reinstated later in the century).

The organization of both riksdag and society according to status and interest groups tended to sharpen social distinctions and make tensions among classes stronger than the rivalries of political parties. This corporative principle, because it applied only to old established groups, also excluded from participation rapidly increasing numbers of merchants, professionals, and other educated "persons of status" (*ståndspersoner*), and the resultant injustice was to plague the country for a century.

The *secrecy principle* was now applied to all actions of the riksdag; no publication was permitted without authorization, thus no public discussion or criticism was possible; even corruption was protected. Corruption was perhaps a more vicious evil in Sweden in the eighteenth century than in contemporary England, for in England the money was English whereas in Sweden it was foreign. Excuses can be offered: Sweden was poor. Many nobles were impoverished, and riksdagsmen could not afford to stay in Stockholm without subsidization. Some of the funds supplied by Russia, France, or England simply enabled men to attend the sessions and to vote as they would have voted without bribes. But the sale of proxies reached large proportions and by 1772 commanded a price as high as 12,000 daler. Buying and selling of offices was common practice in other countries as well as in Sweden. The fact remains that corruption was widespread, demoralizing, and dangerous, as will become evident.

The secrecy principle meant that the proceedings of the riksdag were jealously guarded. Not until 1755, and then only in the Hats' party organ, *Ärlig Svensk* (The Honest Swede), could information about riksdag discussions be mentioned in the press, on penalty of death. In the final years of the Age of Freedom the Caps party succeeded in passing a Freedom of the Press Act (in 1766); this was recognized as having constitutional status, and lip service was paid to it even by Gustav III.[5]

Different principles were emphasized at different periods of the Age of Freedom, but all together the five principles characterize the age. In essence, the constitution of the Age of Freedom created a government in which the sovereignty of the four Estates was embodied in the riksdag. The council became the subservient tool of the riksdag and could not call its soul its own. The king was allowed to remain as titular head of the administration. This constitutional revolution was at once eased and emphasized by the personalities of the monarchs who disliked both the philosophy and its application but were too weak to oppose it effectively. To begin with, Ulrika Eleonora had neither aptitude nor interest in government affairs, and after a year of tension she stepped aside and her husband was elected king as Fredrik I in 1720. (Swedish law forbade a divided rule like that of William and Mary in England.)

A number of separate acts spelled out the details of the new constitution: the *Regeringsform* of 1719, amended in 1720, the riksdag ordinance of 1723, the royal assurances of each new king (1719, 1720, 1751, 1772), plus the freedom of the press act and other reforms of 1766.

The unique body in the riksdag was the farmer Estate, incorporating in the governmental machinery representatives of the large class of landholding farmers, the *bönder*. And this Estate grew in significance as the century advanced. It was composed of about one hundred fifty members, elected one from each *härad* (because of the expense of sending a man to Stockholm sometimes two or more härads combined to send one representative). The riksdag met once every three years. The council, composed entirely of nobles, had been the "king's council" under Karl XI; after 1719 it became the "council of the kingdom."

The new initiatives required of the riksdag encouraged differing opinions and therefore the formation of parties. Lacking, however, well-defined programs, it is not surprising that the parties came to be named, after 1738, simply the Hats and the Caps. The Hats assumed their name for being like the dashing fellows in the tricorne of the day, successors to the empire-minded Holstein party of the 1720s. The Caps were nicknamed because of the charge that they were like timid old ladies in nightcaps. Differences between them were surely no clearer than the differences between Republicans and Democrats in the twentieth-century United States — who also changed with the years.

The "Older Caps," in general followers of Arvid Horn, favored a policy of peace and because of that appeared to be pro-Russian. A majority of them were from Finland and the east coast (except Stockholm) and were interested in Baltic trade. The Hats were sensitive to defense and national prestige, favored strong mercantilist policies, and tended to be pro-French. They came largely from Stockholm and from the west coast. In later years the Hats were identified vaguely with the upper aristocracy and large commercial interests; the Caps with the lower aristocracy, clergy, farmers, and the court, though neither party was pro-royalist. Lines of demarcation were indistinct, as is often the case of politics. The Caps were dominant until 1738, the Hats from 1739 to 1765; then primacy shifted rapidly, with the Caps in power from 1765 to 1769, the Hats from 1769 to the spring of 1772, and the Caps again just before Gustav III's coup. Until the chaos of the final years the parties functioned in highly efficient fashion, with party clubs, whips to keep members in line, and careful advance preparation for elections.

## Foreign Intrigue and Internal Politics

If the picture emerging from the preceding chapter seems dismal, it must be recalled that the situation of Sweden in the 1720s was tragic. The key to both domestic and foreign problems was weakness, weakness of the country economically and militarily, and weakness of the new governmental structure. The constitution of 1720 was an attempt to avoid the evils of absolutism, and this it did: the weaknesses of the sovereigns continued while the determination of the politicians held autocracy at bay for a half-century. But the weaknesses of the politicians produced factional strife, corruption, inefficiency, forays into unprepared and futile wars, plus treasonous dealings with foreign countries. Sweden survived its own weakness only because its opponents, especially Russia, were also weak. These other states, particularly Russia, Denmark, and Prussia, were eager to keep Sweden weak and they cooperated to achieve that goal.

Russia was constantly at the center of the pressures and intrigues against Sweden. The Russians had promised in the Treaty of Nystad to refrain from interference in Sweden's internal affairs, but they interpreted this pledge as their guarantee to protect the constitution of 1720 and thereby to ensure the continued feebleness of Sweden. Their policies in Sweden paralleled their disruptive intrigues in Poland and Turkey. The Russian envoy sent to Stockholm in 1721, Mikhail Bestuzhev-Ryumin, had instructions to support the Holstein faction which favored Karl Fredrik as king to replace Fredrik I. The Russians were particularly worried when Fredrik I roused the peasantry in the interests of a strengthened monarchy, and they staged naval demonstrations in the Baltic. In 1724 they made with Sweden a twelve-year treaty of defensive alliance, presumably hoping to make Sweden a protectorate. Their policy appeared more ominous as Karl Fredrik became a favorite of Peter the Great and in 1727 married the tsar's daughter Anna Petrovna. The possibilities of this marriage were enormous: recovery of Slesvig by Holstein-Gottorp, succession to the throne of Sweden for Duke Karl Fredrik and possibly the tsardom, even a union of Russia and Sweden that would restore the lost Baltic provinces to Sweden. Hope developed that a combination of circumstances might permit Sweden to acquire Norway, thus rounding out a peninsular state. But the inflated dreams of the Holsteiners were not to be realized any more than the royal ambitions of Fredrik I.[6]

The man who shrewdly, cautiously, piloted the Swedish ship of state through the dangers of the 1720s and 1730s was Arvid Horn. Horn, the son of a poor Finnish noble family, had participated in the youthful pranks of Karl XII and had won glory in eight years of warfare abroad, including Narva and Klissow. Karl XII recognized his talent and in 1706 sent him back to

Stockholm, where he soon became a member of the council and its leader and also served as the guardian of the boy Karl Fredrik. Horn realized early that Sweden has lost the power of initiative and therefore favored a policy of peace with English cooperation; he thus came to have a chilly relationship with war-minded Karl XII. His independence at that time gave rise to the story that the king remarked that Horn had grown a head taller in the years he had been back in Sweden (*Se non è vero è ben trovato*). By 1720 Horn was Sweden's leading statesman, to be compared by some with his contemporaries Robert Walpole in England and Cardinal Fleury in France. He was master of the art of the possible. Vis-à-vis Russia he sought freedom without challenge; hence he approved the treaty of 1724. Yet by 1726–27 he was able to get the council to approve the Hanoverian alliance with England and France (by the narrow margin of the king's double vote). He dominated the council and the Estates, even the Secret Committee, and was elected marshal of the realm. Along with being a coldly calculating practitioner of power he was a very pious Lutheran, and he earned the support of the clerical Estate when he sponsored the 1726 Conventicle Decree forbidding nonchurch religious gatherings. Arvid Horn was one of the exceptions to the weakness of the period until he tired with age and was overthrown in 1738. He avoided adventure, preserved peace, and confirmed the authority of the constitution.

Arvid Horn long enjoyed the confidence of the Estates and as chancellor pursued a cautious course, working especially through the Secret Committee. Among his constructive achievements was the codification of the laws in 1734, bringing up-to-date and combining the *landslag* (national law) and the *stadslag* (city law) which stemmed from the Middle Ages. The council contained some opponents of Horn though he succeeded in getting two Holsteiners removed. Gradually more general opposition developed, and in 1734 the riksdag suddenly "remembered" a rule that a councillor of state could not be marshal of the nobility (*lantmarskalk*); thus was Horn divested of his vital posts as chairman of the nobles' Estate and of the Secret Committee. He retained the chancellorship for four years longer.[7]

Horn's diplomatic task was far from simple. The Holsteiners were persistent in their intrigues and were aided by Russian bribes. A strong French faction, supported with French gold, won the sympathies of the restless younger nobles who had not experienced the wars of Karl XII and who longed for revenge against Russia and who were eager for more power. Hence Horn was edged out in 1738 and his Cap colleagues were driven from the council. The war-eager Hats came to office. Rapid shifts of rulers in Russia, after the death of Peter the Great in 1725, encouraged ideas of war and especially the temptations offered by the Russo-Turkish war of 1736–39. The confused situation in Russia, where Elizabeth was seeking to seize power from the regency for Ivan VI, and the outbreak of the War of the Austrian Succession in 1740 made the urge for action irresistible.

In 1738 the riksdag had elected the Hat leader Carl Gustaf Tessin, an enemy of Horn, to the post of marshal and had filled the Secret Committee with men of stronger views. The controversial issues included Horn's moderate policy toward Russia and his unwillingness to support France in a campaign against Russia (which led France to subsidize the anti-Horn party). Further, because he had not wanted to antagonize England, Horn had refused to support the founding of an East India Company, and the Estates created it anyway. Thus the activist, pro-French, ultramercantilist group gradually got the upper hand, which was the reason that in December 1738 Horn at last resigned and Count Carl Gyllenborg became chancellor. Some of Horn's supporters refused to leave the council, but they were tried by the Secret Committee and forced to leave. Until then no clear distinction had been made between legal and political responsibility. The idea of responsibility in the modern parliamentary sense was just emerging, in Sweden as in England.

Tessin succeeded for a time in restraining the revanche-minded Hats, but the riksdag adopted a complex secret plan which authorized the council to make war on Russia if certain advantageous factors should coincide to promise success. Tessin had already negotiated a secret treaty in which France promised subsidies for a war against Russia. War came, but hopes were far from fulfilled. Sweden could in 1741 put 44,000 men into uniform, whereas Denmark-Norway had 57,000, Prussia 83,000, and Russia 200,000. Furthermore, Turkey had made peace with Russia in 1739 and Sweden's small force had to cope alone with the big bear. The war hawks were led on by a three-year subsidy from France, by the prospects of chaos in Russia, and by the general situation of European conflict. But the boldness of the declaration of war in the summer of 1741 was backed only by military unpreparedness, weakness on the battlefield, and bungling in diplomacy.

In November 1741 the Swedes marched with high hopes into Karelia, but after a Russian show of force the indecisive General Carl Emil Lewenhaupt marched them out again. The Russians tried to stir up Finnish opposition, secretly encouraged by the Swedish Caps, and finally invaded the province, hoping to establish Finnish "independence" under Russian protection. The demoralized Swedish army surrendered at Helsingfors and the Russians became masters of Finland. The Hats were in an embarrassing situation and were saved partly at least by the complexities of the dynastic situation.

Ulrika Eleonora's death in November 1741 raised anew the question of the succession, for Fredrik I was childless. Russia now demanded the right to name a crown prince, as a condition for the return of Finland, minus another slice of Karelia. The Danes entered the picture too by nominating the Danish crown prince as heir to the Swedish throne, and the farmer Estate voted in his favor. Karl Fredrik could no longer be considered, for he had died in 1739, but his son Duke Karl Peter Ulrik was an attractive young man and a favorite of Tsarina Elizabeth. Why not curry favor with the tsarina by naming Karl Peter Ulrik crown prince? All four Estates voted for this proposal in 1742, but the election was nullified when Elizabeth, almost simultaneously, named the duke her own heir, and he became Tsar Peter III in 1762. The Russians were in control, for they could use peace-treaty concessions as bargaining items, and they, together with the British and with the Caps in Sweden, favored Adolf Fredrik, prince-bishop of Lübeck and cousin and heir of Karl Peter Ulrik. Above all Elizabeth wanted to avoid the selection of the Danish crown prince, which would probably have led to a new Scandinavian union. However, this possibility appealed to the peasants of Dalarna; their disgust with the government and with the management of the war was aggravated by their depressing economic situation. They became mutinous and finally an army of rebels gathered and marched on Stockholm in June 1743, armed with hunting guns, spiked clubs, and spears. They frightened the residents of the capital, and there was a brief skirmish in the city before the rebels were subdued by a blast of cannon fire.[8]

In the meantime peace had been concluded at Åbo. Russia took a goodly slice of territory off eastern Finland but left the bulk of Finland in Swedish hands, still on the condition that Adolf Fredrik be chosen as crown prince. The Secret Committee had decided to yield to the rebel demands, but the news from Åbo was enough to swing the Estates into line, and both treaty and Adolf Fredrik were accepted on June 23, 1743. The crisis should have been over, but now Denmark threatened war, and the humiliated Hats had to ask for 10,000 Russian troops to camp near Stockholm as protection against the Danes. One consolation for the Swedes was that the crown prince who had been thrust upon them had a few drops of Vasa blood in his veins: he was a great-great-grandson of Karl IX. He was also at the time prince-bishop of Lübeck and guardian of the orphaned son of Karl Fredrik of Holstein-Gottorp.

At this point Sweden appeared to be an abject dependency of Russia, and in 1745 it entered into a new alliance with this traditional enemy. However, Carl Gustaf Tessin, now chancellor, was able to adjust affairs with Denmark, partly through Adolf Fredrik's agreement to drop his claims to Slesvig. A degree of independence toward Russia was also evidenced by the marriage in 1744 of Adolf Fredrik with Louisa Ulrika, the sister of Frederick II of Prussia and a strong-willed woman. When it appeared that the Hats might modify the constitution toward strengthening the monarchy the Russians admonished the crown prince and again displayed their naval power in the Gulf of Finland. The Caps urged the Russians to take more emphatic measures. However, the

Hats were able to withstand all pressures; they made defensive alliances with France and Prussia in 1747 and resumed relations with Turkey. Repeated threats from Russia were politely brushed aside; probably their main effect was to unite the Swedish people behind the government and to enhance Russophobia.

Inspired by his ambitious queen and a small influential court party, King Adolf Fredrik reached for more authority. He declared before the Estates that he had to have the veto power and more voice in appointments, "for in other case I would be less important than the most insignificant inhabitant in this country, who cannot be forced to do anything against his own conscience." [9] The council replied that if the king's conscience should determine law it would be absolutism. The high-handed methods of the Estates, the widespread buying and selling of offices, and the increasing debt of the state led to a strong protest by the farmers in 1756. The struggle became more tense when the king refused to sign measures passed by the Estates, and they reacted by declaring that the council should take the king's name-stamp and use it to sign bills rejected by the king. Inspired by Queen Louisa Ulrika, a tougher character than her husband, the court fought back with a planned coup against the riksdag. But the plot was betrayed and eight of the plotters, including Erik Brahe, were executed outside Riddarholm church. Louisa Ulrika was given a long sermon by the bishop of Västerås, and Adolf Fredrik was given a list of his improprieties against the constitution by the Secret Committee, which told him that if he persisted the Estates would be free of their oath of allegiance. The monarchy was humiliated and the Estates reigned with greater authority than before. A letter was issued on the duties of officials, though most of the reforms suggested were stymied in bureaucratic processes.

Nothing, it seems, could squelch the Swedish urge to reestablish an independent and great power position, to conquer new lands. Perhaps in that viciously competitive era a more passive attitude would have resulted in permanent dependence or even partition. In any event the smaller countries sought both security and opportunity in alliance with the larger powers, among whom warfare was the norm. In the eighteenth century war followed war in rapid succession: the War of Jenkins's Ear and the War of the Austrian Succession, 1739–48; the Seven Years War, 1756–63; the American Revolution, 1776–83; and the wars of the French Revolution and Napoleon, 1792–1815. Sweden's eager search for opportunity (or at least the eagerness of the Hats) discovered something hopeful with the beginning of European war in 1756. An attempt at neutrality in agreement with Denmark failed in 1756, and French persuasion, including a first-year subsidy of 4.3 million livres, brought Sweden into active war against Prussia in 1757. Relations between states are among the most transitory of all relationships. In the diplomatic whirligig of

1756 France became allied with Russia, and Sweden joined with France to help maintain the Peace of Westphalia, "to prevent Russia from acting unilaterally in the Baltic," and to try to expand its territory in Germany.[10]

In this Pomeranian War the Swedes were again sadly unprepared both financially and militarily. The council had to get money through illegal loans from the *Riksbank*, for it dared not call the Estates. The war was fought on Pomeranian and Prussian soil with alternating success and failure but with no decisive action against the great Prussian warrior-king, Frederick II. It was all inglorious and unproductive. When in 1762 Elizabeth of Russia died her successor Peter III hastened to make peace and Sweden was eager to follow suit. Louisa Ulrika was a natural mediator with her brother. Her surprising success in obtaining a treaty restoring the prewar territorial situation was deeply appreciated by the Swedish council and led to a temporary easing of tensions within the government.

In the meantime the riksdag had at last come together in the fall of 1760, and the Hats found it difficult to maintain their position. The Caps were gaining strength everywhere except among the mercantilist upper burghers. One of the chief troublemakers was Carl Fredrik Pechlin, a nobleman of Dutch and Holstein background who had been a Hat leader in the 1750s. In the 1760 riksdag he organized a dissident group (*lantpartiet*), which gained power and for a brief time collaborated with the court. Then, appeased with the payment of a large sum by the French ambassador, he made a deal with Axel von Fersen (the Elder) and the Hats were saved, losing only three of their popularly hated council members. Pechlin, an inveterate intriguer throughout his long career, soon found himself excluded from the riksdag (by a one-vote majority), but he returned and in 1769 joined the Caps. Soon he was the most extreme opponent of Gustav III, always scheming but always consistent in his antiautocratic stance.

The Caps, supported by monetary bribes from Russia and England, in 1765 won their way back to power with majorities in all four Estates. They ousted the nine councillors who had voted to receive French subsidies and ended the pensions and other expenditures on which the Hats had lavished state funds. The Caps' policy was deflationary and included the curtailment of the mercantilist activities of the government, such as loans to factories. Instead of the French connection of the Hats the Caps cooperated with England, but with the goal of maintaining peace. Against the Caps' reforms were the Hats, the court, the bureaucracy, and the prestige and money of France, and they were able to hold power only from 1765 to 1769.

The Caps' most notable achievement of this term was the 1766 Freedom of the Press Act, which became a part of the constitution. Anders Chydenius, the clergyman-economist-riksdagsman from Finland, was its chief proponent.

Political pamphleteering had increased enormously and newspapers were becoming important. Some of the papers such as *Posttidningen* avoided partisanship, but Peter Momma's *Dagligt Allehanda* (Caps) — Sweden's first daily (established in 1767) — the Hats' *Posten*, and Carl C. Gjörwell's royalist *Almänna Tidningar* vigorously argued their political views. The council itself had established in 1755 a weekly to spread the government's (that is, the Hats') position — *Ärlig Svensk* (the Honest Swede); after the legislating of freedom of information in 1766 the riksdag debates were published. Certain topics, such as the monarchy and the church, were still restricted to some extent, but the new liberties were broad. Freedom of the press existed elsewhere only in Great Britain and the Netherlands. Freed from legal restraint, Sweden of the 1760s echoed and reechoed with political debate.

The Caps' program, especially their economic policy, was opposed at every turn. The French withdrew their subsidies, and the Russian minister became the chief governmental adviser. In 1768 matters culminated when the king demanded that the riksdag be called in special session, otherwise he would abdicate. The council refused and King Adolf Fredrik "turned his chair around" to indicate the throne was vacant. For a few days in December 1768 Sweden was without an executive, and the functions of government came to a halt. Crown Prince Gustav was a key figure in urging the king to stand firm, and the bureaucracy supported the crown by refusing to honor the name-stamp. Thus the Caps were forced to call elections and a meeting of the riksdag. They convened the meeting in Norrköping, a place accessible to the influence of the fleets of Russia, Prussia, and Denmark. But reaction to confusion brought the return of the Hats with overwhelming majorities. The foreign powers were intensely interested in developments, and all their ministers were present in Norrköping with their money pouches. In connection with the election of the marshal of the nobles' Estate, according to the English minister, the Russians and the Danes paid out 10,000 pounds in bribes for votes, whereas he restricted himself to 5,000 pounds. But the French were more successful with their 3.5 million livres, paid on condition that the receivers would change the constitution in favor of monarchy.[11] The council of the Caps was dismissed and a new one composed of Hats was installed.

The Hats brought back their extravagant ways, and they also brought definite proposals for the expansion of royal power. They introduced at Norrköping a bill to reduce the council to an advisory capacity and to give the king final decision, except in judicial matters. The Estates were to meet every three years to consider suggestions from the king; they were to act with the king on legislation and declarations of war and were to be responsible for administration and appropriations. The method of selection of councillors was to be reversed, so that the king would make the nominations and the riksdag the final choices. These proposals foreshadowed what was to come in 1772, but they were defeated by a combination of the Caps and Pechlin's *lantparti* faction of the Hats. When the riksdag met in Stockholm in 1770 the French ambassador demanded fulfillment of the pledge to reform the constitution. The Estates by that time were paralyzed with the specter of the chaos in Poland and the fear of foreign intervention in Sweden, and by a vote of three to one they refused to make a change. Choiseul, the French foreign minister, was furious, and recalled his ambassador. Ominously in the background stood Denmark, Prussia, and Russia, who had agreed among themselves to keep Sweden weak by preventing a change in the constitution.

The time of kindly but ineffective King Adolf Fredrik ran out first, for he died on February 12, 1771. But the time of the constitution of the Age of Freedom was running out, too. The Caps, with regained strength among the burghers and the farmers, returned once more to leadership. But the government had changed with the accession of Gustav III, the first Swedish-born king since Karl XII and a more forceful person than any of the recent kings.

It was time for a change. In 1772 Prussia, Austria, and Russia carried through the first partition of Poland, and the Russians and Danes had agreed upon a partition of Sweden in case war should make it feasible. Bribery had risen to an unprecedented level and was corrupting political life. Although corruption may have been as bad in contemporary England the foreign money in Sweden was a more vicious political poison. Both the bitter personal controversies and the self-destructive rivalries of the parties were fueled by ruthless foreign powers. The domestic and international intrigue and kaleidoscopic change are confusing to us, and they were both puzzling and fearsome to contemporaries. We can understand not only why Gustav III felt impelled to change the form of government but why his coup in August 1772 was so readily accepted. Important lessons had been learned, and wobbly steps toward democratic maturity had been taken, but the insidious intrigues of foreign powers, the weakness and bad faith of kings, and the irrepressible yearning for great power status produced such strains that the constitution could not endure. A swing toward autocracy was unavoidable. Yet the Age of Freedom had discovered or reinterpreted certain democratic fundamentals: sovereignty of the people, respresentation of all classes, freedom of expression, and the right and duty of independent judgment by the elected representative. Also temporarily established were some of the institutions natural to a democratic state, as a two-party system and at least the idea of ministerial responsibility. In its eighteenth-century experimental stage the system proved ineffectual and disruptive, although it needs to be recalled that absolutism had proved catastrophic.[12]

## Scientific Achievement

The politicians of the Age of Freedom could not produce order, but order and systematization were precisely the realm within which the great achievements of the period were made. Love of nature combined with the urge for organization in the genius of Carl von Linné (Linnaeus), but he was only the greatest amid a galaxy of scientific talent. The formal gardens of England and of Versailles exemplified a widespread contemporary interest in both the beauties of nature and the imposition of man-made law on the physical universe. The Age of Greatness had brought Swedes into close contact with people and movements on the continent, and the success of Swedish warriors may have emboldened other Swedes to think of themselves as potential equals of the scientists of western Europe.

A revitalization of intellectual life was already evident in the seventeenth century. The University of Uppsala, though founded in 1477, had closed for a long period and then reopened in 1593. As a result of Gustav Adolf's initiative two universities were started in the provinces across the Baltic: Dorpat in Estonia in 1632, Åbo in Finland in 1640. The still older university of Greifswald was acquired with Pomerania during the Thirty Years War. The University of Lund (for southern Sweden) was chartered in 1666. An increasing number of students, after preliminary training in Swedish institutions, found their way for further study and inspiration to the universities of Germany, France, and the Netherlands. And a few bold originators appeared, owing probably more to biological chance than to any of the deep "causes" that we try to find.

Christopher Polhem (1661–1751) was an inventive genius springing from most unlikely beginnings. After the deaths of both father and uncle he was left, at age twelve, completely on his own. As a hired boy on a farm his skill with figures was discovered; soon he had access to a workshop and was making things — everything from scissors to clocks. He yearned for learning and tried to acquire Latin by using a dictionary. At age twenty-five he had at last the opportunity to study in Uppsala where he came to know Olof Rudbeck and other scholars, but demands on his ingenuity in clock repair and the making of machines made study difficult. His mechanical genius brought him to the notice of the Board of Mines (*Bergskollegium*) and of Karl XI and led to a guaranteed annual stipend, a prolonged study trip to England and the continent, and several enticing offers from abroad. But Polhem stayed in Sweden, invented and constructed a siphon-pump for the mines in Falun and a machine for raising ore, planned and started a canal across the country, built a dry dock, invented tools and household utensils, constructed bridges and sawmills — the list is much longer. He built his own workshop at Stjärnsund and taught mechanics to students both foreign and Swedish — one of them was Emanuel Swedenborg, with whom he also discussed metaphysics. Polhem was a mechanical wizard, not a theoretical scholar, and his real concern was to make Sweden a great industrial nation.[13]

The greatest of the purely scientific scholars in the period preceding the Age of Freedom was Olof Rudbeck (1630–1702). He was a versatile and independent researcher, an able administrator as rector of Uppsala University, and an inspiring teacher. His practice of empirical method in anatomical research and his keenness in interpretation led him to the discovery of the lymphatic system and to a more thorough interpretation than that of the Dane Thomas Bartholin, whose discovery came at the same time. Probably his most important contribution was his strong sponsorship of Cartesian philosophy and the freedom of research against the rigidities of scholasticism. Rudbeck it was, too, who constructed the renowned anatomical theater on top of Uppsala's *Gustavianum*. In later life his fervent patriotism and bold imagination ran away with him as he proclaimed in his famous *Atlantica* that Sweden was the original garden of Eden, the vagina of the universe — such absurdities can be forgiven in the light of his substantial achievements.[14]

Urban Hiärne (1641–1724) came under the influence of Rudbeck and Petrus Hoffvenius at Uppsala, traveled on the continent like other aspiring Swedish medics, and received his doctorate in medicine at Angers in France. He became the physician of Karl XI, but his profound interest was in chemical research. He analyzed water, developed and manufactured medicines, and investigated formic acid. Although he was a disciple of Paracelsus and something of a mystic, his laboratory in Stockholm was a most practical stimulus to future chemical research. He was married three times and had twenty-five children; one of his descendants was the eminent historian Harald Hjärne.[15]

Emanuel Svedberg, Swedenborg (1688–1772), was one of the most widely accomplished of the eighteenth-century scientists, although he is better remembered for his religious than for his scientific contribution. His father was a leading churchman — court chaplain, professor, bishop. At Uppsala the son reacted somewhat against religious influences and became enamored with the mechanics of Polhem. When he took his study tour to England and the continent his interest was concentrated on Newton, on clock and instrument makers, and on his own mechanical inventions. Back home he gained a close relationship with Polhem and from 1716 to 1718 edited the first Swedish scientific journal, *Daedalus Hyperboreus*, devoted largely to Polhem's inventions. His eager mind wrestled with the problem of measuring longitude — his solution used the moon, and it satisfied no one but himself. He was experimental and observational in method, but he often reached conclusions too soon. In the field of geology his soundest work was probably the proof that Sweden had once been submerged — by evidence of shell banks on the west coast and fossils at high points. But Swedenborg's intense activity dealt more and more with speculative matters, the attempt to explain the origin of the universe. Most successful, in the light of later investigation, was his theory that the planets had been thrown off from the sun. As he moved on into studies of the human soul he became the first to locate the seat of bodily motor functions in the lobes of the brain, and he thought the soul was also based in the cortex of the brain. He thus united scientific investigation and analysis with visionary theosophy.[16]

Anders Celsius (1701–44) came from academic rather than clerical origins. His father and both grandfathers had occupied the chair of astronomy at Uppsala, but the discipline was in a weak state. When Anders Celsius was given the professorship in 1730 it was partly because of his announced intention of making an early study trip to continental seats of learning. He made enough of an impression in Paris that he was invited to go as a member of a French expedition to measure a meridian of latitude in northern Sweden, part of an attempt to settle the disputed question of the shape of the earth — was it flattened at the poles and bulging at the center? From one July to the next (1736–37), battling mosquitoes in summer and stinging cold in winter, the expedition carried on its work, finally choosing two base points for the triangular measurement on the Torne River. This research team wrestled literally with the cold reality of experimental science. Working together with the well-trained French astronomers was an excellent opportunity for the young Swede. The proof the group sought and found was convincing enough that the opposition was soon silenced. After a five-year absence Celsius took up his duties at Uppsala in 1737, established the first astronomical observatory in Sweden, and developed the 100° thermometer that came to bear his name (although he used 100° for freezing and 0° for the boiling point). His was a productive career though he died at age forty-three.[17]

Medical education in Sweden was in sad condition in the early eighteenth century, and most doctors had to get their training abroad. Nils Rosén von Rosenstein (1706–23), another son of the manse, as a child during the plague was literally snatched from the gravediggers by his mother.[18] He began his teaching at Uppsala in 1731 after studying in Halle, Turin, Paris, Leyden, and other centers and receiving a degree from Harderwijk. He employed clinical methods, practiced dissection and inoculation, and used quinine for malaria. Among his writings were a practical text on anatomy and a large number of scientific and pedagogical works. Internationally he became widely known for his pediatric studies and advice. His articles appeared in the almanacs of the Swedish Academy of Science and formed the basis for his *Instruction on*

*Childhood Diseases and their Treatment*, which was translated into German, English, French, Dutch, and Hungarian. A paragraph from the chapter on nursing may illustrate his direct and popular style:

> If the child is to thrive it must have good and adequate food. Its best food is incontrovertibly its mother's milk; and therefore it is observed that children feel good if they drink their mother's milk even if it does not meet all the requirements which must be met by a wet-nurse's milk before it can be approved; but if another child takes the same milk it immediately begins to feel bad. For that reason mothers who have milk are under an obligation to feed their children with their own milk. The mother wins much by it. She at least has a milder confinement, and the child acquires her dispositions and tendencies. Therefore we see that lion cubs which have suckled a cow or goat have become as though tame, while dogs who have suckled a wolf, on the other hand, have become predatory.[19]

Pioneering in the neglected field of pediatrics, Nils Rosen was far more than a Dr. Spock of the eighteenth century. He practiced as well as preached and had a large clientele in Stockholm, beginning with Fredrik I and continuing up to Gustav III, whom he inoculated as a child.

Carl von Linné (born Linnaeus, 1707–78) was the most renowned and most beloved of Sweden's eighteenth-century scientists. His father, vicar of a small parish in southern Småland, maintained for love and recreation a large garden of flowers. He instilled in his boy such a love of nature that in his early school years he could pay attention to nothing else, and his teachers despaired of him. But his unusually winning personality brough him friends and helpers at crucial moments. After an enriching year at the University of Lund he transferred to Uppsala and the study of medicine, for he had to have a profession. He had acquired a prodigious knowledge of plants, partly through the literature available, largely through his own observations, and it was this knowledge and the passionate enthusiasm that went along with it that brought him into contact with the exceptional theologian Olof Celsius (uncle of Anders Celsius) and with the great Olof Rudbeck. Through them he was invited to lecture on botany in the summers of 1730 and 1731, and his career was assured.

"Introduction to the Floral Nuptials" was the title Linné gave to a paper he dedicated in 1730 to his newfound patron Olof Celsius; title and content foreshadowed the work of his life and the happy, naïve spirit in which he approached it. Here was sketched the theory that plants reproduce like animals through the sex organs, stamens (male) and pistils (female). The idea had been adumbrated but not proved; Linné was to prove it and to base on it his great systematizing contributions. In his binomial system of nomenclature every plant or animal was classified according to species and genera. Thus, for example, the species dog became canis familiaris and the species fox became canis vulpis. The simplicity and utility of the method was a tremendous step forward in organizing knowledge. Though he himself did not consider the sexual system as final and continued to seek a natural system of classification, all botanists after him have been deeply in his debt. His binomial nomenclature is accepted as standard to the present day.

In 1732 Linné began with a journey to Lappland the series of trips to the various provinces of Sweden that was to make known the flora and fauna of the entire country in reports that were scientifically accurate and almost poetically appealing. Linné retained a spiritual feeling for nature and a religious attitude toward life, and he is revered to the present day as the Flower King of Sweden.

When Linné undertook the inevitable trip to the continent in 1735 he took with him many manuscripts still unpublished, and it is not too surprising that he was awarded the doctorate in Harderwijk (where the fees were lower than in Leyden) within a week of his arrival. He quickly made admiring friends wherever he went, and they made possible the publication of one paper after another — fourteen during the three years he was abroad. These included *Flora Lapponica*, the report of his Lappland trip, *Genera Plantarium*, on all known genera of plants, and *Systema Naturae*. The last was a seven-folio-page classification of the three natural kingdoms, including the arrangement of plant species on his sexual pattern. Before his death this work was to reach twelve editions and four volumes in size (2,500 pages).

On his return to Sweden Linné went into medical practice in Stockholm, but he soon accepted a professorial appointment at Uppsala. Rivalry, bitter at first, with Nils Rosén, was adjusted by a division of labor. Rosén was to teach practical medicine, anatomy, physiology, and pathology; Linné was to handle botany, *materia medica*, semiology, dietetics, and natural history. Each man had ample scope.

In 1753 Linné published his *Species Plantarium* describing, ordering, and naming over 8,000 species. In 1758 he followed with a parallel work for zoology. His work was gathering and organizing, only to a limited extent experimental. A popular saying was "God created, Linné organized." His work was also to a high degree inspirational, for both the general public and an extraordinary number of student-disciples.[20]

These disciples of Linné went out into the world to discover life, both plant and animal, and particularly plant life. They sent back specimens by the hundreds and thousands. Linné classified and named them and often grew them in his garden. Fredrik Hasselquist traveled to Palestine and the Near East and died in Smyrna in 1752. Per Osbeck and Olof Torén went to China in 1750, and C. Tärnström journeyed to Cambodia. P. Forsskål visited Egypt and Yemen and created a fine herbarium. P. J. Bergius and Anders Sparrman worked in the Cape of Good Hope and later in the Far East. Carl Peter Thunberg traveled to Holland, then to the Cape, and at last to Japan during a nine-year tour, and soon after his return he took the chair of Linné and continued to teach for forty-seven years. Daniel Solander participated in the first expedition of Captain James Cook (1768–71), and Sparrman in the second (1772–75). Per Kalm visited North America, sent back specimens, and wrote a thorough account of his discoveries and experiences. At the same period the Royal Society in London was doing a similar job of amassing information about the wider world beyond Europe's borders, and the French and others were vitally interested. In the field of botany Linné was the unquestioned leader, and in his day Uppsala was the botanical capital of the scholarly world.[21]

Quite naturally the Swedes regret the sale to England, on the death of Linné's son, of the master's scientific collections, some 15,000 plant specimens and 3,000 items of correspondence, manuscripts, etc., which are now housed with the Linnean Society of London.

In three very different fields significant contributions were made by Pehr Wilhelm Wargentin (1717–83). He studied astronomy under Celsius and made notable studies of Jupiter's moons. When in 1748 he was offered a seat in the Swedish Academy of Science he began the task of organizing and stimulating its activities and cultivating international connections. He was asked to formulate methods to handle vital statistics, and he drew up tables of mortality based on precise methods, particularly valuable because Sweden, earlier than any other country, had begun in 1736 (and more systematically in 1749) to collect rather precise population figures.[22]

Among the fields in which Swedes excelled, along with botany, was chemistry. Torbern Bergman (1735–84) studied insect life and astronomy, began his teaching in physics at Uppsala, shifted to mathematics, wrote a pioneering work in physical geography, and in 1767 won the professorship in chemistry. He reorganized the chemistry department, especially the laboratory work, and founded what is known as chemical analysis. In his own research he showed that platinum and nickel were pure elements and thus ended the controversy over their nature. In his *Meditationes de Systemate Fossilium Naturali* he named and classified, and for compounds he suggested a system of symbols that became the predecessors of our modern, Berzelian formulas. He thus paralleled the work of Linné and was placed by his contemporaries on a similarly high pedestal. Already the Swedes were beginning their astonishingly successful work in isolating the chemical elements.[23]

Whereas Bergman was a broadly educated, wide-ranging, extraordinarily able scientist one of his contemporaries and friends was a genius: Carl

Wilhelm Scheele (1742–86). Scheele was born in Swedish Pomerania, at Stralsund, seventh among eleven children. As a boy he determined to become a pharmaceutical chemist and at age fourteen entered apprenticeship in Gothenburg. His employer had a good laboratory and an extensive stock of materials and for eight years young Scheele made the most of his opportunities and developed a precocious scientific perspicacity. He moved briefly to Malmö, to Stockholm, and then to the Lion Apothecary Shop in Uppsala. His constant experimentation revealed new truths; for instance, he discovered barium as an oxide, and he showed that air was a combination of ''fire air'' (oxygen) and ''foul air'' (nitrogen). In Uppsala he came to the attention of Bergman and the ensuing collaboration between the two was of great help to both men. Bergman helped the brilliant nonacademic to get his first papers published, and Scheele was invited to membership in the Academy of Science at age thirty-two. He discovered molybdic acid and tungstic acid and found that pig iron contained carbon and that phosphorus caused cracks in iron. He discovered manganese, glycerin, and a multitude of other substances essential to chemistry and industry. Although he clung too long to the phlogiston theory and made other errors, his positive achievements provided a basis for innumerable later developments. ''Scheele brought to his science knowledge of a greater number of new substances of fundamental importance than any other chemist.''[24]

Scheele's first chance for independence and financial security came when he moved to Köping to manage the apothecary shop inherited by the widow Pohl. He should have married her at once to ''protect'' her and obtain the apothecary rights. But a rival somehow contracted to lease the shop, and Scheele's business and his experimental laboratory were threatened. It took strong pressure from scientists and the provincial governor to get the widow released from the contract, and at length Scheele was enabled to buy the business. On his deathbed he married Mrs. Pohl. Incidentally, this lady then married the incoming apothecary, Bölckou. When she died Bölckou married a woman who outlived him and married two succeeding proprietors. One apothecary shop, two women, five pharmacists, six marriages![25]

The roster of outstanding scientists might be extended to include Johan Carl Wilcke (1732–96), experimental physicist; Charles De Geer (1720–78), scion of the famous and wealthy De Geer family and himself a famous entomologist as well as industrialist; Axel Fredrik Cronstedt (1722–65) and Johan Gottschalk Wallerius (1709–85), mineralogists and chemists; Samuel Klingenstierna (1698–1765), a mathematician whose most notable work was in geometric optics; and a number of others.

This galaxy of talent appeared with little forewarning, though the inventive achievements of Christopher Polhem and the scientific leadership of Olof

Rudbeck were undoubtedly stimulating factors. The military impact of Sweden during the Age of Greatness made the country widely known and probably enhanced the sense of "can do." The collapse of empire made people of both high and low status feel the prod to realize that sense. Once begun, a kind of chain reaction took hold. The friendly cooperation of men like Polhem and Swedenborg, Bergman and Scheele, as well as the early rivalry and competition between others such as Rosén and Linné was productive interaction, having a multiplying effect like that which made great the Florence of the Renaissance. The effect was heightened by the trips abroad through which keen young men became acquainted with like-minded colleagues and often corresponded with them for decades. The interaction was encouraged by the scientific societies both abroad and at home: the Academy of Sciences at Uppsala was started in 1728, and the Royal Swedish Academy of Science was established in Stockholm in 1739 (Linné was one of the five founders). Many of these Swedes won recognition abroad through memberships in foreign scientific societies and offers of high positions, plus the honors and titles and life-long stipends from the government at home. For the Swedish government, dominated by mercantilist thinking, was quite aware of the economic value of the discoveries being made. The Board of Mines (Bergskollegium) encouraged and subsidized research, and in mid-century Sweden was the leading center for metallurgy. The scientists themselves, however much they loved their flowers and laboratories, were eager to realize the utilitarian value of their research. Bergman, for instance, advised Swedish manufacturers how to get the best results, most cheaply, in the preparation of alum, how to improve poor water, and how to produce mineral waters artificially; he told farmers what mineral substances were necessary for plant health. The great accomplishments of the age were not in abstruse theory but in the discovery and organization of the vast wealth that nature provided, thus strengthening the foundations for future scientific work and industrial exploitation. The amazing productivity of this great epoch could not be maintained, but during and after its flowering foreigners were impressed by the pioneering scientific contributions of the Swedes and invited many of them to become members of their own scientific societies. Travelers from southern Europe were eager to see the laboratories of the chemists and made pilgrimages to the gardens of Linné.

## Population, Agriculture, and Mercantilism

In 1720 Sweden was down on its knees, but not on its back. Eighteen years of war, plus three years in rearguard action against Russian raids along the eastern coast, had taken a horrible toll of human life — mostly young male life. Thousands had died in battle or prison camp; thousands of others had been sold by the Russians to Turkey and by Denmark to Venice as galley slaves. Old noble families were especially hard hit, for the young nobles were the first to go to war; family names were eliminated because brothers and sons were gone and the remaining women married outside noble ranks.

Finland suffered the most, losing 16 percent of its population during the period of the Great Northern War (1700–21), and the rest of Sweden lost 10 percent. The Finnish loss was so severe that the government did not collect taxes there for six years. When perhaps 4,000 men returned to Sweden after 1721 they were mostly impoverished and trained for nothing but war. The dearth of able adult males was such that many farms had to be run by woman power. Within the nobility the proportion of the sexes in the 1720s was five women to three men.[26]

But the resiliency of the human race was quickly demonstrated. Within the fifty years after the end of the war Sweden's population recovered from less than 2 million to about 2.6 million (Sweden proper from 1.5 million to 2 million, and Finland from 300,000 to 600,000). The nobility was replenished with new blood, young men came into the government, farms were pushed out into the borderlands. War had ceased to drain off manpower, and throughout the rest of the century the few wars that Sweden fought were short. Perhaps the most vital factor was that the period was free of plagues and disasters. Bad crop years brought only temporary slowdowns in the rising birth rate and increased the death rate only for the aged and infirm. For the most part mild winters made living easier and increased the grain crops. (It should be kept in mind that population was burgeoning throughout Europe after about 1730.)

Gradually a positive governmental policy developed to increase population — at least to try to satisfy the demand for farm labor. With the coming to power of the Hats in 1738 and with the increasing stress on industry the population problem was looked on more seriously, and by the latter half of the century Chydenius and others were deploring emigration and urging population growth. Pre-Malthusian ideas developed at the end of the century, but until then the problem of Sweden was underpopulation, not overpopulation. Governmental concern with population was evidenced by the establishment of systematic statistical records just before mid-century (see the discussion on Pehr Wargentin in the previous section).

In the long run probably the greatest influence on population growth was the potato.[27] Olof Rudbeck had planted a crop in the Uppsala botanical garden in 1658, and Jonas Alströmer tried in 1724 to persuade farmers of the value of the potato. But conservative tillers of the soil hesitated to change crops or methods. During the Pomeranian War (1756–57) and especially after the failure of other crops in 1771–73 the potato began to be prized. And peoples' eyes were opened wider when in 1748 Eva De la Gardie showed that potatoes were excellent for distilling *akvavit*. Finally, Swedes learned to like the taste of the potato itself so that in the nineteenth century the diet on the farms became "fish and potatos" for one meal and "potatos and fish" for the next.

Gustaf Utterström argues that the increase in population inspired a new form of agriculture based on consolidated and individualized farms. It was also true that the reform in land use made possible the increased population. Traditional strip-farming methods, based on the tiny rural villages, could not utilize to advantage the potential of the soil. Livestock foraged in adjacent woodlands and did not spread fertilizer on the land that needed it most. Ditching was difficult because of the many strips, and all the farmers of the village had to plow and harvest at the same time. Most damaging was that the land had to be divided into narrower and narrower strips as families increased in size, diminishing efficiency just when it needed to be enhanced.[28]

Pressures built up also from outside the farm villages. Cities were growing; for example, Stockholm included around 45,000 people in 1718, 73,000 in 1760. As the smaller towns grew from 5,000 to 10,000 or from 10,000 to 20,000 it became more difficult for the individual urban householder to have his own cows or chickens. Demands on farmlands near the towns therefore increased. Milk, butter, meat, vegetables, and other foodstuffs had to be produced near towns because of the lack of easy transportation. For livestock, fodder had to be specially grown, as foraging in the meadows no longer sufficed. Nor could a third of the land be allowed to lie fallow each year. Crop rotation, use of fertilizers, better plowing (as with the Brabant plow), new products — all techniques had to be tried.

Thoughtful writing on agricultural reform appeared in the 1720s and 1730s, and the Academy of Science turned its attention to problems of farming. The purpose of sending Linné on his tours of the provinces was to learn about problems and processes of cultivation. Men studied the experiments in England by searchers like Jethro Tull and Charles (Turnip) Townshend. Individual landowners tried to train their peasant farmers in improved methods. But progress toward change was slow. Jacob Faggot (1699–1777), director of the Land Survey Office and an officer in the Academy of Science, was an eager apostle of reform. His most notable contribution was his advocacy of the *storskifte* (big redivision) of the strip fields. He hoped that ultimately single-family farms would replace the village system, but he realized that this could not happen at once. Legislation of 1757 permitted such redivision and toward the end of the century Rutger Maclean enforced the system on his own lands in Skåne; not until the nineteenth century was more thorough reform realized throughout the country (see chapter X). For the eighteenth century the reduction was seldom more than from 43 strips to 5 or from 30 strips to 6, but where it was done productivity increased. Occasionally one could see lone houses in the fields instead of the cluster of cottages in the villages, but the real reorganization of rural life did not come in the eighteenth century.[29]

Some changes did come. Sheep raising, for example, was encouraged by the mercantilist politicians who wanted to reduce wool imports. They also stimulated a nationwide program of ditching to drain soggy fields. And the clergy must be credited with spreading information about proper drainage, animal husbandry, crop rotation, and other agricultural innovations; to a considerable extent they accomplished their goals by example, for in the rural districts the pastors were small-scale but enlightened farmers.[30]

Government as directed by Arvid Horn and his cohorts in the 1720s was neither as paternalistic as that under Gustav I Vasa nor as mercantilistic as that of the Hats who followed, but it was pragmatic. To get the country back on its feet the government lent seed and money for rebuilding, relaxed restrictions on guilds, and instituted heavy taxation to pay off the debts of war. The administration issued the product decree (*Produktplakatet*) in 1724 forbidding foreign ships to bring to Sweden goods other than the products of their own country or its colonies; like the British Navigation Acts its objective was to stimulate the regrowth of the Swedish merchant marine, which had declined disastrously during the wars. Positive action was pushed farther afield than before; Sweden made treaties of friendship and trade with Algeria (1729), Tunisia (1736), Turkey (1737), France and Tripoli (1741), the two Sicilies (1742), and Morocco (1763). In 1731 the riksdag chartered the East India Company and in 1738 the Levantine Company was founded for trade in the eastern Mediterranean.

Encouragement of manufacturing became a prime interest of the politicians, and many nobles became directly involved. The House of the Nobles itself owned three-fourths of the factory at Barnängen, and individual nobles invested in the Alingsås factory begun in 1724 by Jonas Alströmer. This enterprising leader had come home after experience in England and convinced officials and riksdagsmen that his plant and his ideas could show the way for a great expansion of Swedish industry. Goods were individually produced — no mass production, no assembly lines. Ribbons, stockings, gloves, hats, pins, dyes, wallpaper — all were made in the same factory. Alströmer used government support effectively, and although his factory did not make money it encouraged others and introduced new methods. Linné visited the factory and wrote of it in lyrical style. In other factories were made wool and silk, glass and china — the most famous factory for china became the Rörstrand factory, founded in 1729. Yet even by 1759 industries employed only 18,000 workers, less than 1 percent of the population.

Moderation marked the mercantilism of the 1720s and 1730s, owing to the dearth of capital and pressing immediate problems. With the coming of the Hats in the late 1730s a more vigorous policy became evident. The riksdag set up a Manufacturing Office in 1739, increased tariffs, and granted privileges to industry: free land for factories, freedom from tariffs on imported raw materials and machines, even freedom from taxes on owners and employees. Home crafts were encouraged, too, and merchants cooperated with peddlers in organized buying and selling of homemade products — spun and woven goods, metal crafts, wood articles.

The government was most interested in the development of industrial technology in such fields as iron production and shipbuilding. Great merchants, shippers, and manufacturers flourished. The social policies of the *bruk*, the decentralized rural-located iron works, were sometimes ahead of legislative controls: the *bruk* paid pensions to the widows of workers and compensation to men injured on the job. Manufacture of iron goods like steel, nails, and tools increased during the 1750s and was later to make Sweden famous. To promote such industries the Ironmasters' Association (*Jernkontoret*) was founded in 1747.

The Ironmasters' Association is an outstanding example of the close cooperation between private business and government. It was started with the blessing of the Secret Committee of the riksdag and promoted everything pertaining to iron, Sweden's most important resource in the eighteenth century. The Association provided advisers (*övermästare*) who helped the members to develop new techniques and new products and so to guide development as to balance supply with demand. Fees collected on the basis of production built a capital fund and enabled the association to arrange for credits for the ironmasters. It served as a kind of bank in cooperation with the Riksbank and was accused of promoting inflation. Despite certain large operations, such as Louis De Geer's munitions works, the bulk of mining and processing of iron was done in small scattered mills and a coordinating body was essential. Kurt Samuelsson for the year 1777 lists 227 iron mills, some of which occasionally combined.[31]

In the 1650s a Dutch-Balt named Johan W. Palmstruch had established a bank in Stockholm, but he had overreached himself. The riksdag then established in 1668 the national bank or Riksbank (300 years later the world's oldest extant bank). It was under careful regulation — at first. But the Hats used the Riksbank to support their subsidies to industry, and when taxes and tariffs were insufficient the printing presses began to roll. Soon inflation created trouble. The Caps came back to office and deflated too drastically. The total effect was monetary confusion which added to the chaos that Gustav

III tried to correct. Part of the difficulty was the attempt to maintain a copper standard and to reconcile the value of the copper and the paper currency of the bank.

Financing was particularly complicated in connection with foreign trade. Producers in Sweden did not have a sufficient capital base to permit them to wait for payment, a process that might be long delayed because of the slowness of transportation. The Riksbank was authorized to lend money on fixed property and iron, later on other products, but this was insufficient for the capital needed. Therefore a system of bills of exchange was developed which meant virtually that some banking house in Hamburg or Amsterdam bought the export product and paid for it before it left Sweden, then collected from the customer in, for example, England. The bill of exchange used in payment could be transferred by the Swedish exporter to an importer who could use it to pay for goods he purchased abroad. The system was of course much more complex than in this simple example, but it worked smoothly and to everyone's satisfaction — the bankers included.[32]

In the eighteenth century Sweden's exports, so dear to the hearts of the mercantilists, consisted largely of iron, copper, and tar; iron accounted for three-fourths of the total. England was the chief purchaser, and it was the favorable balance of trade with England that made it possible for Sweden to buy foodstuffs and other products from eastern Europe and Germany. (See table.) The balance was disturbed toward the end of the century when England tried to free itself from dependence on Swedish suppliers. Swedish controls had pushed prices to high levels, and for the best quality bar iron these prices could be maintained. But the prices also encouraged competitors, especially Russia, to enter the market, and by the early nineteenth century Swedish iron export was in difficulty. Russia was profiting from the expansion of British

Swedish Exports of Bar Iron
(in percentage of total volume)

| Year | Britain | Netherlands | Baltic Countries | Latin Countries |
|---|---|---|---|---|
| 1738–39 | 60.5 | 10 | 19.5 | 10 |
| 1745–49 | 57 | 9 | 24 | 10 |
| 1755–59 | 62 | 7 | 21 | 10 |
| 1765–69 | 56.5 | 8.5 | 22.5 | 12.5 |
| 1775–79 | 53 | 6 | 19.5 | 21.5 |
| 1785–89 | 48 | 4.5 | 15.5 | 32 |
| 1795–99 | 50 | 3 | 27 | 20 |

Source: Kurt Samuelsson, From Great Power to Welfare State (London: Allen and Unwin, 1968), p. 91.

demand, while Swedish sales were dropping off. Sweden sought compensation in the markets of France and Portugal, which bought not only bar iron but hardware and other finished products. Since Sweden's fuel for smelting was limited to charcoal its production was limited to high quality and therefore expensive varieties of iron, a situation that discouraged innovation and that continued until the middle of the nineteenth century when new processes were developed. At least one Swedish critic complained, nevertheless, that Swedish manufacturers and merchants were at fault for failing to adapt their products to what people wanted to buy.[33]

Copper production continued to increase to the 1770s, and prices held up largely because of the Spanish use of copper in coinage. The crown, through its share of mine ownership as well as through taxes, long continued to reap good revenue from copper as well as from iron. In the production and export of tar, important for ship maintenance, Finland was especially important, and again Sweden's monopolistic price policies probably encouraged both Russia and the American colonies to join the competition.[34]

Swedish fascination with the Far East dates far back, and with good reason. As Swedes saw the spectacular profits of the Dutch and the English East India companies they wanted a share of the action and in 1731 founded the Swedish East India Company (*Ostindiska Kompaniet*). It lived on until the Revolutionary and Napoleonic Wars; in 1813 it closed out its business and, horrible for a historian to record, burned all remaining records. Actually, most records were burned year by year to assure secrecy and, probably, to safeguard smuggling operations. In the East India Company's first charter period of fifteen years profits averaged 30 percent per year. By the terms of control its ships had to be built and/or owned in Sweden. During the life of the company these numbered forty-odd and made 132 expeditions. They were built mostly in Stockholm, they had to be sturdy enough for voyages of fourteen to twenty-seven months, and they had to be capacious.[35]

Outbound the ships carried mostly iron, some of which they left in Cadiz and various ports along the way. They picked up as much as they could of Spanish piasters, eagerly sought after in China. "The clank of the piasters is our music," wrote Jacob Wallenberg in his serious-humorous account of a trip in 1769, *Min son på Galejan*.[36] If their sails carried them through the hazards of the sea and the obstacles that might be put in their way by the English or the Dutch they came eventually to Canton. There the supercargo, the real boss of the expedition, would negotiate with the Chinese mandarins for the exchange of goods. In the early years the supercargo was usually a foreigner (Colin Campbell, for example), a man who had obtained his first experience with the Orient in service with the English or the Dutch. Gradually the Swedes themselves learned about the East and replaced the Scots and the Dutch and others. The East India Company provided adventure and served as a school in seamanship, geography, languages, and commerce.

Homeward the ships brought the rich luxury items of the other side of the world: raw silk and silk goods, cotton cloth, lacquer, mother-of-pearl, handsome porcelain often made to order, and, the largest import, tea. One vessel made its way safely out and back but then sank in the harbor of Gothenburg, fully loaded with porcelain; in the twentieth century the cargo was recovered and makes an extraordinary display in a museum in Gothenburg. Most of this fragile beauty has disappeared through the years in the kitchens of Europe. Since the goods of the East Indiamen were expensive luxuries they were sold at great auctions in Gothenburg, to which merchants from the continent flocked.

Tea was a special case. Not only did it comprise half the cargos brought in from the Far East, but some 90 percent of it was re-exported for the English market and it brought as much cash return as all other Swedish exports. The reason was clear. The tea craze had captured England, and their East India Company was granted a monopoly on imports. The government had to cash in on something on which duties could be easily collected; when excise taxes were added the total by 1735 amounted to 100 percent of the value of the tea on entry. Import restrictions further inflated prices. Here was an open invitation to smugglers. When the Ostend Company, ostensibly Austrian but really Scottish, was shut down on English demand, the Scots moved operations to Scandinavia (the Danish East Asiatic Company was founded right after the Swedish company). So these two companies brought from Canton the Bohea tea which was popular with the English, and these two companies imported more tea than did the English. Some tea they sold in their own and continental cities, some they sailed directly to English ports. They collected such vast sums that national finances were strongly affected. And when at last the English lowered their duties (a mean trick), it ruined the smuggling business; that and the Revolutionary wars destroyed the Swedish East India Company and forced the Danish East Asiatic Company to shift its operations into other channels.[37]

A natural complement to the smuggled importation of tea to England was the smuggling out of English exports, especially to the Barbary states with whom, as already noted, the Swedish government made a series of trade treaties. Much of this illicit trade in both directions continued even during the Seven Years War and the other wars of the century — trade was not nationalistic.

These few highlights of economic activity in the eighteenth century illustrate an eager mercantilism in the first half of the century slowly fading into policies of relaxed controls and a philosophy and practice of laissez faire. C. F. Scheffer and others were influenced by the French physiocrats, although probably more strongly by Anders Chydenius. Chydenius anticipated Adam Smith by several years, though his voice did not reach beyond Swedish borders. In the closing years of the century, in Sweden and throughout Europe, the emphasis on economic affairs became overshadowed by the dominance of war and political turmoil.

# X

# THE GUSTAVIAN ERA

ECONOMIC AFFAIRS continued to be debated throughout the eighteenth century, and scientists continued their research. But the atmosphere of Sweden, and the cultural focus, changed dramatically in the early 1770s. Not only did mercantilism yield to more liberal policies in industry and trade but the whole utilitarian emphasis weakened while the fine arts were brought to center stage, and the theater was more honored than the factory or the laboratory. The transformation was brought about by the new young king, Gustav III.

Despite political strife and futile warfare there was an aura that surrounded the Gustavian epoch. Wine glasses with the well-known Gustav III monograms and the furniture of the age are still prized for their nostalgic value, summoning memories of drama and gaiety. (A furniture company, Gustavianska Möbler, had its trucks on the streets of Stockholm in the late twentieth century.) Gustav, like John Kennedy, cast a spell over many of the people about him, a glamor and vitality that roused national pride and that has never been forgotten. The luster of the court was something unique for Sweden, something rare to find anywhere. It was witty, glittering, a bit superficial, in sharp contrast to the scientific seriousness of the Age of Freedom. The atmosphere was charged, as it were, with a current of sparkling energy. Within its own little realm of the court, the aristocracy, and the urban bourgeosie, the Swedish Age of Enlightenment was genuine, perhaps more real than that of Joseph II in Austria or Fredrick II in Prussia — but how can we compare it with France? France, along with ancient Rome, was its inspiration and prototype. It was Gustav who struck the spark and it was the pistol shot in the opera twenty years later that snuffed it out. For after 1792 the Gustavian Age continued, strictly speaking, with Gustav IV Adolf, but the touch of the master was gone, stodginess succeeded brilliance, and by 1809 the dynasty was overthrown.

## *Gustav III (1746–92; King, 1771–92)*

The enigmatic Gustav III has been characterized in words both multitudinous and contradictory: charming, open and natural, domineering, undependable, true-and-false-blended, intriguing, lying, shifting, sanguine, imaginative, liberal, histrionic, effeminate, two-faced, philosopher-king, and so on. No one has called him dull or uninteresting. And no one has quite satisfactorily explained him. Yet he was the star of the show, stamping an age with his name and his personality.[1]

Gustav was five years old when his father came to the throne, and he had ample opportunity to watch the demeaning struggle of the king-in-name with the real holders of power. He was protected and loved by his ambitious mother Louisa Ulrika and most solicitously guided through every hour of the day. The queen mother favored her first-born over the other children, but she "loved in order to master," and the boy came to hate her as well as to love her; he resented her domination and her lapses into indifference. Before he was four years old he was given as governor the wise and kindly statesman Carl Gustaf Tessin, and the boy and the man developed a mutual affection. But within a few years political disagreements caused the Estates to replace Tessin with Carl Fredrik Scheffer, whose concern with economics was not especially to the boy's taste. Olof Dalin was his early tutor in history and geography and evidently made a lasting impression; the prince was specially drawn to the hero-kings of Sweden and to French history and culture. He learned French so well that he always spoke and wrote it better than Swedish. The conflicts and intrigues around him, the divergent attitudes of his royalist mother and the freedom-minded Estates who appointed his instructors taught the sensitive and brilliant child to dissemble, and he never learned to follow a straight path.

From his early years the imaginative prince loved the theater, often provided, through his mother's interest, by visiting French troupes. He loved to act and the theater became his chief recreation, almost an avocation. He wrote plays, directed them, designed staging and costumes, and when he could not carry through completely he drafted plays and had others (Johan Henrik Kellgren and later Carl Gustaf af Leopold) put them in final form. His critics complained that he thought of life as a play and of his job as that of an actor in statecraft; his reign was described as a twenty-year masquerade. "All the world's a stage, And all the men and women merely players." Gustav would have loved to play in life the part of Gustav I Vasa or of Gustav II Adolf. He was proud of the few drops of Vasa blood in his veins and of the fact that he was the first Swedish-born king since Karl XII.

When he reached the throne at age twenty-five the third Gustav was at least well trained for the job. But there were already problems. At five years of age he had been betrothed to Sofia Magdalena of Denmark and in 1766, for diplomatic reasons, the marriage ceremony had to be performed. But Sofia Magdalena was shy to an extreme and nonintellectual, Gustav was cold and undersexed, and although both tried to make something of the marriage it remained always a strained relationship. She was good-hearted, pious, and felt an aversion to the theater that her husband adored. Worst, she was hated by Louisa Ulrika, and "like a pale and silent ghost she wandered about a court that was one day to be her own, unamused by its amusements, and joyless amidst its joys."[2] The son who was to become Gustav IV Adolf was not born until 1778, and then there were nasty rumors about his parentage (rumors that the queen mother believed).

The immediate problem on Gustav's accession was that he was on a trip to Paris when Adolf Fredrik died. He was having a marvelous experience in France, visiting with Louis XVI, conversing with many of the outstanding philosophers of the day (including d'Alembert, Rousseau, the elder Mirabeau, Quesnay), watching theater and best of all establishing acquaintance with the intellectual ladies of the Paris salons. He carried on a lively correspondence for years with the Countess Boufflers especially, and in these letters Gustav's changing ideas of politics can best be observed.[3] The French seemed to be as entranced with the lively Swede as he was with them. During this youthful period he was, or seemed to be, extremely liberal, sincerely concerned with the welfare of the common people, though never of course thinking of himself as one of them. Hence Gustav returned to Sweden glowing with the pleasure of sympathetic and stimulating friendships and with high ideals about the duties of a citizen king.

Before going to France the prince had read P.F.J.H. Le Mercier de la Rivière's *L'Order naturel et essentiel des sociétés politiques* (1767) and had found himself inspired by and warmly in agreement with the thoughts therein about the duties of a hereditary monarch with full executive power and a sense of reciprocal interests between king and nation. Through public education, a free judiciary, and freedom of expression the true happiness of all could be attained. Ideals of responsible monarchy dominated his thinking at the time of his accession. On his way home from Paris he wrote a letter condemning the autocracy of Karl XI and another deploring "anarchy and dissolution" and expressing respect for "liberty, properly understood, founded on reason and humanity." In June of 1772 he wrote Mme. de Boufflers about the "onslaught of Democracy against the expiring Aristocracy, the latter preferring to submit to Democracy rather than be protected by Monarchy, which opens its arms to it."[4] Such statements are in line with two draft constitutions he had drawn up in 1766 and 1768.

Here and throughout much of his reign one seems to sense the king's ambivalence toward the aristocracy — he was one of them, really; he loved them and wanted them to love him. But they foolishly opposed the monarchy in its attempts to move with what he considered the current of the times. Hence, although now he would work with them, he would later feel forced to go against them.

But it was a young and buoyant king who in the spring of 1771 returned to Sweden with renewed French subsidies and encouragement to strengthen the kingship through conciliatory methods. He tried. When the Estates met in June the king, for the first time in 100 years, spoke directly to them. "Born and raised among you I have from infancy learned to love my fatherland, to consider it the greatest good fortune to be Swedish and the greatest honor to be the first citizen among a free people."[5] But the oppositional Caps gained majorities in all except the nobles' Estate of the riksdag. The strong political discontent at the end of the Age of Freedom was directed mainly against the governing aristocracy and was to some extent democratic in spirit. The momentum of this new democracy carried the Caps to stronger and stronger demands. They turned out the Hats, planned a new alliance with Russia, and declared that all men regardless of rank had the right to hold office on the basis of merit. By 1772 two years of crop failures had spread hunger through the land and the new officials did little to help the need. From abroad came the frightening news of the first partition of Poland. Both Russia and Prussia also coveted parts of Swedish territory and Denmark would always be ready to grab its share if opportunity offered. At the moment Russia was involved in a war with Turkey and therefore could not intervene. Gustav III decided it was time to act. He would not even wait for the coordination of Prince Karl's premature revolt in Skåne and the Finnish rising that was being organized by Colonel Sprengtporten.

In the early morning of August 19, 1772 King Gustav took communion and then reviewed the guard. He gathered a small group of officers and asked if they would protect him as he was in danger. They shouted their support and then he got the assent of the troops in the courtyard. There followed a triumphal march through the streets, the arrest of the council, the pledges of support by the administrators, and finally the assemblage of the Estates in the state hall on the twenty-first. In a speech from the throne Gustav condemned the corruption and intrigue of aristocratic despotism, demanded a return to the ancient laws of the realm, and presented a new constitution. The coup d'état was bloodless and complete, immediately accepted by a relieved and hopeful public. The cost of 300,000 livres was paid by France, which sought thereby to strengthen its traditional Swedish ally.

The Gustavian constitution of 1772 was founded upon the ancient maxim:

"The king shall rule the kingdom, he and none other." Yet modifications of this autocratic dictum were significant. The revised form of government, vague in its details, had been composed by Gustav III in consultation with his old tutor and friend Scheffer. The council and all officials were made responsible to the king and could comment but not vote. Some officers were appointed by the king and could be removed by him, though the highest officials had tenure, which was expressly guaranteed in 1786. Promotion was to be based on experience and ability, without respect to favor or birth "when these cannot be found together with ability."[6] Not only in the bureaucracy but also in the riksdag the nobles had to accept limitations, for the new constitution emphasized the provision introduced in 1720 that votes of the four Estates did not have to be unanimous and that even the nobles must bow to a decision approved by the other three Estates (a rule reinforced in 1786). The king might call the Estates when he wished, and he directed foreign policy, but he was not allowed to declare an offensive war without the consent of the riksdag. In judicial processes the king's right was limited; in administrative and economic regulations he had exclusive authority; for general law making, king and riksdag each had initiative and veto power over the other. Return to the laws and customs practiced before 1680 gave the king undefined but important powers in relation to the riksdag, such as naming the speakers for the Estates (except for the clergy, whose speaker was normally the archbishop). The reinstallation of the three-class system in the nobles' Estate was intended to restore preponderance to the upper nobility, from whom Gustav hoped for support. The Secret Committee was abolished and the only important standing committees became the bank committee and the committee of state, each with representatives from the three higher Estates.

Gustav did not shirk the responsibilities he had shouldered but began immediately his work to direct the relief against famine and to bolster Sweden's defenses. Russia and Prussia had promised to block a constitutional change in Sweden, but they were occupied with other problems and were not prepared to use force; only Denmark made threatening military gestures. Gustav rode the *Eriksgata* through the western provinces and strengthened the defense organization as well as national morale. The Danes reconsidered. Once the danger of war had passed Gustav turned his attention to government reorganization. He built a council of men from both parties, forbade use of the old party labels, and the days of the Hats-Caps rivalry were over. Gustav leaned to the nobility in his appointments, especially in the army, but he brought in able younger men and the ideal of service came again to have some meaning.

In an age of enlightened despots Gustav III was by disposition probably as despotic as Catherine II or Frederick II or Maria Theresa, and he was more enlightened. But he was also deeply interested in justice for the individual and he directed reform: during the 1770s the status of illegitimate children was improved, torture was abolished, cases requiring the death penalty reduced, and after an investigation of the actions of judges and administrative officers a number of them were removed from office. After careful preparation the paper currency (in circulation since 1745) was replaced on January 1, 1777 with a silver-based coinage system, whose unit was the riksdaler. Partly for economic reasons and partly in recognition of simple justice, religious freedom was extended in 1781 to foreigners, though not to natives. From Count Gustav Philip Creutz, the Swedish minister in Paris, came an appreciative response: "Your Majesty will be the idol of the people and the hero of humanity." [7]

In 1782 Jews were permitted to build synagogues, but they were restricted to certain cities and could not buy land, marry outside their faith, and carry on handicrafts. In 1781, though opposed by the clerics, the king declared a limited toleration for Christians who were not Lutheran, including Roman Catholics. Excess holidays were eliminated — for example, the third and fourth days after Christmas and Easter — as a measure to increase productivity. In the spirit of the times Gustav tried to inaugurate a national dress for the sake of both economy and national pride, but it was not widely used except for the academic costume that survived in part into the twentieth century. He promoted the building of hospitals, new prisons, dockyards, canals.

One of the really serious problems of the Age of Freedom was the corruption of riksdagsmen and officials by bribes from foreign governments. Sometimes such funds were paid for the deliberate purpose of encouraging party strife and maintaining Swedish weakness. Sometimes it was the reverse, and even Gustav III used French grants to help put through his coup d'état. Riksdagsmen were unsalaried, and often they took foreign money merely to do what they would have done anyway. Nevertheless it was a vicious and demeaning system. Gustav III realized its dangers and by both strengthening royal authority and reinvigorating Swedish pride he did much to diminish if not quite to eliminate this disruptive interference.

Some "reforms" hit the peasantry hard. To protect the king's holdings farmers were denied the right to buy crown lands, and this restriction galled them until it was abolished late in the reign. Most widely annoying was the prohibition of the right to distill privately the beloved *akvavit* or *brännvin* (brandy). This was introduced in 1772 to save grain during a period of famine. By 1775 the hardship had passed but now the government established crown distilleries for the sake of revenue and continued to forbid private operations. The degree of success against home distilling approximated that attained in Kentucky during the prohibition era. The new system was a failure financially, too, for the government had formerly collected more money from taxes than it now did from its own distilleries.

Gustav loved freedom, at least in theory. However, the freedom of the press law of 1766 was too permissive for his taste. In 1774 he issued his own law on the subject. He omitted the paragraphs guaranteeing the right to publish riksdag affairs and to discuss relations with foreign powers, and he made further change easy by giving the act the status of ordinary, not constitutional law. Physiocratic theory guided his action. Anders Schönberg, state historian under Gustav III, wrote of the values of vagueness, and with this Gustav was in full sympathy. As people increasingly used their right to express their dissatisfactions the king grew increasingly sensitive to criticism. In 1780 he issued a decree wherein he affirmed that no individual should be punished for his opinions, but that the guilty one was he who spread criminalities. Therefore the publisher was to be held primarily responsible. The publishers of Stockholm thereupon petitioned for the reinstallation of censorships so that they could know before rather than after what was regarded as punishable. Censorship was not reintroduced, but regulations became tighter and tighter, just at a time when the rest of Europe was approaching the freer position that Sweden had taken in 1766. Gustav III also used the threat of legal process to force people to write his own denunciatory propaganda. He quietly suppressed publication of the riksdag debates. His words were fairer than his deeds, and in actuality writers and publishers were free only in their right to agree with the king.[8]

Gustav's changeable nature is epitomized in his attitude toward freedom of the press, as is also the change wrought by time. In the early years, full of the conviction that he was right and that everyone must recognize his sense of justice and work with him, he moved about among the people, inspired an intellectual court life, and led people by his eager persuasiveness. As problems and antagonisms accumulated he turned to more forceful ways to attain his objectives. He was annoyed by the opposition in the riksdags of 1778 and 1786, and in 1786 he became particularly disillusioned with the attitude of the nobles. These contretemps influenced his shift of interest from domestic reforms to foreign adventure and his attempt to curry favor with the nonnoble Estates, preparing the way for the explosion of 1788–89. Some of the change may have been attributable to the withdrawal of the wise restraining hand of Ulrik Scheffer, chancellor from 1772 to 1783. After the two-year service of Gustav Philip Creutz, poet and long-term ambassador to France, Gustav became his own foreign minister in 1785. Then he could exercise to the full his personal charm and his penchant for intrigue. In both foreign and domestic affairs impulsiveness and unpredictability became more marked. Catherine the Great of Russia wrote to him directly charging, "You are about as reticent as a cannon shot."[9]

Toward the New World Gustav had mixed emotions — admiration for the heroic spirit of the American patriots counteracted by hatred of the revolutionary spirit. A number of Swedes served in the armies of the American Revolution, including Axel Fersen, Curt von Stedingk, two barons Hierta, and Count Adolf Ribbing. Although Gustav prohibited it, Pehr Ulric Lilliehorn served while on leave from the Swedish army. Sweden gained from the war at least a corps of experienced officers. Before the war was over Gustav let it be known that he would like a treaty of friendship and commerce made through Benjamin Franklin, and in 1783 Sweden was the first of the neutral states to make such a treaty with the new republic. Sweden then was happy to receive Franklin's son as its first diplomatic representative from America.[10]

Gustav had long desired a foothold in the western hemisphere and rightly judged that he was most likely to get it through France. The French minister Vergennes was helpful, and after several years of correspondence and negotiation France in 1784 turned over to Sweden the island of St. Bartholomew in the West Indies. France hoped to win gratitude and commerce from its northern ally, and it cost little to part with this undeveloped island. There was a port, now named Gustavia, that had the potential for becoming important especially in wartime trade. Sweden's export to the New World had been mostly herring, but it had dreams of selling iron in quantity. Gustavia became the American base of the Swedish West Indies Company (1786–1805), and during the Napoleonic wars it prospered. As a colony St. Bartholomew was more like the trading posts on the African coast in the seventeenth century than like the mainland bases of the powers, and it bred no illusions of conquest.[11]

The king's attitude toward Russia alternated between fear and friendliness, while his attitude toward Denmark was antipathy occasionally masked by treaty cooperation. Thus in 1779–80 Sweden, Russia, and several other powers, even Denmark to a lesser extent, could cooperate in the Armed Neutrality to protect their common interests against Great Britain. But by 1783 Gustav was attempting to get from the Empress Catherine an agreement that would give him a free hand with Denmark; he wriggled away from Catherine's suggestion for a three-state alliance instead. He wanted Norway and he wanted a "northern system," but not a system dominated by Russia or including Denmark. After he failed in 1783 to win Catherine II away from her alliance with Denmark he turned to the idea of war against Russia, hoping for Polish and Turkish cooperation, with the Porte (Turkey) paying subsidies to

Sweden, the intended result, of course, the reestablishment of the Swedish-controlled balance of power in the Baltic. In November 1787 Gustav visited Copenhagen, trying to get Denmark, already allied with Russia, to join a coalition against Russia. He got assurances of friendship but was left to face Russia alone when he declared war in June 1788. In the meantime he was pressed by internal discontent, including an open attack in the riksdag on his growing despotism.

Would war put discontent to rest and bring Gustav III the glory he craved? In 1783 he had contemplated war against Denmark, but he had to yield to opposition and shelve the idea. He knew that Russia and Denmark were working to undermine the Swedish constitution and the Swedish-French alliance. His hands were nevertheless tied by the constitutional provision that he could not make aggressive war. He had to wait. But not for long. The outbreak of a new Russo-Turkish war in 1787 provided an opportunity that he could not afford to miss. He might after all recreate a defensible frontier in the east by regaining the southeast corner of Finland that had been lost in 1721 and 1743; he might show himself to be a worthy successor of the great warrior-king Gustav II Adolf; and he might thus reestablish the power of monarchy at home. But obviously Russia would not attack Sweden while it was engaged with Turkey and Gustav could not start a war without consent of the Estates. His ingenuity was equal to this problem, for even if his theatricals deluded no one they succeeded: in June of 1788 he had a troop of Swedish soldiers dress up like Cossacks and attack a Finnish position, after which the Swedes took the Russian fortress of Nyslott; the Russians were forced to counterattack, and war was on. Gustav was already in Finland and preparations had been made for a short, decisive war.

Gustav II Adolf might have accomplished it, or Karl XII. Neither Gustav III nor his generals had the foresight or the military daring or the diplomatic skill to carry it through. The big plan for a seaborne attack on St. Petersburg had to be abandoned early and the war degenerated into a series of minor land and sea engagements along the southeast Finnish border. A number of Finnish officers, disgusted with the course of events and antagonized by the king's flouting of the constitution, in August 1788 sent a letter to Empress Catherine II condemning the illegality of the war, asking for the Finnish boundaries of 1721 and for peace negotiations with "representatives of the nation." Organized as the Anjala Confederation 112 officers continued their extraordinary antiofficial diplomacy until the band dissolved in October. Even the king's brother Karl was for a while associated with it. The diverse goals of the plotters, some personally antagonistic to the king, others opposed to the institution of monarchy, still others working for Finnish separatism, weakened the cohesion needed for any kind of success. Some of the conspirators were treasonable in their propositions to Russia, others were within the bounds of legitimate opposition, but the whole affair was too much like those aristocratic confederations that had reduced Poland to chaos and impotence. Fortunately for the king the tsarina did not trust these rebellious and uncoordinated officers, and the only practical result of their activities was to reinvigorate Gustav's depressed spirits and to rally patriotic citizens to the national cause. Only one of the plotters, Hästesko, was executed; Jägerhorn fled to Russia, and several others were exiled.

Denmark did its part in uniting disgruntled Swedes. When Russia, bogged down in its war with Turkey in the south, called on Denmark-Norway for aid against Sweden the Norwegians invaded western Sweden and the Danes threatened Gothenburg. In this desperate situation Gustav III immediately left the Finnish theater of operations, proceeded straight to Dalarna, and in Mora, on the church embankment where Gustav Vasa had spoken, pleaded for a new national rising and for unification against the external and internal threats to national existence. Now he was in his element, dramatizing his troubles, doing what he did naturally and best. As he went about arousing the people they responded with home guard organizations and troops. They shared the king's horror at the treachery of the noble officers of the Anjala conspiracy and bared their teeth in hatred of the aristocracy as a whole and the "treacherous Jutes."

The nobles became fearful, and the turn of events provided a tempting opportunity for Gustav to amend his own coup d'état. The opposition nobility had been maneuvering to create a new constitution to curb the increase of royal power. Now the king could take the initiative and remake the constitution in line with his own changing ideas. Hence he drew up the Act of Union and Security in early 1789, and he considered the time propitious to call a meeting of the riksdag. Through this package of reforms he speeded up the process of equalization among the Estates, to the bitter discomfiture of the nobles. He had already been governing with the advice of commissions rather than the council, and now he simply abolished that ancient body. "Experts," irrespective of birth, would henceforth form the bureaucracy. The king set up a new court composed half of nobles and half of nonnobles and created in the riksdag a smaller Secret Committee, with representatives of all four Estates. To each of the nonprivileged Estates he made various concessions, most significant being the restoration to the farmers of the right to buy tax-privileged (*frälse*) land and to hold all their lands in absolute ownership. Thus the last vestiges of feudal ideas were swept away. Both middle class and peasantry were now free to develop. The king assumed the complete direction of administration, the initiative in legislation, and the right to declare war. The only expansion of the rights of the riksdag was in the realm of financial

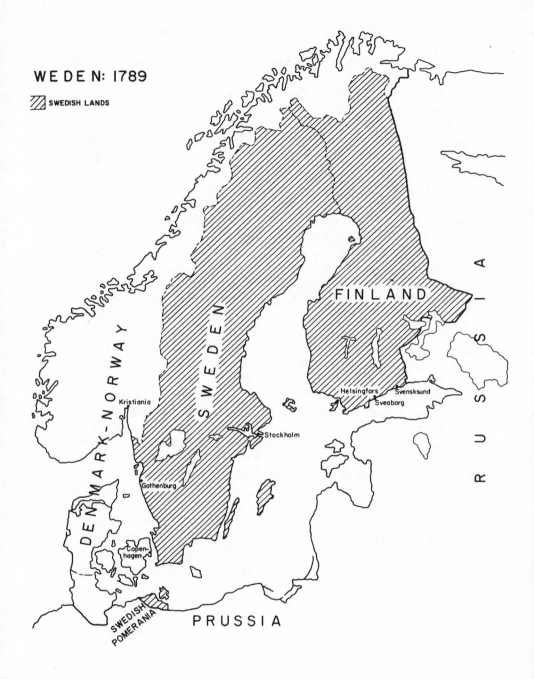

SWEDEN: 1789

SWEDISH LANDS

DENMARK-NORWAY

SWEDEN

FINLAND

RUSSIA

Kristiania

Stockholm

Gothenburg

Helsingfors    Svensksund
        Sveaborg

Copen-
hagen

SWEDISH
POMERANIA

PRUSSIA

control — did Gustav only forget this, or did he plan to care for that problem at a later time?

It was obvious that the nobles would fight these changes that strengthened both the monarchy and the nonprivileged Estates at the expense of the nobility, so Gustav called the riksdag together in plenum to announce the program — not to discuss it. He had carefully laid the groundwork by extensive propaganda against the nobility, and he enforced his will by arresting in advance nineteen of the probable objectors and bribing others. The three lower Estates approved. This extension of the privileges of the lower classes (and of the king) came in February 1789, before the outbreak of the French Revolution. The constitutional changes did nothing to ameliorate the peasants' hatred of the nobility or the nobles' contempt for the peasantry; social cleavages became only more obvious. The antagonism of the nobles toward the king was more bitter.

Gustav's vigorous reaction to crisis and the peoples' strong support nevertheless encouraged outside aid. Turkey finally agreed to offer a subsidy if Sweden would continue the war, and Prussia was ready to help — but Prussia wanted Swedish Pomerania as compensation. The English minister in Copenhagen, Hugh Elliot, charmed by the Swedish actor-king, got Denmark to make an armistice in August 1788 and to declare neutrality in July 1789. A year later (July 31, 1790) England and Prussia joined with Sweden in a treaty of friendship and subsidy. These diplomatic successes made an impression and so did the second naval battle of Svensksund (July 9–10, 1790), where the Swedish fleet, with King Gustav on board, after bravely desperate fighting, gained an unbelievable victory. The Swedes sank fifty Russian ships and killed or captured 9,000 men. At last, and just in time, the man who had dreamed of Sweden's great military heroes was granted a spectacular naval victory — even if personally he had little to do with it. He had had his one war and despite its disasters and disillusionments this piece of success enabled him to come out even. The startled empress Catherine, still fighting the Turks and worried about Poland and Prussia, was ready for peace. It was signed at the border town of Värälä on August 14, 1790. The treaty was negotiated by Gustav's intimate friend and adviser, G. M. Armfelt, nephew of one of the leaders of the Anjala group. No territory changed hands, and amazingly Gustav's largely mismanaged war brought to an end the long Russian interference in Swedish internal affairs. Ignominious beginnings ended in heightened prestige.[12]

Meanwhile the French Revolution was frightening monarchs everywhere. Gustav III was specially sympathetic toward the French royal couple, and his antipathy to revolution was heightened by his own experiences of 1788. Perhaps, thought the king, he could get the cooperation of Russia to help restore the power of the Bourbons! The dream got as far as an eight-year treaty with Russia signed in 1791. But on the domestic scene the superficial calm of the early 1790s was deceptive. The bitterness of the nobles was deep and sometimes pathological. He who wanted "to be loved for his own sake" found himself hated.

Gustav was not a tyrant in the classic sense, yet he had become more unsettled and nervous with age, more distrustful and unpredictable. Always sensitive to criticism, he now became increasingly suspicious. He was "a strange bird," as Beth Hennings has labeled him,[13] theatrical and highstrung, who was confused by ideals of brotherhood and freedom and the contradictory desire to dominate. Ironically, though naturally, it was just among the nobility whom he wanted to favor, provided that they would become a tame court aristocracy, that the opposition became most fanatical. They provided the group capable of conspiracy. Hatred of the king personally and of his despotic rule united men of widely divergent political views. Some were undoubtedly actuated by a patriotic and philosophical hatred of despotism and by a belief in the right of regicide, but the aged and bitter Pechlin was probably the man who organized the irreconcilables for action.

At an opera masquerade on March 16, 1792 the trigger man, Jacob Johan Anckarström, shot Gustav III just above the left hip, and the king died thirteen days later. Forty of the conspirators were found and arrested, and undoubtedly many more were on the fringes of the plot. Yet many of the nobles and the vast majority of the populace, however they had felt about the king before, abhorred the deed and turned their anger against the conspirators and the nobility as a whole. The nobles, fighting both the king and the changing times, had miscalculated the extent of their already diminished prestige. The dead king became a martyr and the plans of his enemies for a new constitution withered and died on his deathbed. Also died with him the spark of cultural revival that he had fanned into flame. The most lasting effect of Gustav's turbulent reign in the sociopolitical sphere was the leveling of the nobles' power, a leveling that Gustav thought it was essential to accomplish by law rather than by revolution. The nobles themselves were not ready to recognize their decline in status. But the fact was that revolutionary tremors were cracking the structure of the Swedish corporate society, as they were more violently overthrowing old institutions on the continent.

## The Cultural Flowering

The Gustavian Age did not achieve its fame from political success or military glory. For the first time in Swedish history the culture of the fine arts burst into bloom. To a certain extent it found its roots in the Age of Freedom with Linné and Dalin and the court life sponsored by Queen Louisa Ulrika. To a much greater extent it was seeded and fertilized from Gustav III's beloved France. Yet a mere imitation of something foreign could gain no fame. The greatness of the age came from the blending of indigenous elements, inspired by France, led by the king, and made Swedish.

Most obvious in their foreign (and chiefly French) origins were the various academies founded in the eighteenth century, some before the time of Gustav III. Best known has been the Swedish Academy (established in 1786). Like its precedent and paradigm in France the Swedish Academy was conceived to preserve the purity of the national language and to compile a dictionary (a task that it has succeeded in extending over a longer period than did the French; in 1975 the dictionary had reached the letter *s*). A more important purpose in Gustav's eyes was to absorb the literary talents of Sweden in the king's service to divert them from the revolutionary tendencies that were attracting continental intellectuals. Of the fixed number of eighteen members the king named the first thirteen. (Election by the Academy itself then became the method of choice.) Nobles and burghers, prestige and ability were well combined. The early programs concentrated on patriotic memorials of national heroes, and Gustav himself wrote a paper (anonymously) on Lennart Torstensson that was critically reviewed. Through almost two centuries the Academy has continued to be a conservative and constructive force in Swedish intellectual life. Since 1901 the world has waited expectantly each autumn for the Academy's selection of the Nobel laureate in literature. This task, which the members treat most seriously, and the accompanying discussion have inspired special interest among the Swedish reading public in the world's literature, for the country as a whole feels an indirect responsibility. Financial backing has been various but ample — including first a newspaper, *Post och Inrikes Tidningar* and salmon fishing rights, later the gift of the Bourse, which happened to be the building in which the Academy had held its first meeting, and a delightful restaurant nearby, The Golden Peace (*Den Gyllene Freden*).

On the same day that he founded the Swedish Academy Gustav established Vitterhets, Historie, och Antikvitets Akademien (Literary, Historical, and Antiquities Academy), which was really a resuscitation of the short-lived literary academy begun by Louisa Ulrika in 1753 as part of her program "to civilize the Swedes." History and antiquities plus philosophy and philology were to be its fields, leaving literature and language to the Swedish Academy. The Academy of Art, building on origins dating from 1735, met first in 1768 and was reorganized in 1773 as the Royal Painters and Sculptors Academy. Music had been favored even before Gustav's time, and the king seemed to be strengthening this tradition when he founded the Musical Academy in 1771.

This, like the Art Academy, was supposed to become a teaching institution, but it was short-lived and had to be reestablished in 1796. The Academy of Science that had been founded in 1739 continued to be active. Governmental initiative and support was vital in each instance. The members of these and other similar academies were the elite who met together in more or less regular sessions, guarded their heritage, rewarded achievement, and encouraged new talent.

A prelude to the blossom-time of Swedish literature appeared with Olof Dalin, who in the 1730s delighted his readers with his imaginative and lightly critical essays in *Then swänska Argus* (The Swedish Argus). He used the Swedish language with a flair and he was so appreciated in the salon of Louisa Ulrika that he was appointed tutor for Gustav, the crown prince, and undoubtedly had much to do with developing the prince's lasting interest in Swedish history and its heroes. Dalin's judicious mind, however, could not accept such nonsense as Rudbeck's Swedish Atlantis: "Where Plato's Atlantis lay, whether in ancient Svea or in the Promised Land or in the philosopher's brain, or if it was drowned in the flood of Old Testament fame, is and shall always remain an uncertain matter."[14] Among the writer's memorable pieces was his satirical "Tale of the Horse," the horse being the Swedish people and his masters the successive kings of Sweden from Gustav Vasa.

Others who were "in at the beginning" included Hedvig Charlotta Nordenflycht (1718–63), inspirer of Gustaf Fredrik Gyllenborg (1731–1808) and Gustav Philip Creutz (1731–85), but above all the extraordinary Carl Michael Bellman (1740–95). Bellman was a man of his time and his city whose rowdy songs are unfortunately almost untranslatable. He portrayed and preserved contemporary life of the streets and taverns in Stockholm, and his characters are real people from the lower fringes of society: Ulla Winblad, of kind heart and flexible morals; Movitz, the amorous jack-of-all-trades; Mollberg, besotted offspring of good family, the two obliging barmaids — they are all made immortal through Bellman's genius. Bellman, himself of good middle-class background, husband and father, maintained in minor government posts through the goodwill of the king, had like his characters too strong a taste for alcohol. He was a leader in their orgies but he interpreted as well as participated. He harnessed his genius by careful workmanship, but he worked only at his poetry, which he loved, not at the office, which he abhorred. When he had money he spent it and a little bit more, so that he served a couple of terms in debtor's prison or in flight and had to be bailed out by friends. One cannot doubt the realism of the life he lived and sang about; Stockholm had 700 taverns for its 70,000 inhabitants, and sorrow was drowned in *akvavit*. Bellman gave his cronies hours of happiness, and he was appreciated in the palace as well, at least by the king. There were fastidious others who lacked understanding of his genius. Sad to say, he was not "respectable" enough to be elected to the Swedish Academy. Greatest of his works is the collection of 83 "Fredmans epistlar" (epistles) wherein we get such gems as

> Let asses groan beneath the yoke,
> Shrewd men scheme till their brains are broke;
> Wine, girls, Fredman's fiddle-bow
> Enchant the night![15]

Bellman mixed humor and pathos, parodied the sacred, shifted suddenly from the sublime to the ridiculous. Two hundred years later his poetry still lives (in Swedish), for he has preserved in it the life of the "other" Stockholm — brothels and brawls, picnics and moonlight dances, graveyards and winter landscapes.

More intellectual and more attuned to the refined taste of the time was Johan Henrik Kellgren (1751–95), a spokesman of the Enlightenment. He was a poet of distinction who for a few years served to put into Swedish the plays that Gustav III drafted in French. Notable among the products of this collaboration was "Gustaf Wasa," a historical drama in the heroic style, very popular for several decades. Kellgren, however, had to do things on his own, so he left the court and in cooperation with C. P. Lenngren founded *Stockholms Posten*. It was Kellgren with his instructive yet bold and entertaining essays who made this the leading newspaper of the day. It was more a journal of opinion than a record of events; it was an outlet for ideas, a critique of the times, and it had a lasting influence on Swedish journalism which to the present day has a strong leaning to social and cultural comment. A measure of Kellgren's greatness is that, although he found Bellman's crudities distasteful, he came to appreciate the rival poet's talent and wrote a sympathetic foreword for *Fredman's Epistles*. Kellgren was thoroughly worthy of his choice as "one of the eighteen" in the Swedish Academy.

Other poets like Anna Maria Lenngren (1754–1817) and Johan Gabriel Oxenstierna (1750–1818) were appreciated by contemporaries but they lacked the purpose and the fire of Kellgren. Much the same is true of Carl Gustaf af Leopold (1756–1829), a man of facile pen who took Kellgren's place as translator and editor for the king.

Carl Christoffer Gjörwell (1731–1811) was a kindly patriarch who wrote delightfully on nature and accumulated a vast store of correspondence. His greatest significance may be that he was the devoted and influential grandfather of C. J. L. Almquist, a controversial genius of the nineteenth century. The entire circle of writers and poets who were stimulated by Gustav

III and by each other included also the social idealist Thomas Thorild (1759–1808), the sentimental poet Bengt Lidner (1757–93), and a number of others who enriched the cultural life of the capital. In yet a different vein, and rather untypical, was the tale of his trip to the Far East by young Jacob Wallenberg (1746–78), *Min son på Galejan*. When he returned on the *Finland* as chaplain Wallenberg described among other things the drinking bouts regularly arranged after the Sunday sermons (a good example of what might be called a "thirst after religion"). The spontaneous and robust realism of the account is like a prose counterpart to Bellman's lusty poetry.

While the literary figures stayed at home with the people who could read their language, artists of other kinds went in considerable numbers to the continent. The "Paris ambassadors" included an unusually able series of men, beginning with Carl Gustaf Tessin and ending in this period with Gustaf Philip Creutz; because of their interest in the arts and their own intellectual qualities and connections, all of them were helpful to visiting Swedish artists. Tessin helped Gustaf Lundberg (1695–1786), portraitist, become the first Swedish member of the French Academy of Art. Alexander Roslin (1718–93) had a brilliant career in France, as did his cousin Adolf Ulric Wertmüller (1751–1811) until the French Revolution drove him to the United States — Wertmüller was certainly one of few who painted both Marie Antoinette and George Washington. To his signature on painting he usually added "Suédois," but like many he was Swedish only in origin. Elias Martin (1739–1818) learned much of his technique and style of landscape painting in England but did most of his work in Sweden.

Art flourished on several levels in the Gustavian Age. The delightful originality and simplicity of peasant art in the rural churches and in the wall paintings in farm homes was the most genuinely Swedish of all art forms; in this genre the art of the eighteenth century was a continuation and expansion of old traditions. The painters were largely self-taught and they depicted biblical or historical scenes with a happy disregard for accuracy of costume or setting. Portraits may have been stiff but they were honest. For furniture and furnishings items were made for simplicity, comfort, and economy. There also flourished for a time the more elaborate designs of *bond-rokoko*.

Comfort in Sweden means warmth in the long winters, and therefore the invention of the *kakelugn*, or tiled stove, was welcomed by thousands. It also became an object of art and spread from cottage to bourgeois apartment and even to the salons of the wealthy and the new opera. The *kakelugn* was developed by Carl Johan Cronstedt, a pupil of Polhem who was designated by the council to find a better method of household heating, largely to save wood. In 1767 Cronstedt demonstrated a stove with spiraling channels in which circulated the heat from a small grate. From a few small sticks the tiled walls of the stove remained pleasantly warm for a full day. The simplest *kakelugn* was a round white tiled stove several feet high, perhaps reaching to the ceiling; beautiful models were also made of pictured tile, both Swedish and Delft.

In the more sophisticated court and the urban centers household decor as well as paintings and sculpture reflected the changing European styles, though they had a Swedish flavor. The greatest artist of the time was Johan Tobias Sergel (1740–1814), who had gone to Rome on a stipend in 1767 and after eleven years was, to his dismay, called home. He had won a place in Italy as the first neoclassicist sculptor and back in Sweden fulfilled many assignments for the king and the riksdag, including a statue of Gustav III and one entitled *Oxenstierna and History*. Carl Fredric von Breda (1757–1818) drew his inspiration from Gainsborough and Reynolds, became a professor at the Art Academy, and painted some 485 portraits in oil.

Gustav III's passion, as mentioned earlier, was theater and opera, and no art form received more thoughtful attention. A French troupe of twenty-five to thirty players had been brought to Stockholm by Louisa Ulrika in 1753 and it had kept the court up-to-date on the drama in Paris. The troupe was dismissed by Gustav in one of his first acts as king, and the reason was simple: he was determined to develop *Swedish* theater. A year later two plays were presented in Swedish and a year after that the first opera. In 1773 came the presentation of "Thetis and Peleus" planned by the king. A climax was reached at Christmas season 1775–76; in a period of two weeks six major tragedies and four minor plays were presented, with the king playing four major roles.

Opera became the favored dramatic form, for singing utilized to best advantage the Swedish language and voices. It was therefore specially satisfying for the king when the magnificent opera house, designed by Carl Fredrik Adelcrantz, opened in 1782 on its impressive site along the Stream (*Strömmen*) across from the royal palace. Every performance, thought the king, should be a "Swedish cultural manifestation," and certainly the "Gustaf Wasa" that he and Kellgren wrote fulfilled the demand — it was patriotic, colorful, and highly popular.

Regular theaters were well patronized in both Stockholm and Gothenburg, and for the court there were theaters at Drottningholm, Gripsholm, and Ulriksdal castles. The Drottningholm theater, with its extraordinarily versatile and well-planned stage, continued in use in the late twentieth century. The Royal Dramatic Theater was started in 1787. Troupes of traveling players carried theater also to several smaller towns. All this activity flourished until the time of Gustav IV Adolf, who refused to spend money on such frivolous luxuries; he once even decreed that the opera house should be torn down, but he was dissuaded and the grand structure survived until 1891, when it was razed to make way for the present building on the same site.

The vigor of the flowering of the fine arts during the reign of Gustav III is as amazing as the outburst of scientific achievement during the Age of Freedom. In each case the government provided initiative and support and in each case resources of talent were on hand, talents that cross-fertilized and reinforced each other. In neither case was the result accidental, for there was purposeful guidance and a willingness to "prime and pump" with large and small government subsidies for factories, theaters and museums, and study trips abroad for young people with promise. Somehow, without benefit of research foundations and fellowship committees, Gustav III and other creative personalities found each other, to mutual advantage.

Cultural developments of the eighteenth century in Sweden entice the interpreter of historical change to try to correlate achievements in the arts and sciences and in administrative and economic activities with the course of political events. Did the atmosphere of freedom stimulate the botanical researches of Linné? Did a new climate of opportunity energize the traders with the Far East? Or was Gustav III's benevolent despotism, his paternal encouragement in the founding of the Swedish Academy, for example, more important for progress? The search is frustrating, for the answers are far from clear. The bursts of activity and accomplishment were not along a broad front of cultural advance but were separate flashes. The population of Sweden was too small to sustain genius in all fields, too poor to support a major breakthrough. Yet individual achievements were notable and were numerous enough to indicate both a favorable environment and a good pool of talent.

Gustav III, though he appeared as a dilettante to many, obtained striking success in two of his major purposes: First, after an unconstitutional and mainly inglorious war, toward the end of his reign, he broke the chains of dependence with which for seventy years Russia had tried to bind Sweden. And, second, although he had built on French patterns and had used French subsidies, personnel, and inspiration, he fostered *Swedish* artistic productivity of high quality. No nation can stand alone in either politics or culture, but at Gustav's death Sweden could feel a self-respecting independence in both realms.

### Gustav IV Adolf (1778–1837; King, 1792–1809)

After the flashing brilliance of the court of Gustav III a cloud of dullness settled over that of the regent Duke Karl, Gustav's brother. Art and drama had vanished from the court, which no longer functioned as the nation's cultural inspiration. Government lost its spark. The duke was lazy, uninterested, and lacking in political insight. He turned over the direction of affairs, in direct defiance of Gustav III's will, to his friend G. A. Reuterholm, a colleague in superstition and the study of occult sciences. Reuterholm was sympathetic to the French Revolution in its early stages, which he had witnessed while living in Paris, and he had been a member of the noble opposition to Gustav III. But when endowed with authority he showed a different face. He was nicknamed The Grand Vizier quite appropriately, for he was by nature despotic and power made him more so. He was willing to see Anckarström scourged and broken on the wheel, but he was lenient with the other murderers of Gustav III; he was also brutal toward his rival G. M. Armfelt and a group of Gustavians who continued to conspire against the new regime. One of his first acts was to issue a liberal ordinance on freedom of the press, but when it resulted in criticism of the government he clamped down viciously. At least he had administrative skill and introduced more systematic procedures in finance and military organization.

In foreign affairs Reuterholm tried to be clever, but others were both stronger and cleverer. He negotiated with changing regimes in France and made Sweden the first monarchic state to recognize the French Republic (in 1795). But nothing was permanent. In between his wooings of France he tried to ally with Russia and arrange a marriage between the youth Gustav IV Adolf and Catherine's granddaughter Alexandra. This foundered eventually on the issue of protection for the princess's religion; in the meantime it created embarrassment and ill-feeling. One of his few foreign policy successes was cooperation with Denmark in the neutrality agreement of 1794. When Gustav IV Adolf reached the age of eighteen and took direction of affairs into his own hands, on November 1, 1796, it was not surprising that he upbraided Reuterholm rather than thanked him, and soon the briefly powerful mystic found himself in semi-voluntary exile.

Gustav IV Adolf was a tragic figure, his reign a disaster, because of an unfortunate combination of external circumstances and his own emotional instability. It may be questioned how much importance should be assigned to childhood difficulties — at the age of two he was taken from his mother to be reared by men; as he grew up he never had a chance to play with other boys; and he was told the rumors that he was not really the son of the king. He was cool toward his mother, worshiped Gustav III, and perhaps was obsessed by the desire to emulate the great Gustav II Adolf and Karl XII. Melancholy and nervous, he lacked both magnetism and self-assurance and took refuge in the rigidities of protocol. The assassination of his father was bound to exacerbate the suspiciousness in his nature, and he gave way easily to outbursts of anger. He was interested in music and he had a good memory but was averse to the philosophical tendencies of the Enlightenment, and especially to Jacobinism. He turned instead to religion and increasingly to pietism. In his early years he envisioned his mission as the protection of throne and altar, later he concentrated on ridding the world of the archfiend Napoleon. The emotional or mental weakness that was obvious in him, and that afflicted his uncle Kristian VII of Denmark, worsened with the buffetings of fortune in the chaotic early years of the nineteenth century.

Unquestionably the young king wanted to "do right," and he at least attempted several positive reforms. In 1808 he approved Baltzar von Platen's plans for a canal across Sweden. He tried desperately to stabilize the finances of the country, first in cooperation with the riksdag and then by himself. He succeeded in reducing by 700,000 riksdaler the debt that had grown during Gustav III's reign from 9 million to 30 million riksdaler, but then the Russian-Danish war wiped out the gains. The mortgaging of Wismar in 1803 for one hundred years and for the sum of 1.25 million riksdaler (it was really a sale, because there could hardly be a thought of recovery) was helpful but insufficient, and the value of the currency continued to decline. In general the economy prospered during the reign, except for crop failures in 1798 and 1799 and the difficulties in export of herring and iron. In Pomerania the abolition of serfdom and other reforms were decreed, but this extension of Swedish law had been long delayed and Sweden was destined soon to lose its Pomeranian foothold on the continent. As chancellor of the University of Uppsala the king was not in sympathy with the intellectual trends and soon turned over that job to Axel Fersen. For formal education, under the influence of the methods of the Moravian Brethren, the king's Ordinance of 1807 was a positive boost, as was the establishment of a professorship in education at Uppsala. But the king doused the cultural sparks fanned by his father — he prohibited the importation of Danish books in 1803 and later of French newspapers and new books; he censored the theater; and he closed the opera, though he did not carry through his threat to raze the opera house where Gustav III was killed.

### Agricultural Reorganization

In agricultural organization Gustav Adolf proved to be a revolutionary, and the enclosure statutes of 1803 to 1807 were surely the most positive achievements of his reign.

The widespread pattern of rural village organization and antiquated agricultural methods was still dominant in Sweden as it was in much of the European continent. In time the process of inheritance had produced more and more complicated division of lands, smaller and smaller strips for the farmer to till. The average farmer in Sweden would have thirty to forty separate pieces of land, sometimes almost one hundred. The diminutive size of the strips and their scattering made cultivation difficult and inefficient. Horses and oxen often could not turn within the width of a farmer's own strip. Every planting and harvesting had to be coordinated with the activities of the village as a whole. The close-built cottages and the little church were picturesque, and the village life was intimate and psychologically satisfying. But productivity was low as in the Middle Ages: grains yielded four and one-half to fivefold at best, and in a bad year like 1812 peas yielded only two and one-half times the seed.[16] In England the enclosure movement had already transformed the medieval structure. In Denmark progress had been made in revamping the old system. In Sweden in the mid-eighteenth century permissive statutes had been passed, largely through the influence of Jacob Faggot, head of the Land Survey Office. This brought some consolidation of the tilled strips. But the dead weight of tradition and inertia prevented significant change.

> Our forefathers, who discovered everything, they were certainly as clever as we. . . . We understand the best ways and methods we are born to and accustomed to, as well as any gentleman in Stockholm who has nothing to do but speculate on things which he doesn't understand as well as an *eng bunne* [meadow rabbit? or meadow (dirt) farmer (*bonde*)?][17]

Because of such attitudes innovation could come only piecemeal and through strong personal leadership. The man who got things moving in Sweden was Rutger Maclean, owner of Svaneholm, an estate of 8,500 acres in Skåne.

Maclean was inspired by what had been done in Britain and Belgium and especially by the example of Denmark, where solid reform had begun in the 1780s. He was impelled by a sense of Sweden's need, acute since the loss of the grain-producing provinces across the Baltic, and by his positive feeling that "out of the womb of the earth is obtained all that is needed for the body of man and the happiness of mankind."[18] Like the enlightened despots of his day who ruled vast empires, Rutger Maclean directed revolution in his estate from above, and perhaps he had more success than his grand contemporaries. He enjoyed the great advantages that his lands were in one piece, that the soil was fertile, and that he could gain governmental cooperation. When he inherited the estate in 1782, at age forty, he had some forty tenants in four villages, plus the manor house, its servants, and its directly operated lands. The semi-feudal tenants in this Danish-influenced part of Sweden owed him as rent a certain amount of fowl each year and day-service at his command. Each of the tenants had rights to sixty or seventy strips of land, about a third of them so distant from his village as to be unusable. Maclean took forceful steps to transform the personal, legal, and economic relationships built up through centuries.

The three essentials of his reform were the consolidation of a farmer's holdings into one piece of land, the abolition of all day-service requirements, and the substitution of money rentals of approximately 100 riksdaler for day-work and previous payments in kind.

He had his entire estate surveyed and redivided into seventy-five single farms, each with about fifty acres arable and fifteen meadow, as nearly as possible rectangular in shape. Then he built roads connecting them. Except for a few persons — craftsmen and those with especially good houses — each tenant was required to move out from the village to his individual farm. Maclean had constructed on each plot a house of timbered construction and a long barn of stamped clay and straw. The barns, built on stone foundations, were both substantial and cheap and some lasted more than one hundred years. Each farm had a two-and-a-half-acre garden plot. The contract required the planting of trees, the use of not more than half the land for grain crops, and included many specific regulations about how the land should be fertilized, fenced, and planted. The agreement with each tenant stipulated fines for nonperformance, and for a definite breach of contract the tenant was supposed to leave his home immediately. Some leases were for a few years but the ideal was a lifetime arrangement.

At first things went rather badly, for about twenty of the tenants left rather than move to isolated farms away from their village attachments. Some stayed only because they were so hopelessly in debt that they could leave only "naked with wife and children." Also the number of farms required twice as many farmers as before, and it was some years before all were permanently occupied. The total population on Maclean's estate fell from 701 in 1785 to 603 in 1786. However, it soon became apparent that a man could raise more crops on his land reduced by half when it was all contiguous and that he could better care for his livestock. Relief from day-work around the manor and from payments in kind made it easier for a man to plan his own work. In brief, Maclean's tenants prospered amazingly, and by 1800 the farms were taken up, and the population had increased to 1,102.

Despite inflation and a number of unforeseen complications Maclean prospered too. On an additional five farms that he operated with hired help he increased production by about 50 percent, using innovative methods intended to stimulate others. He raised a variety of crops such as clover, beets, cabbage, potatoes, and carrots, many of which were used for fodder for his prized livestock. He was careful to keep his fields weed-free. For himself and his people the reason for success lay not only in the plan and the regulations but in the industry and the creative intelligence of the man. He gathered a remarkable library on agriculture, with all the best books in English, French, and German. He built school houses in two villages and sent one teacher to

Switzerland for study with the famous Johann Heinrich Pestalozzi. He inaugurated the use of vaccination and introduced fertilizers and new crops. He designed an improved harness and perfected a light iron plow that could be drawn by two oxen. He carefully ditched his lands. His example was more important than his law. Not only did tenants come in to fill his farms and to practice his techniques, but his skeptical fellow landowners took notice too, and soon all round southwestern Skåne other estates were consolidated and new methods introduced — usually against the stubborn opposition of the peasants. Maclean's ultimate success is attested by the fact that soon after his death, in 1816, most of his former tenants were in a position to buy the farms they had rented.[19]

From the very first, however, Rutger Maclean was concerned not only with his own lands and his own tenants but with the social and agricultural problems of Sweden as a whole. He eagerly showed visiting officials what he was doing, and he had influential friends in Stockholm, though he was himself in opposition to Gustav III and at first to Gustav IV Adolf. Eventually Gustav IV Adolf himself came to approve the reforms that were enhancing the prosperity of Skåne, and he signed the law of 1803 that prescribed the *enskifte*, or single-farm consolidation, for all of Skåne. By 1807, in moderated form, the king extended the new system through most of Sweden (except for Dalarna, Norrland, and Finland). Surveyors were busy for generations, and the local commissions that determined who might stay in the village and who must move to the internal "frontier" became the agents of socioeconomic revolution.

It had to be recognized that different conditions in certain parts of the country required different solutions. In Dalarna, for example, the only fertile land lay in narrow valleys surrounded by forested mountains. So the *laga skifte* of 1827 would later provide for partial consolidation of farms, with some land in the valleys and some in the mountains for each owner, and for the preservation of the traditional villages. Even by 1850 the individualization of the land for the whole country was only half completed. Such a sweeping transformation of a way of life was bound to move slowly. As late as 1967 one farmer in the Lake Siljan area was getting his one thousand separate holdings, some subdivided by inheritance to mere square foot areas, consolidated into a few patches — but this case was the *reductio ad absurdum*.

Loans had to be arranged for farmers who had never really been independent so that they could increase their stock, buy implements, and put up homes and other buildings. Even in long-settled Skåne the process of individualization brought much new land under the plow — from 1805 to 1833 about ten thousand acres per year. Discontent with the destruction of village life, sometimes a feeling of being cast out by one's own neighbors, led to emigration to

Denmark and even to suicide. But the reconstruction of agriculture attracted immigrants, too, from Germany and elsewhere, and enabled the native population to increase and spread out. Frequently the advantages accrued only to the second generation. In Skåne alone the population increased between 1805 and 1850 from 270,000 to 442,000 or 63 percent, as against 44 percent for the kingdom as a whole. Operator ownership of farms doubled in the same period, and the number of sharecroppers decreased, but the number of hired laborers also doubled.[20] Productivity and material progress were enhanced but could not keep pace with the increasing population. This increase was undoubtedly augmented by the greater productivity of the land as well as by the absence of plagues and wars. On balance, conditions were improved, and farmers enjoyed occasional booms and innovations in equipment, such as iron stoves. But along with improvements and reduction of the inefficiencies of the old rural regime the growing population created its own new problems, psychological as well as economic. The advantages of rationalization were partly nullified as more people had to live off the land; the number of cottagers in the country as a whole quadrupled between 1750 and 1860. At the same time there disappeared the neighborliness of the village and some of its festivals and traditions. Some of the former sense of security and stability was lost. The invisible threads that bound human beings to each other were subtly weakened, doubtless helping to prepare the way for the great emigration that was to come.

### The Political-Diplomatic Sector and the Revolution of 1809

While social revolution was sprouting from the soil the political-diplomatic sector was in even more violent turmoil. All Europe was in the throes of change. Gustav IV Adolf's first years as king coincided with the Reign of Terror in France and the spread of war, with the challenge of the masses to monarchs and the very institution of monarchy; it was the trigger of an assassin's gun that gave him an unwanted crown. After the strife-torn later years of Gustav III the accession of this young son was greeted in Sweden with a kind of muted hope, while waves of uncertainty radiated from Paris throughout the continent. Gustav III had eliminated Russian interference in Swedish internal affairs, but Reuterholm had again invited involvement. The youthful Gustav IV Adolf had rigidly asserted Sweden's rights to independence and therefore had given up Princess Alexandra whom he favored for his wife. When he came of age another marriage was soon arranged with Fredrika of Baden. Since Fredrika's sister was married to the Russian heir Alexander the tsar's court could not be too annoyed with the new choice. Actually, Gustav IV Adolf visited St. Petersburg in December of 1800, and he and Tsar

Paul got on famously — they had more fears and hates in common than against one another.

Tsar and king agreed upon another Armed Neutrality, soon to be adhered to by Denmark and Prussia. This put an end to Gustav Adolf's farfetched speculations about an alliance with France that would give him Norway while Pomerania was to go to Prussia and Denmark should be compensated in Germany. Yet nothing lasted long in those chaotic days. Great Britain took offense at the formation of the neutral league; in 1801 its fleet attacked Copenhagen, and it was expected at Karlskrona, where an attack would easily have destroyed Swedish ships and prestige. At the last moment this disaster was averted by the death of Tsar Paul and abandonment by the British of further hostilities — they counted on a change of policy by Alexander I who then came to the throne and in 1802 swung to the English side.

By 1803 the British were again smiling on the Swedes and even requesting an alliance. The brief Peace of Amiens was then over and the British needed an entrepôt to the continent. Swedish Pomerania was about the only possibility left in the north, so the British offered not only a commercial agreement but alliance and generous subsidies and paid up for Swedish ships and cargoes earlier confiscated. Gustav IV Adolf was then on an eighteen-month tour on the continent, and he was close at hand when the Duc d'Enghien was captured in Baden, to be taken to his execution in France. The horror and the brutality of this Napoleonic error struck deep into the king's mind, and to him Bonaparte gradually became the wild beast of the Apocalypse, the Anti-Christ. In October 1805, when the king was home again, Sweden signed the Treaty of Bäckaskog (at that time Field Marshal J. C. Toll's Skåne estate) with Britain, Austria, and Russia, and Gustav Adolf launched his continental crusade against France. It was as disastrous as many other emotional thrusts into the world of power politics.

The resultant Pomeranian War was inglorious and futile and stimulated army and aristocratic opposition to the king. In 1806 Sweden won and lost the province of Lauenburg, and with it 1,000 Swedish prisoners who came under the control of the French Marshal Bernadotte — his odd entry into Swedish history. England was generous with subsidies, but these were of little use, for the decisions of war were made beyond the bounds of this small theater of operations. The battles of Jena and Auerstädt gave Napoleon supremacy in north Germany, and the following year the defeat of Russia at Friedland left Sweden isolated and helpless. Worse than that, Napoleon and Alexander met on the famous raft at Tilsit, and their accommodation had the effect of giving the tsar a free hand in northern Europe.

After centuries of war on the Finnish frontier it was natural for either Russia or Sweden to take advantage of any opportunity to strike at the other. Gustav

III had done so in 1788. Now circumstances favored Russia, and it took a remarkably short time for Alexander to shift from his alliance with Gustav Adolf into a brief period of quiet preparation for conquest and then suddenly to strike in Finland on February 21, 1808, using as justification Gustav Adolf's stubborn adherence to his British alliance. If the conduct of the Pomeranian War caused his closest officials to doubt Gustav Adolf's capacities the Finnish War convinced them fully — though the faults of management were not his alone.

In 1808 Sweden had 66,000 men under arms, and this did not compare badly with the 80,000 that were all Russia could hope to use in Finland. But Sweden had to stand also against Denmark-Norway, now as often allied with Russia (even if the Danes did not push the war very hard). When the Swedes attempted to expand their forces by a *levée en masse* on the ancient pattern, the new troops were depleted by disease induced by bad sanitary conditions — 20 percent of the 30,000 soldiers died. England was Sweden's only ally and the force it sent to Gothenburg under Sir John Moore soon sailed away again with nothing accomplished or even attempted; the situation was made futile by mutual mistrust.

The most tragic and decisive events occurred in Finland itself. The long repetitiveness and strain of wars with Russia bred discouragement. G. M. Sprengtporten, who had led the small separatist sentiment of 1788 and who had been living in Russia since then, reappeared to try to persuade the Finns to make a deal with Russia. (In 1809 Sprengtporten was named governor-general by the tsar.) Many of the people were loyal but resigned. The timing of the Russian attack while the ground was still frozen made defense difficult, and the Swedish army followed its orders to retreat across the country to the Gulf of Bothnia. Occasional engagements gave local victories to the Swedish-Finnish troops, but the combination of strategic plans and overestimation of the Russian strength robbed these successes of significance. The weak and too old Carl Olof Cronstedt, influenced by fear and persuaded by one of his officers who was a brother of one of the Anjala league men, gave a sharp blow to morale when in May 1809 he surrendered the strong fortress of Sveaborg, guarding the sea entrance to Helsinki. He yielded 7,000 men, 2,000 cannon, and 110 ships with hardly a show of resistance. Cronstedt's immediate dismissal and later sentence to death for treason could not reverse the surrender, the most crucial event of the war.[21] Further effort was futile. Gustav IV Adolf took an army to the Åland Islands. One of his errors here was his degradation of all guards' officers for the fault of a few, creating lasting resentment. The king was lacking both in the personal magnetism that leadership requires and in the military skills that he so admired in his great predecessors. He had only stubborn determination. The war was humanized and immortalized in

Runeberg's *Tales of Ensign Stål*,[22] but the mood of the time was more that of
sad desperation than of heroic conflict. Perhaps it was inevitable that Finland
should fall sooner or later to the might of expanding Russia. Perhaps it was
best that the separation came when and as it did. Nevertheless, responsibility
rested on the shoulders of Gustav IV Adolf, and he had to pay for failure.

Steadily the Russian forces advanced until they occupied not only western
Finland but also the Åland Islands and some northern sections of Sweden
proper.

Already in March 1808 Tsar Alexander I had declared Finland incorporated
into Russia. By the end of the year a series of armistices gave Russia effective
control of the entire country. Sweden's power of resistance was broken,
though Gustav Adolf continued to talk of an 1809 campaign. He asked England for new subsidies to meet the renewed attack from Russia, but the
English advised peace, at the same time threatening war if Sweden should
yield to the extent of joining Napoleon's Continental System. Soldiers were
returning to Sweden with disease and frozen feet. Opinion among various
leadership groups began to crystallize against Gustav IV Adolf, and de-
thronement plans developed in the western army, among the Åland troops,
and in civilian groups in Stockholm. Gradually a loose kind of consensus
grew among Jacob Cederström (who had lost his right leg), Hans Järta, and
officers like Carl Henrik Anckarsvärd, Carl Johan Adlercreutz, and Georg
Adlersparre, an officer on the Norwegian front. Adlersparre arranged a vague
standoff agreement with Norway's statholder and commander, Prince Christian August, and then marched with his 2,900 men toward Stockholm, while
Russian forces pressed into Sweden in the north. Meanwhile, on March 13,
1809 General Adlercreutz and six officers simply went to the king's room in
the castle and arrested him. The common folk were shocked, but neither they
nor a single leader made any serious attempt to protect or restore the monarch.
On March 22 Adlersparre entered Stockholm; on the 29th Gustav Adolf
abdicated, though he refused to include his son. After a nine-month detention
at Gripsholm he left Sweden forever on Christmas Eve, 1809. He divorced his
wife in 1812, and for nearly thirty years he wandered in body and mind. He
died alone in St. Gallen, Switzerland, in 1837. His son, who called himself
Prince Gustav af Vasa, remained a pretender throughout his long life, but he
made only a feeble attempt to assert himself. A century and a half later a few
irreconcilable "private Gustavians" still protest.[23]

The temporary government was a "Noah's Ark" of old Gustavians and
revolutionists. Duke Karl, Gustav IV Adolf's uncle, hesitated to proclaim
himself king but accepted the regency once more. Peace was the most urgent
order of business, but peace could come only with a new government. Hence
the riksdag was called for May 1, 1809, and on May 12 a constitutional

committee began its work. Adlersparre was not elected to the committee, but it was an able group of fifteen nobles, including Baltzar von Platen, General A. F. Skjöldebrand, Carl Gustaf Nordin, and the chairman L. A. Mannerheim. Its genius and driving force was Hans Järta, who was the secretary but not a member. He was one of a small group of so-called Jacobins who in 1800 renounced their titles; Järta even took a new name, dissociating himself from the aristocratic Hierta clan. (He preserved the pronunciation but changed the spelling.) Intensive work for fourteen days resulted in a constitutional draft, which was accepted by the riksdag on June 5 and approved on the sixth by Duke Karl, who was immediately elected king (Karl XIII).

War weariness and suspicions among the nobles made further resistance impossible, and Sweden had to accept Russian terms in the Treaty of Fredrikshamn of September 17, 1809. Sweden lost a full third of its territory, including all of Finland, the Åland Islands, and territory in the north to the Torne and Muonio rivers, including even the town of Torneå. Sweden did retain the iron ore districts that were to become so important later. It was a drastic amputation of the kingdom, not only shearing off territory but separating people who had developed together for centuries and who shared a common culture. Finland had been an integral part of Sweden, and meant, and still means, far more to Swedes than merely land and a buffer against the big eastern neighbor. Adjustment to the harsh realities was regarded as necessary, but not necessarily permanent.

Peace with Denmark was signed on December 10, 1809, involving no territorial gain or loss. With France the treaty of January 10, 1810 provided that Sweden should join the Continental System, breaking all commercial ties with England except for the import of salt, and Napoleon returned Swedish Pomerania. Yet neither of these treaties would be permanent.

## The Constitution of 1809

But permanence is just what *did* characterize the constitution of 1809. It was framed in only two weeks of intensive labor but it survived, with some modifications and reinterpretations, until the 1970s. The drafting committee was a reflection of the existing power structure, representing the supreme power of the riksdag: six nobles and three members from each of the other Estates, plus, significantly, the secretary Hans Järta. As Lars Augustin Mannerheim put it, "We were thirty in committee — fifteen members, and Hans Järta, our secretary, who was another fifteen."[24] The document leaned neither to antiquity nor to the ephemeral sentiments of the moment but was a distillation of Swedish historical experience, a blending of elements such as Germanic tradition and Montesquieu. Even its concept of balance of power among executive, legislative, and judiciary was more the result of national experience than of foreign philosophy. Järta summed up his view of the attitude of the group: "The new government was not patterned after any of the social costumes in fashion at the time in the rest of Europe, but after the ancient Swedish dress, with the peasant jacket closest to the body."[25]

The clause in Article IV, "The king alone shall govern the realm," was inherited from the distant past, but it was given up-to-date interpretation. The king had to rule according to the limits set by the constitution, and he had to receive advice from a council of state, which he would appoint. He could not use as advisers "hidden persons without responsibility," and it was provided that he should not appoint close relatives to the council. Of the nine original members three were to have specified functions — the minister of foreign affairs, the minister of justice, and the chancellor. Beyond these nine councillors several secretaries were called to meetings when their problems were under discussion, and gradually new departments were created. Basically the council was an administrative board, appointed individually by the king, responsible individually to the king rather than to the riksdag and concerned primarily with the everyday functioning of government. Appointments to high position were to be made on the basis of merit alone, and thus another privilege of the nobility was canceled; however, in practice nobles continued for a long time to enjoy the top appointments, presumably because of merit. An interesting provision stated that in case of the king's illness or absence for over a year the riksdag should "do what the situation requires," a broad and flexible directive echoing the ancient rule that the Svear could make a king and also depose him.

The current idea of the division of powers was given a special Swedish application. Whereas the executive power was granted solely to the king, the legislative power was vested in both king and riksdag, each with veto power over the other. Approval of three Estates was needed to pass a law and of all four to amend the constitution (in two successive sessions). The riksdag, which was to meet at least every five years, exercised alone the right of the Swedish people to tax themselves, but it proved oddly loath to use this power to coerce the monarchy. Partly this restraint developed because the king received the ordinary income of the state in any case and had the power of economic legislation. The king's powers included the right to name the speakers of the four Estates in the riksdag.

Judicial power was vested in a high court, "independent but not above the law." The court even included the king, with his right to two votes — which he never used. (The right was abolished in 1909.) The court was independent to interpret the law and could declare acts of the riksdag inconsistent with the constitution, yet it lacked real power to call laws unconstitutional, for the riksdag had only to overrule the court at its next session if it wanted to revalidate a law.

Thus the constitution left the kingship strongly entrenched and with the prestige of traditional authority. It also gave the legislature powers that could evolve in time and that enabled it gradually to shift the balance of power in its own favor.

One of the most interesting innovations was the provision for a judicial ombudsman, again an official who had appeared much earlier but had not been given precise constitutional status. He was to be an official of high prestige, with the task of assuring justice to citizens and government employees when the harsh enforcement of rules or the mistakes of officials should create injustice. This *J.O.* (*Justitie-Ombudsman*) increased in importance with the expansion of bureaucracy and became the pattern for similar officials throughout Scandinavia and in several other countries in the twentieth century. He was chosen by the riksdag and was wholly independent. Although he had no enforcement power he was in a position to use persuasion and publicity with maximum effect, and as a last resort he could take a case to court.

Demands of immediacy in the creation of a government mean postponement of many controversial issues — matters often of historical debate and not yet amenable to resolution. One of these sensitive points concerned the taxation of lands long tax-free. Paragraph 114 guaranteed continuation of tax-exemption on *frälse* lands, and the farmer Estate at first accepted the constitution on condition that this article be eliminated. King and nobility were just as adamant for its retention, and on June 27 the farmers yielded. Technically there was a kind of equality, for the farmers or anyone could now buy *frälse* land, and much land came into the possession of nonnobles. It took almost a century longer to establish the principle of complete equality in taxation of land. On various other matters the nobility had yielded inherited privileges — such as their previous exclusive rights to the highest offices, and both burghers and priests also had made concessions. Thus some steps were taken toward full equality.

Another problem left unsolved was the complex of questions involving representation and organization in the riksdag and the desire of the reformers to install a two-chamber riksdag in place of the obsolete four-Estates system. The constitution committee of the riksdag recommended the two-chamber system in 1810, but they did not regard the matter as urgent; it took fifty-five years for realization.[26] The constitution was composed in an emergency situation, and it is a tribute to the committee that it long survived in most essentials. Although there is continuing scholarly controversy about its origins it is clear that the framers were well read in Montesquieu and in works on the constitution of England. They blended the ideas and the experiences of their own time with the long traditions of Swedish government. The emphasis was on the Swedish background but not quite as thoroughly as one observer claimed when he called the constitution an epitome of the history of Sweden put down in legal paragraphs.

The riksdag continued in session, making laws to implement the constitution. Progress was made toward trying to clear up the parlous financial situation, for all foreign subsidies had ceased. An income tax, ranging from .25 percent to 10 percent, displaced the old taxes on such items as windows, carriages, silk, cards, and dogs. Distilling was once more made free — which quickly produced new problems.

The vital thing was that destructive controversy was avoided, the main job got done, and unity was preserved in a time of despair. The overthrow of Gustav IV Adolf and the whole reorganization of government occurred in the period between March and June 1809, while the Russians were still attacking not only Finland but the western shores of the Gulf of Bothnia. No outside help could be found. When the Swedes appealed to Napoleon to help them obtain a reasonable peace he only referred them to ''the spirit of Tsar Alexander.''

## Karl August the New Crown Prince

Because of the age and incapacity of King Karl XIII and his lack of an heir, it was essential to choose a crown prince. King Frederik of Denmark had the inside track, for many hoped through him to regain the advantages of a united Scandinavia. But Frederik insisted on an absolutist regime, and this was absolutely unacceptable to the Swedes. The choice fell on Adlersparre's candidate, Prince Christian August, recently leader of the Norwegian army against the Swedes. The prince thought that he might later transfer the crown to the king of Denmark-Norway and thus unify the entire North. His Swedish backers (Adlersparre, von Platen, and others) wanted a union only of Norway and Sweden.[27] The new crown prince tactfully took the more Swedish name Karl August, and he tried to establish himself and to get acquainted with his new country. But he was not a well man, and on a visit to Skåne he lost control of his horse, fell off, and died in half an hour (on May 28, 1810). Apparently it was a stroke of apoplexy, but rumors spread that it was poison. Suspicion always attends such events, but in this case suspicion was enhanced by distribution of insinuating leaflets. In an atmosphere of chaos and class antagonism it was not difficult to inflame mob feeling. The finger was pointed at Axel von Fersen, a one time friend of Marie Antoinette and now marshal of the realm, whose job it was to lead Karl August's funeral procession in Stockholm on June 20, 1810. There ensued one of the most disgraceful incidents in Swedish history, which illustrated the demoralization that followed defeat and the coup against Gustav IV Adolf.

Fersen's carriage was stoned, and he was wounded; the mob swelled; Fersen left his carriage for the protection of a home along the route, but he was dragged out and slowly beaten to death. Soldiers and police looked on, and when a lieutenant ordered two soldiers to lower their bayonets the order was countermanded by a higher officer and the slow murder proceeded. Recent research indicates that the mob was not riffraff but largely disgruntled clerks in government offices and young men of similar standing, apparently encouraged by higher officials. Who was responsible for the inflammatory leaflets and the callousness and collusion of the authorities was never fully determined. The shock of the event and its lasting shame at least checked some of the bickering and intrigue; the general feeling of revulsion worked especially against those irreconcilable Gustavians who still worked for the return of Gustav IV Adolf's son. (As recently as March 13, 1810 a planned coup had been called off only because King Karl XIII refused to cooperate.) [28]

The historical importance of Gustav IV Adolf lies in his inadequacy. He did promote agricultural revolution, but he failed in the most difficult tasks that fate thrust upon him. His lack of political skill, his futility on the battlefield, and the mess he made of diplomacy — all ending in the loss of one-third of Sweden's territory — led to his overthrow. This produced in turn not only a new dynasty but a modernized constitution and a revitalized political structure. The brutal pruning of the old leadership encouraged new growth.

# XI

# THE BERNADOTTE DYNASTY AND
# THE UNION WITH NORWAY

FOUR REVOLUTIONS marked the beginnings of the nineteenth century in Sweden and put the country on its road to modern redevelopment. In agriculture, constitution, dynasty, and foreign policy the country swung off in new paths. The social-agricultural revolution, prologued by Rutger Maclean and legislated by the land acts of 1803 to 1807, reached to the very roots of Swedish society and stimulated expansion of food production. The constitutional revolution of 1809, important but perhaps least revolutionary of all, codified the past and at the same time built a firm platform for a new political takeoff. The dynastic revolution of 1809–10 discarded the last branch of the Vasas, a family of ofttimes brilliant talent that had at last run out, and gambled on a foreign military figure who founded a line that was to prove both its longevity and its adjustability to change. That third revolution facilitated the fourth, which in 1812 abandoned the well-forged diplomatic links with France and welded an alliance with Sweden's ancient enemy Russia. This dramatic reversal was associated with the transfer of Finland to Russian overlordship and would hardly have been conceivable if the Swedish kingdom had remained intact on Russia's flank. Swedish-Russian cooperation did not perdure, but at least the cession of Finland brought to an end those once-every-twenty-years wars that had characterized relationships for centuries. And Sweden became associated with Norway and permanently oriented toward the west and south instead of being primarily concerned with its eastern border. Economically and culturally the results of the Finnish amputation were incalculable.

The agricultural and the constitutional revolutions have been introduced in the previous chapter as well as the beginnings of the dynastic revolution. It was simpler to overthrow a monarch than to rebuild a government, but constructing a new foreign policy on the wreck of the old was to take time and fresh leadership. Sweden had in many respects in 1809–10 fallen to the nadir of its fortune and spirit. Was it now to go the way of Poland and other states that had been absorbed by stronger neighbors or was it to prove itself still viable? Through the interaction of the four domestic and diplomatic revolutions Sweden was revitalized. Rebuilding was slow but the state survived.

### The Dynastic Revolution: The Second Phase

The forward-looking changes of 1809–10 offered hope, but all was again thrown into jeopardy by the death of Crown Prince Karl August and its aftermath of disorder. Now the old question of the succession became even more acute. Some favored Karl August's brother Frederik Kristian of Augustenburg, about whom little was known. A few preferred King Frederik VI of Denmark, who again avowed his candidacy. All agreed that once again Napoleon had to be consulted. The great emperor, although he still favored his ally King Frederik, was willing to accept Prince Frederik Kristian.

Suddenly a new element was injected into the proceedings. Many people, and especially the younger officers, felt that a strong hand was needed for both the maintenance of internal order and the conquest of Finland. Why could not all purposes be accomplished by electing as crown price a French general who would be able to get Napoleon's cooperation against Russia? Twenty-nine-year-old Lieutenant Otto Mörner decided to act on this program and got himself appointed as a second emissary with duplicate dispatches to Napoleon. Once he had delivered his documents in Paris he discussed his problem with a friend and confirmed his own opinion — a French marshal it should be and specifically Bernadotte.

Jean Baptiste Jules Bernadotte was one in the first group of marshals named by Napoleon in 1804. He had been a soldier of Louis XVI and had risen to the rank of sergeant; with the coming of the French Revolution advancement had carried him through all ranks up to general of division, and he had briefly served as minister of war in 1798 while Napoleon was in Egypt. He had no great strategic victories to his credit, but he had showed himself an excellent tactician and superb in the art of inspiring soldiers. As minister of war and later as supervisor of various conquered territories he had evidenced administrative talent. He had a brief but dramatic experience as French ambassador at the Viennese court. And at one point he had stood in Denmark at the head of an army ready to invade Sweden!

He was in the prime of manhood at forty-seven and cut a dashing figure —

Läckö castle on promontory in Lake Vättern. The thirteenth-century original was rebuilt in the seventeenth century by M. G. De la Gardie. Photo: Erik Jägerblom.

Glimmingehus in Skåne, private stronghold 26 meters high with walls 2 meters thick; begun in 1499. Photo: P. Östner.

Örebro castle, erected in the thirteenth century, made a fortress in the reign of Karl IX, sixteenth and seventeenth centuries. Courtesy of the Swedish Institute, Stockholm. Photo: Åke Ahlstrand.

Late medieval houses on the Great Square, Stockholm. Photo: A.-G. Annerfalk.

The "King's Cottage," a burgher's house in Åhus, Skåne, where Karl XI hid during a Danish raid. Photo: B. Lindström.

Courtesy of the Swedish Institute, Stockholm.

Gustav II Adolf on horseback. Engraving by Crispin van der Passe.

Queen Kristina. Engraving by Petit after
a painting by Sébastien Bourdon.

Axel Oxenstierna. Engraving by
Willem Delff after a painting
by M. van Miereveld.

The *Wasa*, built as Gustav II
Adolf's flagship, 1628, after
being raised from the deep and
before its special museum-house
was built.

One of the many carved figures
recovered with the *Wasa*.

Courtesy of the Maritime
Museum and the Warship Wasa,
Stockholm.

Karl XII

Karl von Linné in Lapp costume

Olof Celsius, Sr.

Gustav III

Carl Michael Bellman and the characters in his writings. Lithograph after a painting by Per Krafft, Sr.

Opposite Page: Karl XII, engraving by Pieter Schenck; Karl von Linné in Lapp costume, engraving by Henry Kingsbury; Olof Celsius, Sr., engraving by Jacob Gillberg; Gustav III, engraving by J. Young after a painting by Carl Fredrik von Breda.

Karl von Linné. Courtesy of the Swedish Institute, Stockholm. Photo: The National Museum, Stockholm.

John Ericsson, inventor

Karl XIV Johan and Desirée

Uppsala University: main building, right rear; Gustavianum, cupola building with anatomic theater in foreground; archbishop's residence, left. Courtesy of the Swedish Information Service, New York.

Hälsingland scene.

Sleighriding in Dalarna. Photo: Alfred Heden.

A peasant quarter in the neighborhood of Hötorget [Haymarket], Stockholm. Woodcut after the drawing by Robert Haglund, 1875.

Stockholm scene (late nineteenth century): Forenoon at Mälar Harbor. Drawing by G. Broling.

tall, with flashing eyes, curly black hair, a captivating smile, and the quick right word. He had married the beautiful Desirée Clary, sister of Joseph Bonaparte's wife Julie, the two of them daughters of a merchant in Marseilles. Bernadotte and Desirée had a handsome young son Oscar. However, although Bernadotte was within the fringes of the extensive Bonaparte clan, some other factors were not so well known.

In 1798 the manipulators of Napoleon's coup had ousted Bernadotte as minister of war. In that chaotic time he was one who respected established authority and the law, and he had looked for the Directory to ask him to protect the constitution. When no such call came he simply stood aside while the bolder man grabbed power. Tension continued between the two ambitious but very different men. Bernadotte had swung with the Revolution but he was not revolutionist. He was a hot-tempered, quick-tongued Gascon but he was as cautious and calculating in action as those sons of the southwest French border. Napoleon was a brilliant and unscrupulous Corsican, eager to take great risks to win great results and respectful only of the law of necessity.

Napoleon claimed that on at least three occasions he would have had Bernadotte shot had it not been for Desirée, his own first fiancée. He resented Bernadotte's legalistic attitude and still more his boasting proclamations; perhaps he feared him as a rival. Yet he knew through experience that he could count on his marshal's loyalty. Only recently the emperor had ordered Bernadotte home in semi-disgrace, although he had only shortly before that granted the marshal a small holding in Italy and the title of prince of Ponte Corvo. When an emergency arose in the Netherlands because of a British military landing and Bernadotte was the general nearest the scene, Napoleon hesitated not an instant in entrusting him with the task of meeting the crisis. In 1810, when Mörner made arrangements to visit him, the marshal was back from this mission but living outside Paris, more or less isolated from events. For the emperor he was too useful and popular to be destroyed, too independent to be absorbed.

Mörner reached Bernadotte through the Swedish consul in Paris, bypassing the ambassador as well as the official Swedish emissaries who had carried the original dispatches. Mörner got from the surprised Bernadotte at least an agreement to consider the proposed candidature. As for Napoleon, when he saw that King Frederik was unacceptable, he suggested Eugène de Beauharnais but Eugène rejected. We do not know what the emperor's thoughts may have been when he learned about the proposal to Bernadotte. Officially he neither approved nor disapproved. Legend has it that at their leave-taking, when the marshal asked the emperor for permission to accept the Swedish invitation, Napoleon asked for a pledge that Bernadotte would never bear arms against France; Bernadotte is reported to have replied that he would have to act in the interests of Sweden, and Napoleon said simply, "Go then, and let our destinies be fulfilled." [1]

In Sweden, meanwhile, the riksdag had been recalled two months after its dissolution, this time to meet in Örebro because of the double dangers in Stockholm of interference by foreign diplomats and of disturbances by obstreperous mobs. Although the tendency in Örebro was to favor Prince Frederik Kristian and the committee at one point voted for him by a majority of eleven to one, it suddenly did an about face. Mörner had been disciplined for his unauthorized approach to Bernadotte, but through others came reports from Paris that Napoleon really preferred Bernadotte and that this prince of Ponte Corvo would bring financial advantages to the depleted Swedish treasury. On August 16, 1810 the committee reversed itself and voted ten to two for Bernadotte, the council approved, and on August 21 the riksdag elected. By October 20, 1810 the French prince-marshal was in Sweden, having accepted Lutheranism on his way through Denmark. And he now took the name Karl Johan — Charles Jean in French and sometimes Anglicized as Charles John. History has no parallel for such complicated and swift procedure and such an unlikely choice.

The desperate circumstances of the country paved the way for a newcomer's success, but it was Bernadotte's own skill that ensured it. He charmed the king and queen, who were delighted to adopt him as their son. He pleased the statesmen and the soldiers. Even Hans Järta, who had had his fill of military interference, could exclaim, "What pleases me most is the conviction that under him the gentlemen lieutenants will remain lieutenants." [2] The prince only once tried to make a speech in Swedish, and the audience's laughter discouraged further attempts. But in French his eloquence was reported to surpass that of Gustav III, and in his greetings to the riksdag he struck the right note:

> Peace is the only glorious aim of a wise and enlightened government. It is not the extent of a state which constitutes its strength and independence; it is its laws, its trade, its industry, and above all its spirit of nationality. Sweden has, it is true, suffered great losses, but the honor of the Swedish name has not suffered by them. May we submit to the decree of Providence and remind ourselves that God has left to us earth sufficient for our sustenance, and iron for our defense. [3]

Desirée did not come to the North with eleven-year old Oscar until December 1810 — not the best month to get acquainted with Sweden. The pretty girl from Marseilles did not adapt to the North (the winter of 1810–11 was unusually cold) and in June she returned to Paris, there to remain until 1823 when the marriage of Oscar brought her north again, this time to stay. Oscar quickly learned to speak Swedish fluently and became the link between the founder of the new dynasty and a whole series of reigns.

It would be fascinating to know clearly Bernadotte's reaction to the Swedish scene in 1810, but we get more evaluations of him than by him. He was too busy to write his impressions, and we must fill in the picture from other sources. Karl XIII was prematurely old, took no forceful part in affairs, and seemed enchanted to have his adopted crown prince assume leadership. King Karl suffered a stroke only a few weeks after the prince's arrival, and through the following eight years of his life Karl Johan was actually, and part of the time legally, regent. The minister of foreign affairs was Lars von Engeström, one of the revolutionists of 1809 who had been minister also under Gustav IV Adolf; he was scholarly and dependable and had thrown his support to Bernadotte's election, but he was perhaps most interested in his own position as chancellor of Lund University. Bernadotte's closest adviser came to be the urbane chancellor of the court, Gustav af Wetterstedt, who in 1824 succeeded von Engeström in the dignity of the foreign minister post. In a more personal way the two counts Löwenhielm became important as advisers and emissaries: Carl Löwenhielm was reputedly a son of Karl XIII; Gustav Löwenhielm served with distinction for several decades after the peace as ambassador in Paris. Hans Järta was a member of the council at first, but he was a highly independent spirit; he soon resigned from the council and in later years became a vigorous opponent of the king.

The various kinds of opposition to royal authority and to him as a person were constant worries to Karl Johan. He was keenly aware that he could not, like a Vasa, appeal for support on the basis of his ancestors' achievements. He knew that all men were fickle, and he had ample evidence of what the Swedes might do if they lost faith in him. Within less than twenty years before he came north had not disgruntled nobles assassinated Gustav III and overthrown Gustav IV Adolf; had not a mob in the streets of Stockholm struck down Axel Fersen?

Karl Johan himself had faced problems of discipline with the aristocratic officers during the continental campaign of 1813. One of the embittered officers who attacked the crown prince for his cooperation with Russia, C. H. Anckarsvärd, became the leader of continuing aristocratic opposition; he was an eloquent rebel of the type common during the Age of Freedom a century earlier. Neither his personal antagonism nor the constitutional objections of the priest F. B. Schwerin could shake the regime in Karl Johan's first or second decade, but the threat grew in the 1830s.

It was understandable that the proud nobility of Sweden did not relish the thought of rule by the son of a lawyer from a foreign country. Tenure based on achievement rather than on inheritance demanded continued success, and Karl Johan realized it. During the campaign of 1813 he had said, "My fate depends on the outcome of a battle. If I lose it no one in all Europe will lend me six francs."[4] Furthermore, Sweden was a troubled and unhappy country in 1810 and for some years thereafter. With such realities constantly in mind, and exaggerated by fears rooted in his ignorance of Swedish language and customs, the crown prince had to face his problems with just the right combination of wisdom and caution and firmness.

Among the problems that the French-born prince saw as crucial, one of the obvious ones was alcohol. He was himself a teetotaler, and he came to Sweden just as the relaxation of restrictions on distilling *brännvin* (*akvavit*) was increasing consumption to over forty quarts per capita per year. Solution had to wait; at the moment all Karl Johan could do was to make the unforgettable statement that "Brännvin will be the ruin of the Swedish people. . . ."[5] The great land reform was already under way; Karl Johan recognized agricultural productivity as a major task, and one of his first acts was to approve the establishment of an agricultural school in 1811. Military training for all men between the ages of twenty and twenty-five was passed unanimously by the riksdag. Another measure influenced by the tensions of foreign affairs was a new law on press freedom that permitted the government to stop publication of any harmful periodical. Proposals were made in 1812 for a revision of the constitution but Karl Johan wisely thought the time inopportune for raising controversial issues. Finance was a realm in which the prince thought himself to be an expert, and the need was pressing, but there is considerable doubt whether Karl Johan's schemes were helpful. Other problems were crucial and immediate: One was that of discipline in the army and order in society. No ruler, least of all a commoner raised to royal rank, could tolerate individual decision making in either military or civil affairs, and Karl Johan's sensitivity on this point was to make the headlines more than once. Even Mörner the kingmaker received small thanks, perhaps partly because he had acted without orders. Restoration of traditional order and respect for law was an imperative for the existence of the state and for its prestige abroad. The immediate overriding problem was indeed Sweden's international position.

## The Diplomatic Revolution

The election of a French marshal as crown prince, together with the recent military and diplomatic catastrophe, raised doubts about whether Sweden even wanted to pursue an independent line. Within Sweden itself it was expected that at the earliest opportunity Karl Johan would get Napoleonic backing for an attempt to reconquer Finland. The French minister, Baron d'Alquier, treated the crown prince as if he were Napoleon's stooge (an attitude that soon led to the envoy's removal by request). The emperor himself could hardly have entertained any illusions about either Bernadotte or the Swedes. Because of his suspicions he brusquely demanded, only a month after the prince left Paris, that Sweden declare war on Britain and enforce the Continental System by excluding British goods from Pomerania. Sweden was hardly in a position to decline. Although Karl Johan abstained from the decision making the government did declare war on its most important trade partner. However, consultations with the commander of the English fleet assured that it would be a phantom war, declared with fingers crossed and fought with hands folded. It would be some months before Sweden's real position could be determined, and it would certainly not be decided on the basis of an emotional crusade.

The determinants of policy were weighed in the scales of calculated politics. If the government were to follow the popular and expected line and make Finland its goal this might indeed prove lucky for Sweden. On the other hand success in Finland would mean continuing enmity with Russia and therefore lasting dependence on France. Karl Johan could hardly envision himself in a position of longtime lackey to Napoleon — of that he had had enough. Furthermore, although Napoleon was in 1810 at the pinnacle of his power, his former marshal had been close enough to realize the instability of that pinnacle. Additionally, he was not swayed either by traditional hatred of Russia or by bonds of sentiment with Finland. He could think coolly of alternatives. The obvious alternative for a prince and a kingdom that had to expand to regain its sense of importance was to move west instead of east. Norway had been on the agenda of Gustav III and on that of Gustav IV Adolf. Norway in Swedish possession would not add to defense obligations but rather would ease them by lessening the threat of the two-front war. This turn westward would please the Russians and might enlist their aid. Because of the maritime relationships involved the acquisition of Norway would require close affiliation with England, which would not be demeaning and should be commercially advantageous. To Bernadotte with his French Revolution-bred concepts of natural boundaries it seemed ordained by nature that the Scandinavian peninsula should be a political unit. Cultural affinities of Sweden with Norway probably had no influence on policy, especially because, in case of a choice, the cultural affinities with Finland were as intimate as could be. That Norway had been long united with Denmark cannot have been perceived as a major deterrent at a moment when revolutionary changes were being forced throughout Europe. National self-determination had not become a sanctified ideal. Sweden's expansion in north Germany, where it still claimed half of Pomerania, was another possibility, but in light of continental conflicts and ambitions it held little appeal. Sweden's new crown prince was therefore actuated by three basic considerations: his recognition that Napoleon stood on feet of clay, his interest in commerce with England, and his desire to win a secure territorial prize for Sweden and thus solidify his position.

In the course of the year 1811 many diplomatic feelers were extended. Karl Johan gave Napoleon every opportunity to assist Sweden in getting Norway from Denmark or Finland from Russia — or both. But Napoleon was concerned with his own problems. More and more as the Swedish policy leaders considered the situation Norway came to be their goal and an anti-French position their means of achieving it. But how could the Swedish people be persuaded to accept this unexpected turn-about? Napoleon himself handed them the solution.

In January 1812 French troops marched into Swedish Pomerania and made the small Swedish occupying force prisoners. The reason was partly that Pomerania was still being used as an entrepôt for British goods in defiance of the continental blockade. More decisive was that Napoleon, before marching to Moscow, had to secure his rear and dared not trust a Swedish continental foothold behind him. The invasion was an act of war as well as an intolerable insult to Karl Johan personally. Immediately the crown prince sent Count Carl Löwenhielm to St. Petersburg to negotiate an alliance with Tsar Alexander, and the diplomatic revolution began.

Alexander, worried about his northern flank in the coming struggle with Napoleon and eager to divert Swedish eyes from Finland, happily signed the treaty that Karl Johan wanted: Russian troops would aid Sweden to wrest Norway from Denmark, *after which* a Swedish force would assist the Russians against the French. This treaty of April 1812 was the keystone for the "policy of 1812" and the model on which other treaties would be patterned. But no one else had as much at stake as did Alexander, and no one else would be quite as generous in his promises. Alexander himself soon had to retract on his troop promises. In August 1812 he invited the new leader of Sweden to meet him in the former Swedish castle of Åbo in western Finland, and there explained that he would need all his soldiers for the defense of Russia against Napoleon. Karl Johan appreciated the situation, for if Russia collapsed Sweden would have no hope of retaining Norway or even its own independence. The two princes of the North actually laid the basis for a long-lasting personal friendship, and Alexander dangled before Bernadotte the possibility of becoming king of France.

It took some months longer for Bernadotte to make peace with England and to persuade the Prussians to accept his terms for cooperation in the great coalition against Napoleonic supremacy. The Austrians never did accept. Diplomacy proceeded in step with military developments, with occasional missteps. As the drama of Napoleonic disaster unfolded in the winter of 1812–13 new hope rose in Europe, which was increasingly eager to enlist the aid of Swedish troops with their experienced general. Prussia in April 1813 agreed reluctantly to Sweden's demand for Norway, as England had done in a treaty of March 3. Britain also of course provided subsidies for the Swedish army. Up to this time it was still the intent that Sweden should win Norway before engaging in action against France, although the English treaty envisioned a campaign in Denmark (vaguely referred to as "on the continent"). Napoleon's calamitous retreat from Russia and the necessity of dealing with him before he could regain strength led nevertheless to shifts in emphasis. For the other allies the defeat of Napoleon was the focus of all their striving. For Sweden and Bernadotte the focus was acquisition of Norway, whereas defeat of Napoleon was incidental. Misunderstandings and recriminations were bound to arise.

Yet again it was only through the success of the larger cause that Karl Johan could hope to gain and hold his compensation. Therefore he yielded to the entreaties of his allies and sent General J. A. Sandels with a Swedish force to reoccupy Pomerania and prepared for his own landing in Germany. At the same time the beginnings of allied success changed the military and diplomatic situation. For a campaign in north Germany Sweden became less important to the allies than Denmark, and Russian diplomatic shenanigans in Copenhagen attempted to win Denmark to "the common cause." Bernadotte had reason to doubt the faithfulness even of his friend Alexander; his fears of a treacherous renunciation of Russian and even British pledges regarding Norway seemed all too close to realization. The prince landed at last in Pomerania in mid-May but was determined not to join battle until the long-promised Russian and Prussian troops were put under his command. It was in these circumstances, where military action and diplomacy had to be juggled expertly, that General G. C. Döbeln disobeyed orders and sent four battalions to the succor of Hamburg. It was only by luck that they did not get caught there by the Danes or the French. Bernadotte was in anguish, and especially disturbed by Döbeln's insubordination. As a lesson to the Swedes he had to discipline an able general. In the Revolutionary army Bernadotte had met the same problem, and it was in 1795 he had said, "An army without discipline can win a victory but cannot make use of it." [6]

Finally Denmark, having refused repeated offers of compromise and territorial compensation, committed itself to the French side. The situation was clarified, and the prince was relieved. Russian and Prussian troops were put under Bernadotte's command, and all was ready for his army to act in both his and the common cause. At just that point, on June 4, Russia and Prussia made an armistice with Napoleon and threw consternation and despair into the

Swedish camp. The general dismay fostered another disciplinary incident in which the Russophobe Colonel C. H. Anckarsvärd wrote a bitter letter to Karl Johan reminding him of the revolution of 1809 and suggesting the possibility of another coup. The colonel was dismissed and became a lifetime antagonist of the prince. Out of the gloom, however, eventuated the participation of Austria in the general alliance and the resumption of war. The respite had at least presented an opportunity for consultation and acquaintance among strangers and former enemies.

At a "summit conference" in Trachenberg, Silesia on July 9–12, 1813 the Swedish crown prince met with the king of Prussia, the tsar of Russia, and a bevy of top-ranking generals and diplomats including Count Stadion from Austria. Political purposes were frankly discussed and a campaign plan was outlined. Although undoubtedly many others contributed ideas Bernadotte was the major author of the so-called Trachenberg Plan. Three main armies would form a sweeping semicircle which would converge on Napoleon. As these armies advanced each would attack when small resistance promised success. When Napoleon himself was present the allied forces should avoid battle, while adjacent armies harassed the enemy flanks, pushing him on until the massed force of all could be concentrated against the military genius. The Austrian-Russian-Prussian Army of Bohemia in the south, 225,000 strong, would be the chief striking force. General Blücher with 50,000 to 80,000 Prussians would move forward from Silesia, and Karl Johan with a 100,000 man army of the North (Swedes, Prussians, Russians, German Legion, etc.) would act on the right flank. "All the allied armies will take the offensive and the camp of the enemy will be their rendezvous." [7]

On August 11 the armistice was denounced, Austria declared war, and a great squeeze slowly brought Napoleon to battle at Leipzig in mid-October. It was a team effort in which the execution followed the plan. Karl Johan's generalship was acknowledged to be superb in the engagements at Grossbeeren (August 23, 1813) and at Dennewitz (September 6) but recriminations were brought against him for exposing the Prussians and saving the Swedes. At Dennewitz General von Bülow's Prussians lost 10,000 men, the Swedes none, and only their artillery was engaged. Karl Johan frankly admitted that he regarded this phase of the war as primarily Prussia's concern and that he had to conserve his Swedes for the accomplishment of their own goal. However justified he was the policy left a bad taste in the mouth, accentuated by later troop dispositions. In the decisive Battle of the Nations at Leipzig (October 16–19, 1813) Bernadotte's army was the last to enter the fray. Suspicion arose that the ex-marshal was not only sparing his Swedes but being tender to the French. Certainly he lacked the eagerness for slaughter shown by Blücher, and it is understandable that he had no taste for leading foreign armies into his former homeland. After the great victory at Leipzig Bernadotte did not join in the common pursuit into France but diverted his own forces northward.

## The Union with Norway

By October 19, 1813 the major object of the alliance had been achieved: Napoleon had been defeated and Europe was free. It was time for the Swedes to act in their own behalf. In late October Karl Johan sent the Prussians and most of his Russian troops forward to clear Holland of the French, and with his own Swedish troops and a corps of Russians he swung off through Hanover into Denmark (Holstein). Opposition on the battlefield was brief, and the Danes were obliged to make first an armistice and finally the Treaty of Kiel (signed on January 14, 1814). Metternich, the great Austrian manipulator, tried by intrigue to undermine Swedish demands during the armistice, but after one resumption of war it was the Austrian Count Bombelles who persuaded King Frederik to yield and thus save his kingdom from utter ruin. By the Treaty of Kiel King Frederik ceded to the king of Sweden and his successors the kingdom of Norway, which should "under full possession and sovereignty belong to the King of Sweden and comprise a kingdom united with the Swedish state."[8] The peculiar phrasing was to stir legal debate for decades to come. Denmark was to get 1 million riksdalers and the province of Pomerania (as soon as Sweden held Norway), and Sweden was to pay Norway's share, in proportion to population, of the Danish national debt (another clause that was to create trouble). Iceland, Greenland, and the Faroes were retained by Denmark, though they were historically Norway's — evidently Chancellor Wetterstedt was not sufficiently aware of his history and did not fight for the overseas territories, for which he was upbraided by the more learned foreign minister von Engeström.

The goal of the Policy of 1812 was attained — but only on paper and at the cost of much bitterness. Now Karl Johan's impatient allies insisted that he hasten to the Low Countries to support the common cause to its denouement. Bernadotte and his army moved on to Liége, but somehow the prince did not find it possible to proceed further. He was still skeptical of his allies as they were of him. He was excluded from the conference of Chatillon and not wanted in the continuing alliance of the major powers. As Castlereagh, the wise English foreign minister, said, not all the small states could be included, and it was therefore a question of four allies or twenty-four, and of course twenty-four was unthinkable. The ex-French general cautiously intrigued for a position of high authority in France, though he turned down a belated offer to be generalissimo for the Bourbons. He shrank back from marching with a foreign army into his native land. Isolated and worried he made an incognito dash to Paris, then darted quickly back to Liége to care for his essential job. He was needed in the North.[9]

The Norwegians resented being handed like so many chattels from one king to another. They cherished the proper historical assumption of being an independent kingdom, and the Danes were quite willing to see them make Statholder Prince Kristian Frederik their king. A constitutional convention gathered at Eidsvold, a pleasant rural estate north of Oslo, and framed a constitution for an independent state. It was a well-conceived document applying to Norway the up-to-date political theories and experience of England, France, and America. On May 17, 1814 the constitution was announced and Kristian Frederik was elected king. That day became Norway's independence day. For Bernadotte and the Swedes it all meant that there could be no peaceful transfer of authority. The army had to march again, and no one's heart was in it. Karl Johan first assured himself of the continuing support of Russia and Britain; from Prussia he did not hope for much, and from Austria he could expect only opposition. His allies did agree to abide by their pledges, and they first tried persuasion on Denmark. But the basic opposition was in Norway itself and was led by young Kristian Frederik. The rapid development and intensity of Norwegian national feeling, the antagonism that had grown toward Karl Johan personally and toward Swedish policy, European sympathy for Denmark, and the desire of all the allies to wash their hands of war left no one eager to aid the Swedish cause.

Bernadotte and the Swedes were of course disappointed that the Norwegians did not wish to unite with them; the pro-union party led in Norway by Count Herman Wedel-Jarlsberg was much weaker in numbers and influence than the Swedes had imagined. Centuries of border warfare had left scars, and although the Norwegians were happy to be rid of Danish tutelage they had no desire to be subjected to another. Perhaps most of all the Norwegians feared the warlike propensities of the Swedes. For the Norwegians no compelling attraction drew them toward Sweden. Economically no great advantage appeared for the Norwegians, or even for the Swedes; the two countries produced timber and other products too similar to stimulate extensive interchange. The Swedish purpose in driving toward union was not economic but strategic and dynastic. Were the possible results worth a long campaign burdensome for both peoples, and bound to destroy property and life, to increase hatreds, and to make reconciliation difficult?

For all these reasons, and for other more complicated ones involving title to Pomerania and possibly his own opportunities in France, the crown prince was eager for a quick settlement. From the end of May he organized new contingents of troops in Sweden and toward the end of July the transports brought home his army from the Low Countries. He had altogether close to

70,000 men, all with training and some with experience, to lead against 30,000 Norwegians, only slightly trained and without experienced leadership. At the end of July the Swedes thrust rapidly into Norway, took Fredrikstad and invested the fortress of Fredriksten. For a week negotiations had been proceeding with Kristian Frederik and on August 14, the same day the Swedes crossed the Glomma River, an armistice was concluded at Moss.

The liberal terms agreed upon at Moss were slowly hammered into a treaty agreement. The armies were sent home, except for a small Swedish force left in Norway. Kristian Frederik left Norway and resigned his powers into the hands of the council and storting. The frontier was demilitarized. Sweden agreed to Norway's retention of the constitution of Eidsvold, making only such changes as were necessary to recognize the king of Sweden as king of Norway. It was a far cry from the absorption of Norway that most Swedes had expected and that had been envisioned in the treaties with Sweden's allies. It was a product of Norwegian action and of Karl Johan's respect for national feeling as well as of his sense of urgency. But the Norwegians were in no hurry. They took skillful advantage of the Swedish sense of haste by forcing concessions, and the points yielded by the Swedes became matters of both psychological and legal importance. Although the Swedes took the view that the Treaty of Kiel was the basis of union the Norwegians insisted that the basis was the agreement made by the storting in November 1814. The differences in legal assumptions continued through the life of the union. Hence the union was a loose-jointed structure, providing for a common king, Swedish administration of joint foreign policy, and otherwise separateness (somewhat like the stipulations in the medieval union under Magnus Eriksson and the later Union of Kalmar). Not even a common defense system was required, and Norwegian military forces could not be taken out of Norway in an offensive war without the consent of the storting.

The Norwegian constitution differed fundamentally from the Swedish. Whereas in Sweden the king had a solid position of authority, in Norway he had only a suspensive veto in the storting, which by passing a law the third time over his veto could override him. The storting itself was a one-chamber body (that divided itself into two parts for ordinary affairs). Sweden retained its four-Estate riksdag, wherein the nobility was still powerful. Norway, with only a few noble families, by 1821 abolished nobility entirely. The king resided in Stockholm except for brief periods in Kristiania and appointed a statholder to represent him in Norway. Since each constitution fairly reflected the nature of each country's society it was clear that disagreements would multiply. For these later disputes the Norwegian insistence on legalities gave them an advantage over Bernadotte and the Swedes, who in 1814 were concerned with practical immediate results.

SWEDEN-NORWAY:
1814 - 1905

K I N G D O M   O F
N O R W A Y   &   S W E D E N

FINLAND
(TO RUSSIA, 1809)

R U S S I A N   E M P I R E

Kristiania

ÅLAND

Helsingfors

Stockholm

Göta
Canal

Gothenburg

GOTLAND

ÖLAND

KINGDOM OF
DENMARK

Copen-
hagen

SLESVIG
HOLSTEIN
(GER. 1866)

MECKLENBURG

PRUSSIA

What had Karl Johan gained? Prestige, to be sure, for himself and for the state that had been defeated and partitioned only four years earlier. The Baltic-oriented state including Finland and constantly feuding with Russia now became a peninsular Scandinavian state looking westward. Also, a unified state had become a dual state (a fact, however, that was less apparent in 1814 than it became some decades later). Swedish Pomerania was passed on to Prussia, and Sweden no longer had either the advantages or the greater disadvantages of continental possessions. Karl Johan was able to make good his claim that Denmark did not deserve Pomerania because of its failure to turn over Norway peacefully; and Prussia paid 5 million riksdalers for the province — 3.5 million to Sweden and 1.5 million to Karl Johan personally — most of which went to recompense his close assistants or to public causes. Overseas the French insisted on return to them of Guadeloupe in the West Indies, which Britain had promised to Sweden; for this Britain compensated Karl Johan personally with 24 million francs, most of which went toward payment of Sweden's foreign debt, while Bernadotte in turn was given a permanent annual grant by the riksdag of 200,000 riksdalers. On the debit side was the Norwegian debt which Karl Johan could not squirm out of paying (Norway assumed it, after reduction to 3 million riksdalers from the Danish claim of 7 million and of course a bitter legacy of ill will in Denmark and elsewhere). Bernadotte had to do something to win the gratitude of the Swedish people and to confirm his dynasty in power and that he did. Nor could Metternich and all his men use the rule of legitimacy to topple the Gascon from his throne in the North. Napoleon and his creations fell from power and vanished. Independent Bernadotte, almost accidentally handed a crown, established a lasting dynasty. Most significant for the future was the detachment from Sweden of Pomerania and from Finland, two longtime sources of military entanglements.

## Note on Finland and Norway

To a twentieth-century observer it seems that Norway should make a more natural partner for Sweden than Finland. But the affiliation of Finland with Sweden in the early nineteenth century was fundamental both legally and emotionally.

The old Sweden had been one state, one church, one culture. We have come to think of Finland as a thing apart largely because of its position and its history since 1809. Before 1809 Finland had been a part of Sweden far longer than had Skåne, Blekinge, and Halland, longer than the unsettled northern provinces and much of the borderland to the west. True there was a Finnish language that was different, and there were separatist movements at various times. But business in Finland as in the other provinces was done in the Swedish language, as were all legal matters. Finnish writers were Swedish writers, on into the nineteenth century. Stockholm was the capital. Finns took part in the riksdag on the same basis as other Swedes. Uppsala was the university of preeminence for the whole state even after the founding of Åbo in 1640. Border problems on the east were problems of the central state, and the armies, whether of Karl XII or Gustav II Adolf or others, were common armies. Antagonism toward Russia was a potent unifying bond. The settlers on the Delaware were a mixture; probably half of them were Finns. There was no single clearcut boundary between Sweden proper and Finland; for example, the breakdown into administrative districts — of church, court, election districts — did not coincide. As for linguistic boundaries, they were either variously local or nonexistent. In Finland were many Swedish-speaking citizens and in Sweden proper a number of Finnish-speaking. Finns became officials in Stockholm and Värmlänningar and Skåningar took posts in Finland. From Sweden proper came much of the capital for Finnish business. Finland, in brief, was much more thoroughly integrated with Sweden proper than was Norway with Denmark.

How can this integrated society of Finland-Sweden be compared with the situation in the new union of Norway-Sweden? Linguistically the Norwegians were of course closer to the Swedes than were the Finns — except that the recognized literary language of Finland was then actually Swedish. On the map Norway looks geographically closer to Sweden proper than does Finland. Yet in the north there was no natural geographic separation between Sweden and Finland. During most of the year it was probably easier to sail across the Gulf of Bothnia or the Baltic than to climb over the mountain range between Norway and Sweden. Whereas the Finns and Swedes had been fighting together for centuries against a common enemy the Norwegians and Swedes had been at each others' throats again and again. Out of a very distant common origin had grown strong differences in cultural development.

Most significant, by 1814 the spirit of nationalism had grown powerful in Norway, first directed against Denmark but easily redirected against Sweden. Hence as the two nations came together, through force, their union was a legal reality but hardly a community of will or common interest.

# XII

## ON THE ROAD TO NEUTRALITY
## AND PEACE, 1810–1914

THE LAST OF THE FOUR REVOLUTIONS of the early nineteenth century involved a complete reorientation of Sweden's relations with its neighbors.
Finland was shorn away; Russia, the traditional enemy, became an ally;
Norway entered into a union with Sweden that lasted almost a century; and
Sweden retired from the continent. Time modified these readjustments, but
fundamental change had taken place: westward leaning replaced eastward
leaning and a basis was laid for a policy of peace.

### A Foreign Policy of Temptation and Restraint

Karl Johan knew the great armies and resources of France and the continent as
a whole; he was probably more aware than any Swede could be of the relative
weakness of his new kingdom. And since, despite his bravado of manner, he
was as practical as any Swede, he carefully set the country on the road to
peace. It was not, however, an unalterable route. Tempting byroads appeared
from time to time before him and his successors. Looking back, we can see
that nineteenth-century Sweden accepted in military and foreign policy the
role of a small and satisfied power, with only occasional yearnings to play a
more ambitious part. The long-lasting era of peace began in 1814, but it
remained a peace backed always by a moderate defensive strength. King and
riksdag were well content with the old *indelta* army apportioned by districts
and locally supported; they rejected suggestions for an expanded and demo-
cratically controlled militia. Policy was influenced by the thought that England would assist Sweden in defense of the Baltic, as it had done in 1808–9,

317

and therefore the Swedish open-seas fleet was combined with its skerries fleet under common direction, and inland strongholds were built rather than coastal defenses.

Nevertheless, Karl Johan watched with fascinated interest the diplomatic developments on the European stage, and for the most part he played in the Russian company. He watched nervously as Napoleon returned from Elba and was shipped to St. Helena, but he did nothing. In the early years of his reign he needed support against the antipathy of Metternich, and he nurtured the bonds struck with Alexander in 1812. For the tsar's sake he even approved the adherence of Karl XIII to the Holy Alliance in 1816 though he had little sympathy with it. He took a pro-Russian line in most of the Near Eastern crises of the 1820s and the 1830s. As late as 1840–41 he was tempted to try to play a role once more in great power politics, but he was dissuaded by his own advisers.

Not always did the relations between the Russian and Swedish monarchs proceed smoothly. Karl Johan hoped for Alexander's support in enabling him to evade payment of Norway's share of the Danish state debt. This he had pledged in the Treaty of Kiel, but when Denmark failed to deliver Norway peaceably into Swedish hands he thought he should be freed of the obligation. He did succeed, as we have already seen, in retaining Pomerania and selling it directly to Prussia. But on the debt question neither Russia nor the other powers would support him, and in bitterness he accepted defeat — though he got the payment scaled down to 3 million riksdalers (even this he had literally to force the Norwegians to pay).

In one of the most irritating and revealing episodes of Karl Johan's diplomatic career he collided directly with Tsar Alexander. The king and his ministers were all involved in the sale of five older naval vessels to Colombia and Mexico in 1824–25. Tsar Alexander's "liberal period" was then long past, and he stood firmly with the king of Spain against the new republics of South America. The republics were ready to pay good silver for whatever ships they could get, and the Swedes could use the money from the sale of the old ships to build two more up-to-date vessels. They dealt through an English firm and thought the British government would back the arrangement. They dreamed beautiful dreams of profit and modernization. But the British did not at that moment want to antagonize the Russians any further. The Swedish position was weakened by a previous agreement they had made not to negotiate with the republics without Russian consent, though the interpretation of this agreement differed between the Russians and the Swedes. The tsar was adamant. The Swedes had to make a humiliating renunciation of contract with the South Americans and pay high damages and, even worse, their bright hopes of expanding trade with the new nations of the west were dashed. The points that pricked Swedish pride were that it had been impelled to make an agreement with Russia in the first place and that Russia alone had the power to interpret it.[1]

Almost immediately after the ship-sale fiasco Alexander died, which eased the solution of a personal problem. For Alexander was guardian of Prince Gustav, son of Gustav IV Adolf and pretender to the throne of Sweden. Karl Johan had been extremely sensitive about the intrigues of the supporters of Gustav IV Adolf and his family and had been highly annoyed when the son Gustav assumed the title prince of Sweden. Karl Johan set the diplomatic machinery in motion in anguished protest, and the new tsar Nicholas was sympathetic enough to help in getting the title changed to prince of Wasa. This cooperation made it easier for Karl Johan to look through Russian eyes at the Turkish war of 1828–29 and at the Belgian and Polish uprisings of 1830 and 1831. Actually, the revolutionary ex-general now abhorred national risings against authority, so his mutuality of feeling was real until he became sickened by the Russian atrocities in suppressing the Poles.

By 1834, in the new Near East crisis, Russian objections to Swedish defense measures led to a Swedish declaration of neutrality in which Sweden-Norway promised to hold open its ports (with a few exceptions) to the navies of all belligerent powers. Such a proposal did Russia no good, for Russia had all the Baltic ports it needed, and its obvious favoritism to England drew protests from the tsar and was a tip-off of the beginnings of a Swedish inclination to the west.

The so-called friendship between the big bear and the little lion was an artificial thing, not based on long-term community of interest even in the days of Karl Johan. Sweden maintained its basic freedom of action and was not lured by fear into the arms of Russia or by economic advantage into the sphere of Britain. Sweden was distinctly uncomfortable as Russia proceeded with fortification work in the Åland Islands, altogether too close to Stockholm. In the later 1830s Sweden began to strengthen its defenses on Gotland and talk began, too, of creating a free port there at Slite or Visby. Since completion of the Göta Canal in 1832 the English had evinced interest in the trans-Sweden shipment of goods and redistribution from a Baltic center to avoid the Danish Sound tolls. But English activity in eastern waters was abhorrent to the Russians, and in 1838 Tsar Nicholas made a special visit to Stockholm and persuaded Karl Johan to drop the plans, at least temporarily. It seemed better to adjust than to annoy.

Another unsettling issue involved the sparsely settled regions of the far north where the Lapps had from time immemorial migrated back and forth with their reindeer. A treaty of 1751 sanctioned these movements, and no boundary was fixed until 1826. Now the Finnish-based Lapps were becoming more interested in fishing in the waters off northern Norway and asked for a place on Varangerfjord where they could build shelters and leave their boats over the winter; at the same time they complained of the damages caused to their settlements by the reindeer of the Norwegian Lapps. The Russians stood behind the Finns, and the Swedes supported the Norwegians (an interesting reversal of position for the Swedes, who had been on the other side of the nonfence in 1751). The stubbornness of each side delayed agreement, and in 1852 the Russians brought pressure to bear by closing the border against the Norwegian Lapps. Behind it all fluttered a shadow of suspicion — were the Russians angling not so much for fishing rights as for an ice-free port on Varangerfjord? No evidence supported this idea, but it was important as a rumor in the period from 1836 to the 1850s; it was reported by J. R. Crowe, British consul in Hammerfest, believed by Lord Palmerston, and used by the Swedes to enhance English concern with northern affairs. Red herrings swam in those cold waters, but obviously the Swedes would allow neither Åland nor Finnmark to become a *casus belli*. The climax in Russian-Swedish relations and the diplomatic revolution came with the Crimean War.

The Crimea was far from Sweden, but the relationship was close. The two points of access to Russia from the west were the Black Sea and the Gulf of Finland. From far back in history wars between the Russians and the Turks roused in Swedish hearts either hope or fear for a second front in the north. When Russia moved against the Turks in the summer of 1853 the response in Sweden was automatic yet restrained. The possibility of a general war was sensed, and at once Denmark and Sweden-Norway agreed upon a proclamation of neutrality along the lines of the declaration of 1834 (but the announcement was delayed until December). During this crisis King Oscar, who had succeeded to the throne in 1844, and many Swedes hoped that the western powers would combine against Russia and that Sweden might take advantage of the situation to regain Finland. For the Finns the sheer necessities of adjustment to the Russian masters brought a degree of acceptance, but the Swedes did not face these necessities and were able to nurture their animosities. King Oscar seemed eager for adventure but had to exercise discretion. Crown Prince Karl was openly bellicose: he took Karl XII as his idol and thought it was his duty to settle the account of Poltava. The French and the English were eager to obtain Swedish aid and deliberately encouraged the Swedish government to think of reconquering its lost province. But how could the Swedes maneuver into a favorable position? The Crimean imbroglio offered the first opportunity since 1809.

In the spring of 1854, even before their declaration of war on Russia, French and British fleets entered the Baltic and during the summer harried the Finnish coast and shipping. They took full advantage of the Scandinavian neutrality declaration which permitted their warships to use Fårösund in Gotland as a base. A force of 10,000 French landed in the Åland Islands and blew up the Russian fortifications at Bomarsund. King Oscar was invited to occupy these Swedish-populated islands, but he would not do so until the allies met his demands for guarantees — and he may thus have lost the only chance to regain at least this portion of the lost Finnish province. Like his father before him, Oscar was bold in speech and hypercautious in action.

As the war progressed the British and French brought increasing pressure on Sweden to join their ranks, but they never put on paper a pledge that Sweden would get Finland. In the meantime Oscar was disgusted that the allies should choose to attack the "giant's little toe" in the Crimea instead of cutting his "throat" at St. Petersburg. At the end of 1855, still hopeful, Oscar drew up a mobilization plan, but to his dismay Austria and France forced the war to a close and their peace arrangements hung on eastern rather than on northern questions. Ironically, Sweden's threatening diplomacy had played a part in inducing the tsar to make peace; he then left Sweden empty-handed.

Although the western powers hesitated to go all the way in bribes and guarantees to Sweden, they did recognize a common interest in blocking Russian expansion in that part of the world. The legal expression of this interest was the November Treaty of 1855, which marked a major reversal of Swedish policy. Sweden-Norway promised not to cede either territory or fishing rights to Russia, and France and England agreed to support Sweden-Norway with force if necessary. Thus came to an end the last vestiges of Sweden's "Policy of 1812"; Sweden renounced its great eastern neighbor and turned westward. The change was not wholly based on the immediate circumstances of the war. Commercial interests and a changing political atmosphere emphasized the increasing importance of ties with Great Britain, whereas the popular antagonism toward Russia, never quelled, made itself felt.

Although Sweden had not quite become a belligerent, Oscar sent an ambassador and a program to the peace conference in Paris. He wanted: limitation of Russian and naval forces in the Baltic and the White Sea; cession of the Åland Islands to Sweden, or at least their neutralization under British and French guarantees; and prohibition of Russian fortifications on the Finnish coast north and west of Sveaborg (Helsinki). But King Oscar I exercised very little leverage, and out of his eager maneuverings all he got was a tiny segment of his second demand: Russia had to pledge not to rebuild the fortifications on Åland. In a more general sense Sweden gained also by the principles of international law enunciated at Paris: "free ships make free goods," to which Britain had yielded in the spring of 1854 because of pressure by the Scandinavian countries and by France and the United States.

The small power had to be satisfied with small gains. It had not dared to take bold risks and had been outmaneuvered by the great states. Economically its "neutrality" had profited both its farmers and merchants. Oscar had played with fire in encouraging the revival of popular hatred against Russia and in taking matters, by personal diplomacy, over the heads of his advisers, but nothing serious had come of either. Sweden had avoided war and after forty years of collaboration with the tsars had used the occasion of the Crimean War to shift its diplomatic allegiances in safety.[2] Although Oscar had played well the game of the possible, now he was sick, prematurely old, and disappointed — and a new threat was building on the southern flank.

The Slesvig-Holstein question exploded with new virulence in the mid-nineteenth century. For centuries these borderlands between Denmark and Germany had played a disturbing role in the history of the entire North, and the legal complications became so involved that Lord Palmerston could all too aptly say that only three people understood them: Palmerston himself, who had forgotten; the Danish king, who had died; and a German professor, who had gone crazy. This is not the place to unravel the skein of confusion. Suffice it to say that the inheritance issue became ominous in January 1848 when Kristian VIII died and Frederik VII inherited as both king in Denmark and duke in Slesvig-Holstein. Frederik had no male heir, and it appeared probable that when he died the succession to the kingship in Denmark would pass in one line, while the succession to the dukedom would pass in another line determined by the Salic Law (requiring inheritance strictly through the male line). This complication occupied the legalists and the great powers and was settled at length by the Conference of London in 1852. The maintenance of Denmark was important for the European balance of power. But for Denmark and Slesvig-Holstein the succession question was only the facade of the controversy. The real conflict sprang from the emotions and ideologies of nationalism.

History had knitted Slesvig and Holstein together and had more loosely connected both with Denmark. Holstein had remained German in population and was a member of the German Confederation. Slesvig, originally Danish, had been slowly infiltrated by Germans. The central portion was mixed, whereas North Slesvig was mostly Danish and rural. In the nineteenth century Germanic nationalism demanded the use of the German language in church and school throughout the duchy and a common constitution for Slesvig-Holstein. This set of demands clashed with Danish nationalism, which insisted on closer integration of Slesvig with Denmark. The majority of Slesvig-Holsteiners sought and won the support of Prussia and other German states; the Danish Slesvigers had the backing of Denmark and of the newly developing pan-Scandinavian sentiment in Norway and Sweden. This sense of Danish nationalism and Nordic brotherhood was illustrated and fostered by the founding in Slesvig, at Rødding, of the first folk high school. Frederik VII tossed fresh fuel onto the pyre when he promised a liberal constitution for the kingdom and proposed to incorporate Slesvig within it. The complex of antagonisms, basically Germanism against Scandinavianism, also involved merchants against farmers, officials against citizenry, and liberals against conservatives. It was all exacerbated by the sweep of revolutions that began in France in February 1848 and spread across Europe. An abscess at the base of the Jutland peninsula affected the entire European political body.

To block King Frederik's plans to assert Danish sovereignty in Slesvig and separate Slesvig and Holstein at the Eider River, an army of Holsteiners marched north into Slesvig, defeated the Danish forces, and threatened Jutland. Must Denmark fight alone against the rebels and their Prussian backers? Romantic Scandinavianism responded to the call, and King Oscar was eager to aid his friend Frederik. The official bodies in Sweden and Norway were skeptical, but they approved of action limited to defense of the borders of Denmark proper. Hence from May to September 1848 a force of 4,500 Swedes and Norwegians sat on guard on the island of Fyn, and 11,000 more waited in Skåne; during an armistice in 1849 another Swedish peace-keeping force occupied Slesvig while the Prussians occupied Holstein. With pressure from Russia and Britain the Prussians were induced to be reasonable, and a settlement of sorts was reached in 1851. But these constitutional agreements were ambiguous compromises, and even the London Protocol of 1852 dealt with the dynastic question (settling on Prince Kristian of Glücksburg as heir) without doing anything to resolve the basic nationalistic rivalries.

Oscar and the Swedes had showed their willingness to cooperate, yet their action was so reserved that the fervent Scandinavianists were disillusioned. They were to be yet more bitterly disappointed. Through the 1850s and in the early years of the 1860s the festering problem of the duchies caused more diplomatic maneuvering among the Great Powers. National sentiment would allow no compromise, and feelings were heated by anti-German demonstrations in 1862 by some 750 Norwegian and Swedish students in Copenhagen. Bismarck frankly played for a settlement in the interest of Prussia.

Karl XV, who succeeded his father Oscar I in 1859, was also a staunch Scandinavianist and rather less cautious. He and his brother, Prince Oscar, paid a cordial visit to Denmark and promised 20,000 troops. The Danish ministers in turn, driven by fear of the Germans, proposed a personal union of the Nordic monarchies. One plan was for Frederik VII to adopt Karl XV so that on Frederik's death the thrones of Denmark, Sweden, and Norway would be combined. Prince Kristian of Glücksburg would then have been allotted Holstein and Lauenburg. Such an arrangement would have violated the international agreement of 1852 and was hardly in the realm of practical politics.

Much as Karl was interested, and although his foreign minister, Ludwig Manderström, supported his Scandinavian policy, other influential ministers were hesitant, like Louis De Geer, or openly opposed, like J. A. Gripenstedt, to an adventurous policy involving alliance and possible war.[3]

Sweden's divided counsels weakened its position, though Manderström tried valiantly to get France and Britain to support Denmark. No one in Sweden, however, was prepared to see his country stand alone at Denmark's side, and the Norwegian leadership was opposed to any policy that might lead to war. With the western powers disinclined to act and with Russia shifting its support to Prussia because of opposition to the Danish liberals, the Scandinavian states became isolated. The Danes nevertheless drove right on to the brink, hoping against hope for the fulfillment of the Swedish promises. They gave up the "Whole State" policy of retaining the loose connection of the duchies with Denmark through a common ruler in favor of the incorporation of Slesvig into Denmark; in November 1863 they announced a constitution that would incorporate Slesvig as far as the Eider. Just at this critical juncture, two days after the promulgation of the constitution, Frederik VII suddenly died. Bismarck and the Prussians were handed their opportunity, for now they could challenge both the constitution and the title of the new King Kristian IX as duke of Slesvig-Holstein.

While Sweden appealed to the Great Powers, the Germans attacked. The Swedish king and prince had promised what they could not deliver, for now both councillors and riksdag refused to cooperate. The Scandinavianists in all three countries became embittered and disillusioned. The defeat of the Danes, left alone to fight both Austrians and Prussians, was inevitable. Because they had overplayed a weak hand they now lost not only Holstein and South Slesvig but the whole of both provinces. The empty promise of a plebiscite in North Slesvig was not fulfilled until 1920, when it came as a by-product of the defeat of Germany by the Allies.

Activist foreign policy led by the king had been rudely slapped down, and in the Austro-Prussian War of 1866 the Swedes quite naturally maintained a position of neutrality. So did they in the Franco-Prussian War, though king and people felt pro-French. In certain circles, however, the success of Bismarck and the strength of Germany so impressed men that they thought of Prussia as the best potential ally of Sweden. In the ensuing years German influence grew in Sweden — in military circles, in business, and in academic life.[4]

Oscar II, ambitious and impulsive, came to the throne in 1872 and yearned to play a large role in politics. In 1873 he gave a clue to his attitude when he wrote of his father Oscar I:

He like us and the great majority longed for the day when Sweden with
advantage and honor could again draw the sword against the ancient
enemy.[5]

Hatred and mistrust of Russia remained the lodestar of his policy, but an
occasion for action never arose. At first he was antagonistic also to Germany,
but his admiration for Prussia grew after 1866. He shared his people's distress
at the defeat of France in 1871, a defeat which among other things nullified
the value of the November Treaty of 1855. Gradually the king became a
profound admirer of Bismarck's conservative firmness. Perhaps the very
powerlessness of Sweden-Norway inspired Oscar to seek influence personally. In 1875 he made a grand tour of European capitals and was free with
advice and comments to his fellow monarchs. He urged the Spanish king to
join with the Central Powers, and he tried to persuade the kaiser to be easier
on France. He expressed approval of the anti-Catholic policy of the Kultur-
kampf and of neutrality for Sweden in cooperation with Germany. Since
pan-Scandinavianism had failed he was ready to accept a more inclusive
pan-Germanism. For such attempts to shape foreign policy on his own he was
severely criticized in the press at home, and his government made haste to
clarify the cautious and true policy of the country and to disavow the king.

Interrelated with foreign policy was defense, specifically the question of
whether Sweden's outmoded military system was strong enough to make of
neutrality a viable policy. Sweden's navy and sea defense were weak. During
the Crimean War it had been happy to lie low behind the British fleet and to
allow foreign warships to use most of its harbors in the Baltic — and especially Fårösund off Gotland. This policy that favored the dominant sea power
did not please others, which was the reason Oscar II had wanted to modify it
in a joint German-Scandinavian-Baltic neutrality. The German involvement
was vetoed by his advisers and by neighboring Denmark. But in 1885–86 the
rules were revised in collaboration with the Danes: fewer ports were to be
available for outside navies and then for only twenty-four hours at a time.
Most important, Sweden decided to build its own fortifications at Fårösund
and to close this vital harbor to outsiders. Both in 1885 and later in 1907
Sweden objected to Russian proposals that would have made the Baltic a
"closed sea." Sweden also opposed all Russian attempts to escape from the
so-called Åland servitude, which had since 1856 forbidden fortification of the
Åland Islands. The Russians lost immediate interest in this demand after their
entente with Great Britain in 1907, and in 1908 the states bordering the Baltic
and the North seas proclaimed the maintenance of the status quo in both
regions. Simultaneously all agreed to the cancellation of the November Treaty
of 1855, which had already withered into inconsequence.

Yet many forces combined to intensify national feeling toward the end of the nineteenth century. The increasing friction with Norway reinforced the Swedishness of the Swedes, the bloodletting of emigration made them fear for their national survival, and the ancient fears of Russian expansion were re-aroused. More positively, the 1890s gave birth to an outpouring of national romantic literature — *The Charles Men* of Werner von Heidenstam (1898) extolling the heroic fortitude of the Swedes in their time of calamitous defeat under Karl XII, *Gösta Berling's Saga* by Selma Lagerlöf (1891), and poems and other works by a brilliant galaxy of writers including Erik Axel Karlfeldt, Gustaf Fröding, and Oscar Levertin which aroused regional interest and pride. Symbolizing it all was Richard Dybeck's stirring national anthem, "Du gamla du fria" (you ancient, you free), originally "Du gamla du friska" (you ancient, you strong), which became popular in the 1890s.

Crises continued to erupt — the Boer War and the Spanish-American War, the Russo-Japanese War and the revolution of 1905 in Finland and Russia, the Balkan crises from 1908 on to 1914, and for Sweden the traumatic experience of Norway's defection. Driven to rely on their own resources, the Swedish people became even more defense-minded than their representatives in the riksdag. They yearned to be let alone; they had cultivated a deep desire to be neutral. They wanted to follow the advice of Foreign Minister Manderström given shortly after the great debacle of the Slesvig-Holstein affair — "to go their way in quiet and calm."

But they would not have a neutrality of helplessness. They would at least defend themselves. And so, by a combination of accident and purposeful restraint the Swedish people and their government gradually forged a consensus: no adventure, no conquest, but plenty of arms for self-defense — if necessary paid for by voluntary contributions.

As far back as the time of Karl Johan there was talk of the advantages of withdrawing from the continent and its strife, of maintaining a neutral stance. Farther back still, dreams of greatness had been renounced. Yet again and again the urge to act had led Sweden almost to the firing line. The Crimean War had offered temptation, but procrastination preserved peace; the Slesvig-Holstein problem twice drew Sweden close to conflict. But the appraisal of resources and possibilities each time produced more caution than daring. With each new crisis and each new decision the idea of neutrality became more firmly fixed. And each time the influence of the elected representatives became stronger. Between 1864 and 1914 no great foreign policy issue (if we except the union question) roused serious activist sentiments among the Swedes.

As the foreign policy of Sweden moves into the new and different arena of the twentieth century it cannot be traced independently of other factors. It is

involved especially with defense problems: the abandonment of the *indelningsverk*, the institution of universal military service, the politics of defense
spending and planning. It is interrelated also with the divorce from Norway
and with the complex of problems connected with World War I. The next
chapter of Swedish foreign policy must be discussed in terms of these topics.

## Dissolution of the Union with Norway, 1905

The peaceful separation of Norway and Sweden in 1905 has been hailed as
one of the great diplomatic achievements, as an example of the way men
should settle their disputes. So it was, but the bloodless conclusion cannot
obliterate the preceding tension or the long-continuing bitterness.

"Almost from the beginning the union distilled the poisons responsible for
its eventual demise."[6] So does Raymond Lindgren epitomize the conflict.
Norway had been forced into the union with Sweden in the early nineteenth
century just when nationalistic feelings, there and elsewhere in Europe, were
reaching a peak of intensity. The manner of the creation of the union, without
consultation with the Norwegians, was a blow to national pride. After four
centuries of subordination to Denmark nationalism had become particularly
strong in Norway. The country was conscious of its poverty compared with
richer and more populous Sweden, conscious also of generations of border
warfare. The Norwegians had tried in 1814 to establish their independence
and they had drawn up their own constitution. As for the nature of their tie
with Sweden a question remained: was Norway connected with the Swedish
government or merely with the king? In practice the Swedish government was
involved in many ways because the king had his main seat in Stockholm and
operated through the government there. Yet he was king of Norway and
Norway's problems had to be handled independently.

The lack of clarity in the relationship may seem puzzling, but as the
Norwegian Gunnar Knudsen said during discussion of the consular government in 1903, "If we come to clarity in interpretation we draw away from
each other; for the clear Norwegian point of view is diametrically opposite the
clear Swedish [point of view]."[7] Because of such attitudes unnecessary decisions were avoided and necessary decisions were delayed as long as possible.

The weakness of the union lay to a considerable extent in the lack of
positive factors encouraging cooperation. The obvious similarities in language
and religion and total culture were so taken for granted that minor differences
were exaggerated. The bodies of law were distinct, though based on similar
ancient foundations. The economies of the two countries in the nineteenth
century were so alike that there was little need, even little possibility, of
profitably exchanging products with one another; the markets for each lay

outside the Scandinavian peninsula. Even the coinage and currencies of the two remained separate until 1875 when a common basis was established among all three Nordic countries, Denmark, Norway, and Sweden. Defense should have been a common concern, but this was a matter to which the Norwegians gave little thought, whereas for the Swedes it was serious.

Cooperation did of course develop in a number of areas. The *Skandinavism* of the 1840s and 1850s drew together both youth and adults of the three neighbor countries; meetings and festivities aroused sentiments of brotherhood. But the harsh realities of war in Denmark and the refusal of the political leaders of Norway and Sweden to come to the aid of their "brothers" brought embittered disillusion to the idealists. In more practical ways Norway and Sweden cooperated in promoting communication and transportation: the Kristiania-Karlstad telegraph in the 1850s, the Ofoten railroad built at the turn of the century to bring over to Norway Swedish iron ore from the Kiruna-Gällivare mines, and the Kristiania-Stockholm railroad established in 1867. Shipping to and from each other's ports grew considerably.

Norway's demands for an independent position, as they intensified in the course of the nineteenth century, were rooted in emotion more than in practical need. The economic disadvantages of the common consular service did create complaints of a practical nature, and the Norwegians, with their large merchant fleet scattered throughout the world, surely needed a good consular corps at their command. However, when the British envoy F. R. Plunkett visited Kristiania (Oslo since 1925) and Trondheim in 1892 the mercantile men with whom he spoke thought that separate consular services would be a mistake; but they were nonpolitical and lacked influence in the storting.

The nationalistic emphasis in Norwegian literature during the nineteenth century was a strong antiunion influence. Henrik Wergeland and J. S. C. Welhaven were its early apostles; Björnstierne Björnson fanned the flames after 1850; he wrote the words to Rikard Nordraak's rousing music for the Norwegian national anthem, *Ja, vi elsker dette landet* (yes, we love this land). And Björnson it was who reduced the union question to its artless simplicity: "In Norway the Norwegian people shall be the masters, they and no others, now and for all times."[8] Wholly emotional was the flag question. Norwegians resented the union insignia in the corner of their national flag; they demanded a "clean flag," and in 1898 the Swedes yielded on this point. The merchant marine could fly a Norwegian flag, and the union mark was required only for state and formal occasions.

Beyond this the Swedes talked of the possibility of compromises. In 1891 Baron Lejonhufvud suggested a basis for Norwegian-Swedish equality in the administration of foreign affairs. Minister Plunkett at that time considered the danger of a breakup of the union was less than that of a combination of Nor-

wegian and Swedish radicals to overthrow the monarchy. Agitation for a republic also worried Kaiser Wilhelm, who in the 1890s thought that Sweden should
maintain the union by force if necessary; he feared a Russian invasion and
partition of Norway. In 1895, on a visit to King Oscar, the kaiser offered his
help to Sweden, but a year later reduced his offer to maintaining a friendly
neutrality. Throughout the whole era of crisis the neighbors of the northern
states were concerned about Scandinavia and about each other. Adolf Hedin,
the radical politician, intuitively feared that Germany might come to think of
Norway-Sweden as a potential ally and that Russia might think of the state
as a potential enemy. Actually the evidence indicates that Russian policy
in the Baltic was only defensive, but Russia watched with care. The Swedes
of course were deeply concerned about the effect of a dissolution on their defensive position.

The essence of the conflict between the two peoples, in both its emotional
and practical aspects, was the struggle for power. Almost to the end of the
dual monarchy the Norwegians insisted they did not want to break up the
union; they wanted only to do things themselves and in their own way. This
involved, for one thing, a parliamentary system of government. When Oscar
II appointed Christian Selmer prime minister of Norway in 1882 the storting
impeached him and his fellow cabinet members for being appointed without
parliamentary approval. The king had to accept the decision and henceforth
cabinets had to be supported by a storting majority. In this political achievement the Norwegians were far ahead of the Swedes.

Power in the control of foreign affairs was the ground on which the final
battles were fought. The Norwegians demanded an independent consular service because the minister of foreign affairs was a Swede residing in Stockholm
and the Norwegians felt discriminated against. What might have satisfied
them was a union foreign minister who could be either Swedish or Norwegian
and responsible to the common king but not to the Swedish riksdag as had
been the situation since 1885. An attempt to reach an agreement on this
problem ended in misunderstanding in 1895, and feelings ran so high that both
Norway and Sweden began military buildups. Sweden's saber rattling and
Norwegian agitation, especially the shrill voices of the *Venstre* (liberal-left)
party created dangerous tension. It was amid these circumstances that the
kaiser had offered his aid to Sweden.

Norwegians were thinking seriously of dissolution of the union and Swedes
were discussing the advisability of using force to make Norway submit.
Swedes wanted to maintain the union partly for the sake of pride, partly out of
respect for aging Oscar II, and partly because of a conviction that power,
peace, and prosperity for both peoples were better assured if they could stay
together. Arguments swirled around the question of the consulates, but it

gradually became evident that this issue was only a symbol and that the *Venstre* group in Norway and the nationalistic newspapers like *Verdens Gang* would be satisfied with nothing less than independence. In the decade after 1895 the Norwegians remained insistent; the Swedes were stubborn and slow to yield. When they did make concessions these had been so long coming that they were not satisfying.

By 1904 Erik Gustaf Boström, prime minister for the second time, attempted renewed negotiations though he regarded them as futile. Indeed, the talks merely hardened the respective positions. In February and March of 1905 Professor Harald Hjärne of Uppsala University published a series of articles in *Svenska Dagbladet* which were significant in the light of future developments. A fatalistic attitude was growing, and these articles suggested conditions for dissolution: razing of the frontier forts, a neutral zone on the border, freedom of transportation and communication, and a treaty that would protect the Lapps and their migrations between Sweden and Norway.

In Norway irritation grew over continued delays, and sentiment crystallized. Fridtjof Nansen, an Arctic explorer and already a national hero, wrote for *Verdens Gang* an article urging that the storting establish a Norwegian consular service and take the consequences whatever they might be. Other intellectuals extended the Norwegian propaganda to Danish, German, and English papers, and soon the Norwegian explorer Nansen and the Swedish explorer Sven Hedin were viciously attacking and defending their respective national positions in articles in *The Times* of London. Governments were being pushed by popular feeling. Both prime ministers were replaced: Boström by the moderate Johan Ramstedt and Francis Hagerup by a similarly moderate but firm Christian Michelsen. The champions were chosen and the decision was clear in March. Norway floated a loan of 40 million kroner to be prepared for any eventuality. The threat of fratricidal war caused many Swedish backs to stiffen, and the Swedish army was clearly superior to the Norwegian. But the danger caused others, including Crown Prince Gustav, to feel that a union that had to be maintained by force was not worth having. He urged that "Sweden should herself propose a divorce rather than to be, so to speak, kicked out of the union."[9]

On May 18, 1905, the day after an emotional celebration of their constitution day, the Norwegians passed the separate consular law. Everything had been foreseen so that when the council in Stockholm received the report and the king refused his sanction, as expected, the Norwegian ministers presented their resignations. Oscar acknowledged that he could not form another government and rejected the resignations. Excitement rose to fever pitch in Kristiania and on June 7 a plenary session of the storting, without a dissenting vote, declared that "the union with Sweden under one king is dissolved in consequence of the king's ceasing to function as king of Norway."[10]

Was this unilateral act by one partner a conclusive decision? Was Norway really independent for the first time in over five hundred years? If so, what kind of government should be set up? Would Sweden go to war? Would the Great Powers involve themselves?

The next months were as hectic as the last few had been. The question of a republic was mooted but did not become a serious issue. But who should be invited as king? The idea prevailed that Oscar should be asked to nominate a Bernadotte. His response was, in essence, if they want a Bernadotte why not I? The next most natural choice was a Danish prince and ultimately the choice fell upon Prince Carl, second son of King Frederik VIII. He was supported by the kaiser and by King Edward of England, his father-in-law, but in both cases after earlier advocacy of a Bernadotte. This note of personal diplomacy was not a decisive element but it is interesting: by its very feebleness it illustrated the fading of monarchic influence in international relations. Even the vigorous shuttle diplomacy of Crown Prince Gustav had little effect, though he journeyed repeatedly, in the spring and summer of 1905, to Kristiania, London, Copenhagen, and Berlin. He received no aid and little sympathy. The chief effect of all his travels was that he felt the pressures for a peaceful settlement.

In the meantime the real decisions were being made in Stockholm and Kristiania. Four Norwegian leaders (Benjamin Vogt, Frederik Wedel Jarlsberg, Halvdan Koht, W. C. Brøgger) went to Stockholm to talk with their varied acquaintances, and their explanations of Norway's attitude were probably significant. Popular reaction was divided as well as outspoken. In Sweden Hjalmar Branting urged peaceful agreement and led 20,000 social democratic demonstrators against war; he urged a strike against the government if war came. The riksdag met in special session beginning on June 27, and feelings were bitter. But the crown prince, taking the place of the king because of Oscar's illness, advised immediate recognition of Norway. Despite this some riksdagmen were vehemently pro-invasion and part of the press was bloodthirsty. The cabinet of Ramstedt proposed recognition of independence and negotiations to settle problems. After a month of furious debate a program was adopted, essentially that proposed by Harald Hjärne: a protest against Norway's unilateral action; the demand that Norway request negotiations; a plebiscite in Norway or a vote on a new storting; and a list of details subject to discussion: razing of the border forts, a treaty protecting the Lapps, rights of transit, a neutralized zone, and a treaty providing for arbitration in the future.

After agreement was reached on this program at the end of July it appeared necessary to replace the weak Ramstedt ministry with a coalition. The leaders

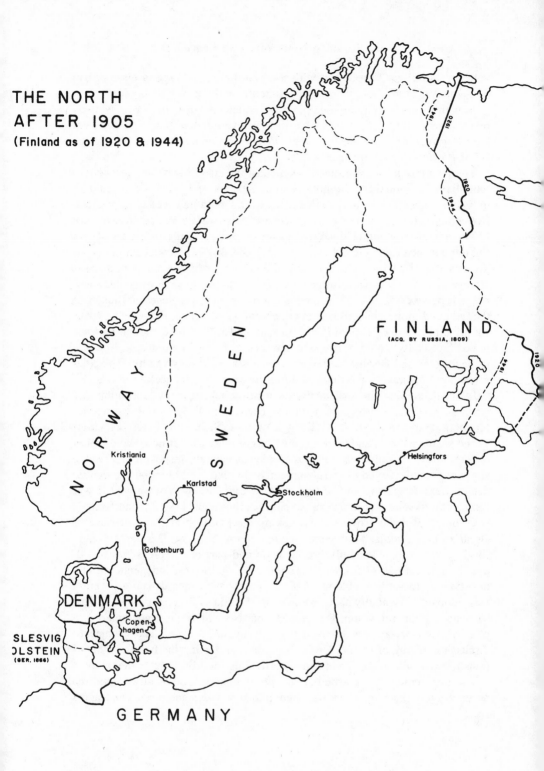

THE NORTH
AFTER 1905
(Finland as of 1920 & 1944)

N O R W A Y

S W E D E N

FINLAND
(ACQ. BY RUSSIA, 1809)

1944

1920

1920

1944

1944

1920

Kristiania

Karlstad

Helsingfors

Stockholm

Gothenburg

DENMARK

Copen-
hagen

SLESVIG
OLSTEIN
(GER. 1866)

GERMANY

became Christian Lundeberg and Fredrik Wachtmeister. Lundeberg wisely decided to add Karl Staaff, a leader of the liberals who was acceptable to the social democrats and already on terms of understanding with the Norwegians.

Norway was obviously winning its case and acted at this stage with restraint. The requested plebiscite was held on August 13 and brought a vote of 367,149 in favor of dissolution to 184 against.

The next step was the meeting of delegations to draw up terms of separation. Karlstad, halfway between Kristiania and Stockholm, was the location. The Norwegians sent Benjamin Vogt, Christian Michelsen, Carl Berner, and Jørgen Løvland, and the Swedes used Lundeberg, Wachtmeister, Staaff, and Hjalmar Hammarskjöld, an international lawyer of distinction. Now the Norwegians made two blunders — they appealed to the powers for support, which affronted the Swedes, and ordered mobilization, which angered them. Lundeberg threatened to break off the talks, and the troop movements were checked.

The final agreement hammered out in strained sessions in Karlstad was essentially the same as the set of terms laid down in July. (It is significant of two ways of thinking that Swedes date the dissolution October 26, 1905 when formalities were completed; Norwegians date the event June 7 when the storting declared the union ended.) Reason won out over passion. The demilitarized frontier between Norway and Sweden stands as a magnificent complement to the Canadian-American boundary — both examples proving that neighbors can live in peace. The fortresses of Fredriksten and Kongsvinger remained as monuments to history, not as barriers between enemies. Acceptance of the agreement was voted 101 to 16 in the storting, unanimously in each of the two houses of the riksdag. Another plebiscite was held to approve Carl as new king of Norway, and he took the old Norwegian royal name of Håkon (and added a VII). Divorce ended a forced and unhappy relationship; like any divorce it represented defeat of cooperation in the existing framework, but it opened the way to voluntary cooperation.[11]

# XIII

## SOCIAL TRANSFORMATION OF
## THE NINETEENTH CENTURY

THE SWEDISH PEOPLE in the nineteenth century turned away from their past; they rejected the traditional society of privilege and deference; they demanded schools and churches that were open to all; they insisted on freedom and equality for the individual based on his rights as a human being. Having discarded the old dreams of glory on the battlefield, though still cherishing the memories of Gustav Adolf and Karl XII, Swedes turned to the more prosaic conquests of countinghouse and factory and farm. The nation was still poor, but social mobility was expressing itself in all sectors, and new ideas were stirring.

### From Society of Status to Class Society

The Swedish status society had taken a long time to develop, and it was firmly anchored. Nobles, clergy, burghers, landowning farmers (*bönder*) — all were aware of their place in the pecking order. Those who were outside the four Estates were not so sure of their place in the social hierarchy, but it did not make much difference because they were politically voiceless. Gradually the situation changed. The voiceless elements that did not fit into the old categories increased in number and influence. Population expanded and functions became more specialized. As diversity increased the privileges and disabilities of different groups had to be redefined. Only the fundamentals remained intact into the nineteenth century, a society of prestige and authority looking down and of deference looking up.

At the top of the social pyramid stood the "persons of status" (*ståndspersoner*), both privileged and unprivileged (*frälse* and *ofrälse*). These included especially the three upper Estates in the riksdag — the nobles, the clergy, and the burghers; together with the unprivileged persons of status, mostly professionals, these upper classes accounted for about 5 percent of the population.

The nobility numbered about 9,000 in the eighteenth century and 12,000 in the mid-nineteenth century. Among them were many gradations of wealth and style. Within the House of Nobles the old distinction dividing the nobles themselves into three classes was again, and finally, abolished in 1809. The difference in status between the higher nobility of counts and barons and the lower nobility, numerous and impecunious, was nevertheless clearly recognized. But whether they lived in simple apartments or small houses or fine palaces hung with Gobelins and paintings, these privileged nobles lived a favored existence.

Until the early eighteenth century and through the time of Karl XII, it was usual that when an outsider rose to high rank in the army or civil office he was given noble status. This upward Estate circulation slowed in tempo but did not cease in the course of the eighteenth century. Since the seventeenth century only nobles could hold the highest offices in the civil service, and after the reduction of their lands many of them had no other means of support. The nobility lost some of their privileges in the "leveling of privilege" of 1789, and they were discredited by the Anjala conspiracy and the assassination of Gustav III (see chapter X). The revolution of 1809 and the new constitution, capped by the election of Bernadotte, emphasized merit rather than birth, and it was then that the *ofrälse* in considerable numbers attained top positions. The nobility as a class was thus emasculated of power, though they still held priorities to a few high offices, including the foreign ministry.

In both Sweden and Finland the great farms with their magnificent manor houses (*herrgårdar* or châteaus) were before the eighteenth century in the hands of the nobility. (The nobles held one-third of the land in Sweden and one-tenth in Finland.) From 1723 other persons of status were permitted to buy such property, in 1789 farmers also might do so. The result of accumulating reforms was that by 1865 the aura of nobility had departed from 60 percent of the tax-privileged lands; only in Skåne and in the Mälar area near Stockholm were there any longer significant numbers of great manor houses (many of them *fideikommiss* [entailed estates]).

The steady erosion of privileges diminished the nobles' prestige as well as their power. They remained at the top, but the pyramid had been flattened. Newer generations tended to concentrate either on land management or on government office rather than on the traditional combination of both. Also, intermarriage increased between nobility and commoners. Whereas in the 1680s only one-fifth of the nobility married outside their own Estate, by the

1860s two-thirds did so — and by the 1960s 90 percent sought brides and bridegrooms from other social ranks. Merchants' daughters married barons, professors married countesses. The ideology and the prestige of blue-bloodedness faded before the social and economic progress of nonnobles and the simultaneous pauperization of many of the nobles. Increasingly sons of the middle class went to the Karlberg Academy and graduated as army officers; more slowly some middle-class sons got into the navy too.[1]

Somewhat apart from the other social groups, so steeped in tradition as to be superannuated, was the military caste of staff and general officers and the widely scattered apportionment (*indelta*) army. This obsolete structure involved somewhat less than 10 percent of the population before it was abolished at the end of the nineteenth century. It was useful only as a security reserve in a state that had renounced conquest. The country could no longer hope to defend itself with an institution that had served well for Karl XI but that was ridiculously out-of-date for the beginning of the twentieth century. To a certain extent it was a refuge for the otherwise unoccupied nobles, who maintained themselves in a majority of the officer's positions; in the lower ranks both army and navy included many nonnobles.

The priestly Estate retained its numbers through the eighteenth and nineteenth centuries but sank by the 1850s to .5 percent of the population. The priests held considerable political power until 1866, when their house in the riksdag was abolished; even after this they retained great influence in the community. They enjoyed tax exemptions on church lands, and as functionaries of the state they were allotted income from taxation. They served the state directly as record keepers of births, deaths, marriages, and the movements of people. As individuals ministers often owned land and encouraged agricultural progress by their experimentation with new crops and new methods. Most important, the priesthood was the learned class, university educated, maintaining libraries and often schools for the parish.

Up to the eighteenth century it was rather common for the priest to marry the widow or the daughter of his predecessor, and for the sons of the manse to follow their fathers into the ministry. But priesthood was not a closed caste; younger sons of the aristocracy frequently became churchmen, and it was never impossible for bright boys from the lower classes to enter the Estate. This became increasingly common in the nineteenth century. But the drawing power of the church declined. Whereas in 1700 57 percent of university students entered the priesthood, by the 1860s the figure was down to 20 percent. Simultaneously children of clerics branched out into other intellectual occupations, becoming teachers, scientists, writers, engineers. Among the clergy as among the other Estates sharp gradations existed. For example, the authority and the magnificence of the bishop in Uppsala or Lund was a sharp contrast to the humble status of the rural pastor in the far north, though even a pastor, with his salary from the state, did not have to suffer all of the hardships of his flock.

Third in rank in riksdag and society was the burgher Estate, representing some 2 percent of the population through both the eighteenth and nineteenth centuries. Foremost among them were the so-called harbor nobility, the *Skeppsbroadeln*, a group of about twenty families, largely foreign in origin (Germans, Scots, Walloons, Jews), who had made fortunes in trade and invested in lands and houses. Gothenburg had a similar group of shrewd merchants with international credit connections. In earlier periods these most successful immigrant merchants often were ennobled, the De Geer family for instance; continuingly they married into the nobility. Just below the great merchants stood the manufacturers and then the lesser merchants and finally the larger numbers of skilled craftsmen. The craftsmen enjoyed the legal advantages of guild restrictions until 1846, although this kind of exclusiveness and regulation could never be fully enforced.

To all these groups must be added the "unprivileged persons of status" made up of the civil officials, military officers, doctors, teachers, lawyers, ironmasters, inspectors, etc. — people of education and standing who were called by title or Mr. and Mrs. (*Herr* and *Fru*). They lacked representation in the riksdag but they were respected members of society. This heterogeneous group, like the burghers, numbered only some 2 percent of the population, but they were vigorous, ambitious, hard-working, to a considerable extent the makers of a new day both politically and economically. This group, along with the burghers, came to be known by the vague but appropriate term "middle class" (a term dating from the 1790s).

By mid-nineteenth century it was the middle class, sons of priests and businessmen especially, that provided most of the administrative, military, and cultural leadership. It was the middle class that had the means to educate their sons. Among the farming population the unprivileged farmers (*ofrälse bönder*) were at the same time taking possession of more land so that by 1865 the nobles held only 40 percent of the tax-privileged (*frälse*) land. Farmers who raised themselves into the well-to-do ranks often became prominent in the riksdag, and they helped to push through the reform of 1865. At the same time there were others who had not attained success, and some who had fallen from a higher position to a lower. Sten Carlsson has most thoroughly analyzed this Estate circulation by which the old society of privilege sank dramatically in power and prestige.[2] The old order became obsolete. In 1866 even the political structure of the four Estates was destroyed. The new class society replaced the Estates or status society. Carlsson lists the six new classes which, though less well defined than the Estates, now characterized the society: (1)

the big-business class, the most prosperous group; (2) the official class of academically educated men in state or municipal service; (3) the civil service; (4) the small businessmen; (5) the farmers; (6) the laborers, consisting of the landless agricultural workers and the industrial workers.

Clearly the new class society represented evolution, not revolution. Even after 1866 the nobles maintained an importance based on tradition, education, and prestige. Of eighty-six top positions in government sixty were held by the sons of officials and eighteen by sons of businessmen. Of the military officers who held the eighty-three top positions, forty-six were from noble families, fifty-two from officers' families (overlapping here, of course), sixty-five from higher officials' families, and eleven from big-business families.

In many countries the military and diplomatic service seem to be the special strongholds of the aristocracy, and Sweden was no exception; breeding, bearing, and fluency in several languages count for much in such milieux. Among officers the nobles remained numerous, and even at mid-twentieth century fully a third of the high-ranking officials in the foreign service were of noble birth. The former status groups were far from being deprived. Further, although the children of lesser civil servants and small businessmen made up one-third to one-half of the student bodies at Uppsala and Lund and would become the leaders of the next generation, the official class was still overrepresented. However, farmers' children made up 30 percent of the priesthood at the beginning of the twentieth century and comprised a large proportion of the teachers and authors. The significant fact was that barriers were breached and that the way into the upper brackets was now open for anyone with the proper combination of background, ability, and will.

## Effects of Population Growth

The nineteenth century was an era of slow transition. In the early years of the century the upper classes included, as was true one hundred years earlier, only some 5 percent of the Swedish people, and the entire population of the cities included only 10 percent. The overwhelming mass of Swedes lived in the country or in rural villages, and to the very end of the nineteenth century these were "the Swedish people." The farmers, the unprivileged fourth Estate in the riksdag, were only the advantaged portion of this great agricultural majority. For four hundred years their Estate was the lowest in the riksdag, never equal in status to the others. Yet they did participate in the political process and enjoyed a higher status than other European peasantry. In 1866 they overturned the obsolete four-Estate structure and in the two-house riksdag they became the mighty ones. However, their period of power was brief. They were succeeded by the industrialists, who were then soon succeeded by the workers.

In the nineteenth century the mass of Swedish people were poor and getting poorer. Their small red cottages that look so picturesque today must have been woefully cramped for their large families, and the poorest shacks of the back-cottagers have disintegrated. In the first part of the century their agriculture was still medieval in technique and organization. They struggled to achieve self-sufficiency in food production, but in frequent bad years they had to import grain. Industry was miniscule. The mines, which had once produced the only exportable surplus and had supported Sweden's Age of Greatness, declined in importance. Copper and silver were almost exhausted; iron ore was plentiful but the iron industry faced severe foreign competition, especially from Russia. Forest wealth was largely unrealized for export because of distance from the markets. Transportation systems had not improved for centuries; what was acceptable in the fifteenth century became less than adequate for an expanded area and a zooming population. The most hopeful part of the picture was that things were so bad that change had a chance.

Fundamental among the forces of change was the steady growth in the number of people. It was like the relentless buildup of the waters of the prehistoric Baltic Sea, which at last created such pressure that the sea burst forth and transformed the geography of Scandinavia. The pressure of population in the nineteenth century became overpowering.

In 1800 the Swedish people numbered 2.347 million; in 1900 the figure was more than double, at 5.136 million. The first big jump came in the 1820s, building upon a surge of births of a generation earlier, in the 1790s. By the 1870s the annual rate of increase had climbed to 1.2 percent. Or to use a different statistical approach, the birth rate stood until the 1880s at more than 30 per thousand, balanced in the early years of the century by a death rate of 25–30 per thousand. Population increase was due primarily to a dramatic decline in the death rate, which was down to 18 in the 1880s (and to 10 in the 1940s).[3]

The causes, as Bishop Tegnér succinctly stated, were "peace, vaccine, and potatoes,"[4] and these same causes were operating through much of Europe. Sweden's land was sparsely settled, but its vast northern area was a poor producer of food crops, and after 1809 expansion into Finland was impossible. Not until late in the century did emigration offer any significant relief; most of the new bodies had to find room in Sweden itself.

Nineteenth-century Sweden was throughout an agricultural society. As of 1800 the population of the rural districts numbered 2.117 million and of the towns only 230,000. Only two towns, Stockholm and Gothenburg, counted more than 10,000. By 1900 the rural population had doubled to 4 million, while the city population had multiplied more than four times to 1.104 million. Urban growth was nevertheless more a portent for the future than a solution for the nineteenth century. At the beginning of the period 90 percent of the population was oriented to agriculture or mining, and by 1900 almost 80 percent still lived on farms or in rural villages. Only in the last quarter of the century was the urbanization really important. As late as 1870 the percentage *directly* involved in agriculture was 72.4. For them the redistribution of land was the revolutionary force in their lives. The village system of agriculture which had come down from ancient times was torn apart. The social pattern of village life was in process of dissolution, although fascinating exceptions left portions of Dalarna, for example, with seventeenth- and eighteenth-century patterns surviving into the late twentieth century. Society was in flux on the farm as well as in the city.

Fortunately the change from the village system to the system of individual self-contained farms brought with it enhanced productivity; otherwise the population surge would have created even greater hardship. (See the section on agriculture in chapter XVI.) The change in system was also accompanied by a basic change in status for large numbers of Swedes. It produced a rural proletariat. In the old community of the village indigent and unfortunate neighbors were carried along without sharp or obvious distinctions in status. Everyone in the parish participated in weddings and in the festivals at Christmas and Easter, at planting and harvest. Men, women, and children worked together in the fields and in the homes. They played together, and they supported one another. But when the individual was put on a farm of his own this support was gone. A man had to do his own work. Even the common woods and fields where his children could pick berries and gather wood and pasture animals were now divided into separate farms. By drainage and cutting new lands had been reclaimed, but this was not enough. Another problem was that, after the individualization of the land a father frequently divided the inheritance among his sons, and farms became too small to support the families. Repeated subdivision caused impoverishment and degradation of status, although because of the growing population it could not be stopped. The process had begun before the reforms of the nineteenth century and now it accelerated.

If for any reason the independent farmer failed he had little choice but to become a sharecropper (crofter) or a landless laborer (*statare*). Anyone without a job for more than eight weeks became ''defenseless'' before the law and was required to take whatever job was offered. He was forbidden to enter a town unless he had a job. The powers-that-be had thus traditionally attempted to reduce vagrancy and begging, and at the same time to assure themselves of a ready supply of labor. In England, when families were forced out of their farming villages by the enclosure system, they could go to the cities and the factories. In Sweden, until late in the nineteenth century, there existed no such alternative. Displaced farmers stayed in the country, lived in tiny shacks in the rear fields, worked as they could for the yeoman farmer or the noble who owned the farm, and reproduced themselves. Only occasionally did the younger generation defy restrictions and move to the cities and overseas.

Although the number of independent farm-owning *bönder* increased, the rise was nothing like the rapid rate of increase of the nonowning, rural workers. (See accompanying tabulation.[5])

| Year | Farmers (owners and renters) | Crofters, Servants, Laborers |
|------|------------------------------|------------------------------|
| 1775 | 1,053, 000 | 549,000 |
| 1870 | 1,396,000 | 1,288,000 |

By 1870 the independent farmers, the sturdy backbone of the Swedish social structure, were practically matched in numbers by the rural landless and dependent groups. As the numbers of landless increased the old controls could not hold. People flocked to Stockholm and to the towns and aggravated conditions that were already bad. Children and women were put to work in factories at low wages, but even then there was not enough work.

The structure of social care developed through generations collapsed under the new weight of numbers. How the pre-Christian community took care of its unfortunates we do not know, but with the coming of Christianity the obligation to care for one's brother became a religious duty. Luther's protest led to a new emphasis on individual responsibility but did not do away with the need for assistance. When Gustav Vasa grabbed the resources of the church he had the decency to recognize the crown's responsibility to the poor and the sick. He forbade begging, even by the dispossessed monks. Gradually the parishes became again the dispensers of aid, and each had to establish a house to take in the poor.

The growing rural proletariat represented a sad aspect of the nineteenth-century social evolution. The patriarchial relationships of the status society were not yet gone, but they were going. There still existed estates of lesser nobles and great farmers on which every family on the estate got a loaf when there was a big baking and on which all enjoyed shares in the slaughter of livestock. Each tenant or worker would have not only his cottage and a pig and chickens but the right to rations of milk, rye, and perhaps a patch of his own potatoes. There were places, like the better plantations of America's Old South, where the lady of the manor was mother and nurse to the dependent cottagers, where all the children, highborn and low, played together, where an attitude of concern and responsibility was answered by respect and loyal service. But the surge in number of people and the rising democratic spirit undermined this old patriarchial pattern. The sense of community could not be as strong where too many shared it nor when, in the expanding *bruk* (ironworks, mines, mills) workers came from different backgrounds with diverse dialects and customs.

At different times and in different parts of the country the problems of vagrancy and begging became serious, and various solutions were attempted. A widespread practice was to allow indigent individuals and families to move from house to house doing what work they could, staying a few weeks with one family and then with another. Often children were placed with foster parents, but this system sometimes degenerated into the selling of children's labor by parents who had more boys and girls than they could use or feed. Sometimes poorhouses were established by the parish, and the old pensioners lived together, as illustrated in Selma Lagerlöf's *Gösta Berling*. Poverty was in any case the responsibility of the community. It became a secular responsibility even when the unit of administration was the parish, which was confirmed by a statute of 1763. Hospitals for the sick, especially for the mentally sick, became a responsibility of the county (*län*); for all who could pay, charges were levied for food but not for care. All who could arrange it were cared for at home. Hospitals were bad, and those for the insane were often barbaric. "The insane in Nyköping's hospital were still locked up in cages with iron bars on their feet in the year 1853, with all the accompanying filth."[6]

Since the communities had to bear the costs of care for the poor they felt it necessary to protect themselves against indigents wandering in from other parishes. The resultant regulation prohibiting a man from moving about without a job, plus the forced labor requirement, often froze a man in his destitution. The alternatives were to join the army or go to jail. Yet these laws could not be regularly enforced and they were moderated in 1819. Wages were still kept as low as possible, and it was taken for granted that the poor deserved their lot or that such was the will of God.

The population spurt and the social distress of the 1830s generated wide discussion. To some extent it was merely the moralizing of the prosperous, but it also considered causes and remedies. The riksdag's poverty committee considered prohibition of marriage before age twenty-five but abandoned the idea for fear of increasing immorality and illegitimate children. The committee was acquainted with Malthus and wanted both to restrict nativity and to educate the working class; it also preached to the well-to-do against luxuries and urged them to save money and lead pure lives for the beneficent effect their example would have on the general public. Public works, from 1840, helped a little as roads were repaired, streams dredged, swamps drained, harbors and canals constructed. Stockholm and some other towns established employment bureaus. Gothenburg had an informal one: people seeking work could stand in line on a particular bridge and wait for an employer to come and find them! Workhouses for the poor drew together too many of the unskilled; sometimes, too, they would bring overproduction and loss. In any case, as E. G. Geijer said, "Nothing is more unfortunate for the workingman than a flourishing workhouse industry." [7]

Reformers persisted at the job and won some revisions of obsolete laws in the 1840s and 1850s. They got the principle established that anyone was free to move into any community in the land until he was fifty-five years of age, and a reaffirmation that the community was responsible for those who could not care for themselves. By 1850 some 3,500 children under fifteen were working in Swedish factories and child labor was a problem because of the long hours (eleven to twelve hours per day) and bad conditions. New laws prohibited employment of children under twelve and night work for all under eighteen, but again neither regulation could be enforced. Only criminals could now be degraded into the "defenseless" category, and forced labor could be required only for a restricted period of time. These ameliorations might have meant little had railway building not begun and had general economic conditions not improved in this period so that workers were more in demand. Relaxed laws and high employment went hand in hand until the crop failures of 1867 and 1868. With 217,000 people listed as needing help in 1869 the burden on the communities was too heavy, and their obligation was reduced to caring for orphans and the insane. However, by 1871 industry had improved enough to absorb some of the excess labor supply, and emigration was beginning to skim off the surplus. At the same time began the really significant shift of population from country to city, from farm to factory. With this shift in population and the growth of industry in the 1870s we can identify the watershed between the old Sweden and the new.

## The Structure of the City

If the nineteenth-century doubling of the rural population created difficult problems consider the complex results of the quadrupling of the city population. Stockholm grew at the average rate, fourfold, as an administrative center with a mixed economy; Borås with its burgeoning textile mills grew eightfold; Eskilstuna built on steel for a tenfold increase; on a combination of industry and commerce Gothenburg expanded tenfold, Hälsingborg fourteen, and Malmö over fifteen. Similar population expansion and tendencies to urbanization were even earlier transforming the societies of England and Germany and the United States — but of course such parallels in no way diminish the importance of these population factors for the Swedish community. (See accompanying table.)

Urban Growth in the Nineteenth Century

| City | 1800 | 1900 |
|------|------|------|
| Borås | 1,800 | 15,800 |
| Eskilstuna | 1,300 | 13,600 |
| Falun | 4,800 | 9,600 |
| Gävle | 5,400 | 30,000 |
| Gothenburg | 12,800 | 130,600 |
| Hälsingborg | 1,700 | 25,000 |
| Karlskrona | 10,000 | 24,000 |
| Malmö | 4,000 | 61,000 |
| Norrköping | 9,000 | 41,000 |
| Stockholm | 75,000 | 300,000 |
| Uppsala | 5,100 | 23,000 |
| Västerås | 2,800 | 12,000 |
| Örebro | 3,300 | 22,000 |

For comparison:

| | | |
|------|------|------|
| Copenhagen (greater) | 104,000 | 370,000 |
| Berlin | 172,000 | 2,000,000 (1905) |
| Paris | 600,000 | 2,600,000 |
| St. Petersburg | 220,000 | 2,100,000 (1914) |
| London (greater) | 960,000 | 6,500,000 (1901) |
| New York | 60,000 | 3,400,000 |

The developing cities offered a life that was harsh and brief, but they attracted people as light attracts moths. Stockholm's population of 75,000 in 1800 was in ensuing years fed by an in-migration of 15,000 per year yet did not reach a total of 100,000 until 1857. Far more people died in the city than were born there. In all the cities of Europe conditions were unhealthful but Stockholm was one of the worst. Even the drastic death rate took a long time to teach people that the sanitation devices of the open country were quite inadequate for the crowded living conditions of a city. Men simply did not know what caused disease until two cholera epidemics, in 1834 and 1853, taught them the hard way. Then the grossest forms of pollution were conquered, the death rate declined, and the population burgeoned; people pushed across the bridges from the central island of Old Town and spread far into Norrmalm and Södermalm and Kungsholm and out toward the military exercise grounds of Ladugårdsgärdet.

From 1725 a builder in Stockholm was required to submit plans for his building. The city was a proud capital that wanted to show a handsome face to the world. In most towns much building was still in wood, for this was the cheap material out of Sweden's vast forests. As a result, fires all too frequently ravaged whole sections of closely built cottages. For example, one-third of Norrköping went up in flames in 1822; fires were frequent in the outlying wood-built districts of both Gothenburg and Stockholm. Stockholm tried to avert this danger by an ordinance of 1763 requiring that all new buildings be constructed of stone, with stone stairways, tiled attic floors, and plastered dividing walls. In accord with the tastes of the times both buildings and streets had to be rectangular to meet the ideals of regularity and symmetry. Revisions of 1842 fixed height at four stories and those of 1876 related height to the width of the street (modern zoning principles were thus foreshadowed).

Wood continued to predominate on the farms and in the smaller towns, and occasionally one can still see timbered manor houses and even rows of small cottages that have survived for centuries, as in the iron *bruk* community of Sandviken. In ancient towns such as Sigtuna and Kalmar one can feel the solid simplicity of real log houses, though these may now be boarded over for the sake of protection or pride of appearance. In some places, too, like Visby, Stockholm's Old Town, and the châteaus of Skåne, stone structures were built several centuries ago that stand today, stuccoed and painted and thoroughly modernized.

In the first four decades of the nineteenth century housing construction in Stockholm was minimal, an average of 7.6 buildings per year. The ideal was to be imposing, to build massively with classic facades after the models of Berlin, Paris, and Vienna. In the period 1840–75 building was more vigorous, at the rate of 41 new structures per year, now up to five stories in height and including a large number of apartments. The city as a whole grew in this densely built style, with outside walls flush with the sidewalk and with small inner courtyards for light and air. Architects were more concerned with facades that were majestic than with interior comforts and the health of the residents. Not until 1860 did even the most luxurious apartments have either an inside lavatory or a bath; the privy was outside behind the building, and baths and laundry were in the attic or other location for group use. Although many of the apartments were large, rows of interconnecting rooms only slowly gave way to a system of hallways leading to wholly individual rooms. As one critic put it, a builder "had on his conscience 20 rheumatic fevers, 15 lung inflammations and 10 eye diseases."[8]

The Stockholm Building Society (established in 1848) contributed to the exchange of ideas and to the general raising of construction standards; the society maintained a library of largely German and French books and periodicals and published a journal of its own. Styles became more eclectic and attention was given to sanitation. A city-plan committee of 1866 urged the creation of parks and broad streets to bring in as much as possible of Sweden's natural advantages and to rid the city of the darkness, unclean air, and all the other evils that weaken bodily health and pollute the soul. As population increased problems grew more complex and the pace of construction accelerated: from 1875 to 1900 builders erected an average of 136 apartment houses per year, until there was actually a surplus of dwelling units.

## Life Styles

Building styles were of course closely related to living styles. One reason that Stockholm became overwhelmingly a city of apartment dwellers was that many of the nobles and government officials had homes in the country. There they could fully enjoy nature and space, so they did not object to less expansive city quarters during the seasons of snow and cold and during those occasions when business or riksdag or society demanded their presence in the capital. Merchants and master craftsmen found it difficult to have apartments large enough or flexible enough to house their apprentices and journeymen, and therefore the guild life was less familial than in foreign cities where the pattern required individual houses. At the same time it was natural for the wealthy, the middle class, and even the less well-off to live side by side in the same building or at least in the same neighborhood. And the "houses" usually had shops on the ground floor, with the living apartments above. One result was that a housewife could do her daily buying in the meat shop, the milk store, the delicatessen, the cobbler's, the bakery — all within her own block — and pick up flowers from the cart on the corner. The master of the house might have his shop and his dwelling quarters in the same building. Each block and each small district of the city tended to become self-sufficient, and a person could live a lifetime without ever visiting other parts of his own city. As the share system of financing became increasingly a cooperative system people tended to become entrenched in the place where they started, though newly built neighborhoods always attracted some families from the older established districts.

In both the towns and the rural areas the servants of the rich, the bearers and diggers and odd-jobs workers, lived in crowded and often filthy conditions. In the company-built row houses, for example, two or three families might live in one room and kitchen. Windows were small, sometimes still covered with animal membrane, though glass was becoming usual in the towns. Down the streets outside sewerage ran in the open to the rivers and lakes from which people took water for washing and drinking — this even in Stockholm, although the larger towns had also their corps of collectors of "night soil" (excrement for fertilizer). Similar conditions existed in all the cities of the continent — pigs ran loose in the streets of New York, too. Disease often spread devastatingly.

Not until 1864 did Stockholm resolve its problem of pure water. In the 1860s and 1870s great progress was made in establishing public facilities for lighting, sewerage, and firefighting. After 1700 pharmacists had to be licensed; public health was publicly regulated, medical service was provided by public physicians (an office which for Stockholm dated back to 1579). State examinations were required of dentists since 1797, although by 1840 only eight licenses had been issued. In this field American influences began to be felt as early as 1825, and these were accelerated a century later. Throughout the Scandinavian countries regulatory practices were similar and spread slowly from the capitals to the towns and rural districts.[9]

Hospitals were for long wholly inadequate and were mainly for the insane and for victims of venereal disease. But in the early nineteenth century each province had at least one hospital, and the principle of public ownership and operation was thoroughly established. Lying-in hospitals and public midwives were regarded as especially important by the mercantilistic leaders of business who wanted as many children born as possible to augment their labor supply. Health requirements were but poorly understood, and the workingman was reported to be bathed only twice in his life — at birth and when laid in his grave. It was fortunate that the vast majority of the people lived in the open country and that the climate was cool.

The cholera epidemic of 1834 highlighted the conditions of the times. The dread disease reached Finland from Russia and the Far East in 1831. King Karl XIV Johan and the governor of Stockholm, Jacob Wilhelm Sprengtporten, ordered safety measures. Nothing happened at once, and precautions were relaxed. Then the plague entered Sweden at Gothenburg, where more than 4,600 died. Stockholm had two hospitals — one for venereal diseases, the other the "Provisional" hospital in a former distillery; some twenty temporary locations were set up with a total of 625 beds. When the blow struck the capital city the death toll jumped to 3,000 in the month of September 1834 and then rapidly declined. Sprengtporten made regular inspections, but the only treatment was with menthol, calomel, camphor, and bismuth. The dead were buried in special cemeteries with gravediggers drafted from the poorhouses. And the experts continued to argue whether the cause of infection was evil particles rising out of the ground and blown by the wind or possibly contagion. Was it necessary to embargo the butter from infected Finland? No one knew. Experience was gained in 1834. Most important, Sprengtporten was able to drive through a general tax for all Stockholm and achieve some degree of centralized control. Until the 1834 disaster the eight parishes of the city had each maintained its separate arrangements for the care of the poor and the ill, because the wealthy parishes had refused to take on the responsibilities of the poorer. The cholera showed them that the city was after all a single community. By the time of the second wave, in 1853, knowledge of public hygiene was sufficient that governments were able to eradicate the disease within the next decade. Leprosy had already been conquered in Sweden, though not yet in Norway.

First paternalism, then mercantilism, and finally a democratic sense of social need supported the public health program, while the sparsity of population in the rural areas, especially of the far north, made private practice unremunerative and therefore unprotesting against "socialized medicine" in its incipient stages.

Life also had its happy aspects. Homes and furnishings were important to people who through long periods of dreary weather had to live indoors. The furniture was simple and mostly of plain wood, with benches along the walls, large rocking cradles, and solid chairs. Utensils of wood and pewter graced the table, where meals would be served out of a large bowl or perhaps from the kettle that had swung in the fireplace. Porcelain was found in the wealthier houses, some with unique designs dating from the eighteenth-century heyday of the China trade. For example, the multidozen service of the Grill family featured the grasshopper design. The original family name was Grillo, meaning grasshopper in Italy from which they had emigrated. In the mid-eighteenth century Claes Grill had become head of the Swedish East India Company and it was natural that he, like many another wealthy merchant and noble, should order from China a personalized table service; what the Chinese imagination did to the grasshopper is delightful to see. Occasionally there was wallpaper, with idyllic or magnificent scenes. Beds were likely to be short, partially closed-in boxes built in along the walls, with straw mattresses and featherbed covers. For heating there was the fireplace and, in the better houses, each room had the plain or tile-decorated *kakelugn*, the porcelain stove which with a little split wood gave off mellow heat for hours.

Food was substantial but not varied. It had been more interesting when the deer, the rabbits, and the birds had been more plentiful. Throughout the nineteenth century the most important single item was the oatmeal porridge; the rice porridge at Christmas time was a rare imported delicacy. Rye and wheat grew in popularity, and the great round sheets of hard rye bread were universal (and easily stored hung from the ceiling on a pole through the center hole). Meat was prized but hard to keep because of lack of refrigeration; it was used at great feasts during slaughtering time in the fall or seasoned heavily to preserve it as long as possible. Fish was a staple along the coast. Milk was usually in the form of buttermilk or sour milk (delicious with a little cinnamon), or preserved longer made into cheese or butter. The stomach-filling innovation of the nineteenth century was the potato, which grew in favor with spectacular speed (44,000 tons in 1802; 626,000 in 1850; 1.63 million in 1900). Although a goodly share of the potato crop was distilled into *brännvin* (*akvavit*) in the early years, much was eaten, too. After around 1910 when the sulphite process was adopted for distilling, the potato was almost solely used for eating. When the emigrants to the United States complained about the dull food they had eaten at home it was either "that eternal porridge" or "nothing but herring and potatoes." In peasant homes vegetables were rare, and fruit even more so.

Variation in diet was deliberately sought, and in 1843 a baker in Borås won a gold medal for making good bread with a combination of rye flour and potatoes. Likewise in 1843 the Royal Academy of Agriculture awarded a silver medal for a process of drying vegetables. Beer had long been used, but the new popular beverage was coffee. Supposedly it was the tragedy of Poltava in 1709 that taught the Swedes to love coffee: the soldiers driven into Turkey with Karl XII learned of it from their hosts and never lost their taste for it. It became so popular in the cities that the government prohibited it in 1794–96 as an economic waste and a danger to health. This led to smuggling and still greater popularity. The use of coffee spread throughout the country and provided the chief substitute for the alcohol that people were trying to resist.

Clothing of course had to be warm and serviceable. The peasants dressed in heavy homespun, while the city-dwellers, especially the more well-to-do, dressed in the fashionable clothing and styles of the European bourgeois. At the beginning of the nineteenth century even the aristocracy abandoned the ruffled and powdered elegance of the eighteenth-century French styles. Textile factories became important and speeded the adoption of international patterns and machine-made clothes. The provincial costumes of the country people became more elaborate and colorful as the womenfolk on the farms were needed less for plowing and chores and had time to indulge their taste for weaving and needlework. These "national costumes" continued to be worn for festive occasions, but their use gradually faded away, surviving into the twentieth century more as tourist attraction than as spontaneous self-expression.

Amusements and recreation were especially affected by economic circumstances and the tone of national leadership. The light and artistic touch encouraged by Gustav III was quickly squelched after his assassination, and Bellman died soon after his beloved king. Theater came back, but its nineteenth-century emphasis was on tragedy rather than on the gaiety and beauty of the Gustavian epoch. Hamlet, for example, had its Swedish premiere in 1819. In the 1850s it became more common for an ambulatory troupe of players to trek from town to town "like proper gypsies." For music the Swedes had the incomparable voice of Jenny Lind, until she went abroad, and they had opportunities to enjoy the famous Norwegian violinist Ole Bull. They had lilting folk songs and the fiddle for the dance and hymns of gripping emotional power. Hundreds of songs were translated from German and from English (Ira D. Sankey was very popular), and the Swedes themselves were productive, not only with psalms such as those in J. O. Wallin's Psalm Book (1819) but also with hymns. Pietists such as Oscar Ahnfelt, the "evangelical troubador," wrote many hymns, as Major Kaleb Johnson of the Salvation Army did later. Linda Sandell-Berg composed one of the most beloved, "Children of the Heavenly Father" (*Tryggare kan ingen vara*), which was sung to a Swedish folk melody; the first two verses illustrate its message:

> Children of the heav'nly Father
> Safely in His bosom gather;
> Nestling bird nor star in heaven
> Such a refuge e'er was given.

> God His own doth tend and nourish:
> In His holy courts they flourish.
> From all evil things He spares them,
> In His mighty arms He bears them.[10]

The Swedish language is clear and strong and lends itself beautifully to song; the great hymns come with such resonance and power that Swedish emigrants found it difficult to believe that God could be worshiped with English hymns.

Social life in the cities concentrated in clubs for men, and eventually the women in self-defense formed their own societies, without the expensive club houses. The world renowned Tivoli opened in Copenhagen in 1843, and a few years later a rather pale imitation started in Stockholm; here were puppet shows and shops, merry-go-rounds, and concerts — a continual carnival. Foreigners came to the country for hunting, but native Swedes still thought of hunting as more for meat than for fun. Skiing and skating were for rural youth. Athletics in the form of sports contests were all but unknown. Gymnastics made headway under the inspirational leadership of Per Henrik Ling, for whom the proper exercises brought harmony and health for both body and soul; Ling was a genius who taught poetry and fencing and the worship of the old Norse spirit all at the same time.

The festivals that had meant so much to the communal village life tended to disappear along with the village itself. The dances and the ceremonies were links with the half-forgotten past, with magical beliefs and fertility rites. When people spread to their individual farms it was more difficult to organize things; when they began to use modern implements, fertilizers, and new crops the old fertility ceremonies were less appropriate; and when half the people moved to the cities the old social bonds were loosened. The local festivals succumbed to progress, but the major national ones survived, especially Midsummer and Christmas, the times when the migrants to the cities came back home nostalgically to relive their youth or at least to remember it.

Midsummer, at the summer solstice, with its eerie light the whole night through, was a time of witchery and romance, of joy in luxuriant nature. Dancing, singing, and merrymaking; maypoles and fine costumes — a festival for all the family. And so was Christmas a family festival, the adapted heathen celebration of the winter solstice, when it was dark outside but warm and bright within. Christmas, along with Easter, was one of the times when all the churches were full. It was families together, bundled against the cold of early morning, sleighing behind flaming torches to the *julotta* (the pre-dawn Christmas service) in the church lighted only with candles. Then followed feasting, gifts, ánd gaiety, still half pagan, half Christian. Through the dark, cold days of midwinter the people moved from one party to the next and feasting continued for a month, from St. Lucia Day (December 13) to Twelfth Night (January 6). Another pagan festival that never died was Walpurgis Night (*Valborgsmässoafton*), the night before the first of May, associated since the Middle Ages with witches, the coming of spring, the lighting of bonfires, the induction into office of new village authorities; more recently it has been made a day of student celebration. In many ways the old lived on within the new.

## Schools

The Latin schools from the Middle Ages and the later gymnasia in the cathedral towns had offered education for a small elite. In the early nineteenth century only about half of the parishes had elementary schools, and these were for only one-half of the population, the boys. The well-to-do could provide instruction at home by parents or by tutors, but the mass of rural youth received no education beyond the catechism. Jacob Letterstedt, growing up in central Sweden in this period, illustrates problems and attitudes. He was one of four children in a family whose ancestors included regimental trumpeters, farmers, ministers, and one district governor. But Jacob's father designated him to carry on the farm, and for that he needed no "superfluous knowledge." Through his mother's manipulations he had one summer in school at age nine and then a year of living in town with an uncle at age thirteen. Otherwise his father kept him home to work in the fields until he was eighteen, and he had to sneak from his father's library the works of Aristotle and Cicero and others to get a partial education. This boy had the spark. He had to abandon his home and move abroad, but he became an inventor, entrepreneur, a wealthy merchant in Cape Town, South Africa, and donor of a major foundation in his homeland (Letterstedtska Fund).[11] Yet even this determined and talented young man suffered from an education that was maimed and inadequate. In the country as a whole, its youthful intellectual potential was being starved.

The liberal reformers, especially a few farsighted farmers, changed the direction of things. The conservatives in the riksdag were divided on the issue, some still thinking that education might create inflated hopes in youth. Others realized that knowledge was necessary for the functioning of a democratic society. They agreed with Bishop Tegnér who declared that in a democracy crudity was unconstitutional and ignorance was treason.[12] Crown Prince Oscar took the lead when he was regent in 1839; among other things he argued for free election of local school board chairmen in the face of the opposition of the bishops who thought a pastor should always hold that office. After careful debate the riksdag passed the landmark act of 1842 which required each parish to establish a common school.

Already Thorsten Rudenschöld, after his university years in Uppsala, had gained experience operating a private school. After failure as a bruksinspector (he was too liberal in his attitude toward the workers), he returned to teaching. When he discovered that the manorial lords thought the infant schools not good enough for their children he decided they weren't good enough for anyone's children and set out to improve them. He developed a school that grew to over two hundred pupils and had to move to quarters in his brother's castle at Läckö. His educational theories led to considerable controversy and helped shape the further course of events.

Rudenschöld might be called a Christian democrat. One day a week he gave over to teaching religion. But he considered it even more essential for the schools to prepare children for the life of the community. For this purpose each child should be educated to the peak of his own capacities and then find the place in society that fitted him. This would mean that some barons' sons would become farmers or mechanics, and some gifted children of the lower classes would become doctors and even officials or artists. Easy social mobility was the key to his philosophy, and no wonder it stirred opposition. For the youngest children he was willing to approve teaching in the homes, through a system of ambulatory schools, but he opposed the rotation teaching through which the more advanced pupils helped the younger while the trained teacher only supervised. He demanded permanent schools with education for all to age twelve, followed by a selection of the most able (regardless of birth) to go on to an elite school from ages twelve to fifteen, and then after further selection to a gymnasium. He would introduce practical work early in the school curriculum. In the riksdag discussions of 1856–58 he promoted his ideas vigorously and traveled widely throughout the country inspecting and advising, and much of his program was adopted then and in the 1860s. For instance, rotation teaching was legally abolished in 1864.[13] However, Rudenschöld could not break down the system of educational dualism which assumed that secondary and higher education were intended primarily for the upper ranks of society and that elementary and practical education were the preserves of the masses.

Another influential figure in the educational debate was P. A. Siljeström, rector of the New Elementary School in Stockholm. He deplored the idea that the elementary school should be a final school for anyone. Siljeström traveled to England and the United States in 1850–51, and this trip strengthened his idea that the schools must train in citizenship, not just in the catechism. He was interested in all aspects of the school situation, among other things in its architecture. He emphasized the need for light, air, and room for equipment and drew a number of plans for school buildings, carefully providing for separate cloakrooms, air circulation, etc. He insisted that the school should be in the center of the town, both physically and ideologically, and that pupils should be taught according to their ability and therefore be prepared to move up or down the social scale.

The significance of the educational discussion in the mid-nineteenth century lies in not only the farsighted views of the educational reformers themselves but the importance allocated to education by the riksdag and the community as a whole. It took many years before the universality of education legislated in 1842 became a reality. Nevertheless, already evident was a public concern with the interplay between the education of the individual and the improvement of society; again and again the same ideas and arguments appeared in the nineteenth century that would be re-expressed in the continuing debate into the later twentieth century.

## The Temperance Movement

Strong drink had a potent appeal to Swedish people; some said the reason was the cold and rainy climate. Unheated churches provided the excuse for men to carry their flasks with them on Sunday for the sake of inner warmth. Most of the drinking was less churchly, and it increased rapidly in the drunken decades between 1810 and 1830. People had discovered the potential of the potato — it was cheap to grow and cheaper to transport the liquid essence than the whole potato. The *brännvin* (*akvavit*) that had been made from grain could now be distilled from potatoes more easily, especially after the government attempts at monopoly were abandoned and home distilling was permitted once more. By 1830 the annual consumption was forty-four quarts per capita; no wonder that Karl Johan thought that alcohol would ruin the Swedish people. Both Gothenburg and Stockholm established temperance societies in 1830, and the Swedish Te.nperance Society was organized in 1837. Norway was a step ahead of Sweden in legislation, but in Denmark early attempts at legislation were abortive.

From time to time another kind of opposition expressed itself. During periods of crop shortages and hunger people occasionally rioted or went on strike against high prices for grain. Repeatedly under these circumstances indignant mobs attacked the distilleries which in the nineteenth century became industrialized and increasingly threatened food supplies and raised food prices.

Leader in the Swedish fight against the spreading social curse was the Lutheran pastor Per Wieselgren. He was in turn stimulated by the visit of an American Presbyterian Sunday School worker, Robert Baird. The movement was backed vigorously by the king, who read the book Baird had written in France about the popular American program and had it translated and given to every pastor in Norway and Sweden. Both temperance and total abstinence were preached, and the need was so imperative that public support grew. In 1847, at the height of the movement, four hundred twenty local societies counted 100,000 members. By the end of the 1840s alcoholic consumption was reduced to about four quarts per capita, less than 10 percent of the consumption two decades earlier. In 1855 home distilling was legally restricted, and the number of distilleries declined drastically. Of course there was apathy and opposition, but the results were amazing, though temporary. The tide of reform had ebbed by 1870.

The late nineteenth-century drive against the misuse of alcohol was even more directly influenced from the United States. Now the demand was not merely for moderation but for total abstinence, and the organizational impulse came through the International Order of Good Templars (IOGT). The Good Templar lodges originated in the United States and at first had connections with the Masonic Order. Olof Bergström, a Baptist preacher and immigrant agent active for a few years in the United States, saw the achievements of the Good Templars in America (where the society had some 400,000 members in 1868, the same year a lodge was founded in England). Bergström failed in his first attempts to organize societies in Sweden, but in 1879 he started the Klippan lodge in Gothenburg. This one took root and spread; eight years later Sweden had 1,519 lodges and 60,000 members; the high point was reached in 1910 with 2,340 lodges and 160,000 members. Meantime the IOGT was expanding around the world, and three Swedes have served as international chiefs.

Within Sweden the Good Templars' influence has profoundly affected not only alcoholism but the democratization of society. The Templars were pioneers in the study circle movement, organizing the first such groups in Sweden in 1902, along with choirs, theater clubs, sport clubs, Boy Scout troops, a large number of youth lodges, and, quite naturally, a cure center for alcoholics. The IOGT was (and is) a grass roots organization through which men could learn to work together for a common goal. They suffered splits and they rejoined in reconciliation, and they maintain even in *brännvin*-loving Sweden a corps of total abstainers. Of course not all men of temperance are members of the IOGT, but 136 out of 383 representatives in the riksdag were teetotalers in 1967.[14]

As of 1909 various temperance societies counted a total of 460,000 members, and during the tense period of the general strike of that year Sweden tried prohibition. A poll in 1910 indicated that a majority favored permanent prohibition, but the realistic leadership was cautious, cognizant of the habits and the demands of the large minority who felt otherwise. Instead of prohibition they adopted for national use a system of rationing pioneered in Gothenburg. Although this restraining method (the Bratt System) curtailed both alcoholism and smuggling it grew more and more unpopular and was at last abandoned in 1955. After a brief binge to enjoy the return of freedom the drinking habits of the people settled back into the old pattern, which meant much heavy social drinking and a high rate of alcoholism. But considerations of health and morality held many people to temperance, and exceedingly strict rules against drinking drivers kept others in line — 120,000 drivers, as of 1959, were pledged to abstinence.

## Religious Awakening

Out of the formalism and the barren overintellectualized theology of the state church sprouted the shoots of religious protest. In the eighteenth century the response was first pietism, strongly influenced by the successive varieties of German pietism and at the end of the century by the "neology" of simplicity and rationalism. All classes of society were affected but in different ways.

Within the state church certain of the new trends found rather mild expression in Archbishop J. A. Lindblom's revised catechism of 1810 and his church handbook of 1811. The ceremony of confirmation for youth was introduced but without the laying on of hands; the ordination ceremony was simplified; in baptism exorcism was abandoned, as was the use of the sign of the cross. In 1819 Johan Olof Wallin, "David's harp of the North," published a new psalmbook, including one hundred fifty hymns of his own composition. He was a preacher of power and a brilliant writer of the new Romanticism; in his hymns he combined, as Alrik Gustafson so well phrases it, "The Oriental magnificence of an ancient biblical tradition with directness, the simple vigor and gravity of a Swedish folk religion." [15] Wallin felt deeply, as did undoubtedly the mass of the Swedish people, that it was wrong to replace the living God with a Supreme Being. One of his finest poems, and one of the most powerful in the Swedish language, was his majestic "Angel of Death," inspired by the cholera epidemic of 1834.

The ritualistic revisions of the early nineteenth century were generally but not universally acceptable. In the far north of Sweden and in other isolated areas where churches were sparse, religious folk movements grew with especial vigor. Active as early as the mid-eighteenth century were the Readers (*Läsare*), small groups meeting in homes to read religious tracts, particularly the writings of Luther. The movement was inspired not only by German pietism in general and by the Moravian Brethren in particular, but it took on its own Swedish flavor. For missionary activity it worked among the Lapps in northern Sweden and Finland, and it emphasized the purification of morals. The Readers remained members of the state church, but their household gatherings emphasized the emotionalism in religion, sometimes becoming fanatical with sighing and groaning among the worshipers as the spirit entered. Of course the meetings violated the Conventicle Decree of 1726 which specifically forbade private religious gatherings. The movement nevertheless continued and spread and in the early nineteenth century took on new characteristics. Among other things it stimulated the peasants to learn to read so that they could study the Bible and tracts at first hand.

The New Readers of the nineteenth century took a stronger stand on salvation by faith and detected in the official handbook and the psalmbook abhorrent tendencies toward an emphasis on works. Their protests were not at first severely dealt with, for the church government was fairly tolerant in the early decades of the nineteenth century; in 1820 it agreed to allow private prayer meetings, and a number of regular ministers led or at least took part in the Reader activities. However, promises were soon forgotten and persecution was resumed.

Two Lund theologians reacted strongly to the popular and low-church movements: Samuel Ödmann (1750–1829), who for forty years preached persuasively from a sick bed, and Henrik Schartau (1757–1825), who propounded with authority a high-church point of view and "strength and reverence apart from sentimentality." [16] The Schartau movement worked within the state church. It was strongly authoritarian and became dominant in the west-coast area; in the later twentieth century it rigidly opposed family planning, the ordination of women ministers, and other modern threats to the established church and the Bible. [17]

Another facet of nineteenth-century religious fervor sparkled in the works of Eric Gustaf Geijer — philosopher, poet, composer, historian, one of the great teachers at Uppsala. His essay "On False and True Enlightenment in Relation to Religion," published in 1811, was highly influential and led at least one of its readers "from an unconscious to a conscious and riper life." [18] Geijer was not ordained and twice he refused a bishopric, but his voluminous writings and lectures reflected his conviction that "history is a continuous manifestation of God." [19]

Among the folk masses religious expression was naturally quite different than among the learned men of Lund and Uppsala. When one group of Readers demanded freedom from the church handbook and were refused, they began not only prayer meetings but at last communion services (in 1848) and their own sect (in 1860). Most of them stayed officially within the state church unless forced out. Foremost among the free-church leaders was Carl Olov Rosenius (1816–68), who came from a north Sweden Reader environment and fell under the influence of George Scott (see p. 359) and Methodism. After 1842 he picked up Scott's fallen torch and for over twenty-five years led the religious awakening in Stockholm and throughout Sweden, inspiring many through his preaching and chiefly his writing. Together with Hans Jacob Lundborg (1825–67) he was a leading figure in the *Evangelical Fosterland Society* (founded in 1856), which from within the state church coordinated the work of numerous Christian groups in home and foreign mission activities. The Board of the Society, composed of twelve Estate-persons (because of their financial contributions), wanted to make it an arm of the state church; Lundborg wanted the church completely freed from its ties to the state, on the model of the Church of Scotland after 1847, and he maintained close relations with the Scots. In the resultant controversy Lundborg lost out, and not even the free churches were able to unite. Soon, too, a large body of the awakened split from the Fosterland Society and formed the Swedish Mission Society (*Svenska Missions Förbundet*; followers in the United States were the Mission Friends, organized in 1885 as the Swedish Evangelical Mission Covenant). Under the inspiration of P. P. Waldenström, a Reader and disciple of Rosenius from Luleå in the far north, this puritanical, democratic, prohibitionist offshoot won a large following in Småland and other emigration-oriented regions and thus eventually gained strong ties with the United States. C. J. Nyvall in Sweden and his son David Nyvall in America exerted great influence in the Mission Covenant Church. Waldenström and the Nyvalls believed not only in God's unshakable love but in a layman's right to administer the Lord's supper and to do so even outside the church. [20]

In the intolerant decade of the 1840s two movements caused particular worry to the conservative church authorities. Lars Levi Laestadius as a youthful scholar traveled in the far north to study botany, and he long continued to do significant scientific work, but he became more interested in people than in plants. For two decades he served as pastor in Karesuando but felt his preaching was futile. In 1845 he went through a profound religious crisis and came out of it awakened, with new insights. He remained within the church, but he now preached with new power, and through the very crudeness of his allegories and poems he reached the simple people who lived in that harsh northern environment. Rebirth, he taught, could come only through public acknowledgment of Christ, not through baptism; public confession of sins was vital. There was hunger, and people who had food brought it to love-feasts where it was shared with others, and the ancient *agape* was preached and experienced. In emotional sessions with shouting and embracing, women tore off their earrings and brooches; all gave up luxuries for the general welfare. They cast aside neckties, tablecloths, and long draperies ("the devil's panties") and damned alcohol. The movement spread across northern Sweden and into Norway and Finland, among both settlers and Lapps. It was a frontier phenomenon that reached also to the United States but had little effect in central and southern Sweden, where people were repelled by its emotionalism and the crudeness of its imagery.

Most violent of these preachers of religious fervor was Erik Jansson, who came from a rural community in Uppland and found his followers there and in Hälsingland. "I am the greatest light since the time of the apostles." "One with the wild beast of the Apocalypse are those false and devilish teachers, the great idol Luther and the soul-murderer Arndt." "The priests are the pillars of hell and the devil's malicious procurers." This extraordinary man, ugly and tense, with weak voice but facile tongue, imbued with a Messiah complex, radiated magnetic power. He answered questions with strings of quotations from the Bible. His meetings violated the Conventicle Decree of 1726 and his attacks on church and clergy were merciless. He persuaded hundreds of enthusiasts to bring their "false" religious books to great burnings. He roused hundreds of people to the sinfulness of their ways but preached the sinlessness of true believers. The archbishop called Jansson a villain, and he was arrested; three days later four unknown men freed him, and he fled, reportedly in female disguise, to the Norwegian border and on to America. About a thousand loyal converts, respectable and propertied people, sold their lands and their belongings and followed him to Bishop Hill in Illinois, there to be joined later by still others to worship God in their own way.[21] (See further, pp. 367–368).

This Swedish Great Awakening was largely a home-grown phenomenon. Yet, just as the old pietism had been nurtured from Germany, so the nineteenth-century manifestations of religious intensity were affected by

British and American ideas and personalities. The first preacher of Methodism in Sweden, for example, was George Scott, born in Edinburgh. He reached Stockholm in 1830, reinvigorated the small group of Methodists already gathered around Squire Samuel Owen, and gained a large following. Scott became a leader in the movements for temperance and in the religious awakening; he was influential with Rosenius and others. But he was an outsider, and during a visit to the United States his sharp criticisms of moral and religious conditions in Sweden angered both the authorities and the people; on his return a riot in Stockholm forced him to give up his work and leave the country.

Later in the 1840s a missionary to the seamen in Gothenburg, F. O. Nilsson, was converted to Baptist beliefs by a German. Nilsson was rebaptized and started a Baptist society in the western province of Halland. Again the authorities clamped down and exiled Nilsson for violation of the Conventicle Decree. He went to Denmark and then to the United States. His sentence was one of the final incidents that mobilized the liberal opposition and won the repeal of much of the old restrictive legislation. Nilsson thereupon returned and founded a Baptist society in Gothenburg but soon thereafter left as a permanent emigrant to America. Both Methodists and Baptists maintained a lively interchange of ministers between Sweden and the United States.

In legislation for freedom of religious expression Sweden lagged behind both Denmark and Norway, but a Society for the Advancement of Religious Freedom, founded in 1851, gradually helped make toleration a reality. None too soon, for as late as 1855 the Readers in Orsa were sentenced to diets of bread and water for up to four weeks and were required publicly to acknowledge the "true faith." Resistance to such tactics increased and even took literary form. Viktor Rydberg's *The Last Athenian* (published in 1859), was a polemic against intolerance not only in fourth-century Greece but in nineteenth-century Sweden. The rigid walls of orthodoxy were breached, piece by piece: In 1855 came the abolition of the requirement for public affirmation of faith, in 1858 the repeal of the Conventicle Decree, and in 1860 the revocation of the pass requirement. In the latter year a new law on dissenters abolished punishment for leaving the state church and in 1870 the qualifications for voting and holding office were made independent of religion. A few restrictions, such as those on Roman Catholics and the existence of monasteries, survived to the mid-twentieth century. A general law of 1873, revised in 1908 and 1931, went far toward guaranteeing full religious freedom, and by 1951 the process was completed. (In the other Nordic countries religious freedom had already been achieved: Norway in 1845, Denmark in 1849, Iceland in 1874, and Finland in 1923.) The last decades of the nineteenth century evidenced wide and varied religious activity. In 1882 the

Salvation Army began its extraordinary growth in Sweden, and the most recent of the major waves of religious enthusiasm came in from the United States after the turn of the century in the form of the Pentecostal movement.

Despite the attacks of liberals, reformers, and crackpots the Lutheran state church stood its ground stolidly. It guarded its position with such rigid insistence that it could not adapt to changing conditions, and the result was stagnation. The slogan of Bishop Gottfrid Billing and his colleagues in the 1870s was to save what was left. Against such reactionism the free churches made strides: in the 1880s both the Baptists and the Methodists doubled their numbers. The socialists, stimulated by men like August Strindberg, vigorously denounced the church, and the liberal student group Verdandi helped provide the philosophical basis for the attack. It appeared that the church was dying.

At the same time the sectarian movements helped in a way to shore up the tottering structure of the state church. Most of the men and women touched by intense religious feelings retained membership in the state church. They helped vitalize foreign mission activity, and in much of the Christian effort in Sweden it became difficult to draw a line between the state church and the dissident organizations. The twentieth-century Young Church movement led by Manfred Björkquist was within the church yet broadly based, and a foundation was established for the ecumenical stress of Archbishop Nathan Söderblom.

For most of the awakened the new sect was something added to enrich their religious life, while they clung to the traditions and the security of the Lutheran state church. Rosenius, for example, took communion in the state church and had his children confirmed therein. For others the opposition to the established church was more deeply felt, and they made a complete break; more often they merely disregarded their old ties and let them die from atrophy. Innumerable gradations developed between formal renunciation on the one hand and dual membership on the other. No one *had* to cut the old bonds to become, for instance, a Mission Friend or a Methodist. And, unless he made a strong case of it, he had to continue paying taxes for the state church.

The revival or awakening of the nineteenth century was not an unmitigated social advance. It did not rejuvenate the church as a whole. Too often it left its devotees uninterested in the "children of the world" who had not been saved; the awakened ones became self-satisfied and aloof from the secular world. The movement led in some cases to ridiculous excesses of ecstatic religiosity. It led many to emigrate, even when they were not as strongly pushed as were the Erik Janssonists.

The awakening grew out of and along with the social developments of the time. All classes of the population were touched by it, but the peasantry were affected most. It was in the beginning a protest against rationalism, a search for a more personal religious faith; it was also a rebellion against pastors who were the petty lords of the parishes and to whom men had to tip their hats. In some ways it was a revolutionary individualism. Even more, however, it was a seeking for the warmth of meaningful human companionship in communities where people were isolated by the breakup of the old agricultural village. It was facilitated by increasing literacy, and it encouraged the reading of the Bible and the tracts. For some it was probably a spiritual substitute for the spirituous, a means of strengthening the resolve to resist alcohol. It was a way of breaking down barriers between the social classes and enhancing a sense of togetherness. The prayer meeting discussions encouraged people to express themselves and thus stimulated progress toward democracy.[22]

### Women, Arise!

In Swedish as in European society as a whole, woman was subordinate to man. On the farms she enjoyed a certain equality in her work in the fields, and often she had the responsibility for taking care of the cows and the honor of handling the keys. In the towns she was virtually a servant of man, and if she was unmarried her position was often dreary and demeaning. She could not be really free for she could not maintain herself economically. Special laws inspired by the gracious charity of men permitted widows to sell tobacco and trinkets, and women were allowed to work in the textile factories. But for the middle-class widow there might be nothing better than retirement to a foundation-home or employment as a household servant. All this unless she could be enough of a genius to rise above her sex disqualification — as did Eva De la Gardie. She was "the first and only Swedish-born woman to be a member of the Royal Academy of Science" and in 1748 published an article on the uses of the potato. Her suggestion that it could be distilled was significant economically and socially as well as scientifically. A few prominent figures of the late eighteenth century became concerned with the question of women's rights, and many men were bothered by the obvious waste of human capacity imposed by the old patriarchal system. Slowly things began to happen.

In 1815 a girls' school was opened in Gothenburg and other improvements in the status of women followed. A notable advance was the law of 1845 equalizing inheritance rights for men and women. In 1846 women gained the right to work in commerce and crafts, and in 1853 to teach in primary schools. The protective spirit was nevertheless evident in the law of 1852 fixing maximum hours of work for women and youth in factories. Meanwhile women were participating almost as much as men in the growing number of discussion associations — the temperance societies and the independent religious groups particularly. Here women's interests were vital and their opinions were listened to.

Not all the discussion about the position of women was calm, and not all of it was dominated by women. In 1839 the erratic genius Carl Jonas Love Almqvist shocked Sweden into attention with his appealing and beautifully written novel *Sara Videbeck* (*Det går an* in Swedish). The story is of a good-looking middle-class girl, thoroughly respectable, who on a trip falls in with a young sergeant. The accidents of life on the road and their mutual attraction lead step by step to the girl's surprising proposal that they live together without the sanctions or the restrictions of marriage, without the obligations of the daily round of household duties, each partner preserving complete independence. The extraordinarily pleasant way in which the tale was told and the reasonableness of the characters gave the novel wide circulation. But the ideas expounded horrified contemporary Swedes and led to Almqvist's destruction — loss of position as teacher and cleric, financial difficulties, charges of murder, and flight into unhappy exile in the United States. Almqvist was far ahead of his time, but his blatant challenge to the institution of marriage and his call for greater freedom for women produced widespread discussion and questioning of the artificial disabilities imposed on womanhood.[23]

Other proponents of women's rights were less revolutionary and perhaps more effective. Fredrika Bremer, for example, argued cogently that women were human beings and that they ought to be educated and treated as the equals of men. In 1828, at the age of twenty-seven, she published *Sketches of Everyday Life*, and she continued to write until her death in 1865. She traveled widely in Europe and the United States and wrote entertainingly and purposefully about the societies she visited. Her letters from America in 1849–50 to her sister, published in three volumes as *The Homes of the New World* in 1853, were widely appreciated in both Swedish and English versions. She spoke directly to people about other people, and she never hid her opinions. However, she would not be accepted as a soul-sister of the feminists of a century later. Her emphasis was not on rights and equality but rather on the special spiritual quality of women; women were the potential saviors of society, and they should have the vote not so much for their own sake as for the ennobling effect this would have on men. In 1856 Miss Bremer published the novel *Hertha*, which was less a story than a preachment, and she raised a storm of protest. It was a generation of reform, and women's rights, urged now by many, became part of the reform legislation. Emancipation was partly a function of the rapidly increasing number of unmarried women.

Women's equality with men in legal and economic status came by slow and reluctant stages. In 1858 unmarried women could be declared of age at twenty-five if they so requested (men attained their majority at age twenty-one); earlier than this all women had been classed in law along with children and the insane; they could not marry or dispose of property without the consent of a guardian or by special dispensation. Increasingly, however, women were needed as teachers in the expanding schools, and hence a training college for women teachers was established in 1861. A year later women were granted rights of suffrage in local affairs. In 1870 women were permitted to take examinations for entrance to the university, although they still had little opportunity to get secondary school preparation; the universities slowly opened their doors except for degrees in theology or law. Since society did not collapse as a result of these not-so-bold measures additional reforms were introduced. In 1884 unmarried women became of age at twenty-one; in 1891 women were allowed to enter the apothecary trade; in 1906 the riksdag agreed to examine the question of women's suffrage, and in 1909 women were made eligible for election to municipal councils.

Individual women were in the meantime making significant contributions. Sofia Gumaelius in 1877 opened an advertising agency that became one of the foremost in Sweden. In the late 1890s Ellen Key shocked the country with her advocacy of free love. In 1909 Selma Lagerlöf was awarded the Nobel Prize in literature. Greta Garbo was soon to appear and other world-famed actresses in her wake. The Swedish woman won the vote immediately after World War I and soon attained high positions in government. Alva Myrdal became an international personality in diplomacy as well as a respected social scientist; Nanna Swartz was a leading physician. In sports and the arts and intellectual activities women came to have unfettered opportunities to use their talents to the full. Most extraordinary of all, they made good their claim to a sex life as free as men's; Swedish women were no longer oppressed.[24]

## Sexual Mores

The world has become deeply interested in the sexual mores of Sweden. Some of the reports have been so sensational that they provoke denunciations of sinful Sweden from one side and happy shouts of enthusiasm from the other. Such reactions are based partly on exaggerations of the evidence and partly on another kind of sin: that of judging the customs of one culture by the circumstances and precepts of another. The pattern of sex practices in Sweden is indeed different from the Victorian standards long preached in England and the United States, and it is a pattern of freedom. It is not, however, an aberration of the twentieth century but is historically rooted in accepted practice and in large part legally recognized.

Kings of Sweden, like those of other countries, frequently had liaisons with women other than the queen. If the illegitimate offspring were competent, and especially if the mother was a woman of some social station, they were accepted and might attain high position. For instance, Count Carl Löwenhielm, representative of Sweden at the Congress of Vienna, was generally believed to be the illegitimate son of King Karl XIII. In the sixteenth century Erik XIV fell in love with the beautiful but low-born Karin Månsdotter and what shocked the court was not the liaison itself but the fact that he married the girl. The nobility was allowed less latitude than the kings, but many nobles — in all lands — were rather free with their affections and so were the wealthier upper-class merchants. At the other end of the social spectrum the peasants and the workers, with no position in society to maintain, were also likely to have few compunctions or constraints in their sexual relationships, at least when unmarried. In Stockholm in the 1840s 45 percent of the babies were born out of wedlock. The maintainers of the moral proprieties (the principles and proprieties of the Christian ethic) were the middle-class citizens who feared financial entanglements and whose ambitions inhibited them from risking a blot of scandal. Even they often yielded to the easier standards of those above and below them on the social ladder. It is important to remember that the overwhelming majority of the people were farmers and farm workers until the end of the nineteenth century and that children were much desired (until the late nineteenth century) as an economic asset in both country and city. Nevertheless there existed wide variations in sexual practices in different sections, even within some parishes.

Reasons for unrestrained romance in the north have been cited as the long dark nights of winter and the light nights of summer; the long distances which prevented the preacher from arriving when wanted; the crowded conditions of the cottages, permitting privacy only in bed (an explanation given also for the bundling in Pennsylvania and elsewhere). But we should consider the more basic reasons. The Swedish peasant was both emotional and pragmatic; his attitude was that sex was natural and that what was natural was right. If there was intercourse in the little room up under the eaves or out in the woodland, but no child, then this might be only an incident.' But the fact of intimacy usually indicated some affection, and if a child was born, then marriage was the natural (though not inevitable) next step. A child needed parents, but otherwise why get married? No responsibility and no sin.

Explanations aside, the historical facts are clear. According to a knowledgeable Swedish sociologist it was true for centuries that the majority of Swedish marriages came only after conception of a child (naturally statistics cannot be wholly dependable in such matters). As a result of the religious awakening of the nineteenth century some change occurred but not much, and religious restraints faded away again in the twentieth century. Statistics have become more complete in recent years, but they do not indicate any fundamental change: in 30 to 35 percent of all Swedish marriages a child is already born or on the way (born within seven months). That premarital sex experience is common is shown by several surveys in the 1960s. Out of a group of 436 draftees 83 percent said they had had intercourse, 7 percent said no, and 10 percent would not answer. In four folk high schools over a period of five years the percentage with sex experience ranged from 37 percent to as high as 87 percent. There is virtually no sense of guilt. In the great majority of cases intercourse is with a steady partner or fiancé(e), rarely with a casual acquaintance. Promiscuity is as rare as chastity, but both do exist. It is probably true that in the 1960s the age of first intercourse definitely dropped to an average of about seventeen years, and much younger among groups like the *raggare* (the wild youth) of Stockholm. Once married, it should be added, and despite the frequency of divorce, Swedish couples seem to be as faithful to the marriage bond as other national groups in western society. While these generalizations appear to be valid for Sweden as a country it must be noted that both ideals and practices vary widely by locality and by segment of the population.

Behind the broad nineteenth- and twentieth-century scene lie the historical, legal, and customary practices, and here is perhaps the chief difference between Sweden (and other Scandinavian countries) and countries such as the United States. Crowded conditions caused families to sleep close-packed and servants of both sexes to sleep perhaps in the hayloft. Fundamental is the old legal recognition in Sweden that a child born to an engaged couple is legitimate, a provision which of course colors the moral attitude. The economic responsibility of the father is also recognized by law, though marriage is not required. Most important is the social attitude that accepts both unwed mothers and illegitimate children as normal members of society. Vis-à-vis the child this is part of the recognition of the rights of personality. Vis-à-vis the mother it is two things: first, it is an attempt to make women's position in society equal to that of men; second, it is the acceptance by a pragmatic society of the reality and naturalness of sex. From the historical point of view what we have, for better or for worse, is the twentieth-century repudiation of the nineteenth-century opprobrium attached to unsanctified sexual relationships and a return to the more quiet acceptance of "the facts of life" as recognized in earlier centuries.[25]

*The Great Migration*

Every route that crosses the ocean
I would mark on the map in red,
For there our hearts' blood flows
From open wounds toward the west.
Look at the brown chests in Gothenburg
That are stacked every day on the quay,
And at the long long lists of passengers
Like death reports from a battle.

Carl Snoilsky (1887)[26]

Snoilsky was reacting emotionally and poetically to the "America fever" that infected hundreds of thousands of Europeans in the late nineteenth century. On the piers of Gothenburg gathered emigrants in homespun, with their sea chests and all their belongings, saying goodbye to the meager life they knew, venturing into the great unknown. The psychological and personal aspects of the story are poignantly told in Vilhelm Moberg's trilogy *The Emigrants, Unto a Good Land*, and *The Last Letter Home*; the sanguine spirits like Karl Oskar seized on the opportunity, whereas the hesitant, like Kristina, had to be dragged along or left at home. They came from the stony farmlands of Småland and Värmland and all about Sweden, from rural villages and crowded cities to sail for England and on across the ocean to the Land of Promise. By 1930 they filled the United States with some 3 million Swedish Americans of first, second, and third generations; Sweden itself then held only slightly more than 6 million. Some went, too, to Canada, Australia, South Africa, South America.

After the seventeenth-century colonization on the Delaware Swedish migration to America never entirely ceased. Per Kalm collected scientific data and Axel Klinkowström made thoughtful observations a generation before Tocqueville,[27] but neither was an immigrant. The young officers who fought in the American Revolution were not tempted to remain. Until the nineteenth century only occasional individuals sought escape from Sweden and haven abroad. Some were rogues and some were saints and most were in-betweens.

Adolph Ulric Wertmüller left Sweden at age twenty-one to study art in Paris with the master J. M. Vien, aided for years by his cousin Alexander Roslin who had already won honors in France as a portrait painter. Wertmüller painted a number of classical subjects, most famous being his exquisite *Danaë and the Golden Rain*, but he earned his living by painting portraits. In 1784 he became a member of the Académie Royale de Peinture et de Sculpture (which became the Académie des Beaux-Arts in 1795). He did a perhaps too true portrait of Marie Antoinette and her children. When the Revolution broke out he was painting the wealthy bourgeois of Bordeaux. As the heads he really wanted to paint fell under the guillotine he moved on to Spain but was still frustrated in his highest ambitions. He fell in with a friend in Cadiz (Henrik Gahn) and they decided to take a trip to America. There he made portraits of several American statesmen, including an excellent one of George Washington. He was not yet an immigrant but he fell in love with the granddaughter of Gustaf Hesselius, foremost painter of the Swedish colony on the Delaware. Wertmüller returned to France and Sweden to put his affairs in order and then, although he was ruinously cheated by a bankrupt brother-in-law, he sailed back to his true love and married her. The couple bought a farm a few miles downriver from Philadelphia and there for the last ten years of their lives they wrestled with the problems of crops and livestock and indentured servants.[28] Wertmüller was unique in talent and experience, but he was also representative of thousands of emigrants in that disappointment and closed opportunities at home set him on the path to America. Incidentally, his friend Henrik Gahn also stayed in the United States, moving to New York and in due course becoming Swedish consul there.

Sometimes the impulse to emigrate was more forceful, as in the case of the "Knave of Fallebo." This consummate rogue was baptized as Carl Johan Nilsson but he assumed a variety of names including Fallenius, Billy Williams, C. W. Hufeland, and finally Dr. C. W. Roback. After Fallenius had swindled a number of Swedes and built up debts he could not pay he fled to Copenhagen and further to Boston. For several years he wandered about the United States and Canada, making patent medicines and exhibiting an alligator which he called a crocodile and said he had caught in Africa. In 1847 he surfaced in Philadelphia as an astrologer, and he made the mistake of appropriating to himself and selling a horoscope developed by a Dr. Hague. Hague exposed him for plagiarism and the unsupportable claims he (then under the name Hufeland) made for his Astrologer's Swedish Consumption Syrup and an amazing electric love powder. The newspapers of Philadelphia, duped for months, turned against him and he was tarred and feathered and driven from the City of Brotherly Love. Soon he was back in Boston, surrounded by mystery and clothed in magnificence, posing as a doctor and magician. He evidently kept clear of the law, hoaxed hundreds, and acquired a small fortune. In his will he provided handsomely for the Roback family in Sweden whose name he had borrowed (they would not accept the money), and he paid off the debts he had left on his hasty departure more than thirty years before. Some of his countrymen were proud of the Swede who had been able to outsmart the Yankees.[29]

Another exceptional emigrant became the leader of the first modern group migration. Erik Jansson, mentioned in connection with the dissenting religious movement, in the years 1846 to 1850 gathered some 1,500 colonists to his Utopian agricultural settlement at Bishop Hill in western Illinois. Many of the group had been prosperous farmers in Sweden and the proceeds from the sale of their farms went into the communal pool through which equipment could be bought and good buildings constructed at once. Careful planning of the whole enterprise assured that masons and carpenters and all necessary skilled workers were on hand. Jansson, as the right hand of God, directed both religious and economic life. The communal organization was held together by religious fervor and the dictatorial rule of the leader, and, in spite of a wave of disease and death and some defections, the colony prospered remarkably. That is, until 1850, when Jansson was killed by a disgruntled husband of a young woman whom the high priest-autocrat would not release from the community. Within a few years Utopia disintegrated without its charismatic leader and prosperity disappeared. The Swedish flavor remained in the town, along with the impressive architecture of the Steeple Building, the church, and the long brick apartment houses on the American prairie. A gallery of primitive but expressive portraits, painted by the blacksmith Olof Krans, have preserved an unusual pictorial record of the citizens and their group activities.[30]

With the exodus of the Erik Janssonists emigration from Sweden began slowly to gain momentum. Dissenters, touched by Methodist, Baptist, and Covenant influences from England and the United States appreciated the more tolerant atmosphere of America. However, the persecution that hounded Erik Jansson and his followers from their homeland was uncharacteristic of Sweden even in the 1840s, and the restrictive regulations that made it possible were gradually eliminated by law. By 1873 the land enjoyed a high degree of religious freedom and freedom of movement, and the religious motivation for leaving the country faded away. Other causes, however, proved still more powerful, and the outward flow of people increased.

On their arrival in America, especially in the years 1845 to 1859, immigrants of all persuasions or none were met in New York by Olof Hedström. Hedström had migrated in the 1820s, married an American girl, and become a Methodist minister. His little church on the "Bethel Ship" in New York harbor was a haven for puzzled Swedish newcomers. The minister not only preached but provided friendly advice on land and the routes west and the purchase of equipment; he was a helpful "saint" to thousands. Others there were, too, who met the ships but took advantage of the innocence of the fresh arrivals for whom God did not supply that instant knowledge of English that Erik Jansson had promised. "Runners" sometimes took the money of the immigrants to buy them railroad tickets but never reappeared, or they led young girls to houses of prostitution. The great majority of immigrants nevertheless found their way to destinations in the interior, to the open lands of Minnesota and the Dakotas, to Texas, to the forests of the Northwest, and to cities that needed builders and craftsmen. Chicago came to have almost as many Swedes as Gothenburg, and a Swedish stamp was put on Rockford, Illinois, Jamestown, New York, and Minneapolis, Minnesota. The Ingrids and the Fridas and the Birgittas, the Oles and Svens and Håkans swarmed in increasing numbers, and as they acquired dollars they sent home money or prepaid tickets for their brothers or their sweethearts to join them.

The Swedes were part of a vast European population movement. Yet this nineteenth- and twentieth-century phenomenon was unlike the mass migrations of the barbarians or the trek of Asian tribes in search of grasslands. The modern migration was a movement of individuals counted in the millions but propelled by individual decisions, although these decisions were affected by general social and economic forces. The difference was that the home society remained intact, it was the surplus that migrated. In the 1850s 30,000 Swedes emigrated; in the 1860s two powerful forces pushed the figure to 146,000. First was the Homestead Act of 1862 with its promise of free or almost free land to settlers in the West; second was the series of disastrous crop failures in Sweden in 1867–69. The pull and the push operated simultaneously. The economic crisis of 1872 in the United States deterred migration temporarily, but a resurgent economy lured a record number in the 1880s — 330,000. The tide ebbed slightly thereafter, but in proportion to its population Sweden sent more of its sons and daughters overseas than did any other country besides Norway and Ireland; 98 percent of the flow went to the United States.

The volume was large: altogether a million and a quarter Swedes succumbed to the America fever in the years 1820 to 1930. Some communities were decimated and some rocky farms were abandoned. Yet even during the record decade of the 1880s the population of Sweden increased by 220,000. Seldom did emigration remove more than half of the annual natural increase. On the other hand it did take young men and women in their most productive years, and it rose occasionally to about 1 percent of the total population. The final turn of the tide came only in 1930.

The causes for this continuing human outpouring from Sweden were multiple and were much the same as the causes affecting other European countries from which multitudes migrated. But proportions and timing were peculiarly Swedish. The nineteenth-century individualization of the land had detached farmers from their ancestral lands and traditional social system. The uprooting was both physical and psychological; once the bonds with neighbors and the old style of life were broken it was easier to move a second time and perhaps a third. On the individual farms families produced more crops and also more children. As the number of heirs increased there was not enough land left to subdivide. The landless, dependent classes grew rapidly. Some found their

Swedish Migration Statistics

| Period | Emigration within Europe | Emigration outside Europe[a] | Immigration from Europe | Immigration from outside Europe | Net Emigration[b] |
|---|---|---|---|---|---|
| 1851–55. . . . . . | 1,503 | 11,241 | . . . | . . . | 22,263 |
| 1856–60. . . . . . | 424 | 3,732 | . . . | . . . | 8,312 |
| 1861–65. . . . . . | 7,272 | 12,544 | . . . | . . . | 23,681 |
| 1866–70. . . . . . | 22,056 | 80,575 | . . . | . . . | 122,646 |
| 1871–75. . . . . . | 22,409 | 42,054 | 11,122 | 3,514 | 57,577 |
| 1876–80. . . . . . | 22,359 | 60,447 | 12,051 | 2,891 | 81,177 |
| 1881–85. . . . . . | 27,209 | 147,619 | 14,208 | 7,172 | 168,930 |
| 1886–90. . . . . . | 21,687 | 179,886 | 14,190 | 12,031 | 178,355 |
| 1891–95. . . . . . | 19,583 | 141,879 | 13,639 | 25,316 | 127,313 |
| 1896–1900. . . . | 22,676 | 62,634 | 17,050 | 22,805 | 53,027 |
| 1901–05. . . . . . | 17,932 | 129,746 | 20,443 | 19,456 | 123,133 |
| 1906–10. . . . . . | 15,692 | 94,297 | 18,989 | 25,536 | 71,721 |
| 1911–15. . . . . . | 15,571 | 63,361 | 16,705 | 22,743 | 39,484 |
| 1916–20. . . . . . | 16,785 | 22,658 | 19,665 | 16,441 | 3,337 |
| 1921–25. . . . . . | 13,166 | 59,438 | 16,602 | 15,074 | 40,928 |
| 1926–30. . . . . . | 9,462 | 46,579 | 14,870 | 15,655 | 25,516 |
| 1931–35. . . . . . | 7,959 | 4,400 | 12,468 | 23,287 | +23,396 |
| 1936–40. . . . . . | 8,820 | 4,584 | 20,114 | 8,753 | +15,463 |
| 1941–45. . . . . . | 10,277 | 1,261 | 46,927 | 1,095 | +36,484 |
| 1946–50. . . . . . | 28,335 | 21,849 | 138,617 | 9,076 | +97,509 |
| 1951–55. . . . . . | 51,291 | 24,264 | 117,387 | 10,536 | +52,368 |
| 1956–60. . . . . . | 56,520 | 18,280 | 115,775 | 12,606 | +53,581 |

*Source:* Compiled for Franklin D. Scott, ''Sweden's Constructive Opposition to Emigration,'' *Journal of Modern History*, 37 (1965): 313.

[a] Total overseas emigration 1851–1950 amounted to 1,190,784, of which 1,141,969 went to the United States.

[b] Including estimates of nonregistered emigration or immigration indicated by +.

way to the towns and took what work they could get, but they were not attached to the city or to city ways and it was easy for them to move on. Emil Tyden may serve as an example. He was one of seven sons on a farm near Gothenburg, a farm that could barely support one family. Young Emil relieved the situation by migrating to America. He got work in a machine shop, invented a lock for boxcar doors, built a factory, and made a comfortable fortune. This kind of example encouraged others, some of whom had similar success, some of whom ended as disastrous failures.

Another cause was dislike of the compulsory military service of thirty days; when it was raised to forty days an extraordinary number of twenty-year-olds chose the moment to emigrate. Young men and women disillusioned in love, or at odds with their parents, left home to escape disappointment or poverty or boredom. And a few fled from the sheriff! Others merely yearned for adventure, went perhaps for a year or two, then stayed a lifetime. Whatever their intentions on the moment of leaving Sweden nearly a fifth of the emigrants returned to their homeland; when they did so they returned not only to Sweden but usually to the communities they had left.

Thousands of the Swedish emigrants had no real stake in the land of their ancestors. They had no homes of their own and little hope of ever having them. They lived in a society of deference and youth was beginning to resent the demeaned status of the unpropertied and the less educated. The Swedes did not depart from a land of the downtrodden; the still poorer peasants of Poland and the Ukraine and the Abruzzi had not yet heard the call to emigrate. The Swedes heard it, for they lived in a society of relative freedom and good communication. They were sufficiently well off that they could dream of being better off. They had the physical stamina to risk the severe ocean voyage and to do the backbreaking work of plowing the new sod and cutting the timber. Most had the rudiments of education and could read and write. Because of the sparsity of cities and specialized industry boys on the farm had learned the diverse skills of carpenter, painter, blacksmith, and animal tender; they were prepared for the demand of the frontier for versatility. They knew how to be independent.

The body of emigrants was not a normal cross section of the Swedish population. In the mid-nineteenth century 60 percent of the migrants were families; by the early twentieth century less than 30 percent were families, instead the great majority were young, single men and women. Families had departed without serious disruption of the age-group pattern in the home society; but when large numbers of young people in the 15–35 age-group bracket left, the balance at home became overweighted with the very young and the very old. This was what disturbed the social analysts and the employers, especially because the drain took vigorous youth just as they were beginning to be able to repay the social cost of their birth and upbringing. Furthermore, in spite of the demand for Swedish maids in upper- and middle-class America, the majority of emigrants were male; the result was a surplus of unmarried women in Sweden, with concomitant social problems, especially of unwed mothers.

Nor was the base of emigration spread evenly throughout the country. The far north did not contribute much. The wide open spaces of Sweden's northland themselves offered an alternative to overseas migration, and this internal frontier grew significantly in population in the 1880s, the decade of largest emigration to America. Nor did the more fertile areas of ancient cultivation in the east and far south add much to the emigrating stream; Uppland, Södermanland, and the rich breadbasket of Skåne could better take care of their own. But the overpopulated and stony provinces of south central and western Sweden sent hundreds of thousands, especially from Småland, Bohuslän, and Värmland. The chief exception to this geographic pattern was Stockholm, from which much of the emigration was second-stage: people moved first from farm to city, then from city to America. Others migrated direct from a farm in Småland to a farm in Wisconsin or Minnesota, or to a city in America rather than to a city in Sweden. As the migration built its own centers across the ocean it was common for a young peasant to have friends or relatives in Chicago or Rockford, though he might know no one at all in Gothenburg or Stockholm. America was close emotionally, though far away geographically.

Letters sent home by emigrant neighbors and cousins enhanced the America fever. Pictures of new homes, even if they looked bleak, excited the imagination, for they represented independence, something owned. Stories of the high wages in the cities sounded fabulous. Accounts of the food — fruit and vegetables and meat in abundance — made Swedish porridge and potatoes unappetizing. News of the schools for children, the cheap rich land and the homestead "free" land, the low taxes, and the potential for an illimitable future — all this was intoxicating and contagious, and the glowing letters of emigrants were read aloud to relatives and friends and often published in the newspapers. Guide books by the dozen and Swedish-English dictionaries were issued to prepare the emigrant for his new life.

George F. Erickson was one of the letter writers. He left Västmanland in 1909, settled in the northern peninsula of Michigan, and for forty years corresponded with a boyhood friend who remained in Sweden. One letter from 1910 read in part:

> I consider myself lucky to get away from there, for there was nothing else to do but stay at home and have nothing to do if I had stayed there. Here in America you don't have to go without work if you want to do something. I never had to look for any work. I got it anyway, so there is certainly a difference here and in Sweden, where you have to go and bow and scrape and ask everywhere and still not get anything. I have it quite good here.[31]

He made a trip back home early in 1914, after he had been in the United States long enough that he would not be picked up for Swedish military service; he wrote his friend that:

> it was hard to leave again but I also thought it was good to get away from everything that was oppressive and all I would have had to do if I was going to stay in Sweden. Here you are in any event a free man in a free land.[32]

The appeal was reinforced by emigrants coming home to visit, wearing their fine clothes, dangling their gold watch chains and boasting of their achievements in the land of promise. Frequently the most expansive of the returnees were agents of railroad companies or steamship lines, eager to sign up new passengers and thus earn their own passage and commission.

One of the more respected agents was Colonel Hans Mattson (some were adventurous scum who preyed on their countrymen), an ambitious boy from northern Skåne who had a little schooling and a year or so of military experience in Sweden. He sensed that a farm boy had little chance of advancement in the Swedish artillery in competition with the sons of the nobility; hence he resigned and with a friend sailed for Boston in 1851. After two years of wandering he reached his future base in Minnesota, where he became a farmer, founder of towns, colonel of a Minnesota regiment in the Civil War, general manager of the Immigration Board of Minnesota, several times Minnesota's secretary of state, editor and cofounder of three Swedish-American newspapers, promoter and immigration agent for the Northern Pacific. His first recruiting trip to Sweden fell in the period of hard times in the late 1860s, and he brought back 800 immigrants. His private banking agency (for the Cunard Line) originated the system of prepaid tickets, whereby settlers could pay in advance for the passage of relatives.[33] As Mattson's story illustrates, emigration was partly spontaneous, but it was partly induced.

Some of the emigrants traveled in tour groups arranged by agents like Hans Mattson. Thus they had help and their initial language problems were minimized. Some even went direct from a Swedish village to a wholly Swedish-speaking community in America, and a few never did learn English. William Widgery Thomas, for example, in the Civil War period American consul in Sweden and later minister, brought a large company of Swedes to northern Maine in 1870; they established New Sweden and other towns, Thomas continued to act as kindly godfather to the settlements, and they maintained their Swedishness for over a century.[34] Emigrants without leaders had to make their own way and take the risk of falling in with questionable company. The usual route in the early years was by way of Gothenburg or Copenhagen to Hull, across to Liverpool, and thence to Boston or New York. Only few shipped direct from Gothenburg. After the founding of the Swedish-American Line in 1905 the connections became more direct.

The combination of the persistent population drain and the continuing discontent in society furrowed the brows of responsible officials. What was wrong with the Swedish state? Individuals had long been writing about the relationship between social ills and emigration. Even in the eighteenth century Chydenius had remarked that people leaving meant people seeking freedom. In the later nineteenth century Knut Wiksell preached a similar doctrine. At length the riksdag itself decided to investigate the problem that threatened Sweden's self-respect and, some thought, its existence. The result was a twenty-one-volume report done with typical Swedish thoroughness; this *Emigrationsutredningen* was nothing less than a sociological analysis of the Swedish community and a mine of information. Directed by the able statistician Gustaf Sundbärg and published in the years 1908–13, it established rather clearly why people emigrated and what they thought was wrong with their country.

The first riksdag proposal for an inquiry, in 1904, was motivated by the concern that

> annually several thousand vigorous young persons leave the fatherland to seek in a foreign country a living which with industry and saving they could as well attain here at home. . . . Information on the dangers of emigration would in large degree check the stream. . . . Another method of checking emigration is to provide a better future for youth here at home.[35]

Another reformer (Ernst Beckman) wanted a study of "American conditions, especially economy and popular education, in order to discover what might be worthy of imitation." He proposed urging emigrants to return so they could infuse Swedish workers with new ideas from abroad and with the American "lust for work," in brief, "to move America over to Sweden."[36]

The compilation and analysis of grievances had a catalytic effect. Although the whole emigration inquiry had little if any effect as a check on emigration, it was a factor of considerable importance in the promotion of social change in Sweden. E. H. Thörnberg, a reformer and an agent of the commission, said frankly, "We reformers used [the inquiry] as a vehicle for social legislation."[37] Interviews with emigrants revealed a whole arsenal of reasons for leaving the homeland: personal dissatisfactions, wanderlust, the urging of relatives already in America, boredom with the dullness of Swedish life, and a pervasive discontent with the social and economic situation. Some mentioned six or eight brothers and sisters and thus indicated there was no room for them at home. Several had emigrated earlier, returned to Sweden for a time, but preferred the greater activity and opportunity in America and were going a second time. Some planned to earn money in America and return to buy a farm, which they could not hope to do while staying in Sweden.

More dramatic than the interviews were the letters to the commission from earlier emigrants settled in America. One had emigrated in 1868, twice returned to Sweden with his savings, but finally settled in America. His reasoning was primarily economic, but his long letter closed with a bitter and revealing comparison: "Here [in America] we have rich men, here we have learned men, here we have 'clever' men, here we have workbosses who sometimes browbeat us — but masters (*herrar*) we do not have."[38] Another closed his equally long letter with advice to Mother Svea:

> When you give your children universal suffrage (for it is at the ballot box that class differences vanish), when you separate church and state, when you modernize some of your antique laws and take education away from the

priesthood, then I shall sell all that I have here and go home to rest in your earth.[39]

An emigrant of 1893 wrote that he had met bad luck and evil in both Sweden and the United States, but he had won out and gained property in America. He had found love of the fatherland was sometimes deeper among emigrants than at home, and he knew many who would be glad to return "if evil conditions were righted." A group of boys in the north of Sweden found a book that painted the hardships and wickedness of America so black that they became suspicious of the author's purpose; they thought it must have been to frighten people and keep them submissive to conditions at home. The boys all migrated. One of them claimed that economic conditions were the least of the causes, for all the boys came from prosperous families; he cited class differences, the suffrage, and military service. From Småland came an embittered young man who had doubtless pulled many a stone from his father's fields. He burst forth with diatribes against potatoes and herring:

> that is what people eat in Småland, along with rye bread as black as the earth and as hard as the stones. God save us from Småland and all that is Swedish. . . . Sweden should have a president instead of a king.[40]

An honest man of the 1880s said he did not know why he had migrated:

> the bread question was much of it, class differences too, and then there was the question of personal worth, for I felt myself valueless for both the community and myself. . . . Still I have nothing to condemn Mother Svea for, because I have at least inherited from her good principles.[41]

This sampling gives only a faint impression of the multiplicity of factors revealed by the letters. The only universal was that each writer had gone to America. Two categories of complaints and demands stood out in bold relief: the demand for greater economic opportunity and the demand for greater democracy.

The economic demand was a craving to earn more than bare subsistence, a protest against no savings, no amusements, no security. But love of home was strong, and again and again an emigrant said he would have stayed in Sweden if he had seen a chance to own his own home. Knut Wicksell remarked that in America a settler might live in a crude sod hut, but he could hope to build a two-story palace; but "he who here in Sweden begins in a sod hunt undeniably has every prospect to end his life in it, or in one like it."[42] Hunger for land and home lured many thousands of Swedes to the prairies of the Midwest. Others were drawn by industry, and they urged Sweden to advance manufacturing. One said it was a question of bread and meat — "bread and meat in America or skin and bones in Sweden."[43]

The letters evidenced a deep resentment against the upper classes of Sweden. The ruling classes were held only partly responsible for economic woes, but they were held wholly responsible for the indignities suffered by the poor. Hence the demand for universal suffrage, with its implicit recognition of the equality of persons. Lack of educational opportunity was rarely offered as a reason for leaving Sweden, but many an American immigrant praised the democratic and broad-based education there and warned Sweden that it must open school doors to more people and provide more practical education. In the whole category of democratic demands the emotional content was clearly greater than the category of economic demands. Economic conditions could be attributed to imponderable fate, but class distinctions and the derogation of personality were man-made and amenable to reform. The acid comments of the emigrants hurt, and they were used as weapons by men who fought for a new order of society. Yet it will remain a puzzling question, how can one weigh the relative importance of these and other weapons in the transformation of Sweden in the twentieth century?

The major continuing organization for counteracting emigration was the National Society against Emigration (Nationalföreningen emot Emigrationen), founded in 1907 and sparked for many years by Adrian Molin, a conservative-nationalist maverick. Molin used both stick and carrot: he condemned the unpatriotic desertion of the fatherland and his vigorous propaganda warned against the dangers of migration; on the positive side he urged reforms to make the fatherland more attractive. Especially he promoted the Own-Home movement, utilizing both state and private support to help families establish small farms of their own, to colonize Sweden instead of America. The Society established or cooperated in funding Own-Home companies in several provinces, and by 1932 it had processed about 200,000 acres of land with a value of some 45 million kronor; one-third of the land was arable and represented about 1 percent of the total of tilled land in the country. The Society was especially successful during World War I, when emigration was shut off by outside forces. Its activity spurred other organizations and business enterprises, and the total impact was to encourage small farmers and to pass ownership into the hands of the operators. Reform came rather rapidly. By 1937 about 90 percent of Sweden's tilled acreage was individually owned, and less than 20 percent of the farms were rented out.[44]

The agonizing reappraisal of Swedish society induced by the threat of emigration, the great "blood-letting of the nation," played a role in the beginning of social reform. Emigration, however, was brought to a halt by events outside Sweden as well as within: World War I, restrictive laws in the United States, and the Great Depression. Sweden was in process of rapid development, not only on the farms, but in the cities where industry was starting to flourish. By 1930, therefore, an era had come to an end, and emigration-Sweden became immigration-Sweden as men left unemployment in America to return to low-paid work — but work and food — in Sweden. Sweden's vigorous economy has kept it a land of immigration.

The impact of the Great Migration was far-reaching and infinitely complex. As the economists reckoned, it did of course deplete the country's youth resources. But Sweden was producing in the nineteenth century far more people than it could support, and the alternative to emigration appeared to be destitution, perhaps ultimately social revolution. The migration peaked in just those years when Sweden was entering the take-off into industrialization, and it acted as a safety valve. Furthermore, large sums of money were sent home by the prospering children of sorely pressed parents; no one can count the five and ten-dollar bills enclosed in Christmas letters nor reckon their importance to the families concerned. Only for money orders is there a fairly clear record; in that medium alone, about $100 million was mailed from the United States to Sweden between 1885 and 1973. Inheritances added further bonuses, amounting to 17 million kronor a year from abroad, mostly from the United States. Between 1906 and 1976 the total of inheritances to Sweden from America was over 500 million kronor.[45] This was at least some repayment for the costs of childhood and rearing.

More intangible but possibly more vital was the intimate personal relationship established between the older, slow-moving society of Sweden and the experimental, rapidly growing society across the Atlantic. In the early years of the twentieth century some Swedish leaders conceived a plan of remigration, eager to bring back to Sweden men and women who had become inoculated with the American eagerness to work. Many did return both to visit and to stay. Just as they had brought to America their own versatile skills and inventiveness so they acquired new experiences and new stimuli in the United States. Migration promoted a salutary interchange of people and ideas that stimulated progress in both Sweden and America.[46]

## A Century of Change

The tone of everyday life had changed repeatedly during the eighteenth century from the harsh conditions during the war-strained times of Karl XII, to the atmosphere of liberty during the so-called Age of Freedom, to the gaiety and sparkle of the unforgettable days of Gustav III. The nineteenth century brought different, more fundamental change. It began with the somberness and deprivations of the period of Gustav IV Adolf; then came economic difficulties, the religious awakening with its moralizing emphasis, the attempt to drown troubles in heavy drinking, and the revulsion that set in against alcohol's excesses. Far-reaching changes resulted from the decline of the village community and the individualization of agriculture, and more from the increasing migration from country to city. Emigration carried over a million Swedes across the Atlantic and created close bonds with a different society. The rapid development of improved means of transportation and communication widened people's vision and stimulated new ideas. The shift in emphasis from agriculture to industry, the spectacular expansion of population, the decline of the old Estate society and the evolution of a new society based on economic classes — these things transformed the structure and the development of society as a whole. The old society had not been static and it had not been truly unified; the new society evolving toward the end of the nineteenth century was, however, frenetic in its activity and heterogeneous in its makeup.

But this kind of summary and analysis tends too much to imply that change was the result of inevitable natural development or irresistible social forces. That this is far from true becomes obvious if we contemplate some of the societies that in the nineteenth century remained nearly static (certain parts of Africa, for example, or of the Far East) or others that changed slowly (including, for example, Bulgaria and Poland). Sweden in the nineteenth century did not develop as rapidly as England, Germany, or the United States, but the tempo of change did accelerate.

Per Henrik Ling helped awaken new ideals for the harmonious development of body and soul. Inspired by Fredrika Bremer and others men saw the injustice of discrimination to women and moved slowly to correct the situation. Guided by educational innovators such as Rudenschöld the Swedes widened the foundations of education. They demanded a warmer and more personal approach to religion and they insisted on freedom and equality for the individual. To some extent these demands were response to the voices the people heard from the French Revolution, from the vigorous new American states, from industrially expanding England. Even more the protests of the Swedish people were the outgrowth of their own experience, the repudiation of restraints and inequities they had long abhorred but had been unable to correct. In the nineteenth century circumstances concurred to make change possible. Changes came neither suddenly nor violently nor with 100 percent completeness. But the old social structure disintegrated under the combination of attrition and attack. Simultaneously basic changes were demanded in the political and economic structure.

# XIV

## THE DEMOCRATIC BREAKTHROUGH·
## OF THE NINETEENTH CENTURY
## I. POLITICAL REFORMS AND
## DISRUPTIVE ISSUES

THE SOCIAL TRANSFORMATION that affected all aspects of Swedish life in the nineteenth century was characterized in the political realm by an irresistible trend toward democracy — slow, blocked at times by the forces of the old order, but always returning to the attack. By the end of World War I the victory was not yet complete, but the "democratic breakthrough" was surging forward on all fronts.

### Political Change in the Early Nineteenth Century

The coup d'état of 1809 had ousted an inadequate king and produced a new constitution for Sweden. But it brought no fundamental change. The king's authority was still defined in ancient terms, and the aristocracy that had conducted the revolution retained its power; the four-century-old riksdag of the four Estates was confirmed in the new constitution. Yet the reformers of 1809 had laid the basis for change. Within a year the incidents of 1809 and 1810 led to the calling of Bernadotte as crown prince.

When this parvenu of the French Revolution became king there was no longer a vestige of either divine right or ancient inheritance; whatever powers might be granted him were his by right of election and approval of the Estates of the realm. Both kingship and aristocracy were challenged by the new doctrines of equality that were spreading throughout Europe. The process of change was slow but thorough, interrelated with developments in the social and economic sectors and affected by external influences from France, Norway, England, and the United States. The constitution of 1809 was repeatedly amended but remained the fundamental law through a century and a half. (The constitution, as it had in the eighteenth century, remained not one document but four: the Instrument of Government, the Riksdag Act, the Act of Succession, and the Freedom of the Press Act.)

Karl Johan, ruler-in-fact from 1810 though he ascended the throne in 1818, was "the last of the 'saga kings.'" His prestige, his force, and his personal magnetism retained for the monarchy more of its glamor and power than the constitution of 1809 intended. He was a law and order man, a rigid disciplinarian who often forgot that he owed his laurels to revolution. Perhaps experience led him to overemphasize the fickleness of fortune. He lived with the results of the revolutionary overthrows in which he had participated and with the consequences of the assassination of Gustav III and the mob murder of Fersen. It was hardly surprising if his suspicious nature exaggerated the threats posed by radical opponents and by the irreconcilable adherents of the Vasas. He felt keenly the antagonism of the Norwegian opposition and tried to suppress national demonstrations. He therefore attempted to restrict the freedom of the press, and he used paid informers and secret police, often only exacerbating the difficulties that any ruler must face. But he realized that vital forces of change were at work.

The council of state, although appointed by the king, was supposed to ensure that the king acted within the constitution. Hence secretaries and councillors displayed differences of opinion and from time to time attempted to check Karl Johan's tendencies toward autocracy. Hans Järta, the brilliant and independent-minded state secretary, resigned his post already in 1811 because the regency, in the king's illness, was handed to Crown Prince Karl Johan instead of to the council as prescribed by the constitution; Järta returned in 1815 only to resign again a year later because he disapproved of the crown prince's financial policy. G. F. Wirsén, one of the ablest of the king's advisers, also resigned in 1816 but soon came back to serve in another post. Never did the council as a whole resign in protest.

Overwhelmingly the nobility supported the monarchy and a conservative philosophy. Many nobles were army officers, and others were civil servants dependent for livelihood and status on their positions in the bureaucracy. The hereditary nobility, in practice if not in law, still were first in line for the higher offices of state. It was not until 1827 that H. N. Schwan, the first commoner, was appointed to the council of state. In brief, the nobility dominated the bureaucracy, and the bureaucracy was the government. The interlocking nature of the system is indicated by the fact that the great majority of the nobles who attended the riksdag were connected with the military or the civil service; in the early nineteenth century fewer than a quarter of them were classed as landowners, ironmasters, or intellectuals. Politically and socially the structure of the establishment was cohesive and almost impermeable — almost, but not quite.

Discontent in the first years of the nineteenth century centered on economic policy, for the country was poor and was making little progress. Karl Johan was proudly convinced of his own financial shrewdness, but his schemes did not succeed. Voices were raised against the government's economic mismanagement and were directed not against the untouchable king but against his advisers. When they proved immovable a tendency grew to reject aristocratic leadership. Yet prominent among the opposition were disgruntled younger nobles. C. H. Anckarsvärd, for instance, a hothead who had tangled with Karl Johan during the campaign of 1813, attacked the government in the riksdag of 1817 and even more sharply in 1823. He was more effective leveling criticism than making constructive suggestion, though he was one of the early advocates of riksdag reorganization; he became enamored of the Norwegian system of one house which divided itself into two. In 1830 he wrote with Judge J. G. Richert a tract based on the theme that "our constitutional system is a deceit and our representation insufferable beyond description."[1] Thus the attacks on economic policy and on the autocracy of the king shifted gradually into a positive program for reform of the four-Estate structure of the riksdag. The process was slow because the system was so deeply embedded in law and tradition and class interest, but time itself was undermining the old edifice.

The three lower Estates, although paid for their attendance, regarded the work of the riksdag as a burden rather than a privilege. The nobles, though unpaid, could more easily afford their temporary residence in Stockholm and could more readily combine attendance at sessions with their work as bureaucrats and with their normal social life. Quite naturally the attendance figure for the House of Nobles was highest — usually at least 100 and on critical occasions as high as 700. Clerical attendance never reached its potential maximum of 70. In the burgher Estate the possible maximum was 106, but only 65 voted in the crucial riksdag reform debate of 1865. The rural districts, of which there were 300, tended even more to combine with one another in choosing representatives to the farmer Estate, where the highest vote recorded was about 150. Election was indirect, as with the other Estates: the farmers of each parish met in the church and chose an elector, who then went to a meeting of all the electors of the *härad* to choose a riksdag delegate. No one could be elected who was eligible for one of the other Estates, hence, unlike the situation in Norway or in England, the farmer representatives were really farmers. The corporate significance of the four Estates was emphasized by the method of reaching decisions in the riksdag — each Estate had one vote.

In 1789 the French had abolished their Estates as the first important act of revolution; in 1809 and 1810 the Swedes feebly challenged their system of Estates, but it took them almost sixty years to accomplish change. In the meantime minor reforms modified the system slightly. The double representation of the nobles on committees was abolished in 1809, and in 1828 committees began to count their votes by individual members instead of by Estate. Almost everyone favored a two-house legislative body, but the riksdag-reform problem was associated with the question of expansion of the suffrage. Anything like a one-man-one-vote principle would give the farmers overwhelming power, hence many proposals for reform were based on the assumption that one house at least must represent property, while the other might represent persons. Some argued that it would be safe to extend the vote widely, for the Norwegian experience demonstrated that the farmers might be expected to elect men of property and position, but no one felt quite sure that this would happen in Sweden. Gradually three shadings of reform opinion became distinguishable:

1. the liberals who favored the Norwegian system — two houses meeting as one on certain occasions, composed of members elected by broad general suffrage;
2. those who feared farmer rule but would approve representation of the more prosperous;
3. the big landowners who wanted to preserve the Estates system at least in part, while broadening the base of suffrage. For them the English House of Lords was the unattainable ideal.

Or we could group "the opposition," as does Douglas Verney, into radical-liberals, economic-liberals, and moderate-liberals. But they did not in any consistent way group themselves.[2]

The so-called liberal movement lacked unity of either leadership or ideology. It drew upon monarchists who hated the king, farmers seeking prestige and power for their class, lawyers and other intellectuals who were denied representation, nobles who were touched with European currents of thought, businessmen who resented the hand of the government in their affairs and inclined to the economic liberalism of the Manchester school and many others. The individualistic diversity of the movement was accentuated by the changes of position indulged in by leaders from time to time: Hans Järta became more and more conservative, E. G. Geijer shifted from conservatism to liberalism in 1838, and even the rebel Anckarsvärd found himself in occasional concurrence with the king. Neither persons nor programs became frozen into position.

The most effective and colorful leader of the farmers was Anders Danielson, a riksdagsman from Västergötland who became so popular that for one session he was elected by twenty-seven *härads* (but he had only one vote). He was in every riksdag from 1809 until his death thirty years later. As early as 1818 he proclaimed that the farmers had grown out of their immaturity, and he identified himself with their demands for recognition and for practical help through reduction of expenses by both state and church. He did favor spending for culture, especially for rural education. Of himself and his inherited means he gave unsparingly and created a kind of personal chancery of secretaries and legally trained assistants. He had the kind of personality that could dominate his own Estate and at the same time work intimately with the reform leaders of the other Estates. One of his tasks was to persuade the farmer-riksdagsmen not to accept the bribes that the government sometimes offered in exchange for their vote. Perhaps it was watching Anders Danielson operate that made some of the conservatives think the farmers could become too powerful.

Newspapers were important in the political discussion, particularly Lars Johan Hierta's *Aftonbladet* (The Evening Paper) founded in 1830. It grew in the 1840s to have the largest circulation of any paper in Sweden — 5,440 copies in 1843, 8,650 in 1848 — but the most significant thing was that about half of the circulation was in the country outside Stockholm. Farmers read it, and one copy was spread among many people, for the cost was over ten riksdaler per year. Hierta was a noble with middle-class interests and connections, versatile in his interests, and blessed with extraordinary energy. His business acumen earned for him a comfortable fortune. Good humoredly but with irony, boldness, and persistence he fought for representational reform, a responsible ministry, women's rights, free trade, and economy. Repeatedly he stepped on the toes of the authorities and they suppressed *Aftonbladet*, but Hierta blandly changed the name: first to New Aftonbladet and, at last, after nine years of persecution, to *Det tjugondeförsta Aftonbladet* (The Twenty-first Aftonbladet). He so discredited the whole system of censorship that in 1845 it was abandoned, and Sweden got a really free press. Hierta's vigorous, French-influenced journalism soon put the rival *Argus*, on which he had apprenticed, out of business. But in Gothenburg in 1832 an even more radical paper was born — *Göteborgs Handels- och Sjöfartstidning* (Gothenburg's Commercial and Shipping News), which fought for freedom in religion and politics and economic life, for reform in riksdag and schools, and for pan-Scandinavianism. It too suffered many suppressions but bounced back and continued to flourish until at last it succumbed in the early 1970s.

There were also conservative papers, though neither so many nor so colorful as the liberal ones. *Post- och Inrikes Tidningar* (The Post and Domestic News) was from 1834 the most significant of these, especially because of the collaboration of August von Hartmansdorff (1792–1856), a learned and independent-minded conservative who occupied a variety of government posts. Many lesser papers struggled briefly and died.

The discontent of the 1830s found no effective expression; it festered in fruitless individual outbreaks. For example, Anders Lindeberg started a newspaper friendly to the government; it failed, and then he was refused permission to start a private theater. He turned rebellious and charged the king with financial interests in the theater monopoly; when he was convicted of libel and sentenced to death he refused to accept a pardon. The government would not let him be a martyr and so declared a general amnesty for political prisoners (he was the only one actually held) and by a trick locked him *out* of the jail. Another unsuccessful editor, M. J. Crustenstolpe, similarly turned in hate against Karl Johan and was condemned to three years in prison. He had such public sympathy that when he was to be transferred from one prison to another a mob of the middle and lower classes rioted and had to be squelched by troops; two people were killed. Other riots broke out in 1838 over the attempt of the government to moderate the anti-Jewish laws, and these forced the government to withdraw some of the concessions. A year later the brilliant romantic author C. J. L. Almqvist turned from fantasy to folk-realism and shocked the country with his novel attacking marriage and appealing for liberation of both women and men from the shackles of forced partnership (see chapter XIII). Almqvist also advocated a kind of socialism and his political views grew more extreme as he was deprived of his teaching position and rejected by society. His tragic end in Germany after a long American exile need not concern us, except to note that he was evidence as well as stimulator of the troubled and protesting spirit of the times.

In a class by himself stood Eric Gustaf Geijer, a literary romantic, a political conservative, and a giant in each of these allied camps. At Uppsala he came to his professorship in history by way of religion and philosophy, and he lectured on the Swedish past to enthusiastic crowds of both students and townspeople. The depth of his understanding gave power to his poetry. He was a close friend of Karl XIV Johan and a pillar of strength to the royalists in the riksdag, where he represented the University of Uppsala. But he respected the criticisms of his friend Hans Järta, and he was sensitive to the new and changing times as well as to the beloved past. He thought long and deeply before he moved, then in 1838 he published a reasoned announcement of a change of faith; he embraced openly the liberalism that had lain dormant within him since his youth. He did not thus reverse his course, but he struck off on a sharply new angle, which appeared sharper to others than to him. Geijer's apostasy (*Avfall*) created an intellectual and political earthquake. His old friends renounced him and his former opponents could not fully accept him. He was isolated but not wholly; the king who had loved him still respected him enough to invite him to sit on the council of state, but Geijer declined. His new program demanded not only a two-chamber legislature and a reform of the suffrage but the separation of the schools from the state, liberal economic regulations, and national unity. The spirit in which he confronted his reoriented life is perhaps best expressed in his New Year's poem of 1838:

> Alone in his frail boat
> The sailor dares to sail the sea;
> The vault of stars above him glows,
> Below the waves his turbulent grave.
> Forward! — this is the bidding of his fate;
> Both in the depths and up in heaven lives God.[3]

Although Geijer and a few others brightened the scene in early nineteenth-century Sweden the overall picture was one of poverty and crime and apathy. Industry continued in the small-shop fashion of earlier centuries and trade was stagnant. Employment could not absorb the expanding population. Europe was moving forward; Sweden was in the economic sense an underdeveloped country, a rural backwater on the margin of the continent. No leader of thought or action could dynamize the people into activity. Denmark and Norway were instituting reforms and the great Bishop N.F.S. Grundtvig was inspiring Denmark with new energy. In Sweden men like Järta and Geijer and Hierta were voices crying in the wilderness. Anckarsvärd, the perpetual protester, simply gave up in 1848. Oscar I was interested in prison reform and in the development of trade, but he was vacillating and basically conservative. Typical of his attitude was his attempt to censor the press in 1853 and, to suppress criticism, his purchase of two socialist papers (*Söndagsbladet* [The Sunday News] and *Folkets Röst* [The Peoples' Voice]).

Among the piecemeal and reluctant reforms were a few that chipped away at significant issues, for example, the extension of women's rights. In the economic realm a number of restrictive laws were abolished by the elimination of guilds in 1846 (in Norway the guilds had been abolished in 1839, in Denmark, 1857); increased freedom was permitted for both external and internal trade by the laws of 1846, 1848, 1857, and 1864; after 1864 a man was allowed free choice of occupation. Meanwhile the decimal system was introduced in 1854 and in 1860 taxes became based on income or wealth rather than status. Ecclesiastical controls were modified between 1855 and 1860, especially with the abandonment of the Conventicle Decree in 1858 and with the granting of permission to leave the state church — if the state approved the church to which a person wished to move — in 1860. Most of the legal discriminations against Jews were removed between 1860 and 1873, despite some popular opposition. Hence progress was being made toward a more just and democratic social order. On the other hand the list of reforms itself indicates the paternalistic nature of the state and that the nobles, the clergy, and the owners of manorial estates who dominated the law-making process were hardly fitted to lead the country boldly into a new industrial age.

A significant forerunner of national reform was the inauguration in 1862–63 of provincial (*landsting*) and city councils (*stadsfullmäktige*). To these bodies were elected a number of nobles, very few clergy, some burghers, and especially persons of status (*ståndspersoner*) and farmers. (Artisans were elected only to the city councils.) The choices indicated what was likely to happen when the riksdag was thrown open to popular election.

However, basic reform of the political system was more important than patchwork improvements. For the building of a functioning democracy the forces of change sketched in the previous chapter were promising developments: the spread of the folk movements (the pietist gatherings, the temperance organizations, the drive for elementary education) which gave the common man experience and training in thinking about social problems and in expressing himself. The ancient guilds had served a similar purpose for their more restricted personnel and the craft societies that replaced the guilds continued the process. Broader-based workers' societies, inspired by Marcus Thrane's societies in Norway, arose in Sweden in the early 1850s. The "association spirit" noted by Geijer in the 1830s and 1840s became an important feature of Swedish society. The total of organizations and people was far less in Sweden than in the United States and western Europe, but in the tightly structured Swedish society the organizations had extraordinary impact, especially within the farmers' Estate in the riksdag. They served as schools of citizenship training and participation among groups who had no other voice in community affairs, and they boded change both in political processes and in the substance of reform.

Land taxes, tariffs, defense, suffrage, and several important but minor issues were all inherently significant. They were also meaningful as causes by which the Swedish people forged their way to a more complete democracy. In the decades between the riksdag reform of 1865–66 and the outbreak of World War I people became steadily more aware of how political decisions affected their lives and they gained the consciousness that they could do something to shape the course of events. They lost the apathy that had brought only 18 percent of voters to the polls in 1867 until, with a vastly expanded electorate, 70 percent voted in 1914. They voted for their own special interests but as time advanced and as economic conditions eased they increasingly were able to think about the welfare of the country as a whole. They respected law and proper procedure, and they gradually established those new procedures by which the will of the people was to become paramount over the will of the man who sat in the royal palace or of his coterie. The politicians fought strenuously among themselves and bargained, and made deals to stay in office or to get things done. Some struggled to attain power, others had to be forced to take office. Some were hesitant to assume responsibility, like the Social Democrats in 1911. Perhaps most important, through this whole period there was amazingly little bribery or corruption in any form or deliberate violation of the law.

## The Riksdag Reform

Dissatisfaction was rife and critics were many, but positive programs were few. Gradually one issue crystallized on which all reform elements could unite: reorganization of riksdag representation. The anachronistic corporative system of the four Estates had been challenged and should have been cast aside in 1809, but the hasty constitution making of that year allowed it to survive. Repeated proposals for change crashed against a wall of conservative opposition. The general consensus favored a two-chamber parliament, perhaps largely because this was the pattern in England, France, and the United States, and Swedes were sensitive to what was done elsewhere. Some favored the Norwegian system which was essentially unicameral. But the problem was not primarily whether the riksdag should have two chambers or four; it was the question of representation by corporate groups or by the people as a whole and therefore voting in four distinct categories or in common.

The four Estates made sense in the fifteenth century when the four rather distinct corporate groups of nobles, clergy, merchants, and farmers fairly well encompassed the entirety of national interests. But the four Estates and the basic corporate idea became obsolete as diversities of occupation and interest increased (see the previous chapter on social change). Even the farmers' Estate was becoming less representative as the number of landowning farmers shrank to one-third of the total and the number of industrial workers increased. Palliative reforms had extended the representation in the clerical Estate to the two universities and the Academy of Science (1823); in the burgher Estate to ironmasters (1830) and to most of the householders in the cities (1858); in the farmers' Estate to farmers owning tax-exempt land (1845) and also to "persons of status" — but the farmers' Estate was an odd location for lawyers and other professionals.

Some riksdagsmen, even among the nobles, came to realize the necessity of change. August von Hartmansdorff, former leader of the conservatives, studied his way to the conclusion that the nobility had played out their role, and he drew up a complicated plan for the reconstruction of the riksdag: five chambers to represent officials, intellectuals, burghers, landholders, and peasant farmers. Reaction against this plan stimulated the formation of the Junker party of true conservatives and friends of the king. Yet something had to be done. King Oscar I, deeply affected by the events of 1848 on the continent, submitted various plans, one providing for a two-chamber riksdag containing a large royal-appointed contingent in the upper house. But 1848 was hardly the moment for such a suggestion. The radicals advocated suffrage for all adult males, also an impossible idea for the time. None of the schemes for patching up the old system could win majority support and by 1854 all of them had been defeated or abandoned. Their only important service was to keep the issue alive.

Steadily though slowly the ancient political structure was being eroded. At length two catalysts appeared, both products of the social and economic transformation that was beginning to reshape Swedish society.

The first of these was Johan August Gripenstedt, who was appointed a consultative minister in 1848 and later minister of finance. Son of a land-owner, he had gone to artillery school and started a career in the army. His normal life was deflected when he married the niece of the aristocratic rebel C. H. Anckarsvärd and became manager and later owner of the Nynäs estates. He supported the king and the royal policies for free trade and railway build-ing. He also had considerable influence among the farmers. He was essen-tially a practical man, and practicality caused him to oppose Karl XV's pan-Scandinavianism and he was able to force the king to renounce, in 1863, his pledge of aid for Denmark against Prussia. On the matter of riksdag reform he stood in the background in the 1850s but he was ready to support the man who would lead the fight.

The second catalyst was Louis Gerhard De Geer, the architect of the great reform of 1865–66. Six generations before him his ancestor Louis De Geer had come to Sweden from Holland, had manufactured munitions for Gustav II Adolf, and had acquired Swedish citizenship, ennoblement, and vast estates. The family proliferated and remained prominent, and this nineteenth-century scion enjoyed all the advantages of high birth and even enhanced his position by marrying Countess Caroline Wachtmeister. He studied law at Uppsala, held judicial and other official positions, and participated in the riksdags of 1853–54 and 1856–58. He authored a book of essays, a couple of novels, and a book on judicial style. His ability and integrity were remarked by Karl XV, who in 1858 persuaded De Geer, then aged forty, reluctantly to accept the post of prime minister. In a short time, despite his comparative youth, his energy and ability made him the leader of the council of state. His authority was all the greater because of the king's indolence and indecisiveness.

Louis De Geer was no revolutionary. In fact it was his fear of radical change that led him to insist on moderate change. Only thus, he thought, could the essentials of the social structure be maintained. He played a leading role in the extension of religious freedom, in the rescinding of the Conventicle Decree and of the pass laws that restricted freedom of movement, in furthering the rights of unmarried women, and in abolishing the employer's right to inflict corporal punishment. His impeccable credentials as a member of the old nobility as well as his intelligence and his persuasive powers enabled him to move minds otherwise immovable. He sensed the vital importance of constitutional reform of the riksdag and when, in the riksdag of 1859–60, the two lower Estates raised this demand anew, he made their cause his own. He wrote Karl XV a blunt memo saying he had to advocate this cause and giving the king six months to accept this or to ask his resignation. For the king the proposal was anathema, but he recognized both the popularity of his minister and the pressure for reform from burghers, farmers, the intelligentsia, and the press. He could not bring himself to request De Geer's resignation. The monarch's acceptance of De Geer's ultimatum enabled the loyal and shrewd minister to issue statements implying that the king favored reform. And Karl XV, appreciating the acclaim that arose from the misconception, had only to say nothing and thus enjoy the people's approval.

The specific proposal, carefully drawn by De Geer, was presented to the Estates in January 1863 to be acted upon at the next session in 1865. It called for the elimination of the four Estates and their replacement by a two-chamber parliament elected by common vote, which would meet annually. The two houses were to be "of equal competence and authority" but different in qualifications and suffrage. The First Chamber would be a conservative stronghold, elected indirectly by the twenty-four provincial councils (as the Senate of the United States was chosen by state legislatures until 1913). Qualifications for membership assured the "propertied conservatism" that De Geer desired — in fact they went beyond his own desires in the form in which the measure was finally passed. Only about 6,000 men could qualify for election. Members were to be thirty-five years of age, homeowners, possessors of property of at least 80,000 riksdalers taxable value (or 4,000 riksdalers income), and they were to serve without pay for a nine-year term. No residence requirement was stated. One member would be elected for each 35,000 of the total population.

The Second Chamber was designed to represent the common people and especially the farmers. The term of members was three years and the minimum age was twenty-five. They were to be elected directly by the voters (with some exceptions), and both voters and members had to meet the same qualifications: male sex, ownership of real estate of 1,000 riksdalers taxable value or rental of farmland (for five years past) of 6,000 riksdalers value or taxable income of 800 riksdalers per year. Members of the Second Chamber had to be residents of the district from which they were chosen. Each member would receive 1,200 riksdalers plus travel expenses but was to have his pay reduced by ten riksdalers for each day of absence during the sessions. One member was chosen for each 40,000 people in the rural districts, one for each 10,000 in the larger cities, and one for each 6,000 in the smaller towns, which might group themselves to make up that figure. In a technical sense this voting structure gave overrepresentation to the towns. But it must be remembered that in 1865 the rural population was 3.6 million and the urban population was only 500,000. Thus the seeming favoritism to the cities merely saved them from being completely overwhelmed.

The franchise was oddly different for the two chambers. The monetary restrictions for the Second Chamber held the number of voters to about 5 percent of the total population or about 20 percent of adult males. But each man had one vote, and voting was in common, not by Estates or classes. For the First Chamber the voting requirements were the same as for the town or provincial councils that chose the legislators, and this meant that the electorate for the First Chamber was twice as large as that for the Second Chamber, although the voting was indirect. Furthermore, for the First Chamber a complicated, graded scale of plural voting permitted wealthy persons and even business enterprises (and thus women as well as men might have a voice) to cast multiple votes, later limited to 5,000 votes apiece in the country and to 100 in the towns. Plural voting could easily nullify the votes of the less well-to-do; wealth was well protected. In fact, "property voted, not persons." This feature disturbed many, and the clergy, particularly, warned that the reform would produce a governing plutocracy. The clergy still favored the corporate principle.[4]

De Geer's plan, put forward as a government proposition and at last positively supported by the king, was neither as revolutionary nor as democratic as it appeared on the surface. The nobility of blood and royal favor were to be unseated as such, the clergy were to be removed from the political scene (they had in 1863 been granted a high degree of ecclesiastical autonomy in a special body), and the roles of businessmen and farmers were to be enhanced. But many of the nobility were already becoming more interested in iron mines and factories than in titles and politics, and those who had wealth could be better represented under the new system than under the old. Aristocratic ties to the monarchy were still strong but weakening. Nevertheless, this belated reform caught the popular fancy and a tidal wave of public opinion eventually pushed it through.

The press was overwhelmingly in favor. Pamphlets pro and pamphlets con were distributed far and wide. De Geer in his memoirs tells of the round of meetings held in Stockholm and throughout the country, of the deputations that came to him and the petitions, one with 60,000 signatures, another from the faculty of Uppsala with 39 names. People awakened through their folk movements were concerned as never before with the problems of their society. They were being informed of the issues and were taking part in a broad-based decision-making process. The traditional deference that muted protest was beginning to disappear, and the pressure for reform became a mighty swell.

De Geer handled the deputations with discretion. He believed that, at one point, he was able to convince a mob leader that the violence he threatened would only delay what was inevitable that year or soon thereafter. The nobles staged two special preliminary meetings, one against the measure and one for it. The proreform meeting was remarkable in that it was called by ten members several of whom were thought to be firm opponents. They motivated their position by announcing that although they personally disliked the proposal they thought its passage was necessary for the good of the country. Such an attitude undoubtedly paralleled De Geer's own feeling. Thus opinions were changing as the momentous decision approached; whereas in October it was reckoned that two-thirds of the nobles were antireform, by early December it was impossible to predict the outcome of the vote.

Long before the day scheduled — Monday, the fourth of December, 1865 — eager reformers flocked into Stockholm by boat and carriage and train. Hotels were filled and restaurants and pubs became political discussion clubs. On that December Monday crowds waited tensely outside the parliamentary halls. The farmers' Estate met at 9:00 A.M. and promptly, without debate, voted unanimously for the government proposal. The burghers met in their hall at 10:00 A.M., all in full dress in honor of the occasion. One negative speech took forty-five minutes, four other members announced their opposition; then the vote was taken, and it was sixty to five in favor. The clergy would have voted no had they possessed the courage of their convictions, but they were afraid they might be the only Estate to oppose, and they dared not risk the popular reaction. Hence they met and decided merely to await the decision of the nobility. As a contemporary paper reported, "The clergy's action deserves no word. The body showed itself unworthy to hold one-fourth of the representation."[5]

Everything depended on the nobles, and their decision remained in doubt for four long days. Debate was vigorous but restrained. Every seat in the house was taken. The Hall of the Nobility was (and is) one of the architectural jewels of the country. Its walls were hung with the coats of arms of ancient heroes, generals of the Thirty Years War, and great officials of the state. It was a handsome symbol of Sweden's Age of Greatness. Over 700 representatives of the foremost families of the land filled the benches and the aisles and the window niches. From nine until three on the first day the nobles bombarded each other with speeches, blending argument and nostalgia. On Tuesday the tension increased. It was a clash of political ideologies, it was partly youth against age, partly mercantile interests versus the interests of the owners of landed estates. And everyone was aware of the upswelling public opinion.

Gripenstedt spoke well for the royal proposition, and so did Ludvig Manderström, who tried to assuage fear: "every light can become a fire, but that is no excuse to continue to sit in darkness."[6] On Wednesday men dependent on the honor of birth saw their cause losing and they thundered their rage and had to be clubbed down by the speaker. By Thursday patience was wearing thin, both in the hall and among the crowds milling outside. De Geer, who had spoken once, appeared again to reason with those who had flayed him. When Baron Klinckowström rose and announced that he would not speak he was greeted with a shout of approval. It was time to vote.

At long last, at 2:00 P.M. on Thursday the noble representatives of the old order filed up to drop their votes in the urns. Counting was slow and hard to keep track of, but when it was finished the tally surprised everyone: 361 "Ja" and 294 "Nej," a margin of 67 votes in favor. The news was greeted with a tumult of joy from the crowd and hurrahs for De Geer, Gripenstedt, Manderström, and the king. That evening processions waited upon the heroes in their residences, and August Blanche, tribune of the people, made grandiloquent speeches. In the meantime, of course, the clergy had voted, anticlimactically and with some bitterness, to accept the unavoidable.

At the beginning of the week the editor of *Dagens Nyheter*, Rudolph Wall, had dramatically declared that "In the space of a couple of days lie future centuries."[7] But the future moved in on leaden feet. No provision had been made for an immediate changeover, and therefore the old Estates stayed on for six months to complete the work of the session; only on June 22, 1866 did they close shop with traditional ceremony, ending four hundred years of their chapter of history. Count Lagerbielke on that final day spoke words that illustrated, at its best, the tone of the occasion:

> Laws can be changed, rights can cease, but there remain the duties to the fatherland. If these duties are fulfilled it matters little to the true nobility *where* in the society its place is located.[8]

Had Sweden achieved a revolution? Or was all the furor only a symbolic victory over an institution already atrophied by time? Was this the end of the old or the beginning of the new? Actually it was something of all these things. The reform of 1865–66 marked a watershed. The old structure of government was a monarchic-aristocratic partnership with a participatory voice allowed to burghers and farmers. It had worked fairly well for several centuries. But in the mid-nineteenth century Sweden was in the doldrums while Europe was edging its way into a new industrial era. Neither the personnel nor the structure of the old Swedish system was suited to these changing times. The nobles' dominance of political life and the archaic four-chamber parliament blocked the road to progress. Their elimination was a prerequisite for the attainment of democracy.

One other relevant fact must be noted well: a fundamental change had been brought about by peaceful means. The old order yielded sulkily but without threats or violence. The reform was moderate enough that it could be accepted, and further change could evolve from there. This moderation was the great service of Louis De Geer, whose calm rationality was one of the most persuasive forces in reaching an agreement. What might have happened had the proposal been rejected we can never know. The king had troops alerted for possible trouble. But there was no trouble, no sense of violence in the air. Reasonableness characterized the transition, and there was therefore no legacy of bitterness to poison the future.

The new riksdag of two chambers was elected in the fall of 1866 but did not meet until January 1867. The new RO (*Riksdags-Ordinans*) of 1866 did not democratize Swedish politics, but it did open the door to the future. For better or for worse, plutocracy had replaced nobility.

### Disruptive Issues and the Struggle for Democratic Government, 1866–1914

Probably everyone was amazed at the makeup of the new riksdag of two houses, especially the First Chamber. The nobility had abandoned its prestigious position and the clergy had all but vanished. And yet, as Sten Carlsson has observed, "The House of the Nobles, with its many landed proprietors and lower public servants was a popular assembly in comparison with [the new First Chamber]."[9] The astonishing fact was that to the so-called upper house of the riksdag, and out of some 6,000 rich citizens qualified for membership, the electing city and provincial councils chose the richest of all to sit. Furthermore, in this "new" First Chamber of 1867, of its 125 members 64 had sat in the Estate of the nobles; 40-odd were counts and barons; 28 were iron masters or factory owners; 95 were current or past servants of the crown — ministers, governors, judges, army officers — providing a vast overrepresentation for the bureaucracy and for the city of Stockholm where most of them lived. Their social and political attitudes were identical with those of the old Estate of the nobility.

The Second Chamber (*Andra Kammaren* or AK) was in its makeup largely a blend of the former burghers and farmers. Of its 190 members in 1867 as many as 107 had served in the riksdag of the Estates: 57 farmers, 31 burghers, 13 nobles, and 6 clergy. (This continuity of personnel should perhaps not seem surprising, for a comparable thing happened in England after the Great Reform of 1832.) The membership was considerably diverse: priests, officials, academics, lower-school teachers, industrialists, merchants, farmers, and 48 high-ranking civil servants. But overwhelmingly (and disregarding overlappings) they were men of the land: 99 were landowners or proprietor farmers; 135 lived in the country, only 55 were from towns. Educationally it was an unusual group for the times, for 73 had completed gymnasium, and 61 of these had university degrees. No laborer was chosen for the Second Chamber until 1878, and there were only 10 in 1905.

In the interrelationship of the chambers certain peculiarities soon became manifest. The most important committees were joint committees, and elections to these were highly valued. It was the practice for consideration of major questions (taxation, finance, defense, etc.) to proceed simultaneously in the two chambers. First voting was by each house separately, but if the two houses disagreed joint voting decided the issue. Since the First Chamber (*Första Kammaren* or FK) was the stronghold of plutocracy and the Second Chamber represented the commonalty, disagreements and resultant joint voting were frequent. Each member's vote was counted, and thus it would be expected that the larger Second Chamber would carry the greater weight in joint votes. The opposite was the case, because the diversity of opinion in the Second Chamber always divided its votes, while the homogeneity of opinion in the First Chamber was able to swing the decision in its favor.

Political parties were slow to develop, in fact De Geer hoped that the new system would prevent their appearance. Men were elected on the basis of personal qualifications, and they found it distasteful to commit themselves in advance to any particular program. Nevertheless common interests and ideas drew men together, at least on individual issues. In the First Chamber it took some time for the "Majority Party" to find itself, but it had little opposition. In the Second Chamber the agrarian interest brought the farmer delegates together and their *Lantmannapartiet* (Farmers' Party) dominated the house for several decades. But these parties remained within the riksdag itself, did not become popular or national, and on different issues different groups formed for varying periods of time. Anything like party discipline was unheard of.

Personalities counted greatly, and one of the most critical but constructive figures of the first generation of the riksdag was Adolf Hedin, an independent spirit who was something of a party himself but more of a stimulator than an organizer. Hedin was a journalist who in the later 1860s made politics his life and social reform his program. A brilliant orator and prolific writer, he was one of the few who could win a hearing both in parliament and among the public. He outlined his program in articles published as a brochure in 1868, "What People Expect of the New Representation," written as fifteen letters to members of the riksdag. He wanted the legislature to take power into its own hands, not leave authority to the king. The interference of officialdom in private affairs must be checked; the overpowering position of the bureaucracy was due to the attitude of the existing government, which "is and considers itself to be flesh of its flesh and bone of its bone, the bureaucracy's finest flower."[10] Parties, he said in contradiction of De Geer, were natural and necessary, though this was not true of meaningless aggregations like the current *Lantmanna* group. Hedin advocated a foreign policy of peace and neutrality but also a strong defense, defense based on universal military service and civilian control. He was a pan-Scandinavian who sympathized with Norwegian demands in the Union. He strongly favored public education and the folk high schools ("Enlighten the people!"), and he proposed factory inspection and old age and accident insurance, urged free trade to lower costs for the poor, and vigorously advocated universal suffrage. After forty years of publicist and political activity this program to which he clung was still not fully realized, but within only a few more years it was all an established part of the Swedish scene. Adolf Hedin was a reasonable, articulate forerunner with a social conscience who realized the issues that had to be met, and he was quite sure of how they should be met.

However, Hedin in those early years stood almost alone. There was little inclination to face issues and still less to transform society. Karl XV wanted to be popular but he could not be bothered with reform beyond that of the riksdag itself (and that had been thrust upon him). De Geer had exhausted his leadership capital in that great effort and by 1870 he was thrust out of office (temporarily). The self-satisfied lords of the First Chamber retained for decades a "dour, pig-headed preoccupation with the retention of the status quo."[11] Hence, odd as it may seem, the new riksdag in its first twenty years did less to change politics and society than did the much-maligned Estates in the period before 1866.

Some issues arose that could not be ducked, and although the first years of the new riksdag were slow-moving they were not barren. One of the difficulties in making progress was, as described by Douglas Verney, the timidity of the farmers in the Second Chamber, who found much to criticize but who were unwilling to assume responsibility for making decisions. Therefore problems of taxation, tariffs, defense, and suffrage remained long unresolved.

## TAXATION

In the late nineteenth century the system that had freed men from taxes on their lands in compensation for their providing horse and armor and service on the battlefield seemed even more anachronistic than the four-Estate riksdag. Nor did substitute service in state offices appear to justify the continuation of tax-privileges on land, especially since men other than nobles had long been permitted to buy such lands. The whole land-tax structure had become unreasonable. The king-in-council would not give relief, and the privileged landowners in the First Chamber joined a minority in the Second Chamber to block parliamentary action. In return for any alleviation of land taxes the defense-minded conservatives demanded support for their military programs. Under pressure from Oscar II, who had become king in 1872, a compromise was worked out in 1873, but in principle only, and implementation was long delayed. Only in 1885 were 30 percent of land taxes rescinded, and in 1892 the remainder, but it was 1904 before they completely disappeared.

A variety of other onerous obligations hung on far past their time: the *indelningsverk*, by which the military were selected and provided with land and maintenance by the citizenry directly (the *indelningsverk* was especially burdensome because it fell unevenly on different areas of the countryside); a parallel system for civil servants and clergy; *skjutsning*, the ancient requirement that farmers along main roads must supply hospitality and transportation for traveling officials. These obsolete and annoying duties were sloughed off one by one in the period from 1878 to 1911.

## TARIFFS

Tariffs hit pocketbooks as hard as did other taxes although their impact was more difficult to understand and particular tariff rates hurt only some people and helped others. Sweden had moved to free trade in the mid-nineteenth century, and the system was confirmed in the most-favored-nation treaty with France in 1865. But conditions changed rapidly. Industry was in its infancy but striving industrialists and eager workers wanted protection, and they were influenced in this direction by the protectionist policies developing in Germany. However, the major push came not from industry but from agriculture. The import of grain from Russia and especially from the United States in the years after the American Civil War drove European grain prices precipitously downward. The grain producers of northern Europe could not compete with the vastness of the American plains and their lush fertility. Danish farmers answered the challenge by shifting to animal husbandry, and some Swedes did the same. The farmers of central Sweden were hardest hit, and as they came to realize what was happening they demanded action from their representatives in the riksdag. The response was complicated by the French treaty with its most-favored-nation clause and by the fact that the urban riksdagmen were happy with lower costs for food. Furthermore, the farmers of southern Sweden were less concerned because of their greater agricultural versatility, and those of northern Sweden were slow to abandon deeply rooted free-trade convictions. The first result of this controversy was therefore a split in the formerly solid *Lantmanna* party. The New Farmers' Party urged protection, the Old Farmers' Party clung to free trade.

Protectionism made steady gains, but in the two successive elections of 1887 (including a special election because of the narrowness of the division) the free traders maintained an edge. However, on the free-trade list for Stockholm one of the twenty-two winning candidates was discovered to have been a few years earlier delinquent in his taxes (by the insignificant sum of eleven kronor). Not only he but the entire list of twenty-two was disqualified and the opposing protectionist list was seated. Thus the protective tariff on grain was instituted sooner than should have been the case, and in succeeding elections protectionists held their majority. In 1892 the manufacturing interests got their protection too.

The tariff controversy was a turning point in both party and parliamentary history. People began to realize the importance for them as individuals of the decisions made in the riksdag and apathy vanished. Parties began to represent something more than the vague class interests that had held together the *herrar* (gentlemen) of the First Chamber on the one hand and the farmers of the Second Chamber on the other. New lines had been drawn on the basis of an issue. In a general way the protectionists tended to be conservative and the free traders tended to be liberal. Most important was the enhanced political interest of the citizenry.

DEFENSE

As a small country that had lost the outlying bastions of its imperial days Sweden had to rethink its strategic position. Therefore in the early nineteenth century it gave up the former concept of peripheral defense; Sweden would henceforth allow an enemy to march if necessary to the central lakes region before it was met in force. In the wars against Napoleon both the Spaniards and the Russians had let the invaders exhaust themselves and stretch their supply lines, and the defenders succeeded then in defeating the intruders.

Why not a similar method for Sweden? The central defense idea was appealing because Sweden could not hope to protect its entire long coastline, especially without subsidies, and during the nineteenth century it had allowed both army and navy to deteriorate. When Karl XV and later Oscar II tried to stimulate defense improvements they roused storms of controversy.

The nobility, traditional guardians of the national safety, favored a strong defense but they did not necessarily agree on how to obtain it. The twelve-day training or exercise period for the militia had been raised in mid-century to thirty days, but it was weakly administered and almost useless for making soldiers. The army of the *indelningsverk* was not much more effective. Its system of maintenance was antiquated and unfair. Yet the system had its stout advocates such as Jöns and Abraham Rundbäck, who helped postpone its destruction. Proposal after proposal for solution to the problem foundered in the conflict over taxation and, as has been seen, even the "compromise" of 1873 remained an empty gesture. Two years after that decision General Baron Hugo Raab suggested universal military service. The riksdag rejected the plan and although it was the unavoidable solution it was not fully adopted until 1901. Controversy continued about the length of the period of liability and the length of the training period as well as about the expense and even the necessity of military service. Some said disband the army, it couldn't defend the country against the Hottentots! One group of young social democrats insisted, like Marxists, that the worker in Sweden had no fatherland and hence owned nothing to defend. The rightists regarded military service as the fundamental duty of every citizen. Baron Ludvig Douglas, of Scottish and German descent, wrote in 1889 a widely read tract entitled "How We Lost Norrland." He pictured a fictional catastrophe in which, after Sweden had rejected an alliance with Germany, it was left alone to fight a Russian invasion; the ill-trained militia troops fired their ammunition uselessly and suffered horrible casualties; the regular soldiers lacked experience and adaptability and could not replace the officers who fell. His conclusion was that all this horror could have been avoided if Sweden had had a strong modern defense.[12]

The roused public interest was inflated by an increase in tensions with Norway, and this enabled Erik Gustaf Boström (prime minister from 1891 to 1900) to win an agreement on a forward-looking defense measure in 1892. Training time for recruits was increased to ninety days, and, to satisfy the free traders, the increased costs would be met through income taxes rather than taxes on consumption goods. However, the defense question became involved with the stepped-up drive for suffrage reform (see the following section on suffrage) and the sharpening of political divisions. Two opinion-oriented groupings formed during the 1890s — the social democrats, led by Hjalmar Branting, who had a rather definite program; and the liberals, composed of a variety of special-interest groups that got together at the turn of the century but never fully coalesced. On the defense question the liberals and social democrats made common cause in arguing that if military service was to be made compulsory those who were subject to service must be given the vote. In 1901 Baron Ludvig Douglas almost succeeded in making a deal whereby the First Chamber would agree to suffrage reform in return for liberal support for the military program. Defense could never be considered on its own merits alone; repeatedly it was paired off against concessions on either taxes or suffrage. In the long run each group of determined advocates achieved its demands, but each was slowed by the other.

Around the turn of the century the problem of preparedness took an ominous priority over suffrage and taxation. The Norwegian partners in the Union were assuming a threatening tone on the west, and on the east General Nicolaj Bobrikov was pursuing a brutal Russification policy in Finland. The Norwegians were reacting sensitively to Gustav Åkerhielm's blustering remark that Sweden should strengthen its military so that it could better "talk Swedish both eastward and westward."[13] The perennial fear of the Russian bear was intensified by the appearance in Sweden of dozens of wandering Russian saw-sharpeners. Almost certainly they were saw-filers and nothing more, but Swedes envisioned them as spies walking purposefully through the land. Thus thousands of Swedes felt endangered from two sides, and parliamentary bargaining was subordinated for the moment. Around 1900 two vital decisions were reached: The first, in 1898, was to build a railway line from Boden (in the far north near the frontier with Russian Finland) through the iron mining country to the Norwegian border. Norway would then build the short line down to Narvik on Ofoten Fjord, from which the ore of the Kiruna-Gällivare fields could be exported to world markets. The related decision, two years later, was to build at Boden what has remained Sweden's most extensive fortification system. This step marked abandonment of the central defense system and return to the peripheral strategy. Each of these projects meant large expenditures and the economy-minded farmers were not happy nor were the radical social democrats. However, the latter still lacked strength in the riksdag (Hjalmar Branting was the sole party-affiliated Social Democrat in the Second Chamber), and the farmers were split. The special opportunities for both protection and development of the northern region were enough to override the commitment to economy. These positive actions on defense and railway were largely due to the leadership capacities of E. G. Boström, for he was a man who could work with the king and who realized his dependence on the riksdag and the parties, a conservative possessed of both tact and firmness.

When Boström resigned in June 1900, presumably from sheer weariness, he was succeeded by Baron Fredrik von Otter. Although von Otter lacked

Bostrom's political talent, it was during his regime that universal military service was at last legislated. The Boer War was in the consciousness of many and added to the fears aroused by Russia and the irritation felt toward Norway. Despite the bitter opposition of the social democrats the attitude of the farmers shifted, and the population of exposed points along the coasts and especially in Gotland and Norrland favored a strong updating of the defense establishment. Popular opinion expressed itself in meetings around the country, and riksdagsmen saw that their constituents were more preparedness-conscious than they. Hence both houses could unite in the reorganization of 1901.

Then for a few years it was defense that was pushed aside, but the liberal and radical elements felt cheated. The military forces had obtained their program, and now every young man faced a service period of 240 days. But only half of the famous slogan "Defense and Reforms" had been realized. The complaint now was that the common man lacked the vote and had no way to make his opinions heard; hence he grew increasingly hostile to the defense establishment. Meanwhile the farmers had been freed from the burdens of both land taxes and *indelningsverk*, and they could indulge in relatively cost-free patriotism.

The burning issue became the construction of a new and larger armored vessel, the F-boat. The Balkan wars, the continuing Russification of Finland, and now the tension between Germany and Russia heightened the nationalistic concerns of the Swedish conservatives. Fear of Russia and admiration for Germany worked together to bolster a big-stick psychology, and the F-boat became the symbol of Sweden's resolve to assert itself. The Conservative government of Arvid Lindman (1906–11), with the German-oriented Arvid Taube as foreign minister, put all its influence behind the F-boat and won the support even of the sober farmers. The liberals and the social democrats vigorously denounced the luxury and the futility of the big warship, and Karl Staaff, the liberal leader, declared that the vessel could not defend as much as Skåne — its only use could be to add a bit of glamor to the life of the bathing resorts at the time of naval visitations. The campaign of 1911 was unusually bitter. The Liberals held their own with 102 seats and Staaff returned to office. But the Social Democrats increased their seats from 34 to 64, and it was they who really caused the downfall of the conservatives. It was the social democrats who were most adamantly opposed to the arms buildup, and some of them went so far as to call for disarmament. Other issues and the widened electorate had also influenced the vote. And the liberals were far from unanimously behind Staaff's critical defense policy. In the new cabinet, nevertheless, both the navy and the army ministers were, for the first time, both civilians. Staaff proceeded further to act on his convictions and in December 1911 he stopped work on the F-boat.

This step produced an amazing popular reaction. The nationalistic young churchman Manfred Björkquist and thousands of others were deeply concerned and in a swift upsurge of feeling 17 million kronor were privately contributed to build the battleship. It was more than enough, the government went ahead with its plans, and in 1915 the *Sverige* was launched. Obviously many Swedes were neither penny-pinchers nor pacifists.

In the meantime a war of pamphlets raged. In 1912 Sven Hedin, an explorer and extreme rightist (only distantly related to Adolf Hedin, the radical), issued "A Warning Word" ("Ett varnings ord"). The essence of the booklet was that Russia aimed to attack Sweden and that therefore Sweden should join the Triple Alliance (composed of Germany, Austria, and Italy) and arm itself. A million copies were distributed and in 1914 Hedin published "A Second Warning." At the opposite end of the spectrum the radical Zeth Höglund published in 1913 the antimilitarist "The Fortified Poorhouse" i.e. Sweden. This gave the doctrinaire Marxist argument against militarism as capitalist business. The moderate conservatives could not accept Hedin, the moderate social democrats could not follow Höglund. Branting took a middle ground and asked that the bourgeois parties get together on some reasonable defense plan.

Prime Minister Staaff himself, as he viewed the worsening situation in the world, had second thoughts. By December 1913 he had changed his mind, and he announced in a famous speech at Karlskrona that he would promote a rearmament program although he did not sanction the extension of the military service term. Staaff's change of mind, however, was not shared by all of his party colleagues in the liberal fold.

Once again a great popular demonstration revealed the deeper currents of opinion among the citizens, and it also produced a constitutional crisis that transcended the immediate conflict. After two months of preparation there descended on Stockholm, on February 6, 1914, the Farmer's March (*Bondetåget*) of 31,000 persons. It was perfectly organized for both transportation and hospitality. Forty thousand more had signed a supporting memorial. All who could do so crowded into the palace yard (*Borggård*) to greet the king and pledge support for his program of defense. It was a huge patriotic binge "With God and Sweden's common people for king and fatherland."[14] King Gustav V, who had come to the throne in 1907, replied in a strong and carefully prepared statement, written largely by Sven Hedin, urging immediate action on rearmament of army and fleet. Those who could not squeeze into the palace yard heard either Prince Karl or the crown prince (later Gustav VI Adolf) read the royal words outside the walls.

The king had shown the speech only to his trusted personal advisers, and they, including the crown prince, advised toning it down. But Gustav, probably welcoming an opportunity for a showdown with the too independent Staaff, "stuck to his guns" in both meanings of this phrase. Staaff was furious that the monarch would speak so positively without consulting his prime minister. He gave the king the chance to explain or modify, but His Majesty was unyielding. He challenged the basic concept of ministerial government. Two days after the Farmers' March Hjalmar Branting organized a march of 50,000 workers pledging support to Staaff in his fight against a return to "personal monarchy." Two days after that a huge student rally demonstrated for the king and defense. The clash was head-on.

The immediate effect was the resignation of Staaff and his cabinet and their replacement by a conservative government headed by Hjalmar Hammarskjöld. The long-term political effect was that the king, despite his promise to do so, never again "spoke to his people." Staaff not only lost his office but was subjected to a vicious campaign of character assassination. He was charged with giving secret information to the Russians; he was labeled a traitor for his cooperation with the social democrats (for they too were called traitors). A year later he died. He had won his point for the long run but not for the short. His Liberal party lost heavily in the special spring election of 1914 and again in the regular fall election, dropping from 102 to 57 seats. It was the Social Democrats who counted the big gains, becoming now the riksdag's largest party with 87 seats. The middle class and the moderate position were being squeezed out and politics was becoming polarized. The effect on the rearmament program is difficult to assess, for within a short time the booming of the guns of August was itself enough to persuade the Swedes to extend military service and build new destroyers.

## SUFFRAGE

The great reform of 1866 had provided for common voting but with limitations, especially the 800 riksdaler taxable income required for voters for the Second Chamber. As of the 1870s less than 7 percent of the inhabitants could vote (22–23 percent of adult males). Both population and eligible voters increased as wages and incomes rose later in the century, but even early in the twentieth century the qualified voters numbered less than 30 percent of adult males. And of the eligibles only 20 percent took advantage of the opportunity for the first several elections after 1866. (In Denmark and Norway the participation amounted to between 40 and 70 percent.) Only gradually did the political apathy of the mass of Swedes become transformed into activity. By 1884, of those entitled to vote, 25 percent went to the polls, by 1896 it was 45 percent, but not until 1908 did the figure pass 60 percent. In the meantime, nevertheless, eager reformers agitated for the elimination of restrictions and the expansion of the suffrage.

The conservative plutocracy remained dominant in the First Chamber and the agrarians ruled the Second Chamber. But the issues of defense, protectionism, and union with Norway affected all citizens and increasing numbers demanded a voice in decision making. Suffrage itself became a key issue as the recalcitrant conservatives opposed all significant proposals for adjustment. The holders of power argued in many ways. One position, expressed by Lektor Teofron Säve, was that the franchise

> is a mandate that the state confers on such persons as are qualified to fulfill it, and it is not a right that is due a person merely because he is born or is a citizen.[15]

Another common argument was that representation should be based on the good of the community as a whole, not on the interests of individuals. Rudolf Kjellén, an internationally known *geopolitiker*, an ideological conservative, and an admirer of German institutions, insisted in a speech of 1896 that

> a politics that seeks to place power in the hands of all is as perilous as it is rootless, for it involves a violation of the order of nature and the organic body of the community of people. On the contrary, in political organization one must seek controls against the confused flood of private interests.[16]

Fundamentally, however, the rigid backbone of opposition was the non-philosophical agrarian majority in both chambers who did not wish to share power with the "lower classes." For them, "private interests" could usually be defined as the interests of the other person.

Diametrically opposed to such views and interests were the liberals and, from their origins in the 1880s, the social democrats. To some extent they based their argumentation on utilitarianism and the ideas of John Stuart Mill that the good of all is best attained through recognition of the self-interest of each and thus through the votes of all. Reference was constantly made to Rousseau and the natural-rights concept of the equality of all men and to the principles enunciated in the American Declaration of Independence. Isidor Kjellberg, a prolific reformist editor who had spent a few years in the American Midwest and then returned to Sweden, was one of the most fervent advocates of electoral reform. In both prose and poetry he attempted to arouse the Swedish people to demand equality and to make "our old dear Sweden as much like America as possible."[17]

The most common bases of reasoning were practical and nonideological. Rights should go along with duties. If a man had to pay taxes he should have a voice in how the funds were distributed; if he had to serve in the army he should be able to participate in policy making. ("One man, one vote, one gun.'') Religious appeals were few, but it was remarked that Jesus's disciples were all poor men. Could it be claimed that because a man did not have 800 kronor in taxable income he was unfit to vote? What about the man who had 799 kronor and was disqualified? What about the man who had 100 fine hogs and could vote, then lost his hogs through the pest and was denied his vote? Did a man with less property have less interest in the community? Then give him the vote and stimulate his interest. The franchise could be both an educational and a nationalizing influence. One writer reminded his readers that it was not 800-kronor men who had followed after Engelbrekt and that it was often the very poor who had fought with Gustav II Adolf during Sweden's Age of Greatness.

Knut Wiksell, a highly respected economist, pointed out that a working-class family who could not qualify under the 800 kroner minimum rule nevertheless paid taxes, both direct and indirect. In total these taxes might add up to 18 percent of their total income and to as much as 52 percent of taxable income, proportions higher than the more prosperous citizens paid. Nonetheless, the working man was excluded from the voting booth until his wages rose higher than 800 kronor.

Although the voting requirements of the 1866 reform favored the farmers, the rural voters were themselves less concerned politically than were the city voters; for example, in 1872 only 16 percent of the eligible voters in the country districts cast ballots but 41 percent of urban eligibles did so, and in 1896 the respective figures were 40 percent and 63 percent.[18] Further extension of voting privileges to the farmers might not, therefore, have been meaningful, although this was the direction urged by conservatives who felt most strongly about the defense question. They thought they could better depend on the rural poor to be sympathetic to a strong defense establishment but feared the negative attitude of the urban working class. For decades the whole matter of franchise was complicated by such conflicting practical considerations. The philosophy of democracy weighed little in the scales of policy making.

When the concept of proportional representation was injected into the discussion similar conflicts of interest appeared. Proportional methods of voting would require enlarged electoral districts, and this would inflict hardship on the sparsely settled areas. Beyond that, proportional representation would encourage the formation of political parties, and this would violate the principles on which De Geer and his cohorts had based the program of 1866. Therefore most though not all of the conservatives at first opposed the proportional idea.

Popular opinion, insofar as it expressed itself in the press and through individuals, strongly and sometimes emotionally favored voting reform. In 1882 a group of students from the University of Uppsala founded the liberal-radical society Verdandi. Although Verdandi was the name of one of the three norns of Nordic mythology, the society looked forward rather than backward; it was interested in suffrage, religious freedom, temperance, union politics, and many other social issues, but most of all it was interested in free discussion of all public problems. There was much sympathetic discussion of the views of Strindberg and Ibsen, and the very freedom of talk at its meetings shocked the conservative authorities and led to disciplinary action by both university and civil officials. Karl Staaff, just beginning his remarkable political career, was the original moving spirit and the society came to be a training ground for many of the liberal and social democratic leaders of the coming generations. The students' concern with education of the citizenry led to the publication of a prolonged series of pamphlets on social questions, offering the students' own liberal views to the community at large. Almost one hundred years later the society Verdandi is still active.

Among the individual activists in the suffrage cause one of the most prominent was Adolf Hedin, publicist, politician, and from 1870 until his death thirty-five years later almost continuously a member of the Second Chamber. He was a thorn in the flesh to Oscar II and the conservatives in general, although on matters of defense he was as nationalist as any. On the suffrage issue he was a persistent gadfly. And there were many others in the riksdag and outside it who could be neither silenced nor diverted. Hjalmar Branting, an honorary member of Verdandi who was to become the great man of the social democratic movement, declared in 1886 that "universal suffrage is the price with which the bourgeosie can buy a settlement through administration in place of liquidation ordered by the court of the revolution." [19]

In 1898 suffrage petitions were drawn up that gained 364,000 signatures, including 63,000 from women. Yet another pressure device was the "folk riksdag," one of which was held in 1893 and another in 1896. In these popular propaganda sessions the representatives were chosen by a universal suffrage system to illustrate how harmless such a method would be. It was a good way to popularize the reform ideas, for the meetings discussed other things as well, but their effect was weakened by controversy. In 1896, of the 145 delegates, 30 were social democrats, and when some of them demanded a general strike to force action the more moderate liberals balked. In a variety of ways the suffrage issue was kept before the public and the riksdag, and sometimes it was the chief issue at elections. But delay and disagreement continued.

The parliamentary maneuvering on this franchise question was far too complicated to trace in detail. Proposals and counterproposals were handled in one riksdag after another. But while Denmark and Norway legislated universal manhood suffrage and Finland went a step further in 1906 and included women, too (the first European country to do so), the Swedish conservatives held the line stubbornly. They could see from the results of the Norwegian move of 1898 that catastrophe did not inevitably follow, but they would not yield. One reason for the failure of the reformers was that even when the liberal forces gained a majority they fell into that all-too-common difficulty of democratic assemblies: they could not agree on one specific program. Votes would be split among three proposals, none having a majority; or the First Chamber would vote for one measure, the Second for another. The opposition could and did find plenty of items on which to confuse and delay the proceedings: the balancing of city and country representation, the precise point at which to put the minimum income requirement for voting, the age limits for voting, the ballot for women, the question of paying national taxes or national *and* communal taxes as a prerequisite for voting, proportional representation in general and specifically for one chamber or for both. The liberals' plan of 1905–6 contemplated single-member districts and the establishment of the Second Chamber as the more representative and the preeminent house. But opinions were badly divided and the outcome was in doubt. At a crucial point in the debate Karl Staaff raised a rhetorical question: what kind of power should rule in Sweden — royal power with people power or royal power with gentry power (*herremakt*)? This comparatively innocent bit of demagoguery brought about the collapse of his liberal reform plan and led to the breakup of his first ministry.

In the elections of 1908 (for the 1909 riksdag) the Conservatives and the Liberals remained the largest groupings but they balanced each other and the solid block of Social Democrats increased their seats from 13 to 34. Weary and worn, everyone realized that the suffrage issue must be resolved. Therefore, under the continuing leadership of Lindman it became the conservatives rather than the liberals who wrote the new franchise law, a compromise that no one really liked: all men over twenty-four could vote for members of the Second Chamber provided they fulfilled certain citizenship requirements, including the payment of taxes. For the First Chamber the property requisites for members were lowered and for the voters a forty-grade scale of income replaced the old tax-rate scale that had been more favorable to the wealthy. The forty-grade scale was an elaborate system of plural voting that allowed men and women of property a number of votes roughly proportionate to their wealth, much as the holder of many shares of stock in a corporation votes according to his share holdings. As for the Second Chamber one effect of the law was to reduce the electoral share of the farmers from 40 percent to 27 percent. The most far-reaching aspect of the bill was its introduction of proportional voting for both chambers, on which the conservatives now insisted (because they could easily foresee, under the revised franchise, their loss of majority status in many districts). Thus was fixed on Sweden the system that Balkanized political parties and virtually prevented a two-party structure. The modest reforms for the First Chamber were sufficient to preserve that body and prevent the Second Chamber parliamentarism that Staaff had hoped to establish.

Full universal suffrage was not yet attained, but the electorate was doubled from 9.5 percent to 19 percent of the whole population, and the barriers were broken. It was enough that the election for the Second Chamber in 1911 sent back to the riksdag 102 Liberals and dropped the Conservatives to 64 while the Social Democrats rose to 64. Staaff came back as prime minister. As for the extent of suffrage a goodly share of the liberals were now probably satisfied. But the social democrats wanted to go the whole way, to wipe away minor restrictions such as the tax-payment rule and to include women in the electorate, and many liberals were in sympathy. Staaff then conceived a clever scheme.

During the second Staaff ministry (1911–14) the suffrage issue became entangled with both defense and temperance. Knowing that he could not get the reactionary First Chamber to agree to women's suffrage for national elections Staaff thought he saw a way to sneak it in through the back door. The temperance issue would be the key to unlock the door to women's suffrage. Sentiment was strong for local option (the "local veto") to permit or prohibit sale of liquor and on this question women should have a voice; therefore why not allow local option on the basis of a general vote of all adult men and women? However, the conservatives were worried about the economic and fiscal effects of prohibition. Therefore, the plan was to offer a bargain: the liberals would go at least part way with the conservatives by supporting military preparedness in return for the conservatives' agreement to the local option plan. This elaborate scheme to solve three problems (defense, temperance, and women's suffrage) in one package became the first casualty of World War I, for before it could be legislated the conservatives knew that war was coming and that therefore they did not have to bargain to get their defense program. Women's suffrage had to wait for the moment of fright at the end of the war, and the temperance issue (see temperance section in preceding chapter) was resolved in an entirely different way.[20]

The account so far of the suffrage campaign has emphasized the offensive by the liberal and socialist groups, but the maneuverings, holding actions, and delays by the conservatives are worthy of notice. Beginning in the early 1880s the reformers got bills through the Second Chamber but never past the First Chamber, which had been deliberately constructed to block hasty action. As long as possible tactics involved flat rejection of change. As pressures for reform grew too strong to disregard the response was to suggest minimal adjustments, such as relaxing the property requirement for voters from 800 kronor to 600 kronor. Another ploy was to demand, in return for concessions, "guarantees for society's calm and orderly development"[21] in the form of raised age limits for voting, tax requirements, proportional voting, and voting by classes. Other guarantees suggested double votes for men over forty and for the educated and, specifically for communal voting, for each krona paid in taxes one vote up to a maximum of ten, thereafter one vote for each five kronor paid. The left parties "had no understanding" for such devices. Yet the "money-idol" basis for the franchise was preserved in some degree down to 1921.

In 1906, when the First Chamber rejected the moderate proposals of the Staaff government, it agreed to an investigation of the question of women's suffrage, a move clearly not intended to produce action (investigations can be very slow). Complete women's suffrage might also be avoided, some thought, by allowing only wives to vote, the idea being that husbands might be able to control them. These squirmings and turnings succeeded in delaying any significant action for twenty-seven years, from 1880 to 1907, and in postponing the final achievement of universal suffrage until the decision of 1918, when world pressures added unanswerable force to domestic demands. Although the suffrage campaign was long-drawn-out it had avoided violence, and in the end it was completely successful.

# XV

## THE DEMOCRATIC BREAKTHROUGH
## OF THE NINETEENTH CENTURY
## II. FOLK MOVEMENTS AND
## POLITICAL PARTIES

ALTHOUGH CERTAIN ISSUES such as taxation and defense were disruptive for the society as a whole they also stimulated popular concern and brought interested groups into closer cooperation. The temperance movement evoked this response in strong measure. Foremost among the organizations that attracted people eager for common action were the trade unions and the cooperative societies. But single-purpose associations had difficulty in attaining majority status; only when people could agree on broad programs encompassing a variety of issues could they organize political parties and attempt to gain power in government. Hence let us focus attention primarily on two of the most influential folk movements and two of the political parties that were dynamic forces in the late nineteenth and early twentieth centuries.

### Folk Movements and Democracy

The participation of hundreds of thousands of plain citizens in social democratic, liberal, labor union, and other political activity in the early twentieth century may seem surprising, a contradiction to the pastoral society of the nineteenth century. In a way it was exactly that and yet it was a natural growth.

The folk movements of the early nineteenth century, especially the temperance societies and the pious "reader" movements, were but forerunners of the great proliferation of societies in the latter part of the century. By the mid-twentieth century there was such a blossoming of interest organizations, clubs, societies, unions, federations, and on and on that people in awed despair spoke of "association Sweden." This organizing obsession played a vital role in the democratic breakthrough. True, the riksdag reform of 1865/66 was forced by well-to-do farmers and the middle class of the cities, and the reformist Liberal party of the early twentieth century was a middle-class phenomenon. But only a step behind came the multitudes of the laboring class, demanding the suffrage and preparing to make their impact on politics. They were more nearly ready than the middle classes could imagine.

In 1846 the laws abolishing guilds had encouraged associations of workers. Workers' societies sprang up in the 1850s, stimulated by the Norwegian example. Culture and pleasure were their primary purposes. Sickness and funeral clubs developed at about the same time as well as the consumers' cooperatives. By the late 1860s the number of organizations was increasing, and in 1864 all restrictions on the founding of societies were removed.

Membership was largely male because of the Biblical and traditional Swedish subordination of women. But the organizations were democratic and increasingly women took part, especially in the religious and temperance societies. Groups were usually small, although there early developed a tendency to build national federations of the local societies devoted to specific causes. Opportunities were ample to discuss problems of common concern, to give talks, to choose officers, to make decisions. And such activities stimulated reading and thinking, and they enriched adult education.[1]

Between 1870 and 1900 the folk movements took hold and flourished. The Methodists organized in 1868, the Baptists in 1872, the Mission Friends in 1878, and the Salvation Army in 1882. After 1900, as the accompanying table indicates, growth slowed but did not stop. Among the temperance societies, of which many were associated with particular groups like women, doctors, railway workers, etc., the largest was the International Order of Good Templars (IOGT), which originated in the United States and continued to be strongly influenced therefrom. In 1900 it had in Sweden 1,624 societies with 95,000 members, and in 1910, when it peaked, it had 2,340 lodges with 160,000 members. The five main temperance organizations had 325,000 members, and they carried on vigorous social and educational programs. Cooperative societies experienced an irregular growth until the national federation, Kooperativa Förbundet (KF) was founded in 1899. In 1904 it included 57 societies and 13,000 members; by 1920 it had 941 societies and 248,000 members. To all these must be added what was to become the greatest of all, the labor unions. The typographers union of 1846 was hardly a real union, but by the 1880s workers' unions counted over 8,000 members and by 1900 the figure was 66,000. In 1920 *Landsorganisation* (LO), the largest federation, reckoned 2,800 member unions and 280,000 individuals; total union membership was 400,000 and growing.

Free Church Societies and Membership

| | 1900 | | 1920 | |
|---|---|---|---|---|
| | Societies | Members | Societies | Members |
| Methodist .................... | 105 | 15,653 | 140 | 16,016 |
| Baptist ...................... | 564 | 40,759 | 669 | 60,913 |
| Mission Friends ............... | 915 | 76,283 | 1,511 | 109,816 |
| Salvation Army ............... | 257 | 12,620 | 261 | 20,304 |

*Source:* condensed and rounded off from Hilding Johansson, *Folkrörelserna och det demokratiska statsskicket i Sverige*, 43.

These organizations represented democracy at the grass roots. Some of them did not profess democracy; John Wesley, for instance, was no democrat and Jabez Bunting said that "Methodism hates democracy as much as it hates sin."[2] Nevertheless the overall tendency was democratic and Hilding Johansson was right when he said that "every society became a pioneer for the democratic system."[3] This was true of the free church groups, the temperance societies, the labor unions, and of course the cooperative societies which were founded on the Rochdale plan of "one member, one vote." All authorities agree that these folk societies were schools of citizenship from which chairmen and board members became officials in communes and state and members of the riksdag. In the management of societies, in the give and take of discussion, men and women learned techniques and built self-confidence. Carpenters could be treasurers, farmers could be secretaries, a railroad worker could be a chairman. The youth clubs associated with the adult organizations gave similar experience to younger men and women who learned early to keep records and manage accounts and to stand up and express themselves. With the strength that comes from group solidarity the representatives of these societies could speak frankly to officials of government and business, and this did something for self-esteem. One young man could bear witness that "Our heroes did not lie in Riddarholm church [the Westminster Abbey of Sweden]; they sat in the directorate of the social democratic youth club."[4]

The cooperative societies deliberately made themselves nonpolitical, but the other large folk movements were all involved in political action. And they won strong representation in the riksdag after the widened suffrage of 1911. The influence of the temperance societies was illustrated by the percentages of teetotalers in the riksdag of 1911: 73 percent of the liberals, 88 percent of the social democrats, but only 22 percent of the conservatives. As to free church affiliation the picture was quite different: 37 percent of the liberals, 5 percent of the social democrats, and 17 percent of the conservatives. All the folk movements were interested in suffrage but, except for the franchise for women that campaign was essentially won by 1911. On other questions they were interested in varying degrees and sometimes in opposite directions. The troublesome issues in 1911–14 were temperance, defense, and the liberal demand for parliamentary government. How would various groups align themselves on issues beyond their primary concerns? They had to decide what must have priority.

The priority for thousands was the antialcohol crusade which swept the country like a great revival in the early years of the twentieth century, quite evidently in response to a deeply felt need. The early nineteenth-century movement had run its course, and the problem was back. In the 1870s a series of local "awakenings" began with the temperance approach; by the turn of the century the demand was for complete prohibition, and the climax came with a voluntary plebiscite in 1909. Voting were 1,884,298 people (men and women), 56 percent of the adult population, and of these 99 percent voted for absolute prohibition.[5] There followed a government investigation of the problem and a recommendation for local option (called in Sweden the local veto) based on popular vote with women to be included in the franchise. (See suffrage section in chapter XIV.) One of the big problems was that liquor taxes provided a significant portion of local revenues (sometimes as much as 40 percent for cities) plus up to 20 percent of the income of the state. The issue became intertwined with economics, women's suffrage, and defense and was therefore stalemated for a time. The solution, if it can be so called, was provided by Dr. Ivan Bratt with a system of rationing that lasted from 1917 until 1955; meanwhile, a plebiscite in 1922 rejected total prohibition.

The great variety of folk movements, the scope of their membership, and the intensity of their purposefulness all illustrate the upsurge of democracy that was transforming Swedish society. They were movements from the depths and they surged through the country and through the twentieth century with the force of the tides of the sea. Two of these folk movements, the trade unions and the cooperatives, deserve more detailed attention.

## THE TRADE UNIONS

Men who worked together, especially in the crafts, had long organized for pleasure and mutual self-help. The medieval guilds shared cultural interests, staged miracle and morality plays, and controlled training and membership within the craft. When in 1846 Sweden abolished the guilds but encouraged associations of workers the artisans continued to organize; the typographers, for instance, did so immediately. Real trade unions of workers in particular branches of industry, organized on a permanent basis for the promotion of their own economic interests, did not appear until the 1870s. First was the union of tobacco workers in Malmö, founded in 1874 by Danish agitators to prevent unorganized Swedes from moving to Denmark and lowering Danish wages.

In the 1870s many strikes broke out but they seldom accomplished much for the workers. The system of employment was patriarchal and so were the attitudes of employers. An incident that caught wide attention and spurred action on the labor front was a famous strike at Sundsvall in 1879. Wages in the sawmills were then at most 2.50 kronor per twelve-hour day, and the owners announced a reduction of 15–20 percent. A committee of workers asked that the former wages be restored but the owners refused, citing hard times. About a thousand workers gathered in a field near Sundsvall (the sharp-shooters' range) and the next day were met by 100 soldiers and the governor of the province who ordered them back to work — "living or dead I will show you that the law will prevail."[6] But there was no law against strikes! The striking workers remained obstinate and their numbers grew to several thousand. An appeal by the governor to the king brought an oft-quoted telegram from Oscar II: "Calm all the right-minded and warn all disturbers, for patience must have a limit. Cannon boats and soldiers are on the way."[7] There was neither violence by the strikers nor shooting by the soldiers, but the governor ordered a thousand workers dispossessed and the leaders imprisoned. Thinking people were disquieted by the high-handed methods used, and the workers learned they were powerless without an adequate organization and the funds to maintain a strike.

Two years later a strike of building workers in Stockholm accentuated the problems that had been illustrated in Sundsvall. The workers lacked a leader of their own but turned to Dr. Anton Nyström, a social-minded medic and author whom they trusted. Because the laborers had no strike fund the sympathetic doctor could only advise them to go back to work, but he issued a call: "Respect for the zealous workman, honor to the well-meaning capitalist"[8] and suggested formation of groups of agents for workers and employers to oversee the interests of each group and of the economy as a whole.

Toward the end of 1881, shortly after the Stockholm strike, the carpenters' union of Stockholm called a meeting at which a fifteen-man committee was chosen to draw up statutes for unions. Besides carpenters the committee included a metal worker, a carpet worker, two shoemakers, a stone carver, and Dr. Nyström. The socialist agitator August Palm was at the meeting, but it was the moderate Nyström who set the tone at this time and wrote the proposed statutes.

This first trial program of 1882 urged establishment of unions within each craft or trade. "Union gives strength." Each union should establish a treasury for pensions and support of injured or unemployed members; encourage education and temperance; set up an executive committee of seven who should mediate disputes between workers and foremen and managers, one or more of whom should represent the union in meetings of other associations. The union should seek peaceful solutions to controversies and should support a strike only after careful investigation of the circumstances.[9]

In succeeding years (1883 and 1886) this program was elaborated to include demands for the establishment of an employment office; increased state travel stipends for workers who wished to study abroad; promotion of good relations between workers and employers and the use of committees of arbitration; universal suffrage; the ten-hour workday and prohibition of Sunday and holiday labor; healthful working conditions; abolition of direct taxes and introduction of progressive income taxes; religious freedom and separation of church from state and school; the single-chamber riksdag; abolition of the standing army and establishment of a citizen militia.

This was an expanded liberal program, wide in scope but not at all revolutionary in tone or content. The socialist tide was soon to swamp its calm reasonableness. A Scandinavian Trade Union Congress met in Gothenburg in 1886 and declared for the socialist program because "the private capitalistic method of production is a permanent hindrance for bringing about prosperity and happiness in the community."[10] Gradually thereafter the liberal influence receded, and although the bookbinders and a few other moderate unions held out for another decade, by 1899 all had yielded to the pressure of the socialists and the call for unity; LO and the social democrats joined hands, and even their formal divorce in 1900 did not stop their living together.

Sweden's trade union history has been dominated by the craft-union idea, by the national federation of these unions, and by the centralization of most of them in LO. Only one persistent competitor has continued, namely the syndicalist SAC (*Sveriges arbetares centralorganisation*), founded in 1910 on the basis of local organizations of all workers in a place (membership in 1970 was 23,700). The main-line development followed the craft structure on which LO was founded, although that structure has been modified in recent years. When it was seen that unified employer organizations had to deal with many different craft unions the LO tried to persuade closely related unions to combine, if possible on the basis of one union for each industry. Resistance was strong and adjustments and compromises were necessary. The lithographers, the painters, the masons, and others retained their individual identities; more combined in industrial unions like the railway workers' union, the metal workers' union, and the seafolks' union that grew out of the seaman's union. This process, beginning in 1912, had by 1954 left seventeen craft unions with membership of 166,000, and established twenty-four industrial unions with membership of over 1 million; three mixed unions had 137,000 members.[11]

Unions developed slowly in Sweden and against much opposition from both government and the general public. The small scale and patriarchal nature of early industry, the scattering of mines, ironworks, and the lumber industries in the *bruk* in sparsely settled woodlands far from ports and cities discouraged labor organization. The Sundsvall strikers, for instance, gathered from many outlying establishments and had no organization. Ordinary middle-class citizens, knowing of labor violence in other countries, feared unions and socialism as challenges to order and to the traditional social structure. The authorities were frightened by strikes and by laborers acting together, and when confrontation was imminent they repeatedly called in the army, thus enhancing the laborers' antagonism toward the military. In 1899 the government affronted unionists by passing the Åkarp law that pledged protection for strikebreakers;[12] the sense of class discrimination and injustice survived for many years, even after the law was emasculated. Employers sometimes fired workers for joining unions. Polarization increased between workers on the one side and employers and officials on the other.

The three-day suffrage strike of 1902 was a flexing of labor muscle, and it encouraged radical elements to try something more extensive. It also led employers to organize the Swedish Employers Federation (Svenska arbetsgivare föreningen — SAF) in the same year. It grew slowly but by 1905 had 236 members who employed 41,000 workers. There were other employers' groups in the metal industry and the building industry. In Denmark a nationwide employers' association had been formed in 1899, and this organization had established a basic agreement (the September Agreement) with labor in 1899, outlining regulations for the relationship between labor and management and setting up a permanent court of arbitration. This was the first such agreement, and it became a guide for Swedish employers, though the accession of labor had to wait.

Industry continued to grow, particularly in the cities, and so did unions. But after 1907 the international economy entered a difficult period and in Sweden wages stagnated. Strikes and lockouts plagued industry through 1908 and 1909. In 1904 and 1907 referenda had been held on the question of a general strike, and in the 1907 vote 70 percent had expressed themselves in favor, the skilled workers showing more hesitancy than the unskilled. The Young Socialists and the Young Democrats, followers of Zeth Höglund, were eager for confrontation despite the depressed state of the economy.

The Great Strike of 1909 was the most dramatic event in Sweden's labor history. Ominous forebodings in 1905–8 gave notice of rising tension. After two lockouts in the metal trades the Metal Trades Employers Association (VF) made the first big-industry nationwide collective agreement, and soon SAF was pushing for collective agreements for all its members, while labor remained reluctant. SAF issued a broad policy statement in 1905 including one paragraph (number 23)[13] that was especially hateful to labor; it stated the employer's right to hire and fire without regard to union membership. This clause was written into agreements with several unions but with a compromise clause recognizing labor's right to organize. The employers wanted uniform national agreements to present a common front against labor's demands and to equalize wages. Hjalmar von Sydow, the new president of SAF, made a study trip to Germany and Denmark and after his return drew up a plan for a basic agreement similar to the Danish arrangements and the Swedish metal trades agreement of 1905. But LO would not consent.

In 1908 anger and frustration rose on both sides. A dock strike raised the question of enforcement of paragraph 23, and disputes over wages and hours disrupted the sugar industry in Skåne and the building industry. The three largest employers associations — SAF, the Central Employers Association, and the Metal Trades Employers Association — combined in a threat of general lockout. LO had decided against a general strike, but the militant Young Socialists and their newspaper *Brand* (Fire) urged mass action. The government entered the conflict and appointed a mediation commission headed by Ernst Guenther, whose compromise proposal was finally accepted. But immediately new disputes arose, first among the bookbinders.

Economic conditions were worsening, to the special disadvantage of the workers. Depression throughout the western world resulted in layoffs and pressure for the lowering of wages. The important export industries were in a far better position than labor, for they had accumulated a backlog of materials to sell which was more than ample for the depressed market.

Dissatisfaction within the ranks of labor was illustrated graphically by the withdrawals from both the trade unions and the Social Democratic party — approximately a third of the membership of each — a year before the Great Strike broke out. Actually, over a four-year period LO membership dropped from just under 200,000 to well under 100,000. Were these defections due to the agitation of the radical youth groups, to lack of appreciation of the efforts of leadership, or simply to the economic difficulties of the times? No one seems to know. In any case the unions were seriously weakened before the big battle began. Nevertheless, Zeth Höglund and the syndicalists gloated over the cancellation of agreements between unions and social democrats. The Young Socialists and the Young Democrats sneered at the parliamentary principle and demanded a thorough shutdown of economic activity.

In the spring of 1909 a series of separate disputes irritated both labor and management. At the Skutskär pulp mill workers struck when employers tried to enforce a leveling of wages. In the clothing industry similar demands raised the question: at what level would wages be equalized? A strike at a power plant on Dalälven, another at the Munkfors ironworks — seven disputes broke out by mid-July 1909. SAF had issued an ultimatum on June 26, had extended the threat on July 14, and on August 2 had ordered a general lockout, involving 100,000 workers. On August 4 LO replied with a call for a general strike, and this involved 300,000 workers. It was the largest strike ever attempted, and it was watched with keen attention around the world.

Work related to public health and safety was exempted from the strike, but nonetheless the public soon came to regard the strike as an attack on both state and community. When the typographers went out the liberals reacted bitterly, for without a free press how could there be reasonable public discussion? The one large group that did not strike were the railway workers, and their abstention was significant: the mine owners and the manufacturers of export products could move their excess stocks to market and thus earn income even while not producing. But general economic conditions remained depressed.

The workers had no inventories to dispose of and their treasuries were rapidly exhausted, along with their small amount of public goodwill. Their hopes for a quick decision were dashed by the railway workers and the shippers. Within a month they had to call off the strike against all except SAF members. Continuing defections of individuals and groups forced a complete retreat by December. It was a severe blow but not a knockout.

The disastrous outcome of the strike taught labor the valuable lesson that it was not strong enough to fight the national community. Those who had dreams of revolution were given clearly to understand that their power was limited by law. The courts declared that even in sympathy strikes unions were responsible for breach of contract. Those like Staaff who advocated regular political action were shown to be right, especially as the new electoral law went into effect that same year; the workers now had the vote and could make their voices heard in the riksdag. The unions and the social democrats perhaps realized the nature of their interdependence more plainly after 1909. On the other side the employers and the state recognized that labor had legitimate complaints against society, that it had power to hurt if not to win, and that it had the will to assert itself. Labor was therefore accepted as a partner in society and reforms were hastened. Within a few years LO was stronger than ever before.[14]

From 1911 the curve of LO membership climbed steadily, past its 1907 peak to 200,000 in 1917, 400,000 in 1925, 1 million in 1941, 1.8 million in 1973. Other national federations (for example, salaried workers, government employees, professionals) added 1 million more, bringing the total union membership to over 2.8 million.[15] About 800,000 of these were women. With a total work force of 4 million this meant that slightly over 70 percent were unionized, making Sweden one of the most highly organized countries in the world. In some fields unionization reached 90 to 100 percent. This was due not to a legal closed shop system but to the tight-knit quality of the union structure, a sense of obligation of one worker to another, a feeling of class solidarity.

The overall guiding instrument of a basic agreement, a kind of constitution for labor-management relations, was finally accepted in 1938 and formalized in what is known as the Saltsjöbaden Agreement. Under the terms of this agreement negotiations covering wages and all the terms of employment are conducted periodically on a national scale.

The negotiation of long-term and far-reaching agreements gave considerable knowledge and power to union representatives and strengthened their position within the unions. This tended to make their continuity in office sometimes extraordinary. For the clothing workers union there was but one change of chairmanship between 1892 and 1945 — not many besides John L. Lewis and Samuel Gompers could challenge such a record! The universal pattern of organization was nevertheless democratic. Representatives elected to the periodic congresses made the important decisions, and on some occasions the referendum was used. In spite of the democratic structure and the common interest the attendance at local meetings did not always reach 50 percent of the membership and was disappointing to the leaders. Enthusiastic pioneers were succeeded by satisfied successors who took everything for granted.[16]

Swedish trade unions have interpreted their mission in the broadest sense. Thus they gradually built a vast educational system, much of it in association with other folk movements like the Social Democratic party, the temperance society Verdandi, the cooperative societies, and others. Together, through the *Arbetarnas Bildningsförbund* (ABF), these societies promote a national network of study circles, lecture series, entertainments, schools, correspondence courses — the gamut of educational activities. One significant institution is the Brunnsvik Folk High School, founded in 1906, and the affiliated LO school, founded 1929. Here much of the leadership of the labor movement has been educated in the social sciences, labor history, Marxism, organizational work, plus public speaking and the humanities. ABF operates about one thousand libraries and offers each year several hundred courses for tens of thousands of students, mostly adults. The trend in subject matter in the courses has been, interestingly, away from the early emphasis on economic and practical subjects toward the humanities. Languages form an important part of the curricula. LO also maintains an extensive archive in Stockholm, and it has an active press and propaganda service. Many unions have their own magazines; one of the best through the years has been *Metallarbetaren*, published by the huge metal workers union.

The characteristics of Swedish trade unionism that stand out are its all-encompassing nature and its cohesion, its hierarchy of organization reaching from the small plant to the central all-inclusive federations. Along with this goes the bond of cooperation between the trade unions and the social democrats as a bloc and a party, a Damon and Pytheas relationship dating from the 1890s and attributable to Hjalmar Branting's insistence that labor is one, with its economic and political interests bound inextricably together. In both unions and party the emphasis has been on practical goals, not on ideology. Their profound interest in education is itself highly practical, although it is a broadly conceived practicality. Mistakes have been made, like the Great Strike of 1909, but they have been rare. Leadership has been farsighted and well balanced. The employers associations have found labor a stiff bargainer but usually reasonable. Hence labor has strongly influenced the national economy and at the same time has increased its own share of the industrial product, all of this through democratic processes and a minimum use of violence.

### ORIGINS OF THE CONSUMER COOPERATIVE MOVEMENT

One of the major popular developments that for many foreigners came to epitomize the Sweden of the modern period was the consumer cooperative movement. Although it walked hand in hand with the trade union movement and the Social Democratic party it remained essentially an independent movement, and its membership grew well beyond both party and unions.

The word *cooperation* was introduced into the Swedish language in 1825 by Erik Gustaf Geijer, who had traveled in England and was concerned with social problems. Cooperation, he wrote, "is a new social order provoked by necessity in the present wilderness of civilization."[17] Some cooperative enthusiasts did indeed dream great dreams of establishing complete fairness in the interchange of goods, eliminating capitalistic exploitation, and creating a society of sweetness and light. But the strength of the cooperative movement in Sweden came to be based less on starry-eyed idealism than on matter-of-fact practicality. Or perhaps it would be better to say that success depended on the effective combination of these two elements.

Cooperation was in the beginning chiefly a way for consumers as a group to buy in quantity and evade the profit taking of the storekeeper. Early projects, such as the "Workers' Rings," gained some discounts from merchants, but such projects were neither demanding nor inspiring, and most of them were dismal failures. Real participation in the distribution of goods required time and energy, capital in at least small quantities, knowledge of merchandise, and the ability of people to work together. Such requirements could be met only on the basis of enthusiastic commitment, and this had to come from within the lower-income groups for they were the people who felt most severely pinched by the existing system.

The pattern of organization that eventually led to success was developed at Rochdale, England in 1844 and reached Sweden some twenty years later by way of Germany. Even then progress was slow. The clientele of the movement possessed meager resources and they were inexperienced in business affairs. Their organizations were local and small. Meaningful savings could come only with large-scale organization. Hence in 1899 interested groups from Stockholm, Gothenburg, and Malmö united to call a General Swedish Cooperative Congress. The Cooperative Union (Kooperativa Förbundet or KF) was founded by the Congress. Through several disappointing years this united wholesale society struggled to serve the local groups and by 1906 it began to show promise. Enough promise that private retail merchants sensed a potential threat and began to strike back. The retailers recognized that they must themselves cooperate to destroy cooperation, and in 1908 they formed a national retailers' association and opened their campaign against the cooperative movement.

Up to this point both the local cooperatives and the wholesaling KF bought their goods as individual merchants from the manufacturers. But now the retailers' association combined to persuade the cartels of manufacturers, first of margarine and then of other products, to refuse the normal wholesalers' commissions to the cooperatives. KF countered by buying a margarine factory to make its own supplies and issued a special appeal to the public to buy stock in the enterprise. The retailers tried to undermine their new competitors by price-cutting as well as by appeals to banks to refuse credit to the cooperatives. The attack against the cooperatives was so strong and so well publicized that its effect, according to Axel Gjöres, one of cooperation's most ardent and effective apostles, was to invigorate the movement rather than to kill it; cooperative members were made more aware of the economies at stake, and they clung all the more loyally to their societies.[18]

Economic advantage was the raison d'être of the cooperative movement, but something of a missionary spirit infused many of the early cooperators. Improving the economic condition of the poorer segments of society was surely a cause worthy of missionary effort. The cooperatives fought against profiteering prices, whether by manufacturers, wholesalers, or retailers. In fact, retailers may have been the least of the "enemies," although their extension of credit to customers was a mixed blessing. The cooperatives discouraged buying on credit, and they encouraged saving by members. They also made people more conscious of the quality of merchandise.

People who owned little else took pride in ownership of the cooperatives, and the principle of one member one vote (regardless of the number of shares owned) maintained democratic control. By the beginning of World War I cooperation in Sweden was a firmly established, growing movement. The war, with its financial strains and commodity shortages, stimulated such further growth that for a time the establishment of new societies had to be forbidden.

Although in the beginning the cooperative movement was often criticized as "petit bourgeois" it was approved by the Social Democratic party congress in 1901. Hjalmar Branting in 1909 regarded cooperation, along with the party and the labor unions, as one of the three chief weapons of social democracy.[19] Yet, although the movement was closely affiliated with both the labor unions and the Social Democratic party through overlapping membership and interlocking leadership, it clung adamantly to the forms of political neutrality. It was nevertheless something more than a mere economic organization. It was a folk movement with many of the characteristics of the free church movement, the temperance movement, and the labor movements, yet it was separate from these. It developed an educational program to instruct members in the principles of economics, and it brought people together to discuss their concerns and to manage their affairs. Young men and women often gained in the cooperative-society discussions their first experience in public speaking, and they were challenged to learn business methods because of the need to keep financial records and to buy goods wisely. Local societies held their members' meetings and chose delegates to regional meetings, and the regional meetings elected representatives to the national congress. The national congress in turn selected the directorate and determined policies. Like other folk movement societies, the cooperatives became schools in democracy. Success in the attainment of practical goals encouraged participation in general political activity and many active cooperators, of whom Axel Gjöres is an outstanding example, went on to attain high offices in the social democratic organizations and in the government. From its beginnings in the simple desire to improve the economic status of the weaker segment of the population the cooperative movement developed political ties and influence within the party that was soon to come to power. It also gained economic importance, especially during and after World War I. But it remained an independent force, and its devoted leadership, working for something more than personal profit, remained true to their primary purpose. The movement was destined to grow still stronger after the end of World War I.

### Political Parties and the Fight
### for Parliamentary Government

Disruptive issues that pulled people apart also provided a basis for special interest groups to associate themselves in pursuit of some immediate purpose. But alignments on questions of taxation or tariffs were frequently different from those on defense, and none of these necessarily brought together the advocates or the opponents of suffrage reform or any other issue. Various folk movements attracted people who were intensely concerned with church activity or temperance or trade unionism or cooperatives or sports or some other special interest. Although many of these interests might overlap, others were contradictory and it was clearly impossible to form any lasting associations on the basis of societies focused on special purposes. Yet for the community as a whole to function, and especially for the government of a democracy to be able to act, means had to be found to build a majority. Not necessarily a permanent majority, but certainly one that could survive through more than one issue.

Political parties are the organizations through which people unite for common action by compromising differences, subordinating lesser issues to greater, and trying to get and hold control of government.

At the time of the great riksdag reform of 1866 Louis De Geer, who abhorred the idea of political parties, thought he had constructed a system that would avoid them. He was soon disillusioned. However, the first parties of the post-1866 period were shifting and amorphous, and they existed only within the riksdag itself and only within each chamber separately. Not until the end of the century did real national parties come on stage. In this, as in many other political matters, Sweden was behind the times, significantly behind its neighbors Denmark and Norway.

The "government," that is, the king and his council of ministers, was supposed to continue after 1866 just as before. Karl XV had made it a condition of his approval of the reform that it would bring no change in relations between the executive and the legislative branches. The king appointed the ministers on the basis of his judgment of their abilities and their loyalty to him. It was immaterial whether they were members of one of the chambers of the riksdag, exactly as it was of no consequence (theoretically) what were their ideological leanings. They were nobles and they were bureaucrats like De Geer and Gripenstedt. As individuals they were appointed and as individuals they were dismissed. Not until 1905 did an entire ministry resign as a group.

An explanation may be useful here of the functions of ministers and their relations with the administrative departments of government. According to long-standing tradition the departments like justice, army, navy, and account-ing were independent agencies, comparable in their independence with the courts in the United States. Each agency was headed by a director-general. This was a prestigious and powerful position and a career post. The ministers, on the other hand, such as the minister of the navy and of education, were not directors of operations or personnel; they were, rather, advisers and policy makers. In the nineteenth century ministers of the council were commonly picked from the departmental bureaucracies; their experience of course stood them in good stead in their advisorial capacity, and they could return to their former posts at their own or the king's pleasure. But as ministers they stood and continue to stand in relation to the administrative departments somewhat as the regents or trustees of a university stand in relation to the operation of the educational program. In this framework it was quite natural to have consulta-tive ministers also, tied to no particular department. The functions of a minis-ter in the Swedish government thus differ from those of a cabinet member in Washington who combines both policy-making and administrative duties.

It was inevitable that this system created for monarchic convenience would be eroded if not smashed. The riksdag was bound to assert itself, and the ministers, although they were responsible to the king, had in their policy-making function to work with the riksdag. Therefore the king tried to appoint ministers who could cooperate, and the ministry as a whole had to be made an efficiently organized body. In 1876 a change was made to give the prime minister greater authority; the minister of state for justice was made prime minister and the justice post was made a separate portfolio. De Geer, now prime minister for the second time, showed great respect for the opinion of the riksdag and so during the 1890s did the quite conservative prime minister E. G. Boström. Most revealing was the situation under Count Arvid Posse, after the farmers' party (*Lantmannapartiet*) brought about De Geer's retire-ment in 1880. Posse was the first real party leader to be appointed prime minister, and he tried to build a cabinet at least partly from his Second Chamber group. But the farmers were timid and overly imbued with the sanctity of the separation of powers; they preferred to remain outside where they could criti-cize but need not share responsibility. Posse therefore ended with a ministry more solidly composed of nobles than the previous ones. And the farmers did indeed remain independent. In 1883 they defeated Posse on the defense question, and this ended Posse's career. The king returned to bureaucrats as prime ministers. Tension continued between riksdag and king and dualism between First Chamber and Second Chamber. The locus of power remained uncertain. The dream of parliamentary government was clearly impossible to realize while two parliamentary houses held equal power and different ideas. The king continued to dominate the government.

Meanwhile grass-roots movements were growing strong (see the previous section on the new folk movements), political concern was rising, and the Norwegian example was stimulating, for in Norway political parties were active and parliamentary government succeeded in 1884. In Sweden, outside the riksdag there were no parties until the social democrats organized in 1889. And this, oddly, was a party with no parliamentary base at all. It was a small but vociferous group with a radical program. At first the social democrats and various groups of liberals cooperated closely, notably in the "folk riksdags" of 1893 and 1896. The liberals encompassed such a broad spectrum of social groups, political philosophies, and special interests that they could not get together.

## THE RISE OF THE LIBERALS

In the Second Chamber the disparate liberal groups were able in 1900 to create, not a solid party, but the Liberal Coalition. Among the total number of groups that agreed to affiliate Douglas Verney identifies five elements: the liberal-minded segment of the farmer representation; the social reformers from a variety of backgrounds; Adolf Hedin and other committed radicals; nonconformist teetotalers; and intellectuals originating in the Verdandi student organization from Uppsala.[20] None of these groups had a solid and disciplined organization, each was open-ended. There was some overlapping of interest but also some conflict. For instance, some of the teetotalers were not in the least radical on anything else, and some of the intellectuals had little in common with the liberal farmers. They could all cooperate only as long as the party promoted their own special concerns. The alliance never "jelled" into a unified force.

The platform of the new coalition, or party, was reformist but mild, deliberately vague to draw in as many reform groups as possible. It succeeded in attracting numbers and this was its strength. But the numbers included such a wide range of opinions that this was also a weakness. The original platform merely called for things like factory inspection, collective bargaining and arbitration, sick pay, a state-supported home ownership plan, the franchise for all tax-paying men over twenty-five, and for Norway an equal voice in the Swedish-Norwegian Union's foreign affairs. Legislative beginnings had been made on several of these items and the list was far from revolutionary. But it did state a definite purpose of progressive change. Karl Staaff, one of the leaders in the organizing move and soon to become the head of the party, introduced an additional program thrust: Second Chamber preeminence and parliamentary government.

Karl Staaff was an initiator, an idealist and a fighter for his ideals. He fought for justice for man in society, undoubtedly strongly influenced by his upbringing in the home of his father, a teacher and preacher. As a student in Uppsala he had shown both his interests and his organizing talent as founder of the activist reform society Verdandi. As a lawyer in the 1890s he practiced the philosophy that everyone deserved a fair hearing as long as there was any chance he was in the right. His own sympathies were never hidden. In one of his most famous trials he came out strongly for the right of labor to organize, and the workingmen never forgot. He stressed the efforts

> To raise the physical-working class to an existence more worthy of their
> character as human beings of invaluable significance to society and cul-
> ture. . . . One of the mightiest levers for this purpose was [is] the building
> of labor unions.[21]

Staaff was brilliant and deeply committed, but he was also very sure of himself and occasionally arrogant. Since some of the other Liberal party leaders were less aggressive Staaff soon stood out as the real leader. In 1905 he was chosen as a consultative minister in the coalition government of Christian Lundeberg (Staaff was the first lawyer to join the king's council). In this interim ministry, chosen specifically to arrange the terms of separation with Norway, Staaff played a foremost role in the delicate negotiations. Oddly, it was the moderate and conciliatory spirit he displayed in this assignment that led King Oscar, albeit reluctantly, to tap him as the next prime minister. In a position where he had power, or at least thought he had, Staaff now showed himself urgent and uncompromising. The result, as noted in chapter XIV, was the defeat of his suffrage proposal and his resignation in the spring of 1906.

Staaff's appointment had been due to the strength of the liberal alliance in the new riksdag (106 seats) and was therefore to some degree a recognition of the parliamentary principle.[22] Similarly, when Staaff's suffrage reform was rejected the king was free to turn to the man he liked and trusted, who represented the conservative wing. "Admiral" Arvid Lindman had been trained as a naval officer and had sailed around the world, but he had left the navy early, had achieved a highly successful career as a "general director" in industry, and had entered the riksdag's First Chamber in 1904. In the Lundeberg ministry of 1905 he had been minister of naval affairs and when he became prime minister the king gave him his admiral's title. As head of government he sailed in heavy seas. His main support was in the First Chamber, and Staaff ridiculed him for trying to operate a "First Chamber parliamentarism." The conservative groups in that chamber were split into several factions, and Lindman's cabinet was a restless and impermanent collection. However, if he was not much of an admiral he was definitely a "captain of industry" and insisted that decisions be reached. He was determined to be no less a reformer than Staaff.[23] In this spirit he drove through the long-debated suffrage reform. Although it really pleased no one it did bring to the polls in 1911 thousands of new voters who (indirectly, of course) voted Lindman out of office, for most of these new voters were liberals and social democrats.

The long-standing cooperation between liberals and social democrats had survived a period of tension at the time of the Great Strike of 1909 (see section on trade unions). Staaff had thought it necessary to make a careful policy declaration in a speech at Eskilstuna on November 21, 1909: Both the employers in their lockout and the workers in their strike had broken agreements and were in the wrong. Society suffered, and loyalty to the whole society was most important; the labor unions seemed to think that loyalty to the laboring class was the highest right. And Staaff criticized the social democrats for supporting the unions in their wrong attitude; he feared that the social democrats had not fully cleaned out the anarchists from their ranks. The typographers' attempt by their strike to paralyze the free press in its job of spreading information and the exchange of ideas was anarchistic. If the social democrats expected to have agreements in the future in their ideal socialist state they must learn to abide by agreements. Liberals must make a choice between anarchy and domestic peace. Staaff answered those who objected that the liberals cooperated with the social democrats by saying that it was everyone's duty to work with others to reach positive goals as long as he did not abandon his principles. The liberals would work for social insurance, but this must be achieved by legal methods, not by anarchy — and anarchy is any attempt to change the social order by any other means than those provided by law.[24]

The speech brought strong rejoinders from the social democrats, including a speech by Branting, and from the radicals within the liberal ranks. Several critics attempted to justify the class-loyalty idea by saying that the time for loyalty to society had not yet arrived. Some defections occurred, but Staaff probably held within his party many others who were afraid that the Liberal party itself had gone too far to the left. Talk there was about a splitoff into a center party, but this soon ceased, for it was seen that it could benefit only the Right.

The upshot was that the Liberal party held together and continued to work for social legislation. The line of demarcation between liberals and social democrats had been drawn, but there was no breach between Staaff and Branting. And although in the election of 1908 the Liberals dropped to 98 seats in the Second Chamber they came back in 1911 with 102. The Social Democrats grew more spectacularly from 34 seats in 1908 to 64, and the conservative groups dropped from 98 to 64. Again the king, now Gustav V, had to turn to Karl Staaff, who offered to share power with the Social Democrats. But Hjalmar Branting preferred to retain a friendly independence. Staaff, with an assist from Lindman, persuaded the king to call a special election for the First Chamber under the new electoral laws, and this cost the right groups a drop in that house from 133 seats to 86 while the Liberals raised their total from 15 to 52 and the Social Democrats from 2 to 12. The Liberals had won a strong position in each house, though not a majority in either.

In defeat as well as in office Staaff remained head of the Liberal party. He was consciously following the British parliamentary example that he hoped to establish in Sweden. In fact, when he returned to the premiership in 1911 he often acted as if that British lower-house parliamentarism had already been attained. Gladstone was his great hero and the House of Commons was his ideal. He tended to forget that Swedish conditions were different. He assumed the superiority of the Second Chamber over the First. But the constitutional equality of the two chambers was solemnly affirmed in the Riksdag Ordinance of 1866, and both Oscar II and Gustav V were on solid ground when they asserted their constitutional right to appoint ministers and direct the government. Gustav, although he doubtless preferred to play tennis or bridge, was a proud monarch in an era of monarchic decline, fighting to maintain prestige and pushed by wife and friends. Staaff was a vigorous reformer, riding a rising tide, but so sanguine that he sometimes got ahead of that tide; he could not be bothered to cajole his king or even to treat him with ordinary respect. Clash of principles and clash of personalities continued to make the Liberal ministries of Staaff (1905–6 and 1911–14) periods of confrontation, the antithesis of the traditional Swedish "politics of compromise."

Nevertheless there was accomplishment, particularly in the field of social welfare. The establishment of the social welfare board and the system of old age pensions financed by a new public enterprise, the tobacco monopoly, laid the foundations of the welfare state during Staaff's period of office.[25] In his first ministry reforms in judicial procedure provided for the indeterminate sentence and conditional pardon. The fuller account of social reform must be considered later although it should be recorded here that it was the liberals who began it before the social democrats had the strength to put things through. In the extension of the suffrage it was the liberals who pushed it so effectively that the conservatives had to pass it, and, ironically, it was just this extension of suffrage that soon allowed the social democrats to oust not only Lindman and the conservatives but also their liberal benefactors. For the decline of Liberal power began in 1911.

The end came swiftly. The reason lay partly in the character of Karl Staaff, still more in a relentless chain of circumstance. Both liberals and social democrats were opposed to the military buildup in Sweden, but the coming of World War I swept the country into a nationalistic fervor and the turbulence of competitive armament. Logically it might be supposed that the current of opinion would have swung most violently against the social democrats, for they were more strongly antimilitarist than were the liberals. However, they were neither damned by being in the position of responsibility nor could they be criticized for being inconsistent; their following was not divided like that of the liberals.

Staaff's problem was that, while he wanted to avoid militarism and to save money for social welfare, the clouds over Europe were gathering ominously in 1911. As Staaff looked at the dark skies above he began to question his own stated policy. So he said he would await the report of a special commission on defense before acting. In the meantime he announced the stoppage of the F-boat construction. Later, as conditions changed he indicated some change of mind. His own party followers became confused and of divided opinions. And the commission whose report he awaited never made a report. Instead, the wave of national sentiment in Sweden that raised funds for the F-boat and that brought thousands to the palace yard to pledge allegiance to the king and national defense, plus the storm that broke over Europe in 1914, revealed Staaff's wavering policy as disastrous (see chapter XIV on defense, p. 400). Hence, as the suffrage issue had brought the collapse of the first Liberal ministry now the defense issue destroyed the second. In the special spring election of 1914 the Liberals dropped to 70 seats in the Second Chamber and in the regular fall election dropped further to 57. Both right and left gained at their expense.

The king's talk in the palace yard had brought things to a head. And the conflict between king and prime minister involved now not only defense but the constitutional question of parliamentary government. Could the king continue to use private advisers like Lindman and Ernst Trygger and Sven Hedin, or must he use only the advisers provided for in the constitutional structure? And was he required to get approval of speeches from the ministry? The issue was now as clearly drawn as Staaff could possibly have wished, yet even he did not realize this for several days. Which was supreme: monarchic independence or parliamentary authority? Staaff fell, but in falling he dramatized this unresolved issue — dramatized it but did not decide it.[26]

## THE SOCIAL DEMOCRATS

Social democracy came to Sweden before the country was ready for it, as Herbert Tingsten notes in his brilliant analysis of the movement.[27] The reason for the premature arrival was a man, a young tailor named August Palm who had been apprenticed at age ten and who soon journeyed to Denmark and Germany and became converted to socialism. He was a stormy petrel and was expelled from Germany in 1877 and imprisoned in Sweden soon after his return. In Malmö in 1882 he launched a socialist newspaper, *Folkviljan* (The Peoples' Will), and when he moved to Stockholm in 1885 he quickly started *Socialdemokraten*, and his penchant for founding newspapers continued to the end of his career. Mercilessly Palm attacked the economic order, the bureaucracy, and militarism. Both church and political authorities were aroused against him. On the constructive side Palm initiated, from prison, the congress of 1889 at which the Social Democratic party was born. He also wrote the party platform which was based on the Danish Gimle program, which in turn was based on the German Gotha statement of 1875. Palm insisted on democratic process as the way to achieve socialism. Nevertheless, he was such a disruptive influence that in 1892 Branting succeeded in having him declared unfit for a leading party position. As father of the Swedish social democratic movement he was an errant parent and in his later years devoted himself largely to campaigning against "temperance fanaticism."[28]

One of the early movers who was shrill without being creative was Hinke Bergegren, really an anarchist. In the socialist youth magazine *Brand*, which he edited, he said that "Our motto is — dagger in the flesh!" At the Social Democratic congress in 1891 he announced that "For my part I think small murders are excellent, and such assassinations put fear in the rulers of society. We should inject the poison named hate, so that we are ripe for whatever violence."[29] Such statements were too strong medicine for the Social Democrats, who disavowed Hinke in 1891 and expelled him from the party in 1906.

As it was August Palm who sparked the movement so it was Hjalmar Branting who tended the fire. In the early 1880s, as a student in Uppsala intimately associated with Karl Staaff, Branting became so concerned about the socialist cause that he left the university without a degree to devote himself full time to the promotion of socialism. He too was full of fiery phrases, and in an important talk of 1886 on "Why labor must be socialist" he took a wholly Marxist line on the class struggle, the materialistic interpretation of history, and the impoverishment of the masses; and he had scathing remarks to make about the "half-liberal eunuchs" who would be moderate. Yet with the passing years he himself moderated his views considerably. He was intelligent enough to see, for instance, that neither in Germany nor in Sweden was the worker becoming more impoverished with advancing industrialism. Nationalism seemed to him to be something worth saving, and therefore defense was necessary; there could be no one-country disarmament. In other words, he was a convinced socialist, but he was an independent thinker and he was definitely a Swede, therefore not doctrinaire and not subservient to foreign ideologies.

Throughout his later years this strong and reasonable man had to carry on a constant struggle with the extremists in his party, but he won an unassailable prestige. The party grew steadily, rapidly, not relaxing its principles but cooperating in constructive ways with Karl Staaff and the liberals. In 1896 Branting was elected to the riksdag on a liberal list. "In the struggle for democratic government liberals and social democrats united in a cooperation that sharpened the social reform will of the liberals and softened the social democrats' demands for social revolution."[30] A comparative biography of Staaff and Branting would probably show that their early acquaintanceship at Uppsala had much to do with shaping that long and fruitful cooperation. Uppsala and the Verdandi Society had at least as great an influence on Sweden as did Eton on England. With regard to Staaff and Branting it was of momentous significance that their differences in outlook were just enough to lead them into two different parties that could each go its own way and yet cooperate.

Branting more than any other determined the character of Swedish social democracy; with firmness he piloted the ship and kept it on course. He could tack in stormy weather, he could yield, but just enough, to the whims of his oft-restless crew. He was strong enough that he could listen to others before making decisions. In him was a touch of greatness: good judgment combined with warmth, human kindness, and cultural interests (he wrote theater reviews). Branting was the first Social Democrat elected to the riksdag, and it was six years later before three companions joined him. His piercing eyes, his bristling mustache, his clear and ready words of wisdom distinguished him at international conferences and led to his becoming head of the first Social Democratic government in Sweden — the first one anywhere to be peacefully elected to office.

Not only Branting but all the leaders and editors of the social democratic papers were profoundly influenced by socialism abroad. They read the theoretical literature and they kept up with events in the countries that were further advanced than Sweden in industrialization and labor organization. They attended international conferences and made friends in other lands. They were perhaps more internationally minded than bankers and businessmen. The Swedes were particularly attracted by the social legislation in Germany and by the German ideologists — so much so that as World War I began the pro-German groups in Sweden were composed of an odd assortment of army officers, aristocrats, some intellectuals, *and* socialist leaders. Branting was one of the few whose strong ties were with Britain rather than with Germany.

The first definitely Swedish social democratic program was formulated in 1897, chiefly by Branting and Axel Danielsson. Its roots lay in the Erfurt program of 1891 but it modified much of that German statement in a Swedish direction, and it modified almost every point of the Marxism it professed. These modifications became more dominant in the coming years. For example, agriculture in Sweden was not moving toward centralization, and the overwhelming numbers of Swedish small farmers could not be disregarded. Nor could they be classed together with the workers in the cities. Even in industry the pattern in Sweden was one of considerable decentralization. Revolutionary rhetoric remained, but the social democratic program turned its attention to improving the life of the poor, providing pensions, social insurance, benefits to the unemployed, temperance, better status for illegitimate children — and a host of similar practical social reform projects.

A factor of supreme importance in the shift of social democratic ideology and tactics was that the leaders discovered that the rulers of the state did not lock the doors against them. The authorities looked askance and were sometimes fearful, but they allowed the radicals to publish their papers and make their speeches; only in extreme circumstances did police and courts intervene. And when Branting took his place in the riksdag a toehold was gained within the structure of the establishment. The dyed-in-the-wool revolutionaries objected to this kind of participation, but they were in a minority. More and more the party leadership became convinced that they could accomplish their objectives by working within the system. Their first and basic demand was for universal suffrage, and they found that the liberals were already working for that; working together they traversed a long distance toward their goal in the period 1907–11. As Branting made clear, socialism would come with social revolution, but this did not necessarily require violence nor did it have to be immediate. The social revolution could be a gradual transformation, an evolution, understood to be under the leadership of the social democratic working class. However, as the party grew it absorbed many who had only the weakest concept of ideology, who were interested only in social improvements.

The idea of the disappearance of the middle class itself gradually disappeared, along with the idea of social catastrophe. Cooperation proved to be possible, first in the folk riksdags of 1893 and 1896, and after that social reformism became the main thrust. Branting came to think of social reform as a way to socialism. Hence, even the necessity of state ownership became questionable. The fundamental thing was improvement of the conditions of life, and the theoretical means to that end became less important than the practical. This line of policy led to the success of the workers' protective laws of 1912, the general pension insurance of 1913, and other constructive pieces of legislation. By gradualism the social revolution was making progress even before 1914.

As for the Social Democratic party itself the statistics tell a dramatic story. Primary membership was in a local society which was in turn a member of a local "commune." Each commune was entitled to send a delegate to the national congress, the supreme authority of the party. It was a well-planned democratic organization. The number of individual members of the party stood as follows:

| | |
|---|---|
| 1889 just above | 3,000 |
| 1892 just above | 5,600 |
| 1895 just above | 10,000 |
| 1905 just above | 67,000 |
| 1915 just above | 86,000 |

And the number of representatives in the riksdag grew likewise.

| | Second Chamber | First Chamber |
|---|---|---|
| 1896 | 1 | |
| 1902 | 4 | |
| 1905 | 13 | |
| 1908 | 34 | |
| 1911 | | 12 |
| 1912 | 64 | |
| 1914 (I) | 73 | |
| 1914 (II) | 87 | |
| 1917 | 97 | |
| 1919 | | 49 |

Basically the party prospered because it represented the rapidly growing and self-conscious industrial worker segment in society. And its opposition became increasingly divided. Growth was not quite as smooth as it looked. Party discipline and esprit de corps were strong, and the social democrats presented through the years a more solid phalanx than either the liberals or the conservatives who split into various combinations and changed their party names from time to time. Nevertheless, despite continuity of leadership and program (or perhaps because of these?) rebellions and defections occurred in social democratic ranks, too. In the 1890s Hinke Bergegren's anarchistic ideas won converts and the congress of 1891 voted against them only 28 to 11, with 12 neutrals. Youth groups had long been more radical than the elders of the party and in 1917 embraced strong impulses from communism. The Left Socialists then split off from the parent party; after 1921, however, those who did not become communist rejoined the fold. Actually, the degree of membership maintenance was phenomenal.

On one ideological point the social democrats never gave up — nor did they succeed in winning it, namely, disestablishment of the state church. Most of the leaders professed themselves to be atheist, and if they nevertheless had their children confirmed in the state church it could be attributed to the fact that this was merely a social custom. But the antireligious propaganda was strong, not only that based on Karl Marx but that based on the pattern of life in Sweden. The church and its ministers recognized a special relationship to the state: they were civil servants both as ministers of the gospel and as registrars of marriages, births, deaths, and migration. Some of them tended to be somewhat high and mighty and to antagonize the laboring lower classes. Church attendance varied greatly in different regions and different parishes, and the taking of communion was rare in some. But at Christmas and Easter people flocked to the services, and in the rural districts at Midsummer also. Most social democrats continued to use Christian services for marriages, funerals, baptisms, and confirmations. August Palm himself had his children baptized. And as late as the 1970s, when a government commission recommended the disestablishment of the church the objections from the general population were so strong that the plan was abandoned — or at least postponed.

The early socialist clubs talked much about the abolition of the state church, and the socialists denounced dogmatic Christianity. Priests were damned for their elitist attitude and for wanting to keep the lower classes in ignorance — not very appropriate propaganda for the Swedish situation. Clerical control of the schools was severely criticized. August Palm talked of the priests as being fat with assured salaries, examples of parasites living off the poor workers. Socialist meetings were often held on Good Friday or on Sundays at the regular church hour. Socialists staged their own burials, but frequently a Christian funeral would follow the next day. It becomes extremely difficult to evaluate the depth and extent of this love-hate relationship between people and church.[31]

The free churches were treated much more gently by the radicals than were the state churches. Naturally so, because the dissenting groups were mainly among the poorer elements of the population and their leaders were completely lacking in the authoritarian manner or elitist attitude. The Salvation Army gained an extraordinary position of strength in Sweden and was clearly sympathetic toward the working classes and the poor.

Churchmen of course fulminated bitterly against the radicals. They abominated the materialism avowed by the socialists and were horrified at the antigodly pronouncements of the wilder ones. While they preached individual loving-kindness they were inimical to attempts by means of social legislation to better conditions of the broad masses. Nathan Söderblom, one of Sweden's greatest theologicans, was one of the few clerics who spoke out against the church as a tool for the wealthy.[32] The churchmen knew that in the regions where socialism was strongest the antagonism toward the church was greatest, and that where socialism was defeated the attitude toward the church was most positive. The feelings of King Gustav as late as 1909 probably reflect the thought of many. Gustav was talking with Staaff and remarked that he was appalled at the thought that the Social Democrats might come into the government and that "This will be impossible with the program they have — republic, denial of God, etc."[33] Staaff could only assure him that it was bound to happen. Gradually the violence of words toned down, but the suspicions and antagonisms remained.

This was, in essence, one of the irreconcilable conflicts because it was based on fundamentally opposite value systems. The best that could be hoped for was a modus vivendi or a hands-off policy advocated by Nathan Söderblom long before he became archbishop. In the 1890s he said that the church should avoid taking a stand for or against opposing political groups so that it would be able to continue to work with whatever kind of government might come to power. The more positive form of Christian socialism did not take root in Sweden but, largely because of the tolerant policy pursued by the liberal and conservative elements, the original materialistic and revolutionary brand of socialism was itself modified.

The relationship of the Social Democratic party and the labor unions has been intimate from the beginnings of each. Social democracy was nurtured within the labor movement, although not all union members were socialists. In 1889 the Social Democratic society of Stockholm invited all labor organizations to send delegates to the congress to create the Social Democratic Workers Party. In 1894, as the idea spread to build a central organization of labor unions, the social democrats worked actively for it, and in 1898 the federation was created — *Landsorganisation* (LO). As of that date the Social Democratic party registered 350 unions as members and 20 political societies. Branting emphasized the singleness of purpose of these two great national organizations, the one in the economic realm the other in the political. And LO voted at its first congress to require all of its associated unions to become members of the Social Democratic party within three years. This "force rule" disturbed many, though Branting spoke of it as "force to freedom." The rule kept some unions from joining the party, and opposition to it was strong enough that two years later the rule was modified into a mere recommendation for collective membership; six years after that permission was given for individual members of an affiliated union to dissociate themselves from the party.

In the 1920s communists and others tried to get a regulation forbidding collective union membership in any political party, but this move did not succeed. In practice it developed that about one-third of local unions affiliated collectively with the party and that of the total membership of the party three-quarters belonged also to trade unions, either individually or collectively affiliated.[34]

The democratic breakthrough, urgently pressed by a minority in the early nineteenth century, won an empty victory in 1866. Stagnation and apathy followed, only gradually to be overcome by new impulses welling up from the masses of the people. Population pressure, vitalizing religious movements, fresh socioeconomic ideas from abroad, vigorous leadership in the liberal and social democratic political ranks, in the trade unions, and in the cooperative movement — these forces and more transformed the political scene in the early twentieth century. Democracy came to life in Sweden. An industrial breakthrough paralleled the political — and perhaps helped cause it.

# XVI

## THE INDUSTRIAL BREAKTHROUGH

THE VIGOROUS MERCANTILE ECONOMY of the early eighteenth century had withered by the early nineteenth century. Progress was apparent in little besides agricultural reorganization and education. Several agricultural and technical schools were started in the 1820s and the 1830s, including the Technological Institute (1825) which became Tekniska Högskolan in 1877. The first folk high school appeared in 1868. A few outstanding personalities in the cultural realm, notably Esaias Tegnér and E. G. Geijer, brightened the scene somewhat. Political protest broke forth occasionally in the press and in some rioting (the *rabulism*) of 1838, but opposition was easily suppressed. The slow pressures of liberalism finally achieved the riksdag reform of 1866, which proved to be a hollow victory. Generally speaking passivity and poverty were the hallmarks of the first half of the nineteenth century.

In the world beyond Sweden's borders stirring developments were changing the material condition of men. Industry was revolutionizing the face of England. In the United States people were taking their covered wagons into the Mississippi Valley and, after 1848, on to the sunshine and the gold fields of California. Steamboats were replacing sailing ships, and railroads were spreading from city to city in Europe and across the plains of America. In Sweden the most obvious area of growth was in population until, some time after mid-century, Sweden too began to move into the modern industrial era.

No beating of drums or ringing of bells announced the industrial breakthrough. In fact, who knows when the catalytic moment occurred? Was it in 1846 when the guilds were abolished? Was it ten years later with the opening of Sweden's first railroad and the establishment of Stockholm's Enskilda Bank? Or in 1866 with the Industrial Exhibition in Stockholm? Or with the production boom of the early 1870s? Perhaps it should date from the

Sundsvall strike of sawmill workers in 1879 or from the founding of the Social Democratic Party in 1889? Or did the moment come with one of the stimulative inventions such as Alfred Nobel's discovery of dynamite in 1863, Gustaf de Laval's steam turbine around 1890, or the successive new methods of smelting iron between the 1850s and the 1890s? This much is clear: industrialization in Sweden lagged considerably behind that in Germany, Britain, and the United States.

Although development was late, with the transition into industrialism coming somewhere in the last third of the nineteenth century (compared with a hundred years earlier in England, at least a generation earlier in Germany and the United States, and a decade or two later in Japan and Russia), it came in Sweden with vigor and with a firm foundation to build on. As in other countries growth was marked by spurts and setbacks, but the trend was strongly positive. To discover the reasons for Sweden's late start and rapid development is difficult. It is nevertheless clear that progress was associated with a growing and industrious population, the presence of basic raw materials in mines and forests, a highly productive agriculture, fortunate investment potential and policies, timely inventions, and entrepreneurial leadership. The very fact that other countries had begun industrialization earlier was a boon to Swedish development — for instance, English demand for Swedish oats, timber, and iron provided profitable markets, while accumulated English and French capital was available for investment in Swedish railways and factories. The process of economic growth became therefore spectacularly successful so that "by the end of the 1920s Sweden had become a fully mature society, ready for the welfare state and the age of durable consumer goods." [1] In a still broader view, one of the poorer countries of Europe in the early nineteenth century became in the later twentieth century one of the most prosperous countries of the world, if not the most prosperous (disregarding some oil-rich sheikhdoms).

How did it happen?

## Population and the Transformation of the Work Force

The Great Transformation was based on a superabundant population searching for the means to support its growth. Even as emigration skimmed off over a million people the vigorous Swedes kept on increasing. No one in the nineteenth century, in contradistinction to the eighteenth and the twentieth, needed to plead for more babies.

The story of population growth is quickly seen in statistics. In the 1750s the birth rate was 35 per thousand, in the 1850s it was 30, and in the 1950s it had dropped to 16. But the death rate was declining even more significantly. In the 1750s deaths were 27 per thousand, in the 1850s down to 22, and in the 1950s to 10. From a slightly different view we can consider the figures for life expectancy: in 1850 about 47 years, in 1900 about 52, and in 1975 about 75 (one of the highest in the world). In absolute figures the population was 1.78 million in 1750, 3.13 million in 1850, 4.03 million in 1900, 7.04 million in 1950, and reached 8.177 million in 1975. Despite minor fluctuations, such as in the disaster years 1867–69, the major trends held steady. The rate of increase was not significantly different from that in other western European countries, but it was felt poignantly in nineteenth-century Sweden because of the meager resources available and the lack of flexibility in the economy. A high birth rate was possible in the early part of the nineteenth century because of "peace, vaccine, and potatoes," and in the later nineteenth century because of the safety valve of emigration. However, before the middle of the twentieth century the problem had reversed itself. Many became frightened at the warnings from Alva and Gunnar Myrdal about declining nativity in Sweden, and Folke Borg published a book entitled *Ett döende folk* (A Dying Nation). The statistics were indeed startling, indicating that Sweden in 1935 held the world's record for low birth rate; it had fallen from 23.6 per thousand in 1920 to 13.7 per thousand, and deaths exceeded births by 3 percent. Further decline was projected to 1990.[2] Actually, total population continued to grow slightly, not because of the birth of Swedish babies but because of immigration from across the Baltic and from southern Europe. The expanding economy required workers for the factories and the service occupations in the cities, and they flocked to Sweden from abroad, until about 10 percent of the population was foreign-born — a spectacular turnabout from the situation in the early years of the century. Certain large industrial concerns, ASEA for instance, found that a majority of their workers were foreigners and that their directions for jobs had to be written in foreign languages, Finnish in particular. In a variety of ways Sweden experienced the problems of immigration that the United States had faced a few generations before.

Occurring simultaneously with the population shifts were significant shifts in the identification of workers with different sectors of the economy, as illustrated in the accompanying table.

This minimization of workers engaged in the primary occupations and proliferation of manufacturing and service workers reveal the revolution that was taking place in the economy and society. Improved technology, especially machines and fertilizers, made it possible for 8 farmers to produce more food than 72 had produced a few decades earlier. But that did not free 64 men to go fishing. The new technology itself required 40 workers to make the tools and supply the fertilizers and the energy that so enhanced the productivity of

SWEDEN'S HISTORIC
PROVINCES

• KIRUNA

LAPPLAND

NORRBOTTEN  HAPARANDA
• LULEÅ

VÄSTER-
BOTTEN

• UMEÅ

JÄMTLAND  ÅNGERMAN-
          LAND
• ÖSTERSUND
          • ÖRNSKÖLDSVIK
    MEDELPAD

HÄRJEDALEN
          • SUNDSVALL
    HÄLSING-
    LAND

• MORA

DALARNA  GÄSTRIK-
• FALUN   LAND• GÄVLE

      • ÖREBRO
VÄRMLAND  VÄSTMAN-   UPPLAND      ÅLAND
• KARLSTAD  LAND    • UPPSALA
                    • VÄSTERÅS
      NÄRKE
DALS-      SÖDER-
LAND      MANLAND  • STOCKHOLM
BOHUSLÄN

          • NORRKÖPING
VÄSTER-  ÖSTER-
GÖTLAND  GÖTLAND
• GOTHENBURG
  • BORÅS
  • JÖNKÖPING
HALLAND        • VISBY  GOTLAND

    SMÅLAND

    • VÄXJÖ
    • KALMAR    ÖLAND

SKÅNE
BLEKINGE
• LUND
• MALMÖ

Distribution of Swedish Population by Occupational Category, 1870–1970

| Year | Population | Agriculture Fishing Forestry | Industry Mining Crafts | Communication Transportation Commerce | Services Professions |
|---|---|---|---|---|---|
| 1870 | 4,170,000 | 72% | 15% | 5% | 8% |
| 1900 | 5,136,000 | 55 | 28 | 10 | 7 |
| 1930 | 6,142,000 | 39 | 36 | 18 | 7 |
| 1950 | 7,042,000 | 25 | 43 | 22 | 10 |
| 1970[a] | 8,081,000 | | | | |
| | 3,404,000 (economically active)[b] | 8 | 40 | 27 | 25 |
| | | 277,000 | 1,373,000 | 906,000 | 848,000 |
| 1870 | | 3,017,000 | 610,000 | 217,000 | 325,000 |
| 1900 | | 2,828,000 | 1,426,000 | 535,000 | 347,000 |
| 1930 | | 2,417,000 | 2,195,000 | 1,117,000 | 413,000 |
| 1950 | | 1,729,000 | 3,007,000 | 1,592,000 | 714,000 |

*Sources:* for 1870–1950, *Historisk statistik för Sverige,* I, p. 29; for 1970, *Nordisk statistisk årsbok, 1974,* Tables 6, 12.
   [a] As of 1970 figures comprising families and dependents were no longer issued; the proportions as shown for the economically active were, however, closely comparable with the earlier figures based on both workers and dependents.
   [b] An additional 9,000 were economically active but it is not known what their occupations were.

Note that if we combine the last two columns in the table the statistics are easily applicable to the schema and terminology of Colin Clark.[3] In this somewhat simplified form we see that the primary occupations (agriculture, fishing, forestry) in 1870 required 72 percent of the work force, the secondary occupations (industry, mining, crafts) used 15 percent, and the tertiary occupations (communications, commerce, services and professions) demanded 13 percent. One hundred years later the primary occupations used 8 percent instead of 72, the secondary 40 percent instead of 15, and the tertiary 52 percent rather than 13.

the remaining 8 farmers; furthermore, it called for 47 assistants and super-visors in the form of government clerks and officials, teachers, doctors, com-munication personnel, and on and on, to keep the complex process function-ing. The earlier so-called Industrial Revolution was mild compared to this sweeping transformation of the economic and social structure. The transfor-mation went beyond expanded population and shifts in occupation. It involved a vast migration from country to city, disruption of long-established relation-ships among people and between people and nature — the social and psychological ramifications have been far-reaching and are only now begin-ning to be understood. Yet the process, though rapid in a historical sense, was not really sudden.

## Progress in Agriculture

In the late eighteenth century and in the nineteenth century the population was uncomfortably large and ways had to be sought to alleviate distress. The response was a drive to make agriculture more efficient. As already discussed, this involved in the first instance replacement of the village system by indi-vidualized farms, but it went farther. There can be little doubt that the changes in farming methods stimulated psychological changes in the farmers them-selves. They were shaken out of their traditional practices, jolted into doing things more on their own initiative. They earned a little money, bought oxen and rented them out, took up handicrafts as business ventures, and adopted more liberal ideas. Such things were instigated by the land surveyors who plotted the new farm units, by ministers and lower officials, and by the spread of education. Thus one kind of change led to other kinds.

As children increasingly grew to maturity instead of dying in infancy, more acreage in crops was required. Therefore in Småland boys were put to work grubbing rocks out of fields, and in Värmland swamps were drained and forests were cut back to make room for potato patches. Farms were sub-divided and the land used for cultivation expanded more than fourfold during the nineteenth century. Gradually mechanization was introduced, especially after 1865. Improved fertilizing methods were introduced. County agricul-tural societies, government-paid research for soil analysis, and direct sub-sidies all helped improve agriculture. Root crops were introduced to make the wasteful fallow period unnecessary. Sugar beets became an important prod-uct, with the annual harvest increasing from a mere 15,000 tons in the late 1700s to 1.767 million tons a century later; this satisfied the Swedish sweet tooth and relieved the burden of importing cane sugar.

As a result of concerted effort cropland use expanded greatly, up to 1920 (see accompanying tabulation). Grassland was simultaneously reduced, until it accounted for only 1.5 percent of area in 1973. Forest and wooded grazing land, on the other hand, increased from 42 percent to 52 percent of total area.

|  | Cropland (in hectares) | Percentage of Total Area |
|---|---|---|
| 1800 | 850,000 | 2.1 |
| 1850 | 2,025,000 | 4.9 |
| 1900 | 3,520,000 | 8.6 |
| 1920 | 3,820,000 | 9.4 |
| 1973 | 2,980,000 | 6.6 |

*Sources: Historisk statistik*, II, p. 33; *Nordisk statistisk årsbok, 1974*, Tables 39, 40.

That land was being utilized more carefully, more scientifically, was indicated not only by expansion of acreage but by the increase of yield in relation to seed. The most notable developments shown in the table on harvested crops are the spectacular increase in wheat raising; the rapid expansion of the potato crop, rising by 1973 to almost 40 times that of 1802 (Swedish potatoes are commonly small and sweet and very tasty with fish); and the sudden expansion of the barley crop in the third quarter of the twentieth century (barley is excellent for feeding pigs).

The livestock census (see accompanying tabulation) displays some extraordinary developments. The small broad-shouldered work horses numbered 400,000 at the beginning of the nineteenth century and 700,000 during World War I; then rapidly the automobile pushed them off the roads and Bolinder-Munktell tractors displaced them in the fields. Goats lost their popularity and dropped from 180,000 in the 1840s to 7,000 by the 1960s, after which the *Statistisk årsbok* neglected the poor beasts altogether. Reindeer declined from about 232,000 in 1900 to about 164,000 in 1940. Sheep for their much-needed wool held their own through the nineteenth century at over a million but in the twentieth century their numbers declined drastically. Cattle were important for both meat and milk products, and their number grew to over 2.5 million in the early decades of the twentieth century, then fell off in the 1960s. Decline in numbers was partially offset by improvement in size and quality.

Butter, cheese, and meat became especially significant because of the changing pattern of international trade. Food products for about a generation earned a large share of Sweden's foreign exchange. In the period from the 1830s to the 1890s Sweden had rather surprisingly become a major exporter of cereals — especially oats for the horses that pulled the trams in London and for the porridge of English industrial workers. In the 1880s wheat from the

Harvested Crops (in metric tons)

| Year | Wheat | Oats | Rye | Barley | All Grains | Yield in Relation to Seed | Potatoes |
|---|---|---|---|---|---|---|---|
| 1802 | 14,000 | 105,000 | 140,000 | 165,000 | 495,000 | 4½ | 44,000 |
| 1820 | 20,000 | 119,000 | 213,000 | 209,000 | 654,000 | 5 | 216,000 |
| 1848/50[a] | 48,000 | 209,000 | 366,000 | 282,000 | 1,090,000 | 6 | 624,000 |
| 1900 | 146,000 | 1,045,000 | 677,000 | 333,000 | 2,641,000 | 7 | 1,630,000 |
| 1950 | 739,000 | 807,000 | 244,000 | 210,000 | 2,689,000 | 9 | 1,734,000 |
| 1973 | 1,335,000 | 1,209,000 | 322,000 | 1,768,000 | 4,800,000 | | 947,000 |

Sources: *Historisk statistik*, II, Tables E16, E19; *Nordisk statistisk årsbok, 1974*, Tables 43, 42.
[a] Annual average for 1848, 1849, and 1850.

rich new fields of America began to reach Europe in quantity and destroyed the markets for the more expensively produced grains of Scandinavia. By the end of the nineteenth century Sweden was importing 30 percent of its grain (especially wheat) and building up a dependence on foreign sources that caused hardship during World War I when the supply routes were disrupted. It was in the changing circumstances of the late nineteenth century, and primarily because of external circumstances, that the Swedes like the Danes (only to a lesser extent) shifted their efforts from grain raising to animal husbandry.

|      | Horses  | Cattle    | Sheep     | Pigs      |
|------|---------|-----------|-----------|-----------|
| 1820 | 416,000 | 1,600,000 | 1,350,000 | 470,000   |
| 1900 | 533,000 | 2,580,000 | 1,260,000 | 805,000   |
| 1950 | 440,000 | 2,650,000 | 280,000   | 1,263,000 |
| 1973 | 52,000  | 1,890,000 | 347,000   | 2,455,000 |

Sources: Historisk statistik, II, pp. 61, 62; Nordisk statistisk årsbok, 1974, Table 46.

The pressures from outside had far-reaching effects on the farmers' position politically as well as economically and involved a whole complex of problems such as emigration, protectionism, and government aid for farm ownership — problems that had to be dealt with separately.

Progress in agriculture was paralleled in almost every sector of economic activity, at first slowly, then in increasing tempo. Stimulating winds of change were blowing.

## Improvement in Transportation

For several generations plans had been mooted to facilitate transportation between eastern and western Sweden, especially between Stockholm and Gothenburg. Christopher Polhem had actually started constructing a canal across the country, utilizing the two great lakes Vänern and Vättern and following the geologic formation through what had been a sound or channel before 7000 B.C. (See chapter I). Karl XIV Johan became interested in this Göta Canal and Baltzar von Platen was ready to undertake the job, which required fifty-eight locks. (It was the great era of canal building in England and the United States; the Erie Canal, for example, was constructed between 1817 and 1825.) The Göta canal was opened in the fall of 1832 and it was for decades an important traffic artery, continuing into the late twentieth century primarily as a leisurely and picturesque tourist route.

Railway building was slow. But at last in 1853 a policy was decided upon and the following year Nils Ericson (brother of John Ericsson of *Monitor* fame) was given the job of directing construction. The state would lay and administer the main lines and leave the building of the branch and smaller lines to private initiative. As it turned out municipalities did more than individuals, who hesitated to invest in such dubious ventures. Ericson, who had worked on the Göta Canal in his youth, proved to be a farsighted planner. He envisioned the entire national system and laid out his lines not merely to connect existing cities with one another but to open up new areas. Railroad building therefore led to locational shifts of population and a broader base for future industrial development. The removal of local tolls and taxes (in 1864) stimulated commercial agriculture and the growth of small manufacturing and service centers at the junctions of developing rail lines, at something like twenty-mile intervals — for example, the towns of Hässleholm, Bjuv, Höganäs, Olofström. When Ericson left his post in 1862 the network of roads was well on its way; the Stockholm-Gothenburg line was complete, as were several shorter routes. For reasons of both defense and expense the line up the east coast was built back from the shore while short feeder lines connected the main line with the towns along the Gulf of Bothnia. Financing proved more difficult than engineering, partly because of lack of experience with large-scale foreign loans. Up to 1914, nevertheless, the state, with the aid of loans abroad, invested 400 million kronor for about one third of the trackage built, and state loans aided a significant proportion of the remaining two-thirds of private lines.

Railroad building had at first surprisingly little effect on the iron and steel industries, for only about 1 percent of domestic iron and steel production was used by the railways. However, this situation changed as construction advanced. Ericson wanted the process of development to aid the total national economy and hence ordered "850 tons of rail from Motala Verkstad at a price that exceeded by 20 percent the price of English rail delivered to Swedish ports in 1861."[4] But Swedish ironworks were small and could not adjust to the irregularities of the orders. Furthermore, the high-quality Swedish pig iron made from charcoal was too valuable for export to be used in steel for rails. In the period 1860–1914, therefore, 86 percent of the rails as well as 95 percent of the coal for the railroads had to be imported. Rolling stock was at first bought from Germany and England, and later Swedish firms copied these cars and locomotives exactly, following the same policy used a bit later by the Japanese. Much of the smaller equipment was manufactured in Sweden where from 15 to 30 percent of the engineering industry was occupied with the railroad program for several years, giving a boost to that industry. The effect on the labor market was considerable, and the new construction jobs slowed emigration to a certain extent. The major periods of railway building occurred in the years 1870–82 and 1897–1910. The densest network was in Skåne, but one of the roads most vital for economic development was that from Luleå through Kiruna and across to Norway to carry the iron ore from the Kiruna-Gällivare mines to Narvik and the Atlantic transportation routes.

The coming of steamships was also slow but further stimulated economic development. The Englishman Samuel Owen put the first steamer on Lake Mälar in 1818 and by 1850 Sweden had 67 steamships, more than any other European country, and was on the way to a gradual changeover from sail (see accompanying table). Soon hundreds of small steamers were plying the inner lakes and the Baltic. Early in the twentieth century the descendants of the Vikings created the Swedish-American Line which until the 1970s carried immigrants and tourists as well as cargo across the Atlantic. The Swedes developed a large general cargo fleet, although never as large as Norway's.

The Swedish Merchant Fleet, 1870–1973 (in metric tons)

| Year | Steam, Motor, Turbine | Sail |
|------|------|------|
| 1870 . . . . . . . . . . | 28,000 | 254,000 |
| 1890 . . . . . . . . . . | 141,000 | 320,000 |
| 1900 . . . . . . . . . . | 325,000 | 289,000 |
| 1910 . . . . . . . . . . | 593,000 | 177,000 |
| 1920 . . . . . . . . . . | 712,000 | 121,000 |
| 1930 . . . . . . . . . . | 1,144,000 | 72,000 |
| 1940 . . . . . . . . . . | 983,000 | 64,000 |
| 1950 . . . . . . . . . . | 1,432,000 | 49,000 |

*Source: Historisk statistik,* III, p. 65.

With the arrival of the automobile age two Swedish companies, Volvo and SAAB, made cars for the Swedish market first and soon began to compete vigorously for foreign sales. SAAB, incidentally, was an offshoot of the firm that built planes for the Swedish air force.

The new means of transportation, railroads especially, had been looked forward to by the peddlers and the handicrafts people who anticipated ease in reaching wider markets. To their chagrin they discovered that the improvements were so great that they threatened the existence of the peddlers; they encouraged mass production and large-scale shipments which outcompeted the operations of small businesses — just one example of how invention and development may produce surprising results.

### Forest-based Industry

An essential precondition for take-off into the industrial age was the development of one or more substantial manufacturing sectors. Sweden produced two, the first of which was timber. The forests had stood there for centuries, pine and spruce and birch stretching for miles after miles. The wood had been used for buildings and ships and furniture and toys and fuel, even for plows and spoons. But it had not been exported in quantity, partly because other countries too grew trees and their need for import was small. England's greater need for wood (for houses, pitprops, masts, and other items) could be met by Norway and Canada, both of which were more accessible than Sweden to this market.

But by the mid-nineteenth century, with the growth of population and industry in western Europe, additional supplies were required. The limited resources of Norway were being used to the limit, and Britain and other countries had to look farther afield — to Sweden, Finland, and Russia. Sweden was ready to respond. Steamships were making transportation cheaper and more dependable, railways were improving land transport. Sweden's northern rivers were peculiarly well suited for flotation of logs. Trees could be cut in winter and the trimmed logs taken to the river banks or onto the ice. Since the rivers flowed southeast the ice melted first in the lower regions, gradually farther and farther upstream, thus releasing the logs in an easy and steady sequence so they could be "harvested" downstream. The major problem was to clear the streams for the driving of the logs. Steam sawmills were established, beginning in 1848, especially at the mouths of the rivers, and the forests provided ample wood for fuel to produce the steam. Water power was also used. For transport to foreign markets Sweden's growing fleet of steamships, 368 by 1870, was ready.

Thus the processing and export of sawn and planed lumber boomed; after doubling in the years 1832–50 export quintupled between 1850 and 1875 and doubled again from 1875 to 1900. Safety matches were invented by Gustaf Pasch in 1846, at first hand-manufactured by teams of men, women, and children, and became an important export in the 1860s. A mill for mechanical wood pulp was in operation at Trollhättan in 1857 and chemical pulp was developed in the 1870s. Manufacture of paper became significant by 1870. All this development was aided by the abolition of British preferential tariffs on wood in 1842 and the Swedish abandonment of restrictions on sawing in the same year. The industry grew so rapidly that more and more capital was needed, and this led to the building of share-capital corporations; Korsnäs was created in 1855, Mo and Domsjö and others in the 1870s. To indicate how rapidly the Swedes took to the ways of industrial capitalism it might be added that there were proposals for cartelization, and in 1883 the Swedes tried to get a production-limitation agreement with Finland and Russia.[5]

Obviously the early products of this burgeoning timber industry were only a short step removed from the raw material stage, but their production required improved transportation, aggregations of capital, and a sizeable labor force.

# NORTHERN RIVERS

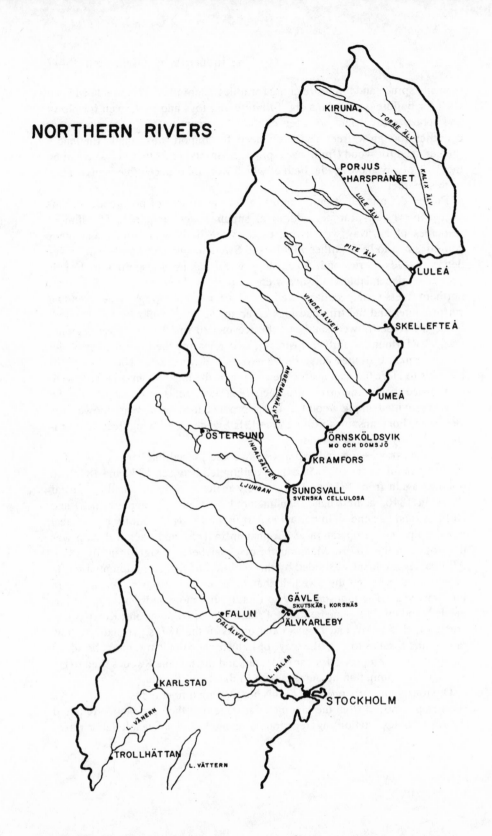

KIRUNA•

TORNE ÄLV

KALIX ÄLV

PORJUS
•HARSPRÅNGET

LULE ÄLV

PITE ÄLV

•LULEÅ

VINDELÄLVEN

•SKELLEFTEÅ

ÅNGERMANÄLVEN

•UMEÅ

•ÖSTERSUND

•ÖRNSKÖLDSVIK
MO OCH DOMSJÖ

INDALSÄLVEN

•KRAMFORS

LJUNGAN

•SUNDSVALL
SVENSKA CELLULOSA

GÄVLE
SKUTSKÄR; KORSNÄS

•FALUN

•ÄLVKARLEBY

DALÄLVEN

L. MÄLAR

•KARLSTAD

STOCKHOLM

L. VÄNERN

TROLLHÄTTAN

L. VÄTTERN

There was a rapid, large-scale trend toward increased, refinement of the raw material in Swedish factories, especially as pulp and paper (see accompanying tabulation).

|  | Value of Exports (in kronor) | |
|---|---|---|
|  | Pulp (all kinds) | Paper (all kinds) |
| 1921/25 (annual av.) | 206,000,000 | 108,500,000 |
| 1950 | 1,120,000,000 | 544,000,000 |

Source: Historisk statistik, III, pp. 37, 38.

Around the turn of the century the demand for Swedish timber diminished while the supply of large trees was becoming exhausted. Fortunately another demand rose rapidly, one that could be supplied better by smaller trees that could be grown faster: the expansion of size and circulation of newspapers required ever larger quantities of paper. Inventions by C. D. Ekman and C. D. Flodquist improved the processes of making sulphite pulp and enabled pulp exports to rise tenfold in the period 1894–1913. The sulphite process using spruce and the sulphate method using both spruce and pine together made possible thorough utilization of the forests; even some birch and aspen could be blended with the other woods. As Swedish industry proceeded to the manufacture of newsprint, kraft paper, and fine writing paper, the total of paper products accounted for 9 percent of Swedish exports by 1950.

## Iron Ore, Iron, and Steel

Sweden's second major manufacturing sector was based on iron. Iron had been found and worked in Sweden for centuries, taken from bogs before it was discovered in mines. The swords of the Vikings and the cannon of Gustav II Adolf attested to its quality and its skillful processing. Ironworks of varying size were widely scattered through central Sweden. The farmers produced pig iron, but for processing bar iron capital was necessary. Sweden sold its iron to many countries but particularly to the Netherlands (in the 1620s), then to England. During most of the eighteenth century more than half of Swedish exports of bar iron went to England. However, when the English developed the puddling process in the 1780s they surpassed the Swedes in iron production. This and Russian iron threatened Swedish export. Each country had to use for fuel what it had: the English were forced to use coal and coke, the Swedes to use charcoal. Charcoal produced a finer product but a more expensive one and the Swedes had to learn to make the most of their quality iron and steel. Increasing quantities were used at home for manufacture of tools and machines, but the major share of this high quality product continued to be exported.

Iron was so important in the Swedish economy that the government repeatedly intervened in its control. The quality standard of the export product was a matter of national concern and each shipment was carefully scrutinized. Not only was the munitions industry of the early seventeenth century eagerly nurtured by the state, but standards of competence for workmen were decreed in 1637 and maintained for two hundred years. Skilled workers were recruited from Germany but the most important contingents were the Walloons, brought in during the early seventeenth century.

The iron workers were given special privileges such as freedom from military service and even from taxation. They were customarily provided housing, with garden plots and grazing rights, and these benefits were made legally mandatory in 1766. The smiths knew they were better off than farm workers and were surrounded by an aura of superiority. Therefore they tended to pass on their jobs to their sons, and families continued in the ironworks for generations. The whole structure was patriarchal, including provision for the aged and the ill. The ironmasters, sometimes nobles, sometimes "persons of status," were prestigious members of society, and the brands they stamped into the bars of iron (frequently their own initials) were guarantees of quality and also marks of distinction like coats of arms.

The so-called German method of processing iron ore was still in use in the mid-nineteenth century, but demand had increased and improved methods were needed. Sweden's product of bar iron increased from 90,000 tons in 1846 to 137,000 tons in 1860, only 10–15 percent of which was kept at home. The iron was produced in about four hundred small and scattered ironworks, scattered partly because of the huge demand for wood and charcoal and the expense of transporting them. When the Englishman Henry Bessemer developed a process of purifying steel ingots by blowing out extraneous matter in a converter, the Swede G. F. Göransson (founder of Sandvik Steel Corporation) made the method practicable at Edsken (1858). However, this method did not notably improve the quality of the steel and its use gradually ceased, though the last furnace did not shut down until 1964. The Lancashire method was widely adopted in the 1860s and dominated until the 1890s. A real breakthrough came with the Siemens-Martin process (1868) which could use both pig iron and scrap iron. Since its economical use required larger units, the number of ironworks was soon reduced by half and was further decreased from 211 works in 1896 to 74 in 1933. Production costs were lowered because of these consolidations and because by the 1870s the railroads made transportation cheaper and more efficient. The "basic" process, developed in the 1870s, combined features of the other methods and was the one generally in use by the time of the major expansion of the 1890s. Electric processing did not become important until the World War I period.[6]

In the later nineteenth century much of Swedish export of iron and steel went to England, and high quality soft iron from the Lancashire process was then often re-exported to India for use in the village smithies. After the 1890s, however, about half of the iron product was retained in Sweden for its own industries.

As for iron ore, its export had been prohibited until the 1850s and then began slowly. Transportation costs were themselves a prohibiting factor. In the early 1870s ore export amounted to some 21,000 tons annually. But soon, with heavy demand from the industries of Belgium, Britain, and Germany, export increased phenomenally. The new processes made more feasible the use of ore with phosphoric content (and the Germans particularly made use of this phosphoric bonus for fertilizers). At the same time the extension of railways, first from the Grängesberg field to Oxelösund and later the lines in the northern part of the country, gave access to markets. In 1888 the railroad from Gällivare to the Gulf of Bothnia at Luleå started ore on its way to world markets, and in 1902 the difficult road over the mountains from Kiruna to Narvik in Norway opened a still more direct route. Foreign capital in the initial stages of both mining and railway construction and later the Swedish state's participation in the building of the railway created Sweden's most important single industrial institution. The Luossavaara-Kiirunavaara Aktiebolaget, LKAB for short, which operated the great northern iron ore mines (largest being the open pit at Kiruna), was responsible for 8 percent of Swedish export in the years just before 1914. It was nevertheless the kind of export that had no multiplier effect on the nation's economy; that is, it stimulated no additional home industry. The governments of Norway and Sweden owned the essential rail line, and the Swedish state held half the shares in LKAB with an option to buy the remainder (which was exercised in 1957).

Iron ore was the giant, but Sweden had a wealth of other ores as well. Iron ore weighed in the millions of tons, copper weighed in the thousands, and silver and gold in kilograms, but they were all valuable. Stora Kopparberg, the great copper producer of earlier centuries, showed a remarkable talent for adapting to the depletion of the copper ore, first by utilizing by-products, especially the red paint for the cottages that dot the Swedish countryside, then by exploiting its forest resources and processing timber, paper, and steel. Therefore Stora Kopparberg, which claims to be the oldest corporation extant (existing in 1288, chartered 1347), remains one of the great ones even without copper. Its plants and mines and forests are scattered across a wide belt that spans central Sweden. Like other big concerns such as Uddeholm and Åtvidaberg, it is a vertical combination based on mines and forests, with sawmills, forges, foundries, and workshops for its processsing plants.

Although most of the large mining and manufacturing companies are out-

Production and Export of Iron Ore and Iron in Sweden, 1836–1950 (in metric tons)

| Year (annual average) | Ore Production | Ore Export | Pig Iron Export | Ingot, Sheet Steel Export |
|---|---|---|---|---|
| 1836–40 . . . . . . . . . . | 251,000 | | | |
| 1861–65 . . . . . . . . . . | 453,000 | | | |
| 1871–75 . . . . . . . . . . | 785,000 | 21,000 | 54,000 | 151,000 |
| 1886–90 . . . . . . . . . . | 930,000 | 97,000 | 59,000 | 219,000 |
| 1891–95 . . . . . . . . . . | 1,517,000 | 522,000 | 67,000 | 196,000 |
| 1901–05 . . . . . . . . . . | 3,563,000 | 2,540,000 | 85,000 | 215,000 |
| 1911–15 . . . . . . . . . . | 6,759,000 | 6,440,000[a] | 208,000[a] | 264,000[a] |
| 1936 . . . . . . . . . . . . . | 11,250,000 | 11,198,000 | 113,000 | 120,000 |
| 1938 . . . . . . . . . . . . . | 13,928,000 | 12,685,000 | | 146,000 |
| 1945 . . . . . . . . . . . . . | 3,930,000 | 1,229,000 | 6,000 | 80,000 |
| 1947 . . . . . . . . . . . . . | 8,894,000 | 8,504,000 | 26,000 | 63,000 |
| 1950 . . . . . . . . . . . . . | 13,611,000 | 12,943,000 | 69,300 | 167,340 |

Source: Historisk statistik, III, Tables 1, 17.
    [a]For 1913.

growths of older *bruk* (works), an important exception is the Boliden Company which began at the end of the World War I and had remarkable success in finding ores in the vast Norrland area lying between Stora Kopparberg tracts and the Kiruna-Gällivare iron-ore area. Boliden engineers, utilizing the latest scientific techniques for locating deep-lying minerals, searched especially for copper, the discovery and exploitation of which have far exceeded the production of the Falun copper mountain. In addition the Boliden explorers found valuable quantities of gold, silver, nickel, lead, and other ores.

## Invention and Manufacturing

Sweden was endowed with fertile plains in Skåne, with water power in magnificent falls in the north, with boundless dark green forests, and with a wealth of minerals underground. The challenge to the people was to learn how to use these gifts of nature. Selling timber and iron half-processed left the major gains of manufacturing for the English, the French, and the Germans. To make things themselves the Swedes had either to copy the products of others or invent products of their own; they proved adept at both. In the processing of iron, for example, they mostly adapted to their own circumstances the techniques discovered by others. But they showed also that Christopher Polhem was not the last inventive genius born under the north star.

Gustaf de Laval (1845–1913), descendant of a French ancestor ennobled in Sweden in the seventeenth century, was a many-sided inventive genius. His 1878 invention of the cream separator spread rapidly around the world, and the company he organized to make it (Separator, later Alfa-Laval), with its daughter companies in other countries, made him wealthy. The cream separator enhanced the efficiency of the cow, and it could be used as a small hand-operated device or as a power-driven machine. De Laval's other invention of primary importance was the steam turbine, which he made practical and usable, and again he founded a company for its manufacture.

Lars Magnus Ericsson (1846–1926) invented the first table telephone and founded in 1876 the L. M. Ericsson Company, which manufactures telephone equipment for markets throughout most of the world. Sven Wingquist (1876–1953) perfected the modern ball bearing and founded Svenska Kullagerfabrik (SKF) in 1907. The safety match was developed in the 1840s and three decades later Alexander Lagerman (1836–1904) constructed a machine for mass production of matches — long before the fantastic financial edifice that Ivar Kreuger built of matches. Alfred Nobel (1833–96) patented dynamite and left his resultant fortune as a foundation that honors men of achievement in peace, science, and literature. Baltzar von Platen (1898–   ), descendant of the canal engineer, invented the gas-driven refrigerator that was exploited by the Elektrolux Company. Gustaf Dalén (1869–1937) made a series of basic inventions for the use of gas, was longtime director of the AGA company, and won the Nobel prize in physics in 1912. Carl Edvard Johansson (1864–1943), "master of measurement," developed a method of precision measurement of great importance for the armaments of World War I and for mechanical manufacture in general. The list goes on and on of the constructive geniuses on whose inventions have been built the great Swedish manufactories and multinational corporations. In weaponry, electronics, gas lighting, airplane and automobile manufacturing, in chemical industries — especially those dealing with cellulose and other wood products — in machine tools, and a host of other items Swedes have made noteworthy inventions and created producing organizations.

Some of the characteristics of Swedish economic developments are well illustrated by the history of one of the older middle-sized companies — the Åtvidaberg complex in south central Sweden. It dates back to a medieval copper mine in Åtvid's parish in Östergötland. Much later, in 1761, a company was formed to rebuild the mine and to buy up supporting forests and water power. The company ceased to exist when Johan Adelswärd bought up the shares of his partners and organized a *fideikommiss* (entailed estate) which was chartered by Gustav III in 1783. The farsighted Adelswärd encouraged experimentation and invention and prospered. Generation followed generation on this estate. The widow of the past generation moved out of the main manor house to a smaller house somewhere on the estate, and younger sons had other houses and held employment in the *fideikommiss* according to their interests and their abilities. Here was created a miniature principality both innovative and paternalistic. The latest techniques in smelting were complemented by provision for medical care for the workers, pensions, and a home for the aged.

Production from the copper mine continued through the nineteenth century, sometimes rivaling Stora Kopparberg in output. Here was built one of the first railways in Sweden. In 1883, when the copper was beginning to thin out, a twenty-three-year-old Theodor had to abandon his projected study trip to the United States and take over the responsibilities of management. New activities had to replace copper mining. After a fire in 1903 the Bersbro mine and the Forsaström works withdrew from the *fideikommiss* and the copper-mining concern was reorganized into a corporation. The *fideikommiss* remained for the property as a whole — the extensive farms, forests, and waterfalls.

In its search for new sources of income the institution began to make office furniture and wagon wheels and started other enterprises including a dairy, a slaughterhouse, a mill, a brewery, and a laundry. In 1906 these were all combined in Åtvidaberg United Industries. Experiments were made in producing electricity from water power, and when Crown Prince Gustav visited Åtvidaberg and Forsaström in 1903 he could admire electric power at work in the mines and factories. A Finnish professor, Selim Lemström, came to the estate to experiment with the use of electricity to stimulate plant growth; the idea had already been tried in England and Germany, and here too the results were unsatisfactory. Experimentation was necessary but could not always yield positive results.

Plans were made to gain more power by rebuilding three falls into one, and a noted architect, Professor I. G. Clason, was hired to build the power station. Theodor Adelswärd's dream was to make Åtvidaberg a model garden city. In 1911 copper mining was completely abandoned and the Forsaström Power Company was created, retaining the rights of the *fideikommiss*. Demand for power increased and the Company acquired additional waterfalls. When drought dried up the supply in the early 1930s the Company had to buy electricity from outside and then build a steam power plant. It made itself a power distribution center for a wide area south of Linköping. As part of social democratic policy to eliminate the old entailed estates the institution of *fideikommiss* was abolished in 1963, with distribution of each estate to be required on the death of the last owner. The Adelswärd barony was transformed into a shareholding company (Baroniet Adelswärd Aktiebolag), and thus the aggressive and adaptable concern has continued to function.

In the meantime other adjustments had been made to the changing times. Åtvidaberg United Industries was sold by the Adelswärd family in 1917 to a consortium, and when this corporation failed in 1922 it was reorganized as Åtvidaberg Industries. The new company expanded and flourished for half a century, acquiring or spawning a number of subsidiaries such as Facit (calculating machines — later bought by Electrolux), Halda (typewriters), furniture factories, machine shops, even secretarial schools. It had offices throughout Sweden and agencies in 109 foreign countries. Despite crises and changes most of the operations continued and prospered.

The long history of Åtvidaberg embodies many of the characteristics that apply to the Swedish economy as a whole: the utilization and exhaustion of natural resources along with adaptability to change; entrepreneurial and technical experimentation and initiative; patriarchalism and cooperation; fusions and partitionings and reorganizations.[7]

Some Swedish industries grew in a quite different way, out of popular homecrafts (*slöjd*, becoming *sloyd* in English) which had been practiced for centuries and out of hundreds of small industrial concerns. Most notable was probably the textile industry, long prominent in the region around Borås (about 35 miles inland from Gothenburg). This industry was given a boost by the cheap cotton available from America. In this area of poor land the farmers found they could supplement their meager income with crafts — wood working, glass blowing, spinning, and weaving — the latter two done mostly by the women. Peddlers then hawked the products far and wide. Women who made hair ornaments sometimes crafted as they traveled and peddled. The quality of Swedish handicrafts was so high that customers long had a prejudice against factory-produced articles (which, indeed, in the beginning years were frequently inferior). The province of Dalarna was famous for its metal crafts and for wooden articles (such as the toy wooden horses loved by tourists and their children), clocks, and furniture. The number of handicraft

| Increase in Value of Swedish manufactures, 1836–1950 (in millions of kronor) | |
| --- | --- |
| 1836/40 | 20.1[a] |
| 1861 | 74.6 |
| 1871 | 105.2 |
| 1881 | 168.0 |
| 1891 | 287.8 |
| 1901 | 1,025.2 |
| 1911 | 1,651.1 |
| 1921 | 4,119.0 |
| 1931 | 4,356.0 |
| 1941 | 9,412.0 |
| 1950 | 23,822.0 |

*Source: Historisk statistik*, III, pp. 6, 12.

[a] Annual average.

workers increased from approximately 60,000 in the 1850s to over 90,000 in the 1890s. Gradually industrialization created more jobs and handicrafts declined in relative importance. They nevertheless retained prestige, and societies for the preservation of traditional skills became popular.[8]

Interestingly the industrialization of textile and clothing manufacture concentrated in the same region where the handicraft production had been strongest, in and around Borås. In some areas and with some crafts the handicraft system survived into the late twentieth century (for example, leather manufacturing around Malung in Dalarna), illustrating again the established specialization by town and district.

## Energy

Energy is the all-important prerequisite for modern industry. Sweden lacks both coal and oil; it is blessed with a good supply of timber for the production of steam and with water power, although the fickleness of rainfall makes for undependability. As far back as the thirteenth and fourteenth centuries water power was used in iron making, but for centuries to come the power had to be used at its source. With the harnessing of electricity and the invention of the three-phase system (partly by the Swede Jonas Wenström and the Croatian-American Nikola Tesla), electric power could be transmitted over distance.[9] Beginning in 1893 power stations were built for individual plants and towns. Early in the twentieth century larger plants were constructed, such as the one at Trollhättan, and power companies distributed electricity over extensive areas. The government built large hydroelectric plants at Porjus in the north and at Älvkarleby, while Stockholm and other cities built their own (see map of northern rivers). After World War I the competing companies discovered that it was beneficial to all to connect their lines so that they could interchange power to meet emergencies or special load demands. Storage of water helped to even out the supply. In the 1930s the great power resources of the Norrland rivers began to be harnessed by combinations of steelworks, pulp companies, and municipalities. Two hundred twenty thousand volt lines carried electricity to Stockholm and to south Sweden. Finally the government decided to take complete responsibility for further installations. Despite protests about the effect on the ecology, a huge station was built at Harsprånget, with a six-hundred-mile transmission line to carry 380,000 volt current far to the south. Other plants in the south were linked with these northern producers into an integrated nationwide system which was in turn connected with Danish and Norwegian power lines so that electricity could be switched back and forth between these northern neighbors and with sources and markets to the south in Europe.

As the power of a waterfall depends on the height of the fall and the amount of the water flowing per second, it is essential to locate power stations in river valleys where, within reasonable geographical distances, the difference in water level above and below the station is as great as possible. In Sweden the altitude of the mountains in the northwest is comparatively low and the distance to the sea is long. Therefore, most rivers slope gently from the source to the mouth, leaving only a few real waterfalls with a sufficiently great drop for economical power construction. To harness the most power in the rivers where they form rapids special methods had to be found. Swedish industries and power companies early developed a system with relevant machines and tools to drill, blast, and excavate the solid rock which was mainly granite and gneiss. The rocks were found to be strong, homogeneous, and highly suitable for tunnel construction. Nature was surprisingly cooperative in placing at the disposal of engineers excellent building materials from early geological periods.

A dam was built across the river and just above the dam a shaft or tunnel was dropped straight down to a power station blasted out of the rock. There the water was fed into the turbines driving the electric generators. After it had done its work the water could be allowed to flow off gently through another tunnel or tail race to rejoin the river below the rapids. Sometimes these tail races were several miles long. The rapids almost disappeared in this process but the riverbed was still there. Flumes had to be constructed around the drop shaft and provided with at least a minimum of water to carry floating logs. Likewise water ladders had to be installed to allow fish to swim or jump counter-current.

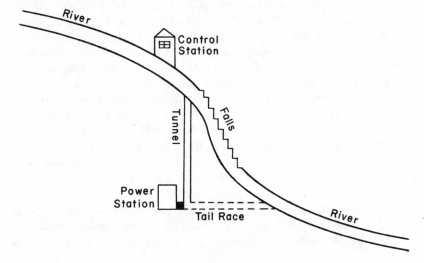

Not all of the picturesque rivers of the northland have been harnessed to the present. Sportsmen, recreationists, ecologists, and environment protectionists have fought stubbornly to preserve nature's balance and beauty. By the 1970s about half the water power that nature offered was utilized, and in 1976 a couple of rivers were still intact.

Water power transformed into electricity lighted the homes and stores of the cities, heated the ovens of the steel mills, drove the trains, and ran the machines in thousands of factories. But, vigorously as the production of electric power was pushed, it could not keep up with the voracious demand for energy, which on a per capita basis was matched only by the United States, Great Britain, and Canada. Quantities of coal, coke, and oil had to be imported, at steadily increasing cost. Sweden was thus driven to build nuclear power plants, the first in 1963. By this time oil supplied nearly 75 percent of the energy demand; electricity from water power supplied 14 to 20 percent of requirements and it was reckoned that nuclear power would eventually supply another 20 percent. However, the dangers inherent in the use of nuclear energy caused questioning and delay and political controversy.

## Finance

Another kind of energy was also indispensable: finance. Just as local merchants extended credit to home craftsmen so the larger mercantile houses were helpful in making advances to the ironmasters and the timbermen whose operations were always greedy for capital. Mines and forges and lumbermills required large financial outlays, and because most of their products were exported a long waiting period between production and payment was unavoidable. After crises in the early nineteenth century and the rapid expansion of production, the merchants alone could no longer satisfy the demand for credit. Sweden had some commercial banks in the early nineteenth century built on the British model, issuing notes and located in the towns. But they were small, too often involved in politics, and could not attract capital from a wide public. In 1856 a group headed by André Oscar Wallenberg (1816–86), a banker and merchant from Sundsvall but well known in Stockholm, obtained a charter for Stockholms Enskilda Bank (SEB).

The SEB, definitely a family bank, the creation of A. O. Wallenberg, continued from the mid-1880s under the leadership of his sons Knut Agaton (1853–1938) and Marcus L. (1864–1943), grandsons Jacob (1892–  ) and Marcus (1899–  ), and great grandson Marc (1924–71). The founder was a man of wide vision and many activities, a journalist, politician and member of the riksdag from 1853 to his death, and especially a promoter of industry. He conceived of the bank as an institution to gather deposits of individuals' savings and to use those resources constructively. He took risks and in periods of crisis was occasionally in tight corners. The basic program of the bank was to investigate carefully each new enterprise and its promoters and, when it approved, to give full support with both money and advice. When a company was thoroughly established the bank would pull out its capital, to be transferred to another new venture. Occasionally, as with the big electric firm ASEA, the bank found itself holding complete ownership. Funds were obtained not only from deposits but from extensive borrowing abroad and the issuance of notes and bonds. The purpose and the result was to assure the effectiveness of large-scale industries and to keep them in Swedish ownership (in contrast to the situation in Norway). From the mid-1890s SEB was concerned primarily with Lappland ores (LKAB), the electrical industry, and timber. K. A. Wallenberg and Marcus held about 30 percent of the share capital of the bank and were careful to maintain the proportion when capital was increased to meet new requirements. SEB was particularly eager to finance new enterprises that were controlled by members of the family, and whenever its funds were involved the bank exercised guidance in the choice of management. Banking thus became the headquarters of the capitalist structure, foreseeing and directing development, taking risks and profits.[10]

Another important early bank was Skandinaviska Kreditaktiebolaget (The Scandinavian Credit Share Corporation), which became Skandinaviska Banken in 1939 and was merged with the Wallenberg bank in the 1970s to form the Scandinaviska Enskilda Bank. It was the first share-bank and shortly after its founding in 1863 it came to fulfill the central banking services that the Riksbank as much as possible avoided. Its capital was about two-thirds foreign, but when international unrest led investors to pull back the opportunity was seized to make it a truly Swedish bank, and A. O. Wallenberg succeeded in getting its headquarters placed in Gothenburg instead of in Copenhagen. Although the bank tried to resist long term investments, it lent much capital to railroads. The Skandinaviska bank absorbed a number of provincial banks and became the largest in Sweden. Sorely pressed by the bankruptcy of Ivar Kreuger concerns in 1932, the bank nevertheless received aid from other banks and from the government and came through the crisis without loss.[11]

As a footnote to the financial history of Sweden it should be mentioned that for almost fifty years, 1875–1924, the three central Scandinavian countries — Sweden, Denmark, and Norway — maintained a monetary union, based on a common value for the krona (Swedish) or krone (Denmark and Norway). The names remain, but the values have diverged.

Sweden was fortunate that the large capital funds needed for development were readily available. This was an advantage gained by the lateness of its entry into the industrial age, after Germany, Britain, and France had had time to accumulate capital and become happy to lend it. Mortgage funds for Sweden had been obtained abroad since 1846, chiefly from Hamburg, and went largely to rural mortgage societies. After 1861 these borrowings were concentrated in the Mortgage Bank founded that year. The amount outstanding rose to 400 million kronor in the mid-1880s. By the 1890s foreign investment in Sweden amounted to over one-third of domestic accumulations. The funds for the homeowner and farmer were far surpassed by the loans to industry. The railway development that began in the 1850s was financed largely by government borrowings abroad. The first such Swedish loan in forty years was made by a German consortium. In the 1870s heavy borrowing began in England and later France played the leading role; by 1913, when Sweden had outstanding foreign debts of 900 million kronor, the French held notes for two-thirds of the total. The French policy was to finance other countries' development rather than to push its own further. Loans came from Britain also, but the British had other outlets for their capital, and the Wallenberg connection was primarily with France; he acted as intermediary for many of the loans both governmental and industrial.[12]

An often forgotten source of funds, though on a scale less extensive, were the remittances from America, and these, being gifts from emigrated sons and daughters, did not have to be repaid. The amount was about 500,000 kronor in the year 1885, 38 million in 1910, from 30 million to 35 million each year from 1923 to 1930. In dollar terms the annual average from 1906 to 1930 was $8 million to $10 million. For the nine years from 1922 to 1930 remittances from America amounted to 25 percent of Sweden's balance of payments (that is, 25 percent of the excess of the value of imports over exports). To this sum should be added the grants for research made by the Rockefeller Foundation and others. These funds were valuable pluses for the Swedish economy.[13]

In the nineteenth century the large capital funds needed for railway construction were obtained largely by the government through foreign loans. The demands of the timber and iron industries were met by the borrowings of private concerns both at home and abroad. The rapidly proliferating manufacturing enterprises obtained their money more from individual savings. These savings were surprisingly large for a variety of reasons. Foremost was the fact that Swedish exports in the period 1860–1914 expanded in quantity and enjoyed unusually advantageous prices on the world market. The total national income rose 400 percent in that half-century. The effect of this growth was accentuated because domestic prices in Sweden increased only 25 percent. Thus farm workers whose income rose by 200 percent and industrial workers whose income rose by 275 percent were both happily better off. The nation's wage bill remained far less than the 400 percent increase in national income;

the margin of 125 to 200 percent could be labeled "savings without pain." Officials and professionals were doing comfortably well and did not exhaust their incomes by spending. Merchants were inclined to plow their profits back into their businesses. Tax policy favored personal accumulations, for there was no progressive tax on incomes until 1909 (then in the form of a surtax). It is understandable that personal bank deposits grew from 18 million kronor in 1860 to 6.8 billion kronor in 1945. Commercial banks doubled their assets in the brief span from 1900 to 1913, and industries obtained funds for expansion.[14]

The total effect of foreign loans, domestic savings, and investment gave Sweden a rich flow of invigorating capital and combined with other factors to make its industrial development unusually rapid, even if belated.

### Foreign Trade

But Sweden, like any small country with a limited variety of resources, was dependent on foreign trade for prosperity. The country could exist with minimal trade, but the existence too would be minimal. As new ambitions awakened to life the Swedes reached out eagerly for expanded contacts. Circumstances were favorable.

During the early period of the industrial breakthrough, when Sweden had to borrow heavily from abroad, it was fortunate to have that long period from about 1830 to the late 1860s when it could produce a surplus of grain and sell it abroad at good prices. By the time that opportune market had been destroyed by imports from the lush wheat fields of the American West the Swedes were in a position to shift their efforts into animal products from the farms and industrial products from the factories. Hence a fair degree of economic balance was maintained.

From 1860 to 1875 Sweden's terms of trade improved; export prices rose more rapidly than import prices. During the later 1870s economic conditions were bad, but thereafter lower transportation costs helped reduce import prices while exports held their own. About half of the exports were raw materials, a proportion that increased with the expansion of ore shipments in the 1890s. Timber exports increased as Britain and France lowered their tariffs. All in all, Sweden was able to import more goods and at the same time pay off the debts for railway construction and industrial installations. And people lived better than ever before.[15]

World War I severely disrupted commerce, and although Sweden was not directly involved it lost thousands of tons of shipping and hundreds of lives. By the end of the war the country was fortunate in being able to replace the lost tonnage but the regular flow of trade was reduced drastically. Neverthe-

Value of major imported and exported Swedish products, 1871–1950
(in millions of kronor)

| Year (annual average) | Agriculture and Animal Products | | Forest Products | | Paper Industry Products | | Textiles | | Minerals and Nonmetal Products | | Metals and Metal Products | |
|---|---|---|---|---|---|---|---|---|---|---|---|---|
| | Imports | Exports | Imports | Exports | Imports | Exports | Imports | Exports | Imports | Exports | Imports | Exports |
| 1871/75 | 97 | 52 | 2 | 88 | 2 | 4 | 47 | 2 | 21 | 5 | 28 | 48 |
| 1891/95 | 131 | 83 | 6 | 119 | 6 | 31 | 62 | 9 | 44 | 27 | 40 | 40 |
| 1901/05 | 197 | 59 | 6 | 159 | 8 | 54 | 58 | 3 | 86 | 54 | 76 | 72 |
| 1911 | 238 | 118 | 16 | 180 | 10 | 120 | 82 | 5 | 95 | 98 | 99 | 127 |
| 1916 | 333 | 232 | 16 | 334 | 17 | 288 | 100 | 24 | 321 | 170 | 183 | 409 |
| 1921 | 430 | 152 | 16 | 194 | 25 | 291 | 132 | 26 | 161 | 128 | 216 | 247 |
| 1931 | 363 | 117 | 22 | 174 | 20 | 347 | 225 | 15 | 201 | 138 | 272 | 278 |
| 1941 | 281 | 73 | 13 | 213 | 20 | 280 | 267 | 1 | 418 | 228 | 394 | 510 |
| 1950 | 1,323 | 435 | 88 | 670 | 38 | 1,763 | 806 | 101 | 942 | 598 | 1,379 | 1,505 |

Source: Historisk statistik, III, p. 58 (cf. tables of production of particular commodities, Historisk statistik, III, pp. 1–12).

less, the price situation was such that exported iron ore and iron brought extraordinary prices, and since imports were restricted there was only one way to spend the profits — paying off debts. Sweden's export surplus for the years 1914 through 1918 totaled 1.345 million kronor. Sweden therefore emerged from World War I freed of its burden of external payments and on the plus side with a small body of investments abroad. The advantages were accompanied by disturbing rises in prices and by deficiencies in imports, for instance fertilizers. Dependence on foreign trade led to strained relations with both Germany and Great Britain and to long-drawn-out and tense negotiations (see chapter XVII).

Cooperation during the war had been advantageous to all the Scandinavian countries and they sought to continue that cooperation after the war. In 1930 the three Nordic neighbors Denmark, Norway, and Sweden joined with Belgium, the Netherlands, and Luxemburg in the Oslo Group (and Finland associated itself in 1932) to promote freer trade among themselves. However, Great Britain objected that those agreements violated the most-favored-nation clauses in the treaties these countries had with Great Britain and that the Oslo Group arrangements had to be abandoned. Only after World War II could a tariff-reducing effort, now including Great Britain, be realized (EFTA; see "Nordic and European Cooperation" in chapter XIX).

Until World War II, which produced changed relations, Sweden's chief trade partners were Germany and Britain. With Germany Sweden bought more than it sold; with Great Britain the pattern was the reverse, Sweden exporting more to Britain than it bought in return (See accompanying table). With the other countries of the North Sweden maintained for the most part a favorable balance of trade; with the United States it was usually unfavorable; with Russia trade was comparatively small. Sweden's total exchange of goods was spread widely around the globe.

## The Bases of Sweden's Economic Accomplishment

The foregoing account documents an amazing achievement for a country that as late as 1850 had to be described as undeveloped, economically backward. Even in the next few decades Sweden's development was slower than that of its neighbors Denmark and Norway. How was it possible for Sweden then to forge ahead so strongly? What were the bases of its economic accomplishment?

In the first place, two kinds of inheritance stood Sweden in good stead: A long history of peace and still longer freedom from invasion left the country with a solid inherited investment in houses, churches, castles, furniture, art — innumerable items that it did not have to create anew. In the early years of

Swedish Trade with Selected Countries
(in millions of kronor)

| Year | United States | | Germany | | Great Britain | | France | | Denmark, Norway, and Finland | | Russia | |
|---|---|---|---|---|---|---|---|---|---|---|---|---|
| | Imports | Exports | Imports | Exports | Imports | Exports | Imports | Exports | Imports | Exports | Imports | Exports |
| 1905 | 41 | 10 | 220 | 85 | 140 | 160 | 16 | 30 | 70 | 90 | 29 | 7 |
| 1910 | 53 | 23 | 230 | 124 | 164 | 190 | 28 | 42 | 81 | 95 | 32 | 18 |
| 1915 | 322 | 24 | 251 | 486 | 214 | 330 | 24 | 31 | 132 | 97 | 24 | 76 |
| 1920 | 780 | 129 | 500 | 185 | 915 | 825 | 96 | 187 | 440 | 390 | 2 | 22 |
| 1925 | 219 | 143 | 378 | 206 | 291 | 367 | 49 | 84 | 196 | 180 | 3 | 32 |
| 1930 | 229 | 161 | 533 | 225 | 263 | 395 | 56 | 93 | 180 | 243 | 13 | 31 |
| 1935 | 189 | 156 | 358 | 187 | 285 | 322 | 49 | 56 | 170 | 190 | 16 | 10 |
| 1940 | 310 | 55 | 794 | 494 | 170 | 120 | 25 | 18 | 167 | 328 | 42 | 11 |
| 1945 | 201 | 239 | 90 | 1 | 75 | 282 | 8 | 67 | 168 | 624 | 30 | 3 |
| 1950 | 681 | 369 | 662 | 733 | 1776 | 880 | 424 | 246 | 541 | 973 | 43 | 113 |

Total of Trade with All Countries
(in millions of kronor)

| Year | Imports | Exports |
|---|---|---|
| 1905 | 574 | 450 |
| 1925 | 1,446 | 1,360 |
| 1950 | 6,000 | 5,700 |

*Source: Historisk statistik*, III, pp. 52–54.

464

industrialization it had the advantage also of inherited tendencies of thrift so that spending increased more slowly than profits, and there was a surplus to apply to new enterprises. It had also an elite cadre of highly educated leadership.

A long-continuing decentralization of industry in the early decades of development was of vital importance for both industry and society. Decentralization was influenced by the historic pattern of the *bruk* and by the scattered location of resources — ores and timber and waterfalls — resources best used where they were found. The layout of railway lines planned to serve many and new communities promoted the growth of medium-sized towns. In the infancy of industrialization these factors helped keep management and labor a little closer to each other than where great factories drew hordes of worker˙ into strange and crowded cities. In a *bruk* like Sandviken, for example, families suffered in unsanitary and inadequate housing, but space and open air were all about and the situation was far more tolerable than in the tenements of Manchester.

Agriculture too was more widely scattered than normal, with farmsteads spread far apart in a rocky and wooded terrain dotted with lakes. Scattering encouraged farmers to develop a versatility of skills; they had to be carpenters, masons, blacksmiths, roadbuilders, everything. They became adaptable and accustomed to hard work. These inbred qualities they took to the factory and eventually to the city. They had talents and a sense of personal worth and of their individual importance in the productive process. They made an unusually effective labor force.[16]

One cause must probably be ascribed to accident, but it was a vital force: the land was blessed with a galaxy of inventive geniuses — de Laval, von Platen, Nobel, the Ericsson brothers, and many more. Some of them created things, some perfected the incomplete inventions of others. The number of machines they developed to the point of usability is extraordinary. In spite of the fact that Sweden had to import a large proportion of its chemicals, the country produced several world-famous chemists. After Scheele and Berzelius and other early greats came at the end of the nineteenth century Alfred Nobel; he founded the explosives industry at Bofors, where both munitions and industrial and pharmaceutical chemicals are still manufactured.

Hand in hand with the idea-men came the practical manufacturers who could make the telephones and the refrigerators and the turbines and the separators that other talented ones invented. It was important also that Sweden had much of the basic raw material out of which to manufacture the invented products: for example, steel-making capacity unsurpassed, wood and pulp and just the right kind of wood (aspen) to make the safety matches that Gustav Pasch invented, water power, and capital, the life-blood of enterprise.

How this poor country on the margin of Europe came to have the requisite capital carries us beyond domestic causes. The inflow of capital was due in the first instance to external factors such as the expanding population of Europe and the industrialization in England and Germany and elsewhere that demanded quantities of iron ore and iron and steel, timber and paper and pulp. Lennart Jörberg says that the industrial development before the 1870s "was to a considerable degree an adaptation to what was happening outside its borders and to a lesser degree an independent economic expansion."[17] Highly important was the fact that the terms of trade were solidly in Sweden's favor — export prices were higher than import prices. Of course the Swedes had to organize the production and export of their goods, and they had to learn how to manage the income therefrom. Again, as with inventors, the financial wizards were also available, especially long-lived shrewd men like the Wallenbergs, who were eager both to make money for themselves and to promote the greatness of Sweden. Such men believed in planning and they oiled the wheels of progress by injections of funds at the right time and place. Water power, for instance, Sweden possessed in good measure, but for centuries it had been tumbling unproductively into the sea; at last the techniques were available to harness this white power. To call it all a fortuitous concatenation of circumstances would be to overemphasize the element of chance — but luck was a factor.

Along with bold new venturing the Swedes also evidenced conservative tendencies. For instance, they never abandoned the homecrafts that in many countries were so thoroughly overwhelmed by machines. Pride in hand skills remained as a challenge to the machine. Caution was also displayed in leaving firms that originated new products, be it telephones or vacuum cleaners or whatnot, with a monopoly or at least a quasi-monopoly of the domestic market; they had ample competition on the international market, while locally they enjoyed free opportunity. Protective tariffs, introduced in the 1880s, gave a degree of advantage to home industry without seriously restricting imports. Both government and business realized that national prosperity could be won only through international activity, which explains the large number of Swedish-based multinational corporations.

Those who think that only a socialist state can organize productivity for the national good should recognize that the building of a prosperous Swedish community took place under a thoroughly capitalist system. But it was a system, be it noted, in which government cooperated wholeheartedly with business. Private concerns could not marshal the funds necessary for the exploitation of the northern ore fields; the governments of Norway and Sweden built the railway that opened the fields to use and the government of Sweden owned half of the LKAB mining concern until 1957, since then all of it. Government borrowed money abroad to build the railroads, and in innumerable ways the state encouraged the industrial sector. From the time of Gustav Vasa in the sixteenth century and the mercantilists of the eighteenth century Sweden was a "mixed economy."

Thus Sweden, though it had copious supplies of two basic raw materials, did not become merely an exporter of nature's gifts; rather the presence of these raw products stimulated the development of manufactures and a home market. The rapid industrial breakthrough from the late nineteenth century to the mid-twentieth century was produced by a combination of individual genius, labor, government, technical, financial, and economic forces working together as a team in a world that offered unusual opportunities. Pervading the whole society was a deep national pride and a will to achieve.

# XVII

## SWEDEN AND WORLD WAR I
## 1914–18

SWEDEN, DURING THE WORLD WAR I YEARS 1914–1918, engaged in a determined holding action. The will of the country as a whole was to stand aside, to maintain a strict neutrality. Neutrality in "thought, word, and deed" proved impossible for the United States, but Sweden came closer to attaining it. Two years before the outbreak of war, on December 21, 1912, Sweden, Denmark, and Norway had issued a declaration of agreement on the principles of neutrality and had pledged to notify each other of any departure from these principles. On August 3, 1914 Sweden proclaimed complete neutrality and immediately took defensive military measures. On August 8 Sweden joined with Norway in a common declaration of neutrality.[1]

Knut A. Wallenberg, the prominent banker and at this time foreign minister, would have gone further in cooperating with Norway. In August he obtained Norway's agreement to a defensive alliance, hoping by this step to deter any Swedish "policy of adventure" in collusion with Germany. But his colleagues in Stockholm held to the policy stated by a riksdag commission in 1905, the year of separation — a "defensive alliance is for Sweden more unfavorable than no union. . . . Sweden should under no circumstances assume a responsibility that might, against her own interests, involve her in Norway's possible conflicts with foreign countries."[2]

Nevertheless, Nordic cooperation in neutrality was close. The three kings came together in Malmö in December 1914, the first time since 1905 that Gustav and Håkon had met. They met again in 1917, this time in Kristiania (Oslo). Repeatedly Sweden, sometimes in collaboration with its neighbors, appealed to the United States for common action to uphold the principles of neutrality and to invervene "against every attempt, whencever they come," to nullify the international rules built up through centuries.[3] Hjalmar Hammarskjöld, the prime minister, was a widely known authority on international law and lent a special respect to the Swedish position. But the United States, operating from a different base of power and responsibility, did not respond, and the situation changed after April 1917 when this western great power became a belligerent.

While the United States listened to the call to "Save America by aiding the Allies," in Sweden the Entente sympathizers called only for neutrality. The interventionists among the Swedes were pro-German. They were few but purposeful and highly placed. One of the most active was Count Arvid Taube, Swedish envoy to Berlin, whose erroneous idea that Swedes were "absolutely pro-German" had to be counteracted by none other than Helmuth von Lucius, the German Minister to Stockholm. The marshal of Sweden, Ludvig Douglas (more German than Scottish despite his name, and related to the Swedish queen), was strongly in favor of a German alliance. The queen, Viktoria of Baden, great granddaughter of Gustav IV Adolf and granddaughter of Kaiser Wilhelm I, was proud to be honorary colonel of a German regiment and was thoroughly German in her orientation. So were Sven Hedin, the world-renowned explorer of Central Asia, and Rudolf Kjellén, the noted geopolitician.

Rather oddly, as viewed from a later perspective, a number of social democrats were also outspokenly pro-German. They admired the German social-security program and were impressed by Germany's scientific and industrial achievements. The most vocal of these pro-German activists had to pay for their opinions by "excommunication" from the Social Democratic party (Otto Järte, Yngve Larsson, Gustaf Steffen). Järte and Larsson were among the contributors to a book published in June 1915 by Adrian Molin, *Sveriges Utrikespolitik i världskrigets belysning* (Sweden's foreign policy in the light of the world war), which advocated "courageous lining up on Germany's side."[4] The rank and file of the social democrats were neutralists if not pacifists, as had been illustrated during the crisis of the Norwegian separation. Hjalmar Branting, leader of the party, was influenced by French and German socialism but even more strongly by British social and political ideals.

The social democrats' interest in peace was real but utterly inadequate. In the early years of the war the internationally minded social democrats of many European countries were active in attempts to end the fighting. Branting in the summer of 1915 visited his party associates in several belligerent capitals to sound the possibilities. But while Thorvald Stauning of Denmark pressed for a laying down of arms Branting emphasized less the immediate urgency and more the need to establish lasting foundations for a just and peaceful world, including national self-determination and democracy.[5] Yet neither social democracy nor Christianity, among either the warring or the neutral nations, despite their common commitment to peace and the brotherhood of man, was able to agree on any effective program to settle the conflict except by force. Sweden, at least, was not going to be drawn in.

In November 1915 Prince Max von Baden, the queen's cousin, visited Stockholm with tempting though somewhat vague proposals from the kaiser's government: if Sweden aligned itself with Germany against Russia it might hope to gain not only military supplies and support but autonomy for Finland and annexation of the Åland Islands, together with leadership of a Scandinavian *Bundesstaat* and future cooperation with Germany; Russian expansion could thus be checked. For Swedish nationalists such a program had strong appeal, and two of them had an audience with the king on December 1, 1915. Otto Järte, a social democrat at the time and later a conservative, with the maverick conservative editor Adrian Molin,[6] appealed to the king not to delay too long in leading Sweden into the war; the people might seem opposed to involvement, but as soon as the troop trains moved they would be united behind royal leadership; otherwise, "If the entente wins, ideas of republicanism and parliamentarism will win the ratification of world history." The king must "lift the people up from the quagmire of party degradation."King Gustav V, who had been at first reserved, now (according to Järte's account), "stated repeatedly *that he was of the same opinion as we*." (Järte's italics.) National unity was essential and would come with a German invasion of Finland. Gustav admitted that he could not, as a constitutional monarch, make binding promises, but he had assured Max von Baden that when Germany entered Finland "he would speed into action" and that he was sure the people would follow him.[7]

The parliamentary and cabinet leadership held quite different views on both desirabilities and possibilities. Hammarskjöld held strongly to neutrality (benevolent toward Germany, strict toward the Allies), Wallenberg inclined toward the Entente but with no idea of fighting on their side. The people as a whole were undoubtedly more firmly determined in their peace-mindedness than Adrian Molin had thought. Acquisition of the Åland Islands and autonomy for Finland were deep-seated national desires, but Molin was probably right in suspecting that by the fall of 1915 the most favorable moment had passed. The submarine warfare, the execution of Edith Cavell, and the ruthlessness of the war were turning German sympathizers into opponents.

The German reaction to Swedish attitudes, and especially the king's, was pungently expressed by the kaiser in one of his famous marginalia, dated December 30, 1915 (after Max von Baden's return from his Swedish visit): "In the exhibit of spineless princes the Rumanian Ferdinand and Gustav of

Sweden must take First Prize! They will wreck themselves on hyperconstitutionalism.''[8]

Sweden's real problems during the war were economic, especially the feeding of its people. British restrictions on trade, imposed as early as August 20, 1914, began the erosion of the maritime laws of war. On September 21 iron ore was declared conditional contraband, but Sweden succeeded in getting ore removed from the list. In October Germany began to seize neutral ships in the Baltic and to take them to German ports for search. On November 12 Denmark, Norway, and Sweden joined in sending identical notes to Britain, Russia, France, and Germany, protesting the closing of shipping routes by mines, the extensions of search, and the free interpretation of contraband. Sweden then imported about one-third of its cereals; but by prohibiting re-export and buying from the United States it was able to get sufficient foodstuffs up to the fall of 1916.

Actually Sweden enjoyed an economic bonanza in the first two years of the war, but conditions worsened as the fighting grew more desperate. German submarines took a serious toll. In the course of the war Sweden lost, from all causes, over 200,000 tons of shipping and 800 lives. British action was not as costly in lives, but the policy of forcing Swedish ships to stop in British ports disrupted supply routes. Cargoes had to be discharged and examined and frequently were retained for British use; the British controlled the seas and they rationed the neutrals according to their conception of the neutral's needs. Soon Britain began the practice of holding each Swedish ship until another arrived, because it feared that the ships would stop coming altogether. Both Germany and Britain prohibited the export of coal, and Sweden could get essential fuel only by giving ''compensations'' in return: pitprops, iron, steel, dairy products, paper, horses.

Germany's unrestricted submarine warfare in 1917 brought traffic with Britain almost to a halt. Peacetime imports of coal and coke had amounted to 5 million tons but this was reduced to less than half in 1917; and whereas 90 percent normally came from Britain, in 1917 only 25 percent was British. Whereas in 1913 Sweden had exported 22,000 tons of pork, meat, and butter to Great Britain and only 3,000 tons to Germany, by 1916 the figures were completely reversed, with 30,000 tons going to Germany and only 61 tons going to Britain.[9] These spectacular shifts were caused by the combined influence of war and geography: Germany blocked Swedish trade with Great Britain; Britain blocked Swedish commerce with the West; but it was difficult for Britain to stop Swedish trade in the short haul to Germany, a trade which was highly profitable in the early years of war. Germany desperately needed Swedish foodstuffs and iron ore, and it could in turn supply Sweden with coal even though this had not been a regular trade item in peacetime. Sweden's "compensation" trade with Britain was made up largely of lumber and paper. Thus survival trade was based on a kind of barter system, loosely controlled by occasional safe-conduct agreements and by licensing. In June 1915 the Swedish government set up a State Trade Commission to regulate the supply of economic needs. In October 1915 a joint-stock company called Transito was established, nominally owned by a Swedish merchant but actually by the British government and controlled through the British embassy in Stockholm.[10] Transito gained great power, arranged for various kinds of balanced trade, and forced merchants to promise not to re-export to the enemy — which roused howls of protest. The United States, after entering the war, rivaled Britain in prohibitions on trade. Trade with Russia practically vanished, and there was no access to Dutch ports. Manufacturing concerns that could not get raw materials had to close down (refineries, margarine factories, rubber plants). Everyone had to tighten his belt.

The rules of neutrality that favored neutral commerce were disregarded by Germany and increasingly flouted by Britain after 1916. The United States reversed its support of neutral rights after it became a belligerent. To some extent the warring powers winked at certain prohibited trade, for it was not in their own interest to choke the neutrals to death. It should be noted that a dissenting opinion came from Rear Admiral M. W. W. P. Consett, a British naval attaché in Scandinavia from 1912 to 1919 who resented the bluster of the Nordics and judged it would have been better if they could have been treated as enemies and their coasts closed to German traffic;[11] but Consett was overruled. General intra-Scandinavian trade diminished, yet Swedish imports of food from Denmark doubled between 1917 and 1918 — including butter, pork, cheese, and eggs (75 million of them!). From Norway 54,000 tons of salt herring proved to be an ample supply of that commodity, and Norway also provided 18,000 tons of nitrate fertilizers. Sweden reciprocated with lumber, paper, glassware, and brick.

Protracted and tense trade negotiations with Great Britain evidenced Sweden's attitudes and problems during the latter half of the war. Hammarskjöld felt perhaps more strongly than anyone else in the government that Germany would win the war and that Sweden must maintain good commercial and political relations with the Central Powers. He approved the mining of the Kogrund passage, keeping Allied shipping out of the Baltic and favoring German interest. In the negotiations with the British, seeking relaxation of their trade restrictions, it was Hammarskjöld who dictated terms bound to be unacceptable and the negotiation collapsed in February 1917. Knut Wallenberg, as foreign minister, had more faith in the British and their allies and more feeling for the needs of Swedish industry to obtain raw materials from the west and for the people to obtain cereals. But his prime minister outmaneuvered him.

However, by March 1917 the debate within the Swedish political leadership forced Hammarskjöld's resignation; he had lost the confidence of his conservative colleagues. He was followed by a conservative regime headed by Carl Swartz with Arvid Lindman as foreign minister. This was the month of the Russian Revolution, which raised hopes among the radical elements in Sweden, as elsewhere, and fears in the upper echelons of society and politics. Early the next month the United States declared war on Germany. The complexion of the war was changing and no one could predict what might eventuate.

The British watched the situation in Sweden closely. They no longer feared as much as they had previously that Sweden might join Germany in the war, and they tended to take a stiffer stance against Sweden's commercial demands. They had disliked the Hammarskjöld policies and they saw little change with the coming of Swartz and Lindman. They were not interested in resuming trade negotiations and gradually developed a policy to bring down the Swedish government in the hope that a succeeding liberal regime would be more friendly to them. The means they used was the notorious Luxburg affair.

The Swedish government, in one of its unneutral "benevolences," permitted Germany to use Swedish channels for diplomatic cables. The British intercepted and deciphered some of these cables, notably one from Count Luxburg, the German minister in Argentina, in which he suggested that two Argentinian ships enroute to Europe with supplies should be sunk without trace (*spurlos versenkt*). Publication of the cable was withheld until just before the Swedish election in September. It was then released in the United States and it exploded the myth of strict Swedish maintenance of international law and neutrality.[12] The immediate effect on the elections was probably slight, but the governing conservatives dropped from 86 to 57 seats in the Second Chamber — a defeat influenced primarily by the economic discontent. The combination of election losses, economic distress, and the disgrace of its own unneutral deceit forced the resignation of the Swartz-Lindman government at the end of September.

The government formed in October 1917 marked some new departures. Although the Social Democrats had earlier refused to accept joint responsibility with the Liberals, they did so in 1917, producing the first such coalition. Nils Edén, a veteran liberal and a professor of history at Uppsala University, took the post of prime minister on condition that no personal or unstatutory advisers would come between him and the king — a specific reference to the courtyard crisis of 1914 that now fixed in constitutional practice the rules of parliamentary government. The Liberals held seven posts, the Social Democrats four; among the latter was Hjalmar Branting. However, Branting was so uncomfortable in his finance position that he departed in a few months, being replaced by Fredrik Thorsson. Johannes Hellner, a nonparty moderate and Entente-oriented, became foreign minister. Although the government was now more responsible to the riksdag, and especially to the Second Chamber, the First Chamber continued to represent "the rich, the wise, and the good" and could block action by its legislative partner.[13]

Two particularly complicated problems involving foreign affairs faced the new government. The first was in the East, where the Bolsheviks grabbed power in Russia on November 8, and where a month later Finland declared independence on December 6. By January civil war broke out in Finland. Strategic considerations were vital for Sweden, and its traditional ties with the Finns were of psychological importance. But the Swedes were badly divided on what action to take — the conservatives wanted to help the White forces, the leftist elements were eager to aid the Reds. A strong Swedish position on either side might lead to civil strife within Sweden itself, and therefore the government had to tread gingerly. The time seemed propitious to many for a Swedish takeover of the Åland Islands, overwhelmingly Swedish in language and sympathies. The Germans were eager to see the Swedes become thus involved, but caution restrained the northern neutrals.

The second matter of utmost importance was resumption of the trade negotiations with the western powers. This time Marcus Wallenberg, stepbrother of Knut Wallenberg and a member of the 1916–17 delegation, returned to London as head of the new delegation. From December 1917 until June 1918 the strenuous discussions continued, made more difficult by the addition of the Americans. Britain and its allies wanted to make sure that vital supplies did not reach Germany, and they desperately needed ship tonnage. The Swedes, like the Norwegians and others, were in dire need of foodstuffs that could come only from the Americas through Allied-controlled seas. Sweden's need was the more desperate in 1917–18 because of an unusually poor harvest. At Christmas 1917 a gift from the United States was welcome: 2,500 tons of coffee and 5,500 tons of kerosene — in return for 13,500 tons of Swedish shipping. It was an arduous task to work out the necessary concessions and compromises, which also had to be acceptable to Germany. After a *modus vivendi* agreed on in January-February 1918 the final terms provided that Sweden would reduce its iron-ore shipments to Germany from 5 million tons to 3.5 million tons; Britain would buy 2 million tons. The Allies agreed to facilitate Sweden's import of grain, fodder, coal, textiles, rubber, and coffee. Sweden in return put 400,000 tons of shipping at the disposal of the Allies. The agreement was in itself a tacit admission that the Allies had the power, if not the right, to determine Swedish trade relations even with Germany. The terms were the most favorable granted to any neutral, partly because the British were interested in upholding the moderate Edén government. The close connection between domestic politics and the trade negotiations had been a prime factor throughout. In this aspect the United States was fundamentally ignorant of the Swedish situation, depended on the British for information, and in general followed the British lead.

The agreement did not eliminate Sweden's hardships, although it must be kept in mind that hardship in Sweden was not at all comparable to that in the warring states and among many of the neutrals. Sweden did have to ration bread, milk, potatoes, and even textiles; coffee also was rationed, which was a serious thing for the heavy-coffee-drinking Swedes. And prices rose to two and one-half or three times what they had been in 1914. One of the casualties of the war was the Scandinavian monetary union which had been established in 1873 but ceased to function in 1917 because of the changed and unbalanced currency situation in the three countries. Despite the rise in prices Sweden maintained a strong currency until 1919.[14]

All in all Sweden came through the war remarkably well. Shipping losses were replaced by the end of the war. Because its exports earned extraordinarily high prices and its imports were reduced by necessity its balance of payments was highly favorable. Excess earnings enabled Sweden to recapture bonds and pay off about two-thirds of its foreign indebtedness. At the same time a number of foreign-owned establishments in Sweden were taken over by Swedes. From an economic point of view neutrality had paid well. In the political realm the war speeded up the process of democratic change.

# XVIII

## DEMOCRATIC SWEDEN, 1918–45

How Did Sweden achieve democracy in politics? It was not easy. Democracy is easy neither to attain nor to hold. After the aristo-democracy of Sweden's Age of Freedom had been overthrown by the enlightened despotism of Gustav III, participation in national political life had remained limited to certain segments of the population. Local government had been more susceptible to popular influence. Even the great reform of 1866 had merely shifted power in the riksdag from an elite of nobility to an elite of landed wealth. General manhood suffrage was attained very slowly, through the spread of liberal ideas, the growth of a demanding industrial labor class, and the practical cooperation of liberals and social democrats. The next step to truly universal suffrage was managed with an assist from a world war and the fright that its upheavals sent through the body politic. It was during that war, too, that the principle of ministerial responsibility to parliament was at last recognized. The problem of the postwar era was therefore to realize in practice on the gains made in law. It was an uncharted course, and it was not surprising that the going was rough.

Rough indeed was the path to democracy in the fourteen years between 1918 and 1932, with minority governments, frequent changes of leadership, no clear-cut decisions on policy. With the introduction of universal suffrage (1918–21) the social democrats became the largest single party in each chamber of the riksdag, but not until 1941 did they gain a clear majority in the Second Chamber; they dropped in 1945 to exactly half, 115 out of 230 seats, and it was twenty-four years before they once more enjoyed a majority position. The politics of compromise was forced by the electoral situation, not by the fact that Swedes loved compromise. The necessity of gaining support through coalitions or through persuasion of individual members of other parties meant that no intemperate partisan measures could be passed. It also became clear that each time the social democrats moved strongly toward socialism they lost votes in the next election. The electorate wanted moderation, and even the strongest party learned to be cautious.

## Building a Viable Democratic Political System

The foundations of the new political structure were laid during World War I, which had speeded the natural process of change. The war had been a shattering experience, psychologically if not physically, for all the neutral border states. The rapid wind-down in the fall of 1918 and especially the disruption in Germany and the wave of revolution in Russia frightened the forces of order everywhere. In Stockholm the left-wingers among the social democrats grew more blatant in their demands for the abolition of the monarchy, of military service, and of the capitalist system. Two days after the armistice of November 11 worker demonstrations in Stockholm demanded a general strike, establishment of a socialist republic, and organization of workers' and soldiers' councils. The prosperity that had come to business had not filtered down to the workers, who suffered from rising prices and shortages of food. Their resentment expressed itself in such un-Swedish forms as food riots and looting of stores. It looked for a moment as if revolution might come in Sweden as well as in Germany and Russia.

In this high-pressure atmosphere the government brought forth a proposal for a sweeping suffrage reform. Under the chairmanship of Hjalmar Branting the "third special committee" of the riksdag debated the proposal in feverish haste and reached the dramatic day of decision on December 17, 1918. One of the left social democrats spoke of "unavoidable conflict" if the government proposal was not accepted, and Gustav Möller declared that "no power can stop a change."[1] It was hinted that the coup d'état of 1809 was not so terrible and might be repeated. The conservatives objected to threats, but they were ready to yield a great deal, and Branting was able to maintain some reasonableness of discussion. The suffrage question was important for its own sake and even more for the effect it would have on the First Chamber, where the power of property had been ensconced since 1866. The indirect method of selection, with the communal and city councils choosing the members of the First Chamber, was retained, but the qualifications of voters for the local councils were, by the reform, made the same for the councils as for the Second Chamber.

The conservatives on the committeee readily accepted the principle of one man one vote and thus the ending of the forty-grade scale (see the section on suffrage in Chapter XIV). More difficult was to allow a man to vote if he still owed taxes or if he was not on the tax rolls. Women's right to vote was not as divisive a question as might be expected, for women had long enjoyed a minimal suffrage, in communal elections only, if they had owned sufficient property. Women's suffrage was coming rapidly in other countries. Hence tax restrictions, property restrictions, and sex restrictions were all abandoned (except for people on poor relief), and the voting age was set at twenty-three for both communal and national elections. Since these changes involved constitutional revision they were held for final action by a second riksdag, but the decision was made in 1918, and popular agitation was calmed. By 1922 the military service prerequisite for voting was abolished, and the two houses could select their own speakers (royal appointment had lasted a long time!).

Gone was the character distinction between the two houses of the riksdag, an essential ingredient of the 1866 reform. No longer would the First Chamber be likely to veto important acts passed in the Second Chamber, for their clientele was now the same. Henceforth the party divisions in the two chambers were similar, though the longer terms of First-Chamber members meant a lag in change in that body. The immediate effect was a drop in conservative representation in the First Chamber from 87 to 38 (in the Second Chamber they dropped from 86 to 57). From 1919 until the introduction of the unicameral system in 1970 the two houses were equal not only in power but in "character." Remaining insignificant restrictions on suffrage were removed in 1945 and 1953, the age limit was reduced to twenty-one (1945), then to twenty (1965), and to eighteen (1976).

Victory at long last in the suffrage campaign confirmed deep-seated change in Swedish society. Yet the wonder is that the left political groups did not become more radical. In Norway the Labor party joined the Comintern in 1919 and was called the "most radical socialist party in western Europe";[2] only four years later did it withdraw from this communist affiliation. In Finland destructive civil war between left and right tore the country apart. But in Sweden during the early years of the war the social democrats liked to think that the regulatory practices installed through necessity were peaceful steps toward their goal of socialization. Toward the end of the war they disabused themselves of this illusion and when they joined with the liberals in the Edén coalition government their perspective changed. Responsibility both gave encouragement for the distant future and induced restraint for the present.

The party as a whole followed the lead of Hjalmar Branting and Gustav Möller. These were practical-minded men and their policies succeeded not only in winning participation in government but also, in the fall of 1918, in achieving that definitive breakthrough of democracy: universal suffrage. Success had come slowly, but it had come without violence, through the unique cooperation between reformist socialism and radical liberalism. This success was due in large measure to two strong men and their understanding cooperation: Karl Staaff the liberal (who had died in 1915) and Hjalmar Branting the social democrat. Their close association dated from Uppsala student days and their ideals remained similar although their methods and their affiliations were different.

Hjalmar Branting was a remarkable personality, a man "created to impose, to convince, to win," according to a contemporary appraisal when he was a young man. He was quick with the right and kindly word as well as able to flare in righteous anger. He came from an academic family; his father was principal of a secondary school and received the coveted professorial title. Like many others of the Swedish socialist leadership he sprang not from the slums or the rural shacks but from the upper-middle-class elite, a fact of significance for the whole movement. As a young man Branting became absorbed in the struggle for social justice, but it was justice through law that he demanded, not the justice of the barricades. His culture, his humaneness, his international acquaintanceships and outlook made him in later life a revered figure in socialist circles both at home and abroad.[3] To Hjalmar Branting must go the lion's share of the credit for holding the reform movement within bounds during the postwar chaos of hope and desperation. He was strong enough and clever enough to maneuver so that the extremists did not have to be condemned and extruded but left the party voluntarily, some to become communists, but others, in disillusionment with communism, to return later to the social democratic fold.

However, the long and fruitful period of cooperation between social democrats and liberals was bound to come to an end. Once their common goal of democratic political processes was achieved their fundamental divergences on other issues had to assume priority. In this new situation the Swedish community had to build a viable system based on a weakened monarchy and a more responsible riksdag. At the same time the government had to face difficult economic adjustments exacerbated by postwar problems in the outside world and finally a worldwide depression; it had to chart a new course in foreign affairs; and it had to plan a sweeping program of social reforms. The shuffling and juggling among these problems of government, the economy, foreign relations, and social reform become intricately confusing if dealt with chronologically, as can be sensed from a study of the accompanying list of ministries and tables of election results. Hence let us approach these main problems one by one for the period between the world wars.

Party Strength in the Second Chamber of the Riksdag: Delegates Elected 1911–48
(Total membership of the Second Chamber throughout this period was 230)

| Year | Conservatives (Högern) | Farmers (Bondeförbundet) | Liberals[a] | Social Democrats | Socialists | Socialists-Communists | Communists | Of which Women of All Parties |
|---|---|---|---|---|---|---|---|---|
| 1911 | 65 | | 101 | 64 | | | | 1 |
| 1914 (Mar.-Apr.) | 86 | | 71 | 73 | | | | |
| 1914 (Sept.) | 86 | | 57 | 87 | | | | |
| 1917 | 59 | 12 | 62 | 97[b] | | | | |
| 1920 | 70 | 30 | 48 | 82[c] | | | | |
| 1921 | 62 | 21 | 41 | 99[b] | | 7 | | 4 |
| 1924 | 65 | 23 | 33 | 104 | | 5 | | 3 |
| 1928 | 73 | 27 | 32 | 90 | | 8 | | 3 |
| 1932 | 58 | 36 | 24 | 104 | 6 | | 2 | 5 |
| 1936 | 44 | 36 | 27 | 112 | 6 | | 5 | 10 |
| 1940 | 42 | 28 | 23 | 134 | | | 3 | 17 |
| 1944 | 39 | 35 | 26 | 115 | | | 15 | 18 |
| 1948 | 23 | 30 | 57 | 112 | | | 8 | 22 |

*Source: Historisk statistik*, III, pp. 268–269.
  [a] Before 1924 they were called "Liberala"; between 1924 and 1932 they were divided into two groups, "Liberala" and "Frisinnade"; after their reunion in 1935 their party was called the "Folkparti."
  [b] Includes Left Social Democrats.
  [c] Includes Left Social Democrats and Communists.

Party Strength in the First Chamber of the Riksdag: Delegates Elected 1911–50
(Total Membership of the First Chamber throughout this period was 150)

| Year | Conservatives (Högern) | Farmers (Bonde-förbundet) | Liberals (Liberala Frisinnade) | (Folk-parti) | Social Democrats | Left Socialists | Socialists-Communists | Communists | Of which Women of All Parties |
|---|---|---|---|---|---|---|---|---|---|
| 1911 | 87 | | 51 | | 12 | | | | |
| 1919 | 38 | 19 | 41 | | 49 | 2 | | 1 | 1 |
| 1921 | 41 | 18 | 38 | | 50 | 2 | | 1 | 1 |
| 1922 | 41 | 18 | 38 | | 50 | 2 | | 1 | 1 |
| 1923 | 44 | 17 | 36 | | 50 | | 3 | 1 | 1 |
| 1924 | 44 | 18 | 35 | | 52 | 1 | | 1 | 1 |
| 1925 | 46 | 17 | 34 | | 51 | | | 1 | 1 |
| 1926 | 49 | 16 | 32 | | 52 | | | 1 | 1 |
| 1928 | 48 | 14 | 30 | | 52 | | | 1 | 1 |
| 1929 | 49 | 17 | 31 | | 52 | | | 2 | 1 |
| 1930 | 49 | 17 | 30 | | 52 | | | 1 | 1 |
| 1931 | 50 | 17 | 28 | | 54 | | | 1 | 1 |
| 1932 | 49 | 19 | 26 | | 55 | | | 1 | 1 |
| 1933 | 50 | 18 | 23 | | 58 | | | 1 | 1 |
| 1934 | 49 | 19 | 20 | | 61 | | | 1 | 1 |
| 1935 | 48 | 20 | | 19 | 62 | | | 1 | |
| 1936 | 46 | 22 | | 16 | 65 | | | 1 | |
| 1937 | 45 | 22 | | 16 | 66 | | | 1 | |
| 1938 | 43 | 23 | | 17 | 67 | | | | |
| 1939 | 41 | 24 | | 15 | 69 | | | 1 | |
| 1933–40 | 36 | 23 | | 15 | 75 | | | 1 | |
| 1941 | 35 | 24 | | 15 | 75 | | | 1 | |
| 1935–42 | 31 | 21 | | 15 | 82 | | | 1 | |
| 1936–43 | 30 | 21 | | 15 | 83 | | | | |
| 1937–44 | 30 | 21 | | 14 | 83 | | | 2 | |
| 1937–45 | 28 | 21 | | 14 | 84 | | | 3 | |
| 1939–46 | 26 | 21 | | 14 | 86 | | | 3 | 2 |
| 1940–47 | 25 | 21 | | 16 | 85 | | | 3 | 2 |
| 1941–48 | 24 | 21 | | 18 | 84 | | | 3 | 2 |
| 1942–49 | 23 | 23 | | 20 | 81 | | | 3 | 4 |
| 1943–50 | 22 | 25 | | 20 | 79 | | | 4 | 4 |

Source: Historisk statistik, III, p. 267.

# Government Ministries in Sweden, 1914–45

| Dates | Party | Prime Minister | Other Significant Ministers (FM = Foreign Minister) |
|---|---|---|---|
| February 1914–March 1917 | Nonparty | Hjalmar Hammarskjöld | K. A. Wallenberg (FM) |
| March 1917–October 1917 | Conservative | Carl Swartz | Arvid Lindman (FM) |
| October 1917–March 1920 | Liberal-Social Democratic | Nils Edén | Johan Hellner (FM)<br>Hjalmar Branting<br>Östen Undén |
| March 1920–October 1920 | Social Democratic | Hjalmar Branting | Erik Palmstierna (FM)<br>Östen Undén<br>P. A. Hansson |
| October 1920–.October 1921 | Nonparty | Louis De Geer<br>Oscar von Sydow | Herman Wrangel (FM) |
| October 1921–April 1923 | Social Democratic | Hjalmar Branting | Rickard Sandler<br>P. A. Hansson<br>H. Branting (FM) |
| April 1923–October 1924 | Conservative | Ernst Trygger | C. Hederstierna (FM) (to Nov. 1923) |
| October 1924–June 1926 | Social Democratic | Hjalmar Branting (to Jan. 1925)<br>Rickard Sandler | Östen Undén (FM)<br>Torsten Nothin<br>P. A. Hansson<br>Ernst Wigforss<br>Gustav Möller |
| June 1926–October 1928 | Liberal Coalition | C. G. Ekman | Eliel Löfgren (FM)<br>Felix Hamrin |
| October 1928–June 1930 | Conservative | Arvid Lindman | Ernst Trygger (FM) |
| June 1930–September 1932 | Liberal | C. G. Ekman<br>Felix Hamrin | |
| September 1932–June 1936 | Social Democratic | P. A. Hansson | Rickard Sandler (FM)<br>Per Edvin Sköld<br>Östen Undén<br>Ernst Wigforss<br>Gustav Möller |
| June 1936–September 1936 | Farmers | Axel Pehrsson | K. G. Westman (FM) |
| September 1936–December 1939 | Social Democratic-Farmer coalition | P. A. Hansson | Rickard Sandler (FM)<br>K. G. Westman<br>A. Pehrsson–Bramstorp<br>Gustav Möller<br>Ernst Wigforss<br>Per Edvin Sköld |
| December 1939–July 1945 | Coalition | P. A. Hansson | Christian Günther (FM)<br>F. Domö<br>K. G. Westman<br>Per Edvin Sköld<br>Gustav Möller<br>Ernst Wigforss<br>Gösta Bagge<br>A. Pehrsson–Bramstorp<br>Bertil Ohlin |
| July 1945–October 1951 | Social Democratic | P. A. Hansson (to Oct. 1946)<br>Tage Erlander | Östen Undén (FM) |

## Political Readjustment

Political parties are fundamental to the workings of proportional representation and parliamentarism, but parties are never static. Splinterings and regroupings, growth and decline are inevitable, and changes of party names complicate matters further. But since World War I there has usually been a five-way division in the parties of Sweden (and of the other Nordic countries): conservative, liberal, agrarian (farmer, later "center"), social democratic, and communist.

The three nonsocialist parties, which stood in varying degrees for the maintenance of the existing order, were weakened by the differences among them and within them. The liberals were split among themselves on issues such as temperance, the free church movement, and defense. Diverse groups of farmers only slowly united in *Bondeförbundet* and remained concerned almost wholly with agricultural problems. The conservatives (*Höger*) were interested in defense, monarchy, and business and were fairly solid among themselves. These three "bourgeois" party groups lacked the kind of common concerns that could enable them to work consistently together. Their agreement on general principles such as individualism and the rights of capital lacked impelling and harmonizing power.

The social democrats, on the other hand, had a cohesive philosophy, influenced by Marxism and international socialist thought — especially German, French, and English — although carefully and thoroughly adapted to Swedish conditions. A certain degree of influence emanated from Scandinavian experience, too: it is of interest that Willy Brandt spent the years 1933 to 1945 in Norway before becoming the socialist leader in Berlin and Germany; and Bruno Kreisky served on the scientific staff of the cooperative society in Stockholm from 1938 to 1946 before returning to Austria and becoming chancellor. The social democrats of the North had a mission: to change society. Internal differences of opinion about methods and the speed and extent of socialization caused occasional splinter groups to break off, but common purpose and intelligent leadership held the party together. Party discipline was strictly commanded on pain of expulsion. Gustav Möller stood firmly against the leftists' demand for social revolution; socialization, he insisted, must come gradually, and this policy was accepted by the party. The basic demands for democracy and social control of the means of production fused and expanded into a broad program of welfare and equality (*jämlikhet*).

Near the end of World War I (1917) a dissident group of Left Social Democrats built their own party, and in 1921 the majority of this group became communist. One faction among them consisted of moderate communists, and when their leader, Zeth Höglund, failed in his attempt to maintain freedom from Moscow, they returned in 1926 to the social democratic fold. The iron-willed, hammer-and-sickle communists remained a small group, but they pounded continuously at the social democrats.

The two major aggregations of political opinion, the socialists and the nonsocialists or "bourgeois," represented diametrically opposite ideologies. It is impossible to find a suitable term to apply to the three parties on the right. The conservative wing took for itself the name Right *(Höger)* but eventually renamed itself Moderate. The farmers were surely not "bourgeois," nor were many of the liberals. "Nonsocialist" is clear enough, but the negative connotations of the term are hardly justified. "Rightist" or "right-wing" is not quite accurate. All these terms will be used, but they are not wholly correct. The socialist left prefers to call the other parties "bourgeois," while these parties themselves use the term "nonsocialist." The problem is not one of translation, for the Swedes themselves have not come up with a satisfactory term; this is perhaps a key to understanding the difficulties they have in cooperation with one another. The socialists and nonsocialists divided the electorate almost evenly between them; on two occasions in later years parliamentary strength was precisely balanced. Power fluctuated back and forth until 1932, and for decades thereafter neither side had sufficient power to push an extreme program or ride roughshod over the opposition. Political change was therefore gradual, not spectacular, but change there was.

The intentions of the social democrats had never been secret. In 1919, while they shared the government with the liberals, they demanded a series of tax reforms: progressive property taxes, increased taxes on business and rents, and agreement on an income tax. A year later, when the party drew up a wide-ranging program of reforms, they listed also such items as a steep inheritance tax, unemployment insurance, a republican form of government, more state control of private business, the right of expropriation and forced purchase of large estates — in other words, full socialization. In such a program the liberals were quite unwilling to cooperate, and the Liberal-Social Democratic partnership ended soon afterwards. When in March 1920 the Edén government resigned, Hjalmar Branting came in as prime minister of the first Social Democratic government in the world to reach power by peaceful processes. Erik Palmstierna became foreign minister, and the cabinet included Per Albin Hansson, Fredrik Thorsson, Rickard Sandler, and Torsten Nothin. As a single-party, minority government it had little chance for a long life, but it gave experience to young men who would be heard from again and again. It set up commissions to investigate such problems as the referendum, industrial democracy, state control of trusts, and the socialization of natural resources and production. On the immediate problem of tax policy the government proposals were too severe for the liberals and the farmers to accept, and many social democrats thought the ministry should resign. But the king had acquired great respect for Branting and urged him to stay, partly because of the Åland problem (see section on foreign affairs in this chapter).

The autumn election in 1920 produced a swing to the right in the Second Chamber and then Branting had to resign. A caretaker government under Louis De Geer (the younger) came in for a few months, being succeeded by a similar government under Oscar von Sydow. In 1921 the new electoral law became effective, with the electorate expanded from 1.2 million to 3.2 million. Although the majority of eligible voters were now women, only 47 percent of them voted, compared with 62 percent of men; four women were elected to the Second Chamber. The new voters reversed the trend of the previous election: the social democrats added 17 seats for a total of 99 and became the largest single party in the Second Chamber. Branting returned as head of his second minority government (October 1921–April 1923), but stability could hardly be expected. Unemployment and strikes became disruptive issues, played upon by the communists. When the First and Second Chambers disagreed on a policy of assistance to strikers the government resigned. A conservative-farmer ministry headed by Ernst Trygger tried its hand, pledged to "intelligent adjustment." Dissension over a military bill and an unclear mandate in the 1924 elections led to the resignation of the Trygger government and the return of Branting for a third time.

When the "grand old man" died early in 1925 the social democrats continued briefly with Rickard Sandler as prime minister. In May Fredrik Thorsson, another of the veterans, died. The charter members of the party were gone and the leadership team of 1925 was composed of a new group, mostly men in their forties: scholarly Rickard Sandler; his rival, strong man, and clever tactician with the folksy touch, Per Albin Hansson; social theoretician and finance expert Ernst Wigforss; strict constructionist Östen Undén; Gustav Möller, the poor boy who became party secretary and architect of social reforms; Torsten Nothin, minister of justice. Per Edvin Sköld, able and versatile, was added in 1932. These were the men who would lead the way to the welfare state, and it was an extraordinarily able and committed group.

However, in the 1920s the social democrats continued to suffer from the frustrations of their inadequate power base. Having the largest single party in the 230-member Second Chamber was not enough, and opinions were so divided that no coalition of parties could long survive. C. G. Ekman, leader of the *Frisinnade folkpartiet*, which had split from the other liberals in 1923, upset the Sandler government in 1926; this group then formed a minority coalition ministry with the *Liberala*, their former party mates (these two groups reunited in 1935 under the name *Folkparti* [Peoples' party]). It was a labor issue that wrecked the Sandler government in 1926. A long strike at the Stripa mine in central Sweden led to a directive by the riksdag that the miners who refused work that was offered should receive no unemployment benefits; the cabinet denounced this rule and resigned. Ekman became prime minister although he had a backing of only 32 members in the First Chamber and 33 in the Second. He governed as "balance-master," seeking support first from the bourgeois majority, then from the social democrats, as circumstances required. With social democratic and farmer support the government passed a school reform in 1927, and with rightist cooperation it established in 1928 a labor court — an institution that labor at first opposed but gradually came to appreciate.

The campaign of 1928 became a clear-cut struggle between left and right. Social democrats and communists cooperated to a certain extent, and the social democrats' proposal for increased taxes on inheritance, income, and property to equalize wealth antagonized the bourgeois. One sentence in the tax motion read: "poverty is accepted with equanimity when it is shared by all." [4] This apparent defeatism shocked the liberals and conservatives, who also blamed the social democrats for reducing the military establishment. The result was an increase of 11 seats for the bourgeois parties and a loss of 14 by the Social Democrats (the Communists increased by 3). Since the big gain was for the conservatives the Ekman government reluctantly left office. Conservative Arvid Lindman became prime minister for a second time; Ernst Trygger joined the government as foreign minister.

The good economic conditions and sunny prospects for the conservative government were soon clouded by the international depression sweeping in from the United States and by the difficulties of agriculture, suffering from external competition. Again it was C. G. Ekman who wrecked the ministry and again he was called to be prime minister, but with a still smaller parliamentary cohort: 23 in the First Chamber and 28 in the Second. He refused to build a coalition with the social democrats and the farmers, and the other liberal group refused to join with him. Despite the weakness of his position Ekman carried on for two years (1930–32), and some things were accomplished under steadily worsening conditions. However, eight changes of government in the twelve years from 1920 to 1932 indicated uncertainty in policy at a time when firm direction was needed.

The elections of 1932 were influenced by the depression and gave the Social Democrats 104 seats in the Second Chamber, still 12 short of a majority, but enough to give confidence to the sanguine leaders of the party. Nevertheless, they would have to have allies to be able to govern vigorously. Because of their strong ideological position they could not expect cooperation from other parties of principle. But the farmers had a party of interests rather than principles and with them a bargain might be struck. Especially the younger elements among the farmers were ready to support certain parts of the social democrats' program in return for advantages to agriculture. Thus a notorious horse trade (in Swedish, *kohandel* [cow trade]) was arranged: the farmers got higher prices for dairy products and protection against imported grain, and the social democrats compromised on their unemployment program. The arrangement worked out advantageously for the country and established a precedent for closer cooperation in the future, notably in the Social Democratic-Farmer coalition governments of 1936–39 and 1951–57. This was the practical politics of men like Per Albin Hansson and Axel Pehrsson–Bramstorp, the upcoming leader of the farmers' delegation. Because of this intermittent collaboration the Social Democrats were enabled to hold power from 1932 into the 1970s with only a break of a few months in 1936. Only twice during that entire period did they enjoy a majority of their own in the Second Chamber (1941–45 and 1969–73).

With the coming of World War II the luxury of domestic political wrangling was laid aside. From December 1939 until the end of July 1945 the cabinet included representatives of all the major parties, although the Social Democrats retained the most posts and kept the premiership in the hands of Per Albin Hansson. This ability to set aside partisan politics in an emergency was illustrated less happily in World War I and in the denouement of the Union crisis in 1905, but during World War II it functioned moderately well.

We must not overestimate the confusion caused by frequent changes of government. In Sweden the cabinet ministers were policy makers rather than administrators, whereas in the United States their opposite numbers in the president's cabinet combined both policy-making and administrative functions. In Sweden the day-by-day business of government could go on indefinitely through the powerful bureaucracy of administrative boards and commissions. The age-old institutions such as the Board of Commerce and the Office of Mines and the newer instrumentalities such as the Labor Market Board and the Telecommunications Administration were practically independent forces. They functioned according to law and established procedures irrespective of changing party power and personnel. The general directors of these bodies held practically indefinite tenure and high prestige. Although personal and political favoritism inevitably affected their appointment, there was no such thing as a spoils system. Men and women of ability were chosen without overmuch regard for their social origins or political tendencies. The fine traditions, the security and prestige of the civil service continued to attract persons of education and standing, the scions of the great families and the impecunious aristocracy. The class which in England and other countries went into the army or the church had less opportunity for such outlets in Sweden, especially in recent years when the army did not offer much challenge and the church had lost its power. Foreign-service appointments, particularly, usually went to men of the upper social and income level who had the education and the language skills to fit the positions, although the assignments were made by a Social Democratic administration. Governors and other officials tended, once appointed, to become nonpartisan. Throughout the civil service standards of honesty and performance were high; corruption was almost unknown. Swedish officials had the chance to work for the community without the turmoil and uncertainty of political strife or the competitiveness of business. The civil service in Sweden had, in brief, something of the nimbus of the courts in the United States.

Bureaucracy was nevertheless bureaucracy and people complained bitterly of *krångel Sverige* (harassment Sweden). Assiduity and precision were characteristic of Swedish officialdom. And it was the officials who brought government closest to the citizens whether they were social workers or police, teachers or postmen, judges or clerks or inspectors.

Gradually the social democratic leadership became aware of the fact that although riksdag and government represented labor more than other classes, the bureaucracy and the diplomatic corps were filled with people from the so-called upper classes. Even then, however, the response was not "Let's appoint more social democrats and representatives of social classes III and IV." The solution to the problem of building social balance into the bureaucracy was to democratize education so that young people of all social classes would be equally well prepared for government positions.

### Economic Adjustment, 1920–40

After World War I economic decline followed the wave of wartime prosperity. The foreign market for iron ore and iron vanished in 1918, and the high 1917 output of iron was not matched again until the 1940s. The deflation of 1921–22 was a disaster, though short-lived. The wholesale price index (on the basis of 1913 = 100) fell from 376 to 163. In January 1922 the unemployed numbered 163,000, and one of every three union members was out of work. Real taxes for wage earners doubled and businesses went bankrupt. The economic distress goes far to explain the Social Democrats' victory at the polls. During 1922 conditions began rapidly to improve: export of iron and iron ore and wood products resumed, and communal and cooperative construction helped put people back to work. By 1924 Sweden was able to be the first country in Europe to return to the gold standard.[5]

However, unemployment plagued Sweden intermittently through the 1920s and early 1930s. The causes could be blamed on external factors because world markets for the products of mines and forests were irregular. Disruptive strikes made the situation worse and raised the question in 1923 of unemployment assistance to strikers — an issue played upon by the communists and which led to disagreement between the First Chamber and the Second and to the short-lived ministry of Ernst Trygger. Soon an agrarian crisis was added to the industrial, as imports reduced the price of grain. The first relief was for the government to buy up domestic grain at fixed high prices and to control imports through a half-state, half-private organization (a plan suggested by Per Edvin Sköld and implemented by the government).

Depression continued to deepen in 1931, and the worse it became the more strident grew communist agitation. The most serious example of tension occurred in Ådalen in Ångermanland, northern Sweden. After a strike of several months' duration at last strike breakers were hired. The communists called for a general strike, the workers demonstrated, a company of soldiers was called in, stones were thrown, the military answered with shots, and five people were killed. In the riksdag the heated charges of the communists were answered with defense of the right to work. Arthur Engberg, one of the leading social democrats, called the soldiers murderers and the strike breakers vermin.[6] Violence in labor disputes was sufficiently rare that the Ådalen affair stirred up a strong polarization of feeling between labor and the general population.

By September 1932, when the Social Democrats returned to office, both the agricultural crisis and industrial unemployment had become serious, and during the following winter both grew worse. So much worse, indeed, that in desperation the stage was set for the collaboration of the party of labor and the party of the farmers, mentioned earlier. Their combined action was successful partly because of the existence of the reserve fund built up through the liquor control system. There were still arguments about whether governmental support should be used for major construction projects and labor paid at regular (unskilled) rates or whether assistance should be given as a dole. It was the same problem that faced governments in the United States and other industrial countries during the depression. In Sweden both systems were used and it was fortunate to be able to pull rapidly out of the slump.[7]

Another factor of prime importance was monetary policy. In September 1931 Sweden followed Great Britain in abandoning the gold standard; throughout the period of crisis the English and the Swedish monetary policies harmonized well, which eased the problem for Sweden. The Riksbank restored its foreign assets, which had fallen to 49 million kronor in 1931, to 717 million kronor in 1936; it increased its gold reserves in the same period from 206 million kronor to 529 million kronor. Sweden became a capital-exporting country during a time of world crisis. Devaluation of the krona reduced the cost of Swedish pulp, iron ore, iron, and steel enough that the export of these basic products could be approximately doubled between 1932 and 1936. Prices of import products increased, but the amount of imports was reduced so that no trade crisis developed; from 1932 to 1936 the country was able to hold the balance of trade almost even.

A major disaster threatened at one point to wreck the entire recovery program. Shock waves ran through Sweden and the whole financial world at the death of Ivar Kreuger and the collapse of his vast financial empire. In the 1920s, when not only Sweden but the developing countries of eastern Europe and Latin America were thirsting for capital, Kreuger became the angel who got money and lent it. Although his father was a match manufacturer Ivar Kreuger's career began with a construction business (Kreuger and Toll, founded in 1908), based on a light concrete method that he learned on a trip to America. Soon the firm moved into the match business, too, and by 1923 Kreuger teamed up with Lee, Higginson, and Company of Boston to found the International Match Company. By the late 1920s Kreuger controlled over half the world's production of matches and held monopolies in several countries to which he granted loans. He was called a financial wizard. In 1927 he loaned the French state $75 million and a year later $125 million to Germany. He bought the Boliden mining company of northern Sweden from Skandinaviska Kredit AB and launched a massive building program which might have exhausted the ore within ten years. Evidently he planned to sell the company while its production was at its peak, and several parties were interested in the purchase (the Swedish state, Stockholms Enskilda Bank, and some English concerns). Kreuger's complex financial skyscraper might have stood somewhat longer had boom conditions continued but instead the worldwide depression created unusual strains. Kreuger had difficulty getting new extensions of credit, and on May 12, 1932 he was found shot dead in his Paris apartment, presumably a suicide. His grand construction turned out to be a house of cards. His chief Swedish bank, the Skandinaviska Kredit AB, was flattened and only government assistance could save it. His bookkeeping was found to be so complicated and deceptive that it took years to straighten the accounts. Thousands of investors were wiped out, and confidence in Swedish honesty was given a serious blow. The revelation that Prime Minister Ekman had received from Kreuger at least two 50,000-kronor gifts (one of which he falsely denied) forced Ekman's resignation in August 1932, and other repercussions were felt around the world.[8]

Devastating though the Kreuger crash seemed at the time, its long-term effects were less catastrophic than was at first feared. It probably reinforced the social democratic predisposition for government controls. Encouraged by the "Stockholm School" of economists and the ideas of John Maynard

Keynes the Swedish government continued to spend its way out of the depression. According to this new way of looking at finance, public expenditures could be regarded as stimuli to the economy in a recession period and as a means of increasing employment and productivity. The government therefore developed two budgets, the operating budget, which had to be tight, and the capital budget, which could be expansive. For its antidepression campaign the government was fortunate in having at hand a large fund accumulated by the liquor monopoly.

Sweden's unusually rapid recovery from the depression was attributed by Arthur Montgomery primarily to the Riksbank's cautiously expansionary monetary policy, assisted by the government's expansionist policy in the public works and other unemployment relief, programs that were wise from an economic point of view and essential as social policy. Montgomery emphasizes also that Sweden's recovery was greatly aided by improvement in foreign economies, especially in England and in Germany. Most things worked together for good: vigorous individual effort, decisive governmental action, and the happy coincidence of foreign demand for Swedish products. All in all, the decade of the 1930s was a period of vibrant activity in Sweden. Industry was "rationalizing" its processes by electrification, mechanization, and scientific improvements so that by 1935 its productivity was 20 percent greater than in 1929, with a labor force only 2 percent larger.[9]

Both economically and socially one of the important activities of the 1930s was the housing program. In 1930 a housing exhibition in Stockholm displayed exciting new designs partly indigenous, partly inspired by German functionalism. The emphasis was on utility, efficiency, and the elimination of elaborate decoration. It was an architectural and artistic event for furniture as well as for home construction and helped to build the reputation of the "Swedish modern" style, soon to enjoy a worldwide vogue. The construction and equipment of the new-style homes fit the simpler taste of the twentieth century. The labor-saving devices for housekeeping, especially in the kitchen, encouraged homebuilding for young families in which both husband and wife worked outside the home. Many people hoped that easier living conditions might arrest the alarming decline in births, to which the Myrdals called attention. Housing was also closely associated with the renewed vigor of the cooperative movement.

### The Cooperatives — a Buyers' Democracy?

It was in this period between the two world wars that cooperative housing became a giant and the cooperative movement reached maturity. Individual housing cooperatives had long existed but in 1923 the HSB (Hyresgästernas

Sparkasse- och Byggnadsförening — the Tenants' Savings and Building Society) was founded in Stockholm. In its first decade the HSB was responsible for the building of over 8,000 dwelling units, mostly in large blocks but ranging in size from 4 to 400 units each. HSB, as its name indicated, emphasized both savings and building; it established a savings bank, sold its own bonds, and worked together with the cooperative insurance company to amass capital. An individual normally joined the society and began to save for his down payment before he got an apartment, but from the beginning he had a voice in planning and management. He could expect the most up-to-date floor plans; the most efficient methods of handling garbage; space and equipment for special child-care rooms, recreation rooms, outdoor playgrounds, cooperative stores, carpet-beating rooms, laundries, and so on. HSB even built summer colonies. This Stockholm society proliferated branches through the country, in 60 towns by 1940. In each community a parent society was responsible for building programs, each building had its own "daughter" society, and all were linked into the national organization.

Location of construction, planning, and financing were all complicated, but the complications inherent in such matters were eased in the Swedish situation where legislation favored the savings and building cooperatives, and municipalities aided the projects. Sometimes construction was arranged in partnership with labor unions. And although HSB was the largest of all the organizations many local societies remained unaffiliated. In 1940 another national housing cooperative was organized, Riksbyggen (National Building), owned in a three-way partnership by KF (Kooperative Förbundet — the Cooperative Union), the Confederation of Trade Unions, and the National Union of Construction Workers. Riksbyggen had by 1974 built 200,000 dwelling units, 55 percent of them cooperatives; HSB had built somewhat more, and these two big institutions managed about two-thirds of the half-million cooperative housing units in the country. (Since ownership of each dwelling is commonly vested in the individual, these would be called condominiums in the United States.)

Cooperation also took hold in other sectors of the economy. An association for handling gasoline and automotive accessories began in 1915, and others followed, many of them later associating themselves into Bilägarnas Inköpscentral (IC — Auto Owners' Purchasing Central) or Oljekonsumenternas förbund (OK Union — Oil Consumers' Union). After 1960 these two combined under the name OK Union, absorbed KF's fuel business, and joined with similar operations in Denmark and Norway. Membership grew to 660,000, and in 1974 the OK had 14 percent of the market for heating oil and 21 percent of that for gasoline. KF inaugurated Folksam, a fire insurance company, in 1905 and gradually moved into car and life insurance. By the

1970s Folksam was the third largest insurance company in Sweden, being especially strong in the group life and group health insurance field.

The cooperative movement frightened private businessmen but it did not drive entrepreneurship from the market place. Individual retail stores continued to exist alongside the cooperative Konsum and Domus stores and nationally to outsell the cooperatives. The independent local cooperative societies registered as of 1974 some 1.72 million members, and in that year they handled 18 percent of the total retail trade, with special strength in the food business. Members of course bought many items outside the cooperative facilities, and nonmembers shopped in cooperative stores and gas stations. In foods and other everyday consumption goods the miscellaneous independent stores were slowly falling behind, dropping from 39 percent of the market in 1970 to 31 percent in 1974. In the same period the KF stores held even at 31 percent. The association of approximately 5,000 private merchants who began in 1930 to organize the ICA (Inköpscentralen), and who later established supermarkets and shopping centers after the American pattern, increased their share from 31 percent to 37 percent. A third nationwide system was organized in 1972 to serve as wholesaler for the independent stores not members of either KF or ICA; it was known as DAGAB, an abbreviation for *Dagligvarugrossisternas Intresse AB*; it permitted independents to realize the advantages of large-scale purchasing while they remained independent. DAGAB grew with amazing rapidity to include most of the previously unaffiliated food stores. Nevertheless, growth potential seemed to reside primarily in the ICA group, and cooperation appeared to have leveled off. The leveling nevertheless left KF alongside Volvo as the largest single business enterprise in Sweden, with close to one and one half billion dollars in annual turnover. Since 1950 the number of stores was sharply reduced, but membership and volume of business continued to increase. The movement was still strong, although the fervor of the pioneers was gone and private enterprise was also strong.[10]

That the cooperative movement was not entirely national and self-centered was indicated by its international connections. Not only did Rochdale supply the inspiration and the organizational pattern, but relations with the English movement were continuingly nurtured by visits and personal acquaintance. Within the North the Swedish societies developed close relations with the societies in Finland, Denmark, and Norway, and through a joint inter-Nordic society formed in 1918 they combined in large-scale buying on the foreign market, especially of coffee, fruit, and other "colonial products." The Swedish cooperators collaborated actively with the international cooperative movement. They aided the development of societies in Asia and Latin America and, perhaps most significantly, in East Africa, where since 1967 they have acted together with the other Nordic countries' cooperatives in education, advice, and technical assistance. They plan and collaborate closely with SIDA (the Swedish International Development Agency).

The Swedish cooperative leadership of the twentieth century was composed of shrewd and careful men who were aware of the too sanguine hopes and the mistakes of their nineteenth-century predecessors. Albin Johansson, managing director of KF in the crucial 1930s and 1940s, was said by some outside the movement to be the ablest businessman in Sweden. The opposition of private interests alerted the cooperative people to the need to be cautious. Hence they restricted their field of operation to certain sectors of the economy and felt their way. They specialized in food and everyday needs, only gradually expanding into other people-related businesses, particularly fuel, housing, and insurance. They built some factories, but only after they found that the existing price structure for the goods to be made was unreasonably burdensome. Thus they were able to bring prices down and realize a profit as they broke monopolies in margarine, galoshes, flour, and electric lamps. Marquis Childs in *Sweden, the Middle Way* (1936) has told dramatically how the Luma lamp factory won victory over the European lamp trust and reduced prices for the people of all northern Europe. Occasionally some particular combination of need and opportunity opened up an unusual endeavor, as when KF took over the ceramics plant at Gustavsberg when it was about to close.

The Swedish cooperatives threw down the gauntlet to private business where it was vulnerable; they maintained high standards of management and good quality in products; they clung to sound business practices but they were consumer-oriented rather than profit-oriented; they kept management democratic; and because of their methods and their ideals they enjoyed the good will of the labor unions and the social democratic government. Hence they built a secure place for cooperation within the mixed Swedish economy but did not attempt to destroy the private sector.

In brief, the cooperatives served in practice as brake and corrective on private business, while in philosophy the movement was a fundamental challenge to the concepts of entrepreneurship.[11]

## Progress toward Social Reform

Favorable economic conditions facilitated progress in meeting insistent social demands. The social democrats were the foremost spokesmen for social reform, but most members of other parties also recognized that justice and national well-being required some fundamental changes in society. There was of course much outright opposition to the proposals and the ideology of the social democrats, but practical politics prevailed and the function of the nonsocialist parties in the riksdag came to be that of restraining and modifying rather than of negating and destroying. Even the conservatives who rejected the philosophy of state intervention found themselves helping to shape programs of social reform; the liberals tended to approve the goals of reform if not the methods; the agrarians took the practical position that they would trade support for social reforms in return for specific gains for the farmers; the communists felt that everything being done was only weakly palliative, but they lacked the strength to achieve revolution. Hence reforms were accomplished gradually, step by step, with compromises and half-measures. The demands for reform covered the entire gamut of social discontents.

The alcohol problem had concerned Sweden for centuries and attempts at control had taken varied form and had achieved little success. Concern was widespread. In 1922, against the wishes of the conservatives, the government held a plebiscite on prohibition (consultative only and on the basis of manhood and women's suffrage). Strong sentiment among the social democrats and an important segment of the liberals was not enough, though the vote was close: 889,000 for and 925,000 against (59 percent of women voted for prohibition). Examples from the United States and Finland were not encouraging, and Sweden had already developed a compromise method of liquor control. The so-called Gothenburg system was based on the idea of separating profits from the sale of liquor; it had been tried in Gothenburg since 1865 and in Stockholm since 1895. Dr. Ivan Bratt emphasized rationing also and this system under a public-controlled monopoly was introduced in Stockholm in 1913 and in the kingdom in 1917, combined with local option (as applied to restaurants and bars) by decision of local governing bodies. The liquor ration book (*motbok*) remained in use from 1917 to 1955 when the control system was abolished. After a brief flurry of extraordinary consumption the country settled down to normal drinking habits, although alcoholism continued to be a serious national problem.

In the 1920s, while parties and governments were shuttling back and forth, only minor reforms were accomplished, for example, increases in sickness insurance and a law on arbitration in labor disputes. When the social democrats and the farmers began to work together in the early 1930s, the social democrats were enabled to promote home building and public works, to provide unemployment insurance, and to increase the income tax by 20 percent. When the farmers objected to Wigforss's demand for "death duties" (a charge on an entire estate), the social democrats compromised with higher taxes on individual heirs. Old-age pensions were expanded in 1935 and 1937; provision was made for motherhood benefits, marital loans, grants to widows and children, and subsidies for school lunches; twelve-day paid vacations were ordered for workers.

Difficulties arose when the social democrats attempted to bargain between defense and reform, as had been done by Boström in 1892. Per Albin Hansson was willing to offer support for the defense program of the bourgeois parties in return for acceptance of increased taxation for pensions. Firm resistance to this proposal led to the resignation of the Hansson cabinet in June 1936 and to the "vacation government" of the Farmers from June to September — the only gap in Social Democratic parliamentary leadership for many decades.

The setback was perhaps healthy, and the Social Democrats' platform for the 1936 elections was marked by moderation. Their appeal in the campaign was for welfare, especially higher pensions for the elderly. Voters disregarded the conservatives' warnings about defense and their condemnation of socialism, and 75 percent of them went to the polls. They reduced the Conservative seats from 58 to 44 and raised the Social Democrats' seats from 104 to 112 — still not a majority, but a significant indication of public opinion, especially if the Socialist party's 6 and the Communists' 5 were added. Per Albin Hansson was the winner and heir to the personal popularity of Hjalmar Branting. Per Albin calculated carefully and finally invited the Farmers party (Bondeförbundet) to join a coalition with the Social Democrats; he thus broke the bourgeois majority in the First Chamber and won a strong backing in both houses.

The shift of political emphasis was not merely moderation. It was a profound readjustment in attitude and it was associated with the responsibility of power. For an opposition party theories might be sufficient, but for the party directing government practical problems and solutions demanded priority. The economic crises of the early 1930s confronted political leaders with situations not envisaged in abstract theoretical formulations. And the social democrats of Sweden, practical men that they were, adapted policies to need rather than to ideology. Ernst Wigforss judged that the success of his party was due to the belief that the Social Democrats were the only politicans capable of acting with energy (*handlingskraftiga*).[12]

The Marxist principle of class struggle, for example, was abandoned and the new program was couched in terms of social equalization and building a happy and cooperative Swedish national community, the people's home (*folkhem*). Welfare rather than socialism became the emphasis, though it was felt that since socialism's purpose was welfare, whatever was done for welfare had to be socialism. There thus remained a fundamental difference between the contemporaneous programs of the social democrats of Sweden and the New Dealers of Franklin D. Roosevelt's United States, each of which influenced the other. Whereas the Swedish program aimed in the long run to transform society, the American program was designed to shore up and preserve the old social structure.

Therefore the Swedish government vigorously took initiatives both to meet immediate problems and to build the new society. When the leaders realized that they could not accomplish things alone they frankly made a "deal" with the farmers. But when the farmers entered into the political coalition of 1936 the "great farmers" (*storbönder*) moved over into the ranks of the conservatives. The smaller farmers, working together in producers' cooperatives, were becoming more sympathetic to the group activities of the industrial laborers, less antagonistic toward government interference and high tariffs — for these measures brought them higher prices.

One long overdue reform was the abolition of the *statsystem*, in which since the mid-eighteenth century the lowest class of farm laborers on the larger estates had been maintained in abject conditions, paid by meager wages-in-kind. The kindly paternalism that sometimes characterized relationships between landlord and crofter seldom affected these poor itinerant and exploited rural workers (the *statare*). With little chance to acquire either money or education they remained improverished and ignorant. Through the nineteenth century their plight was depicted in literature by E. G. Geijer, Fredrika Bremer, C. J. L. Almqvist, August Strindberg, and many others. Strindberg "prophesied that a time would come when the peasant lost his crofter, the gentleman farmer his *statare* and the townsman his servant. 'And the present slave-state will disappear, and a just society begin.'"[13] In the twentieth century literary attacks on the system became stronger and occasionally unionization made headway, one spectacular example being in Uppland, under the leadership of Oscar E. Sjölander. His union, independent from 1918 to 1930, at last joined the national organization, *Svenska Lantarbetarnas förbund*. LO, which had at first concentrated on industrial workers, became increasingly interested in the rural labor force.

The real breakthrough on the *statare* problem came as a result of further literary exposures, supported now by the social democrats and the small farmers. A few of these *statare* struggled and rose above their fellows. Most important of the new writers of this group was Ivar Lo-Johansson, himself the son of a *statare*. He told with vivid detail of the lives of ordinary workers both on the farm and in the city, vignettes of poverty and of the suffering from arrogant masters, of motherhood in misery, of feeding the pigs and of carrying heavy sacks of coal. He made his readers feel the oppression that deprived the laborer of both dignity and hope, that made him think himself incompetent. As critic of this labor system Lo-Johansson proved that it need not be politicians that originate reform. With the biting words of his novels he roused indignation and sympathy in the consciences of citizens and legislators.[14] The demoralizing *stat* system was ended by law in 1945.

Urban labor was in a different situation, being both more concentrated and more organized. The individual unions and their federation, LO, were well established before World War I, even though they had suffered from the loss of the 1909 general strike. Thereafter labor steadily increased its organizational strength and recruited beyond factory and wage workers. In 1931 salaried employees in private employment founded a union called Saco; in 1937 the salaried workers in government formed TCO (Tjänstemans Central Organization), and in 1944 these two merged into the new TCO, which became a potent union. The most important step was taken in 1938 when LO got together with the employers' association, SAF, through negotiations at Saltsjöbaden in a basic agreement that became a charter regulating the relationship between labor and management. (The labor background for this agreement is discussed in chapter XV, pages 412–419.) Both parties felt the threat of governmental intervention in the interest of the public if they could not reconcile their own disputes. The comparable September Agreement in Denmark had been effective since 1899. The Saltsjöbaden Agreement laid the basis for increasingly broad national negotiations on wage and employment problems. Specifically it set up a six-member Labor Market Board composed of three from each group, restricted strikes affecting essential public services, and established principles to guide relationships between labor and management. It inaugurated a system in which the leaders of labor and the leaders of industry came to know and understand each other. Their fundamental differences remained and each group fought for its own concerns in the division of the income from production. But acquaintanceship and trust undoubtedly reduced both the number of strikes and their bitterness and destructiveness.

Underlying the agreement itself and the human relationship growing out of it was the understanding on both sides of the bargaining table that labor and management had not only conflicting interests but common interests in the productivity and prosperity of the country — a solid fact perhaps easier to recognize in a small country than in a large one and a fact that some foreign observers have found it difficult to appreciate. Obviously it was to the advantage of everyone to compromise differences peaceably rather than engage in destructive strife.

In the two decades from 1919 to 1939 Sweden moved in noteworthy fashion, even if by short steps, on the road to social democracy. World War II put a temporary halt to social progress, and it might be well to pause and pull together some of the complex strands of the period. Between 1919 and 1939 Sweden changed course. The shift began with the achievement of universal suffrage (only a few minor restrictions were left to be eliminated during succeeding years). Then, having obtained political democracy, the social democrats pushed on for social democracy. In the first hectic decade the new direction was not clear. The fluctuating balance of parties meant repeated transfers of power. The social democrats increased in popular support and in self-confidence until they overreached themselves and in 1948 were "contained" by the resurgent liberals led by Bertil Ohlin. The rather even division of political opinion then and for decades to come tended to check extremism of any kind and to enforce a "politics of consensus." The social democrats were full of ideas and energy and they supplied most of the dynamism of politics. The bourgeois or nonsocialist parties did not attempt to stand in adamant opposition but considered it their role to criticize, moderate, revise, delay. Thus progress was made in a broad program of social reform, hesitatingly in the 1920s, decisively in the 1930s. But it was not yet the welfare state.

As the social democrats began to accomplish their goals, and especially after they achieved the leading position in government, they modified many of the positions they had taken so absolutely in the earlier period. The demand for abolition of the monarchy and the introduction of a republic they allowed to stay on the books, but they did not press it. At one point Per Albin Hansson asked that the topic be deleted, but his followers would not go that far. They pushed for disarmament but in the light of world conditions later compromised on that issue. They continued to talk about the nationalization of industry, but they pursued the idea only weakly. The nonsocialists, for their part, went along with most of the welfare program advocated by the social democrats. All groups agreed, with amazingly little dissent, on the policy of neutrality.

## A New Course in Foreign Affairs

World War I dramatized the increasing interdependence of Sweden and the world beyond. After the war it was an international body that judged the Åland Islands issue, and the economic situation in Europe and America determined prosperity or distress for the vital export sectors of the Swedish economy, employment or unemployment for thousands of Swedish workers.

This interdependence was frankly recognized in the prolonged debate on entry into the League of Nations, conducted while the Edén government was still in power. The parties on the right tended to be antagonistic, leaning toward isolationism. All agreed that the faults of the Covenant were serious, but the left groups convinced themselves that this was at least an honest attempt to create a peaceful world and that Sweden should participate. They considered that they were yielding the Swedish desire for neutrality, but they hoped the result would justify the sacrifice. The conservatives, including Hjalmar Hammarskjöld, looked at the League as a power instrument in the hands of the Allies and feared that the former neutrals would be called on to enforce against Germany the harsh terms of Versailles. Some wanted to delay decision on membership until they could be sure the United States would join; most assumed that it was only a matter of time until the United States did so. Debate raged until, on March 3 and 4, 1920, the First Chamber voted 86 to 47 and the Second Chamber 152 to 67 in favor of joining. Although all the Scandinavian states eventually entered they all registered skepticism. The decision was hard to make, but once made it was firm.

The willingness of the Swedes to submit their national interests to an international rule of law was given an immediate and severe test. The Åland Islands were of prime strategic concern to Sweden and they were inhabited by a Swedish-speaking population. But in 1809 they had been taken over, along with Finland, by Russia. The Swedes thought that the islanders should be granted the much-talked-of right of self-determination, and the Ålanders officially requested this right. In a plebiscite of 1919 they voted 95 percent for reunion with Sweden. Finland rejected the Swedish arguments, stood on the legal rights of continued sovereignty, and at length sent troops to Åland. Finland also objected at first to submission of the question to the League, but the League assumed its competence to handle the issue and before its final judgment both Finland and Sweden agreed to accept the League's decision. A three-man commission made a study of the situation and recommended to the Council of the League that the Ålands should belong to Finland. The Council so decided.

On the Åland issue the various Swedish parties and the press had come into fundamental agreement in favor of annexation. Hjalmar Branting had taken a leading part in the Swedish campaign, and in his capacity as Swedish delegate to the League he had the sad duty of announcing that his country would loyally accept the Council's determination. Disappointment was general and was seasoned with a sense of disillusionment in the workings of international justice. But there was no attempt to deny the legality or the finality of the judgment, and the Åland Islands case stands out as one of the unquestioned successes of the League. By treaties among the Baltic states and action of the Finnish government the islands were neutralized and the population granted special rights such as the use of the Swedish language in the schools, local self-government, and no military service. Later, hindsight persuaded many Swedes that the result was actually best for Sweden.[15]

While Branting served as delegate to the League his personality and wide acquaintance made him an effective spokesman for the small states. He and the Swedish government opposed the French invasion of the Saar and objected to Italian action in Corfu. Swedes had at the end of World War I come to sympathize with the Allied cause but did not forget their respect for German science and social programs nor their sense of what was right. They strongly disapproved the harsh terms of the Treaty of Versailles. In *Social-Demokraten*, for example, appeared in 1923 an all too prophetic warning: "Encircle Germany with zones . . . treat her as the dangerous lunatic of Europe, take every precaution against her, and one day Germany will break out of her cell with the demoniac force of the lunatic." [16] Hence Branting and Östen Undén, who succeeded him at the League in 1925, urged just treatment for Germany and for the German minority in Poland.

Among the many constructive influences of Sweden in the League was its self-denying action concerning its nonpermanent seat in the Council, to which the country had been elected in 1922, representing in reality Scandinavia as much as itself. Undén, an expert in international law, was convinced that the number of permanent seats should not be enlarged. In connection with Germany's projected entry into the League, however, Poland, and later Spain and Brazil, demanded seats. Sweden therefore voluntarily yielded its seat so that Poland might have a semi-permanent place and thus put an end to one of the dangerous prestige-rivalries.[17]

Sweden was beginning in the 1920s to practice the "active neutrality" that was later so named. It played an influential role in the Turkey-Iraq border dispute. In relation to the Geneva Protocol for international disarmament and guarantees Sweden declared in 1924 that the country was ready to apply sanctions of economic and financial character but not military. The Swedes urged establishment of an organization for arbitration of international disputes, and the four Nordic states agreed to arbitrate their own differences.[18]

Strict recognition of law and treading with caution are the best defenses for small countries. Acceptance of this principle by the Swedish government and people forced the resignation in 1923 of the foreign minister in the Trygger government, Carl Hederstierna, because in a public speech he had advocated a defensive alliance with Finland against Russia. His successor arranged for recognition of the Soviet state and a commercial treaty, though fears of the great communist power had certainly not abated. Intelligent self-interest led the Scandinavian states to do all in their power to strengthen the international machinery of peace, but they saw it steadily eroding because of the unreadiness of the Great Powers either to compromise their own conflicting interests or to discipline those who asserted the law of force. Baron Fredrik Ramel, foreign minister, went hopefully to the disarmament conference in Geneva in 1932. But it was futile. No effective action was taken against the Japanese invasion of Manchuria (1931–32) or the Italian attack on Ethiopia (1935). The smaller states were annoyed and alarmed, and in 1936 the Scandinavians together with Spain, Switzerland, and the Netherlands declared their own right to decide, as the Great Powers were doing, when and how they would apply sanctions. In 1938 the states of the Oslo Group withdrew completely from the sanctions system of the League. It was a gesture of dismay and defeat. (On the Oslo Group see p. 463.) The nazi drive for their "thousand year Reich" followed shortly thereafter (in 1939).

As tension and lawlessness spread and as Germans showed renewed and suspicious interest in the Baltic, Sweden and Finland thought it would be good to free themselves from the rigid demilitarization of the Åland Islands. All ten states signatory to the Åland Islands agreement indicated approval of the Swedish-Finnish plan, but Russia interjected a *nyet*.

Sweden worked persistently to strengthen its own security and that of the Nordic area. Together the Scandinavian states worked out a system by which one of them would always have one of the nonpermanent seats on the Council of the League of Nations, and their foreign ministers held preparatory meetings before each League session. They drew up a revised set of neutrality rules in April and May 1938, pledging to keep out of Great-Power combinations and war and forbidding military-plane overflights of the Nordic lands. On some delicate matters each country had to go its own way, as with the nazi nonaggression pacts. President Roosevelt triggered these treaties when, after the *Anschluss* with Austria and the invasion of Czecho-Slovakia he asked if Hitler's other neighbors felt secure. The nazi fuehrer took the opportunity to invite each of these countries to sign a mutual nonaggression treaty. Among the northern states Denmark thought it impossible to refuse, Norway said no, Finland excused itself because of its friendship pact with Russia, and Sweden negotiated its way out of any commitments. With its neighbors across the Baltic Sweden avoided entanglement, although Estonia, Latvia, and Lithuania, and Finland too, were eager for association with the Scandinavian countries.

In the early 1920s, during the era of hope after World War I, the left parties in Sweden had pressed for continued reduction in the military establishment. After the indecisive election of 1924 the social democrats and the liberals cooperated to drive through a significant curtailment of the defense program, eliminating some of the historic regiments. Civilian service was permitted for conscientious objectors, and the length of the military training period was shortened (although not much for students, who were expected to become officers). The law aroused a storm of protest, magazines were founded in support of the military, and a "National Association for Sweden's Defense" was established. In a few years their propaganda could say "We told you so." The balance of Swedish opinion swung toward defense.

Whereas Denmark made a definite decision to spend its money on welfare rather than armament and Norway did little to maintain a defense establishment, Finland and Sweden determined to build up their defenses. The threatening militarization in both Germany and Russia and the equally ominous peril of fascist ideology destroyed the dream of a peaceful world. Some 350 Swedes responded to the crusading urge and went to fight for the loyalists in the Spanish Civil War. At home the social democrats argued no longer for disarmament, though Sköld and Wigforss tried strenuously to keep the defense budget under restraint.[19] In the defense commission of 1930, which made its report in 1935, only one member retained the pacifist stance. Rickard Sandler, the Social Democratic prime minister in 1925–26 who was responsible for the great arms reduction, himself became in the late 1930s a vigorous advocate of a renewed military buildup and a joint Swedish-Finnish defense of the Åland Islands.

To an astonishing extent defense was treated as a domestic political issue, the conservatives making it the most solid plank in their platform, the left parties consistently opposing military expenditures and the military establishment. How much, one wonders, were these attitudes conditioned by the close identification of the upper classes with the officer corps and of the laboring classes with the "cannon fodder"? (The fact that the younger officers, as in Karl XII's army or among the British forces in World War I, suffered in war greater casualties than the common soldiers was not generally recognized.) Or was the divergence of views determined by the greater interest of the educated and wealthy segments of society in foreign affairs and the concentration of the worker element on domestic concerns? In any case both sides played politics with "defense or reform."[20]

Hence during the period when communism was violently asserting its grip on Russia and Germany was girding for war and disaster, Sweden was trying to forge a nonrevolutionary middle way, cautiously but constructively. Then the affairs of Sweden — and the world — were rudely interrupted again by war.

## World War II

In World War II Sweden was the only one of the Nordic states to avoid direct involvement, and even the Swedes found themselves threatened and circumscribed by the conflagration around them. The immediate reaction of Sweden and all its neighbors was a declaration of neutrality. But pronouncements on paper did not halt the march of armies.

Russian demands on Finland in the fall of 1939 roused Sweden to danger. Sweden was tied to Finland by bonds of tradition and sentiment, and this former eastern province was still regarded as a buffer against the age-old enemy, Russia. The smaller Baltic states were being absorbed into the Soviet system beginning in the summer of 1939, and in October the Soviets asked

Finland to grant them military bases in return for territorial concessions. A week later the Swedes, Danes, and Norwegians joined in a declaration to Russia that a blow against Finland would be regarded as a blow against the entire North. On October 18 the heads of the four northern states, with their foreign ministers, met in Stockholm and pledged solidarity, although they made no military commitments. When the Russians struck on November 30 feeling ran high in Sweden.

Although Denmark and Norway declared neutrality Sweden did not and in the coming weeks sent large quantities of arms and ammunition to Finland from its own armories. Foreign Minister Rickard Sandler wanted Sweden to take this occasion to fortify the Åland Islands, according to a plan previously discussed with the Finns. But the cabinet refused to risk a war with Russia, and Sandler left the government. More than 8,000 Swedes volunteered for service in Finland, and the government answered Russian protests by saying that this was all done within the rules of international law. Beyond this the authorities in Stockholm would not go. Östen Undén expressed in the League of Nations the sympathy of the Nordic peoples for the plight of the Finns but would not join in a call for sanctions. The League, in its boldest and final gesture, banished the Soviet Union from membership, but the guns were not silenced. The heroic resistance of the Finns in that bitter winter of 1939–40 roused admiration and sympathy around the world, but it was impossible to send effective aid.

The southern routes were blocked by Germany, the northern by Russia, and the middle route across Norway and Sweden required consent of these nonbelligerents. Neither would give it because they did not wish to become theaters of a war between outside powers. They felt sure that the proposed French and British aid would be insufficient and futile and would lead to a British or a German takeover of the iron mines. On March 12, 1940 Finland yielded and signed a treaty of peace with Russia.

Four weeks later Germany pounced on Denmark and Norway, and warned Sweden to keep out or else! Swedish intelligence reports enabled the Swedish government to warn their friends a few days in advance of the attacks, but neither the Danes nor the Norwegians would believe them. After April 9 the Swedes were again confronted with a soul-searing decision, in fact an entire sequence of decisions. Should Sweden try to remain neutral? Should the Swedes voluntarily come to the aid of their neighbors — neighbors who had failed to maintain for themselves respectable defenses? What could the country do after half-emptying its own arsenals in aid to Finland? And its position vis-à-vis Germany was more vulnerable than toward Russia. Again there were strong feelings among the people toward their brother-Nordics, but the government realized that a restraining hand was necessary. Sweden assumed a posture of firm defense of its own territory and strict neutrality toward Germany, Denmark, and Norway.

To maintain the position of legalistic neutrality was extremely difficult, with Germany constantly demanding concessions and with Norway expecting friendship rather than rigid application of rules. Through the first two months the situation was fairly clear. Sweden refused to permit German military equipment to be sent north on Swedish railways to the soldiers fighting in northern Norway but did allow a trainload of hospital supplies to go through, and probably illegal materials and even personnel were included. Swedish guards both then and later sometimes winked at German violations of transportation regulations by both rail and ship. There was much openly avowed flouting of neutrality in favor of Norwegian soldiers who sought refuge in Sweden and were provided with lodging and food in mountain cabins near the border. But other incidents occurred such as detention of refugees, and these actions the Norwegians deeply resented.

One potentially unique arrangement barely failed of realization. Hermann Göring, "the big nazi," had been in Sweden frequently with his first wife and presumably retained affection for the Swedish people. Therefore, in the early days of the war, when the fighting in the northern part of Norway was on a fairly even basis, a Swede proposed to Göring that both German and Norwegian troops should withdraw from the Narvik area and allow that region to be occupied by Swedish soldiers as trustees until a total decision was attained. Both parties examined the idea and approval was obtained from London. On June 3 the Norwegian foreign minister, Halvdan Koht, and his Swedish counterpart, Christian Günther, signed an agreement at Luleå, and it was sent to Germany for formal ratification. However, military events moved faster than the diplomatic. On June 7 the Norwegian government fled to England, and an interesting experiment never came into being.

The Germans now insisted that Norway was conquered and therefore the Swedes should permit transit through Sweden of supplies and of German soldiers on leave from occupation duty. However, Norwegian forces were still fighting, and Sweden puzzled over the German request and delayed giving an answer. They inquired of the British government what might be expected in Norway and received the ominous reply that Great Britain might have to make peace, that Britain would be guided by common sense, not bravado (June 18). It was indeed a dark moment. The Netherlands and Belgium had fallen. Italy had declared war on France and Britain (June 10), and the Germans had taken Paris (June 13). Could Sweden stand against the German juggernaut? Under these circumstances Sweden made its first major concession; it allowed the German "leave soldiers" to travel to and from Norway through Sweden and permitted general goods, not war materials, to be shipped on Swedish railroads. To the Norwegians Sweden explained that "all neutrality policy had its limits in the possibilities open to the neutral state."[21]

More nonneutral concessions were made in response to German pressure when in June 1941 the war was resumed in Finland. Not only did Sweden permit the entire German Engelbrecht Division to cross northern Sweden for the Finnish battleground, it also yielded to German demands for the use of Swedish water and air passage for transports to Finland. These unneutral concessions were excused as being assistance to the Finns, but the more important reason was certainly fear of German retaliation in case of refusal. The concessions were hedged about with limitations, and as much as possible they were hidden from the public. King Gustav, Foreign Minister Günther, and Gösta Bagge, leader of the conservatives, were all in favor of granting the permissions, and it may be that the king suggested that he might resign if the demands were refused. Certainly the facilitation of German transport to the Finnish front was a highly important service; rejection might well have brought German military action, and definitely it would have created an acute governmental crisis in Stockholm. There were some, like Wigforss, who would have stood on principle and risked refusal. Others favored not only granting nazi demands but thought of the possibility of fighting alongside the Germans against Russia. General Olof Thörnell, commander of the Swedish forces, said in a report to the government on April 4, 1941 that for the sake of Sweden's future position and prestige in northern Europe it would be natural to

> make preparations so that participation [by Sweden against the Soviets] be as effective as possible from the beginning, so that the land war can be held at a distance from our borders.[22]

On July 19, 1941 Thörnell suggested further that for both political and strategic reasons perhaps Sweden should contribute to the defeat of the USSR; this would be for the sake of Finland, but "I never pressed for active participation."[23] Judging from the strong popular reaction against the passage of the Engelbrecht Division through Swedish territory, a movement that could not be hidden, it seems doubtful that the country would have tolerated intervention. The traffic concessions in and over the Baltic were as much as possible kept from becoming public knowledge. Everything boiled down to the fact that in the spring and early summer of 1941 it looked quite probable that Germany would win the war, and Sweden dared not defy it.[24]

Aid in the other direction, warmly supported by the majority of the citizenry, included shipments to Norway of food, prefabricated houses, hospital supplies, maps, and other necessities. Hundreds of young Norwegians were sent on from Sweden for training in Camp Little Norway in Canada or were trained in Sweden as ''police'' to take control in Norway after the war. When the nazis attempted to round up the Jews of Denmark Swedes rallied to the cause and helped about 8,000 escape to Sweden where they and some 7,000 other Danes lived through the latter half of the war, many in private homes. From the Baltic states, especially Estonia, some 35,000 refugees fled to Sweden. About 70,000 Finnish children were received in Swedish foster homes. Count Folke Bernadotte arranged near the end of the war for the release of 19,000 Danish and Norwegian prisoners from German concentration camps. Innumerable acts of mercy can be attributed to people who did not talk much of sentiment but whose sense of human brotherhood counteracted the restrictions of neutrality.

Although Sweden suffered less in World War II than it had in World War I, the effects of the war were profound. Greater self-sufficiency and careful planning avoided the desperate shortages of food, though the lack of fuel and coffee and other ''colonial goods'' were hardships. Limited amounts of trade were permitted by the warring powers; the Germans allowed five ships per month to trade with the West out of Gothenburg, but occasionally they abruptly stopped the traffic; this trade cost the Swedes at least 11 ships and 100 lives. The British permitted the Swedes to ship iron ore and ball bearings to Germany but pressed steadily for reduction. By 1942 both imports and exports were down to less than half of their normal levels. Smuggling became respectable; a small fleet of fast motor boats carried ball bearings to England and courier planes flew high between Stockholm and London.

The old favoritism toward Germany suffered shock upon shock and vanished almost completely during World War II. The attacks on Denmark and Norway and the continuing threat against Sweden, together with the abhorrent doctrines of nazism, forced the Swedes to maintain a strong defense. The military budget rose from $50 million in 1938 to $400 million the next year and $600 million before the end of the war. Constant alert was necessary and several times the full complement of 600,000 soldiers and 110,000 women in the Lotta Corps was mustered. Sweden's Bofors antiaircraft guns were perhaps the best to be had, and they were used and manufactured under license also by the United States. The small naval force was strengthened and it tried to watch against the intrusion of submarines from either Germany or Russia. In a widely disseminated pamphlet, ''Directions for Citizens of the Kingdom in Event of War,'' the Swedish government proclaimed to all that ''Resistance shall be made in all situations. Any announcement that resistance shall be abandoned is false.''

From time to time German invasion forces were reported poised to strike at Sweden. Probably the most dangerous occasion was in the spring of 1943, although the general population had hardly an inkling of the threat. The nazi strength in Norway had been built up by 25 panzer divisions and the total of German troops to 400,000. In the fall of 1942 Hitler had said that the security of the northwest flank was more important than the coming spring offensive in Russia. The plan was to strike in force from Norway through central Sweden toward Stockholm and to occupy the capital. A German military estimate reckoned that, although the people were 80 to 90 percent pro-Ally in senti-ment the officer corps was presumed to be 70 percent pro-German, and that the commanding general, Olof Thörnell, was both pro-German and defeatist; therefore the Germans hoped that the military leadership would bring about a Swedish surrender before a battle for Stockholm could materialize. They may well have been mistaken. In 1943 Sweden had 185,000 men under arms, but only 50,000 were field-trained soldiers. The Germans counted on their superiority in the air to disrupt further mobilization of Sweden's full potential. It was distant developments that parried the nazi threat: the Allied invasion of Italy, the fall of Mussolini, the rising pressure against France — all combined to make Hitler withdraw troops from Norway to France instead of opening a new front in the North. Neither the attitudes nor the capabilities of the military and the people of Sweden were ever put to the acid test.[25]

The press in Sweden was for the most part both free and outspoken. A few papers sympathetic to Germany, especially Torsten Kreuger's *Aftonbladet* and *Stockholms Tidningen*, were far outnumbered by the independent press, some of which (most notably *Trots Allt* and Torgny Segerstedt's influential *Handels- och Sjöfartstidning* of Gothenburg) lashed out steadily at the nazis. Some issues were confiscated, but the attacks continued. The Germans writhed and protested and called the Swedes "swine in dinner jackets,"[26] but they could not frighten or choke off the vehement opposition. The tiny Nazi party in Sweden was not able to elect a single delegate to the riksdag. The atmosphere of freedom along with the key geographic position of Stockholm made the city an active center of espionage, like Lisbon in the south.

As the tide of war turned and it became obvious that the nazis could not realize their dream of a "thousand year Reich," Sweden's policy shifted. Neutrality had always been the art of the possible, frankly unheroic. In trade negotiations with the Allies the Swedes were blamed by Dean Acheson for being difficult to deal with and, along with the Swiss, "among the most independent-minded, not to say stubborn, people in the world."[27] And he had reason to complain that despite solemn promises to the contrary the Swedish ball bearing company, SKF, increased exports to Germany. Erik Boheman, who came to Washington on a special mission in 1942, had counter-complaints; he found Americans woefully ignorant of Swedish conditions and unwilling to believe in Sweden's readiness to defend itself against Germany. In August 1943 Sweden placed new restrictions on freight traffic via Sweden between Germany and Norway, and from September 1944 only hospital cars could pass from Finland through Sweden to Germany; in 1944 at last the export of ball bearings was severely curtailed. Cessation of credit and insurance stopped the ore trade with Germany. Sweden closed its waters to German warships and forbade foreign trade in its Baltic ports. Supreme caution had paid off, but now caution could be relaxed and Sweden could hasten the end of the war by new kinds of restrictions. By bending first one way and then the other before the changing winds of war the Swedes were able to save themselves from involvement. Their justification was that they had done nothing to start the war and could not be held responsible for fighting it.

King Gustav V, who had been pro-German during World War I, was a strong influence for neutrality in World War II, but the major architect of policy was Per Albin Hansson, Social Democratic prime minister in the coalition government. But no one in government had any real difficulty in leading the people in a neutrality policy. On this there was almost unanimous consensus. Many were uncomfortable as they watched the suffering of their neighbors, but few indeed were those who thought they could accomplish good by interfering. Fears and friendships, hates and hopes, were all subordinate to the conviction that Sweden must remain out of the conflict.

Kurt Samuelsson points out some of the social and psychological effects of the war, especially the new acquaintanceship and close cooperation among people in all walks of life. In the emergency situation bankers and railroad workers, professors and farmers worked shoulder to shoulder and came to know each other as human beings, not as mere cogs in a social and economic structure. New bases were established for understanding and cooperation and for solidarity. The arrogance of class could never be the same after sharing in the same mess line or standing guard together through the long night watch. The severe taxes to which everyone yielded accustomed people to new levels of public expenditure and made it easier to accept the heightened postwar charges for social services. And major programs of social aid were regarded as essential to avoid the economic fluctuations that had followed World War I. Hence it became acceptable that increased old-age pensions, free lunches in the schools, free textbooks, and family allowances would double the welfare costs of government from around 5 percent of the net national income to around 10 percent soon after the war.[28]

The decades of depression and war left Sweden superficially unscathed, yet deeply changed. Government had become more democratic and more pervasive, industry had grown strong, the social democrats had inaugurated a program of social reforms that indicated the direction for more sweeping change, and Sweden had developed a new consciousness of its place in the world.

# XIX

# THE ERA OF THE WELFARE STATE

AFTER THE ENFORCED PAUSE OF WARTIME an almost feverish urge propelled Sweden into reforms in every major sector of society: expansion and internationalization of the economy, democratization of education, revision of the constitutions of national and local governments, increased freedom of religious choice, assertion of "active neutrality" in international affairs — nothing was left unquestioned or untouched in the drive for social equalization and improvement. People seemed to sense that a moment of opportunity had arrived and must be seized. The social democrats held the leadership role. Immediate reform and long-term planning vied with each other for precedence. Diplomatic, social, and economic problems had to be faced simultaneously in practice, but for our understanding they had best be dealt with separately.

## Active Neutrality

At first glance it would appear that in foreign affairs change was less dramatic than in home affairs. Certainly the basic policy of neutrality remained as firm in 1946 as in 1939. But the world had changed and Sweden had perforce to respond to new situations. Since Sweden was not a belligerent its statesmen were not involved in the construction of the United Nations, but the country now did not debate the question of membership as it had with the League of Nations. Sweden now deliberately abandoned absolute neutrality, joined the United Nations in 1946, and participated fully in a variety of international associations, including the Organization for European Economic Cooperation (OEEC; later OECD) and the Council of Europe. Being a nonaligned and small state, its diplomats and other personnel were in demand at points of tension around the world. Swedish civil and military cohorts were used in peacekeeping and humanitarian aid in Korea (1953), the Middle East (1956–57), the Congo (1960–64), Cyprus (in the 1960s), and the Sinai (in the 1970s). When Sweden held a seat on the Security Council of the United Nations, its position was sometimes that of the western democracies, sometimes that of the Soviet group. The Swedish attitude was often puzzling from the political point of view, simply because it was based on juridical rather than political considerations. In 1975, for example, Sweden angered Israel, with whom relations had been close, by voting to allow the PLO (Palestine Liberation Organization) to be heard in the United Nations. Increasingly it became clear how much the Swedes were concerned not only with international law but with fundamental problems of human rights. Since Sweden had no overseas territories and no alliances, its government assumed that it could view the conflicts of other states in an impartial and judicious spirit. Out of concern for peace and right the government therefore spoke out strongly on many occasions. Russia, for example, was condemned for the foul attack on Czecho-Slovakia in the spring of 1948, and the popular reaction to that event was sharply reflected in the autumn elections when the communists dropped from 15 seats in the riksdag to eight. On its own account Sweden protested repeatedly to the Soviet government against strange submarine incursions into Swedish waters and against the shooting down of Swedish planes over the waters of the Baltic. Both popular and governmental feeling was strong against the Soviet invasion of Hungary in 1956. Outspoken opposition was expressed against race discrimination in South Africa and in the United States. In the 1960s and the 1970s the Swedes reacted stridently to what they regarded as imperialistic and unjust actions by the United States in the Vietnam war.

The American government and many of its people resented these bitter criticisms from a friendly country, and they led at last to the verge of a diplomatic break. It was a situation in which the overwhelming majority of the Swedish people agreed with their government's position, as did millions of Americans who nevertheless did not like to be lectured by foreigners. Olof Palme had taken a leading part in demonstrations and statements while he was a cabinet minister and continued when he became prime minister in 1968 both to condemn and to maintain the right of Swedes to express their opinions. For example, in an interview in *Le Monde*, he declared

> For us neutrality does not and cannot signify isolation, silence. We remain
> neutral vis à vis the military blocs but we cannot be indifferent to the prob-
> lems of the world we live in.[1]

This was the justification of "active neutrality." It expressed itself not only in denunciations of the actions of others but in positive terms. Immediately after World War II the Swedes contributed heavily to the rebuilding of Norway, with food, prefabricated houses, and other essentials. There were those who attributed such generosity to the guilt complex that Sweden felt for not being a partner in the war. Perhaps this was part of the reason, but it must be recognized too that a missionary urge had evidenced itself long before. For example, the Swedes had built hospitals and nutrition centers, agricultural training schools, and other institutions in a number of places in Africa, notably Ethiopia. Their concern for the welfare of others and for the rights of man found practical expression in a level of aid to developing countries that surpassed what any other people offered. The national goal was to give in foreign aid 1 percent of the GNP; in the mid-1970s the figure attained was .75 percent, which was the highest rate for any of the industrialized lands, except Norway. It amounted to 2.9 percent of the 1976 budget. To that extent Sweden recognized the responsibility of affluence.

That neutrals can also have their heroes is illustrated in the lives of two self-sacrificing Swedish humanitarians. One was Folke Bernadotte (1895–1948), who toward the end of World War II not only saved thousands of Danes and Norwegians from nazi concentration camps but who kept on with dangerous assignments until his death. He helped to arrange the peaceful surrender of the German forces in Norway after the war and he worked unremittingly to assist the Russian prisoners in northern Norway. As head of the Swedish Red Cross, succeeding his uncle Prince Carl, he was active on many fronts. In May 1948 he accepted an urgent appointment by the United Nations to go as mediator into the tense, hate-filled Middle East. Because there appeared to be a chance that he might succeed, he was cut down by gunfire from an Israeli terrorist gang in September 1948, only 119 days from the start of his mission.[2]

Second of the notable Swedish martyrs to the cause of world peace was Dag Hammarskjöld (1905–61), who tried to make the United Nations a greater power than the Great Powers wished it to be and who met his fate in the heart of Africa while attempting to resolve another of the irresolvable human conflicts. Born into the proud public service tradition of the Hammarskjöld family and brought up under the intimate influence of Archbishop Nathan Söderblom, one of the world's great churchmen, it was not strange that Dag Hammarskjöld should enter public service. Nor was it surprising that a Swede should succeed a Norwegian as secretary-general of the United Nations, for its leadership had to come from the neutral and smaller states. But this man added an unexpected touch of greatness and devotion to a task too heavy for any man. Neither the tribes of Africa nor the nations of the world outside were ready for the mutual give-and-take processes of peaceful and constructive international relations. The downing of his plane in the forests near Ndola signaled not only the personal fate of Dag Hammarskjöld but a disaster for humanity, a disaster presaged in his own thought and poignantly expressed in one of his "Markings" dated July 6, 1961, two months before his death:

> Tired
> And lonely,
> So tired
> The heart aches.
> Meltwater trickles
> Down the rocks,
> The fingers are numb,
> The knees tremble.
> It is now,
> Now, that you must not give in.[3]

Another whose work was not interrupted by martyrdom was Elsa Brändström, "The angel of Siberia," who did extraordinary work as a Red Cross nurse among the war prisoners in Russia in World War I. After the war she continued service for the children of deceased prisoners, establishing a home for them in a Saxon castle and acquiring support from both Sweden and the United States.[4] These are a few examples of how the critical and negative aspects of active neutrality were counterbalanced by positive and constructive action.

## Nordic and European Cooperation

Less dramatic, but stamped also by idealism and hope, were the efforts to build workable cooperation among the Nordic peoples themselves. Swedes were not always the initiators in these endeavors but they eagerly participated. In 1948 it was Sweden that attempted to draw Scandinavia together in an alliance to defend neutrality. Denmark and Norway, however, with all-too-fresh memories of the nazi invasion, were dubious about the possibility of Norden standing alone, and Sweden made it clear that its proposal precluded any commitments or dependence for supplies on any non-Nordic power. Norway therefore chose affiliation with NATO (The North Atlantic Treaty Organization) and Denmark followed. Sweden refused to compromise its own nonaligned position and remained alone.

In 1952 Denmark suggested the creation of a Nordic Council which would, without any military obligations, provide for discussion of common problems in economic, social, and cultural matters. The Nordic Council, which included Iceland and Finland as well as the three central Scandinavian states, institutionalized the cooperation that had developed through the nongovernmental Norden societies of each country (1919–　). Investigations were conducted for the council on all conceivable questions of common interest — the bridge over Öresund, education in its many facets, pollution of air and water, patents, the social rights of seamen, health, transportation, consumer services, laws on the press — producing twenty to thirty carefully prepared reports each year.

The result of this cooperation and other patterns of interchange of people and ideas was that the Nordic countries had more laws in common than did the states of the United States. Frequently discussions between bureaucrats and legislators across national lines developed the actual detail of laws that were thereafter passed in the different countries in identical form. The language of the commission reports, incidentally, was the language of that particular commission's chairman or secretary (with the Finns, however, normally using Swedish, the Icelanders Danish). The council meetings, held for a week once each year, moved from one capital city to another; the delegates were representatives of both the executive and the legislative branches and were balanced according to party strength in the parliaments.

This kind of voluntary cooperation, with each country preserving freedom of action, was highly successful. More binding types of cooperation repeatedly ran into snags. But when the European Economic Community (EEC — the "Common Market," later known simply as the European Community, EC) was established with its six original members, a group of another seven (Denmark, Norway, and Sweden, plus Great Britain, Portugal, Switzerland, and Austria — "The Outer Seven") got together in the European Free Trade Association (EFTA) in 1959. Finland joined as an associate member in 1961. Success in reducing tariffs and increasing trade among themselves was phenomenal: in the first ten years commerce within EFTA grew 186 percent; that among the Scandinavian countries alone grew 284 percent. This evidence of the advantages of customs-free trade tempted even the Swedes to consider joining the still larger EEC. However, Sweden worried about the political overtones in EEC; it would not yield its neutrality. (Nonalignment is the more precise and accurate term for Sweden's peacetime policy, which becomes neutrality during war periods. Neutrality and neutral are nevertheless words commonly applied and they are satisfactory if properly understood.)

One *ad hoc* negotiation showed the far-reaching possibilities of cooperation. During the multinational meetings of the "Kennedy-round" for the relaxation of trade barriers, in 1966–67, the Scandinavian states were relegated to secondary status as small powers. However, they realized their importance as a group and they agreed to act together with the skillful Swedish diplomat Nils Montan as their spokesman. The effect was impressive. Montan, representing an association whose total trade with EEC was larger than that of the United States, was able to gain concessions that none of the states could have acquired acting alone.

The urge to maintain both neutrality and close cooperation in the North produced another stillborn plan for a Nordic economic union, Nordek. Olof Palme, the new prime minister of Sweden, was eager for the realization of this organization, and in February 1970, at a meeting of the Nordic Council in Reykjavik, he was able to get unanimous approval by the five states. Immediately after his return to Sweden Palme undertook a trip to the continental capitals. Was he, as the Finns seemed to suspect, hoping to use Nordek as a means of bargaining with EEC? In any case, Finland quickly withdrew its support of Nordek, sensing inevitable Soviet disapproval of any kind of Finnish association with the Common Market. Without Finland Nordek was dead.

Long-drawn-out negotiations with EEC on a country-by-country basis ensued. Norway held a plebiscite which voted against adhesion, and the government had committed itself to accept the result. Denmark held a plebiscite that favored accession to EEC and Denmark therefore followed Great Britain into the Common Market. In Sweden the negative decision was made by the government itself after many months of anguished debate. The social democrats put the danger to neutrality ahead of economic considerations; the business community, in the main, argued that entrance into the European Common Market was essential for Swedish prosperity. Ultimately what happened for Sweden, as well as for Norway (in separate arrangements), was a trade agreement with EEC that provided most of the economic advantages of membership but prevented the country from being a participant in the community's decision making. EFTA survived only as a feeble remnant of its former strength.

Relations with EEC were vital because of the fundamental importance of foreign trade for the Swedish economy and national welfare. The basic outline of the industrial breakthrough has been traced in chapter XVI, and this achievement was of course due primarily to Swedish efforts. However, the dependence of the Swedish economy on trade with other countries can hardly be overemphasized. By the 1970s one-fifth of Sweden's total production was exported, and this in time paid for a similar share of imports. Commerce was the key to Sweden's burgeoning prosperity. Without demand in Britain and Germany and elsewhere for Swedish goods Sweden would have remained impoverished. Export of products not only supplied funds for buying imports but production for the foreign market reduced the unit costs of making items like automobiles and thus enabled this small country to support its own manufacturers.[5]

## The Economy and Economic Democracy

In the period after World War II Sweden experienced both a dramatic increase and a structural change in foreign commerce and in the production apparatus that supported that commerce. These developments went well beyond the "breakthrough" previously described. For centuries the basis of Swedish exports was raw materials and semi-processed goods — ore, pig iron, rolled steel, wood, pulp, paper. Changes accumulated in the late nineteenth and earlier twentieth centuries. After world War II change occurred with a rush, first in that harvest-time burst immediately after the war, then in a prolonged surge of expansion. The products of mines and forests continued to be important, but the emphasis came to be on refinement of those products, their manufacture into office machines, steam turbines, automobiles, ships, medical equipment and supplies, textiles, plastics, telecommunications equipment, furniture. Forty percent of this industrial output was exported. These highly sophisticated products required other components than Sweden itself could produce and led to increased imports. Foreign trade expanded in closely parallel fashion in both export and import. Workers were in such demand that foreign labor was called in from Finland and Denmark and from as far away as Italy and Jugoslavia and Greece. After 1930 Sweden became a country of net immigration instead of emigration, with the great influx coming after World War II. By the 1970s some 70,000 Finns had taken Swedish citizenship and 200,000 more came as temporary workers. Occasional unemployment was inevitable, but the Finns, particularly, supplied a fortunate degree of flexibility in the labor market, for they could go home when work grew slack.

Improved techniques, fertilization, mechanization, and rationalization (see p. 517) brought a reduction of the farm labor force to 6 percent of the total number of workers and simultaneously raised the amount of food production. Even the cows and the chickens were more productive than ever before. Self-sufficiency in food supply was in the 1970s about 85 percent, but the national goal was to reduce this to 80 percent, maintaining home production at this level for the sake of national security. Amalgamation reduced the number of farms and this process was to be continued until only about 100,000 farms remained (in 1944 there were 406,000; in 1972 there were 144,000). Farms were being enlarged, but acreage was also being reduced. Small farmers in Småland, for example, were forbidden to sell their farms for agricultural use. Much land was put back into forest. It was a reversal of the nineteenth-century process of drainage and clearing, for it had been discovered that the trees that produced good lumber were more valuable than the potatoes that grew poorly in the rocky soil. The planned process of change also reduced the number of cattle and sheep and allowed for thousands more hogs. For the future, it was planned that Special Rationalized (SR) farms would be created: small ones with 70 to 120 acres of arable and 250 to 400 acres of forest, with 25–30 cows, to be worked by man-and-wife teams putting in about 3,000 hours per year; and larger farms with one "hired-hand" added and an expected total of 5,000 hours of work.[6]

## THE PARALLELISM OF GROWTH
## OF IMPORTS AND EXPORTS

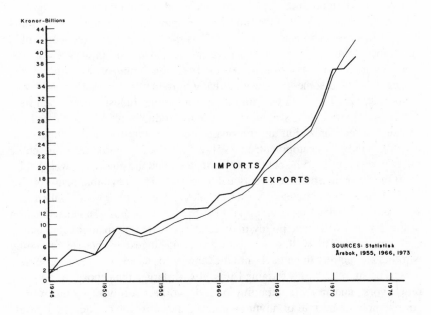

Up to 1975 agricultural output was still on the increase, and industrial production was about ten times that of 1900. Because of changes in products, in methods of recording statistics, and in the value of money it is impossible to be precise concerning rates of growth. Yet every method of measurement tells an impressive story: In the late 1830s the average annual manufacturing production amounted to 20 million kronor; in 1871 it passed the 100 million mark; in 1900 it reached 1 billion kronor; in 1950 the figure was 24 billion kronor; and by 1973 the total passed 147 billion kronor. For a shorter span of time and figuring in terms of fixed monetary values (the 1959 krona), the value of exports increased between 1947 and 1967 by over 7.5 percent per year, or for the twenty-one years a total of 161 percent. In terms of current krona values for the same twenty-one-year period the increase was from 2.5

billion kronor to 23.3 billion kronor. The figures for wages in that period from 1947 through 1967 averaged an increase of over 8.7 percent annually or a total of 184 percent. If one turns to the growth rate of the total GNP, the results show an annual expansion of 3.3 percent in the 1950s and of 4.5 percent in the 1960s. Figuring in terms of volume and for the years 1960–75, the Swedish achievement averaged about 4.3 percent per year — slightly better than the American experience, slightly less than that of West Germany, Italy, or France.[7]

This growth in productivity was accompanied, in both industry and agriculture, by a steady decline in the number of workers employed. Working hours were further reduced because since 1953 workers enjoyed a three-week, paid vacation, in the 1960s a four-week vacation, and by the mid-1970s a five-week vacation was envisioned. As of 1975 the hours of work per week averaged 40, and some firms were already introducing the 36-hour week and the 6-hour day. The trend was similar to that in other industrialized countries, but it was particularly strong in Sweden. Productivity was enhanced, of course, by mechanization and rationalization. A simple example may illustrate the kind of development: in 1950 a forest worker produced one cubic meter per day; in 1975 he cut five cubic meters, and the prediction was that by 1980 the amount would be twenty cubic meters. The inevitable result of this kind of increased efficiency was technological unemployment; skilled and semi-skilled workers were being laid off by the thousands. The combination of this process with state policy in agriculture meant that many people had to seek new jobs. The welfare state considered itself responsible for retraining workers and getting them back into the labor force as soon as possible in new jobs. The number being retrained was always larger than those doing mere relief work, and in their retraining periods workers received regular wages. An unemployment rate of anything above 3 percent was considered serious, and it seldom reached as high as 4 percent; in 1975 it was 1.75 percent. The trend in employment was away from industry and agriculture and into service functions.

The dramatic and often disturbing shifts in the use of the work force can be seen most clearly in the accompanying tabulation indicating developments within only a decade and a half in the recent twentieth century. Put in percentage terms, and if we take into account the expansion of the work force by 420,000, the number employed in the private sector decreased in 15 years from 88 percent to 75 percent, while those employed in the public sector increased from 12 percent to 25 percent of all employed persons. The most spectacular changes were in agriculture, where the number of workers was down to less than half, and in the service occupations, all of which were up, but especially in the public sector, where the increase was more than double.

Since productivity increased despite the decrease in the number of production workers, it was obvious that the significance of these shifts was not so much economic as social, and of course technical.

| Workers in: | 1960 | 1975 |
|---|---|---|
| Agriculture, fishing | 475,000 | 209,000 |
| Forestry | 114,000 | 61,100 |
| Industry | 1,040,000 | 1,039,000 |
| Electricity, gas, water | 27,000 | 28,500 |
| Construction | 307,000 | 332,000 |
| All goods and power production | 1,963,000 | 1,669,600 |
| Trade | 446,700 | 508,100 |
| Traffic | 247,500 | 270,400 |
| Private services | 496,800 | 557,400 |
| State service | 145,900 | 236,800 |
| Communal service | 271,400 | 747,700 |
| Total service functions | 1,608,300 | 2,320,400 |
| Total workers | 3,571,400 | 3,990,000 |
| in private sector | 3,154,100 | 3,005,500 |
| in public sector | ' 417,300 | 984,500 |

Source: Långtidsutredningen 1975 (SOU 1975: 89, p. 173).

In the realm of business organization it was notable that consolidations and mergers were taking place in almost every economic sector. The old neighborhood milk stores and tobacco shops, the little grocery stores with their big coffee-grinders and their gossip-corners gave way to chain stores and supermarkets as in the United States and elsewhere. The total business mergers numbered 70 in 1959 and 340 in 1970. Companies like Electrolux and Volvo grew internally, then because of their strength absorbed smaller companies ("Unto him who hath shall be given, and from him who hath not shall be taken away that which he hath"). But the process was more than the strong absorbing the weak. The strong wished to be stronger to compete in the world arena. For Sweden, despite its small size, was participating in world enterprise. The Lamco iron mine in Liberia was but one example.

When the magazine Fortune in 1972 listed the 300 largest industrial concerns outside the United States it found that 15 of them were Swedish. This same proportion continued, as Fortune found that in 1975 out of 500 of the largest companies 25 were Sweden-based. Japan led the way with 122, Britain had 84, Germany 72, France 44, Canada 38; then came Sweden ahead of Switzerland, the Netherlands, Belgium, and all others. Notable among the Swedish giants were Volvo, SAAB-Scania, ASEA, Electrolux, L. M. Ericsson, SKF (ball bearings), Svenska Tändsticks (matches) — companies that not only sold their products abroad but often had plants in other countries. There were also other companies formed as combinations, especially the state-managed industries in the Statsföretag group. In relation to its size Sweden had more multinational concerns than did the United States, and its overseas operations were growing rapidly. Swedish employees abroad numbered 35,000 in 1965, 183,000 in 1970, and 286,000 in 1974. These same corporations in 1974 employed 432,000 workers in Sweden. Almost two-thirds of their sales were to foreign markets. The Swedes had the technological and the business know-how to back up these ventures, and they possessed the "planetary appetite." They were in full agreement with the attitude expressed by the president of the IBM World Trade Corporation: "For business purposes the boundaries that separate one nation from another are no more real than the equator." [8]

The advantages of bigness impressed the managers of domestic enterprises, too. Banks, stores, and industries surveyed the advantages of large-scale operations and gave up cherished rivalries. In the early 1970s some of the country's largest banks merged, including Stockholms Enskilda Bank and Skandinaviska Banken, which formed the new Skandinaviska Enskilda Banken (S E Banken). Soon thereafter two government banks, Postsparbanken and Kreditbanken, joined to form PK Banken. The two largest department-store chains combined to form one all-inclusive chain, although the employees fought hard to prevent this merger with its inevitable reduction of staff.

An ample supply of funds was essential for the vast technological improvements in all branches of the economy. Forestry and agriculture were becoming capital-intensive as were the engineering industries. Construction and the building of energy sources required massive investment. Sweden's demands for energy made it the world's largest per capita importer of oil, for its supply of water power met only one fifth of the need. The rising cost of oil was therefore a serious drain on the country's money supply. The Norwegian oil strikes in the North Sea encouraged Swedes to hope that Sweden might obtain oil and gas from the Norwegian fields and that Swedish interests might have a chance to join in prospecting and development of fields farther north. Nuclear power also became one of the hopes of the future, and several plants were constructed. However, fear of leakage and accident caused agonized debate and created a divisive political issue. On this the social democrats and the conservatives found themselves together on the positive side, and the center was strongly negative; but all parties were split among themselves. The issue was crucial in the election of 1976 but future policy was not yet rigidly determined.

The nature of the relationship between government and business was one of the most fascinating aspects of the Swedish economy. Both government and business emphasized that 90 percent of business was in private hands. While technically this was true the statement obscured the amount of control which the government exercised and the amount of voluntary cooperation between business and government. Mutuality of interest was recognized. Companies like Volvo, ASEA, L M Ericsson, and others were national assets. They gave employment to thousands and they brought in large amounts of foreign exchange. It was literally true that what was good for the big manufacturers was good for the country and vice versa. In the 1970s the government engaged in extraordinarily complicated maneuvers to make sure that the shipbuilding companies could continue to operate and thus maintain employment. ASEA-Atom, which built the nuclear plants, was owned half by the state, half privately, and it in turn bought heavy equipment from a consortium composed of the private Uddeholm Company, the American Combustion Engineering Company, and the Swedish government.

The cooperation between big business and big labor was institutionalized in the Saltsjöbaden Agreement of 1938. In rather oversimplified terms it might be said that industry and labor (SAF and LO) sidestepped state regulation by making the state a silent partner in the concerns that affected them and all of society. Heated debate preceded the adoption of a policy that came later to be known as "Harpsund democracy." Harpsund was a pleasant rural estate given to the Swedish government in 1952 and used for conferences and entertaining by the prime minister, an ideal place for shirt-sleeve diplomacy both foreign and domestic. There the leaders of business and the leaders of labor could get together under the informal auspices of government to work out their problems. Some observers saw in the system ominous collusion between people who should be fighting each other; others saw it as a rational way to preclude destructive strife. In the early 1970s wildcat strikes broke out in northern Sweden, labor protesting against its own officials thought to be too friendly with management. At the other end of the employee-management relationship some industrialists objected to what they regarded as fraternizing with labor.

There can be no doubt, however, that this three-way cooperation strengthened the national economy. It fitted in with the social democrats' penchant for state action, yet it fell short of socialization. In the 1970s the most urgent demands for change were calls for more state participation. Something of this was being accomplished through financial operations.

The General Pension Fund grew during the 1970s into an immense reserve of capital, amounting in 1976 to approximately \$25 billion (100 billion kronor) and scheduled to rise to approximately \$35 billion by 1980. Sweden was accumulating the contributions paid for future pensions instead of using the pay-as-you-go system adopted by the United States. At first investments of these funds were made in home mortgages and loans to agriculture and industry; purchase of stocks was prohibited because of ideological objections to acquiring ownership of business. Later these restrictions were modified so that a certain percentage of shares could be bought. It appeared likely that further relaxation would permit larger investment in industrial and commercial enterprises, for the pension funds would soon amount to two-thirds of all national savings. The placement of investments from these funds would determine the course of the country's economic development. The financial managers would decide who would grow and who could not grow.

A second large aggregation of capital was the body of investment reserves built up by business. In 1938 a law was passed giving tax advantages to companies that set aside investment reserves in the Riksbank; experience led to strengthening of the law in 1963. A company could allocate up to 40 percent of its pre-tax profits to an investment fund, and 46 percent of this amount was to be deposited in the Riksbank. At a later time the Riksbank could release these funds for construction or other specified purposes. Use of the fund acted to stabilize fluctuations in the business cycle, to absorb excess liquidity in boom periods, and to stimulate employment in periods of depression. Further, it enabled the Riksbank to direct the expenditures into distressed areas and thus to aid regional equalization. Even businessmen were happy because of the tax savings they enjoyed.[9]

The allocation of investment became a significant aspect of social policy, involving both the placement of funds and their ownership. In Denmark the labor unions proposed using their accumulating dues to purchase shares of stock but bowed before a storm of protest and dropped the scheme. The Swedes considered using this method to gain worker control of their industries, but the idea of labor becoming involved in the capitalistic system aroused vigorous opposition within the unions as well as in the bourgeois sector. Since the late 1940s the conservatives had discussed what came to be known as owner democracy (ägardemokrati), the idea being to encourage citizens to own their own homes and to buy shares in corporations. In the 1970s a new impetus for broad-based stock ownership came from a different direction and with a different purpose.

Rudolf Meidner, chief economist for the labor federation (LO), brought forth a specific proposal for the gradual acquisition by the labor unions of ownership of the Swedish economic structure. In what some called the most radical LO congress ever held, in the spring of 1976, the LO itself approved the general idea. The plan was that 20 percent of the post-tax profits of the larger corporations should be set aside by law not for the wage account but for the purchase of stock in the name of the unions.[10] Thus the workers would gain ownership of the means of production. They would become in effect their own employers. The reaction against the proposal was strong. Many workers approved purchase of stock but thought the shares should be owned by individual workers rather than by the already overpowerful unions which threatened thus to become a state within a state. A task force representing industry had already accepted the idea of employee funds, but insisted that participation should be both individual and voluntary, not fixed by law as in the Meidner plan.[11]

Immediately after the approval of the Meidner scheme by the LO congress, *Svenska Dagbladet*, the conservative daily, conducted a poll with the aid of Sifo, a major polling organization. The two questions as they were posed in bold simplicity undoubtedly influenced the answers, but the results were nevertheless both surprising and significant. When asked, "Are you for or against that Sweden be socialized?" 16 percent replied "for" and 65 percent replied "against"; 19 percent were doubtful. The most startling statistics were among the social democrats, who voted only 24 percent for socialism, 49 percent against. When the question was directed specifically to the Meidner proposal — "Are you for or against that labor unions should take over ownership of all enterprises?" the result showed only 12 percent in favor, 69 percent opposed, and 19 percent in doubt. On this the social democrats voted 22 percent in favor, 49 percent against, and 30 percent doubtful.[12] The interpretation one must place on such answers is that the Swedish people wanted social reforms and social welfare without socialism. But it remained strange that approximately half the voters sent to the riksdag social democratic and communist representatives. The only thing certain was that debate would continue on this and other socialist proposals. Meidner advised his supporters to be patient; his proposal would come up again at the next LO congress, in 1981.

The plan as adumbrated would require several decades to produce effective ownership control for the unions. Pension funds had already begun to buy stocks, but these funds were not owned directly by either unions or individuals. In the United States pension funds were commonly owned by unions; the Teamsters, for example, had some billion and one-half dollars in pension funds. Altogether hundreds of workers' pension funds in thousands of businesses amounted in 1975 to about 30 percent of the total value of American commercial stocks. By the year 2000 these funds would hold about 60 percent. These amounts were far higher than those about which the Swedes were debating. The pension funds of course belonged to the workers who contributed to them, and they could easily be used for control if ownership were not so widely dispersed. In practice the accumulated moneys were invested in a great variety of enterprises, with no one fund having a controlling interest in any particular industry; frequently it was required that no more than 5 percent of a fund be invested in the stock of one corporation. The possibilities of purposeful control lay only in the future, both in the United States and in Sweden. Nevertheless, the situation led Peter Drucker, an American management and financial writer, to refer to the United States as the most socialized country in the world, although neither Swedes nor Americans seemed to realize the fact.

Drucker condemns the Swedish plan because (1) it would confine stock purchase to the nation's own companies at a time when worldwide scope for investment is essential for profitability and security; (2) it would "freeze the economy and ensure that a substantial part of the pension-fund assets will be misinvested in the old, declining, obsolescent, or obsolete industries, to the detriment of economy and pension plan participants alike"; and (3) for political reasons the fund could not sell the stock of declining companies, and hence would lose value.[13]

Oddly, this vast American system had developed with no thought of its socializing potential — it had been urged originally by the president of General Motors — while the more modest Swedish proposal was conceived deliberately as a means of transferring ownership from capitalists to workers. The effective result in each case was to be ownership by the workers of the means of production, except for agriculture. Either system differed from a state take-over of industry, the old idea of what socialism involved. Furthermore, in each case ownership was in the beginning highly decentralized and did not bring with it management or control. As to what might happen in the future one had to consider the vision of Ernst Wigforss who some years earlier wrote of the "socialistic desire that ownership of the means of production should pass to the community" to achieve greater economic equality. Wigforss wanted "a democratic organization of economic life wherein wage earners through their labor organizations exercise a direct influence."[14]

This latter idea of worker participation in decision making was separate from the matter of ownership. The shop committee of labor was an established device for handling suggestions and complaints at the immediate and everyday level. Workers came to want more than that, to help determine company policy on wages and working conditions as well as on broader questions involving products and sales. Codetermination by capital and labor, only rarely conceived of in the United States, was being adopted widely in West Germany and elsewhere in Europe. In Sweden the system came step by step in the 1970s, and by January 1, 1977 all concerns with more than twenty-five employees were required to have employee representation on boards of directors. Employees had the right to demand information and to be able to negotiate on all matters affecting activities and conditions of the workplace. If the boards of directors used a language other than Swedish (many used English), adequate translation had to be provided. Heavy penalties were prescribed for violation of the rules, whether by employers, unions, or individual employees. The immediate goal of representation was achieved; the goal of worker control of economic life was a dream for the future, and it was a dream not shared by all wage earners. A serious question was: how many workers wanted to participate in the responsibilities of ownership and management?

The movement toward worker participation in ownership and management offered a socialist alternative to the nationalization of industry and a way to avoid giving overweening power to the state. The danger feared by many was that it would, instead, merely give overwhelming power to the unions.

## The Restructuring of Society

The demand for improvement of the conditions of life went beyond the bounds of economic arrangements either foreign or domestic. The glow of hope in the immediate postwar period 1946–51 was labeled the "harvest time," though it was hardly that. More appropriately it might be labeled the "seed time," for the reforms of that epoch proved to be the beginnings of vaster changes yet to come.

Pensions were increased, but more significant than the increases was the fact that pensions were made independent of the amount contributed. Grants were made for child allowances, and support was increased for vacation trips for mothers and children. The period of paid vacations for workers was successively increased. A national system of health insurance was instituted. Courts were expanded and the prison system was remodeled. Whereas in the nineteenth century the single-cell system (influenced by American example) was considered especially humane, now it was regarded as brutal; open wards were introduced, and family visitation was permitted. Religious freedom was provided for all who wished to opt out of the state church, free church pastors were permitted to perform marriages, and cloisters were permitted for the first time since the Reformation. To make higher taxes bearable provision was made for withholding at the source. For agriculture subventions were voted in an attempt to equalize the income of farmers with that of workers in industry. Shop committees were established in factories to give more voice to labor. Fundamental decisions were made for a gradual transformation of the educational system and the powerful influence of the pastors in the school system was abolished. In government structure the multitudinous small rural communes (2,300) were amalgamated into 800 (eventually to 270).

After this dynamic five years of change the process of self-examination and reform continued more slowly. Many brains were at work in government bureaus and research institutes, seeking to identify injustices and inefficiencies and to recommend correctives. Everything was under scrutiny, imperfections were recognized but perfectibility was assumed. Long-term plans succeeded each other at five-year intervals, and plans were followed by action. No longer was it a matter of mere social reforms, patching and repairing an outworn social structure. Gradually a new purpose and a new design emerged. The old society would be replaced by a new "welfare state." The helpless individual would no longer be left to fend for himself in a ruthless competitive system. The state would look after its people, see to it that they had health care, housing, jobs, and cultural advantages — everything they needed. The goal professed was unfettered opportunity for the individual, the method was oversight by the government to provide that opportunity and to prevent interference. A few broad categories of programs may illustrate the dynamic action that was transforming a once passive society.

Health of the citizenry early became one of the prime concerns of the state. S. A. Hedin introduced a health insurance proposal in the riksdag in 1884, and from then on laws followed one another in steady succession attempting to alleviate the distress of sickness from birth and childhood on through old age. Advice and prophylactic treatment for prospective mothers, health instruction and examination in the schools, district health officers and child welfare boards, required doctors in factories, health and accident insurance, ample hospital facilities — these things were provided at nominal fees or no fees at all. Medicine became preventive as well as curative. Except for insurance programs general taxation bore the burden. Hospitals were not only publicly owned and excellent but they provided, as of the early 1970s, 149 beds per ten thousand inhabitants (compared with 111 in the Soviet Union and 75 in the United States). Infant mortality in the first year of life was reduced to one-half of that in the United States and was the lowest in the world.[15] Longevity was the highest in the world. Abortion was controlled but was available practically on demand. The health program was supported by highly efficient research, often aided by grants from such institutions as the Rockefeller Foundation. Closely related to matters of individual health were other programs such as careful regulation of housing, provision of recreational facilities, control of pollution and other ecological problems. The health of the individual was regarded not only as a personal matter but as a social good.

Decentralization of government and business was conceived as an absolute necessity. Despite mobility by car and train and plane (or because of it?)

The Romanesque cathedral in Lund. Courtesy of
the Swedish Information Service, New York.

Courtesy of
the Swedish Institute,
Stockholm.

Windmills at Störlinge on the
island of Öland. Photo: AKA.

A *fäbod* dairy in Härjedalen.
Photo: S. O. Håkansson.

Stigbergsgatan in Stockholm South, with old houses preserved. Copyright Bildtjänsten.
Photo: A.-G. Annerfalk.

Midsummer in Dalarna. Photo: B. Dahlin.

In the Stockholm skerries. Photo: Gösta Lundquist.

Dramatic Theater, Stockholm. Courtesy of the Swedish
Institute, Stockholm. Photo: Arne Enander.

Winter at Skansen, Stockholm.
Courtesy of the Swedish Information
Service, New York.

Carl Milles's statue of Neptune at
Skeppsbron, Stockholm. Couresty of
the Swedish Institute, Stockholm.
Photo: A.-G. Annerfalk.

Aerial view of "The City between the Bridges," Old Stockholm, with the royal castle in center. Photo: Bror Karlsson.

The Council Chamber in the royal palace. The Gobelin tapestries were a gift from Louis XV of France to Gustav III.

A Swedish day-care center. Courtesy of the Swedish
Information Service, New York. Photo: Bertil Forsén.

Edward Hald, artist, with the blower, Herr
Bergquist, at Orrefors. Courtesy of Orrefors
Glasbruk.

The open prison, Tillberga. Courtesy of the
Swedish Information Service, New York.
Copyright Saxon-Bild. Photo: Pelle Arfvidsson.

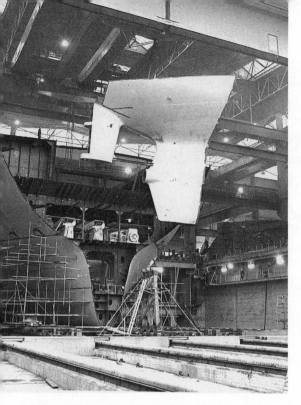

Ship under construction at Götaverken's Arendal shipyard. Courtesy of the Swedish Information Service, New York.

Pulpwood coming to the Jössefors bruk in western Sweden. Courtesy of the Swedish Information Service, New York.

Equipment for mining iron ore, Kiruna. Courtesy of the Swedish Information Service, New York. Photo: Börje Rönnberg.

The "tipper trolley" which facilitates stand-up work, Volvo's Torslanda plant. Courtesy of Volvo of America.

Täby, a Stockholm satellite community. Photo: Erik Claesson.

Biskopsgården, Gothenburg. Photo: Stig Sjöstedt.

The Stockholm City Hall, 1923; architect, Ragnar Ostberg. Sculpture, *The Sunboat*, 1966, by Christian Berg. Photo: A.-G. Annerfalk.

Stockholm, the new "City" skyscrapers, 1959–     The Concert House, Stockholm, by Ivar Tengbom, 1925. Photo: Bror Karlsson.

Nils Nilsson Skum, Snow landscape with Lapps herding reindeer. Courtesy of The National Museum, Stockholm.

Ernst Wigforss. Courtesy of the Social
Democratic Party. Photo: Hans
Malmberg.

Hjalmar Branting. Photo: Henry Goodwin.
Courtesy of the Royal Library, Stockholm,
Photographic Collections.

Thorbjörn Fälldin. Photo: ReTeam Foto.

Olof Palme. Courtesy of the Social
Democratic Party.

August Strindberg. Photo: Herman
Hamnqvist. Stockholm, 1901. Courtesy of
the Royal Library, Stockholm,
Photographic Collections.

Alfred Nobel. Courtesy of the Royal
Library, Stockholm, Photographic
Collections.

Silvia and Karl XVI Gustav, 1976. Photo: Lennart Nilsson.

people crowded insistently into urban centers. Bureaucratic expansion and factory productivity seemed to require large concentrations of workers. But these concentrations grew so large that they choked the streets with automobiles and forced people to live in congested apartments. After a certain point inefficiency and depersonalization destroyed the advantages of concentration. Hence the government took the lead by sending many of its bureaus and offices to smaller towns outside Stockholm — the agricultural and forestry boards, for instance, moved to Jönköping, various defense offices to Karlstad, and some pension and insurance offices to Sundsvall. Industries found it advantageous to establish their factories in communities outside metropolitan areas. Population trends in cities and small towns began to be reversed, though the process was often painful for families rooted in their localities.

"Humanizing of the workplace" became both a slogan and a program in the early 1970s. It involved lounges and light and beautification, but especially reorganization of work patterns. Volvo, for example, was plagued with absenteeism and high turnover. Both Volvo and SAAB therefore experimented with abolition of the assembly-line monotony in which a worker did nothing but twist a particular bolt all day. They adopted systems of teamwork for the manufacture of a large section of a car, the members of the team varying their tasks and planning how best to do them and learning varied skills. There was even consideration of a plan to allow one small group to build an entire car, but this idea was abandoned as uneconomical. The concept of giving workers a greater sense of significant participation was applied in many factories.[16]

In the late 1960s and early 1970s the cry of the new forces was for *jämlikhet*, a word which has to be translated as equality but which also has connotations of social solidarity.[17] The goal was to eliminate the class distinctions that had segmented Swedish society for generations. Methods of accomplishing this broad social purpose included several of the matters discussed above such as regionalism and representation on boards of directors. They involved also educational policy and the rights of women. On an immediately practical basis the drive was for equalization of wages between, for example, factory workers and office personnel, blue collar workers and white collar workers. The proposal, conceived during an inflationary period, advocated significantly higher wages for the blue collar group and only a meager improvement for the white collar personnel.

The professional workers decided they could not submit to this kind of discrimination and declared a strike in February 1971. It began with about 2,500 members of the professional union (SACO) and soon spread to include workers belonging to the Federation of Government Officers (SR). The response was a lockout that included some 20,000 teachers. Railroads and industries were crippled, as were schools and social service agencies. When the Government Service Board ruled the lockout legal the Collective Bargaining Office decided to lock out most of the officers in the military. Forty-seven thousand workers were out, and the jobs of twice that number were threatened. This escalation of conflict frightened the country. Perhaps the right to strike, or lockout, must have limits? The riksdag finally voted by a large majority to declare a six-week moratorium on all strikes and lockouts. This period passed without final agreement, and a general strike was threatened to begin on the Midsummer weekend. Concessions on all sides averted disaster but at a cost of wage increases for laborers averaging more than 9 percent per year for three years.

The meaning of the conflict and its resolution was that the separate branches of the labor force could argue about their respective shares of the wage krona but that their government would not tolerate a breakdown of the socioeconomic structure; for *their* government was now responsible not only for the interests of labor but for the welfare of the country as a whole. The practical needs of society were paramount. It was a most uncomfortable realization for the ideological social democrats. The *folkhem* ideal could not eliminate rivalries within the family. Perhaps the differences in interests between different segments of the working population had become sharper than the differences between labor and management, or at least more emotion-laden. Unauthorized strikes in the iron mines also manifested a dissatisfaction with union leadership, a feeling that labor officialdom had lost touch with the rank and file and identified more with fellow-officials of government and industry than with the worker ranks from which they had sprung. Equality was hard to attain.

On the purely social level equality was achieved more easily. The stilted traditional style of speaking to one another in the third person and with constant use of titles ("Would the professor like another cup of tea?" "I would suggest to Herr Svensson") — such usages rapidly disappeared in the mid-twentieth century and were commonly replaced with the intimate *du* (you), previously used only within families and between close friends. Long gone was the practice of tipping one's hat to one's "betters," such as the pastor or the factory owner; no longer did one admit to having "betters."

There were other practical aspects in the program of achieving equality of opportunity for every member of the community. For instance, those living in the distant and rural districts were admittedly short-changed on the cultural amenities such as access to theaters and museums and sometimes the availability of the simple necessities. Therefore the government's program was to make sure that hospitals, schools, museums, shops, theaters, and so on were within reach of everyone and to subsidize bus transportation where necessary. A major governmental industrial enterprise, Norrbottens Järnverks

Aktiebolag (NJA) was supported to build a huge steel plant at Luleå in the far north and thus provide jobs and an industrial base in a region where private capitalism could not justify investment. For similar reasons a new university was established at Umeå. Such projects were helpful to this sparsely settled area, but they could not completely overcome the disadvantages of distance and harsh climate. In 1970 the State Company (*Statsföretag*) was created as a holding company to centralize control over a number of establishments that the state was taking over; it could then transfer funds from profitable concerns to unprofitable ones and thus maintain employment even in distressed areas. The State Company took over several companies that were in trouble and by 1973 it had 37,000 employees in thirty-one companies. Its overall achievement had to be measured in social terms more than in economic success. The mix in Sweden's mixed economy was becoming weighted toward the state side. These concerns were separate, at least for the time, from the railways, post office, telecommunications, and other public utility operations.

Equal status for women had been on the reform agenda since the mid-nineteenth century, and legislation had gone far to remove traditional disabilities. But Utopia was not yet attained. For example, although women were permitted to become ministers in the state church there was still strong opposition from within the church itself. Principle and practice were at variance in Sweden as in most western countries. Day-care centers were provided for children so that mothers could work outside the home. There was also a systematic attempt in the schools to give boys as well as girls training in the care of children and in cooking and the maintenance of the household. Fathers, whether married or not, were legally obligated to help support their children, although if they did not do so society assumed the responsibility. One home for mothers with fatherless children, with which I am acquainted, was so pleasantly comfortable that it was difficult to get the mothers to move out when their children grew up.

In their political position women in the nineteenth and early twentieth centuries enjoyed neither equality nor liberation, as amply attested in law and literature; their situation was much the same throughout the western European world. The franchise came gradually, with final full equality at the ballot box in 1918–21. Individual women made their mark in public affairs in many ways: Selma Lagerlöf won the Nobel Prize for Literature in 1909; Kerstin Hesselgren became housing inspector for Stockholm in 1906 and was then school inspector, factory inspector, and in 1921 the first woman member of the riksdag; Nanna Swartz was named professor in the Caroline Medical Institute in 1937; Karin Kock became a cabinet minister in 1947; Alva Myrdal opened her extraordinary career in 1934 with publication (in collaboration with her husband Gunnar) of the book on the population crisis, *Kris i befolk-*

*nings frågan* (*Nation and Family* [1941]), which shocked Sweden into action against the fear of death by decline of population; Mrs. Myrdal went on to become an international leader in social and disarmament matters in the United Nations, ambassador to India, and cabinet minister.

But outstanding individual cases do not obscure the fact that real equality was still an ideal rather than an actuality. Wages, for example, were supposedly equalized but women's average pay was less than men's. And women, although they may have appreciated their status of legal equality, did not push for complete realization of their opportunities in public life. Certain physical and psychological differences between the sexes remained — a situation with which most people were quite content (*vive la différence!*). But women as managers in business were becoming more common, and in the riksdag the number of women steadily increased from 5 in 1922 to 26 in 1950 and 75 in 1977. The question of female succession to the throne was complicated by the social democrats' proposal to get rid of the monarchy entirely. When in 1975 it was proposed to set up an investigative commission on the question of female succession, one Social Democratic woman representative deserted her party's position to vote for the proposition, and party discipline operated to exclude her from the riksdag list in the next election.

New groups in the community who required special consideration were the immigrants. They were given conscientious attention, provided with information booklets and free instruction in the Swedish language. Often special housing was arranged. No foreign workers from outside Scandinavia were allowed to enter the country unless they had work permits issued with the approval of the LO (an interesting instance of the use of a nongovernmental organization to carry out a government function). Hence unemployment among immigrants was seldom a problem. Normally they had to accept the more menial jobs in restaurants and factories, and even then there was sometimes resentment against them on the part of Swedish workers. Furthermore, Sweden was an ancient society that had never sloughed off its built-in class distinctions and inherited traditions. It was not a society closed to foreigners, many of whom had through the years been fully accepted. Yet the process of assimilation was slow and often disheartening. At an earlier period Swedish visitors and immigrants to the United States had complained that although it was easy to make acquaintances in America, it was difficult to make friends, to get beneath the surface of human relationship. Immigrants to Sweden likewise found it difficult to get beyond the superficial cameraderie of the workplace with their Swedish fellow workers.[18]

If the immigrants were the newest inhabitants of Sweden the Lapps were among the oldest. For centuries they had followed their reindeer in the seasonal migrations across the cold tundra or from the forests down to the seashore. The boundaries drawn by land-conscious nation states meant little to these nomads of the North as they crossed freely back and forth within the territories of the Lappmark that are now Swedish, Norwegian, Finnish, and Russian. These people adapted themselves remarkably to the demands of their bleak and imposing environment. In the Middle Ages the *Birkarlar* traded among them for furs and collected taxes. Miners tried to use them as laborers and met with frustration. Missionaries attempted the difficult task of Christianizing and educating them; they built chapels in the wilderness and held school in tents, but with only slight success. The Lapps (or *Samer*) long remained the racial and cultural minority in an otherwise homogeneous society.

Slowly but irresistibly, as population increased in the south, land-hungry settlers pushed into the grazing lands of the reindeer, the economic foundation of Lapp life. Roads and eventually railways cut across the routes of the animals' migration; the waterfalls of the rivers were harnessed and electric power lines were strung through the forests; the forests themselves were cut for timber. Governments were torn between the needs of expanding agriculture and industry and their sense of responsibility for the rights of the original inhabitants. Yet numbers increased, and in the 1970s the Lapp population was reckoned at about 2,000 in Russia, 3,000 in Finland, 22,000 in Norway, and 10,000 in Sweden. These small and widely dispersed groups clung long and tenaciously to their ancestral and independent ways, but their cause was hopeless in confrontation with the mechanized and ordered civilization of the twentieth century. They represented the Scandinavian parallel to the American Indians.

A blow to the old culture was the convention of 1919 between Norway and Sweden that closed the Norwegian border to most of the Swedish Lapps for the crossing of their reindeer. Swedish policy was to force the Lapps to accept a money economy, with emphasis on slaughtering. In the 1970s the Lapps had some 250,000 deer, and the annual product of meat and hides was valued at more than 7 million kronor. Domestication had largely replaced the seasonal migration to new feeding grounds, and modern methods of husbandry had superseded the old. Now snowmobiles were used for herding and airplanes for communication.

Increasingly both the Lapps of the fjeld and the Lapps of the forest were abandoning their ancient culture, moving southward and settling in established communities. Less than a third of Sweden's 10,000 Lapps still depended on reindeer. The state required children to attend school. It built old people's homes in the possibly mistaken belief that it was more humane to let the old and worn-out sit and stare rather than to be left behind in the annual trek with only a knife in hand.

Integration into the Swedish culture proceeded inexorably, ameliorated by the Lapp administrative agency of the national government which built bridges, established a reindeer institute, and built a folk high school in Sorsele in 1942 (transferred to Jokkmokk in 1945). The Lapps themselves, traditionally individualistic and living in more or less isolated small groups, had never learned the political arts. Beginning in 1904 various attempts were made to organize them, but no permanent assembly was achieved until 1950 in Jokkmokk with the so-called Lapp riksdag; thereafter this consultative assembly met yearly. Other unifying and energizing institutions were developed by a few Lapps and sympathizers. In 1919 a Lapp newspaper was founded by Torkel Tomasson, and in 1960 this was taken over by the dedicated native Lapp school inspector, Docent Israel Ruong. Three special radio stations came to serve the Lapp communities. Several native artists have brought honor to their people, perhaps most notably Nils Nilsson Skum (1872–1951), who portrayed reindeer and their herding with rare artistic skill and fidelity. But to gain acceptance and equality the Lapps needed both purposefulness on their own part and all the strength and resourcefulness of the special ombudsman appointed in 1962 to represent their interests. For the tendency of the Lapps was to accept their fate and of the government to disregard them.[19]

## Democratizing Education

The school is an integral part of society, one function among many others. It is therefore necessary that the school at all times should reflect in its own functions the development and tendencies of the society which it is to serve, and preferably also help to further that development.[20]

To put this philosophy into practice the Swedish reformers of the post-World War II era pushed through a systematic and thorough reconstruction of the entire educational system. The fundamentals of political democracy had been established, and thus the doors had been opened to social democracy and economic democracy. However, each of these facets of democracy was incomplete, as is indicated by the need to precede each by a qualifying adjective which emphasizes its segmental character. The realization of total democracy could be achieved only when all citizens were fully informed and able to communicate intelligently among themselves. Democracy in education was therefore a sine qua non for the fulfillment of democracy in all sectors of society.

A beginning had been made in 1842 with the compulsory education law, but this had applied only to elementary education. Advanced education remained the province of an elite, especially the children of the already educated. An aristocracy of learning controlled the educational process itself as well as the higher offices of the state, the professions, and big business. The prestige of the educated class was maintained by a deep popular respect for learning and for the teachers who bore and spread that learning. No position in society, unless possibly that of the general directors of the government's main administrative boards, enjoyed a prestige as high as that of the professor. As of the mid-twentieth century almost all children got at least some schooling and the literacy rate was close to 100 percent. But children were separated at an early age in school largely on the basis of probable future occupation. A bright child from whatever background *might* go far in school; he could be seen through university and graduate school on government loans. But it was rare for the child of a farmer or a laborer to go beyond elementary school — he would be forsaking his proper place in society. A statistical survey published as late as 1976 indicated, for instance, that if a policeman's daughter and a professor's daughter got the same good grades in secondary school the policeman's daughter would probably continue schooling to become a nurse, whereas the professor's daughter would study to become a doctor.[21]

In the towns schools were differentiated so that one school took children who would presumably complete their education with the elementary school and take up unskilled work; one took children preparing for clerical work, trades, and semi-skilled occupations; a third was for those who wanted scientific or classical studies and would be ready to go on to the university. The latter group would proceed through a rigorous course of study in the gymnasium to about age twenty and at the end pass an intensive examination known as *student-examen*, capping an education roughly comparable to that of an American student at the end of two years of college. He was then ready for "life" or for his chosen discipline in the university.

Who was it who attained the high status of *student* and the privilege of university admission? In the first place the total number was small. In spite of the fact that those who took the *studentexamen* doubled between 1930 and 1951, still less than 5 percent of the twenty-year-olds in 1951 did so. For comparison it might be mentioned that at that time more than 10 percent of American youth had at age twenty completed two years of college. Furthermore, the social distinctions in the Swedish student cohort were startling. The majority of students came from the small upper class of wealthy and academic families.

In the period around 1950 there was much use, for statistical purposes, of the "Social Groups," and the accompanying short tabulation portrays the relation of social classification and higher education. Social Group I, 6 percent of the population, was made up of the wealthier merchants and landowners, high officials, professionals, and intellectuals; Social Group II, 37 percent of the population, included farmers, skilled craftsmen, teachers, office personnel, etc.; Social Group III, 57 percent of the people, included farm laborers and renters, fishermen, miners, and the host of unskilled workers. The student group represented an almost exact inversion of the Social Group proportions.[22]

| Social Group | Percentage of Population | Percentage of Students |
|---|---|---|
| I | 6 | 58 |
| II | 37 | 36 |
| III | 57 | 6 |

The meaning of these proportions was obvious, and it disturbed the liberals and social democrats profoundly: the two upper social groups with 43 percent of the population had 94 percent of the personnel trained for leadership roles. From the majority of the people, the lower-income portion, only 6 percent were prepared to take higher offices in government or business, to become ambassadors or general directors or party leaders. Higher education was restricted to a self-perpetuating elite. The early leaders of the Social Democratic party, including Hjalmar Branting, had come from this elite, even later ones like Olof Palme. But this was not a situation to gladden the hearts of social reformers, and it could not be depended upon to continue to produce effective leaders. The lower income groups must produce their own educated leadership. What was required, therefore, was a thoroughgoing reform of the entire educational system.

Demands for such reforms began in the nineteenth century. Ellen Key, who in 1900 published "the only Swedish pedagogic writing that has become a world sensation," favored the comprehensive school idea: all children should attend the same school to age fifteen "to learn to respect each other."[23] Anders Fryxell, J. O. Wallin, Thorsten Rudenschöld, and Fridtjuv Berg were all of the same mind. But the elite system was deeply entrenched.

The process of reform began, as was the Swedish custom, with the appointment of a series of investigative commissions. Experimentation and change began in the early 1950s. Studies were made of the educational systems of other countries — England, Germany, Russia, and especially the United States. Educational leaders were sent on examining trips, many reports were written. Public discussion groups, in some of which I was privileged to participate, argued the merits of the old Swedish system and the proposals for revision. Interest was intense, sometimes overheated. The press was filled with columns of debate. The push for reform came from the social democrats and some liberals who wanted to obtain the same kind of education for the lower-income groups as for those of higher income and established position, to introduce more citizenship training and less religious instruction, to reduce the classical emphasis and increase the number of "practical" subjects, to promote equality and social solidarity.

The philosophy of John Dewey was influential. One bitter opponent of change, a teacher of German, complained of the

> relapse into the culture and moral-degrading American individualistic psychology. . . . [The fault lies in the atmosphere, which] is poisoned by a spirit which cripples the mind. And this spirit has come here with the Gulf Stream, that is sure.[24]

Educational conservatives were sure that discipline, not freedom, was needed. University professors argued against the new proposals which were sure to weaken the academic preparation of university students, and the association of secondary school teachers long remained bitterly opposed. Social conservatives attacked the reforms because of their leveling purpose. But powerful political elements had decided on the democratization of education and it proceeded irresistibly.

The principles actuating the architects of the new school policy were stated as imparting knowledge and training skills to develop "harmonious individuals, and useful and responsible members of society." Nothing revolutionary in that! But also in the report of the 1957 Schools Commission, adopted by the riksdag in 1962, was the bold statement: "the school system should promote an equal appreciation of all occupations, a realization that every occupation without exception is as important as any other."[25]

Changing policy was accompanied by increased enrollment: in the elementary school it rose from 79 percent of the child population in 1950 to 99 percent in 1970; in the nineteen to twenty-four age group enrollment jumped in the same period from 5 percent to 30 percent. Differentiation in the elementary grades was abolished in favor of the comprehensive school (*enhetsskolan*), which brought all children together under the same roof for all the earlier years. Textbooks and lunches were provided free. The curriculum in the first six grades was general and was taught by the classroom teacher, while in grades 7–9 teaching was done by subject-matter teachers. Choices were available in the upper grades. For instance, all studied English, but for a second foreign language they might choose German, French, or Russian. (National needs required a wide spread of language ability.) Classes were "de-sexed" and Sten and Knut took up happily the study of cooking, serving food, and homemaking, while Ingrid and Kerstin indulged in carpentry and similar subjects. Religious instruction was retained, but it was based no longer on the Lutheran catechism but rather on the Sermon on the Mount, and at the upper level it became an objective general treatment of religions of the world.

Realistic sex education was taught in graduated steps, but thoroughly, in coolly physiological terms. One comment was that the Swedes wanted sex to be a wholly private matter but that they had "publicized the privacy all out of it."[26] In the ninth grade two weeks of practical job experience were required (an interesting innovation although hardly comparable to the two years required in China).

Stringency of discipline was replaced by a more relaxed atmosphere in which there was an attempt to inculcate a sense of individual responsibility. Enjoyment of school was one goal and it was being attained. New school buildings were designed specifically for the comprehensive school, without rigid division into separate rooms and with facilities for team teaching. Control from Stockholm was reduced in budget and classroom matters and each local school was left free to plan its own curriculum and methods. Pupils were encouraged to express themselves. The old authoritarianism was gone — to the continuing distress of conservative older parents and teachers and to the seeming delight of pupils and younger teachers.

Building upon the reform in elementary education came reforms also in the secondary schools, which after 1966 provided for a three-year theoretical course in preparation for the university, a presumably terminal two-year theoretical course, or a two-year practical course. The gymnasia and vocational schools which in 1950 enrolled 33,000 students, by 1972 enrolled 235,000. This augmentation of numbers among younger students had its effect on universities, too, where matriculations rose rapidly to 90,000 in 1967, to 120,000 in 1970, but then dropped to 106,000 in 1974. Medicine and other scientific fields restricted admissions, and one result was inflation in the humanistic and social science fields until the job market was oversaturated (a phenomenon not unknown in the United States and other affluent countries).

The university curriculum was basically professional and assumed that the general cultural foundation had been laid. Students entering the university at the usual age of twenty to twenty-one were expected to plunge at once into the study of medicine or law or a specific humanistic or scientific field. Increasingly they were expected to complete their studies within a comparatively short time. The old pattern of joyous years of social life with education as a by-product was frowned upon in the post-World War II epoch and would not be subsidized. The atmosphere of university life was academically purposeful, for higher education had become a concern of society, not something involving only the individual and his family.

Sweden went exceptionally far in making education at all stages possible for everyone. Work experience as well as school records might count for admission to higher educational institutions. All students in secondary schools were given grants of about $25 per month, and those over twenty years of age received $45; if they had economic need they might get additional grants of up to $70 a month plus loans of up to $1,600 per year. At the university level grants began at about $450 per year and could rise with loans and child support to over $2,500 per year. Graduate school scholarships and other support might give a research student as much as $5,000 per year tax free. (These figures are all for the early 1970s.) The criteria for determining grants and loans were combinations of merit and need. The purpose was clearly that no able and industrious student should be held back in his education because of economic need. That the program of widening educational opportunity was popularly approved is attested by the expanding enrollments at all levels.

To absorb the influx of students at the university level the older institutions at Uppsala, Lund, Gothenburg, and Stockholm proved insufficient. Perhaps also the aura of the past clung too persistently in the hallowed halls of the traditional institutions, and they were not located conveniently for some students. Hence an elaborate plan was developed for decentralizing higher education, for bringing universities, especially in the early years of study, to people in all parts of the country. A university was created at Umeå in the far north and at Linköping, and university branches were established in Örebro, Karlstad, and Växjö. More branches were projected, but before they could be established the great wave of enrollments subsided, and the future was uncertain. Along with the attempted geographic redistribution of university education went a redistribution of authority. In the 1970s the traditional academic control was being diffused among citizens of the community, and within the universities new governing bodies included students and staff members as well as professors. While the pressure for entrance to the university was growing another reform attempted to shorten the period of study, especially at the doctoral level. This was called "internationalizing" the doctorate, by reducing its requirements to what were regarded as the norms in other countries.

Universities, for all their importance, were far from being the only institutions of advanced education. There were the great medical schools such as the Caroline Medical Institute in Stockholm, the technological institutes in Stockholm, Gothenburg, Lund, and Linköping. The folk high schools had perhaps outlived their greatest usefulness, but their enrollments increased into the 1970s; they were in their very essence democratic, and the one at Brunnsvik was famous for training radical political leaders. Correspondence schools and study circles (136,000 in 1968–69) and a great variety of adult education programs blanketed the country, especially those sponsored by the Workers' Cultural Society (ABF). The Swedish Broadcasting Corporation experimented not only with televised adult education programs but with classes for the schools. All these institutions and television programs received state subsidies; education in Sweden was almost entirely public as well as co-educational. About 10 percent of the national operating budget went to education, nearly 5 percent of the GNP. Even the few private schools (about 30, of which 9 were boarding schools) received state aid. Two of the notable secondary schools were in Sigtuna: Sigtuna Skolan and Humanistiska Lärover-ket.

The goals of education were carefully thought out: the individual goal of personal development; the goal of productive citizenship; the general social goal of greater equality among all Swedes. In the twentieth century the government was exerting its authority to direct the entire educational process for purposes of the organized society, for *jämlikhet*. What effect this would have on education and on society in the future was yet to be seen.[27]

## The New Constitution and Political Change

Fundamental change in the form of government is always slow and difficult, but the constitution of 1809, frequently amended in detail, was recognized as in need of thorough revision. A commission of investigation was named in 1954 and through the next two decades a new constitution was gradually created. The "Instrument of Government of 1974" contains thirteen chapters, each including from seven to nineteen articles. Along with bringing many items up-to-date, two major changes were introduced. First was the abolition of the two-chamber parliament that had been instituted in 1866 and establishment of a single-chamber riksdag of 350 members. The number was changed to 349 in 1976 because the first of the single-chamber elections had produced an even split, 175 to 175, between the socialist and the nonsocialist parties. This division necessitated a lottery system to decide a number of closely contested decisions, and this gambling procedure seemed hardly a proper way to run a government. The single-chamber idea had long been advocated by the liberals and was only rather reluctantly accepted by the social democrats, who had enjoyed a continuing majority in the slow-changing First Chamber. But the unicameral system was at last agreed upon and took effect in 1971.

The second major change was the curtailment of royal power. The king had in practice already lost most of his authority but had retained the nominal right to appoint the ministers of state and to preside over the cabinet; his intimate knowledge of the affairs of the kingdom gave him influence. But the republican principles of the social democrats could be assuaged, and the monarchy retained as an institution, only by stripping the king of the last vestiges of authority. In the new constitution the king was deprived of all but his public relations functions. The proud but obsolete phrase that "the king, he and none other, shall rule the kingdom," was stricken and replaced by the statement:

"All public power in Sweden emanates from the people." This first article on basic principles continues: "The Swedish democracy is founded on freedom of opinion and on universal and equal suffrage and shall be realized through a representative and parliamentary polity and through local self-government." Article 4 confines itself to stating that "The king is the head of state," and Chapter 5 adds only some general specifications regarding tenure and duties. Article 5 declares that "The government [cabinet] rules the country. It is responsible to the riksdag." When Article 3 further prescribes that "The riksdag is the principal representative of the people," it is obvious that with the change of a few words the king could be dropped and someone else named head of state. Chapter 2 is a thoroughgoing guarantee of "fundamental freedoms and rights": freedom of assembly, of expression and of the press, of association, of religion, and of movement. Careful provision is made for the functioning of government and riksdag, of the committee structure that is of vital importance, and of the courts.

For the monarchy, the Act of Succession of 1810 was still valid into the later 1970s, but revision was under consideration, especially concerning the possibility of female succession. Popular sentiment as indicated in polls expressed itself strongly for retention of kingship as an institution, but no one fought to give the monarch power.[28]

For the riksdag, proportional representation is so arranged that 310 of the riksdagsmen are chosen for "constituency seats" and the additional 39 are then selected for "adjustment seats" on the basis of the total votes obtained by the parties nationally (but all delegates are assigned to constituencies). Only parties that obtain at least 4 percent of the votes can win representation.

Local government has long been important in the Swedish political structure and in recent years has become increasingly integrated with the national government, even in matters of taxation, which allow for a lessening of the national tax burden when the local taxes are abnormally high. About 40 percent of public administration is conducted by the municipalities. Since the mid-twentieth century local and national elections have been held simultaneously, with terms of office running for a uniform three years.

A third fundamental constitutional change, abolishment of the state church, was advocated by a commission headed by Alva Myrdal, then head of the ecclesiastical department in the government. Popular opinion on this matter was so strongly opposed to change that the reform was quietly laid on the shelf. Some churchmen, nevertheless, thought it might be healthy for religion if the church was forced to be independent.

In a provision that looks cautiously but hopefully toward a more integrated and peaceful world community the Instrument of Government (chapter 10, article 5) permits the riksdag to entrust certain decisions and/or functions "to

### Prime Ministers, 1917–77

| Dates | Prime Ministers | Parties |
|-------|-----------------|---------|
| 1917–20 | Nils Edén | Liberal-Social Democratic |
| Mar. 1920 | Hjalmar Branting | Social Democratic |
| Oct. 1920 | Louis De Geer, O. von Sydow | Caretaker government |
| Oct. 1921 | Hjalmar Branting | Social Democratic |
| Apr. 1923 | Ernst Trygger | Conservative |
| Oct. 1924 | Hjalmar Branting | Social Democratic |
| June 1926 | C. G. Ekman | Frisinnade-Liberal |
| Oct. 1928 | Arvid Lindman | Conservative |
| June 1930 | C. G. Ekman (F. Hamrin, Aug.-Sept. 1932) | Frisinnade |
| Sept. 1932 | Per Albin Hansson | Social Democratic |
| June 1936 | A. Pehrsson | Farmers |
| Sept. 1936 | Per Albin Hansson | Social Democratic |
| Dec. 1939 | Per Albin Hansson | Coalition (wartime) |
| July 1945 | Per Albin Hansson (Tage Erlander after Oct. 1946) | Social Democratic |
| Oct. 1951 | Tage Erlander | Social Democratic-Farmers |
| Oct. 1957 | Tage Erlander | Social Democratic |
| Oct. 1969 | Olof Palme | Social Democratic |
| Oct. 1976 | Thorbjörn Fälldin | Center-Liberal-Moderate |

another state, to an international organization, or to a foreign or international institution or community."

More meaningful than technical modifications in the constitutional documents were the profound shifts in attitudes and customs which grew almost imperceptibly through time. Joseph Board has put his finger on a significant aspect of these shifts. He speaks of the breakdown of "the Athenian model" of Swedish politics, by which he means the older pattern of "harmony, compromise, extensive consultation of interest groups, deliberation, restraint, pragmatic bargaining, consensus, balance, and stability."[29] All this, including the deference paid to experts, made up the reputation of Swedish politics. And it did not entirely disappear. However, the element of consensus, which perhaps best epitomized the reputed ideal, was weakened by a new aggressiveness on the part of the radicals among the social democrats. Their ideas were probably no more radical than those of older statesmen like Ernst Wigforss. But the older group recognized that progress had been attained in cooperation with the liberals and that time would favor reform. The young radicals were impatient, in a hurry for Utopia now. They pushed the party leaders to take strong positions, and for a time politics was confrontation rather than consultation and compromise. After the extremely close election of 1973 Prime Minister Olof Palme was successful for a time in leading the way back to a more cooperative position but tension remained high.

Tensions and problems previously identified came back into focus in the electoral campaign of 1976 and resulted in a shift of power. The margin was slight: the bourgeois parties together won 50.7 percent of the popular vote and 180 seats in the riksdag; the Social Democrats dropped to 42.9 percent of the popular vote but remained the largest single party and held 152 seats; the communists polled 4.7 percent and took 17 seats. Small parties that won no seats polled 1.7 percent. The bourgeois margin of victory was small but clear, and the Center, the Folk party, and the Moderates subordinated their differences, pooled their interests, and built a coalition government with Thorbjörn Fälldin of the Center party as prime minister. Fälldin was a shrewd and strong politician but a plain man of the people, a pipe-smoking sheep farmer from the north of Sweden, earthy in wisdom, slow of speech, a sharp contrast to the intellectual and quick-tongued Olof Palme. Fälldin's appeal as a person lay in his transparent sincerity; he was a man to be trusted. To some extent the cause of the changed balance was a pervasive unease, a vague sense that the great achievements of social reform may have gone far enough and that the time had come for a pause. Forty-four years of virtually continuous power and success had bred in the social democrats a degree of self-righteous arrogance, a feeling that the government belonged to them. This attitude seemed to be exemplified in the arbitrary handling of the tax cases of Astrid Lindgren and Ingmar Bergman. Citizens were beginning to fear the intrusion of government into their private lives and to sense that they were being deprived of the opportunity to make their own choices. Worries that had long been common among the bourgeois element spread further through the body politic, especially among the youth.

Among specific concerns were the steadily rising tax burden and continuing inflation. Even labor unionists realized that the Swedish wage level threatened to price Swedish goods out of world markets and that a slow-down in wage increases was inescapable. One of the most heatedly debated issues was the expansion of nuclear energy plants. The social democrats and the conservatives considered nuclear power essential, the liberals were of diverse minds, and the centrists were opposed. Center party leader Thorbjörn Fälldin pledged to stop nuclear plant construction and halt production unless absolutely safe methods of waste disposal could be found. This may have been the crucial issue on which the nonsocialists won the election, and when Fälldin became

## The Second Chamber of the Riksdag
### (single chamber after 1971)

| Year | Conservatives | Farmers | Liberals | Social Democrats | Left Social Democrats | Socialists | Communists | Of which Women of All Parties |
|---|---|---|---|---|---|---|---|---|
| 1915 | 86 |  | 57 | 87 | 11 |  |  |  |
| 1918 | 57 | 14 | 62 | 86 | 5 |  |  |  |
| 1921 | 71 | 30 | 47 | 75 | 6 |  | 2 |  |
| 1922 | 62 | 21 | 41 | 93 |  |  | 7 | 4 |
| 1925 | 65 | 23 | 33 | 104 |  |  | 5 | 3 |
| 1929 | 73 | 27 | 32 | 90 |  |  | 8 | 3 |
| 1933 | 58 | 36 | 24 | 104 |  | 6 | 2 | 5 |
| 1937 | 44 | 36 | 27 | 112 |  | 6 | 5 | 10 |
| 1941 | 42 | 28 | 23 | 134 |  |  | 3 | 18 |
| 1945 | 39 | 35 | 26 | 115 |  |  | 15 | 18 |
| 1949 | 23 | 30 | 57 | 112 |  |  | 8 | 22 |
| 1953 | 31 | 26 | 58 | 110 |  |  | 5 | 28 |
| 1957 | 42 | 19 | 58 | 106 |  |  | 6 | 29 |
| 1959 | 45 | 32 | 38 | 111 |  |  | 5 | 31 |
| 1961 | 39 | 34 | 40 | 114 |  |  | 5 | 32 |
| 1965 | 33 | 35 | 43 | 113 |  |  | 8 | 31 |
| 1969 | 32 | 39 | 34 | 125 |  |  | 3 | 36 |
| 1971 | 41 | 71 | 58 | 163 |  |  | 17 | 48 |
| 1974 | 51 | 90 | 34 | 156 |  |  | 19 | 50 |
| 1977 | 55 | 86 | 39 | 152 |  |  | 17 | 75 |

*Sources: Statistik årsbok, 1973, p. 405; Historisk statistik, III, p. 269.*

prime minister he was obligated to fulfill his pledge. His colleagues in the ministry, however, demanded compromises. With divided opinions on this and other issues, and a narrow majority of seats, the nonsocialist coalition faced a serious problem of survival.

The new government's statement of policy, dated October 8, 1976, read like an American party platform. Fälldin promised therein decentralization of governmental authority and of economic enterprise, security for all generations and groups, promotion of economic competition, employment for everyone, reform of tax policy, guarantees of civil rights and liberties, a foreign policy of peace and security, expanded industrial democracy and a five-week paid vacation to begin in 1978, sex equality and shorter working hours for parents of young children, improved housing opportunities, new guidelines in agricultural policy, and an environmental and energy program based on ecological principles. A special commission would study the problems of nuclear energy and prepare a plan for phasing out nuclear power if safety in waste disposal and reprocessing of nuclear fuel could not be guaranteed; if riksdag opinions were hopelessly divided a national referendum might be held. In welfare and health services the aim would be to expand noninstitutional care. Greater local control of education was envisioned and closer contacts between schools, working life, and the general community. Support for cultural activities would be increased and decentralized.

In short, the government undertaking stressed improvement, not curtailment, of the programs developed by its social democratic predecessors, with special emphasis on decentralization and the control of nuclear power. The trend toward socialization would of course be slowed. The policy makers were new and if they could cooperate effectively they would have three years to show that a nonsocialist coalition could function. The personnel of the administrative bureaucracy would remain almost intact, but new committee appointments would bring changes in the tone of government.

## Summation — the Nature of the Welfare State

The Swedish welfare state was both an institution and a mentality. In both capacities the historical period of gestation had been long. Precedents included the ancient close-knit peasant community, the district defense system of pre-Viking times, the Christian parish of the Middle Ages with its care for the weak, the paternalistic monarchy of Gustav Vasa, and the mercantilism of the eighteenth century. The increase in numbers of people and their mobility and the complexities of modern society required new forms of social organization. Sweden's response was the welfare state.

As an institution the welfare state was in the 1970s functioning very well. It was efficient, honest, all-embracing. The trains ran on time, the streets were kept clean, poverty and slums were eliminated. Material well-being was provided in exceptional measure. Discussion of public issues was completely free. The political skill of the social democratic leadership had enabled it to stay in power for an extraordinary period of 44 years (with one insignificant break), so long that the majority of the Swedish people had never known another government. And therein lurked danger.

Inevitably the long tenure in office bred in politicians and bureaucrats a sense of permanence and of the rightness of the regime and its policies. They were doing good things for people and therefore they knew best. And the people were pleased with the benefits they enjoyed. A welfare mentality pervaded both officialdom and citizenry and resulted sometimes in administrative agencies permitting their own interests to take precedence over the interests of the people they supposedly served.

Throughout this treatment of the welfare state of the second half of the twentieth century, a treatment basically positive, it will have been recognized that Swedish problems were similar to the problems of other industrialized countries. To some extent other countries worked out similar solutions. If there was something unique in the Swedish situation it was the forthrightness with which Sweden faced these problems and the forcefulness of the role played by government. Nevertheless, neutrality was probably the only issue on which there was genuine consensus. Occasionally the government could act directly contrary to public opinion; for instance, shortly after a consultative referendum decisively rejected a changeover from left-hand traffic to right-hand the government simply went ahead and accomplished it, and with excellent results. Many decisions were made by the narrowest majorities in the riksdag, and as we have seen, in the 1970s a number were made by lot. Opposition never retired, and often it was effective in holding reform programs within reasonable bounds.

Ideological opposition toward government intervention was strongest within the business community and among ideological conservatives. Gösta Bohman, leader of the *Moderater*, at a party youth conference in 1975 denounced the social democratic "closed society" and called for an "open society." He complained that social democrats did not understand the relation between democracy and freedom and insisted on the right of the individual to be independent and to watch over those who had set themselves up as guardians in a closed society.[30] The conservative youth organization declared for the "right to be a minority."[31]

Attitudes on the meaning of freedom differed fundamentally. Olof Palme, for example, considered that "freedom has to do with the social and economic environment. If you build up your social programs you build up freedom, if you take away the fears of unemployment, of hospital costs, of old age, you build up freedom."[32] Yet these things hardly represented the classic concept of freedom as understood by the Greeks or the Swedish conservatives — or the American frontiersman who wanted to put on his own shirt rather than have someone do it for him. Fundamental objections were voiced on the dangers of bureaucracy and the emphasis on materialistic values in the reform programs. Fears of the demoralization of the work ethic caused by the benevolent policies of government were frequently expressed, though so far they lacked significant foundation in fact.

A caustic attack on the welfare state was written recently by the English journalist Roland Huntford, who thoroughly damned the "new totalitarians" who exercised authority in Sweden. He wrote of economic security bought with political servitude; he condemned the system in which "directors general are the everyday rulers of Sweden"; he mentioned repeatedly the meek submission of people to governmental power; he claimed that the "legislature has been consigned to impotence"; he abominated the idea that labor and management could make an agreement without fighting.[33] Perhaps the largest blind spot in Roland Huntford's views was his failure to realize that the institutions of social relations need not necessarily apotheosize antagonism. Although labor-management relations and the courts of the United States, for example, operated on a frankly adversary system which has worked fairly well, there can be other and perhaps better ways of conducting human affairs. The Swedes are among those who for centuries have prized adjustment rather than conflict among themselves. In brief, Huntford's analysis was one-sided and exaggerated; it built up a distorted caricature, and yet there was half-truth in his argument.

Not only in Sweden but throughout the world the "free market" had vanished; everywhere government was asserting a strong leadership role. Controls piled on top of one another not only in communist lands but throughout the so-called free world. But, although government aid was denounced as policy, it was constantly sought by both individuals and companies in trouble. Antiplanning attitudes remained popular while planning increased.

Planning and controls were often irksome. It was hard to escape from uniformity in the design of apartments and houses. And a man could not paint his home until he had obtained official approval of the color. What was for his neighbors a protection was for him a restraint. The restrictions of both law and tradition enfolded all Swedes. So far it was impossible to say that the regulations of social welfare had stifled initiative or industry, but one must question Albert Rosenthal's statement that "there is no evidence in Sweden today that the development of the social programs has lessened the freedom of the individual."[34] Freedom of thought and expression has not been curtailed, but freedom of action, certainly. The controls that hedged an individual about were supposed to enhance his freedom in other aspects of his life. However, the good of society took precedence over the good of the person. Things were done *for* the person, which diminished the things to be done *by* the person.

Another notable aspect of the welfare state was its materialistic emphasis. As Gunnar Adler-Karlsson put it:

> In Sweden all the parties of the economic process have realized that the most important economic task is to make the national cake grow bigger and bigger, because then everyone can satisfy his demanding stomach with a greater piece of that common cake. When instead there is strong fighting between the classes in society we believe that the cake will often crumble or be destroyed in the fight, and because of this everyone loses.[35]

This "functional socialism" illustrates the Swedish pragmatic approach and the rejection of the doctrinaire.

The power of labor was shown in the steady increase of wages, an increase that gave the Swedish worker in the 1970s the highest wage scale in the world. Adler-Karlsson remarked that labor was "more active in dividing the GNP than in making it grow."[36] The national wage bill plus the cost of the social programs were major factors helping to produce an unusually high inflation. The inflation in turn threatened to price Swedish goods out of their world market, although this disaster had not yet eventuated in the mid-1970s.

What were the outstanding characteristics of Swedish welfare society? One no longer clung to the past but sought new and different ways. *Change* was the feature, the index, of the time. Change was exemplified in major alterations and expansions of government policies as well as in practical matters like the relocation of government offices and the de-urbanization of industry, in the abandonment of left-hand traffic that had ruled since the days of Karl XII, in the adoption of new family names, and in the revolutionary informality of personal address wherein everyone became *du*. The static and the passive were eschewed. No longer did anyone declare that "whatever is, is right."

Second only to change as a characteristic of the period was the *centrality of government*. Government involved itself in all aspects of society. Only in connection with the church did it attempt withdrawal, and in this popular opposition defeated government purpose. Government conducted investigations regarding scores of public questions and followed investigation with legislation. The judicial ombudsman was busy protecting the citizen from undue interference by other governmental agencies, and the system proliferated so that there appeared even an ombudsman for consumer problems. The strong state did not nationalize prospering big industries, but it hedged them about with restrictions and it began to operate smaller industries on its own.

The state formulated educational policies to conform to its political ideals. It assumed oversight over all significant aspects of national life.

In governmental stimulus for change *planning* was essential. In 1944 a broad-based planning commission was established, representing all major sectors of the community — government, business, industry, labor, women, agriculture, the cooperatives, and others. Organizations projected short-term and long-term prognoses, and the Social Democratic government itself brought forth a grandiose ''Regional Plan for the 1970s.'' This called for increased citizen participation in planning processes and laid down guidelines such as redistribution of industries to equalize employment opportunities in different regions, location of cultural facilities within reach of all, control of pollution and conservation of natural resources, and above all recognition of the principle that future development must be determined with a view toward the good of society as a whole.[37]

Pervading the purpose and planning of the welfare state was the concept of *social justice*. The word-slogan of the late 1960s was *jämlikhet*: ''All individuals have an equal right to live a rich and evolving life,''[38] in the words of the 1969 report of the Social Democratic-LO task force. *Jämlikhet* meant security, freedom, happiness, the right to cultural opportunities, employment, and influence in the community. And it meant an approach to equalization of income and therefore social solidarity in the congenial Swedish *folkhem* (peoples' home). The point of the program was directed against the privileged for the advantage of the underprivileged and the bettering of their conditions of life.

Sweden's progress in the twentieth century was extraordinary, especially in the material realm. The Swedes achieved one of the highest standards of living in the world. The individual enjoyed an exceptional degree of security. But crime rates were rising. Alcoholism and mental illness were serious problems. Youth was restless. Remnants of autocratic rule remained in certain corporations and rural *bruk*. The privileged classes were unhappy at the threat to their privileged status. An establishment still existed — no longer that of the court or the nobility, nor that of a wealthy plutocracy, but a new establishment based on position. It included the magnates of business and finance, the top generals and professors, the heads of the great newspapers, the cabinet ministers and leaders in the riksdag and the directors-general of the great state institutions, the ambassadors, and the heads of the labor unions and the federation of employers. This was the actual fraternity of power.[39]

Like all ambitious programs that of the Swedish reformers was neither perfected nor perfect. The bureaucracy was huge and powerful. It was sometimes overeager, sometimes apathetic. Denunciations of the ''Big Brother'' complex were overdrawn but not wholly lacking in justification. The tyranny of the masses and the arrogance of social planners could become as oppressive as the tyranny of kings or plutocrats. The safeguard was only that as long as the machinery of democracy remained intact the citizens had the power to make changes.

*Political democracy* had been obtained at the end of World War I. Its partner, parliamentarism, became complete in the 1970s with the abolition of the last vestiges of royal authority; the new constitution affirmed the sovereignty of the people. *Social democracy* was realized almost as fully as law could achieve, though it was clear that class distinctions had not been eliminated (can they ever be in human society?). The third phase in the process of equalization was on its way. Workers were sensing the varied taste sensations of *industrial democracy* in the "humanizing of work places" and the responsibilities of decision making in directors' board rooms. And in Sweden as elsewhere there had arrived an extraordinary, only half-appreciated, equalization of privilege, what might be called a *utilitarian democracy:* the availability of public services, education to the highest level, information and art and literature and medical services — even the privilege of flying through the country or to the far corners of the earth on the magic carpets of their own Scandinavian Airlines (SAS) which represented not only high technical and business achievement but an unusual cooperation among three brother-peoples of the North.

# XX

## THE MULTIFACETED CULTURE OF THE
## TWENTIETH CENTURY

IN ECONOMIC AND POLITICAL LIFE the Swedes in the twentieth century moved
from freedom to regulation; in social and cultural life they went from regulation to freedom. The controls that hedged people about in business did not halt
economic progress, and in the sphere of mind and spirit these controls had no
relevance. The breakdown of traditional restraints to self-expression, whether
in literature, arts, science, or social relationships, stimulated cultural ferment
throughout the life of the nation. The accompanying economic prosperity
enhanced opportunities in the noneconomic fields. But freedom was the fun-
dament on which culture built.

### Sweden Writes

The paradigm and prototype of this self-assertive freedom was August Strindberg (1849–1912), rebellious and tortured soul, Sweden's outstanding literary genius; he was both realist and dreamer, with an imagination that flew
off in all directions. His versatility was such that he might have become a
musician or painter and he fancied himself an inventive scientist. But he made
words his medium, writing poetry, novels, dramas, and history in amazing
profusion. He was a bitter social critic who unmasked the pretensions of his
contemporaries and exposed not just their foibles but their meannesses and
deceits. In a violence of words he struck at persons and institutions that did
not live up to his standards, often most harshly against those he held most
dear. It was hard to be a friend, or a wife, of August Strindberg. He was an
antifeminist and at the same time an idealizer of womanhood. He attacked

549

marriage but he tried it three times — and failed three times. With feverish intensity he wrote, and as a critic aptly put it, "no one has a shorter way from the blood to the ink." [1] He said of himself that he was born without a film over his eyes and that he could see right through things.

The brash realism with which he treated national heroes in his most important early play, *Master Olof*, won him no acclaim at the time, but in 1879 his realistic novel, *The Red Room* (*Röda rummet*) immediately procured his reputation. It was gentler in tone than much of his later writing but nevertheless an unforgettable satire of the Stockholm "establishment" of his day. Its success stimulated both Strindberg himself and other authors, but the increasing bitterness displayed in works such as *The New Kingdom* (*Det nya riket*) created deep enmities and led to his temporary move to the continent, where he flitted restlessly from place to place. His enemies in Sweden brought charges of blasphemy against him; he returned for trial and was acquitted, but the experience left deep scars.

Much of Strindberg's writing was autobiographical and so realistic that it only aggravated his tragic marital relationship with Siri von Essen. Shortly after a divorce in 1891, a second marriage collapse (with Frida Uhl), and repeated failures in his scientific experiments, he went through a period of theological speculation, intense introspection, and mental imbalance that he labeled the Inferno. He kept moving about and kept on writing, writing, writing. Psychological searching, usually within the realm of his own experience, characterized his greatest dramas such as *The Father* and *Miss Julie* and the autobiographical prose works *The Son of a Servant* and more directly *The Inferno*. Few victims of schizophrenia and paranoia have had either the keen intelligence or the mastery of expression to be able to analyze their own disease as did Strindberg. Dr. Franklin S. Klaf has hailed him as the first psychologist in modern drama and has drawn significant comparisons between Strindberg and Eugene O'Neill, who was strongly influenced by his Swedish predecessor. [2]

Strindberg's works would be occasionally calmly natural, like *The Natives of Hemsö* (Hemsöborna), sometimes mocking criticism, especially of Ibsen, but often vitriolic and brutal. The realism of the subject matter was matched by conciseness of form, rapidity and clarity of action, uncompromising analysis of character. It was Strindberg who set the tone and style of Swedish letters for the twentieth century. He antagonized the old guard, he shocked the moralists and embittered churchmen, he irritated women. At the same time he fascinated all, and for those who did not have to absorb his barbs he was an inspirer and a support. His angry protest was both personal and social, and it touched sympathetic chords in youth and in the radical labor movement. Before his death he became the idol of just those groups who loudly denounced idolatry. He roused Swedes to think, to reexamine their ethical and social patterns of thought. No one could match his fire, his versatility, or his productivity, nor his unique combination of naturalism, fantasy, and invective. He became the most world-renowned of Sweden's literary figures.

One side of this genius's interest and production attracted little world attention, for it was definitely Sweden-focused, namely his historical writing. The historical work of his early years was attacked by professional historians as amateur and inaccurate, but when he moved into historical drama he had a medium in which he was master and in which interpretation of character could be more personal. His first important historical play was *Master Olof*, a drama of Gustav Vasa and his religious leader, too daring in its psychological realism for Sweden of the 1870s and 1880s but nevertheless Sweden's first great drama. Much later, in 1899, appeared four historical plays that the author had been laboring on for years: *The Saga of the Folkungs*, *Gustav Vasa*, *Erik XIV*, and *Gustav Adolf*; seven more followed soon after.[3]

Strindberg, like many of his contemporaries, was fascinated by the legends and historical records gathered and written up in popular style by Anders Fryxell (1795–1881) in forty-six volumes of *Berättelser ur svenska historien till ungdomens tjänst* (Stories from Swedish History for the Service of Youth). Dependence on these uncritical tales did not enhance the historical value of Strindberg's dramas, but they were nevertheless highly interesting studies in both personality and situation, and they made good theater. Both Fryxell's early nineteenth-century writings and Strindberg's later works grew out of the national romanticism of the nineteenth century which gained added poignancy in the decades around the turn of the century.

In this period when emigration and the secession of Norway were forcing Swedes to self-examination and intensified nationalistic feeling, writers in all genre naturally responded to the call of national need. Regional nostalgia and national patriotism blended in a variety of publications. Verner von Heidenstam emphasized the heroic steadfastness of the Swedish people in the somber years of trial during the long-drawn-out campaigns of Karl XII in *The Charles Men* (*Karolinerna*). Heidenstam felt deep pride in his own ancient and aristocratic heritage, but this pride was mellowed by his humanistic temperament, and he was able to describe the brutishness of the half legendary Folke Filbyter as honestly as the development of a more noble society under the later Magnus (in *The Tree of the Folkungs* [*Folkungaträdet*], 1905, 1907). In 1899 he published a series of poems, *One People* (*Ett folk*), directly concerned with the national problems of the day. His was a sober nationalism (at least in his later years), but no less moving for that, and his works were highly popular. He was in a way the Sir Walter Scott of Sweden, certainly the country's greatest writer of historical-heroic fiction.

In a different method and spirit Selma Lagerlöf (1858–1940) expressed her national feeling. Her first major work and perhaps her greatest was *Gösta Berlings Saga* (1891), appearing early in the nationalistically self-conscious decade of the 1890s. She drew her inspiration from the tales and legends of her beloved province of Värmland, and although her purpose was a moral one she made the escapades of the twelve cavaliers of Ekeby so engaging that readers lost themselves in sheer enjoyment. More profound is the Lagerlöf treatment of Dalarna in the novel *Jerusalem* (1901–2), concerning first the rural religious-minded community in western Sweden, then following the pious emigrants to the Holy Land. In later years she wrote memories of her childhood and novels of Italy, but her enduring fame rests with Gösta Berling and Nils Holgersson. *The Wonderful Adventures of Nils* (*Nils Holgerssons underbara resa*) finds a bored country boy magically reduced in size, riding on the back of a great goose from one end of Sweden to another. Miss Lagerlöf's superb story telling has illuminated Sweden's geography for school children through generations. It is places rather than people but highly entertaining; it is low-key, natural nationalism.

Selma Lagerlöf clung tenaciously, if also with difficulty, to moral purpose and optimism. She exemplified a side of Swedish character rather different from that seen in other writers. And she won justified acclaim both in Sweden and abroad; she was awarded an honorary doctorate, given the Nobel Prize in literature for 1909, and was elected as the first woman member of the Swedish Academy in 1914.

Another brilliant *Värmlänning*, contemporary with Heidenstam and Lagerlöf, was Gustaf Fröding (1860–1911), little known abroad because his career was brief and his medium was poetry (always difficult to translate). In Sweden he was almost worshiped for his deep humanity and the powerful beauty of his verse. He had noble dreams for man's future, but he too early fell victim to disabling schizophrenia.

Fourth in the group of great ones in the early twentieth century was Erik Axel Karlfeldt (1864–1931). He typified that "fascination which [Sweden's] ancient folk life exercised over the cultural life of the day."[4] Causes of this emotional reaction lay in the idealization of a way of life that was disappearing as well as in the affront of the Norwegian withdrawal from the union and the departure of the emigrant horde to America. Men had to cling fast to what they held dear. Karlfeldt gave them Dalarna, his own and what has been called the most Swedish of all Swedish provinces. His "bucolic humanism" was deeply appealing. The poetry of his Fridolin's songs roused emotional responses of identification in readers from all parts of Sweden. Love, nature, and tradition were recurring themes; whimsy and sincere depth of feeling were characteristics of his contribution. He was healthy and strong and much beloved. He too was a member (and a long-time secretary) of the Swedish Academy and was awarded the Nobel Prize posthumously the year of his death.

Hjalmar Bergman (1883–1931), a genius and a bundle of nerves who was able to look on his fellow humans with understanding and pity, put in many of his novels the people of his hometown of Örebro (Wadköping). He blended the hilarious and the psychologically dramatic, as in *God's Orchid* (*Markurells i Wadköping*) through which he captured popularity. His *Clownen Jac* is partly introspective criticism, partly portrait of Charlie Chaplin and satire of America. Ellen Key (1849–1926) was an idealist, a feminist, and an advocate of woman's role as mother in society, and an early proponent of the comprehesive, or unified school. Albert Engström (1869–1940) was a versatile cartoonist, writer of short stories and sketches, who made sober Swedes laugh at themselves.

Categorizing Swedish literature either chronologically or topically is difficult, for there was much overlapping and individual authors displayed different faces at different times, though perhaps none in such great variety as Strindberg. However, besides the national nostalgia around the turn of the century a few other emphases can be identified, especially the proletarian and the antifascist.

Most consistently representative of the proletarian school was Ivar Lo-Johansson (1901–76), who has already been mentioned in connection with the campaign to destroy the *statare* system on the farms. Several other writers of more or less proletarian origin and reformist purpose included Martin Koch (1882–1940), who in the wake of the general strike of 1909 wrote *Workers, a Story about Hatred* (*Arbetare, en historia om hat*) and a few years later *God's Beautiful World* (*Guds vackra värld*) in which he narrated the exploitation and progressive degradation of a family through two generations as it moved from a rural to an urban milieu.

Eyvind Johnson (1900–1976) came out of a boyhood of little schooling and the meanest kinds of hard work in Sweden's far north. But he had within him the spark of genius and will that took him at age nineteen to Stockholm, then on to the continent. He fell under the spell of Proust, Gide, and Joyce, absorbed inspiration and style, and adapted and invented for himself. At first he wrote mainly of his own Norrland, notably of the darkness of life in the northern town of Boden — *City in Darkness* (1927). As he returned to Sweden in 1930 he shed some of his negativism, or at least added to it a redeeming glint of hope, as indicated in his *Farewell to Hamlet* (1930). He identified himself with the social democrats and wrote sharp criticism of capitalism and industrial society. Still thinking of the north he wrote the autobiographical Olof series. One of the most poignant sub-stories therein is the tale of the mother in the foggy swamps whose children died one after another of tuberculosis. In the deepness of her grief she got the idea that the fogs from the swamp actually were her children, so she breathed their poisonous vapors and died. But more and more Johnson turned from his regional proletarian themes to national and international matters. In the ideological conflicts of the 1930s and later he aligned himself wholly with the West against the brutality of nazism and communism. Allegory, satire, narrative — he used them all with purpose and effect.

Vilhelm Moberg (1898–1973) sprang from the peasant proletariat of Småland in the south, the province that gave birth to thousands of emigrants, including all of Moberg's many uncles and aunts. He is most widely known for his great trilogy on the migration (*The Emigrants, Unto a New Land*, and *The Last Letter Home* — actually a tetralogy in the original Swedish version), which was made into two successful movies. The first volume gives an unforgettable picture of life in nineteenth-century rural Småland, a rugged life he had already indelibly etched in his novel *Raskens*. Moberg was another largely self-taught genius, and his range covered far more than the emigrant epic. He was strong in body and spirit, a vital son of the soil who advocated a republic and who lashed out against privilege and injustice. During World War II, for instance, he wrote a gripping novel, *Ride This Night*, about resistance in Sweden in the seventeenth century, which drove daggers into the nazis of the twentieth century. At the time of his death he was working to finish what he called "My History of Sweden," a very personal view of Sweden's past, meant to emphasize the part played by the common people rather than the kings and the magnates.

Harry Martinson (1904–78), also of proletarian origin, was a sensitive and unusually gifted poet. His haunting *Aniara*, the tale of a huge spaceship that escapes the atomic destruction of the earth but goes off course and sails endlessly in space, a blend of scientific drama and Nordic mysticism, was made into an opera and presented on television. *The Road*, a novel in prose, grew out of the author's tramping experience and, like all his writing, breathed a thoughtful humanism. His was a genuine poet-nature.

The galaxy of talent in the mid-twentieth century and its productivity and variety is all but overwhelming. Agnes von Krusenstjerna (1894–1940) composed novels about the degeneracy of the upper class in which she was born. Gunnar Ekelöf (1907–68), experimental and psychological, dealt in surrealism and was a highly versatile poet. Stig Dagerman (1923–54) specialized in portraying the horrors of war. Artur Lundkvist, charged with creative energy, was both poet and critic. Pär Lagerkvist (1891–1974), brilliant, philosophical, was one of the giants. His publication began with a condemnation of the superficiality of Swedish literature of 1913. He offered his own thoughtful questioning with two collections of poetry, *Anguish* in 1916 and *Chaos* in 1919, influenced by the tragedy of war. *The Hangman* (1933) was inspired by the brutalities of Hitler. Throughout his career Lagerkvist was searching for the relationship between God and eternity.

> Around me lies eternity,
> Around me you keep silence, God
> What is vast and empty as eternity,
> What is secretive, mute, as you, O God?

in another example:

> I walk in darkness. I wander under the stars.
> I know man's humbleness before eternity. I know
> the chill of night, which surrounds me.[5]

His most widely acclaimed works were *The Dwarf* and *Barabbas*, the gripping story of the sinner in whose place Christ was crucified. These brought him the Nobel Prize in 1951.

Birger Sjöberg (1885–1929) provided a lighter touch until he grew introspective and dark. Karin Boye (1900–41) appealed for a sense of responsibility, then finally yielded to despair and committed suicide. Evert Taube, who died in 1976 at age 85, was the perpetual troubadour, light-hearted and loved by all. Gustaf Hellström (1882–1953), was long enough abroad as journalist in Paris, London, and New York to gain perspective on his native land, and he could look with understanding amusement at the family ambitions of Lacemaker Lekholm (*Snörmakare Lekholm får en idé*). Frans G. Bengtsson (1894–1954) had a first-rate historical mind but also a racy pen and he entertained with tales such as the bold Viking novel *The Long Ships*. Bertil Malmberg (1913–58) was one of the few Swedish writers who went to Germany at the end of World War I and remained strongly German-influenced; the overwhelming majority of his writing contemporaries found their external influences in France, Britain, and the United States. Anders Österling (1884-1981) was one of those especially under the spell of the Anglo-Saxons and the love of nature; he was dedicated, restrained, dignified. Hjalmar Söderberg (1869–1941) helped balance the rural regionalism of the Värmland, Dalarna, Norrland, and Småland writers with a touch of "sophisticated urban regionalism" in his portrayals of the spirit of Stockholm, especially as reflected in the witty restaurant conversation of the writing fraternity and in the moods of the streets and the waterways. One of his popular novels was *Martin Birck's Youth*.

Important among the poets of the 1930s was Hjalmar Gullberg (1898–1961), who in everyday terms interpreted deep religious experience, and Johannes

Edfelt (1904–  ), who expressed a profound sense of human brotherhood, fighting to overcome frustration. For the 1940s the great name was Erik Lindegren (1910–68), who with passion and learning helped introduce foreign literature to the postwar generation. Among the younger poets were Tomas Tranströmer (1931–  ) and Lars Forssell (1928–  ). Forssell cultivated disengagement but also indulged in social satire and won his way into the elite ranks of "the eighteen" in the Swedish Academy.

Sven Delblanc (1931–  ) wrote out of the turmoil of the 1960s in Berkeley, California his caustic *Åsnebrygge* (*Bridge of Asses*). Per Olof Enquist (1934–  ) criticized Swedish neutrality in World War II in his *Legionärerna*, motivated by his observation of the demonstration marches in the American South. Astrid Lindgren made up stories for her daughter about Pippi Longstocking (*Pippi Långstrumpor*), the lonely but perky and charming gamine. Then the stories were published and translated into at least thirty-one languages until they entranced children all the way from France to Japan.[6] Astrid Lindgren became so popular that her taxes in 1976 climbed to 102 percent of her income and this led to the use of her imaginative talent in a biting exposé of the stupidities and arrogances of bureaucracy in a not-wholly-fancied dictatorship — *Pomperipossa i Monosmania*. Another significant writer was Sara Lidman (1923–00), who in *The Tar Still* and *Cloudberry Land* revealed a fresh insight in dealing with life in the far north.

These and many more comprise a remarkably varied assortment of authors. Clearly the proletarian authors loved to write about their own lives, and they merged the personal into the regionally nostalgic and the socially critical. Sometimes their writing became, as with Strindberg, introspective and psychologically probing, and it frequently wrestled with fundamental problems of good and evil. Writers traveled and lived on the continent, and they were fully aware of general European and American trends in literature. But they seldom ventured to deal with European topics. They remained Swedes and wrote either on regional-national subjects in Sweden or on the universals of the human condition. Many started from Marxist origins and were sharply critical of the existing social order. Yet they loved Sweden and were profoundly affected by the glories of Swedish nature: the whispering woodlands, the beauty of blue sky and clear water, the dramatic changes of the seasons with the long, light nights of summer and its brilliant flowers, the moody darkness of winter and the quiet stillness of the snow.

The Swedes both write and read not only the output of Swedish authors but literature from around the world, in both the original languages and Swedish translations. Their reading is stimulated by the responsibilities of the Swedish Academy, which each year must choose the winner of the Nobel Prize in literature; hence their fare and their taste have become cosmopolitan. All of this, in turn, acts to encourage Swedish writers to appeal to this knowledgeable home reading public. Writers are also encouraged by the generosity of annual grants from the government. These grants, incidentally, were supported by a system in which the government assigned a small royalty each time an author's book(s) was borrowed from a public library. The ubiquitous reading circles throughout the country devour and discuss books ceaselessly. In brief, literature is popular, and the writer is respected. Sweden vies with Iceland and its other Scandinavian neighbors as being among the most literate and most eagerly book-consuming countries in the world.

Newspapers, also, are unusually popular with Medelsvensson (Mr. Average Swede) and his family. To a large extent the daily paper in Sweden provides not only news but the kind of material supplied in the United States by magazines of culture and opinion. Articles of historical and general cultural interest are regular features and frequently are written by the foremost scholars and writers. The major papers are usually politically affiliated, and *Aftonbladet*, the Stockholm evening tabloid, has been owned by LO since 1956; it competes with *Expressen*, the still more popular liberal paper. The leading morning papers in Stockholm have been for several decades the liberal *Dagens Nyheter* and the conservative *Svenska Dagbladet*. In Gothenburg the leader is *Göteborgsposten*, a liberal paper. Among the provincial press, aside from the purely local papers, the most significant are *Uppsala Nya Tidning* and Malmö's *Sydsvenska Dagbladet*. Within recent decades a number of medium-sized dailies have died because of inability to compete for advertising with their more successful rivals. However, over 100 papers remain, and the total circulation has increased phenomenally since 1920, amounting in the 1970s to over 4.5 million for the population of 8 million.

The press reflects definite political opinions, but its political influence is open to serious question. The social democrats, for instance, publish about 20 percent of the daily papers and get about 50 percent of the votes; the liberals have about 50 percent of the press and get about 20 percent of the votes. The conservatives have another 20 percent plus of the circulation. Perhaps people like to read some political slants different from their own, but probably the main reason for the dominance of the liberal press is that these papers enjoy more thorough advertising coverage, and they provide better sports and feature reading. Common practice is for these papers to include columns with excerpts from papers of opposing opinions. Weeklies with diverse social attitudes are widespread — *Metallarbetaren* of the metal workers' union, *Vi*, the organ of the cooperative societies, and *ICA-Kuriren* for the independent retailers. The avid reading public can get what it wants.[7]

## From Theater to Television

In 1921 Agne Beijer rediscovered the charming little theater in Drottningholm that had been constructed for court use in 1766 but had fallen into disuse. It was put in order for summer presentations and became symbolic of a sweeping theatrical regeneration. New decor changed the appearance of the Dramatic Theater and the Opera in Stockholm. But leadership came from Gothenburg, where the country's first theater-in-the-round was built in 1916 — the Lorensberg, which emphasized the unity of scene and lighting and play. The new concept was that the theater did not need to attempt an impossible replication of reality; it could be frankly theater. Hence fresh artistic effects could be sought in stage equipment and scenic background and better use made of the potential of electric lighting. Influences from France and England and especially from Germany through Max Reinhardt were warmly embraced. Deeply involved in the theatrical renaissance after World War I were Pär Lagerkvist (1891–1974) and other writers, especially Ingmar Bergman (1918–   ) as both writer and dynamic director.

This renaissance did not restrict itself to Gothenburg, Stockholm, and the court but spread rapidly throughout the country. Theaters became centers of popular interest and pride. City theaters were inaugurated in Hälsingborg (1921), Gothenburg (1934), Malmö (1944), Norrköping and Linköping together (1947), Uppsala (1951), Borås (1954), Stockholm (1960), and Luleå (1967). Even more important for the nationwide extension of dramatic art was the establishment in 1933 of the National Theater (*Riksteatret*), which sent touring troupes throughout the country and inspired local repertory companies.

In Sweden as everywhere the repertoire of both theater and opera was cosmopolitan, perhaps more so in Sweden than in most places, although opera was usually translated and sung in Swedish (a language notable for its clarity and adaptability to singing). Opera was sometimes presented in the language of origin, and I recall one truly international case when the Italian opera *Madame Butterfly*, which has a Japanese setting and an American hero, featured a visiting Japanese singing the title role in French while the other characters and chorus sang in Swedish. It was common practice to adapt Swedish novels as plays, such as Hjalmar Bergman's *Markurells i Wadköping*, and the dramatic works of Strindberg, Lagerkvist, Martinson, and others were very popular. Hjalmar Bergman ranks second only to Strindberg as a dramatist; his *Swedenhielms*, the great Swedish national comedy, continues to delight audiences as they laugh and cry at the same time. But the Swedes also staged a great deal of Shakespeare and both the classic and modern playwrights of other countries — Sartre, Anouilh, Brecht. They had a special affinity for Eugene O'Neill, who so openly avowed his debt to Strindberg; the world premiere of O'Neill's posthumous *Long Day's Journey into Night* was specifically assigned to Stockholm.

Radio, with radio theater, was introduced in 1925, demanding new techniques owing to its dependence on sound alone. At first the brief daily time allotted was devoted mainly to news broadcasts, but it gradually broadened to include a wide range of offerings. Radio service was kept under control and guidance by the state. The management was private, but the state appointed two members of the board, the press three, and the radio industry two. After 1955 a second program was introduced, with Program One on the light side, Program Two more serious. After television was launched in 1957 its popularity spread rapidly. Both radio and television were used extensively for instruction in the schools. The decision was made early that no commercials be permitted. Expenses were covered by license fees; within seven years of the beginning of television people had taken out some 2 million licenses. Objections rose loudly against the leftish tendencies in the programs, tendencies that were irrefutable (especially in Program Two) but that were due to the inclinations of the program managers and personnel, not to pressure from the government.

A medium in which Sweden attained international eminence was the cinema. Sound film began in 1901 with film synchronized with gramophone, and the technique for regular sound movies was exhibited for the king in 1921. However, the early silent films, initiated by Victor Sjöström and Mauritz Stiller, had become so popular in Sweden and had built up such an excellent export business that the promoters were reluctant to shift to sound. The coming of radio in 1925 provoked a crisis for the movie houses, and *Svensk Film* responded by producing a series of good comedies in the 1930s, not yet venturing into more serious subjects. In 1936 Ingrid Bergman made her mark in the Swedish film *Intermezzo*. When World War II dried up the sources of foreign films the home industry was given a boost and a push into more serious subject matter and a real involvement in aesthetic and social problems. As writers and directors Ingmar Bergman (1918–   ), Arne Sucksdorff (1917–   ) and Alf Sjöberg (1903–1980) showed special talent. Pictures such as Moberg's *Ride This Night,* Lo-Johansson's *Only a Mother,* and Lagerkvist's *Barabbas* showed the capabilities of the industry. Alf Sjöberg's presentation of Strindberg's *Miss Julie* shared the grand prize in the Cannes Festival of 1951.

Most innovative proved to be Ingmar Bergman, who posed existentialist and profound psychological problems in films such as *The Seventh Seal* and *Wild Strawberries* and created powerful impact with techniques of sparsity. He sought truth in the human face — ''The human psyche became the stage for his conflict-motif. He used the camera with the same precision as a researcher used his scientific instruments."[8] Bo Widerberg's (1930–    ) *Elvira Madigan* and Jan Troell's (1931–    ) masterful filming (with Liv Ullmann and Max von Sydow) of Moberg's emigration epic added luster to the Swedish reputation in motion pictures.

The film business was threatened by the competition of television and by special taxes. In 1963 the tax burden was reduced and five years later *Film House* was started, housing among others a Dramatic Institute for all categories of theater, including television, radio, and film. Sweden has given Hollywood and the world a surprising number of stars in the film acting field, with Greta Garbo and Ingrid Bergman heading the list.

## Painting, Sculpture, and Architecture

Painters were the first and most uninhibited promoters of national romanticism — after their return from France. They went to the continent as young students with talent, supported by government grants. They studied the classic art of Rembrandt and Rubens, and they imbibed inspiration from Courbet, Manet, Matisse, Corot. Particularly they were influenced in the 1880s and 1890s by the Barbizon School and by periods of residence in Grez-sur-Loing, south of Fontainebleau, where Carl Larsson, Strindberg, and others learned to paint nature intimately.

Ernst Josephson (1851–1906), one of the ablest of the late nineteenth-century painters, displayed both fancy and realism in portraits and in his best-known work, *Strömkarlen* (*The Water Sprite*), now in Prince Eugen's museum at Waldemarsudde. Unfortunately he, like his contemporary Carl Fredrik Hill, was disabled by schizophrenia at the height of his creative powers. Gustaf Cederström (1845–1933) was best known for his military-historical works, especially the heroic and moving *Funeral Procession of Karl XII*. The spirit of his work coincided with that of Heidenstam in literature. A wholly different kind of national feeling was evoked by the new generation of painters who focused attention on the beauties of the peaceful homeland.

Four great ones, all close personal friends, were Carl Larsson, Bruno Liljefors, Gustav Fjaestad, and Anders Zorn. Carl Larsson (1853–1919) was a Stockholm lad who adopted the upcountry province of Dalarna and gave its nature the quiet, realistic-romantic treatment he had learned at Grez. He drew the milking of the cow and the crayfish parties down by the lake. Fully as appealing were his portraits of his family and their home, done with love and decorative detail. He made the traditional simple furniture and decorations of

Dalarna popular patterns even for city living. Larsson was the foremost Swedish representative of *l'art nouveau*.

Bruno Liljefors (1860–1939) concentrated largely on Uppland, just north of Stockholm, and painted the robust outdoors with hunters and deer, with foxes running by the fence, with little birds in the bushes. Again, realistic, beautiful, nostalgic.

Gustav Fjaestad (1868–1948) was painter preeminent of snow, and he never lacked material: pure white snow, the essence of stillness and peace, covering fields and trees and stretching to the limits of vision.

Anders Zorn (1860–1920) could preserve in etching, watercolors, painting, or sculpture what his eye saw, and thus he was a superb portraitist, with many American portraits to his credit. He immortalized the healthy, full-bodied Dalarna maiden; he painted the rustic equivalents of Susanna in the bath, but with vitality and movement. Largely self-taught, he was a natural genius, and he made his own style. In sculpture Zorn's most significant work is probably his statue of Gustav Vasa in Mora.

Prince Eugen (1865–1947), youngest son of Oscar II and Queen Sofie, industrious and talented scion of the Bernadotte clan, belonged with the above group of four outstanding artists. Eugen specialized in monumental landscapes and scenes of Stockholm and painted a number of murals for schools and public buildings in what might be called the national-lyrical style. He was of significance also as a patron, and his villa at Waldemarsudde, along the harbor leading into Stockholm, he made into a museum of high quality. At the other end of suburban Djurgården Ernst Thiel did not paint, but he befriended artists and bought their work and gathered another exceptional collection of turn-of-the-century paintings — Larsson, Fjaestad, Zorn, Liljefors, and others; the Thielska Gallery is a Swedish treasure house, taken over by the government in 1924.

A quite different school of art, popular in the early years of the twentieth century, was that of the followers of Henri Matisse. Outstanding among them was Isaac Grünewald (1889–1946) who loved to fill great spaces with color and form and whose decorative art was in demand for halls and theaters.

The prime genius of Swedish sculpture was Carl Milles (1875–1955), who learned impressionism under Rodin but later developed his own more vigorous style. His powerful monumental statues, including *Europa and the Bull*, *Folke Filbyter*, *Gustav Vasa*, and the *Orpheus* group at the Concert House in Stockholm are found throughout Sweden, twenty-odd in Stockholm alone. In 1929 Milles migrated to the United States and became the leading figure at the Cranbrook school near Detroit. He maintained connections with Sweden and left his home in the Stockholm suburb of Lidingö to the state as a museum. In the

United States he created the handsome *Meeting of the Waters* in St. Louis and monumental fountains in several cities.

The artists who came to the front in the mid-twentieth century, and there were many, abandoned the strong national and regional impulses of their great predecessors and followed both individual and international patterns. People were still eager to have paintings in their homes and some culture-minded business concerns such as chocolate manufacturing Marabou decorated factory gardens and public rooms with first-class painting and sculpture, just as likely to be Italian or Spanish as Swedish. The government encouraged this semi-public art by requiring that for all public buildings 1 percent of construction costs must be used in artistic decoration.

In public architecture the dominant trend through most of the nineteenth century was cosmopolitanism. Even for the National Museum (built in 1866) the architect was German and the style was like the bourse in Frankfurt and the opera in Budapest. Similarly, the main university buildings in Lund and Uppsala were cosmopolitan and Renaissance in style. Toward the end of the century the national spirit began to affect buildings as well as literature and painting. In the transition period Isak Gustaf Clason constructed in stone the handsome Nordiska Museum (1890–1907) in Renaissance style with some Vasa touches; the building was, as Elias Cornell says, "a patriotic triumph in cosmopolitan style," with evidences of influence from Denmark, France, Germany, and England.[9] Here Clason cooperated with Artur Hazelius (1833–1901), whose life was devoted to the creation of this Nordic museum and its open-air counterpart, Skansen, dedicated to memorializing the peasant life of Sweden and the North.

Ragnar Östberg (1866–1945) became spokesman for a greater infusion of the national inheritance in his masterwork, the Stockholm City Hall, which occupied him from 1911 to 1923. Here he succeeded in combining elements from Läckö castle and other traditional Swedish buildings with the great "Blue Hall," its colonnade and its grand staircase inspired by the doge's palace in Venice; it made a marvelous locale for the Nobel dinner and other festive occasions. Furniture and decor in various parts of the building gave many interior decorators an opportunity to express individually their own views of the national spirit.

Even in a century when religious interest was on the wane a number of unique and impressive new churches bore witness to a continuing faith and architectural novelty. Engelbrekt's church in Stockholm, standing high at the end of a rocky ridge, is both delicate and stately. The Masthugg church in Gothenburg (1910–12) dominates a cliff from which it can be seen far out at sea; despite its size its body and massive tower are reminiscent of the small stone churches of the Middle Ages.

The active interest in theater has challenged architects to produce a variety of original and highly successful buildings in Gothenburg and Malmö and smaller towns. Imaginative construction in business blocks was illustrated by a shopping mall in far northern Luleå; open-air walkways were not practical because of the long months of snow and cold, so the entire mall was enclosed and well lighted.

But such innovative and reasonable ideas had been slow to develop. In the early years of the century, when cities were pushing beyond their ancient boundaries, the best that people could do in Sweden, and in most other industrializing countries, was to extend streets in long straight lines, past rectangle after rectangle of factories or houses, regardless of the shape of the terrain or of the views from the homes, whether of picturesque waterways or of dull railroad tracks. Residences of the ordinary folk were apartments large or small encased in massive buildings standing tight against the sidewalks and stretching block after block, perhaps with inner courtyards paved with stone. No wonder the urban Swede had to have his extra cottage in the skerries or up in the mountains. Yet some city planners in the mid-twentieth century actually wanted to tear down the Old Town of Stockholm, the "City between the Bridges," and rebuild it in square blocks. Fortunately, before this proposed reconstruction became a real threat more artistic and more humane ideals began to take hold in the 1960s and 1970s; remodeling of interiors saved handsome exteriors and preserved the historic heart of the city. In another central section of Stockholm a large area was razed and a row of skyscrapers built to form "The City"; this entire section was transformed in a modern and international style, with a cultural center, a new steel-and-glass building used temporarily for the riksdag, and two levels of shops and offices.

Escape from darkness and overcrowding was possible for the more affluent when *villa städer* (garden towns) developed in districts outside the main city, as in Djursholm outside Stockholm. But these spacious homes, expensive to heat and maintain, could not be the solution for the majority. Carl Larsson showed how a mere cottage could be made beautiful and comfortable and preached the message in his book of 1899, *A Home*. Yet this ideal, too, presupposed space and was more suitable for the small town than for the large city. Carl Westman and Ragnar Östberg urged the values of the small home built for one's own family, its own interests, and its own needs, not for friends and not for show. Their doctrines were warmly greeted by Adrian Molin who promoted the "Own Home" movement in an attempt to counteract emigration.

Soon new forces were operating that would radically change public architecture as well as housing design: electricity and the housekeeping appliances it made possible, poured concrete or light concrete blocks and steel reinforcement, the automobile and buses, the crowding of people into cities. Buildings either public or private had to be functional; it was an international demand. Among the originators of functionalism in Swedish architectural design were Osvald Almqvist (1884–1950), Gunnar Asplund (1885–1940), and Gregor Paulsson (1889–1977). Almqvist built in the 1920s a symbolic and at the same time practical power station at Hammarfors. Asplund designed the unusual Stockholm City Library in a modernized Egyptian style; it may remind one of John Ericsson's "cheesebox on a raft," but it remains both attractive and utilitarian. Paulsson was concerned with city planning and housing and the importance of artistic design in the little implements of everyday use. He, as director, and Asplund, as architect, collaborated in the revolutionizing Stockholm Exhibition of 1930, introducing to Sweden functionalism in home architecture and household equipment and furniture. The designs of houses and furnishings there exhibited went beyond the continental examples and achieved worldwide fame. The emphasis was on utility and the abandonment of decorative frills; external appearance was ruthlessly sacrificed for the sake of efficiency and comfort. The use of the most modern equipment was presupposed. But beauty in simplicity was emphasized; *vackrare vardagsvaror* (more beautiful everyday things) became a popular slogan. This kind of architectural and furnishings revolution had implications not only artistic but social; with this kind of house and equipment a woman could get her work done without a maid and go out to a job beyond the home.

However, the urgency in the demand for housing, especially after World War II, led to unfortunate compromises and economies. Barrack-like structures sometimes eight to ten stories in height were erected in the outskirts of cities and towns. Their gray massiveness in the empty space between city and forest was a shock to the eye and an odd contrast to the planned efficiency of internal design. Protest against the drabness and uniformities of these mass housing ventures led to the introduction of color and other modifications, but similar buildings continued to be constructed long after the pressures for facilities had eased. A more satisfying home plan was the single-family house on a small but independent lot, even if the expense required that these be built dozens in a row and according to identical architectural design. At least children did not have to ride an elevator to go out to play. Too often, however, economy became the ruling factor, and imagination and variety had little chance.

In tune with the spirit of the welfare state was the building of large planned communities, especially in the outskirts of Stockholm — Vällingby, Farsta, Täby, and others. These ultramodern suburbs, each with complete facilities for everyday living, were linked to the central city with a rapid-transit subway system which helped alleviate the congestion that otherwise threatened to choke the city to death. Individual home garden plots were too expensive, but attempts were made to preserve patches of rock and green and open space between the concentrations of reinforced concrete. However cold and uninviting were the exteriors of these self-contained suburbs the dwelling units were scientifically engineered for comfort and efficiency. An innovation in some of the large complexes was a system of trash removal by long suction conduits. Provision was regularly made for playrooms and playgrounds, and attempts were made to hold auto traffic and parking outside the living areas as, for example, in Baronbackarna in the outskirts of Örebro. The common practice of cooperative ownership required at least a minimum of acquaintanceship among the occupants and helped establish some community feeling.[10]

Modern art went beyond both utilty and decorativeness. Whatever the medium — painting, photography, sculpture, architecture — it sought self-expression, psychological interpretation, and social effectiveness. It was profoundly individualistic, no longer national. Scores and hundreds of Swedes made individual contributions, but it was too early to assess leadership in this highly personal field. No Swede stood out as prominently as the Swedish-American, Claes Oldenburg. Swedishness, in any event, was no longer valued, for art no longer paid attention to national themes or characteristics. This was one realm in which patterns and tastes had found a world base. The Museum of Modern Art in Stockholm displayed the works of artists from everywhere. It also served a social purpose and represented par excellence the goals stated by the riksdag — "Cultural policy must assist in creating a better social environment and be conducive to equality."[11] Temporary exhibitions were used to stimulate people to take an active part in "democratic cultural life." The "Ararat" exhibition of 1976 was an impressive illustration of the devastating effects of pollution and the exploitation of human and other natural resources and of the potential in the positive uses of nature, for example, in the harnessing of solar energy. Art, in brief, was being directed to social purposes. Museums were not to be permitted to be graveyards of art. The Scandinavian open-air museums of social history, Skansen in Stockholm being a superb example, had proved the value of the "living museum" idea, and the modern museums carried the idea further and made themselves constructive teaching institutions.

Throughout the western world the style and purpose of art and architecture were revolutionized in the twentieth century, and the Swedes stood in the forefront of development.

## Music for All the People

Music has been important in the folk life of the Swedes for generations — the country fiddler at the dance, the ballads, the student songs, the hymns of the churches, the ever-popular choral societies. Jenny Lind, "The Swedish Nightingale," unforgettable legend of the nineteenth century, had charmed Sweden, England, and America, and P. T. Barnum offered her to the multitude. Later came Kristina Nilsson, Jussi Björling, Birgit Nilsson, and many more who gained international fame as singers. Among composers of high rank were Franz Berwald (1796–1868), Hilding Rosenberg (1892–1985), and Karl-Birger Blomdahl (1916–68). The rich productivity of recent composers included several operas based on the work of Swedish authors: Rosenberg made an opera for P. D. A. Atterbom's *Lycksalighetens Ö (The Isle of Bliss)*; Gösta Nystroem (1890–1966) was strongly influenced by Pär Lagerkvist in his *Sinfonia espressiva* and other works; Lars-Erik Larsson (1908–1985) based his *Förklädd gud (God Disguised)* on a text by Hjalmar Gullberg; Karl-Birger Blomdahl touched upon the space age in utilizing electronic music for the opera *Aniara,* based on Harry Martinson's epic.

Although lacking any single genius with the reputation of the Finnish Sibelius, the Norwegian Grieg, or the Danish Nielsen, Swedish musicians in the later twentieth century were nevertheless attracting international attention, and radio and television were making the Swedish people more music-conscious than ever before. In fact, probably the most significant aspect of music in Sweden in the twentieth century was its rapid spread in the people's consciousness and activity. Perennially appealing to the religious element were the hymns of Lina Sandell, along with the Moody-Sankey hymns and other imports. For the less religious the music that enthused the crowds was as un-Swedish as could be imagined, for example, the Afro-American contributions of Dizzy Gillespie in the 1940s and of Louis Armstrong in the 1960s and 1970s.

Another kind of musical expression sprang from the musically interested and politically aware youth of the 1960s and after. Dissatisfied with the older forms of music and the grip of commercialism on the art, diverse groups organized music festivals associated with political activism, especially opposition to the war in Vietnam. The influence of the Beatles and of rock and pop music from America was strongly felt. Yet an urge to get back to Swedish elements challenged the foreign importations. Rival summer festivals appealed to youth and the activists gathered thousands of participating musicians, each with his own instrument. Smaller groups formed to play and to make records of the ancient folk music. Fiddlers blended the old folk music with pop and they played in restaurants and pop clubs, traveling as the troubadours had done. Imbued with a new musico-political ideology the new genre began to make their own "noncommercial" records.

Government, too, assumed the initiative for promoting nonpolitical musical appreciation in the schools and among the wider public. Cities established orchestras and choruses and the Swedish Radio encouraged maintenance of the traditional music as well as composition of new contributions. The national government subsidized eight symphony orchestras, three opera stages, and a number of ballet troupes and indirectly sponsored orchestral tours through the country. The Institute for National Concerts was funded generously by the government for about 90 percent of its expenses, but management was left as much as possible to local arrangers. Concerts and explanatory talks were given for schools, hospitals, trade unions, immigrant groups, community centers, hospitals, and people in the far corners of the land who were more or less shut off from cultural offerings. Pop, classic, contemporary, and folk music were all included in the programs. Many of the musicians came from the former Military Music Corps, in 1971 demilitarized as the Regional Music Organization. Beyond this, however, one purpose of the plan was to stimulate local talent particularly among the youth. It was teaching as well as entertainment, based on the concept that music was a common language, a means of communicating with everyone everywhere.[12]

### Changing Styles in Handicrafts

The things which surround us at home, outside, and at work, all have significance not only in the functions they fulfill but in their aesthetic qualities, i.e. the impression they make on our senses. . . . The people who have given them form and colour represent a complete spectrum of applied artists, practical artists, designers, or whatever we choose to call them, who, in the words of August Strindberg, are concerned with 'everything separate and movable which makes a house a home for living things.'[13]

Long before the specialization of labor that set artists apart from other workers the making of things for the home and the family was done in the home. Home crafts are common throughout the world but perhaps they were especially important in the northern countries — well-made clothes were essential because of the climate; much living was done indoors in the long dark winters; and convenient utensils and furniture were necessary. Also, there was time to design and to fabricate during the months when little could be done outdoors. Traditions of exquisite workmanship for the swords and shields of warriors and the dress and jewelry of women date from ancient times. The colorful provincial dress for both men and women, with distinctive patterns for each locality, originated in the sixteenth and seventeenth centuries and spread more widely during the nineteenth-century upsurge of national feeling.

Even before the middle of the nineteenth century people who prized fine workmanship and national tradition began to worry lest cheap manufactured goods from Germany and England would inundate the country and choke the skilled home crafts. Nils Månsson Mandelgren therefore founded as early as

1845 the Swedish Handicraft Association (*Svenska Slöjdföreningen*) and a year later the school that was to become the State School of Arts, Crafts, and Design (*Konstfackskolan*). The purpose of encouraging the continued production of high-quality homemade clothing and furnishings was gradually modified into training artists and designers to work in industry, to assure that machine-made articles would also be tasteful and of high quality. This drive fused with the national romantic movement in art and literature and the cause was promoted by Artur Hazelius (1833–1901), who founded the Nordiska Museum in Stockholm and the open-air living museum, Skansen. There cottages and manor houses, barns and livestock, were brought in from all parts of the country to illustrate how people lived a generation or so previously; men and women "lived in," dressed in provincial costume, and used the customary implements of the different communities.

Since 1884 the Handicraft Association has published materials propagating its causes: especially *Form*, a magazine published since 1932 which now has ten issues a year; and *Kontur*, a magnificent annual through the prosperous years 1950–66. The home architectural and furnishings exhibit of 1930 was only the most extensive of a number of exhibitions staged by vigorous leaders of the movement. Åke Stavenow, director of the Association from 1936 to 1949, took traveling exhibits to the continent and the United States. To an unusual extent the Swedish people were educated to appreciate the cultural values of their handicraft traditions. The result was not only preservation of home crafts but strong pressure for the maintenance of taste and quality in factory-made articles. The slogan of the 1930s, "More beautiful everyday things," had a real impact on industry. Laminated plywood, for example, was used in furniture designed for comfort to spread the vogue of "Swedish Modern." Märta Måås-Fjetterström (1873–1941) was a leader in the 1920s and 1930s in creating textile designs that broke with conformity, frequently using Oriental motifs.

More and more emphasis came to be placed on quality, as was particularly evident in the creation of art glass. Edward Hald (1883–1980) and Simon Gate (1883–1945) went into the Småland woods and at Orrefors (Woodcock Falls) developed new art glass of beauty unsurpassed in the modern world. Kosta, dating from 1742, Strömbergshyttan, and additional rivals expanded the Swedish production of decorative glass and fine table services. In other long-established plants new forces were at work. Excellence in design was given new emphasis at the Rörstrand porcelain factory and at Gustavsberg, which was taken over by the cooperative society in 1937. But conflict developed between the quality ideal which meant designing and making for the affluent and compromise ideals in mass production for the common man. By the 1960s a revolt against the restrictive insistence on quality led to greater artistic freedom, even an attempt to idealize the primitive and the childlike. Social consciousness injected itself into art and pop art became popular.

During the 1960s frustrations and restlessness roused protest and rebellion in Sweden as well as in the United States and around the world. Young people became conscious of environmental threats and of the futility of simply following old patterns. They became anti-individualistic and wanted to work in groups. Above all, perhaps, they wanted to do their own thing, not merely follow the paths of the past. They tried strong, bright colors, and bold designs that were "no longer 'tasteful,' . . . but attempt rather to militate against all that might be described as aesthetic or integrating."[14] They rebelled against convention. They became interested in folk arts and folk music and they felt kinship with the folk art of Africa, Asia, and South America, and the blue jeans culture of the United States. Some moved to the country. They were dissatisfied with the workings of the profit system and wanted to deal constructively with social problems. In the field of industrial design the new spirit led to the formation of groups such as the Ten Swedish Designers and the six in the Program Group, Inc. Another group formed the Collective Workshop, which rented an old factory in Stockholm and experimented with technical equipment. By cooperative endeavor, together with attention to the needs of manufacturers and consumers and the community as a whole, groups such as these created improved designs for specific items like hospital stretchers, and they redesigned inner courtyards of housing complexes. They added color and play equipment and got people to work together. They wanted to redesign things to redesign living. The younger students of design eschewed grades and degrees and preferred anonymity. But they were eager to produce. They brought a new spirit into the venerable State School of Art and Design (*Konstfackskolan*) and other design schools and urged that a number of such schools be scattered throughout the country, not be concentrated in Stockholm and Gothenburg. A Design House was established in Lidköping, led by Carl-Harry Stålhane, formerly with Rörstrand. Similar institutions sprang up in Umeå and other cities.

In the 1970s concern with quality was returning because of disgust with the shoddiness of many factory products. But it was realized that factory-made articles could be of high quality and that new materials such as plastics and new textiles could provide tasteful and useful items for a mass market. Designers who had gone off on their own began to come back to cooperate with industry, and older designers continued to be innovators. One of these, Bruno Mathsson, long a student of posture, became a designer for Dux, Sweden's largest furniture manufacturing company. The young HI group created comfortable and handsome chairs in tubular steel, new kinds of stackable chairs, upholstery in thermo-plastic, utilizing new materials in attractive form.

Swedish artistic design and technological inventiveness have remained alive and responsive to new tastes in ceramics, silver, glass, textiles, wood, steel, plastics, producing for both a Swedish and an international market. In many areas of activity, notably weaving, exquisite articles are still being created within the home.[15]

## Sports and Recreation

Per Henrik Ling had popularized gymnastics in Sweden in the nineteenth century, and the tradition survived for generations. Ling's son opposed the trend toward competitive sports; so did church groups who objected to violation of the Sabbath and radicals who objected to royalist and militarist tendencies in the new sports. But the competitive appeal of soccer and hockey, and of swimming, skiing, and skating was irresistible. Viktor Balck (1844–1928) was a vigorous promoter of international gymnastic and sports activities and from 1894 to 1920 a member of the International Olympic Committee. Sigfrid Edström (1870–1964), who became head of the large ASEA concern, succeeded Balck as the great leader of Swedish international sports. Fire and police departments and industrial establishments organized athletic teams and soon sport became a national passion. In 1913 the riksdag began giving financial support for athletics. On a Monday morning as much as 20 percent of the daily newspaper text might be devoted to the results of the weekend contests, with full pictorial coverage of the heroes and dramatic incidents. Armchair sports enthusiasts could have their vicarious thrills.

In the years after 1900 sports gradually won a place in the schools. School athletic associations, beginning in 1916, grew to 50,000 members in 1936 and almost 450,000 in 1966. National contests were held in swimming and other sports. Outside the schools associations were formed for all conceivable sports, bandy (a kind of hockey), handball, badminton, tennis, bicycling, boxing — and the Swedish Sports Federation, founded in 1903, in 1974 counted 3.4 million members (including many duplicate memberships).

Sports interest was stimulated by surprising Swedish successes in the Olympic games in 1906 and 1908 and especially by the games held in Stockholm in 1912. Support came from the national lottery after 1934, and by 1967 the state backing of 26 million kronor helped to build stadiums and swimming pools, to provide equipment, and to pay for instruction. Soccer, which the Swedes call *fotboll*, was the most popular sport, with about 3,000 clubs; it involved thousands of boys from the early grades up, with emphasis on the team aspect of the sport. Ice hockey was a close second in public favor. Extent of participation was spectacularly illustrated by the famous Vasa ski race, dating from 1922, staged in memory of Gustav Vasa's reputed flight on skis four centuries earlier and the ensuing race to catch him and bring him back. This became a popular annual ski event, largest of its kind in the world, attracting up to 10,000 skiers, both Swedish and foreign, for its fifty-five-mile course through the woods of Dalarna. Orienteering took people of all ages from goal to goal over unknown terrain and back again, making a game out of hiking. Popular also were hunting and skating, boating and swimming, cycling and motoring — out of doors in the ruggedness of winter or the warmth of summer. And tennis, indoors in the tennis halls in winter, outdoors in summer. King Gustav V continued his tennis past the age of ninety; Björn Borg while still in his teens won international fame; in 1975 Sweden won the Davis Cup competition.

Both participator and spectator sports occupied an extraordinarily high place in Swedish life. Both were thoroughly organized, bureaucratized, and subsidized. Factories used athletic teams as a means of advertising and to promote morale. Perhaps more important, sports became an expression of Swedish nationalism. A gold medal in European or Olympic competition was prized as highly as knighthood in the Middle Ages. While the emphasis in government programs was on team and group activities successful international champions became popular heroes. Ingemar Stenmark was idolized for his success as a skier, his team spirit, and the modesty of his manner. Björn Borg, a more individualistic contender, was a close second in national favor. Basketball was in the 1970s winning a popular place, stimulated by professional players and coaches from the United States. In ice hockey the migration was the other way around, with some of Sweden's best players being lured to the teams of the United States and Canada.

Perhaps it belongs with sports to mention "free time" activities such as tending the colony gardens, sailing, and the tourism which draws Swedes to follow the route of Nils Holgersson around their own country or to travel to sunny strands in Rhodes or the Canary Islands. With lengthening vacations and security of income the possibilities for all forms of recreation are almost limitless.[16]

## Religion in the Twentieth Century

The state church of Sweden was in a critical position at the turn of the century. Churches were becoming emptier and emptier. Biblical criticism, the scientific spirit, the aloofness of the clergy, and a growing materialistic outlook all contributed to lessening man's feeling of dependence on religion. But the romantic nationalism that flowered during the 1890s gave impetus to a folk-church ideology. At the same time the liberal theology freed the church from the old Lutheran concept of the ordered society where the church served as the governing element. The foundation was laid for a movement that could reach all parts of the population with the gospel dressed in nationalistic and sentimental garments.

This Young Church movement drew its ideology from the romantic concept of history that recognized Christianity as the world's foremost cultural force: God was the primary force in the world and thus ethical norms and religious faith became prerequisites for all purposeful activity, individual as well as political. The future became a sacred concern. Whereas the "free church" theology held that God's forgiveness was for believers only, Bishop Einar Billing (1871–1939) insisted that the Christian message was for everyone, not just the "awakened." Thus the young clergy and theologians had a platform from which they could reach out to all the people full of hope and faith for the future.

This hope soon found concrete expressions: under the leadership of young Manfred Björkquist, then a theology student at Uppsala, a revival swept the university. Two by two or in larger groups, the students went on "crusades" visiting the parishes around the university town, preaching and explaining the new winds that were blowing. This spontaneous evangelization soon found institutional expression in a student association, in the magazine *Vår Lösen* (*Our Watchword*), and in the Sigtunastiftelsen (The Sigtuna Foundation, 1917) and its significant conference center.

The outstanding personality of this exciting period in Swedish church history was Nathan Söderblom (1866–1931). Born in a conservative and biblically faithful family, he, during his years as a student in Uppsala, went through a religious crisis where he rid himself of his fundamentalism without losing his belief. He was stimulated both in faith and in ecumenical outlook by participation in the 1890 Christian student convention in Northfield, Massachusetts, and he became a source of inspiration first to the church and later to his students when he served as professor. In 1914 he was installed as archbishop. Ecumenical striving, Söderblom believed, could be used as a vehicle for promoting peace and so he called an ecumenical meeting in Uppsala in 1917, at the height of World War I. The result was disappointing. But his hope was fulfilled with the Stockholm Meeting of 1925. The Roman Catholic Church was not represented but the Greek-Orthodox was and therefore Christianity as a whole was better represented than at any time since the ecumenical councils of the church fathers. The Life and Work section of the World Council of Churches came into being at Stockholm and was the outcome of Söderblom's efforts. Other influential religious leaders included Gustaf Aulén (1879–1977), professor at Lund and later bishop of Strängnäs, ecumenical, musical, a prolific author still writing in his nineties; and Anders T. S. Nygren (1890–1978), another Lund professor and bishop whose writings on love and ethics were translated into many languages.

In the turbulent first decades of the twentieth century the movement to separate church and state gained momentum. This had been a plank in the Social Democratic platform at the end of the century, but now it was expressed in legislation. In 1908 civil marriage was introduced as an alternative to the church ceremony. The church's monopoly on funerals was abandoned in 1926. It can be added, though, that very few took advantage of the new alternatives, as the old customs were deeply ingrained in the social pattern. One of the hotly debated issues was the question of the place of religious instruction in the schools. In 1919 a coalition of liberal state church theologians and free church leaders succeeded in eliminating the catechetical instruction, perhaps just as much for its being an outdated form of instruction as for its religious essence. In place of this rote learning a broader study of the Bible was instituted with emphasis on the Sermon on the Mount, and the time for this instruction was reduced from six to two hours per week. At this same stage it was stipulated that the instruction was to be objective, something long discussed in the school curriculum debate.

Not until 1951 did complete religious freedom become a reality. Before that date one could leave the state church only if he became a member of some other Christian church. But in 1951 this last restriction was abolished and one could leave the church by simple declaration. Only a fraction of 1 percent took advantage of this possibility in spite of vigorous propaganda by the radical clergy who wished to break down the routine and meaningless acceptance of Christianity.

The so-called free churches, which had been so significant in the nineteenth century and had taken such an active role in the temperance movement and other social causes, continued to grow until about 1930. Popular evangelism was a force, and the free churches provided a religious base for those political and social radicals who retained faith in Christianity but could not tolerate the Lutheran state church. These dissenter churches of various denominations encouraged participation in political life, and their members continued to be represented among the riksdag's social democrats and liberals far beyond their natural proportion in parties or population. However, the fires of faith began to burn lower toward mid-century. Membership declined drastically: Missionsförbundet (its offshoot in the United States known as the Mission Covenant Church) dropped from 114,000 members in 1930 to 85,000 in 1972, the Baptists from 63,000 to 25,000, the Methodists from 17,000 to 9,000. The Pentecostals, on the other hand, increased from 25,000 in 1925 to 93,000 in 1972, and the Roman Catholics in the latter year numbered 59,000. The Salvation Army, long exceptionally strong in Sweden, almost held its own with 36,000 members in 1972.

The gradual loosening of the state church's control over the population and the development toward a less rigorous religious discipline brought on a reaction in the 1920s. A high church movement began to gain momentum. Its supporters favored a more catholic tradition and laid heavy emphasis on priestly authority and the individual's religious faith. This group soon came into conflict with the low church and folk church groups who were more concerned with social and missionary work. Another group put faith in the disciplinary role of the church and the leadership position of the ministers, namely the extremely low church Schartau group on the west coast. Strange bedfellows indeed, these and the high church people, although both were authoritarian and motivated by tradition.

The question of women priests gravely damaged the Swedish church, pitting clergy against other clergy and clergy against their congregations. In 1951 a committee led by a bishop found no theological objections to women as priests, and the government in 1957 presented The Church Meeting with a positive proposal. (The government could do this since the Church of Sweden is a state church without its own legislative organ, the power of The Church Meeting being chiefly advisory.) The Meeting was badly divided on the matter and asked for respite until the next assembly, which normally would be in five years. Everyone hoped that some of the heated feelings would have cooled by then. But the government was impatient and sent the proposal to the riksdag, which passed it, and a new Church Meeting was called for in 1958. This extraordinary procedure served only to harden attitudes. Immediately a group of clergy and laymen with Bishop Bo Giertz of Gothenburg as their leader formed a group known as "church union around Bible and faith" which aimed to guard the literal interpretation of the Bible and the church's confessional writings. The group received the bulk of its support from the low church revivalist areas of the west coast and Småland and from the high church groups throughout the country. The alliance was a shaky one, the strongest common interest being dread of women in front of the altar, the one group otherwise being fundamentalist and suspicious of everything modern and catholic while the other stood very close to the Roman tradition.

When in 1960 the first women priests were ordained, the group declared open hostilities against the rest of the church and instructed its supporters not to attend services led by women priests or in any way to support them. This refusal of the clergy to cooperate was an expression not only of antagonism toward women priests but also of opposition to state intervention in church affairs. Under the new regulations laymen gained greater participation in the governance of the church. Clergy who refused to marry divorcees, since they believed this to be against the word of God, were convicted in the courts since the government took the view that the clergy in performing marriage ceremonies acted as civil servants and not as priests. The hope came to be that the Church Meeting, with its new majority of laymen, would be the highest legislative organ in the church and that control of the church would thus pass to the people themselves. This order of things was ardently favored by liberal churchmen. Support was less enthusiastic among the high church and other conservative groups who argued that a truly democratic church government could be realized only when none but practicing Christians would be allowed to participate in elections bearing on religious matters.

The central debate regarding religious questions in Sweden revolved around the church's relation to the state. In 1968 an official committee which had investigated the matter for a decade presented its conclusions. It proposed four possible solutions ranging from the status quo to abolition of the official religion and confiscation of all church property. Both these extremes were rejected and the possible choices were narrowed to two: either the state religion could be preserved, but with the church having freedom from the state in decisions concerning the church's own affairs, or else the official religion could be abolished and the church lose its right of tax support. In the latter case the state church would be placed on the same footing as the free churches, and no one would automatically be a member at birth. This was the position favored by yet another uneasy combination of forces in Swedish church history: liberal theologians and some fundamentalist groups. The vast bulk of the population favored a continued church-state relationship, not so much on religious grounds as out of habit and because the church was a part of the society that could not be done without at weddings, baptisms, and funerals, those occasions which always have been connected with the memorable moments in the peoples' lives.

This was the background for the howls of protest that were voiced when the government commission headed by Alva Myrdal recommended disestablishment of the church as a provision of the constitution of the 1970s. Opposition was so general that the government quickly shelved the proposal. Nevertheless in the 1970s the church in Sweden was again in a critical situation. Church attendance and popularity were at low ebb. Some of the New Testament salt had lost its savor. Christians who yearned for personal worship and those who emphasized social action had trouble finding common ground. Yet both low church and high church factions were eager to make the church once more an effective force in Swedish society.[17]

## The Intellectual Scene

Small size and geographic isolation may be disadvantages for intellectual achievement, but in Sweden these disadvantages were overcome by frequent travel, by subsidized study on the continent, by the high social value placed on learning, and by a few dynamic, energizing personalities. Governmental stimulus was often, though not always, a prodding factor. Social need was a frequently impelling force, as it was in the scientific flowering of the early eighteenth century. The challenging circumstances of the late nineteenth century again found talent to respond, and a period of unusual achievement followed.

The way was prepared by institutions founded in the eighteenth and early nineteenth centuries: The Academy of Sciences, the Swedish Academy, the Academy of Letters, History and Antiquities, and the universities and research institutes. The universities of Uppsala and Lund had long maintained basic educational facilities and sound academic programs. Demands for urban counterparts to the idyllic situations of these traditional centers of learning resulted in the establishment of parallel institutions in Stockholm and Gothenburg at the end of the nineteenth century. The initiatives for new cultural achievement came directly from individuals, but those individuals had drunk from the Pierian springs of the universities.

An illuminating example of the place of seminal personalities is provided by the Nordenskiölds (the clan includes three branches with three spellings of the name: Nordenskiöld, Nordenskjöld, and Nordensköld). From the genes of this family came a galaxy of outstanding talent in geology, geography, archaeology, and ethnology; the urge to explore and to analyze was deeply ingrained. Adolf Erik Nordenskiöld (1832–1901) got his early education in Finland but moved to Sweden as a young man because of his opposition to Russian rule. His passion for natural science, especially geology and geography, took him first to Spitsbergen and Greenland, but his great desire was to conquer the dangerous Northeast passage. In the *Vega*, with Louis Palander as captain of the ship, he led an expedition of eighteen men from northern Norway through the frozen waters north of Siberia, through Bering Strait, then around Japan, India, through the Suez Canal, and back to a hero's reception in Stockholm (1878–80). It was the first time man had been able to circumnavigate Asia. His example and inspiration sent his son Gustaf (1868–95), primarily a mineralogist, off to Greenland and to Colorado, where he pioneered the study of the Mesa Verde cliff dwellings. Another son Erland (1877–1932), ethnologist, studied Indian life all the way from Patagonia to Panama. A nephew Otto (1869–1928) explored the Antarctic as well as Peru, Greenland, and the Klondike.

Spitsbergen was a favorite laboratory for the nineteenth-century scientists — its flora, its fauna, its rocks; several traveled to Greenland as well.

They did not confine themselves to the far north, but this was their natural bailiwick. Alfred Gabriel Nathorst (1850–1921) started his paleobotanical researches in Greenland and Spitsbergen. Gerard De Geer (1858–1943) was led by his investigation of glacial melting on Spitsbergen to trace thoroughly the chronology of the recession of the Ice Age in Sweden. He confirmed his methods and results by studies in glaciated regions in eastern North America. Lennart von Post (1884–1951) studied quaternary geology and invented the pollenanalysis method of tracing the history of climates and vegetation. Hans W:son Ahlmann (1889–1974), geographer and glaciologist, helped expand knowledge of the polar regions both south and north and of the geography of Scandinavia.

The urge to explore what lay beyond took Salomon August Andrée (1854–97) and his companions Nils Strindberg and Knut Fraenkel on a balloon trip to the North Pole in 1897. Tragically, after a three-day flight the balloon came down in the Arctic ice east of Spitsbergen. During a three-month hike the explorers worked their way to a small island near Spitsbergen. They died slowly, presumably of trichinosis contracted by eating diseased polar bear meat. Andrée's diary and Fraenkel's meteorological observations, along with photographs and most of the equipment of the expedition, were recovered in 1930; they provide a remarkable record of the dramatic but ill-fated mission.[18]

Among the explorers with broad-ranging interests in everything new to be found was Sven Hedin (1865–1952). Hedin had something of the flair and the vitality of Theodore Roosevelt. His will, his eternal boyishness, and his genius with languages enabled him to become intimately acquainted, in a series of five expeditions, with the people and the deep interior of central Asia. Although he made friends with strange peoples he felt a conscious superiority and habitually wore European clothes. The same attitude made him an admirer of the nazis, despite (or because of?) his mother's Jewish origin.

One of the greatest of Sweden's great quadrumvirate of chemists (Bergman, Scheele, Berzelius, and Arrhenius) was Jöns Jacob Berzelius (1779–1848). He was perhaps the last for whom it was possible to carry all existent chemical knowledge in his head. He wrote textbooks as well as articles, and he put later generations in his debt by simplifying the system of classification and symbols for chemical elements and compounds. Berzelius helped prepare the way for the later flourishing of Swedish chemistry, and he did much to train young medics in laboratory work.

Of the later group of chemists Svante Arrhenius (1859–1927), a versatile genius, is given foremost place. His interest was not so much in practical applications as in theories and hypotheses. He developed the theory of electrolytic dissociation and the theory of volcanism, and he revolutionized electrochemistry. The Nobel Prize was awarded him in 1903. Theodor (The) Svedberg (1884–1971) was innovative and wide-ranging, enjoying constructive hobbies like botany and photography; his photography made legible the writing in the famous *Codex Argenteus* (*The Silver Bible*) in Uppsala. Svedberg's Nobel Prize came for his early work in colloid chemistry, a field in which he inspired many students in both Sweden and the United States (after his visit to the University of Wisconsin in 1923). For the measurement of the velocity of sedimentation he invented the ultracentrifuge with a centrifugal force a million times the force of gravity; the sizes of molecules are measured in "Svedberg units." Of far-reaching significance was his discovery that the molecules of several proteins are of uniform size. Later Svedberg became interested in nuclear chemistry. Others whose work has spread the reputation of Swedish chemistry are Hans von Euler and Hugo Theorell, both of whom were given Nobel honors for enzyme research; and Arne Tiselius received one for molecular chemistry.

In physics the great nineteenth-century name was Anders Jonas Ångström (1814–74), notable for his *Optic Researches* of 1853 and the *Recherches sur le Spectre Solaire* of 1868. The "Ångström Unit" of ten millionths of a millimeter for the measurement of light is properly named for him. Manne Siegbahn (1886–1978), who became chief of the research institute in physics at Uppsala in 1937, is known especially for his X-ray spectroscopic work in the measuring of wavelengths and for his atomic physics. Gustaf Dalén (1869–1937) was one of the more practical scientist-engineers who in 1906 joined Svenska Gasaccumulator (AGA) and three years later became its director. He perfected acetylene lighting, built a good household stove, and won world renown for the Dalén light, or Agafyr, used for coastal beacons, for it bursts into flame automatically at dark and extinguishes itself at dawn.

Hannes Alfvén (1908–    ) conceived constructive theories in the field of magnetism and plasma physics. He also played a leading role in the campaign against expansion of nuclear energy. The astronomer Bertil Lindblad (1895–1965) was widely recognized for explanations of the peculiarities of the Milky Way and the structure of galaxies. The interplay of both rivalry and cooperation among the Swedish chemists and physicists was a continuing stimulus to themselves and others.

In the field of medicine Swedish doctors have not only maintained a high level of medical service within Sweden but have developed techniques and ideas which have spread far beyond. The Caroline Medical Institute in Stockholm is a center of pioneering cancer research, partly supported by the Rockefeller Foundation. Herbert Olivecrona (1891–1980) became one of the world's great brain surgeons. Clarence Crafoord (1899–1984) constructed a heart-lung machine and advanced thoracic surgery. Nils Alwall (1904–1986) invented the artificial kidney machine. Robin Fåhreus (1888–1968) made significant discoveries concerning the precipitation of the blood. Jan Waldenström (1906–    ) contributed to the understanding of blood illnesses and metabolism.

Swedish science has made obvious contributions to human betterment and is widely known and appreciated. Work in the humanities has been more culture-bound and therefore less well known abroad. There have been exceptions, such as the archaeological investigations in Italy carried on by King Gustav VI Adolf, the Sinology of Bernhard Karlgren (1889–1978), the Semitic and Iranian researches of H. S. Nyberg (1889–1974), and the Greek and Mycenaean work of Martin P. Nilsson (1874–1967), Axel W. Persson (1888–1951), and Arne Furumark (1903–1982), and the more recent studies of the Dead Sea Scrolls.

More thorough and more distinctive activities have been conducted within the Scandinavian area. Departing from the concentration on wars and national heroics modern archaeologists and historians have unearthed surprising facets of the Nordic past. The archaeologists Oscar Montelius (1843–1921) and Hans Hildebrand (1842–1913) utilized the methods of natural science and developed carefully periodized chronologies of the Bronze Age in the North. Montelius later extended his chronological system in time and to cover Britain, western Europe, and Egypt. Excavations at the commercial site of Birka in Lake Mälar were begun by Hjalmar Stolpe (1841–1905), and still more exciting finds were uncovered at nearby Helgön (Holy Island) and analyzed under the direction of Wilhelm Holmquist (1905–    ) (see chapter I). The glories of the art and material culture of the early Viking period were revealed by Sune Lindquist (1887–1976) and those of the Iron Age on Öland by Mårten Stenberger (1898–1973). Sven B. F. Jansson (1906–1987), who became the world's first professor of runology, led in the preservation and interpretation of Sweden's treasure of runestones. He was such an eager collector that he could only be delighted when a house burned down, enabling him to acquire for the museum a runestone imbedded in its chimney.

In spite of the heightened national consciousness at the end of the nineteenth century historical scholarship in its many ramifications moved far from the fileo-pietistic emphasis of Fryxell, for example, to a more scholarly and critical approach. The history of literature was represented by able scholars such as Henrik Schück (1855–1947), Martin Lamm (1880–1950), and Victor Svanberg (1896–1985). In the history of art two of the notable contributors were Johnny Roosval (1879–1965) and Henrik Cornell (1890–1981).

Tension developed between some of the strong personalities leading different schools of historical writing, one represented by conservative Harald Hjärne (1848–1922) of Uppsala and his followers, another by the Weibull "dynasty" in Lund. Martin Weibull (1835–1902) illustrated strong interest in both provincial Skåne and Scandinavian history, inclinations that continued with his sons, especially Lauritz (1873–1960)[19] and Curt (1886–    ), and on to grandson Jörgen (1924–    ). The four Weibulls were professors of history, all imbued with the ideal of hard-headed source criticism, yet able to popularize their scholarship with students and the general public. Gottfrid Carlsson (1887–1964) of Lund passed the torch to his son Sten Carlsson (1917–      ), who became professor at Uppsala, a prolific scholar, and promoter of research in social history and the history of Swedish emigration. Two of the leading historians of the twentieth century won their way into the elite circle of "the eighteen" in the Swedish Academy: Nils Ahnlund (1889–1957) of Stockholm, specialist on the seventeenth century and historian of the early centuries of Stockholm, and Erik Lönnroth (1910–   ) of Gothenburg, who began as a medievalist but broadened his research to other fields. Recent trends in Sweden as elsewhere tend to emphasize quantitative methods.

Among political scientists the leading figure was Axel Brusewitz (1881–1950), who occupied the chair and the quarters in Uppsala honoring the tutor of Gustav II Adolf, Johan Skytte. Brusewitz was active in government commissions and highly influential as a teacher and a writer on constitutional problems and constitutional history. More widely known was Herbert Tingsten (1896–1973), first as professor and then as editor of Stockholm's *Dagens Nyheter,* a prolific and stimulating writer who had a strong impact on Swedish thought and politics.

In economic history the pioneering figure was Eli F. Heckscher (1879–1952), who broke paths for a whole generation of able scholars who devoted themselves to completing and criticizing his work. In the broader area of social science two of the precocious scholars are Gunnar Myrdal (1898–1987), whose field of research included not only the social problems of Sweden but those of the United States and of Asia, and Alva Myrdal (1902–1986), specialist in population and peace, diplomat, and administrator.

Sweden's economists have won attention and respect both in Sweden and abroad. Knut Wiksell (1851–1926) was a social radical and an original thinker who developed significant and internationally applicable theories on capital, prices, and taxes. It was he who had that simple answer for the nationalists who complained about emigration: the way to stop emigration was to stop having babies. The internationally known Gustav Cassel (1866–1945) combined profound scholarship, especially in matters of price and finance, with a talent for publicizing his views; in the columns of *Svenska Dagbladet* he persistently campaigned against state intervention in economic life. A different emphasis was introduced by Bertil Ohlin (1899–1979), who believed strongly in the values of a free economy and feared socialism yet thought that occasionally circumstances demanded government action; private ownership of business must be accompanied by a sense of responsibility for the general welfare. This "social liberalism" became the policy of the Liberal party in which Ohlin was a leader from his early years. But the well-reasoned middle position was hard to maintain against pressures from both right and left.

This sampling of a portion of the independent and constructive scholars of Sweden is meant only to give a glimpse into the scope of their activities and the principles that guided them. They represent, in general, values common to the scientific spirit of the twentieth century, perhaps intensified by a sense that because they lived in a small country they had to attain an especially high standard to win international attention.

## On the Characteristics of Swedish Society

The most essential characteristic and component of twentieth century Swedish society is democracy — "the fragile and indispensable compact of trust and individual reliability which makes freedom possible, limits powers and demands accountability."[20] This realistic definition fits the Swedish attitude and situation like glove on hand, epitomizing "the shared conception of the enterprise of which they [the Swedes] are all a part."[21] Democracy has been a slow-growing historical development, but from the realization of independence under Gustav Vasa, to the pride in power under Gustav Adolf and Karl XII, on through the disappointments of military defeat and economic backwardness, and into an epoch of scientific, economic, and political achievement the Swedes have always been aware of their Swedishness. They have experienced at least a vague sense that the fate of each was bound up in the fate of all. The institutions of democracy, fragile though they be, represent the ideals that the twentieth-century national spirit struggles to protect.

Swedish nationalism has its own special emphasis. One of the unmistakable shared attitudes of the Swedes is their love of the country itself — the changing beauties of summer and winter, the woods and lakes, the birds and flowers, the wild animals. Literature and art have romanticized Swedish nature: nature is good and beautiful, and anything natural is right. Linné was a product of this love of nature, and a stimulus to its further development. The endemic love of flowers and knowledge about them is a manifestation of the attitude toward nature as a whole. It has often been remarked that the reserved Swedes find it easier to love inanimate nature than all-too-animate human beings. They like to say it with flowers, and florist shops do a thriving business the year around; flower stands in the streets have sprigs and bouquets for guests to hand to their hostess.

Homes are not only kept fresh and attractive with flowers but with art on the walls and with furniture made for both beauty and comfort, fulfilling the demands voiced in the 1930s for "more beautiful everyday things." Pride in the home is second only to the love of nature. Homes and towns and cities are carefully planned and kept clean and neat; if some un-Swedish Swede happens to be careless or slovenly he is sure to be brought to task by his neighbors.

Medelsvensson, the average man, likes to think that he is not nationalistic. It reminds one of Benjamin Franklin's shrewd comments on the man who claimed to be wholly modest — but he was proud of his modesty! The Swede is proud of being a Swede. Even the emigrants who chose to leave the homeland retained nostalgic memories. The ones who stayed home sang the national anthem with feeling — "Du gamla, du fria,"

> You old, you free,
> You high-fjell Northland,
> Quiet and joyous and beautiful
> I hail you, loveliest land upon earth.

and provincial songs with gusto:

> Ack, Värmland du sköna . . .
> (O, Värmland, you beautiful . . . )

Whatever their political opinions Swedes, like Americans, tend when abroad to defend their country's policies. And perhaps it is significant that at Christmas time they love to decorate the Christmas tree with strings of small Swedish flags of the golden cross on the field of blue. One peculiarity might seem to confirm the Swedish denial of nationalistic sentiment: he tends to prize things foreign and to think of the foreigner as a superior being (up to a point!). Americans are acquainted with such phenomena, for they too often think of foreign imports as automatically better than their own products. The Swede also wants to be thought of as up-to-date and cosmopolitan. For instance, a few years ago government and business launched a campaign to retire the picturesque Dalarna wooden horse because it was thought to be a symbol of an antiquated rural culture, too quaint for the desired modern image. Sweden spends large sums on propaganda (or "information") in foreign countries. The information is voluminous, accurate but not critical, attractively packaged, and most helpful to those who teach or write about Sweden. It is also recognized that its purpose is to win foreign approval of Swedish policies and products. For Sweden, nationalism is not only sentimental, it is also practical.

Swedish nationalism is not militaristic as it was in the times of Gustav II Adolf, Karl XII, and Gustav III. With some severe lessons well learned the Swedes have abandoned ideas of conquest. But not the conviction that they know how the world had best be run. The government is prepared to lecture other states for their follies and even to sponsor boycotts of regimes that make mistakes — Spain and Chile are recent examples. The people of the country largely approve such measures and hope that their moral impact may have some effect even if they cannot apply other pressure. Demonstrations and declarations give some sense of satisfaction in that the country is making its influence felt. And the Swedes help developing countries generously with financial and technical assistance.

Supportive of nationalism is the Swedish striving for excellence and demand for quality — in clothes for warmth, wear, and appearance, in bridges for beauty as well as strength, in foods for the irresistible smörgåsbord, in utensils and automobiles and art and literature and medicine. The stress placed on perfection and precision has proved its value in the production of high quality steel, machines, and tools, in extraordinary achievements in chemistry and other scientific fields, in invention of new devices and techniques.

It leads one to wonder if Alfred Nobel was an accidental genius or if he was a natural product of his environment? Were his prizes for superior achievement a consequence of his realization that Swedish culture put an extraordinary value on superior achievement? It was not wholly accidental that the peace prize was put in Norwegian hands while Swedish institutions were made the high courts to decide on excellence in scientific and literary fields. The democratic Swedish people share vicariously in the responsibility for these prizes, and through the prizes they have created a world nobility of the intellect.

The drive to excel and the striving for status have long been aspects of the Swedish society. Rivalries have thus been intense in government and business and education. Vicious public competitions for precious professorships, conditioned by both their scarcity and their prestige, have long poisoned the academic scene. Until recent reforms scholastic pressures were intense among both faculty and students even at the secondary school level. The extreme demand for excellence and the virulence of competition led ultimately to a reaction, to a call for changed emphases. Radical social change resulted, at least on the surface. The society of deference, of titles and ceremoniousness, that up to the middle of the twentieth century made this an exceptionally status-conscious community, was challenged and defeated. The telephone catalog that had alphabetized subscribers by title began to list the Anderssons, the Olssons, etc., by first names alphabetically. The awkward method of individual address in third-person formalities suddenly changed to address in the intimate *du* (you) form. Hosts and hostesses became embarrassed to enforce the rigid protocol of the *skål* at dinner, and drinking patterns were relaxed. Dress patterns became less formal. In the universities, except for traditional Uppsala where the cannon salute still greeted new doctors, the elaborate ritual of graduation gave way to simpler ceremonies. In the secondary schools both the strictness of grading and the elite distinction of the student cap were abolished (at least officially). The de-emphasis on rank and formalities came because of the democratizing urge that seized the socialists and the young. Partly this was in response to the more democratic practices of other countries and the feeling that Sweden must cast off the vestiges of its aristocratic past.

These changing patterns of life were not merely rejections of tradition, they were affirmative responses to new social ideals. They were epitomized in two words: *folkhem* (the people's home) and *jämlikhet* (equality). Both were old words that expressed ancient longings. *Folkhem* was the ideal of the "peoples' home," where all members of the community should live in harmony, where consensus should reign with no antipathy among social classes. *Jämlikhet* called for the elimination of social classes; it meant both equality and social solidarity; it demanded positive action and became the popular slogan of the late 1960s. In 1969 a joint committee of LO and the Social Democratic party published a program intended "to counter a concentration of privilege and power in groups favored by tradition and to give the masses an increased share of material well-being, cultural possibilities, and democratic influence. All people have the same right to live a rich and developing life."[22] The committee's report denied the risks of uniformity and insisted that individual differences rooted in factors like health or intellectual handicaps must be minimized by a generous social climate; the most disadvantaged groups must be given the top priority in adult education.

Such a program marked approval of the school reform that was proceeding and that removed the ingrained elitism of the educational system. It assumed the equality of men and women and the correctness of the view that all occupations were of equal worth. And it assumed a society of peace and justice guaranteed by institutions such as the ombudsman who protected the citizen against administrative inequities. The extent to which the ideal of equality was realized in the 1970s may be illustrated by the fact that King Karl XVI Gustav had for the first time in 1976 to pay taxes on his income like any other citizen.[23] When he married a commoner, Silvia Sommerlath from Germany, on a beautiful day in June 1976, the whole country warmed to the charm of the young queen, and monarchy won enhanced popularity.

The relationship between individual and government is one of the most interesting aspects of the Swedish scene. Unlike the attitude more or less prevalent in the United States that government is a thing apart from the person, perhaps even his enemy, the dominant attitude in Sweden is that government is the agent of the people, an institution created to do their will. A corollary of this attitude toward government is the profound respect for law, a living inheritance from the distant past. Expectations of assistance from government are realized in manifold forms. Not only are hospital and health care practically free for the citizen (and of high quality), but government support is generous for students, for artists and authors, for sports associations, for businesses in trouble, and for the unemployed. The costs of these benevolences involve high taxes and they involve government controls. Do these controls violate individual freedom and stifle initiative?

From business entrepreneurs and others come anguished complaints against government regulations, but the fact that government has not slain all the giants of industry is indicated by the many great multinational corporations based in Sweden. Nor have artists and authors been lulled into inactivity because the government grants them annual stipends and promotes the distribution of their works. Rather, removal of economic handicaps appears to have freed the individual for creativity. And the work ethic is not dead. Government subsidies to theater and opera appear to produce results as good as those obtained by systems of private philanthropy. The reason is that government attempts to support but not to regiment.

However, the dangers of huge centralized power have not been exorcized. Lurking in the shadows is always the threat of abuse of authority and the more subtle threat of assumption of the leadership role by a self-satisfied ideological elite. Undoubtedly some people find their hopes thwarted (which happens elsewhere, too). Some feel frustrated simply because everything is so neatly organized and planned. Yet the high degree of innovation, of literary and artistic productivity, of scientific achievement, and of economic progress all indicate that the time of disaster has not yet arrived. Certain checks are built into the structure of the Swedish government — for example, the ombudsman and, most important, the universal observance of democratic processes. Things can be changed and are steadily being changed by continuing processes of self-examination and re-examination. Tendencies toward socialist authoritarianism have not destroyed the basic institutions of democracy.

Socialization is both long established and yet incomplete. A kind of socialization has existed for centuries: in 1542 Gustav I Vasa declared, for instance, that the vast empty areas of northern Sweden "belong to God, to the King, and to the Swedish crown, and to nobody else."[24] Government traditionally owned vast properties. The second modifying element is that in the late twentieth century Swedish business, in assets and sales, is about 90 percent privately owned and managed. The proportion is slowly changing, but for the most part the socialist government up to 1976 was satisfied to control and to guide without outright nationalization. Competition and entrepreneurship survive. But the individual does not have to operate wholly alone.

Organizationalism is so typical that Swedes speak of their own "Association-Sweden." Laborers are organized, employers are organized, and so are teachers, nurses, engineers, and women. In the early 1970s the economically active population numbered 3.4 million while the five major labor organizations (LO, SAC, SR, TCO, and SACO) counted 2.74 million members; adding the membership in associations of merchants, doctors, and the like it is obvious that practically all people who work belong to a worker organization. In some industries membership was 100 percent. Few countries can show such solidarity in organization, and in few countries are the organizations and the folk movements so directly influential in government. Even culture was organized on a vast and elaborate basis; in 1969–70 the adult-education associations had some 54,000 circles studying literature, art, music, theater, etc., with 563,000 participants.[25] The National Council for Cultural Affairs and the Swedish Institute together compiled in 1973 an elaborate plan for a national cultural policy. Public expenditure for cultural programs was given as 942 million kronor for 1973/74, projected to increase to 1.952 billion kronor in 1981/82; the state's share of the expense would increase from 45 to 50 percent, the county councils' share from 4 to 7 percent, and the municipalities' portion would decrease from 51 to 43 percent.[26] The largest increase recommended was for the support of literature, press, films, and scholarships — "the privately operated cultural sectors" — from 4 percent to 24 percent. Here were three hallmarks of Swedish society in one package: organization, planning, and social consciousness.

Last but not least must be emphasized that among the people runs a deep current of social concern and responsibility, a current springing from a strong Christian tradition and conditions of life that have demanded mutual helpfulness. It moderates and sometimes contradicts the likewise powerful sense of individualism. It infuses the thinking about social welfare at home and the strong programs of aid to developing countries.

Out of this blend of idealism and self-centeredness, of love of country and planned purpose the modern Swedish community has been forged.

# Epilogue

## SWEDEN AND THE CRISIS OF THE WELFARE STATE

### *Steven Koblik*

WHEN FRANKLIN SCOTT completed writing *Sweden: The Nation's History* in 1976, a historic event had just occurred: the creation of the first nonsocialist majority government in Sweden since the 1920s. The departing Social Democratic prime minister, Olof Palme, publicly proclaimed that the new government would find the country in perfect running order. Indeed, a general optimism existed that Sweden had somehow avoided the worst effects of the '73–'74 recession and had created a unique and superior set of social and political institutions and traditions: "the Swedish model." That Sweden had already plunged into a severe economic crisis, was about to experience a political turbulence unimaginable in Sweden in the early postwar period, and would undergo a major economic and social transformation were not understood by most Swedes—including the members of the new nonsocialist coalition.

To understand the nature of the crisis Sweden faced, and the assumptions and policies with which the Swedes tried to meet this crisis, we must remind ourselves of some of Professor Scott's insights. The Swedish welfare state was a postwar phenomenon. Its antecedents lay deep in Swedish tradition, but the political, ideological, and economic conditions necessary for its creation came together only after 1945. Different ideological and political notions existed about the nature of the welfare state. The initial set of reforms passed by the Riksdag drew support from a broad coalition of parties usually including the Social Democrats, the Liberals, the Farmers, and the Communists—often the Conservatives as well. Programs were created slowly, only after long, in-depth study by parliamentary commissions that included political officials, experts in the field, and representatives of various interest groups—workers, employers, housewives, and so on. Consensus seeking was preferred to confrontation, and pragmatism ruled. What solutions would best address a given problem? Testing and altering policy after implementation were integral parts of building the postwar welfare state. Increased "security" *(trygghet)* and equality of opportunity, particularly in education and employment, were emphasized. As Tage Erlander said more than once, "We were aware that we could not achieve everything at once; we had to establish priorities and try to achieve as much as possible."

## Labor, Economics, and Politics

Equally important to Sweden's success in the fifties and sixties were a disciplined labor market and a Western economic boom. The Saltsjöbaden agreements of 1938 between LO and SAF established a formal system for labor market relations and, perhaps more importantly, a framework for elite bargaining between powerful leaders of organized labor and organized management. The agreements removed the government from any formal role in the labor market and reinforced hierarchical structures within LO and SAF. Local unions as well as local employers were not permitted to negotiate directly with one another until their representative organizations had reached an agreement in principle concerning the form of a general labor contract. Power accrued to the leaderships of the labor market partners, encouraged interest-group representation and representative democracy, and limited the independence of individual entrepreneurs and workers. "The spirit of Saltsjöbaden" came to symbolize a willingness on both sides of the labor market to find accommodation and agreement.

Sweden's success in maintaining labor market stability between 1950 and 1970 was remarkable. The United States, for example, averaged more than six times the number of work stoppages per 100,000 employees each year during this twenty-year period. This relative labor peace depended upon a variety of factors including discipline within each labor market organization, knowledgeable and mutually sensitive negotiators, and a general recognition of Sweden's need to remain competitive internationally. This last factor led LO as well as SAF to push for increasing worker efficiency and productivity through rationalization, technological innovation in production, worker retraining, and a supportive political and economic environment.

The most important impetus for Sweden's economic growth was an overall boom in the Western economic system. Sweden's performance in economic terms was neither unique nor particularly distinguished. What was important for Sweden's development was that the government and the labor market parties took advantage of the growth to establish a more democratic and equitable society. The birth and infancy of the Swedish welfare state occurred at a time when the Swedish economy flourished and money was available to fund new public programs, such as national health care, expanded educational opportunities, better pensions, and improved housing. No attempts were made to nationalize industry or seize control over individual assets — the time-honored system of entail was abolished in 1963 but in such a way that aristocratic families could maintain control, if not ownership, of most of their family's traditional holdings. As Sweden's economic pie enlarged, the growth provided the financial resources for the establishment of the welfare state. Few Swedes could feel that the welfare state robbed them of what was rightfully theirs. Even the growing tax burden could be accepted (grumbling about taxes became a national pastime second only to discussions of the weather) because a majority of Swedes believed that every citizen is entitled to a moderate level of security and opportunity.

Two different issues in the fifties illustrated Sweden's response to economic growth and the limits of consensus on the welfare state: the active labor market policies and the supplementary pension system. Two labor economists, Rudolph Meidner and Gösta Rehn, encouraged the government in the mid-fifties to inaugurate a series of programs to stimulate employment opportunities. These programs, which included worker retraining, a sophisticated information system concerning job opportunities, and worker relocation schemes, were established in the late fifties and early sixties. LO and SAF also agreed to accept these policies. They provided a positive atmosphere for improving the quality of the work force, reinforced the commitment to full employment (Sweden had a shortage of workers during much of this period), and buttressed the geographical movement of Swedes from rural to urban areas, from small communities to large ones, especially Stockholm, Göteborg, and the Skåne region. Only in the late sixties, after a period of dramatically enhanced standard of living, were significant questions raised about these policies in terms of "quality of life." Critics within the labor movement itself and the Center party claimed that the active labor market policy served primarily the interests of large corporations and forced workers to uproot themselves from their traditional and preferred environments. Workers' physical standards of living improved, it was argued, but their quality of life worsened. They lost the intimate contact of small communities and their closeness to nature. Yet full employment was maintained, large numbers of women were drawn into the work force, and foreigners were recruited to meet the shortfall of available workers.

The debate on the supplementary pension system (*Allmän tilläggspension* [ATP]) demonstrated the boundaries of broad consensus on the welfare state and laid the foundation for a new political alignment in Swedish politics that continued until the late 1980s. The general pension in Sweden had been raised after the war, but it, like most social security schemes in Western states, did not provide most retired people with incomes similar to those they had earned during their active years in the marketplace nor with a growth of incomes consistent with that for the actively employed. Public pensions provided only the bare minimum; the question was how to insure that people who had worked diligently and lived frugally all their lives did not sink into poverty because of retirement, old age, or illness. Could private insurance provide the needed security or was some sort of public scheme, either voluntary or compulsory, needed? No agreement between the political parties could be reached. In 1956 the pension question surfaced as a major issue and remained an important one until the early sixties.

The ATP debate as it evolved had a number of critical foci: how the new system should be managed; how the system would be financed; and how to sustain cooperation between the two governing parties, the Social Democrats and the Agrarians. A nonbinding referendum was held in 1957 which provided voters with three distinct choices. The first was a labor-supported alternative that made the system compulsory and public. The system was to be financed directly by employers on actuarial principles similar to private insurance, and the funds managed by special boards controlled by representatives of government, labor, and management. A second Agrarian alternative opted for a purely voluntary system with an emphasis on increasing the basic pension. The third alternative supported by the Conservative and Liberal parties, as well as SAF, argued for a system established through labor market agreements, based on actuarial principles and controlled by employers. The referendum did not clarify the issue: the first alternative received 45.8 percent of the vote, with the second and third getting 15 percent and 35.3 percent respectively. The green-red coalition collapsed. The Social Democrats formed a single-party government that set as its first task the resolution of the ATP question. By a margin of one vote, after a special parliamentary election in 1958 and the abstention of a Liberal member of parliament, ATP on the lines of the first alternative became Swedish law in 1960.

As a result, Sweden has two pension systems of contrasting character. The normal pension resembles the American social security system. It provides minimal levels of subsistence and is funded by current taxation. The supplementary pension offers additional security approaching an income maintenance policy and is funded actuarially. Neither program is free from financial difficulties, but the latter is in potentially greater difficulty due to the age distribution (low fertility and high longevity) and sluggish economic growth after 1975. ATP was not simply a major new step in the evolution of the welfare state. It also began the realignment of Sweden's five political parties into a two-bloc system. Prior to 1957, the key to political stability in Sweden had been cooperation between the Agrarians and the Social Democrats; after 1957, the Agrarians renamed themselves the Center and began their attempts to become the largest nonsocialist party in Sweden. The continued governance of the Social Democrats and economic growth in the sixties and early seventies, however, led to a new outburst of legislative activity.

The keys to what could be termed the second phase of the Swedish welfare state were Alva Myrdal's 1970 report to the Social Democratic party, *Toward Equality*,[1] and a new set of party leaders. The Myrdal report went well beyond what had heretofore been the central thrust of the welfare state. It posited "equality" *(jämlikhet)* as the main goal and discussed a wide variety of social and economic issues. Its agenda was at once more radical and difficult to achieve than previous party policies. It presented the kind of program that appealed to the new Social Democratic leader, Olof Palme, who replaced Tage Erlander after the Social Democrats' large victory in the Second Chamber elections of 1968.

Palme was accompanied by a new generation of Social Democratic leaders: Ingvar Carlsson, Thage Petersson, Kjell-Olof Feldt, among others. They were anxious to establish their own identity and to increase the pace of change in Sweden. They accepted notions of Sweden's progress and uniqueness more common to a growing number of social scientists outside Sweden than to the leadership groups they were replacing. They had more extensive educational training and less contact with the working life of their country than had Erlander's generation. They also seemed in a hurry.

The reforms of the first Palme government were enacted more quickly than earlier reforms. Administrative commissions often replaced parliamentary ones. Alternatives were not carefully tested; ideology overruled pragmatism. The results, such as the reform of higher education, were frequently disappointing, neither resolving the identified problem nor avoiding the creation of new ones.

The most significant changes occurred in labor market relations. A new trade union leadership wanted significant changes in working conditions, wage differentiation, hiring and firing practices, decision making within firms and institutions, and in ownership. They talked of establishing "economic democracy." LO proved ineffective in getting SAF to accept these new ideas and turned to the political arena for support. "The spirit of Saltsjöbaden" languished and was replaced by a more confrontational relationship that was fought out in the political system rather than in labor market negotiations. The one major exception was wage differentiation, which was decreased through a policy of "wage solidarity" in labor market negotiations. The continuing labor peace masked deep unhappiness especially within SAF as bills passed parliament often with broad support from nonsocialist parties as well as from the Social Democrats and Communists.

An occupational safety law, a job security law, and the codetermination act of 1976 were the main pieces of legislation. The first gave increased power to the shop stewards for organization of the workplace and protected workers from work-environment risks. Its effects on the whole have been positive, and employers have adjusted and utilized the talent of the work force more effectively. The job security act has been more controversial. Its proponents claim that it has provided necessary security for workers and modified the active labor market policies. Opponents argue that it has introduced harmful rigidities into Swedish economic life and that it leads to increased unemployment, especially among young people. The codetermination act eliminated the exclusive right of employers to hire and fire, but its impact has not been as extensive as both opponents and proponents had assumed.

There is little doubt that one of the ramifications of these laws was to change the style of management in Sweden. Managers could no longer arbitrarily make decisions. More often than not, they must convince other individuals within the firm. Knowledge necessary for intelligent decision making was required by law to be shared with union officials. A successful Swedish employer has had to learn to be both an entrepreneur and captain of a team of powerful representatives. In effect, he must be capitalist and politician simultaneously. Typical of this new breed of managers is Sweden's most well-known employer Pehr G. Gyllenhammar, president of Volvo, a multifaceted company that produces 10 percent of Sweden's GNP.

A few have argued that these changes in the structure of Swedish firms have caused an increased "bureaucracy," slowness in decision making, and a greater tendency to risk-aversion, but on the whole the Swedes seemed to have taken advantage of these changes. Consensus building was a well established cultural tradition; its application to industry did not occur in a vacuum. Once the economic crisis of the last decade was apparent, a sense of a shared responsibility between management and labor grew. In cooperation with successive Swedish governments, the labor market partners played an instrumental role in responding to the crisis of the welfare state.

The one major program advocated by the labor movement that was not made into law during the seventies was "employee funds." As originally proposed, these funds appeared to be an attempt to democratize ownership of private firms but to leave the exercise of those democratic rights in the hands of representative institutions, most importantly the trade unions. Only after the Social Democrats returned to power in 1982 was a law passed establishing the funds. By this time, the funds were designed to have far less impact on the Swedish economy than their architect, Rudolph Meidner, had intended. The issue remains an open one in the late 1980s with the nonsocialist parties pledged to eliminate the funds if elected to office, and the Social Democrats unsure of their position after 1990.

The Social Democrats were not the only party to experience a change in leadership. All other parties had new chairmen and were trying to find programs that would attract voters in the seventies. The Conservatives changed their name and called themselves the Moderates in an attempt to avoid the pejorative connotation of the word conservative. Gösta Bohman, their new leader, demonstrated considerable political ability and made the party by 1979 the largest nonsocialist vote-getter. The Liberals had the greatest difficulties sustaining their leadership and political profile. Three men led the party in the seventies: Gunnar Helén, Per Ahlmark, and Ola Ullsten. The Center party became the largest nonsocialist party after the 1968 election and its new chairman, Thorbjörn Fälldin, became the dominant nonsocialist politician during the seventies despite a consistent reversal in Center party electoral fortunes after 1973. Even the Communists had a new leader, Lars Werner. Taken together, these figures were the first truly postwar generation of Swedish politicians.

The issue that attracted the most consistent public attention during the seventies was nuclear energy. Sweden's experience with the development of nuclear energy reflects significant contrasts between the Sweden of the fifties and sixties and that of the seventies and eighties. Immediately after World War II, Swedes viewed nuclear fission as a challenge to their scientific community, offering opportunity for Sweden's economy. Sweden's economic growth has been dependent upon the importation of energy sources. Nuclear energy provided the possibility of becoming less energy dependent and was enthusiastically supported by all political parties and the labor market partners.

The first ten years of research and development, conducted through cooperation between the government and private industry, did not differentiate between nuclear power and the building of a nuclear arsenal. Between 1955 and 1959, an intense debate developed on the question of whether Sweden should be nuclear armed. A combination of women's organizations and influential Social Democratic politicians, especially the foreign minister, Östen Undén, successfully stopped the development of a Swedish atom bomb. Parliament unanimously ratified that decision in 1968. Sweden was one of the first countries to decide voluntarily not to build an atomic bomb. Undén hoped that Sweden's policy would encourage other nations to do the same and prevent the spread of weapons. Sweden's self-restraint and its technological capabilities allowed it to become an active force in international negotiations on arms control and disarmament. A commitment to the development of nuclear energy, however, grew dramatically in the late fifties.

A half-public, half-private corporation, ASEA-ATOM, became the industrial heart of Sweden's rapidly expanding nuclear energy industry. Sweden's energy consumption per capita trebled between 1945 and 1973 as its economy flourished; nuclear energy, it was argued, would be cheaper, would reduce Sweden's energy dependence, would provide jobs, and would establish a new industrial sector to compete in the marketplace. Nuclear energy was to be the new economic growth sector for the late twentieth century and into the twenty-first.

It was only in 1970 when two female Center party members raised the question of the safety of the nuclear energy plants that the issue moved slowly into the political arena. Birgitta Hambraeus, a Center party member of parliament, asked the government in 1972 to defend the safety standards of the nuclear plants. A year later the Center party decided to oppose all use of nuclear facilities until or unless the safety issue could be resolved. Fälldin made the question an important issue in the campaign of 1973.

By 1975, the debate on nuclear energy had become the dominant media question in Swedish politics. Many influential writers had sided against nuclear energy, as had the Communists. Public opinion surveys suggested both deep divisions within the Swedish public and great concern over the safety question. Party affiliations, normally very strong, were much weaker and the question seemed to have the capacity to split the Swedish electorate along nontraditional lines much as membership in the European community had divided Denmark and Norway. A firm parliamentary majority, the Social Democrats and Moderates, remained committed to an expanding nuclear energy program; the Liberals tried to establish a quota of ten reactors but no more. Nuclear energy was the key to the victory of the nonsocialists in 1976. For the first time in 44 years a majority nonsocialist government could be formed. It could not have occurred at a worse time.

The Center-Liberal-Moderate government headed by Fälldin was unaware of the severity of the economic crisis. The so-called bridge-building economic policies of '74 and '75 (a product of cooperation between the Social Democrats and the Liberals—including the Center only in 1974) combined with labor market agreements that inflated Swedish wages and dramatically placed Sweden in a precarious economic situation. In addition, the rapid increase in the price of oil and the rise of industrializing countries along the Pacific rim with their ability to produce steel and ships threatened the competitive international position of Sweden. Those few Swedes who recognized the seriousness of Sweden's problems either could not make themselves heard or remained silent for political reasons.

The coalition wanted most of all to demonstrate that they were a credible alternative to Social Democratic governance. After all, most Swedes had never known a nonsocialist ministry. Protection of, and if possible expansion and refinement of, the welfare state became a central concern of the new government. Clearly there was resistance in accepting that Sweden must change to meet new economic realities. With tax levels already over 50 percent of GNP, any belt-tightening measures would be politically difficult and potentially destructive to the nonsocialist alternative.

In fact, there was no hope for the Fälldin government. The three parties were irreconcilably divided on nuclear energy. Negotiations on the coalition's governmental statement almost collapsed over nuclear energy and were salvaged by postponing the question. This compromise resolved none of the intergovernmental differences and gave the Social Democrats an opportunity to attack Fälldin for what was called "his perfidy." The positions of each of three coalition parties hardened; no possibility of compromise existed between Center and its two partners. The government collapsed in October 1978 — the first majority nonsocialist government in a half-century had survived for two years! A minority Liberal government headed by Ullsten took its place.

Many of the Liberal leaders hoped to establish a new alignment in Swedish politics. They believed that a coalition between the Social Democrats and themselves was possible. The problems of the economy and nuclear energy were more easily compromised between the two parties than between the three nonsocialist parties. However, the nuclear energy issue undermined such thoughts. In March 1979, the Three Mile Island nuclear power plant accident became public knowledge; its impact on Sweden was dramatic. The Social Democrats suddenly decided to accept a referendum, and the Liberals and Moderates followed suit. None of these parties wanted the issue to overshadow the September elections.

The election of 1979 was a troubled one. The three nonsocialist parties carried the burden of their governmental failures. The Social Democrats scored them on their economic policies. In turn, the Social Democrats were handicapped by their continued commitment to the employee funds that were not popular. The Moderates argued for a reduction of the marginal tax rates and gained more seats than any other party. The Social Democrats increased their popular vote by 0.5 percent, but the three nonsocialist parties held a slight majority of the seats in parliament. The Center suffered the greatest loss of votes.

A new party coalition government under Fälldin was formed. With nuclear energy to be resolved in the 1980 referendum, the primary task of the government was to deal with the economic crisis. The first Fälldin government tried to meet the worst of the crisis by successive devaluations, by borrowing money, and by taking over weak companies to sustain full employment. Sweden quickly accumulated a huge foreign debt.

General Government Fiscal Information, 1977–1984 (in millions of crowns)

| Year | Net balance | Total State debt | Foreign debt |
|------|-------------|------------------|--------------|
| 1977 | 6,218 | 82,340 | 5,066 |
| 1978 | − 1,928 | 105,238 | 11,203 |
| 1979 | − 13,618 | 139,086 | 14,876 |
| 1980 | − 19,663 | 192,088 | 32,105 |
| 1981 | − 28,232 | 252,968 | 46,721 |
| 1982 | − 39,844 | 319,686 | 62,536 |
| 1983 | − 35,124 | 407,325 | 81,427 |
| 1984 | − 18,152 | 482,636 | 102,947 |

*Sources:* For fiscal information see *Yearbook of Nordic Statistics* and the English summary of *The Swedish Budget,* published annually.

Interest payment on the state debt grew from 4 percent of the national budget in 1975–76 to 29 percent for 1984–85. Government takeover of many failing industries was also costly. Over 15 billion crowns were spent between 1977 and 1979 on shipbuilding and steel making alone. Total company-specific subsidies in the decade of the seventies reached approximately 26 billion crowns, nearly all after 1975. Corporate tax revenues by comparison totaled 15.2 billion. The nonsocialist government created more publicly owned enterprises in terms of numbers of employees in two years than the Social Democrats had done in 44.

The second Fälldin government continued the policies of its predecessors with large expenditures for direct support of industry, increasing public deficits, devaluation of the crown, and the maintenance of full employment. Sweden's unemployment rate stayed below 4 percent, while many European countries experienced double digit figures. The government also began to increase public support for research and development, especially for energy related projects.

The referendum on nuclear energy, held in 1980, seemed to resolve the issue. Once again the electorate faced three alternatives. The Center and Communists advocated a rapid dismantling of Sweden's nuclear facilities, while the Social Democrats, Liberals, and Moderates supported more cautious programs to phase out nuclear energy production. While none of the alternatives received a majority, the accepted interpretation of the referendum's results was that Swedes wanted to end nuclear energy production in Sweden. The parliament and future governments would have to decide exactly how. In the eight years between the referendum and 1988, the parliament did not fix a precise schedule for the phase-out, although the Social Democratic government claims that by the year 2010 no nuclear plants will be in operation. The accident at Chernobyl in 1986 reinforced public support for a phase-out, but considerable problems related to energy production remain.

The changing nature of energy production/consumption in the shadows of the nuclear energy debate and the economic crisis reflect some important shifts in Sweden between 1973 and 1987. Energy conservation, declining use of oil, increased support for energy research and development, increased efficiency — all have been major aspects of these changes. Total energy consumption declined by 14 percent between 1973–74 and 1985, despite a 7 percent growth in industrial production. Oil consumption dropped by nearly 50 percent in the same period, and now accounts for approximately 50 percent of all Sweden's energy needs. The greatest energy saving occurred in industrial usage, especially in pulp and paper manufacturing. Nuclear energy production accounted for over 40 percent of the electricity produced in 1984. Phasing out nuclear energy presents a real challenge to Sweden, and successive governments have increased support for research and development in the field, from 40 million crowns in 1980 to 483 million in 1984. At the same time, Sweden is trying to solve its own energy problems and to develop new internationally competitive industries. These policies have begun to pay dividends: heat pumps, trash conversion, peat energy production, and wind energy are but a few examples of areas where Swedes have made real advances.

The second Fälldin government proved to be no more successful than the first in maintaining internal cooperation. Tax policy led to its collapse in 1981. Nominally the division between the Center and Liberals on one side and the Moderates on the other was the former's agreement with the Social Democrats for a three-year gradual reduction of marginal tax rates. The Moderates wanted immediate and significant tax relief. However, at its heart, the collapse of the second Fälldin government symbolized a new era of Swedish domestic politics in which the Moderates were attempting to become the dominant nonsocialist alternative, as had occurred in Norway.

Popular support for the Moderates had risen steadily in the seventies until they had become the largest nonsocialist party. The major appeal of the party was a demand for tax reduction, but in order to be consistent, the party had also to propose cuts in public spending. Their dilemma was to identify expendable or grossly inefficient programs. Swedes wanted their taxes cut yet supported all the major social welfare programs. In addition, fully 38.2 percent of the entire work force was employed in the public sector (up from 20.2 percent in 1965 — the growth had occurred almost entirely within the county or communal institutions). These individuals represent a potent part of the electorate and could not be expected to vote to eliminate their own jobs. It was nearly impossible for the Moderates to take positions similar to those of President Ronald Reagan or Prime Minister Margaret Thatcher. They had to find a way to stop the growth of the welfare state without appearing to suggest that they opposed it in principle.

The 1982 elections produced the return to power of the Social Democrats and the continued growth of the Moderates—the Center and Liberals who had governed the country since 1981 in the third Fälldin ministry suffered considerable losses. The Social Democrats took advantage of perceptions of mismanagement, especially of the economy, on the part of the nonsocialist governments, while the Moderates focused on the proclaimed danger of the employee funds to a free economy. A new party, the Ecology party, made its debut and received slightly less than 2 percent, not enough to be represented in parliament. Interestingly, the single issue that had hurt the governing parties most during the election was an attempt by the government to cut spiraling medical costs by limiting wage compensation during the first days of illness. There was, in short, little in the results of 1982 that gave substance to the notion that Swedes were willing to reconsider the welfare state. Could the Social Democrats restore the health of the economy and the confidence that had characterized Sweden in the early seventies?

The first task of the new government was to fulfill its promise to establish employee funds. Little enthusiasm existed within the government for the idea, and a majority of the public remained hostile. Nonetheless, a bill passed parliament establishing the funds as of January 1, 1984. The enacting legislation established a full review process and a commitment to reexamine the question in 1990. Although the nonsocialist parties remain adamant that they will dismantle the program on return to office and large-scale public demonstrations occurred in 1983 and 1984 against the funds, it is unclear what the future holds for them. The parliamentary bill was a pale reflection of the initial Meidner proposals. It no longer sought to gain worker control over private enterprise. The employee funds were much more a program to increase savings, to provide more risk capital, and to give the unions something in return for their cooperation in no-growth wage agreements. The Social Democrats wanted to reestablish their credibility as the governing party of Sweden.

The new government consisted entirely of post-Erlander Social Democrats. Headed by Olof Palme, the key minister was Kjell Olof Feldt, Minister of Finance, who dominated the myriad economic issues as his predecessor, Gunnar Sträng, 1956–76, had once done. Feldt talked of a "third way" for Sweden to follow between "Thatcherism" and communism—in essence a return to the economic strategies of the fifties and sixties managed by a powerful, careful, and cooperative Minister of Finance. An immediate 16 percent devaluation followed the election victory. Direct subsidies to company-specific industries all but disappeared. LO agreed to show wage restraint. White-collar unions proved more difficult to control. Few new spending measures were allowed. Feldt even published a book in which he questioned the conventional Social Democrat wisdom that the public sector must have a monopoly on essential social services, for example, day care. While he received bitter criticism from some Social Democratic groups, especially the women's organization, the very fact that he had dared to raise the issue demonstrated that the Social Democrats had returned to a more pragmatic course than that which they had followed after 1968. Efficiency became an important element in the provision of public service. Private business had no difficulty appreciating Feldt's policies. The stock market soared and many of Sweden's key industries registered record profits.

The ability of the Social Democrats to remain in power in 1985 depended to a great extent on Feldt's success. This election marked the initial culmination of the Moderates' growth and to a great extent focused upon explicit Moderate party suggestions to change the direction of the Swedish welfare state. Palme attacked the Moderate leader, Ulf Adelsohn, for wanting to dismantle the welfare state. Adelsohn stumbled in his response, and the new Liberal chair, Bengt Westerberg, found a large group of nonsocialist voters to attract to his party. The Liberals more than doubled their percentage of the electorate and registered the second largest gain in an election since 1945. Westerberg's message underscored knowledgeable solutions to Sweden's problems. He successfully presented himself as a nonsocialist version of Kjell-Olof Feldt. Thorbjörn Fälldin's popularity declined, and in the wake of Center's poor showing, an in-house revolt led to his resignation. Karin Söder became the first woman to lead a Swedish political party.

The new Social Democratic government had few personnel changes. Most importantly Sten Andersson, party secretary from 1962–1985 and minister of social welfare from 1982–1985, became foreign minister. Feldt continued to dominate economic policy and maintained his cautious neo-Keynesian ways. The great trauma for the government and country came on February 28, 1986, when the prime minister, Olof Palme, was assassinated in a Stockholm street. Politically the transfer of power to his successor, Ingvar Carlsson, occurred without a hitch. Psychologically, Sweden was deeply shaken.

The Palme murder was unsolved as of the winter of 1987–1988. Despite enormous expenditure of resources, Sweden's attempts to find the responsible parties has resembled more Peter Seller's Inspector Clouseau than the fictional Swedish policeman, Martin Beck. It seems likely that the crime was not simply the act of a disturbed individual. Swedes have had to face the reality that their politicians are no longer safe alone on the street—Palme had attended a movie with his wife and was walking unguarded home from the theatre. Sweden's secret service had demanded that they be allowed to provide adequate protection for the nation's leaders. These demands in turn threaten the approachability of politicians, a traditional element in Swedish politics. Carlsson reluctantly allowed the secret service to establish a secure prime minister's apartment in the old city of Stockholm. A blue-ribbon parliamentary committee is now trying to decide how to balance security needs with political tradition.

Emotionally the Palme murder caught Swedes unprepared. The outpouring of bipartisan acclaim would have surprised anyone who had months or years earlier witnessed the wide-spread criticism of Palme. Brilliant, outspoken, and combative, Palme was a controversial figure. As leader of the dominant political party, he naturally appeared to be the most important political figure in the country. Actually, his most distinct contributions came in the field of foreign affairs.

Sweden maintains a nonpartisan foreign policy. There is unanimous agreement among Swedish parties that the country should be nonaligned in peacetime in order to maintain neutrality in case of war. Sweden's nonalignment is affirmed by a strong and independent defense and active participation in international bodies, particularly the Nordic Council, the United Nations, and the OECD. In addition, Sweden has committed itself to an extensive aid program for developing nations; the annual target of 1 percent of GNP has been set by parliamentary vote. Despite general agreement on these pillars of Swedish foreign policy, there have been many occasions where individual goals could have been pursued more aggressively or the specifics of a particular policy could have been debated.

For example, on the question of aid to developing countries, disagreements have arisen over which countries should receive aid, how much, and in what form. Although the parliament has established certain guidelines on these issues, the Swedish International Development Agency (SIDA) is supposed to set general policy as well as administer aid programs. In particular, aid to Cuba was questioned in the light of Cuban military involvement in Africa and eventually cut dramatically. The longest standing debate concerned aid to Vietnam, which has received relatively large amounts of money for the building of a paper and a pulp industrial complex at Bai Bang.

Public discussion of important foreign policy problems is often stylized and incomplete. Issues related to the credibility of Swedish defense policy have not been discussed thoroughly despite a decline in relative expenditures for defense, the growing difficulties of the development of new weapons systems (especially fighter aircraft), and the changing strategic situation in northern Europe. Until the mid-seventies, defense policy was based on the idea that no attack on Sweden would occur in isolation, that any conflict in northern Europe would likely follow an outbreak of hostilities elsewhere (presumably in central Europe), and that any attacker would have limited military means. Swedish defense therefore simply had to be credible in the context of meeting a limited threat and a willingness to use it against any aggressor. Significant shifts in strategic relations between NATO and the Warsaw Pact countries were visible by the mid-seventies, but a Soviet submarine—a nuclear armed, Whiskey class—stuck deep within a well-defined security area in 1981 forced a reexamination of Sweden's defense policies.

The response of the Fälldin government to the submarine crisis fell within the traditions of Swedish neutrality. All major actions were approved unanimously by the parliamentary committee on foreign affairs. A strongly worded protest was lodged, and an insistence on interrogation of the officers of the vessels was sustained. The Swedish navy eventually moved the vessel from Swedish waters into open sea. Public demands for stronger action, including military boarding the ship, and/or taking control of the vessel and using it as a bargaining chip (such as for the release of Swedish diplomat Raoul Wallenberg, who rescued large numbers of Jews in Budapest in 1944 and who was arrested by Soviet authorities in 1945), were not seriously considered. Few public figures in Sweden saw anything to be gained from extending the crisis. The real problem was the increasing Soviet submarine incursions in Swedish territorial waters.

A special parliamentary commission examined the incursions, confirmed their significance, and offered a variety of possible explanations for their occurrence. Palme as prime minister tried to maintain the view that only in a few cases could Sweden be totally sure of the nationality of the submarines. His position was neither accurate nor forthcoming, but probably reflected his concern to normalize relations with the Soviet Union as quickly as possible and to gain support for other international initiatives he had undertaken (see below). What had become clear in Sweden and elsewhere was that the strategic assumptions of Swedish defense policy were no longer as convincing as they once were.

It is now possible to imagine an initial strike in Scandinavia either as a bargaining strategy or as a first stage of an envelopment of central Europe. It is also possible to see Scandinavia as a critical geographical element in terms of defense in missile exchanges, forward bases for missile attack, and as a critical element in control of the north Atlantic. Both NATO and the Soviet Union have increased their military strength and readiness in the region. The northern European sector, once perceived as a backwater, may be the most sensitive in all of Europe. This fact creates great challenges for Sweden's defense and perhaps its neutrality. Yet, in 1987, a parliamentary coalition of Liberals and Social Democrats passed a new defense bill that allocated moderate increases in defense spending and that did not challenge conventional wisdom. It seems unlikely that Sweden would embark on any major changes in its traditional nonalignment and defense policies.

The evolution of the European Community (EC) has also provided a new set of problems for conventional Swedish neutrality. During the fifties and the sixties, Sweden not only refused to join France, Italy, the Federal Republic, and BENELUX in creating the European Communities (the Coal and Steel Community, the Common Market, Euratom, and so on) but actively worked against it through the EFTA. When Denmark, Great Britain, and Ireland joined the community in 1971–72, Sweden faced the choice between full membership and a trade agreement. Only the latter was consistent with nonalignment, and therefore the choice was rather simple. However, integration within the community has fitfully progressed and the community has enlarged. What are the implications of this development for Sweden's future economic well-being?

Nordic cooperation has been viewed since World War II as a critical element in Swedish foreign policy and a partial balance to Sweden's nonmembership in EC. Denmark as an EC member served as something of a representative for the other Scandinavian states and was the community's most reluctant partner. Denmark appears, however, to be reevaluating its community policies. Nordic cooperation, significant as it may be, seems to have real limits whether in defense or economic terms. Sweden's devaluations have often occurred without informing the other Scandinavian states and partially at their expense. During 1987, public discussion both in Sweden and Norway indicated a growing recognition that community evolution might force a serious reevaluation of current policies. What one can be sure of is that Sweden will attempt to maintain its traditional nonalignment and to protect its economic markets within EC.

In all these issues of foreign policy, there is great stability and continuity. Individual prime ministers or foreign ministers impact Swedish policy marginally. Olof Palme brought enormous energy and knowledge about foreign affairs to the prime minister's office as well as a determination to serve effectively as his own foreign minister and to achieve for Sweden and himself a higher international profile.

Much of Palme's sense of social injustice and political commitment came from his personal experiences as a young man traveling in the United States and the Third World. His passion to try to find ways to help poor, frequently small, countries was uncommon for a Western statesman and clearly appreciated by leaders of developing nations. As a former prime minister between 1976 and 1982, he participated in the United Nations commission on North-South relations under the chairmanship of Willie Brandt. Palme chaired a similar commission on security questions. He also served as an unsuccessful mediator for the United Nations in the Iran-Iraq conflict. His own international profile had already been well established by his opposition to American involvement in Vietnam. One of his last international efforts was a six-nation call for international peace and reconciliation which attempts to bridge gaps between North and South, East and West.

While there can be no doubt that Palme was the most recognized Swedish politician of this century, his impact on the mainstream of Swedish foreign policy does not loom large. As international tributes poured into Stockholm following his assassination, Sweden went into mourning. Small mountains of flowers appeared at the site of his murder. Normally dour Swedes cried openly in the street. His funeral became a celebration of his commitment and his accomplishments. It also reflected a sense of the country's lost innocence. Sweden's foreign policies would not change, but it seemed unlikely that such a small country would soon again produce a leader of international repute.

Ingvar Carlsson was well prepared to become prime minister, having been Palme's handpicked successor since 1968. Carlsson had broad experience and was, in fact, more acceptable to various sectors of the labor movement than Palme. His foreign policy experience was limited. His style was less combative, more cooperative, and more traditional than Palme's. In the aftermath of the assassination a deliberate attempt to lower the level of hostility between the parties succeeded. Two parties changed leaders: Carl Bildt replaced Adelsohn, while Olof Johansson took over for Karin Söder after her health deteriorated. Only Lars Werner remained from the seventies. The tone of Swedish politics has changed; compromise and problem solving rather than ideologically driven solutions have become more dominant.

Sweden had not solved its economic problems by 1987. Indeed there was much to worry about including the debt, difficulties in maintaining full employment, inefficiencies in the public sector, and tax reform. Yet there is an air of cautious optimism. The old spirit of shared responsibilities seems to have been reestablished. Hard problems are being addressed; different alternatives are being examined. LO for example has cooperated actively with SAF in the implementation of robotics in the work place. Sweden now has the highest per capita number of robots of any country. It also has one of the largest research and development commitments per capita in the world. Enormous efforts (institutional, individual, and governmental) are made in programs of "continuing education" to sustain a highly educated, flexible, and competent adult population. The Liberals and the Center have shown a willingness to work with the Social Democrats on issues ranging from defense to taxes. Sweden's ability to control its economic problems has become the subject of international scrutiny and praise.

In March, 1987, *The Economist* called Sweden "an economic paradox:"[2] "It has the biggest public sector of any industrial economy, the highest taxes, the most generous welfare state, the narrowest wage differentials, and powerful trade unions. According to prevailing wisdom, it ought to be suffering from an acute bout of 'eurosclerosis,' with rigid labour markets and arthritic industry. Instead, Sweden has many large and vigorous companies, and one of the lowest unemployment rates in Europe."[3]

A 1987 Brookings study equally praised Sweden's abilities to approach its problems effectively. OECD has made similar observations. Of course, these international observers see the problems as well, but they too appear to share Swedish optimism that the country can maintain its course.

## Social Change

Yet Sweden's ability to prosper in the future is not based simply on its economic and political institutions. It is perhaps based on its most important resource, the Swedish people. The past twenty years have witnessed a dramatic change in the nature of Swedish lifestyles. How will changes in attitudes toward women, marriage, and work and growing cultural heterogeneity affect the nature of the welfare state?

Perhaps most important, the pace of change in Swedish family structure has accelerated. It is difficult to understand fully why these changes occur or their ramifications. The evidence does, however, clearly indicate that the traditional Swedish family is under great strain:

Marriage Stability (Medians per year per indicated period)

|  | 1921–30 | 31–40 | 41–50 | 51–60 |
|---|---|---|---|---|
| Marriages | 39,234 | 51,497 | 60,446 | 52,132 |
| Divorces | 1,813 | 2,926 | 6,082 | 8,622 |
|  | 1961–70 | 71–75 | 76–80 | 1984 |
| Marriages | 53,983 | 41,154 | 39,575 | 36,849 |
| Divorces | 10,209 | 19,385 | 20,524 | 20,377 |

Source: Yearbook of Nordic Statistics.

We can see three rather distinct periods: pre-war, immediate postwar, and post-1970. Today Sweden has the highest divorce rate in Europe. A number of factors may have contributed to this increased instability.

Attendance in the Swedish state Lutheran church has been declining since the thirties. The teaching of religion was dropped from school curricula in the early sixties. Most Swedes' contact with the church comes at Christmas, at a baptism, perhaps at a confirmation, or at a funeral. Whatever institutional or social role the church played in sustaining traditional family values has dissipated if not disappeared. It may, however, be incorrect to place too much emphasis on religious practice.

The church's influence in providing moral guidance seems to have been on the wane since the late nineteenth century. The free churches were more dynamic than the state church and integrated into the other "people's movements" (unions, cooperatives, prohibition, Liberal and Social Democratic parties) that were instrumental in modernizing the country. The moral tenets of Christianity became integral elements within these groups and have been sustained in the welfare state. One need only to read the popular press, listen to political debate, or examine primary and secondary curricula to recognize that Christian values are firmly entrenched in the society. Granted these values do not include what most Americans think of as Christian attitudes toward sex, and most younger Swedes probably do not realize that the value system they receive from parents and social institutions is religiously based.

Swedish sexual behavior historically has had little to do with "normal" Christian expectations. Premarital sex was common in preindustrial Sweden. In the nineteenth century, a significant percentage of women were already pregnant when they got married. That number has increased in the twentieth century. Attitudes toward children born out of wedlock have also been more liberal in Sweden than in most other Western societies. The Swedes have not wanted to place the "sins" of one generation onto another. Public support for children has not been dependent upon the circumstances of their birth.

Divorce simply seems to have become more acceptable in the postwar period. The rise in the divorce rate in the immediate postwar period occurred before dramatic changes in women's participation in the work force. Perhaps the divorce rate in this period reflects the growing urbanization and mobility of Swedish society. Marriages were more likely to be sustained in small towns and villages where extended relationships existed. The rapid growth of post-war greater Stockholm and other urban areas undoubtedly proved a difficult adjustment for many. The growth in crime rates also reflects the anonymity of the urban landscape.

Many observers have argued that the increased divorce rate is attributable to a change in women's roles.[4] The number of women in the work force has increased steadily since 1960. In the age group of 25 to 64, the employment to population ratio of women grew from 52 percent to 79 percent between 1963 and 1984. Much of that growth has come in public sector jobs. These women, however, work nearly one-fifth less time per week now than women did in 1963. A general reduction in working hours is partially the reason for this decline, but the variety of tax and social incentives also provides part of the explanation. Has the working woman per se contributed to the decline in family stability?

Women have become more independent. Beginning with the family social reforms of the thirties, the Swedish state—with the support of all the political parties—has intervened by encouraging family growth and by providing equal opportunities for all children regardless of birth. Changes in the tax laws during the sixties made being a housewife an economic disadvantage to most Swedish women. Direct subventions for child allowances as well as growing day-care opportunities increased rapidly, especially after 1970. The goal of the day-care programs is to provide a place for every child by 1990—although there is much political disagreement over this issue and how it should be achieved.

It seems reasonable to conclude that the combination of a growing independence of women along with the substitution of state-supported child-care programs has contributed to increased family instability. We should remind ourselves, however, that the philosophy of the welfare state is to provide security, independence, and greater equality. Equality for women is far from complete, and its price may be a restructuring of traditional social institutions.

Sweden's reputation as a pioneering country for women's rights is only partially accurate. Voting rights came after World War I, and prominence in party leadership has been slow. The number of women representatives in parliament increased significantly only in the last ten years. Women have had little impact on the trade union movement, despite their increase in numbers. Women's educational rates, although improving, lag behind men's. The 1980 Act of Equality established a series of equity measures including a "comparative worth" standard for employment. But women's incomes continue to be lower than men's.

1983 Income Earned: Men, Women, and Average (in crowns)

| Age | Men | Women | Average (both sexes) |
|---|---|---|---|
| –19 | 19,200 | 17,500 | 18,300 |
| 20–24 | 55,800 | 50,400 | 53,100 |
| 25–34 | 82,500 | 57,300 | 70,300 |
| 35–49 | 103,800 | 64,600 | 84,900 |
| 50–64 | 99,600 | 60,900 | 80,300 |
| 65– | 65,200 | 40,200 | 51,000 |

Moreover, evidence suggests that what women have in fact accomplished is to add their workplace responsibilities to their traditional "duties." Despite efforts to encourage men to share household and child-rearing activities, there is little to suggest that major changes have occurred. Men seem to want to maintain their traditional roles, while women struggle for equality and independence.

Political-cultural trends have also contributed to this process. The independent, professional, or working woman became a symbol for advocates of the welfare state—Alva Myrdal would be a good example—and a character in modern literature and films. Young women were told that personal fulfillment came from education and a satisfying job, just as for men, as well as from a meaningful relationship with a member of the opposite sex. Formal marriage became passé in the late sixties, which means the marriage-divorce statistics for the past 15 years underestimate dissolution of pair-relationships. By 1984, fully 46 percent of all children were born out of wedlock. Swedish law has been changed to equate legal marriages with a relationship with "a significant other" — *sambo* in Swedish, which literally means "person with whom you live."

The decline of the Swedish family has become a popular topic among American sociologists. A 1987 *Wall Street Journal* article was entitled, "Sweden's Disturbing Family Trends"; while David Poponoe concluded in an article for the *Journal of Marriage and Family* that "family dissolution is one of the few classically defined social problems that is getting worse in Sweden."[5] Swedes, interestingly enough, do not see the issue in the same light. Newspapers have sometimes focused on the abuse of power exercised by local social welfare boards in removing children from their parents; Jan Myrdal wrote two devastating critiques of his mother's child-rearing activities;[6] and Ingmar Bergman's films often illustrate a deep frustration among his female characters. Swedes will complain about the growing power of the state, yet little evidence exists that these complaints will generate strong political change. The trade unions and the Social Democratic party have made increased support for child rearing their most important priority for the early nineties. Why don't Swedes seem to fear the changes in family structure as much as outsiders?

The question is easier to pose than to answer. The answer must combine social-economic-political values with psychological needs. As for the former, the increased independence and equality provided by the welfare state is approved by nearly all adult Swedes. For many, the traditional family was an institution of inequality and, in some cases, oppression. Nor is it clear that the traditional Swedish family successfully met the psychological needs of its members. "Duty" often was the strongest bonding agent, rather than mutual respect or emotional interdependence. Children were taught their place in a hierarchical order headed by career-oriented males. Contemporary Swedes seem willing to test new forms of interrelationships to better harmonize their values and needs.

Divorce is not as legally, economically, or emotionally traumatic as it is in the United States. Moreover, adult Swedes appear to realize that children are potentially the greatest losers in divorce cases. Custody issues are more easily resolved—perhaps because the children themselves have a legal right to be involved in the decision. Whatever emotional damage is caused by a divorce, Swedes try to minimize it. Former spouses with their children and extended families, even their new partners, will occasionally spend traditional holidays together. Textbooks, especially those written for younger children, have been redesigned so that students living with one natural parent will not feel deprived. The smallness and interconnectedness of Swedish society provides a cultural and emotional safety net for these experiments. To outsiders, it often smacks of the Brave New World.

## Crime

Crime in Sweden has risen sharply since 1950. According to conventional wisdom among Swedish criminologists, crime is primarily the product of poor socioeconomic conditions. They argued that the development of the welfare state would improve standards of living and therefore reduce crime levels. In theory and practice the values of the Swedish welfare state were incorporated into the criminal justice system: individuals were not solely responsible for their actions—society, too, carried a responsibility; most offenders could be rehabilitated; and treatment of individual criminals should be designed with the specific person in mind.

Model Swedish prisons and rehabilitation techniques attracted considerable international attention. No Swedish prison holds more than five hundred inmates; the overwhelming majority contain fewer than one hundred. It is forbidden by law that any prison should be more than 85 percent filled in order to provide room to separate young and old, drug and nondrug offenders. Prisoners have a series of rights including conjugal visitations, leaves under certain circumstances, and the opportunity to work for market pay rates. Capital punishment does not exist, and the longest actual served sentences are between seven and twelve years.

Sweden has spent considerable sums of money to rehabilitate offenders and to eliminate presumed causes of crimes. Yet the statistical record gives little solace. Since 1950, every major category of crime, except rape, has seen a 400 percent increase.

Crime (Reported)

| Year | Murder | Assault | Rape | Theft | Fraud |
|------|--------|---------|------|-------|-------|
| 1950 | 105 | 7,395 | 350 | 110,470 | 18,820 |
| 1960 | 133 | 8,711 | 512 | 203,675 | 23,969 |
| 1970 | 218 | 18,385 | 692 | 390,523 | 71,029 |
| 1980 | 394 | 24,668 | 885 | 514,130 | 96,701 |
| 1984 | 479 | 30,785 | 995 | 574,533 | 88,814 |

*Source: Yearbook of Nordic Statistics.*

How are we to interpret this record? Even given some quibbling over the meaning of the data, one can hardly conclude that a more equitable distribution of the goods and services in society, the elimination of the worst forms of poverty, and an increase in the standard of living have prevented a dramatic growth in crime rates. Conventional wisdom on the relationship between socioeconomic conditions and crime needs some serious reconsideration.

The relatively low levels of crime before 1950 might have been more a reflection of the nature of Swedish society and cultural values than anything else. In small urban settings and in rural communities, grass-roots social control may have restricted criminal behavior. Rapid postwar urbanization and the relative anonymity of the large cities diluted this control, especially over young people. What is noteworthy is that crimes of violence and property are matched by so-called middle-class crimes, such as fraud. Swedes have prided themselves on their honesty. Visitors to Sweden before 1960 were often struck by Swedes' honesty. Historically, there are surprisingly few examples of graft or corruption in government. Yet in 1987 alone the president of a major Swedish corporation resigned after it was disclosed that he deliberately broke the law with implications that public officials were also knowledgeable. One of the ombudsmen has also resigned because of alleged improprieties. A convicted spy took advantage of a home visit to escape the country; the ensuing scandal led to the resignation of the minister of justice and much embarrassment to the Social Democratic government. *The New York Times* published an article accusing a large group of civil servants as well as the government of obfuscation and deliberate procrastination in the investigation of the Palme murder.[7]

Economic crimes have also caused increasing concern. In the late seventies, Gunnar Myrdal suggested that Swedish tax laws were turning Sweden into a nation of tax dodgers. Estimates of the illegal exchange of goods and services range from 10 percent to 25 percent of GNP.

Swedish respect for the law has changed—how much is difficult to measure. However, at least in one area, drinking and driving, Sweden appears to have successfully wedded a strong legal proscription and social acceptance. Swedish law treats drunk drivers strictly and automatically. Persons who serve alcohol can be held liable, as well as the individual who consumes it. Swedes have adjusted their patterns of drinking and transportation. At a typical Swedish party one person will not be drinking so that he or she can drive the others home, guests may use taxis or other forms of public transport, or everyone will be invited to stay the night and sober up.

No doubt many factors contributed to an increase in crime in Sweden besides rapid urbanization and a decrease in social control. The welfare state in and of itself does not seem to have either a positive or negative influence. To complicate matters further, crime rates throughout Europe vary greatly from country to country, even among those nations with similar socioeconomic systems. Norway, for example, has much lower rates than all other Scandinavian states, as does Austria. Norway and Austria are two of the most traditional societies in Europe. Perhaps for this reason they have been more successful in maintaining a spirit of community and self-control.

The presence of foreigners has often been associated with increases in crime, especially drug-related offenses. Available data for Sweden on this topic are less than complete, although it is clear that foreigners compose a disproportionate number of lawbreakers. Using statistics related to criminal offense and admittance to prison, the highest percentages registered by aliens have tended to be for drunkenness. They also reflect relatively higher numbers in crimes of violence:

Foreigners Incarcerated in Swedish Prisons by Types of Crime (in percentage)

|               | 1975 | 1981 | 1983 | 1985 |
|---------------|------|------|------|------|
| Violent crime | 15   | 23   | 23   | 21   |
| Narcotics     | 5    | 18   | 17   | 15   |

These figures may reflect that native Swedes are able to avoid incarceration for the same crime more easily than foreigners. While it is hard to draw conclusions about the role of aliens in crime rates, it is easier to observe that immigration has changed the face of Sweden since 1960.

## Immigration

Since 1930 Sweden has been more of an immigrant country than a source of emigration. The total number of aliens in Sweden has grown from 35,111 in 1945 to 421,667 in 1980. Immigrant population more than doubled in the sixties, from 190,621 in 1960 to 407,808 in 1970. The immigrants came from various countries and often during specific periods. Germans for example arrived immediately after World War II. Finns have immigrated to Sweden in large numbers since the fifties; they comprise nearly 45 percent of all aliens in the past decade. Yugoslavians, who make up the second largest foreign element, came in large numbers in the sixties, and 38,272 retained their Yugoslavian citizenship in 1984. The primary cause of this immigration has been economic. People either sought jobs or were recruited to fill vacancies. Since the economic difficulties of the mid-seventies, immigration has been strictly limited, with, of course, the exception of Scandinavians (who have freedom to move among the five Nordic states). Sweden's foreign element has grown from 2 percent of the population in 1950 to 5 percent in 1980. Moreover, many aliens have been naturalized. Approximately 4 percent of the population are naturalized citizens. The total percentage of foreign-born in Sweden appears to be approximately 9 percent of the entire population. In addition, this group is younger relatively than the Swedes and has higher fertility rates.

Swedes before 1945 enjoyed a long period of cultural insularity. Proud of their culture and unused to people with different values and ideas, their initial attitude was that either the immigrants would assimilate and become "good Swedes," or they would return to their homelands once the economic circumstances changed. The immigrants were well treated in terms of economic and social services, but their own cultures were ignored. By the late sixties, pressure from the immigrants themselves, especially the Finns, led to a reversal of policy. Instead of assuming a total immersion in Swedish culture, official policy now recognized the uniqueness and worth of each culture. Symbolic of this new policy was the commitment to teach the children of immigrants their own language in Swedish schools. Every immigrant child was promised four hours of instruction per week in his or her parents' native tongue. Cultural diversity became the standard and blended well—at least theoretically—with a commitment of higher education to "internationalize."

In reality, the experience of immigrants in Sweden has been only marginally different than in other Western countries. Recruited to do jobs that Swedes themselves do not want to do, they are to be found predominantly in industrial and lower level, service-sector jobs. With the exception of the Finns and a few well-educated political refugees, immigrants seldom occupy high-ranking positions. Well-treated institutionally, they have found a Swedish society that is not notably flexible. Anti-foreign graffiti began to appear in the sixties. Divisions between the "foreigners" and the Swedes at schools became common. Sporadic violence occurred in a few towns where there were high concentrations of aliens. The foreign language program for children is a sop, perhaps more useful for the jobs it provides immigrant teachers than for the value of the language training.

All immigrants receive extensive Swedish language training, and thus full exposure to Swedish values and principles. That these values stand in direct contrast to many immigrant values was unappreciated until recently. Imagine the dilemma of a woman from a Mediterranean culture who is told in school by Swedes that she is independent and equal to her husband and then goes home to a family that expects her to fill the subservient role of women in her native society. The situation is fraught with difficulty, and it is the immigrants who somehow must resolve the dilemmas. The same is true with the children whose identity as outsiders is reconfirmed by the native language training and, if they are to remain in Sweden, who must compete with their peers in Swedish. The good intentions of official Sweden should not blind us to the real problems of immigrants in Swedish society.

## Education

Education is another area where great change has occurred but not necessarily envisioned. Sweden altered its educational system through two major reforms: the comprehensive school reform that began in 1950 and the reform of postsecondary education that began in 1968. The primary purpose of both of these reforms was to democratize education. Greatly disproportionate numbers of upper-class and urban middle-class children took advantage of the educational opportunities provided by the pre-reform, rigid, elitist system.

The Social Democrats and the Center wanted to change the system so that the people they represented could receive the benefits of a good education. In terms of the comprehensive school reform, fully in place by the late sixties, the rigid stage-examination system was eliminated, curricula were altered, separate schools for academic and trade-oriented students were merged, and the level of classwork was set for average rather than bright students. The advancement of the best students was partially sacrificed so that more students could receive a better education and presumably better employment after school. Jobs in Sweden are frequently awarded on the basis of formal "merit" (i.e., specific qualifications), not necessarily on potential or experience, which means that there is a much higher correlation between specific forms of advanced education and employment opportunities.

The obvious next step was to change postsecondary education. The purpose of postsecondary education in Sweden is educational-employment specific. There is no notion of a broad and "liberal arts" university education. From the outset of their postsecondary educations, students study narrowly defined subjects with the presumption that a set of jobs will be available at the conclusion of their work. Given society's need for well-trained people and the limited resources of a small state, this system was cost-effective.

A coalition of Social Democrats and the Center attempted to increase equality and democracy in higher education after 1968, with mixed results. The reforms of postsecondary education struck at a number of traditional elements: institutions increased in number and the power of the older universities declined; student enrollment grew; decision making within institutions weakened the power of professors within their disciplines; and curricula modification occurred. There was the hope that the social bias of the university student population would be undermined, and that the curriculum would not reflect what was presumed to be the conservative values of the professoriate. New problems began to surface almost immediately.

More students meant that job opportunities for graduates decreased. The quality of many programs declined. Professorial power often found new outlets, and the democratization process had less impact than had been intended. An example of unexpected difficulties was a new system for university admissions. Applicants with work experience were given advantages over students applying directly from gymnasium. This system was intended to encourage "late bloomers" and "second careers." When, however, a forty-five-year-old engineer began his medical studies, it became obvious that the program had to be modified. Sweden could not afford to train older people who would retire before they could "repay" society. Admission policy became even more sensitive when the total number of university places became restricted and competition more rigorous.

Swedish postsecondary education today is not as different from that of the sixties as educational reformers had hoped. A disproportionate number of upper-class and middle-class students continue to exist. Many of the most radical governance changes have settled in and professors' power has grown again. Moreover, there are some new issues related to the schools of technology, which by international standards have traditionally been extremely good. There are questions about the quality of incoming students and about a tendency of some of the best students to seek employment outside Sweden. The potential loss of technocrats bothers a country whose economic well-being depends on its technology and its ability to adjust constantly to a changing international marketplace.

One other area of education deserves notice: continuing education. Swedes are life-long learners. Parliamentary legislation has established guidelines for paid educational sabbatical leaves for all employed persons. Private firms encourage both management and workers to participate in various educational activities. Most major organizations offer a broad variety of evening classes, weekend seminars, and study visits. The range of opportunities for nondegree, self-motivated learning is astounding. Certainly a significant segment of the populace participates yearly in one or more such programs. This fact guarantees a continuing investment in and revitalization of Sweden's human resources.

## Sweden Today

English-speaking writers and politicians talked of the crisis of the welfare state in the late seventies and early eighties. Their claim was that the welfare state had stifled initiative through high taxes and over-bureaucratization. The market was too constrained and inefficient. Swedish economists and others agreed that Sweden had to change course. In many ways, Sweden has changed but not at the expense of the welfare state.

Sweden today is a different country from that a decade ago. It has undergone a structural economic change. No longer are the iron mining, shipbuilding, textile, wearing apparel, shoe making, and timber industries the significant employment sectors. Between 1960 and 1980 there were 150,000 fewer jobs in mining and manufacturing. Employment in agriculture fell by over half in the same period. The greatest growth has been in the service sectors—both public and private. Service-sector jobs employ more people than mining and manufacturing and provide over 36 percent of jobs. Moreover, even in traditional industries such as steel manufacture, production levels have been retained or increased with fewer workers and greater efficiency. Sweden's economic future depends upon its ability to remain competitive in a rapidly changing international marketplace. To do so means that Swedes must innovate new products, control production costs, improve productivity, and market effectively.

There seems to be good evidence that Sweden can meet this challenge. A joint LO-TCO-SAF report published in 1987 underscores the point that if Sweden wishes to avoid increased unemployment and stagnation, wage increases must be minimal over the next decade and any wage increase must be tied to increases in productivity. The ability of the labor market parties to agree on how Sweden must deal with the immediate future is another sign that "the spirit of Saltsjöbaden" has been restored after the turbulence of the seventies. Of course, severe economic problems remain.

The debt question is the most problematic. Despite a decline in the size of the yearly deficit, the total debt continues to grow. Future Swedish governments must begin to reduce the size of the total debt, which can be accomplished primarily by controlling public spending relative to increases in tax revenues. Thorough reexamination of existing programs with consideration for efficiency and effectiveness, as well as a cautious approach toward new reforms, has already begun and will become even more common. Pragmatism has returned to the evolution of the Swedish welfare state after a decade of ideological wishful thinking. There are some hard questions to resolve.

Wage solidarity may be one of the most difficult. The unions have insisted for fifteen years that the incomes of better paid workers grow slowly so that the worst paid could improve their standards more quickly. This policy may also have had the effect of helping strong companies and driving weak ones from the marketplace. Criticism of wage solidarity has been growing from some economists since the early eighties; even Kjell-Olof Feldt has worried publicly about its effects. The issues relate to incentives for key elements of the labor market— highly skilled technocrats and managers, and to productivity. Representatives of white-collar sectors have been particularly insistent on reexamining "wage solidarity." Labor unrest in the eighties has come, to a considerable extent, from white-collar groups, particularly the public sector. Will this unrest continue and will the discipline and hierarchical structure of the unions weaken or collapse? Much of the health of Sweden's economy depends on the answers to these questions.

Indeed the future evolution of the public sector has been a trying dilemma. Frustration over bureaucratic interference and restrictiveness has increased since 1970. Public-sector efficiency is often hard to measure. Yet an effective bureaucracy and public sector are essential. How to eliminate bureaucratic inefficiency while providing needed services will be a delicate problem. Even more difficult to foresee are the consequences of on-going social changes in Swedish society, particularly in the areas of family structure and the impact of a more heterogeneous society. Will the sense of Swedish social solidarity weaken? Will the work ethic be less important? Can Sweden undergo major sociocultural transformations without eroding the foundation of the welfare state itself?

John Logue, a distinguished scholar of modern Scandinavia, has suggested that perhaps the welfare state can work well only for one generation: As the values for individual responsibility and collective solidarity weaken, the ability of the society to sustain the welfare state lessen. It seems clear that both values and norms will continue to change, but it is not necessarily so that these changes will undermine the welfare state — although reform continues to be an on-going process. It is easy for outside observers to miss the fundamental consistencies in Swedish life and to exaggerate the impact of change.

The particular blend of individualism-social solidarity in Sweden has deep roots and shows little sign of being undermined. There has been, and remains, widespread appreciation of the fact that without a strong sense of social solidarity, few opportunities for individual growth exist. Labor market relations, family structure, and treatment of immigrants — all reflect attempts to link the two as society changes. Disagreements naturally exist over how best to achieve a balance in the context of Sweden's need to be competitive internationally. Yet few fundamental questions are raised about the principles.

There have probably been some shifts in the work ethic. Some of these changes were certainly positive. People no longer need to work if they are ill. More people are participating in the form and structure of their work activities and have influence over what constitutes a major portion of their adult life. Some take unfair advantage of the security programs, but personal fulfillment through one's work remains a strong ideal in Sweden. Nor has social solidarity perceptibly weakened.

The Swedish education system from the day-care centers to the universities emphasizes the importance of social solidarity. All the political parties and institutions of society do so as well. The degree of solidarity can be argued and may indeed change on the margin, but, here too, there is little to suggest that it will decline or disappear. On the contrary, individual freedom has grown since the advent of the welfare state. The problems lie with specific programs, their effectiveness, efficiency, and their cost.

No western society is flourishing in this age of constraints and change. Yet Sweden has managed to provide opportunities for its people to work at levels higher than almost any other society and in jobs that are meaningful and well paid. It has sustained basic security for all its citizens. It has encouraged individual growth through education and leisure time activities. It has survived a major economic transformation in a relatively healthy state. Many of its problems are linked to the larger world and shared within it. Specific programs within the system will change and fiscal constraints will make themselves felt. Yet the strength and the wisdom of the linkage between social solidarity and individual liberty remain fundamental in the Swedish welfare state.

Notes and Selected Bibliography

## Abbreviations Used in Notes and Selected Bibliography

| | |
|---|---|
| AHR | American Historical Review |
| ASR | American-Scandinavian Review |
| DSAH | Den svenska arbetarklassens historia |
| DSH | Den svenska historien |
| DSUH | Den svenska utrikespolitikens historia |
| HT | Historisk tidskrift |
| JMH | Journal of Modern History |
| SEHR | The Scandinavian Economic History Review |
| SFGT | Svenska folket genom tiderna: vårt lands kulturhistoria i skildringar och bilder |
| SHGT | Sveriges historia genom tiderna |
| SHVD | Sveriges historia till våra dagar |
| SOU | Statens offentliga utredningar |
| SPHQ | Swedish Pioneer Historical Quarterly |
| SS | Scandinavian Studies |
| SU | Svensk uppslagsbok |

# NOTES

Full references for citations given in shortened form in the notes are provided in the bibliography, which lists general sources and chapter-by-chapter recommendations for further reading.

## Chapter I

1. Gerard De Geer, "Förhistoriska tidsbestämmningar," *Ymer*, 45 (1925): 1–34. Summarized in Jalmar Furuskog, *Vårt Land*, 59–61.
2. Curt Weibull, "Goternas utvandring från Sverige," *Scandia*, 23 (1955–1957):161–186; J. Svennung, "Goternas utvandring — och Vagi Fluvius hos Jordanes," *HT*, 87 (1967): 78–92; J. Svennung, *Zur Geschichte des Goticismus*, in Skrifter utg. av K. humanistiska vetenskapssamfundet i Uppsala, 44: 2B (Stockholm: Almqvist & Wiksell, 1967); Carl-Axel Moberg, *Innan Sverige blev Sverige* in Det levande förflutna, no. 14, 64–70. See also two articles by Lauritz Weibull, "En forntida utvandring från Gotland," *Scandia*, 15 (1943): 267–276, and "Jordanes framställning av Scandza och dess folk," *Nordisk historia*, 1: 43–68.
3. An intriguing theory connecting the Herules with the Icelanders is developed by Barthi Gudmundsson in his *The Origins of the Icelanders*, trans. and ed. Lee M. Hollander (Lincoln: University of Nebraska Press, 1967), 141–142, 165–166.
4. Howard L. Adelson, "Early Medieval Trade Routes," *American Historical Review*, 65 (1960): 271–287. Cf. Sture Bolin, "Olika slag av myntfynd," and "Skattefynd som historiska källor," *Ur penningens historia* (Stockholm: Aldus/Bonnier, 1962), 32–64. See also Gunnar Ekholm, "Handelsvägarna mellan Skandinavien och det Romerska riket," *Scandia*, 10 (1937): 149–164; Sture Bolin, "Muhammed, Karl den Store, och Rurik," *Scandia*, 12 (1939): 181–222.
5. See Sune Lindqvist, *Uppsala högar och Ottarshögen*, Arkeologiska monografier utg. av K. vitterhets, historie och antikvitets akademien no. 23 (Stockholm, 1936).
6. See Jerker Rosén, *Svensk historia*, 1, *Tiden före 1718* (Stockholm: Bonnier, 1962), 89; Elias Wessén, *De nordiska folkstammarna i Beowulf*, in K. vitterhets och antikvitets akademiens handlingar, 36: 2 (Stockholm, 1927); Bernice Grohskopf, *The Treasure of Sutton Hoo* (New York: Atheneum, 1970); R. L. S. Bruce-Mitford, "The Sutton-Hoo ship-burial," appendix to R. H. Hodgkin, *History of the Anglo-Saxons*, third ed. (Oxford: Clarendon, 1952), 2: 696–734.
7. *DSH*, 1: 124–133; Wilhelm Holmqvist et al., *The Golden Age of Viking Art in Sweden* (Stockholm: Historiska museet, 1964 [guide to a traveling exhibit]); Holger Arbman et al., *Vendel i fynd och forskning* (Uppsala: Upplands fornminnesförening, 1938); Haakon Shetelig,

*Classical Impulses in Scandinavian Art from the Migration Period to the Viking Age* (Oslo: Aschehoug, 1949).

The Lapps of the far north lived an existence separate from the Scandinavians, yet they had early developed a culture suited to their needs. Artifacts, pictures, and descriptions in ancient sources such as Procopius, Diaconus, Adam of Bremen, and others show that the Lapps had skis from as early as 1000 B.C. (one is dated by pollen analysis to about 2000 B.C.) and reindeer sleds (Ernst Manker, "Förhistoriska fynd från Samernas land," *Svenska Dagbladet*, April 17, 1968).

8. Shetelig, *Scandinavian Art*, 10.

9. Wilhelm Holmqvist, *Helgö: den gåtfulla ön*.

## Chapter II

1. Holger Arbman, "Forntiden," *SHGT*, 1: 115.

2. Robert Latouche, *The Birth of Western Economy. Economic Aspects of the Dark Ages.* Trans. E. M. Wilkinson (London: Methuen, 1961), 211–235, 309–310; *DSH* 1: 140–175.

3. The Finns to this day call Swedes *Ruotsi*, a word stemming from their word for rowers. Probably the Slavic term *Rus* is but a contraction of *Ruotsi*, although some Russian historians claim the original Rus were a non-Scandinavian people from deep within Slavic lands.

4. Sven Tunberg, *Rod och roslag i det gamla Sveariket*, 4.

5. *Ibid.*, 4–51. Erland Hjärne confirms this interpretation when he writes, "The division into ledung districts was from beginning to end the ledung ship structure imposed upon the community in arms." (Quoted in *HT*, 90 [1970], 291.)

6. In *Heimskringla* Snorri Sturluson says this fateful battle was fought by Olof Skötkonung and Sweyn Forkbeard against Olav Tryggvason in the sea off Rügen. Having weighed the evidence, Lauritz Weibull locates the scene near the island of Ven in Öresund, as Adam of Bremen had stated. (Lauritz Weibull, *Nordisk historia*, 1: 313-330.)

7. Varangian probably meant "oath-sworn" (that is, "men sworn to support each other"). It was used first among the Byzantines, then came to serve throughout the eastern lands as another term for the Rus. See "Varjager" in *SU* and the extensive explanation in the introduction to *The Russian Primary Chronicle* (Laurentian text), trans. and ed. Samuel Hazzard Cross and Olgerd P. Sherbowitz-Wetzor (Cambridge, Mass.: Medieval Academy of America, 1953), 35–50.

8. *The Russian Primary Chronicle*, 58–61.

9. For a treatment much broader than that indicated by the title see Alexander A. Vasiliev, *The Russian Attack on Constantinople in 860* (Cambridge, Mass.: Medieval Academy of America, 1946); S. H. Cross, "Scandinavian Infiltration into Early Russia," *Speculum* 21 (1946): 505–514; George Vernadsky, *The Origins of Russia* (Oxford: Oxford University Press, 1959); Stuart R. Tompkins, "The Varangians in Russian History," *Medieval and Historiographical Essays in Honor of James Westfall Thompson*, ed. J. L. Cate and E. N. Anderson (Chicago: University of Chicago Press, 1938), 465–490; A. Ya. Gurevich, *The Campaigns of the Vikings* (Moscow: Science Publishing House, 1966); Nicholas V. Riasanovsky, *A History of Russia* (New York: Oxford, 1962), 25–30.

10. For an elaborate paean of praise for this bold Viking see C. Raymond Beazley, *The Dawn of Modern Geography* (New York: Peter Smith, 1949), 2: 103–104.

11. John Geipel, *The Viking Legacy*.

12. Sven B. F. Jansson, *The Runes of Sweden*, 135; Jansson, *Svenska utlandsfärder i runinskrifternas ljus*, in Svenska spår i främmande land (Gothenburg: Riksföreningen, 1956), 3: 5, 18, 23, 45.

13. Quoted in A. C. B. Mercer, "Vikings in Ireland," *The Norseman*, 10 (1952): 11.

14. From the *Hávamál*, ancient Norse proverbs, quoted in a slightly different translation by Henry Goddard Leach in his *Pageant of Old Scandinavia* (Princeton: Princeton University Press for the American-Scandinavian Foundation, 1946), 36.

15. Eric Linklater, *The Ultimate Viking* (London: Macmillan, 1955), 8–11, 63, 124.

16. *Kristin Lavransdatter*, trans. Charles Archer (New York: Knopf, 1923) and *Origin of the Icelanders*, trans. Lee M. Hollander (Lincoln: University of Nebraska Press, 1967).

## Chapter III

1. A different and thought-provoking theoretical and comparative approach to the ancient religion of Scandinavia is provided in Georges Dumézil's *Gods of the Ancient Northmen*. Dumézil's intensive research has, in the words of Einar Haugen (who edited the English translation), "restored to Scandinavian and other Indo-European mythologies their backward perspective, revealing them as indigenous products with roots going back to the parent society of the Indo-Europeans" (p. xx).

2. Sven B. F. Jansson, *The Runes of Sweden*, 90. See also *DSH*, 176–180, for more information on the runes and good illustrations.

3. Rimbert, *Anskar: The Apostle of the North, 801–865*. See also Lauritz Weibull, "Ansgarius," *Nordisk historia*, 1: 175–190 (same article published in *Scandia*, 14 (1942). Weibull emphasizes the diplomatic activities of Ansgar, who was an emissary of the emperor as well as of Christ in the north German area.

4. *History of the Archbishops of Hamburg-Bremen by Adam of Bremen*.

5. One of the most interesting and imposing of the stone churches still standing is found at Husaby near Skara in Västergötland; it dates from the eleventh and twelfth centuries. But its predecessors were evidently continental rather than Anglo-Saxon.

6. Quoted in Adolf Schück, "Den äldre medeltiden," *SHGT*, 1: 169.

7. Adam of Bremen, *History*, 203.

8. *Ibid.*, 205.

9. *Ibid.*, 210.

10. G. Hafström, *Land och lag* (Stockholm: Geber, 1959), 14.

11. Jansson, *Runes*, 93.

12. *Ibid.*, 94.

13. *Ibid.*, 100.

14. Kenneth Scott Latourette, *A History of the Expansion of Christianity, II. A Thousand Years of Uncertainty*, A.D. *500*–A.D. *1500* (New York: Harpers, 1938), 79, 139–145, *passim*.

## Chapter IV

1. *Svenska medeltids rimkrönikor*; Ingvar Andersson, *Erikskrönikans författare*, in Svenska Akademiens Minnesteckningar (Stockholm: Norstedt, 1958); R. Pipping, *Kommentar till Erikskrönikan*, Skrifter utg. av Svenska litteratursällskapet i Finland, no. 187 (Helsingfors, 1926).

2. Quoted in Gerhard Hafström, *Land och lag* (Stockholm: Geber, 1959), 17.

3. *Ibid.*, 37–38.

4. *Ibid.*, 39.

5. A *husaby*, though with variant spellings, was found in each of the ten hundreds of Tenhundredland and in each of the eight hundreds of Eighthundredland. Symbols on shields from these places were often dogs, punning on the similarity between *hund* (dog) and hundred, and the kings were called *Hundekonger*. The husaby system of organization was borrowed from Sweden by both Denmark and Norway. See Asgaut Steinnes, "Hundekongen," *Historisk tidsskrift* (Norwegian), 1958: 301–322.

6. Eli F. Heckscher, *An Economic History of Sweden*, 59–60.

7. From an unnamed medieval skald, E. Ingers, *Bonden i svensk historia*, 1: 28.

8. A dramatic account of the spread of the plague and its effects on people's bodies and minds is found in Vilhelm Moberg, *A History of the Swedish People: from Prehistory to the Renaissance*, 123–150.

9. Sven Tunberg, in *SHGT*, 2: 21.

10. This section on law is adapted from the article in *SPHQ*, October 1967, 209–220.

11. Ingers, *Bonden*, 1: 31–32.

12. Quoted in Hafström, *Land och lag*, 19.

13. *Västgötalag*, *passim*. The best modern edition of this and other provincial laws is *Svenska landskapslagar*, edited by Åke Holmbäck and Elias Wessén.

14. *Ibid.*; Stig Jägerskiöld in *DSH*, 1: 256–259.

15. *Dalalagen*, in Holmbäck and Wessén, eds., *Svenska landskapslagar* and cf. vol. 17 of *Corpus Codicum Suecicorum medii aevi*; see also Hafström, *Land och lag*, 65–66.

16. *Ibid.*

17. *Hälsingelagen*, in Holmbäck and Wessén, eds., *Svenska landskapslagar*, 6: 304.

18. Magnus Eriksson's *Landslag* is commonly cited as MELL and the city laws (*Stadslag*) as *MESt*; both edited by Åke Holmbäck and Elias Wessén in *Rättshistorisk bibliotek*, 6 (1962) and 7 (1966).

19. See discussion in Holger Arbman, *Birka, Sveriges äldsta handelsstad* (Stockholm: Thule, 1939); Nils Ahnlund, *Stockholms historia före Gustav Vasa*, 143–147.

20. Sidney Cohen, "The Sea Laws of Visby," paper presented at the American Historical Association meeting in San Francisco, December 1965.

21. Ernst Ekman, "Olaus Petri's *Domareregler*," paper presented at the American Historical Association meeting in San Francisco, December 1965.

22. Ingers, *Bonden*, 1: 53.

23. Hafström, *Land och lag*, 45.

24. Ivan Svalenius, *Gustav Vasa* (Stockholm: Wahlström & Widstrand, 1950), 122.

25. Erik Lönnroth, *Från svensk medeltid*, 13–87; Erik Lönnroth, *Statsmakt och statsfinanser*.

26. The name Folkung is usually applied to the dynasty begun by Birger Jarl and his son Valdemar, which survived until the fall of Magnus Eriksson in the latter half of the fourteenth century and the death of Olof in 1387. Some historians insist that the "genuine Folkungs" were members of a powerful family of the period 1180–1250, descendants of Folke the Thick. This family provided the leadership of the magnates and especially the almost hereditary jarls, most notable being Birger Brosa (1180–1202), Ulf Fasi (?–1248), and Birger Jarl (1248–66). Lawman Eskil and two bishops were older brothers of Birger Jarl. Another theory holds that Folkung originally meant simply folk-king and that the original Folkungs comprised not a family but the members of a petty kings' or magnates' party. It seems quite possible that the latter two meanings were not mutually exclusive. Further it seems possible that Birger Jarl obtained his office through family and/or party support, opposed to strong kingship and to church influence; that he then, when his son Valdemar was made king, solidified his own and Valdemar's position by an alliance with the church and by a Scandinavian dynastic policy. In other words, he was a proper heir of the "genuine" Folkung tradition, but opportunity led him to adopt a new policy, and he made the name Folkung stand for the opposite of what it had meant. See further Erik Lönnroth, "De äkta folkungarnas program," in *Från svensk medeltid*, 13–29; and Sture Bolin, "Folkungarna," *Scandia*, 8 (1935): 210–242.

27. The first Swedish *drots* was named in 1276, and the title was used through the fourteenth century for the king's viceroy or first assistant, with his duties only vaguely defined. From the fifteenth to the end of the eighteenth century the title was used from time to time for the highest judicial officer or occasionally for the head of the law-enforcement administration.

28. This book was a revision for Swedish purposes of Egidio de Colonna's *De Regimine Principum*, which argued the values of absolutism — but not tyranny. Birgitta's visions tended to take the point of view of the magnates among whom she had been brought up. The problem of government by one or by many was a perennial issue and led to the publication of this work in 1634, during Queen Kristina's youth (see Nils Runeby, *Monarchia Mixta* [Uppsala: Svenska Bokförlaget, 1962], 222–224).

29. *Svenska medeltidens rim-krönikor*, ed. A. Rydfors.

30. On Gotland and Visby during this period see *DSH*, 2: 48–69; *SU*, "Gotland"; Johnny Roosval, *Den gotländske ciceronen*, (Visby: Gotlands Turistförening, 1926); Bengt Thordeman, *Korsbetningen*, in Svenska fornminnesplatser (Stockholm: Wahlström & Widstrand, 1932).

31. This section on Birgitta and the section following on Margareta are adapted from "A Saint and a Queen: Two Indomitable Figures of the Fourteenth Century," in *Scandinavian Studies*, ed. Carl F. Bayerschmidt and Erik J. Friis (Seattle: University of Washington Press/American-Scandinavian Foundation, 1965), 373–384.

32. For a thorough discussion of Birgitta's attitude toward the king see Ingvar Andersson's

essay on Birgitta's revelations as a source for Magnus Eriksson's history in *Källstudier till Sveriges historia, 1230–1436* (Lund: Lindströms Bokhandel, 1928), 108–150.

33. See *DSH*, 2: 125–133; Adolf Schück in *SHGT*, 1: 309–316; Conrad Bergendoff, "A Critic of the Fourteenth Century. Saint Birgitta of Sweden," *Medieval and Historiographical Essays in Honor of James Westfall Thompson*, ed. James L. Cate and E. N. Anderson (Chicago: University of Chicago Press, 1938), 3–18; T. Andrae, *Birgitta*; Yngve Brilioth, "Birgitta som religiös personlighet," in [festskrift] *till G. Aulén* (Stockholm, 1939), 52–68; and especially Birgitta's "revelations" — *Himmelska uppenbarelser*, 4 parts, trans. and ed. Tryggve Lundén (Stockholm: Allhem, 1958–1959).

34. This bunglesome title was of course used only for legal purposes. From the first Margareta was known as queen, though her German enemies often referred to her as "Mr. Queen" or "Madame King."

35. These understandings, however, were not in writing, and Michael Linton insists that Margareta did not make any binding promises. See his *Drottning Margareta, fullmäktig fru och rätt husbonde*, Studia historica Gothoburgensis, no. 12 (Gothenburg: Akademiförlaget, 1971), 166–185.

36. Quoted by Sven Tunberg in *SHGT*, 2: 325.

37. Quoted by Halvdan Koht, *Drottning Margareta och Kalmarunionen*, 80.

38. Gösta Johanneson, *Historiska urkunder* (Stockholm: Svenska Bokförlaget/Bonnier, 1957), 1: 140–143. Cf. Tunberg, *SHGT*, 2: 322.

39. *Drottning Margareta och Kalmarunionen* (Stockholm: Natur och Kultur, 1956), 97–123.

40. "Kalmarunionen," in Lönnroth, *Från svensk medeltid*, 94.

## Chapter V

1. Jerker Rosén, *Svensk historia*, 1: 170, 221, 294, 322, 400–401. Among the differing authorities see especially K. G. Westman, *Svenska rådets historia till år 1306* (dissertation; Uppsala, 1904); K. E. Löfqvist, *Om riddarväsen och frälse i nordisk medeltid* (dissertation; Lund, 1935); F. Lagerroth, *Den svenska landslagens författning i historisk och komparativ belysning* Skr. utg. av Fahlb, stiftelsen, no. 32 (Lund, 1947). Löfqvist particularly emphasizes the distinction between the magnates of independent position and the "king's men" who were knights and squires in his *hird*.

2. *DSH*, 2: 299.

3. Sven Ulric Palme, *Sten Sture den äldre*, 292.

4. On the Bloodbath see N. Skyum-Nielsen, *Blodbadet i Stockholm og dets juridiske maskering*. On general developments see, in addition to the citations above: Gottfrid Carlsson, *Medeltidens nordiska unionstanke*; *DSH*, vol. 2; Jerker Rosén, *Sveriges historia*, vol. 1; Erik Lönnroth, "Den svenska riksdagens uppkomst," *Scandia*, 15 (1943): 1–18; Lönnroth, "Kalmarunionen," in *Från svensk medeltid*, 88–101; Lönnroth, "Engelbrekt," *Scandia*, 7 (1934): 1–13; and the general bibliography for the chapter.

5. Carl Grimberg, *Svenska folkets underbara öden*, 1: 449.

6. See Erik Lönnroth in *The Cambridge Economic History of Europe* (Cambridge: The University Press, 1963), 3: 361–396.

7. Charles Edward Hill, *The Danish Sound Dues and the Command of the Baltic. A Study of International Relations* (Durham: Duke University Press, 1926), 28–29.

8. Sven Tunberg, *Riksdagens uppkomst*, 60.

9. *DSH* 2: 240, 260. Dorothea's morning-gift from King Kristofer included the castle of Örebro together with Närke and Värmland. When Kristofer died and Dorothea married the new king, Kristian of Oldenburg, the legal and political problems became acute. See Erik Lönnroth, "Den svenska riksdagens uppkomst," *Scandia*, 15 (1943): 1–18.

10. Tunberg, *Riksdagens uppkomst*, 48; Gösta Johannesson, ed., *Historiska urkunder*, 1: 144–145.

11. Condensed from A. Rydfors, ed., *Svenska medeltidens rim-krönikor*, 31–32.

## Chapter VI

1. Ivan Svalenius, *Gustav Vasa*, 81.
2. *Ibid.*, 122.
3. *Ibid.*, 122.
4. Nils Ahnlund, in *Tradition och historia*, 45.
5. Olaus Petri, *Skrifter i urval*, 101.
6. *Ibid.*, 53–68, *passim*.
7. Ahnlund, *Tradition och historia*, 43–53; *DSH*, 3: 46–54, 55–56; Conrad Bergendoff, *Olavus Petri and the Ecclesiastical Transformation of Sweden, 1521–1552*; Alrik Gustafson, *A History of Swedish Literature*, 56–62; Olaus Petri, *Skrifter i urval*; Petri, *En swensk cröneka.*
8. Svalenius, *Gustav Vasa*, 187; cf. Sven Lundqvist, *Gustav Vasa och Europa*, 107–121.
9. Alf Åberg, *Nils Dacke och landsfadern*, 69.
10. Quoted in Svalenius, *Gustav Vasa*, 236–238 (here somewhat abbreviated in translation). Cf. Gösta Johannesson, *Historiska urkunder till undervisnings tjänst*, vol. 2 (Stockholm: Bonnier, 1957), 18–20.
11. On some of the earlier protests that were answered with armed force see, for example, Tom Söderberg, *Stora Kopparberget under medeltiden och Gustav Vasa* (Stockholm: Pettersons, 1932), 275; *DSH* 3: 86–91; Bertil Boëthius, *Gruvornas, hyttornas, och hamrarnas folk*, in *DSAH*, 77. Åberg's *Nils Dacke* is the scholarly revisionist work. A treatment that is emotionally sympathetic to Dacke and antagonistic toward the "tyrant Gustav Vasa" is Vilhelm Moberg's chapter "The Dacke Rising — Our Greatest Popular Revolt," in his *A History of the Swedish People: from Renaissance to Revolution*, 219–268.
12. Svalenius, *Gustav Vasa*, 256; on Gustav's accumulating wealth see also Michael Roberts, *The Early Vasas*, 177–187.
13. Svalenius, *Gustav Vasa*; Lundqvist, *Gustav Vasa*; Erik Lönnroth, "Gustav Vasa," in his *Från svensk medeltid*, 180–184; Roberts, *The Early Vasas*; Lars-Olof Larsson, "Gustav Vasa och 'den nationella hären,'" *Scandia*, 33 (1967): 250–269; Wilhelm Tham, in *DSUH*, vol. 1, part 2 (1560–1648), 9–35; Nils Ahnlund, *DSUH*, vol. 1, part 1 (tiden före 1560).
14. The best general accounts of the successors of Gustav Vasa are in Sven Ulric Palme, "Vasasönerna," in *SFGT*, 2: 161–286; and Roberts, *The Early Vasas*, 199–469. For Erik XIV see the excellent biography by Ingvar Andersson, *Erik XIV*.
15. Birgitta Odén, "Striden om myntregalet," *HT* (1964), 129–184.
16. See Julian H. Franklin, *Jean Bodin and the Rise of Absolutist Theory* (Cambridge: The University Press, 1973); Nils Runeby, *Monarchia mixta*, 4, 7, 80–81, 121; *DSH*, 3: 260–262.
17. See the four-page essay on "Tre kronor" in *DSH*, 2: 84–87.
18. Roberts, *The Early Vasas*, 250–272; 394–403; Wilhelm Tham, *DSUH*, vol. 1, part 2, 9–100.
19. Oskar Garstein, *Rome and the Counter-Reformation in Scandinavia*, I (1539–1583), Scandinavian University Books (Oslo and Bergen: Universitets forlaget, 1963).
20. Eli F. Heckscher, *Sveriges ekonomiska historia från Gustav Vasa*, I (Stockholm: Bonnier, 1935). See also the condensed English version, *An Economic History of Sweden*, 3–78. A more detailed treatment of the social aspects of the economic life is given by Heckscher in *Svensk arbete och liv, från medeltiden till nutiden* (Stockholm: Bonnier, 1941). An enlightening personal illustration of sixteenth-century economic life from a foreigner's diary is provided by Birgitta Odén in "A Netherlands Merchant in Stockholm in the Reign of Erik XIV," *SEHR*, 10 (1962): 3–37. On general developments the best treatments are Roberts, *The Early Vasas*, and *DSH*, 3.

## Chapter VII

1. Sven Ulric Palme, *Kungligt och kvinnligt*, 109–110; Nils Ahnlund, *Gustav Adolph the Great*, 98–104, 121. And see the characterizations of Hjärne, Martin Weibull, Michael Roberts.
2. Ahnlund, *Gustav Adolph*, 102–103.
3. *Ibid.*, 98.

4. Quoted from *Atlantica*, I, 57, 58, in Ernst Ekman, *JMH*, 34 (March 1962): 61.

5. From Axel Oxenstierna's first foreign policy statement as chancellor, March 1612, quoted in Wilhelm Tham, *DSUH*, vol. 1, part 2 (1560–1648), 96.

6. Sven Lundkvist, "Rörlighet och social struktur i 1610-talets Sverige," *HT*, 94 (1974): 192–258; Jerker Rosén, *Svensk historia*, 1: 502.

7. See map in Michael Roberts, *Gustavus Adolphus: a History of Sweden, 1611–1632*, 1: 80.

8. Roberts, *Gustavus Adolphus*, 2: 331.

9. *Ibid.*, 2: 424.

10. Carl Hallendorff, ed., *Tal och skrifter av konung Gustav II Adolf* (Stockholm: Norstedt, 1915), 114–118 (condensed in translation).

11. The *Wasa*, in its specially constructed museum, became a prime tourist attraction, illustrating early seventeenth-century clothing, food, tools, as well as naval construction. See, for example, Georg Hafström, *En bok om skeppet Wasa* (Stockholm: Christofers, 1959).

12. Sven Lundkvist, "Slaget vid Breitenfeld 1631," *HT*, 83 (1963): 1–38; Roberts, *Gustavus Adolphus*, 2: 537.

13. Ahnlund, *Gustav Adolph*, 298.

14. *Ibid.*, 299. For a survey of recent literature see Ernst Ekman, "Three Decades of Research on Gustavus Adolphus," *JMH*, 38 (1966): 243–255.

15. Roberts, *Gustavus Adolphus*, 1: 278.

16. *Ibid.*, 1: 332.

17. Sven Nilsson, "1634 års regeringsform," *Scandia*, 10 (1937): 1–37.

18. Alf Åberg, "Arms and the Men," *Industria International, 1962*, 146.

19. Roberts, *Gustavus Adolphus*, 2: 7–8.

20. Alf Åberg, quoted in *Nordisk tidskrift för bok- och biblioteksväsen*, no. 3 (1965), 65.

21. Kurt Ågren, *Adelns bönder och kronans*; Bertil Boëthius, *Gruvornas, hyttornas och hamrarnes folk*, 220; Harold R. Shurtleff, *The Log Cabin Myth, a Study of the Early Dwellings of English Colonists in North America* (Cambridge: Harvard University Press, 1939).

22. Amandus Johnson, *The Swedish Settlements on the Delaware, 1638–1664*, 2 vols. (Philadelphia: University of Pennsylvania Press, 1911); abridged as *The Swedes on the Delaware* (Philadelphia; Lenapé, 1914); Israel Acrelius, *A History of New Sweden; or, The Settlements on the River Delaware*, trans. William M. Reynolds (Philadelphia: Historical Society of Pennsylvania, 1874); Nils Jacobsson, ed., *Per Lindeströms resa till Nya Sverige, 1653–1656* (Stockholm: Wahlström & Widstrand, 1923); *DSH*, 4: 182–187; Allan Kastrup, *The Swedish Heritage in America* (St. Paul: Swedish Council of America, 1975), 18–55, and see the bibliography therein.

23. Roberts, *Gustavus Adolphus*, 1: 369.

24. *Ibid.*, 1: 361.

25. Wilhelm Edström, in *Svenska Dagbladet*, January 21, 1975.

26. David Gaunt, *Utbildning till statens tjänst*.

27. Sforza Pallavicino, as quoted in Curt Weibull, *Drottning Christina*, 2nd ed. (Stockholm: Natur och Kultur, 1934), 94 (and see the English ed., 60).

28. Weibull, *Christina of Sweden*, 63 (and see the Swedish ed., 99).

29. Christina, *Självbiografi och aforismer*, 77–112, *passim*.

30. Sir Bulstrode Whitelocke, *A Journal of the Swedish Embassy in the Years 1653 and 1654*, rev. ed. by Henry Reeve (London: Longman, Brown, Green, & Longmans, 1855).

31. Two volumes of historical fiction that are sensitive and interestingly interpretive are Ruth Stephan's *The Flight* (New York: Knopf, 1956) and *My Crown, My Love* (New York: Knopf, 1960).

32. Weibull, *Drottning Christina*, 132.

## Chapter VIII

1. Nils Sylvan, *SHGT*, 3: 46.

2. Curt Weibull, "Tåget över Belt," *Scandia*, 19 (1948–1949): 1–35.

3. See also Finn Askgaard, *Kampen om Östersjön 1654–1660* (Köpenhamn: Nyt Nordisk Forlag, 1975); Sven Ingemar Olofsson, *Karl X Gustaf*; B. Kentrschynskyj, *Karl X Gustav inför krisen i öster, 1654–1655* (Karolinska Förbundets Årsbok, 1956), 7–140; Georg Landberg, *DSUH*, vol. 1, part 3 (1648–1697).

4. F. Lagerroth, *Frihetstidens författning* (dissertation; Lund, 1915), 173.

5. Landberg, *DSUH*, vol. 1, part 3, 125–153.

6. Sylvan, *SHGT*, 3: 84.

7. Michael Roberts, "Charles XI," *History*, 50 (1965): 160–192 (also in Roberts, *Essays in Swedish History*, 226–268). This is a strong appreciation of the achievements of a methodical, obstinate, far from brilliant man. Roberts quotes the declaration of the principle of sovereignty of 1693: Karl XI "is by God, Nature, and the crown's high hereditary right . . . an absolute sovereign king, whose commands are binding upon all, and who is responsible to no one on earth for his actions, but has power and might at his pleasure, as a Christian king, to rule and govern his kingdom." For a nineteenth-century appreciation see "Geijers föreläsningar över Karl XI:s historia," *Geijerstudier*, II (Uppsala: Almqvist & Wiksell, 1955). For an excellent study of one of the most influential advisers of the king in his early years see Göran Rystad, *Johan Gyllenstierna*. See also Alf Henrikson, *Svensk historia*, 2: 608–612.

8. Sam Clason, *Till reduktionens förhistoria*, 198.

9. Under "reduce" Webster's second edition lists as meanings obsolete or rare "to bring back," or "to restore." It is in this sense, stemming from the Latin *reducere*, that the Swedes used the term *reduktion*. It seemed also to connote "to bring into a certain order, arrangement . . . to bring under rules." Hence it is best to retain the Swedish term instead of translating to the less accurate "redemption" or "reversion."

10. *SU*, "Reduktion," 991.

11. Sylvan, *SHGT*, 3: 123.

12. John Robinson, *An Account of Sweden*, 2nd ed., 41, 42. For the most thorough treatment of the early phases of the reform see Stellan Dahlgren, *Karl X Gustav och reduktionen*; and for the later phase see Ola Lindquist, *Jakob Gyllenborg och reduktionen*, Bibliotheca historica Lundensis, no. 4 (Lund: Gleerup, 1956).

13. Roberts, "Charles XI"; S. Ågren, "Karl XIs indelningsverk för armén" (dissertation; Uppsala, 1922).

14. Erik Dahlberg, *Suecia antiqua et hodierna*.

15. Jerker Rosén, *DSUH*, vol. 2, part 1 (1697–1721), 41.

16. Sylvan, *SHGT*, 3: 154.

17. Claude Nordmann, *Grandeur et liberté de la Suède*, 222, 224; Otto Haintz, *König Karl XII von Schweden*; Ragnhild Hatton, *Europe in the Age of Louis XIV* (New York: Harcourt, Brace & World, 1969); Hatton, *Charles XII of Sweden*; John J. Murray, "The Görtz-Gyllenborg Arrests — A Problem in Diplomatic Immunity," *JMH*, 28 (1956): 325–337.

## Chapter IX

1. Holstein-Gottorp was a patchwork of lands at the base of the Jutland Peninsula that was, for the Swedes, the back door to Denmark through which they had repeatedly invaded (most notably in 1643 and 1658), and the Danes had ample reason to dread an actual union of the duchy with Sweden.

2. *Frihetstidens författning*.

3. Michael Roberts, *Swedish and English Parliamentarianism*, 10, 28–29, 35; see also Ludvig Stavenow, *Frihetstiden: dess epoker och kulturliv*, 152–153.

4. Sten Carlsson, *Byråkrati och borgarstånd under frihetstiden*, 139–152.

5. Roberts, *Swedish and English*, 31, 37.

6. Claude Nordmann, *Grandeur et liberté*, 248–266; H. Arnold Barton, "Russia and the Problem of Sweden-Finland, 1721–1809," *East European Quarterly*, 5: 431–455.

7. Birger Sallnäs, in *DSH*, 6: 70–73.

8. Barton "Russia and the Problem"; *DSH*, 6: 110; Olof Jägerskiöld in *DSUH*, vol. 2, part 2 (1721–1792).

9. Quoted by Walfrid Holst, "Frihetstiden," in *SHGT*, 3: 369; see further F. Lagerroth, *Frihetstidens författning*, 421.

10. Barton, "Russia and the Problem," 444.

11. Stavenow, *Frihetstiden*, 123–134.

12. On this period of exceptional confusion see, in addition to the works cited above, Alf Henrikson, *Svensk historia*, 686–687; Gunnar Olsson, "Fredrik den store och Sveriges författning," *Scandia*, 27 (1961): 337–366; Nordmann, *Grandeur et liberté*, 276–280; Beth Hennings, *Gustav III som kronprins*, 335–373. Prince Gustav as early at 1768 considered that revolution was the only way to achieve an effective government.

13. P. Gunnar Andersson, *Svenska snillen*, 98–144.

14. Nils von Hofsten in *Swedish Men of Science*, 33–41.

15. Sten Lindroth in *Swedish Men of Science*, 42–49.

16. Walfrid Holst in *SHGT*, 3: 34–343; Lindroth in *Swedish Men of Science*, 50–58; Bryn J. Hovde, *The Scandinavian Countries* (Boston: Chapman, Grimes, 1943), 27, 123, 304.

17. Andersson in *Svenska snillen*, 145–172; N. V. E. Nordenmark in *Swedish Men of Science*, 66–73.

18. Nordmann, *Grandeur et liberté*, 319.

19. Quoted by Wolfram Kock in *Swedish Men of Science*, 78.

20. Nordmann, *Grandeur et liberté*, 314–317; Arvid Hj. Uggla, *Linnaeus*.

21. Hans Krook, "En Linnaean i Japan," *Svenska Dagbladet*, August 6, 1975; Per Kalm, *Resa till Norra Amerika*; Raymond Phineas Stearns, *Science in the British Colonies of America*.

22. Lindroth in *Swedish Men of Science*, 105–112; Andersson in *Svenska snillen*, 215–243.

23. Hugo Olsson in *Swedish Men of Science*, 131–140; Andersson, *Svenska snillen*, 244–268.

24. Lars Ohlon in *Swedish Men of Science*, 149.

25. *Ibid.*, 141–150; Andersson, *Svenska snillen*, 269–317.

26. Ragnhild Hatton, *Europe in the Age of Louis XIV*; Kurt Samuelsson, *From Great Power to Welfare State*; *DSH*, 6: 12; Stavenow, *Frihetstiden*, 64.

27. See William L. Langer, "Europe's Initial Population Explosion," *AHR*, 69 (1963): 1–17.

28. Utterström, "Population and Agriculture," *SEHR*, 9 (1961): 176–194; Gunnar Olander, "Hemmansklyvningen i Skaraborgs län vid mitten av 1700-talet," *Scandia*, 20: 118–126.

29. E. Ingers, *Bonden i svensk historia*, 2: 11–311; Samuelsson, *From Great Power*, 72; Stavenow, *Frihetstiden*, 286–287; Bertil Boëthius, *Gruvornas, hyttornas och hamrarnas folk*, 268, 274.

30. Hovde, *The Scandinavian Countries*, 80–88.

31. Samuelsson, *From Great Power*, 92; see also Gunnar Arpi, "The Swedish Ironmasters' Association," *SEHR*, 8 (1960): 77–90; Sigvard Montelius, et al., *Fagerstabrukens historia*.

32. Samuelsson, *From Great Power*, 96–101.

33. *Ibid.*, 88–93; F. D. Scott, ed., "Swedish Trade with America in 1820: a Letter of Advice from Baron Axel Klinkowström," *JMH*, 25 (1953): 407–414.

34. Eli F. Heckscher, "Den svenska kopparhanteringen under 1700-talet," *Scandia*, 13 (1940): 22–89; Sven-Erik Åström, "The Transatlantic Tar Trade," *SEHR*, 12 (1964): 86–90; cf. Herbert Osgood, *The American Colonies in the Eighteenth Century*, 4 vols. (New York: Columbia University Press, 1924–25), 1: 495.

35. *DSH*, 6: 158–167; Eskil Olán, *Ostindiska compagniets saga*; G. K. Troili, *Ur handelns och sjöfartens häfder*.

36. Excerpts are given in *DSH*, 6: 156–157.

37. H. S. K. Kent, *War and Trade in Northern Seas*, 112–129.

## Chapter X

1. See, e.g., Georg Landberg, *Gustav III inför eftervärlden*, 2nd ed. (Stockholm: Proprius, 1968), 11–12.

2. Robert Nisbet Bain, *Gustavus III and His Comtemporaries*, 37–38.

3. Beth Hennings, *Gustav III och Grevinnan de Boufflers: En brevväxling från vänskapskultens tidevarv*.

4. H. Arnold Barton, "Gustav III and the Enlightenment," *Eighteenth Century Studies*, 6 (1972): 10, 11.

5. Beth Hennings, *Gustav III. En biografi*, 55.

6. Sten Carlsson, *Svensk historia*, 2: 204.

7. Photocopy in Amandus Johnson Collection, American Swedish Historical Foundation, Philadelphia, dated February 26, 1779.

8. Stig Boberg, *Gustav III och tryckfriheten, 1774–1787*.

9. Paul Britten Austin, "The Fatal Day of Axel Fersen," *Industria International 1962*, 134–138.

10. H. Arnold Barton, "Sweden and the War of American Independence," *William and Mary Quarterly*, 3rd series, 23 (1966): 408–430; Adolph B. Benson, "Our First Unsolicited Treaty," *ASR* 7 (1919): 43–49; Harald Elovson, "De svenska officererna i nordamerikanska frihetskriget," *Scandia*, 2 (1929): 314–327; Allan Kastrup, *The Swedish Heritage in America*, 84–102.

11. Ingegerd Hildebrand, *Den svenska kolonien S:t Barthélemy och Västindiska Kompaniet fram till 1796* (Lund: Lindstedt, 1951). Creutz to Gustav III, March 7, 1779 (Amandus Johnson Collection, American Swedish Historical Foundation).

12. Erik Lönnroth, "Gustav III of Sweden: the Final Years. A Political Portrait," *Scandinavica*, 6 (1967): 16–25.

13. Hennings, *Gustav III*, 90.

14. Alrik Gustafson, *A History of Swedish Literature*, 119.

15. Paul Britten Austin, *The Life and Songs of Carl Michael Bellman, Genius of the Swedish Rococo*, 112 and frontispiece; *DSH*, 7: 255.

16. *Historisk statistik*, 2: 45, 46. See also E. Ingers, *Bonden i svensk historia*, vol. 2.

17. Quoted by Lauritz Weibull, *Scandia*, 23 (1955–1957): 215.

18. *Ibid.*, 217.

19. Ingers, *Bonden*, 2: 460.

20. *Ibid.*, 492.

21. Carlsson, *Svensk historia*, 2: 285-286.

22. Johan Ludvig Runeberg, *The Tales of Ensign Stål* (New York and Princeton: American-Scandinavian Foundation, 1938). See also Gustafson, *History of Swedish Literature*, esp. 221–229.

23. Harald Hultman, *Prinsen av Vasa* (Stockholm: Bonniers, 1974).

24. Quoted by Lydia Wahlström, *SHGT*, 3: 614.

25. Quoted by Sam Clason, *SHVD*, 11: 113.

26. H. Arnold Barton, "Late Gustavian Autocracy in Sweden: Gustav IV Adolf and His Opponents, 1792–1809," *SS*, 46 (1974): 272.

27. H. Arnold Barton, "The Swedish Succession Crises of 1809 and 1810, and the Question of Scandinavian Union," *SS*, 42 (1970): 309–333.

28. H. Arnold Barton, *Count Hans Axel von Fersen*, 362–403.

## Chapter XI

1. Torvald Höjer, *Carl XIV Johan*, 2: 31–34.

2. *Ibid.*, 29.

3. Sam Clason, *SHVD*, 11: 189n.

4. Höjer in *SHGT*, 4: 48.

5. See Franklin D. Scott, "American Influences in Norway and Sweden," *JMH*, 18 (1946): 38–39.

6. Höjer, *Carl XIV Johan*, 1: 57.

7. Franklin D. Scott, *Bernadotte and the Fall of Napoleon*, 90.

8. Höjer, *Carl XIV Johan*, 2: 228–231; cf. Scott, *Bernadotte and the Fall*, 144–148.

9. F. D. Scott, "Bernadotte and the Throne of France," *JMH*, 5 (1933): 465–478; Scott, "Karl Johans kandidatur till franska kronan 1814. Några dokument," *HT* 54 (1934): 271–280; Scott, "Benjamin Constant's 'Projet' for France in 1814," *JMH*, 7 (1935): 41–48.

## Chapter XII

1. *DSUH*, vol. 3, parts 1–2 (1792–1844), 241–254.

2. *DSUH*, vol. 3, part 3 (1844–1872), 62–118; Paul Knaplund, "Finmark in British Diplomacy, 1836–1855," *AHR*, 30 (1925): 478–502; Edgar Anderson, "The Crimean War in the Baltic Area," paper read at Second Conference on Baltic Studies, San José, California, 1970 (see *Summary of Proceedings, Association for the Advancement of Baltic Studies*, 1971, 168–169); Sven Eriksson, *Svensk diplomati och tidningspress under Krimkriget* (Stockholm: Norstedt, 1939); C. F. Palmstierna, *Sverige, Ryssland och England, 1833–1855 Kring Novembertraktatens förutsättningar* (Stockholm: Norstedt, 1932); Paul Knaplund, "Nye oplysninger om Novembertraktatens forhistorie," *Historisk Tidsskrift* (Norwegian), 5.r.,6.b. (1924): 213–258; C. F. Palmstierna, "Sweden and the Russian Bogey," *The Nineteenth Century and After*, 113 (1933): 739–754.

3. An interesting contemporary expression of pan-Scandinavianism combined with an appeal for action against Russia is G. Lallerstedt, *La Scandinavie, ses craintes et ses espérances* (Paris: E. Dentu, 1856). See also *DSUH*, vol. 3, part 3, 15–20, 119–122.

4. Lawrence Steefel, *The Schleswig-Holstein Question* (Cambridge: Harvard University Press, 1932); *DSUH*, vol. 3, part 3, 21–61, 119–234.

5. *DSUH*, vol. 3, part 4 (1872–1914), 326.

6. Raymond E. Lindgren, *Norway-Sweden: Union, Disunion, and Scandinavian Integration*, 28.

7. Jörgen Weibull, *Inför unionsupplösningen 1905*, 152.

8. Quoted by Wilhelm Keilhau, *Det norske folks liv og historie* (Oslo: Aschehoug, 1935), 10: 117.

9. *Ibid.*, 281.

10. Lindgren, *Norway-Sweden*, 131.

11. On the problems of the union and its dissolution, out of the voluminous literature in memoirs and historical writing and in addition to the titles mentioned above and in the bibliography, see: Stig Hadenius, *Fosterländsk unionspolitik. Majoritetspartiet, regeringen, och unionsfrågan, 1888–1899*; Sune Jungar, *Ryssland och den svensk-norska unionens upplösning. Tsardiplomati och rysk-finländsk pressopinion kring unionsupplösning från 1880 till 1905* (Åbo: Åbo Akademien, 1969); Johan Ernst W. Sars, *Norges politiske historie*, 1815–1885.

## Chapter XIII

1. Sten Carlsson, *Ståndssamhälle och ståndspersoner 1700–1865*, especially 192–194.

2. *Ibid.*

3. *Historisk statistik*, 1: 36–47.

4. Arthur Montgomery, *Svensk socialpolitik under 1800-talet*, 19.

5. Arthur Montgomery, *Rise of Modern Industry in Sweden*, 60–62.

6. Montgomery, *Svensk socialpolitik*, 87.

7. *Ibid.*, 83.

8. See especially Birgitt Gejvall-Seger, "Stockholms hyreshusbebyggelse på 1800-talet," in *Historia kring Stockholm. Från frihetstiden till sekelskiftet* (Stockholm: Wahlström & Widstrand, 1967), 98.

9. Brynjolf J. Hovde, *The Scandinavian Countries, 1720–1865*, 576–582.

10. From *The Covenant Hymnal* (Chicago: Covenant Press, 1973), hymn no. 382 (see *SPHQ*, 25 [1974]: 110).

11. Franklin D. Scott, "Jacob Letterstedt and Nordic Cooperation," in J. Iverne Dowie and J. Thomas Tredway, eds., *The Immigration of Ideas* (Rock Island: Augustana Historical Society, 1968), 15–28.

12. Christina Stael von Holstein Bogoslovsky, *The Educational Crisis in Sweden in the Light of American Experience* (New York: Columbia University Press, 1932), 103.

13. Hilding Danielson, *Till Carl Rudenschiölds Biografi* (Lund: Gleerup, 1922); Rolland Paulston, *Educational Change in Sweden* (New York: Teachers College Press, 1968).

14. Frederic Fleisher, *The New Sweden* (New York: David McKay, 1967), 24.
15. Alrik Gustafson, *A History of Swedish Literature*, 187. See also John Wordsworth, *The National Church of Sweden*.
16. Wordsworth, *National Church of Sweden*, 365.
17. Berndt Gustafsson, *Socialdemokratien och kyrkan, 1881–1890*; Carl-Henrik Brodin, manuscript of 1969.
18. Wordsworth, *National Church of Sweden*, 366.
19. *Ibid.*, 367.
20. David Nyvall, *My Father's Testament* (Chicago: Covenant Press, 1974); Bengt Sundkler, *Svenska Missionssällskapet, 1835–1876*.
21. See Paul Elmen, *Wheat Flour Messiah* (Chicago: Swedish Pioneer Historical Society, 1976); Olov Isaksson and Sören Hallgren, *Bishop Hill, A Utopia on the Prairie* (Chicago: Swedish Pioneer Historical Society, 1969).
22. *DSH*, 9: 84–87.
23. *DSH*, 8: 192–195; Gustafson, *History of Swedish Literature*, 204–213.
24. *DSH*, 8: 281–282, 284–289 and 9: 192–195; Gunnar Quist, *Fredrika Bremer och kvinnans emancipation* (Gothenburg: Akademiförlaget, 1969); Greta Wieselgren, *Den höga tröskeln*. *Kampen för kvinnas rätt till ämbete* (Lund: Gleerup, 1969). The latter two items are, respectively, no. 8 and no. 7 in Kvinnohistorisk Arkiv.
25. Maj Gullstedt in *Svenska Dagbladet*, August 1, 1968; Lars Gurmund, interview, 1953; Franklin D. Scott, *Scandinavia*, 85–87; and on the situation in the mid-twentieth century the best treatment is Birgitta Linnér, *Sex and Society in Sweden* (New York: Pantheon/Random House, 1967). See also Richard F. Tomasson, "A Millennium of Sexual Permissiveness in the North," *ASR*, 62 (1974): 370–378.
26. *DSH*, 9: 35.
27. Franklin D. Scott, *Baron Klinkowström's America, 1818–1820*.
28. Scott, *Wertmüller: Artist and Immigrant Farmer*.
29. Sten Almquist, "The Knave of Fallebo," *SPHQ*, 27 (1976): 6–25.
30. See note 21.
31. H. Arnold Barton, ed., *Letters from the Promised Land*, 268.
32. *Ibid.*, 275.
33. Lars Ljungmark, *For Sale — Minnesota: Organized Promotion of Scandinavian Immigration, 1866–1873* (Chicago: Swedish Pioneer Historical Society, 1971).
34. Allan Kastrup, *The Swedish Heritage in America*, 275; W. W. Thomas, *Sweden and the Swedes* (Chicago: Rand, McNally, 1892).
35. *Emigrationsutredningen: Betänkande*, 3.
36. *Ibid.*, 6–11.
37. Brynjolf J. Hovde, "Notes on the Effects of Emigration upon Scandinavia," *JMH*, 6 (1934): 268 n. 51.
38. *Emigrationsutredningen*, 7: 144.
39. *Ibid.*, 150.
40. *Ibid.*, 229.
41. *Ibid.*, 176.
42. Knut Wicksell, *Om utvandringen* (Stockholm, 1882), 97.
43. Eli F. Heckscher, *Svenskt arbete och liv* (Stockholm: Bonnier, 1941), 340.
44. Scott, "Sweden's Constructive Opposition to Emigration," *JMH*, 37 (1965): 328–330.
45. *Svenska Dagbladet*, January 19, 1976.
46. Some of the rapidly expanding publications on Swedish emigration have been mentioned in these notes and in the bibliography for the chapter. Space is lacking here to list much of this new research, which happily departs from the often fileo-pietistic emphasis of earlier writings and assumes an objective tone, frequently putting stress on quantitative methods. In the 1960s and the early 1970s an extensive Migration Research Project at the University of Uppsala resulted in a number of doctoral dissertations, notably Sture Lindmark's *Swedish America, 1914–1932* (Uppsala and Chicago: Swedish Pioneer Historical Society, 1971) and Ulf Beijbom's *Swedes in*

*Chicago. A Demographic and Social Study of the 1846–1880 Immigration* (Uppsala and Chicago: Chicago Historical Society, 1971). Several of the later studies are epitomized in *From Sweden to America. A History of the Migration*, ed. Harald Runblom and Hans Norman (Uppsala and Minneapolis: University of Minnesota Press, 1976), a volume which also contains an extensive bibliography. For the more recent American publications the best source and guide is *The Swedish Pioneer Historical Quarterly* (1950 to the present).

## Chapter XIV

1. Quoted in Douglas V. Verney, *Parliamentary Reform in Sweden, 1866–1921*, 21.

2. *Ibid.*, 35; Berit Borell, *De svenska liberalerna och representationsfrågan på 1840-talet*, 36 and *passim*.

3. Cf. Alrik Gustafson, *A History of Swedish Literature*, 176, for another translation.

4. Verney, *Parliamentary Reform*, 50; Stig Hadenius, ed., *Kring demokratins genombrott i Sverige*, 13; Brynjolf J. Hovde, *The Scandinavian Countries, 1720–1865*, 572; Nils Edén, *Den svenska riksdagen under femhundra år*, 258.

5. Erik Lindorm, *Carl XIV Johan — Carl XV och deras tid, 1810–1872*, 428.

6. A feature article in *Dagens Nyheter*, November 14, 1954, gives a vivid description of both riksdag and city during the days of the voting.

7. *Ibid.*

8. Louis De Geer, *Minnen*, 2: 37.

9. *DSH*, 9: 12.

10. Adolf Hedin in Valfrid Spångberg, ed., *Tal och skrifter*, 10.

11. Kurt Samuelsson, *From Great Power to Welfare State*, 171.

12. *DSH*, 9: 208–209; Ebbe Gyllenstierna in *Svenska Dagbladet*, May 16, 1956; Lars Danius, *Samhället och försvaret* (Stockholm: Medborgarskolans förlag, 1956).

13. Stig Hadenius et al., *Sverige efter 1900*, 24. The remark about "talking Swedish" created such an uproar in Norway that it led to the dismissal of Åkerhielm.

14. Sven Ulric Palme, *På Karl Staaffs tid*, 117–121, which is one of the best accounts of this tense period.

15. Quoted by Torbjörn Vallinder in Stig Hadenius, ed., *Kring demokratins genombrott*, 25–26.

16. *Ibid.*, 26.

17. *Ibid.*, 51.

18. *Historisk statistik, III*, 270.

19. *DSH*, 9: 162.

20. *Ibid.*, 212–227; Sven Lundkvist, "Popular Movements and Reforms, 1900–1920," in Steven Koblik, ed., *Sweden's Development from Poverty to Affluence*, 180–196.

21. Edén, *Den svenska riksdagen*, 275.

## Chapter XV

1. Hilding Johansson, *Folkrörelserna och det demokratiska statsskicket i Sverige*, 59.

2. *Ibid.*, 52.

3. *Ibid.*, 59. See also Sven Lundkvist, "Popular Movements and Reforms, 1900–1920," in Steven Koblik, ed., *Sweden's Development from Poverty to Affluence*, 177–193.

4. Quoted in Johansson, *Folkrörelserna*, 78.

5. *DSH*, 9: 165–168.

6. Torvald Karlbom, *Den svenska fackföreningsrörelsen*, 21.

7. *Ibid.*, 21; *DSH*, 9: 160.

8. Karlbom, *Fackföreningsrörelsen*, 26.

9. This and other documents are reproduced in Karlbom, *Fackföreningsrörelsen*, 28–30.

10. *Ibid.*, 35.

11. *Statistisk årsbok för Sverige* (Stockholm: Norstedt, annual), 1954: 221; 1970: Table 234.

12. *DSH*, 9: 160, 248.
13. This paragraph later became number 35, and in the 1970s it was known as paragraph 32.
14. The most thorough study of the background of the General Strike is Bernt Schiller, *Storstrejken 1909: förhistoria och orsaker*. See also Kurt Samuelsson, *From Great Power to Welfare State*, 202, 219–220.
15. For the early years see Karlbom, *Fackföreningsrörelsen*, 261; for the later, *Statistisk årsbok 1973*, 239.
16. Jörgen Westerståhl, "Demokrati och fackföreningsrörelser," in Stig Hadenius, ed., *Kring demokratins genombrott i Sverige*, 136–173.
17. Axel Gjöres, *Co-operation in Sweden*, 22.
18. *Ibid.*, 46–47.
19. Herbert Tingsten, *Den svenska socialdemokratiens idéutveckling*, 2: 371–400.
20. Douglas V. Verney, *Parliamentary Reform in Sweden, 1866–1921*, 137–158.
21. Leif Kihlberg, *Karl Staaff*, 1: 178.
22. First choice for the premiership was Alfred Petersson of Påboda, usually known simply as Påboda, who had been minister of agriculture in the Lundeberg cabinet. Påboda was the first peasant farmer to serve as a minister, and in the course of his career he was four times minister of agriculture. He was a strong, dependable personality who liked to retain more independence than he could enjoy as a member of the ministry, and hence he was something of a problem to his various prime ministers; in part this was also because he started out as a good conservative but swung toward the liberal camp.
23. Ivar Anderson, *Arvid Lindman och hans tid*, 111.
24. Sven Ulric Palme, *På Karl Staaffs tid*, 157–164.
25. Douglas V. Verney, "The Foundations of Modern Sweden: The Swift Rise and Fall of Swedish Liberalism," *Political Studies*, 20 (1972): 56.
26. See Johan Hellner in W. Odelberg, ed., *Minnen och dagböcker*, 191–229; see also Playford Thorson, "The Defense Question in Sweden, 1911–1914" (unpublished manuscript).
27. *Den svenska socialdemokratiens idéutveckling*.
28. *DSH*, 9: 161. Cf. article by Tage Erlander on August Palm in *SU*.
29. *DSH*, 9: 224.
30. Tingsten, *Socialdemokratiens idéutveckling*, 1: 78. See also Jean Braconier, "Till minnet av Hjalmar Branting," *Sydsvenska Dagbladet*, February 16, 1975.
31. See Berndt Gustafsson, *Socialdemokratien och kyrkan, 1881–1890*.
32. K. J. Höjer, *Svensk socialpolitisk historia*, 51–52.
33. From Staaff's diary, quoted by Axel Brusewitz in *Scandia*, 23 (1947): 181.
34. Raymond Fusilier, *Le parti socialiste suédois: son organisation*; Karlbom, *Fackföreningsrörelsen*; O. Fritiof Ander, *The Building of Modern Sweden*; Donald Blake, "Swedish Trade Unions and the Social Democratic Party: The Formative Years," *SEHR*, 8 (1960): 19–44.

## Chapter XVI

1. Walt W. Rostow, "Rostow on Growth," *The Economist* 192 (August 15, 1959): 413. See also Rostow's controversial *Stages of Economic Growth*, 2nd ed. (Cambridge: Cambridge University Press, 1971).
2. Alva and Gunnar Myrdal, *Kris i befolkningsfrågan* (Stockholm, Bonnier, 1934), translated as *Nation and Family: the Swedish Experiment in Democratic Family and Population Policy*; Folke Borg, *Ett döende folk* (Stockholm: Geber, 1935).
3. Colin Clark, *The Conditions of Economic Progress* (London: Macmillan, 1940).
4. Hans Modig, *Järnvägarnas efterfrågan och den svenska industrin, 1860–1914*, 136; Ernst Söderlund, "The Placing of the First Swedish Railway Loan," *SEHR*, 11: 43–59; Bengt Holgersson and Eric Nicander in *Economy and History*, 11: 3–51; Sverker Oredsson, "Försvarsintresset omkring 1890, järnvägsbyggandet och Sveriges strategiska läge," *Scandia*, 34 (1968): 287–310.

5. See especially Lennart Jörberg, *Growth and Fluctuations of Swedish Industry, 1869–1912*; Ernst Söderlund, *Swedish Timber Exports, 1850–1950*; Söderlund, "Företagsorganisation och företagsledning inom trävaruindustrin," in Ragnhild Lundström, ed., *Kring industrialismens genombrott i Sverige*, 51, 59.

6. S. Montelius, "Recruitment and Conditions of Life of Swedish Ironworkers during the 18th and 19th Centuries," *SEHR*, 14 (1966): 1–17; *Sveriges industri* (1967): 37–39.

7. Gösta Adelswärd, *En historia om forskraft*; Adelswärd, *Hans Majestäts skål i Åtvidaberg: Oscar II inviger en järnväg* (offprint from *Östergötland 1972* [Meddelanden från Östergötlands och Linköpings stads museem], 1972); Adelswärd, *Varaktigare än kopparn. Åtvidaberg, 1413–1963*.

8. Tom Söderberg, *Hantverkarna i genombrottsskedet, 1870–1920*; Kurt Samuelsson, *Hur vår moderna industri vuxit fram*.

9. See Filip Hjulström, "Elektrisk kraftöverföring och elektrifiering av stor industri," in Ragnhild Lundström, ed., *Kring industrialismens genombrott*, 144–156.

10. Bertil Boëthius, "Jernkontoret and the Credit Problems of the Swedish Ironworks: a Survey," *SEHR*, 10 (1962): 105–115; Olle Gasslander, *History of Stockholm's Enskilda Bank to 1914*; J. Potter, "The Role of a Swedish Bank in the Process of Industrialization," *SEHR*, 11 (1963): 62–72.

11. Bertil Boëthius, "Skandinaviska Banken i det svenska bankväsendets historia, 1864–1914," *HT*, 84 (1964): 483–487.

12. Kurt Samuelsson, *From Great Power to Welfare State*, 195–196; Potter, "The Role of a Swedish Bank," 65; Frank W. Fetter, manuscript of 1969, "The Swedish Experience."

13. Erik Lindahl et al., *National Income of Sweden, 1861–1930*, part 1, 79, 87, 151, 237, 271; part 2, 589. See also Franklin D. Scott, "American Influences in Norway and Sweden," *JMH*, 18 (1946): 46.

14. Samuelsson, *From Great Power*, 162–64, 202; Jörberg, *Growth and Fluctuations* and the review of this book by Sven Lundström in *HT*, 82 (1962): 330–333; Söderlund, *Swedish Timber Exports*, 172.

15. Eli F. Heckscher et al., *Sweden, Norway, Denmark and Iceland in the World War* (New Haven: Yale University Press, 1930); Lennart Jörberg, "Structural Change and Economic Growth," in Steven Koblik, ed., *Sweden's Development from Poverty to Affluence*, 89–135.

16. Kurt Samuelsson makes much of one rather dubious advantage enjoyed by the Swedes: poverty. The argument is that an excess population of impoverished farm workers was forced to migrate to the towns and there became the sinews of the new industrial machine. The idea would seem to have more validity if it were not that many other peoples have had sufficient poverty without developing industry and future prosperity. (Samuelsson, *From Great Power*, 165–184).

17. In Jörberg, "Structural Change," 106.

## Chapter XVII

1. United States Naval War College, *International Law Documents*, (1917), 183ff; (1918), 150–159; W. M. Carlgren, *Ministären Hammarskjöld*, 45.

2. *Ibid.*, 91.

3. United States Naval War College, *International Law Situations*, (1932), 132–133; Philip C. Jessup in *Neutrality: Its History, Economics and Law*, 4: 166–170; see also *Foreign Relations of the United States*, 1914 Supplement: 151, 159ff, 360, 465–466, 472–474; 1915 Supplement: 7–8, 296–298, 500; 1916 Supplement: 689, 691.

4. Torsten Gihl, *DSUH*, 4: 109, 113–114; Elis Håstad, *Sveriges historia under 1900-talet*, 20–24.

5. Martin Grass, *Friedensaktivität und Neutralität. Die skandinavische Sozialdemokratie und die neutrale Zusammenarbeit im Krieg August 1914 bis Februar 1917*.

6. Adrian Molin was editor of *Det Nya Sverige* throughout its entire existence, 1907–28, a periodical expressing his brand of conservatism, strongly infused with both nationalism and socialism. He claimed in 1936 that he had been a fascist before fascism, a boast supported in large

measure by his *Svenska spörsmål och kraf* (Swedish issues and demands), a book published in 1905 adumbrating ideals of the national community and of the "blood and soil" bond, of the strong state, and of the futility of parliaments (Stockholm: Geber).

7. Franklin D. Scott, "Gustaf V and Swedish Attitudes toward Germany, 1915," *JMH*, 39 (1967): 113–118.

8. W. M. Carlgren, *Neutralität oder Allianz*, 236.

9. Steven Koblik, *Sweden: the Neutral Victor*, 21. See also Eli F. Heckscher et al., *Sweden, Norway, Denmark, and Iceland in the World War*.

10. Jessup, in *Neutrality*, 4: 188–189.

11. Montagu William W. P. Consett, *The Triumph of Unarmed Forces (1914–1918)*, 109.

12. Steven Koblik, "The Politics of Swedish Neutrality," *HT*, 92 (1972): 52–71; Koblik, "Failure and Success," *Scandia*, 38 (1972): 82–112; Koblik, *Sweden: the Neutral Victor*.

13. See Östen Undén, *Minnesanteckningar* (Stockholm: Bonnier, 1966), 41, *passim*. A significant inquiry into the political forces and trends at work in the Sweden of 1917 is Steven Koblik's essay, "Between Reform and Revolution," *Scandia*, 42 (1976): 115–132.

14. Edgar Turlington, in *Neutrality*, 3: 101–111; *DSH*, 9: 311, 314; Heckscher, *Sweden, Norway, Denmark, and Iceland*.

## Chapter XVIII

1. Nils Herlitz, "Författningsrevision 1918," *Svenska Dagbladet*, December 12 and 18, 1958.

2. Richard Tomasson in Introduction to Herbert Tingsten, *The Swedish Social Democrats*, xvi.

3. *DSH*, 9: 338–339; Jean Braconier, "Till minnet av Hjalmar Branting," *Sydsvenska Dagbladet*, February 16, 1975.

4. *DSH*, 10: 67–71. In Swedish the offensive phrase read: "Fattigdomen fördrages med jämnmod, då den delas av alla," (see p. 71).

5. Ernst Söderlund, "The Swedish Iron Industry during the First World War and the Post War Depression," *SEHR*, 6 (1958): 53–94, especially 78–83; *DSH*, 10: 23–24, 29; *Historisk Statistik*, 3: table 17.

6. *DSH*, 10: 76–77.

7. Arthur Montgomery, *How Sweden Overcame the Depression, 1930–1933*.

8. *DSH*, 10: 78–80; Jan Glete, *Kreugerkoncernen och Boliden*. Two additional studies were in 1975 nearing completion, all three studies being financed by the Riksbank's 300th anniversary fund (see *Svenska Dagbladet*, November 22, 1975).

9. Montgomery, *How Sweden Overcame the Depression*, 84–85, 53–54.

10. See *Dagligvaruföretagen*, SOU 1975: 69, 110–111.

11. In addition to the items listed in the chapter bibliography see *Vår Bostad* (Stockholm: HSB, 1934), especially pp. 39–41; Mauritz Bonow, *Kooperationen och folkförsörjningen* (Stockholm: KF, 1936); The Swedish Institute's Fact Sheet, *Consumers Cooperatives in Sweden* (Factsheet 43 d Om) (Stockholm, 1974); Anders Hedberg, *Swedish Consumers in Cooperation* (Stockholm: KF, 1937).

12. Ernst Wigforss, *Minnen*, vol. 3; Herbert Tingsten, *Den svenska socialdemokratiens idéutveckling*, 1: 383.

13. Lars Furuland, *Statarna i litteraturen*, 427; see also Curt Johanson, *Lantarbetarna i Uppland, 1918–1930*.

14. Ivar Lo-Johansson, *Statarna*; Lo-Johansson, *Stockholmaren*; and other works. See also Jan-Anders Paulsson, "Ivar Lo-Johansson: Crusader for Social Justice," *ASR* (Spring 1971): 21–31.

15. Herbert Tingsten, *The Debate on the Foreign Policy of Sweden, 1918–1939*, 83–137.

16. Quoted in Tingsten, *Debate*, 28; Östen Undén, *Minnesanteckningar*, 67–68, 71–72.

17. Undén, *Minnesanteckningar*, 108–112.

18. Erik Lönnroth, "The Diplomacy of Östen Undén," in Gordon Craig, ed., *The Diplomats*, 86–99; *DSH*, 10: 42–43.

19. Wigforss, *Minnen*, 3: 83–84; Lars Danius, *Samhället och försvaret*.

20. Åke Thulstrup, *Reformer och försvar*.

21. Franklin D. Scott, *Scandinavia*, 233–234.

22. Interview with General Thörnell, *Svenska Dagbladet*, March 7, 1976.

23. *Ibid*.

24. Åke Thulstrup, "Gustav V:s roll under midsommarkrisen 1941," *HT*, 92 (1972): 72–79; Per Andreen, "Politiska handlingslinjer i midsommarkrisen 1941," *HT*, 93 (1973): 38–65; Kent Zetterberg, "Marskrisen — en alternativ tolkning," *HT*, 94 (1974): 59–81; Göran B. Nilsson, "Midsommarkrisen 1941," *HT*, 91 (1971): 477–532.

25. Carl-Axel Gemzell, "Tysk militärplanläggning under det andra världskriget: fall Sverige," *Scandia*, 41 (1975): 199–248.

26. For example, the *Danziger Nachrichten*.

27. Dean Acheson, *Present at the Creation: My Years in the State Department* (New York: Norton, 1969), 50–52, 58–59.

28. Kurt Samuelsson, *From Great Power to Welfare State*, 246–248.

## Chapter XIX

1. Nikolaj Nejland in *Sydsvenska Dagbladet*, March 2, 1973.

2. Ralph Hewins, *Count Folke Bernadotte, His Life and Work*.

3. Dag Hammarskjöld, *Markings* (New York, Knopf, 1964), 213. Quoted by kind permission of the publisher.

4. *DSH*, 9: 298, 300.

5. Frantz Wendt, *The Nordic Council and Co-operation in Scandinavia*; Stanley V. Anderson, *The Nordic Council, A Study of Scandinavian Regionalism*; Royal Ministry of Foreign Affairs, *Sweden in Europe 1971* (Stockholm: Swedish Institute, 1971); Mats Bergquist, *Sverige och EEC*; *EFTA Bygger ett frihandelsområde i Europa*; Emile Benoit, *Europe at Sixes and Sevens: the Common Market, The Free Trade Association, and the United States*; *Expanded Nordic Economic Cooperation*.

6. *Svensk ekonomi 1971–1975, med utblick mot 1990*, SOU 1970: 71.

7. *Ibid*., especially p. 24. The similar report for 1975, seventh in a series that began in 1948, is entitled *Långtidsutredningen 1975*. *Huvudrapport* (see especially the tables therein, pp. 111–122); *Historisk Statistik*, 3: tables 5, 6, 8; *Yearbook of Nordic Statistics 1975*, 97; Assar Lindbeck, *Svensk ekonomisk politik* (1968 ed.), 200, 201, 203. Two recent studies utilize new methods of measurement for economic growth and should be consulted by those interested in careful detailed appraisals: Östen Johansson, *The Gross Domestic Product of Sweden and Its Components, 1861–1955* (Stockholm: Almqvist & Wiksell, 1967); and Olle Krantz and Carl-Axel Nilsson, *Swedish National Product, 1861–1970. New Aspects on Methods and Measurement* (Lund: Gleerup, 1975).

8. *Fortune*, August 1972, 152–159 (the full Swedish list of multinationals is reproduced in Franklin D. Scott, *Scandinavia*, 169); *Fortune*, August 1976, 232–242; Birgitta Swedenborg, *Den svenska industriens investeringar i utlandet, 1970–1974. Forskningsrapport no. 5* (Stockholm: Industriens Utredningsinstitut, 1976), tables 9, 11; Richard J. Barnet and Ronald E. Müller, *Global Reach. The Power of the Multinational Corporations* (New York: Simon & Schuster, 1974), 14.

9. Swedish Institute, Fact Sheet 51 f Qa.

10. *Metallarbetaren*, no. 13, March 12, 1976; nos. 26–27, June 25, 1976.

11. *Svenska Dagbladet*, May 5, 1976.

12. *Ibid*., June 24, 1976.

13. Peter Drucker, *The Unseen Revolution. How Pension Fund Socialism Came to America* (New York: Harper & Row, 1976), 154, 38–40.

14. Ernst Wigforss, *Minnen*, 3: 418, 429.

15. WHO, *World Health Statistics Annual 1971*, vol. 3 (Geneva, 1975), 169–176; *Statistisk årsbok för Sverige* (Stockholm: Norstedt, annual), 1970: table 460.

16. In 1974 a group of six Swedish specialists held one-day seminars at several institutions in the United States, including UCLA, on Swedish experience with "Humanizing the workplace."

Among the relevant materials distributed were issues no. 2, 12, and 13 of *Current Sweden* for 1973 and the Ministry of Labor's booklet of May 1974 on the *Workers' Protection Act and the Worker's Protection Ordinance*.

17. *Jämlikhet*. Första rapport från SAP-LO:s Arbetsgrupp för Jämlikhetsfrågor (Stockholm? 1969).

18. David Schwarz, *Svensk Invandrar- och Minoritets-politik, 1945–1968*; Schwarz, ed. *Svenska Minoriteter*. See also the perceptive article by Jane Kramer, "Invandrare," in *The New Yorker* for March 22, 1976.

19. Israel Ruong, *The Lapps in Sweden*; Björn Collinder, *The Lapps*; Asbjørn Nesheim, *Introducing the Lapps* (Oslo: Tanum, 1963); Ernst Manker, in *DSH*, 16: 119–123, 234–237. See also the classic older account, Johannes Schefferus [John Scheffer], *The History of Lapland. Wherein are [sic] shewed the original, manner, habits, marriages, conjurations, etc., of that people* (Oxford, At the Theater, 1674 [Facsimile ed., Stockholm: Rediviva, 1971]).

20. Jonas Orring, *School in Sweden* (Stockholm: Skolöverstyrelsen, 1969), 37.

21. *Svenska Dagbladet*, February 12, 1976.

22. Franklin D. Scott, *The American Experience of Swedish Students*, 11.

23. *DSH*, 9: 235.

24. Karl Larm, "Kromosompedagoger och Standardbarn," *Aftonbladet*, (January 14, 1953).

25. Quoted in Orring, *School in Sweden*, 41, 39.

26. Deane William Ferm, in *Christian Century* (January 14, 1970), 45–48.

27. For general coverage on education see also the several items listed in the chapter bibliography and the fact sheets on education issued by the Swedish Institute.

28. *Constitutional Documents of Sweden: The Instrument of Government, The Riksdag Act, The Act of Succession, The Freedom of the Press Act* (Stockholm: The Swedish Riksdag, 1975).

29. Joseph Board, "A New Look at Swedish Politics: Compromise and Change," *SS*, 46 (1974): 1–19.

30. Quoted in *Svenska Dagbladet*, November 23, 1975.

31. *Ibid*.

32. Interview reported by Bernard Weintraub, *New York Times*, November 12, 1972.

33. Roland Huntford, *The New Totalitarians*, 78, 88, 166–181.

34. In his *The Social Programs of Sweden*, 157.

35. Gunnar Adler-Karlsson, *Functional Socialism. A Swedish Theory for Democratic Socialization* (Stockholm: Prisma, 1967 [1969 actual]), 18.

36. *Ibid.*, 27.

37. *Svensk ekonomi 1971–1975 med utblick mot 1990. 1970 års långtidsutredning. Huvudrapport* (Stockholm: SOU 1970: 71); Lars Nabseth et al., *Svensk industri under 70-talet med utblick mot 80-talet* (Stockholm: Utredningsinstitut, 1971 [same as SOU 1971: 5]). See also *Långtidsutredningen 1975* (Stockholm: SOU 1975: 89).

38. *Jämlikhet*, 10.

39. Kurt Samuelsson, *From Great Power to Welfare State*, 281–282.

## Chapter XX

1. Quoted in Alrik Gustafson, *A History of Swedish Literature*, 255.

2. Franklin S. Klaf, *Strindberg: The Origin of Psychology in Modern Drama*.

3. Excellent translations of the series of Strindberg's historical dramas have been made by Walter Johnson and published by the University of Washington Press and the American Scandinavian Foundation.

4. Gustafson, *History of Swedish Literature*, 325.

5. Quoted by Åke Janzon in *Svenska Dagbladet*, July 12, 1974.

6. Ralph Slayton, "The Love Story of Astrid Lindgren," *Scandinavian Review*, no. 4 (1975): 44–53.

7. The evidence for this section lies primarily in the writings themselves, a few of which are listed in the bibliography of this volume. The best of the general surveys is Alrik Gustafson's *A*

*History of Swedish Literature*, mentioned above. *DSH* is also a good reference, especially 9: 230–233, 235 and 10: 163–167, 172–176. In English some greater detail may be found in *Scandinavia Past and Present*, 2: 909–950, 1064–1079.

8. *DSH*, 10: 95. On the general subject matter see also pp. 87, 189–192.

9. *DSH*, 9: 154.

10. See Elias Cornell, "Svenskt bygge från 1860-tal till 1920-tal," *DSH*, 9: 145–157; *Scandinavia Past and Present*, 2: 1096–1098; *Painting and Sculpture at Freia and Marabou* (Oslo-Stockholm, 1955); *Sweden in Brief* (Stockholm: Swedish Institute, 1974); Carl G. Laurin, "A Survey of *Swedish Art*," in *Scandinavian Art*, 128–237.

11. Quoted in Nils Göran Hökby, "What is the Position of the Swedish Museums Today"? *Current Sweden*, no. 83, July 1975.

12. H. Törnblom, "Den nyare svenska musiken," *DSH*, 10: 81–83; *Sweden in Brief*, 51–53; Per Svensson, "New Developments in Swedish Pop and Jazz — Alternatives to the Commercial Music Movement," *Current Sweden*, no. 84, August 1975; Claes M. Cnattingius, *Contemporary Swedish Music* (Stockholm: Swedish Institute, 1973); *Tradition and Progress in Swedish Music* (a special edition of *Musikrevy* [Stockholm, 1973]).

13. Sven Erik Skawonius, quoted in Erik Zahle, *Scandinavian Domestic Design* (Copenhagen: Hassing, 1961), 54.

14. Beate Sydhoff, "The New Printed Textiles," *Current Sweden*, no. 68, April 1975, 3.

15. In addition to the magazine *Form* and the annual *Kontur* mentioned in the text see Arthur Hald and Sven Erik Skawonius, *Contemporary Swedish Design* (Stockholm: Nordisk Rotogravyr, 1951). On early developments a good brief treatment is Anna Houg Rutt, "Why Sweden leads in Design," *American Magazine of Art* (April, 1933), 169–180. The Swedish Institute has published a number of up-to-date items on design, especially *Design in Sweden* (1972), with articles by specialists; and in the *Current Sweden* series of leaflets Beate Sydhoff's "The New Printed Textiles" (no. 68, 1975), and "Contemporary Woven and Free Textiles in Sweden" (no. 69, 1975), and Kerstin Wickman's "Attitudes are changing in Swedish art handicrafts" (no. 100, 1975).

16. *Sweden in Brief* (1974), 61–63; Jan Lindroth et al., in *DSH*, 10: 177–186.

17. Berndt Gustafsson, *Svensk kyrkohistoria*; Carl-Gustaf Andrén, "Svensk kyrkokunskap," in Sven Kjöllerström, *Praktisk teologi*, 2nd ed. (dissertation; Lund: Gleerup, 1967); Per-Erik Persson, *Kyrkorna i världen* (dissertation; Lund: Gleerup, 1967); Carl-Gustaf Boëthius, "Religionen i 1900-talets Sverige," in *DSH*, 10: 62–66; Bengt Hägglund, *Teologiens historia*, 2nd ed. (dissertation; Lund: Gleerup, 1963); *Svenska kyrkan och staten. Slutbetänkande*, SOU 1968: no. 11.

18. Per Olof Sundman, *The Flight of the Eagle* includes a factual introduction preceding the fictionalized account of the flight.

19. Birgitta Odén's *Lauritz Weibull och forskarsamhället* offers an in-depth and wide-ranging analysis of Weibull's work and influence on scholarship.

20. Robert Kirsch, in a review of *Nightmare* in the *Los Angeles Times*, January 25, 1976.

21. John W. Gardner, in "The Antileadership Vaccine," *Annual Report of the Carnegie Corporation of New York* (1965), 12.

22. *Jämlikhet* (Stockholm: SAP-LO, 1969), 9.

23. *Svenska Dagbladet*, January 27, 1976.

24. Quoted by Gunnar Jarring in *Grit*, January 3, 1960.

25. *Statistisk årsbok för Sverige* (Stockholm: Norstedt, annual), 1973: 52, 239.

26. *New Cultural Policy in Sweden: A Proposal*, 148–150.

## Epilogue

1. Alva Myrdal, *Toward Equality* (Lund: Prisma, 1971).

2. *The Economist,* March 7, 1987, 21.

3. Barry Bosworth and Alice M. Rivlin (eds.), *The Swedish Economy* (1987).

4. For an interesting study on the situation of women in Sweden, see Mary Ruggie, *The State and Working Women* (1984).

5. *The Wall Street Journal,* June 24, 1987, 23. David Poponoe, "Beyond the Nuclear Family: A Statistical Portrait of the Changing Family in Sweden," *Journal of Marriage and Family* (forthcoming).

6. Jan Myrdal, *Barndon* (1982); and *En Annan Värld* (1984).

7. Richard Reeves, "The Palme Obsession," *New York Times,* Sunday Magazine, March 1, 1987, 20.

# SELECTED BIBLIOGRAPHY

## General

Andersson, Ingvar. *History of Sweden*. 1956. Reprint. Westport, Conn.: Greenwood Press, 1975. The best one-volume history for the pre-twentieth century.

————. *Skånes historia: till Saxo och Skånelagen*. Stockholm: Norstedt, 1947.

Andrén, Nils. *Government and Politics in the Northern Countries*. Stockholm: Almqvist & Wiksell, 1964.

Carlsson, Sten, and Rosén, Jerker. *Svensk historia*. 2 vols. Stockholm: Bonnier, 1960–1962. Standard Swedish textbook; Rosén authored vol. 1, Carlsson vol. 2. See also *Den svenska historien*.

Edén, Nils. *Den svenska riksdagen under femhundra år*. Stockholm: Norstedt, 1935.

Furuskog, Jalmar. *Vårt land*. Stockholm: Bonnier, 1943. Cultural geography.

Geijer, Erik Gustaf. *Svenska folkets historia*. 4 vols. Malmö: Världslitteraturens, 1928–1929.

Grimberg, Carl Gustaf. *Svenska folkets underbara öden*. 9 vols. Stockholm: Norstedt, 1925–1926. The classic "everyman's" history.

Gustafson, Alrik. *A History of Swedish Literature*. Minneapolis: University of Minnesota Press for the American-Scandinavian Foundation, 1961. Encyclopedic coverage, readable style.

Guteland, Gösta; Holmberg, Ingvar; Högerstrand, Torsten; Karlquist, Anders; Rundblad, Bengt. *Ett folks biografi*. Stockholm: LiberFörlag, 1975. Historical sociology.

Heckscher, Eli F. *An Economic History of Sweden*. Cambridge: Harvard University Press, 1954. This pioneering work in economic history is somewhat outdated but still valuable. A translation of *Svenskt arbete och liv*. Stockholm: Bonnier, 1941.

————. *Sveriges ekonomiska historia från Gustav Vasa*. 2 vols. in 4. Stockholm: Bonnier, 1935–1949.

Henrikson, Alf. *Svensk historia*. 2 vols. Stockholm: Bonnier, 1963. The anecdotal and gossipy side of history.

Herlitz, N. *Grunddragen av det svenska statsskickets historia*. 5th ed. Stockholm: Norstedt, 1957.

*Historisk statistik för Sverige. Historical Statistics of Sweden: I. Befolkning. Population, 1720–1950*. Stockholm: Statistiska centralbyrån, 1955.

*Historisk statistik för Sverige. Historical Statistics of Sweden: II. Väderlek, lantmäteri, jordbruk, skogsbruk, fiske t.o.m. år 1955. Climate, land surveying, agriculture, forestry, fisheries — 1955*. Stockholm: Statistiska centralbyrån, 1959.

*Historisk statistik för Sverige. Historical Statistics of Sweden: Statistiska översiktstabeller utöver i del I och II publicerade t.o.m. år 1950. Statistical survey. Tables not published in Volumes I & II.* Stockholm: Statistiska centralbyrån, 1960.

Hovde, Brynjolf J. *The Scandinavian Countries, 1720–1865.* 2 vols. 1943. Reprint. Ithaca: Cornell University Press, 1948. First-rate social history.

Ingers, E. *Bonden i svensk historia.* 3 vols. Stockholm: Lantbruksförbundets tidskriftsaktiebolag, 1948.

Jägerstad, Hans. *Sveriges historia i årtal; koncentrerad historisk uppslagsbok.* 3rd rev. ed. Stockholm: Prisma, 1965. Chronology.

Jörberg, Lennart. *History of Prices in Sweden, 1732–1914.* Lund: Gleerup, 1972.

Koblik, Steven, ed. *Sweden's Development from Poverty to Affluence, 1750–1970.* Translated by Joanne Johnson in association with the University of Minnesota Press and Steven Koblik. Minneapolis: University of Minnesota Press, 1975. Swedish history from the eighteenth to the twentieth century; topical essays by outstanding Swedish authorities. Translation of, *Från fattigdom till överflöd.* Stockholm: Wahlström & Widstrand, 1973.

Laurin, Carl; Hannover, Emil; and Thiis, Jens. *Scandinavian Art.* New York: American-Scandinavian Foundation, 1922.

Lawerys, J. A., ed. *Scandinavian Democracy: Development of Democratic Thought and Institutions in Denmark, Norway, and Sweden.* Copenhagen: Danish Institute, 1958.

Lindorm, Erik. *Ny svensk historia.* Stockholm: Wahlström & Widstrand, 1938–1947. Compilation of newspaper articles and illustrations representing contemporary history. Includes: *Gustaviansk, 1771–1810; Carl XIV Johan — Carl XV och deras tid, 1810–1872; Oscar II och hans tid; Gustav V och hans tid* (4 vols.).

Lindroth, Sten. *Svensk lärdomshistoria.* 2 vols. Stockholm: Norstedt, 1975. Intellectual history covering Middle Ages, Reformation, and Age of Greatness.

Malmgren, Robert; Sundberg, Halvar G. F.; and Petrén, Gustaf. *Sveriges grundlagar och tillhörande författningar med förklaringar.* 9th ed. Stockholm: Norstedt, 1967.

Mead, W. R., and Hall, Wendy. *Scandinavia.* New York: Walker, 1972.

Moberg, Vilhelm. *A History of the Swedish People: from Prehistory to the Renaissance.* New York: Pantheon, 1972. A "popular history of the Swedish common man." Translation of *Min svenska historia,* by Paul Britten Austin. Stockholm: Norstedt, 1970.

———. *A History of the Swedish People: from Renaissance to Revolution.* New York: Pantheon, 1973. Continuation of his 1972 work given in the previous entry and all that he completed before his death in 1973. Translation of *Min svenska historia,* II, by Paul Britten Austin. Stockholm: Norstedt, 1971.

Molin, Adrian. *Landskapskynnen.* Stockholm: Norstedt, 1930.

———. *Svenska spörsmål och kraf.* 2nd ed. Stockholm: Geber, 1906.

Nordic Council (Nordiska rådet). *Yearbook of Nordic Statistics. Nordisk statistik årsbok.* Stockholm, 1962– .

Oakley, Stewart. *A Short History of Sweden.* New York: Praeger, 1966.

Rosén, Jerker. (See Carlsson and Rosén.)

Samuelsson, Kurt. *From Great Power to Welfare State: 300 Years of Swedish Social Development.* London: Allen & Unwin, 1968.

*Scandinavia Past and Present.* Edited by Jørgen Bukdahl et al. 3 vols. Odense: Arnkrone, 1959.

Scobbie, Irene. *Sweden.* New York: Praeger, 1972. Recent, accurate, readable, brief.

Scott, Franklin D. *Scandinavia.* Cambridge: Harvard University Press, 1975.

*Statens finanser.* Stockholm: Riksrevisionsverket, 1976.

*Statens offentliga utredningar.* Stockholm: Norstedt. Reports of government investigating commissions, regularly used as bases for legislation. Unusually thorough and wide-ranging. Cited by year and number, for example, SOU 1975: 49.

*Statistisk årsbok Statistical Yearbook.* Stockholm: Norstedt, annual.

*Svensk uppslagsbok.* 2nd rev. and enlarged ed. 32 vols. Malmö: Norden, 1947–1955.

*Den svenska arbetarklassens historia.* 9 vols. Stockholm: Tiden, 1941–1955.

*Svenska folket genom tiderna: vårt lands kulturhistoria i skildringar och bilder.* Edited by Ewert H. G. Wrangel. 13 vols. Malmö: Allhem, 1938–1940.

*Den svenska historien.* 10 vols. Stockholm: Bonniers, 1966–1968. An expanded, illustrated version of Sten Carlsson and Jerker Rosén, *Svensk historia*, 2 vols. Excellent. Includes many contributions by topic specialists.

*Svenska män och kvinnor, biografisk uppslagsbok.* 8 vols. Stockholm: Bonnier, 1942–1955.

*Den svenska utrikespolitikens historia.* 5 vols. in 10. Stockholm: Norstedt, 1951–1961.

*Sverige: land och folk.* 3 vols. Stockholm: Natur och kultur, 1966. Superbly illustrated geography.

*Sveriges historia från äldsta tid till våra dagar.* 6 vols. Minneapolis: Svenska Amerikanska Postens förlag, 1900. Covers period from 1060 to 1875.

*Sveriges historia genom tiderna.* Edited by Harry Maiander. 5 vols. Stockholm: Saxon & Lindström, 1947–1948.

*Sveriges historia till våra dagar.* Edited by Emil Hildebrand. 14 vols. Stockholm: Norstedt, 1919–1926.

*Sveriges Riksdag: historisk och statsvetenskaplig framställning, utgiven enlig beslut av 1926 års Riksdag.* Edited by Nils Edén. 8 vols in 17. Stockholm: V. Petterson, 1931–1938.

Swedish Institute. Stockholm. *Current Sweden* and numerous pamphlets and fact sheets on specific topics.

Weibull, Lauritz. *Nordisk historia: forskningar och undersökningar.* 3 vols. Stockholm: Natur och kultur, 1948–1949.

## Bibliographies

Bring, Samuel E. *Bibliografisk handbok till Sveriges historia.* Stockholm: Norstedt, 1934.

Collijn, Isak. *Sveriges bibliografi intill år 1600.* 3 vols. Uppsala: Svenska litteratursällskapet, 1927–1938.

*Excerpta historica nordica.* Copenhagen: Gyldendal, 1955– Published under the auspices of the International Committee of Historical Sciences. Summaries, usually in English, of recent historical publications in northern Europe. Biennial or triennial.

Geete, Robert. *Fornsvensk bibliografi.* 3 vols. Stockholm: Norstedt, 1903–1948.

Groennings, Sven. *Scandinavia in Social Science Literature.* Bloomington: Indiana University Press, 1970. English language literature; quite thorough, up-to-date publication. Includes index of authors.

Holmbäck, Bure. "About Sweden, 1900–1963: a Bibliographical Outline." In *Sweden Illustrated.* Stockholm: Sweden Illustrated, 1968. Lists 5,000 books in English under about 180 subject titles. Sponsored by the Swedish Institute.

*Offentliga utredningar i Norden. Katalog 1975.* Stockholm: Nordiska rådet och Nordiska ministerrådet, 1976.

*Statens offentliga utredningar, 1960–1975. Katalog.* Stockholm: LiberFörlag, 1976.

*Suecana extranea.* Stockholm: Kunglig Biblioteket, 1963– . A bulletin of the Royal Library, Stockholm, listing new books on Sweden in various non-Swedish languages. Since 1967, issued twice yearly.

*Svensk historisk bibliografi.* Stockholm: Svenska Historiska Föreningen. Annual.

*Svensk historisk bibliografi: systematisk förteckning över skrifter och uppsatser som röra Sveriges historia.* 6 vols. Stockholm: Norstedt, 1907–1968. Svenska Historiska Föreningen. Books concerning Swedish history published from 1771–1960. Includes index of authors.

*Den svenska historien.* 10 vols. Stockholm: Bonnier, 1966–1968. Each volume contains lengthy, detailed bibliographies arranged by subject.

Warmholtz, Carl G. *Bibliotheca historica sveo-gothica.* 15 vols. in 8. 1782–1817. Reprint. Copenhagen: Rosenkilde og Bagger, 1966–1968.

## Periodicals

*American-Scandinavian Review.* American-Scandinavian Foundation. New York, 1913–1974. (See also *Scandinavian Review.*)

*Artes. Kvartalskrift för konst, litteratur och musik.* Musikaliska akademien, Konstakademien, Svenska akademien. Stockholm (Norstedt), 1975– .
*Economy and History.* Institute of Economic History and the Economic History Association, University of Lund. Lund, 1958– .
*Emigranten; Bryggan/The Bridge.* Samfundet emigrantforskningens främjande. Karlstad, 1971– .
*Form. Svenska slöjdföreningens tidskrift.* Stockholm, 1905– .
*Historisk tidskrift.* Svenska historiska föreningen. Stockholm, 1881– .
*Kontur. Swedish Design Annual.* Svenska slöjdföreningen. Stockholm, 1950– .
*Lychnos. Lärdomshistoriska samfundets årsbok.* Stockholm, 1936– .
*Metallarbetaren.* Svenska metallindustriarbetareförbundet. Stockholm, 1890– .
*News from Sweden.* Swedish Information Service, New York, 1941–1976.
*Nordisk kontakt.* Nordiska Rådet. Stockholm, 1955– .
*Nordisk tidskrift för vetenskap, konst, och industri.* Letterstedtska föreningen. Stockholm, 1878– .
*Personhistorisk tidskrift.* Personhistorisk samfundet. Stockholm, 1899– .
*Scandia. Tidskrift för historisk forskning.* Historiska institutionen. Lund, 1928– .
*The Scandinavian Economic History Review.* Scandinavian Society for Economic and Social History and Historical Geography. Stockholm [and other Scandinavian cities], 1928– .
*Scandinavian Journal of History.* The Historical Associations of Denmark, Finland, Norway, and Sweden. Stockholm (Almqvist & Wiksell), 1976– .
*Scandinavian Review.* American-Scandinavian Foundation. New York, 1975– . (See also the *American-Scandinavian Review.*)
*Scandinavian Studies.* Society for the Advancement of Scandinavian Study. Lawrence, Kansas, 1911– .
*Scandinavian Times.* Copenhagen, 1969– . Issued as *Scandinavian Times News-Magazine*, 1963–1968.
*Svensk tidskrift.* Stockholm, 1911– .
*Sweden Now.* Ingenjörsförlaget. Stockholm, 1967– .
*Swedish Pioneer Historical Quarterly.* Swedish Pioneer Historical Society. Chicago, 1950– .

### Newspapers and Weeklies

*Dagens Nyheter.* Stockholm, 1864– .
*LO Tidningen. Fackföreningsrörelsen.* Stockholm, 1921– .
*Svenska Dagbladet.* Stockholm, 1884– .
*Sverige-nytt/Swedish Digest.* Stockholm, 1948– .
*Sydsvenska Dagbladet.* Malmö, 1848– .

# SUGGESTED READING BY CHAPTERS

## Chapter I

Almgren, O. *Sveriges fasta fornlämningar från hednatiden.* 3rd ed. Uppsala: Lindblad, 1934.
Arbman, Holger. *Birka: Sveriges äldsta handelsstad.* Från forntid och medeltid 1. Stockholm: Thule, 1939.
———. "Forntiden." In *SHGT*, vol. 1. Stockholm: Saxon & Lindström, 1947.
*Beowulf: with the Finnesburg Fragment.* Edited by C. L. Wrenn. Fully revised by W. F. Bolton. New York: St. Martin's, 1973.
Bibby, Geoffrey. *The Testimony of the Spade.* New York: Knopf, 1956. Popular-scientific archaeology dealing with the entire North.
Bruce-Mitford. R. L. S. *The Sutton Hoo ship-burial.* vol. 1. London: The British Museum, 1975. With tables, graphs, maps.

Chambers, R. W. *Beowulf: an Introduction to the Study of the Poem*. Cambridge: Cambridge University Press, 1959.
*Fornvännen: tidskrift för svensk antikvarisk forskning*. Utgivet av Kungl. Vitterhets historie och antikvitets akademien under medverkan av Svenska fornminnesföreningen. Stockholm: Almqvist & Wiksell/Geber, 1906–
Fredsjö, Å.; Janson, S.; and Moberg, Carl-Axel. *Hällristningar i Sverige*. Stockholm: Forum, 1956.
Holmqvist, Wilhelm. *Helgö: den gåtfulla ön*. Stockholm: Rabén & Sjögren, 1969.
Klindt-Jensen, Ole. *A History of Scandinavian Archaeology*. Translated by G. Russell Poole. London: Thames & Hudson, 1975.
Leach, Henry Goddard. *Pageant of Old Scandinavia*. Princeton: Princeton University Press for the American-Scandinavian Foundation, 1946. A fascinating anthology, largely from eddas and sagas.
Moberg, Carl-Axel. *Innan Sverige blev Sverige*. Stockholm: Geber, 1951.
Munch, Peter Andreas. *Norse Mythology: Legends of Gods and Heroes*. New York: American-Scandinavian Foundation, 1954.
Näsström, Gustaf. *Forna dagars Sverige: kulturhistorisk bilderbok om Hedenhös och medeltid*. 4 vols. Stockholm: Bonnier, 1948– .
Nerman, Birger. *Sveriges första storhetstid*. Stockholm: Skoglund, 1942.
————. *Die Verbindungen zwischen Skandinavien und dem Ostbaltikum in der jüngeren Eisenzeit*. Stockholm: Akademiens förlag, 1929.
*Nordisk kultur*. 30 vols. Stockholm: Bonnier, 1930–1956. See, for example, articles on Hedeby and Birka.
Saxo Grammaticus. *The First Nine Books of the Danish History of Saxo Grammaticus*. Translated by Oliver Elton. Folklore Society Publications, no. 33. 1893. Reprint. Liechtenstein: Kraus, 1967.
Shetelig, Haakon, and Falk, Hjalmar. *Scandinavian Archaeology*. Translated by E. V. Gordon. Oxford: Clarendon Press, 1937.
Snorri Sturluson. *Heimskringla: History of the Kings of Norway*. Translated by Lee M. Hollander. Austin: University of Texas Press for the American-Scandinavian Foundation, 1964.
————. *Ynglingasaga*. Edited by Elias Wessén. Stockholm: Svenska bokförlaget, 1952.
Stenberger, Mårten. *Det forntida Sverige*. Stockholm: Almqvist & Wiksell, 1964.
Svennung, Josef. *Zur geschichte des Goticismus*. Stockholm: Almqvist & Wiksell, 1967.
*Svenska fornminnesföreningen*. Stockholm, 1871–1905. A journal.
*Tor: Meddelanden från institutionen för nordisk fornkunskap vid Uppsala universitet*. Stockholm: Almqvist & Wiksell, 1955– . A journal.
Weibull, Curt. *Sveriges och Danmarks äldsta historia*. Lund, 1922.

## Chapter II

Anderson, Sven Axel. *Viking Enterprise*. New York: Columbia University Press, 1936.
Arbman, Holger. *Svear i österviking*. Stockholm: Natur och kultur, 1955.
————. *The Vikings*. London: Thames & Hudson, 1961.
Arbman, Holger, and Stenberger, Mårten. *Vikingar i västerled*. Stockholm: Bonnier, 1935.
Arne, T. J. *Svenskarna och Österlandet*. Stockholm: Natur och kultur, 1952.
Bengtsson, Frans G. *The Long Ships*. New York: Knopf, 1954. Historical fiction.
Blegen, Theodore C. *The Kensington Rune Stone*. St. Paul: Minnesota Historical Society, 1968.
Brögger, Anton Wilhelm, and Shetelig, Haakon. *The Viking Ships*. New York: Twayne, 1971.
Brøndsted, Johannes. *The Vikings*. Translated by Kalle Skov. Middlesex: Penguin, 1965.
Davidson, Hilda R. Ellis. *The Viking Road to Byzantium*. London: Allen & Unwin, 1976.
Ekholm, Gunnar. *Forntid och fornforskning: Skandinavien*. Stockholm: Bonnier, 1935.
Foote, Peter G., and Wilson, David M. *The Viking Achievement*. New York: Praeger, 1970. Emphasis on home and social background.
Geipel, John. *The Viking Legacy: the Scandinavian Influence on the English and Gaelic Languages*. Newton Abbot: David & Charles, 1971.

Jansson, Sven B. F. *The Runes of Sweden*. Translated by P. G. Foote. Stockholm: Norstedt, 1962.

Jones, Gwyn. *History of the Vikings*. London: Oxford University Press, 1968.

———. *The Norse Atlantic Saga*. London: Oxford University Press, 1964.

Kendrick, T. D. *A History of the Vikings*. London: Methuen, 1930.

Klindt-Jensen, Ole. *Vikingarnas Värld*. Stockholm: Forum, 1967.

Klindt-Jensen, Ole, and Wilson, David McKenzie. *Viking Art*. Ithaca: Cornell University Press, 1966.

Leach, Henry Goddard. *Angevin Britain and Scandinavia*. Cambridge: Harvard University Press, 1921.

Linklater, Eric. *The Ultimate Viking*. London: Macmillan, 1955. Fictional but essentially correct.

Olrik, Axel. *Viking Civilization*. Revised after the author's death by Hans Ellekilde. New York: American-Scandinavian Foundation/Norton, 1930.

Skelton, R. A.; Marston, Thomas E.; and Painter, George D. *The Vinland Map and the Tartar Relation*. New Haven: Yale University Press, 1965. Despite the challenge to the authenticity of the Vinland map, this remains a valuable book.

Tunberg, Sven. *Rod och roslag i det gamla Sveariket*. Stockholm: Geber, 1947. Outdated but useful.

Turville-Petre, G. *The Heroic Age of Scandinavia*. London: Hutchinson, 1951.

*Varangian Problems: Report on the First International Symposium on the Theme the Eastern Connections of the Nordic Peoples in the Viking Period and Early Middle Ages*. Moesgaard, University of Aarhus, October 7–11, 1968. Copenhagen: Munksgaard, 1970.

Williams, M. W. *Social Scandinavia in the Viking Age*. New York: Macmillan, 1920.

Wilson, David McKenzie. *The Vikings and Their Origins*. New York: McGraw, 1970.

## Chapter III

Adamus Bremensis. *History of the Archbishops of Hamburg-Bremen by Adam of Bremen*. Translated with an introduction and notes by Francis J. Tschan. New York: Columbia University Press, 1959.

Craigie, William A. *The Religion of Ancient Scandinavia*. London: Constable, 1906.

Dumézil, Georges. *Gods of the Ancient Northmen*. Edited by Einar Haugen. Berkeley: University of California Press, 1973.

Floderus, E. "Från hedendom till kristendom." in *SFGT*, vol. 2.

Grønbech, Vilhelm. *Religionsskiftet i Norden*. Copenhagen: Gyldendal, Nordisk forlag, 1913.

Macculloch, John A. *The Celtic and Scandinavian Religions*. London: Hutchinson's University Library, 1948.

Nerman, Birger. *När Sverige kristnades*. Stockholm: Skoglund, 1945.

Palme, Sven Ulric. *Kristendomens genombrott i Sverige*. Stockholm: Bonnier, 1959.

Rimbert, Saint. Archbishop of Hamburg and Bremen. *Vita Anskarii*. English translation, *Anskar: the Apostle of the North, 801–865* by Charles H. Robinson. London: Society for the Propagation of the Gospel in Foreign Parts, 1921. Bishop Rimbert was Ansgar's fellow missionary and successor.

Ström, Åke V. "Germanische Religion." In *Die Religionen der Menscheit*. Stuttgart: Kohlhammer, 1975.

Ström, Folke. *Diser, nornor, valkyrjor: fruktbarhetskult och sakralt kungadöme i Norden*. Stockholm: Almqvist & Wiksell, 1954.

———. *Nordisk hedendom: tro och sed i förkristen tid*. Gothenburg: Akademiförlaget-Gumperts, 1961.

Turville-Petre, E. O. G. *Myth and Religion of the North: the Religion of Ancient Scandinavia*. New York: Holt, Rinehart & Winston, 1964.

Weibull, Lauritz. "Ansgarii skrift om den påvliga legationen över Norden." In *Nordisk historia*, vol. 1. Stockholm: Natur och kultur, 1948.

Wordsworth, John. *The National Church of Sweden*. The Hale Lectures, 1910. London: Mowbray, 1911.

Chapter IV

Ahnlund, Nils. *Stockholms historia före Gustav Vasa*. Stockholm: Norstedt, 1953.

Andræ, Tor. "Birgitta." In *Essäer*. Stockholm: Bonnier, 1948.

Cornell, Henrik. *Den svenska konstens historia*. vol. 1. Stockholm: Bonnier, 1944.

*Corpus codicum suecicorum medii aevi auspiciis principis hereditarii regni Sueciae Gustavi Adolphi editum* . . . 18 vols. Copenhagen: Munksgaard, 1943-1965. Facsimiles of important medieval documents.

Hafström, Gerhard. *Land och lag*. Stockholm: Gebei, 1959.

*Hansestaederne og Norden*. Det nordiske historikermøde i Århus, 7-9 August 1957. Århus, 1957.

Hildebrand, Hans Olof H. *Sveriges medeltid: kulturhistorisk skildring*. 3 vols. Stockholm: Norstedt, 1879-1903.

*Historiska urkunder*. Edited by Gösta Johannesson. 3 vols. Stockholm: Svenska bokförlaget/ Bonnier, 1957-1960. Selected source materials.

Holmqvist, Wilhelm. *Sveriges forntid och medeltid*. Malmö: Ljustrycksanstalt, 1949. Abundantly illustrated; by a leading Swedish authority.

Ingers, E. *Bonden i svensk historia*. vol. 1. Stockholm: Lantbruksförbundets tidskriftsaktiebolag, 1949.

Jörgensen, Johannes. *Saint Bridget of Sweden*. Translated by Ingeborg Lund. 2 vols. London: Longmans, Green, 1954.

Koht, Halvdan. *Drottning Margareta och Kalmarunionen*. Stockholm: Natur och kultur, 1956. A great Norwegian scholar's treatment of an extraordinary woman and the brief period of Nordic union.

*Kulturhistorisk leksikon for nordisk middelalder fra vikingetid til reformationstid*. 19 vols. Copenhagen: Rosenkilde og Bagger, 1956-1975. This multivolume work is completed through "Vidisse," with one volume yet to come.

Kumlien, Kjell. *Sverige och hanseaterna: studier i svensk politik och utrikeshandel*. Stockholm: Wahlström & Widstrand, 1953.

————. *Sverige och den tyska hansan*. Stockholm: Geber, 1943.

Lindblom, A. *Sveriges konsthistoria*. vol. 1. Från stenåldern till Gustav Vasa. Stockholm: Nordisk rotogravyr, 1944.

Linton, Michael. *Drottning Margareta: fullmäktig fru och rätt husbonde*. Stockholm: Akademiförlaget, 1971.

Lönnroth, Erik. *Från svensk medeltid*. Stockholm: Aldus/Bonnier, 1959.

————. *Statsmakt och statsfinanser i medeltida Sverige*. Gothenburg: Elander, 1940.

————. "Unionsdokumenten i Kalmar 1397." *Scandia* 24 (1958): 32-67.

Magnus, Johannes. *Historia de omnibus gothorum sveonumque regibus*. Basiliae: Ex officina Isingriniana, 1558.

Magnus, Olaus. *Historia om de nordiska folken*. 5 vols. Uppsala: Almqvist & Wiksell, 1909-1951. Social history; translation of the original Latin edition, published in 1555. Fascinating woodcuts.

*Magnus Erikssons landslag*. Modern Swedish interpretation by Åke Holmbäck and Elias Wessén. Rättshistoriskt bibliotek, vol. 6. Stockholm: Nordiska bokhandeln, 1962.

*Magnus Erikssons stadslag*. Modern Swedish interpretation by Åke Holmbäck and Elias Wessén. Rättshistoriskt bibliotek, vol. 7. Stockholm: Nordiska bokhandeln, 1966.

Moberg, Vilhelm. *Ride this Night!* Garden City: Doubleday, Doran, 1943.

Musset, Lucien. *Les Peuples Scandinaves au Moyen Age*. Paris: Presses Universitaires de France, 1951. The best one-volume treatment of the Middle Ages in the North.

Nash, E. Gee. *The Hansa*. London: John Lane the Bodley Head, 1929. Popular.

Nordström, Johan. *Johannes Magnus och den götiska romantiken*. Stockholm: Almqvist & Wiksell, 1975.

Petri, Olavus. *Olai Petri svenska krönika*. Edited by G. E. Klemming. Stockholm: Klemming, 1860.

Rydberg, Olof S. *Om det från unionsmötet i Kalmar år 1397: bevarade dokumentet rörande de nordiska rikenas förening*. Stockholm: Norstedt, 1886.

*Svenska landskapslagar.* Interpreted and explained for present-day Swedes by Å. Holmbäck and E. Wessén. Series 1–5. Stockholm: Geber, 1933–1946. Includes Västgötalagen, Östgötalagen, Dalalagen, etc.

*Svenska medeltidens rim-krönikor.* Edited by A. Rydfors. Stockholm, 1925. Includes Eriks-krönikan, Karls-krönikan, and Sture-krönikan.

*Svenskt diplomatarium.* 9 vols. & supplement. Stockholm: Norstedt, 1892–1970. Documents covering the period 817–1368.

Westman, Knut Bernhard. *Birgitta-studier, 1.* Uppsala: Akademiska boktryckeriet/Berling, 1911.

## Chapter V
### (see also bibliography for Chapter IV)

Ahnlund, Henrik, ed. *Historia kring Stockholm före 1520.* Stockholm: Wahlström & Widstrand, 1965.

Ahnlund, Nils. *Engelbrekt.* Stockholm: Svenska kyrkans diakonistyrelses bokförlag, 1934.

Andrae, C. G. *Kyrka och frälse i Sverige under äldre medeltid.* Stockholm: Svenska bokförlaget/Norstedt, 1960.

Arnoldsson, Sverker. *Ericus Olai och periodindelingen i Sveriges historia.* Gothenburg: Wettergren & Kerber, 1953.

Brilioth, Yngve Torgny. *Den senare medeltiden, 1274–1521.* Vol. 2 of *Svenska kyrkans historia.* Stockholm: Svenska kyrkans diakonistyrelses bokförlag, 1941.

Carlsson, Gottfrid. *Engelbrekt, Sturarna, Gustav Vasa: undersökningar och studier.* Lund: Gleerup, 1962.

———. *Medeltidens nordiska unionstanke.* Stockholm: Geber, 1945.

Hill, Charles Edward. *The Danish Sound Dues and Command of the Baltic. A Study of International Relations.* Durham: Duke University Press, 1926.

Kumlien, Kjell. *Med svenskarna och Engelbrekt: ett 500-års minne.* Stockholm: Norstedt, 1935.

Lundegård, Axel Wilhelm. *Om Engelbrekt, Erik Puke och Karl Knutsson som blev kung.* Stockholm: Aktiebolaget Ljus, 1913.

Lundholm, Kjell-Gunnar. *Sture den äldre och stormännen.* Lund: Gleerup, 1956.

Moberg, Vilhelm. *A History of the Swedish People: From Renaissance to Revolution.* Stockholm: Norstedt, 1971.

Palme, Sven Ulric. *Sten Sture den äldre.* Stockholm: Walström & Widstrand, 1950.

Skyum-Nielsen, N. *Blodbadet i Stockholm og dets juridiske maskering.* Copenhagen: Munksgaard, 1964.

## Chapter VI

For this period, see also relevant volumes or sections in the following multivolume works: *DSUH, SHGT, SHVD,* and Geijer, E. G. *Svenska folkets historia.*

Åberg, Alf. *Nils Dacke och landsfadern.* Stockholm: LTs förlag, 1960.

Ahnlund, Nils. *Tradition och historia.* Stockholm: Norstedt, 1956.

Andersson, Ingvar. *Erik XIV: en biografi.* Stockholm: Wahlström & Widstrand, 1935.

Bergendoff, Conrad. *Olavus Petri and the Ecclesiastical Transformation in Sweden, 1521–1552: a Study in the Swedish Reformation.* New York: Macmillan, 1928.

Hallgren, Sören, and Söderberg, Bengt G. *Mellan himmel och helvete.* Stockholm: Rabén & Sjögren, 1970.

Hammarström, Ingrid. *Finansförvaltning och varuhandel, 1504–1540: studier i de yngre Sturarnas och Gustav Vasas statshushållning.* Dissertation. Uppsala, 1956.

Heckscher, Eli F. *Sveriges ekonomiska historia från Gustaf Vasa.* 2 vols. in 4. Stockholm: Bonnier, 1935–1949.

Hildebrand, Emil. *Svenska statsförfattningens historiska utveckling från äldsta tid till våra dagar.* Stockholm: Norstedt, 1896.

Holmquist, Hjalmer. *Reformationstidevarvet, 1521–1611*. Vol. 3 of Svenska kyrkans historia. Stockholm: Svenska kyrkans diakonistyrelses bokförlag, 1933.

Kjöllerström, Sven. *Striden kring kalvinismen i Sverige under Erik XIV: en kyrkohistorisk studie*. Lund: Gleerup, 1935.

Lönnroth, Erik. *Statsmakt och statsfinanser i medeltida Sverige*. Gothenburg: Elander, 1940.

Lundkvist, Sven. *Gustaf Vasa och Europa*. Stockholm: Svenska bokförlaget, 1960.

Ödberg, Fridolf. *Om stämplingarna mot konung Johan III åren, 1572–1575*. Stockholm: Fritze, 1897.

Odén, Birgitta. *Rikets uppbörd och utgift: statsfinanser och finansförvaltning under senare 1500-talet*. Bibliotheca historica Lundensis, 1. Lund: Gleerup, 1955.

Palme, Sven Ulric. *Sverige och Danmark, 1596–1611*. Uppsala: Almqvist & Wiksell, 1942.

Petri, Olaus. *Skrifter i urval*. Edited by Gunnar T. Westin. Stockholm: Natur och kultur, 1968.

———. *En swensk cröneka*. Edited by Jöran Sahlgren. Uppsala: Sveriges kristliga studentrörelses förlag, 1917.

Roberts, Michael. *The Early Vasas: a History of Sweden, 1523–1611*. Cambridge: University Press, 1968.

Runeby, Nils. *Monarchia mixta: maktfördelningsdebatt i Sverige under den tidigare stormakstiden*. Uppsala: Svenska bokförlaget, 1962.

Schück, Henrik. *Olavus Petri*. 4th ed. Stockholm: Geber, 1922.

Söderqvist, O. *Johan III och hertig Karl, 1568–1575*. Uppsala: Almqvist & Wiksell, 1898.

Sommarström, Hugo. *Finland under striderna mellan Sigismund och hertig Karl, 1*. Stockholm: Björck & Börjesson, 1935.

Svalenius, Ivan. *Gustav Vasa*. Stockholm: Wahlström & Widstrand, 1950.

Yrwing, Hugo N. *Gustaf Vasa, kröningsfrågan och Västerås riksdag 1527*. Lund: Gleerup, 1956.

## Chapters VII and VIII

Ågren, Kurt. *Adelns bönder och kronans: skatter och besvär i Uppland, 1650–1680*. Uppsala: Svenska bokförlaget/Norstedt, 1964.

Ahnlund, Nils. *Gustav Adolph the Great*. Princeton: Princeton University Press, 1940.

Bengtsson, Frans G. *The Life of Charles XII, King of Sweden, 1697–1718*. Stockholm: Norstedt, 1960.

Boëthius, Bertil. *Gruvornas, hyttornas och hamrarnas folk*. In *DSAH*.

Christina. *Självbiografi och aforismer*. Stockholm: Natur och kultur, 1957.

Clason, S. *Till reduktionens förhistoria: gods- och ränteafsöndringarna och deförbudna orterna*. Stockholm: Beckman, 1895.

Dahlberg, Erik. *Suecia antiqua et hodierna*. 3 vols. in 1. Stockholm, 1667–1716.

Dahlgren, Erik Wilhelm. *Louis De Geer, 1587–1652: hans lif och verk*. 2 vols. Uppsala: Almqvist & Wiksell, 1923.

Dahlgren, Stellan. *Karl X Gustav och reduktionen*. Uppsala: Svenska bokförlaget/Norstedt, 1964.

De Geer, Louis. *Brev och affärshandlingar 1614–1652*. Edited by E. W. Dahlgren. Stockholm: Norstedt, 1934.

Gaunt, David. *Utbildning till statens tjänst: en kollektivbiografi av stormaktstidens hovrättsauskultanter*. Stockholm: Almqvist & Wiksell, 1975. The education of officials in early modern Sweden, 1600–1800.

Haintz, Otto. *König Karl XII von Schweden*. 3 vols. Berlin: Gruyter, 1958.

Hatton, Ragnhild. *Charles XII of Sweden*. London: Weidenfeld & Nicolson, 1968. Most modern treatment.

Herlitz, Nils. *Från Thorn till Altranstädt: studier över Carl XII:s politik, 1703–1706*. Stockholm: Norstedt, 1916.

Hjärne, Harald. *Gustaf Adolf och andra svenska minnen*. Stockholm: Bonnier, 1932.

———. *Karl XII omstörtningen i Österuropa, 1697–1703*. Stockholm: Bonnier, 1932.

Jonasson, Gustaf. *Karl XII och hans rådgivare: den utrikespolitiska maktkampen i Sverige, 1697–1702*. Stockholm: Svenska bokförlaget/Norstedt, 1960.

Landberg, Georg. In *DSUH*, vol. 1, part 3 *(1048–1697)*.
Nilsson, Sven A. *På väg mot reduktionen: studier i svenskt 1600-tal*. Stockholm: Natur och kultur, 1964.
Nordmann, Claude. *Grandeur et liberté de la Suède (1660–1792)*. Paris: Béatrice-Nauwelaerts, 1971. An interpretive narrative, well written.
Olofsson, Sven Ingemar. *Carl X Gustaf: hertigen-tronföljaren*. Stockholm: Norstedt, 1961.
———. *Drottning Christinas tronavsägelse och trosförändring*. Uppsala: Appelberg, 1953.
———. *Efter Westfaliska freden: Sveriges yttre politik, 1650–1654*. Stockholm: Almqvist & Wiksell, 1957.
Oxenstierna, Axel Gustafsson. *Rikskanslern Axel Oxenstiernas skrifter och brefväxling*. Utgiven af Kungl. Vitterhets historie och antikvitetsakademien. 21 vols. Stockholm: Norstedt, 1888–1956.
Palme, Sven Ulric. *Kungligt och kvinnligt*. Stockholm: LTs förlag, 1958.
Petrén, Sture; Jägerskiöld, Stig; and Nordberg, Tord O:son. *Svea hovrätt: studier till 350-årsminnet*. Stockholm: Norstedt, 1964.
Platbarzdis, Aleksandrs. *Sveriges första banksedlar*. Stockholm: Sveriges riksbank, 1960.
Roberts, Michael. *Essays in Swedish History*. London: Weidenfeld & Nicolson, 1967. On Charles XI, Christina, and special subjects.
———. *Gustavus Adolphus: a History of Sweden, 1611–1632*. 2 vols. London: Longmans, Green, 1953–1958.
———, ed. *Sweden as a Great Power, 1611–1697*. New York: St. Martin's Press, 1968. Collection of documents.
———, ed. *Sweden's Age of Greatness, 1632–1718*. New York: St. Martin's Press, 1973. Essays by Swedish specialists.
Robinson, John. *An Account of Sueden: together with an Extract of the History of that Kingdom*. 2nd ed. London: Printed for Tim Goodwin, 1711.
Rosén, Jerker. *Svensk historia*. vol. 1. Stockholm: Svenska bokförlaget/Bonnier, 1962.
———. *DSUH*. vol. 2, part 1 *(1697–1721)*.
———. *Från Sveriges stormaktstid*. Lund: Gleerup, 1966.
Rystad, Göran. *Johan Gyllenstierna*. Stockholm: Wahlström & Widstrand, 1957.
———, ed. *Historia kring trettioåriga kriget*. Stockholm: Wahlstrom & Widstrand, 1963.
Sjödell, Ulf. *Kungamakt och högaristokrati. En studie i Sveriges inre historia under Karl XI*. Lund: Gleerup, 1966.
Stolpe, Sven. *Drottning Kristina*. Stockholm: Bonnier, 1960.
*Svenska kungatal: tal till rikets ständer av Gustav Vasa, Gustav II Adolf och Gustav III*. Stockholm: Bonnier, 1914.
Sylvan, Nils. "Karolinska tiden." In *SHGT*, vol. 3.
*Tal och skrifter av konung Gustaf II Adolph*. Edited by Carl Hallendorff. Stockholm: Norstedt, 1915.
Weibull, Curt. *Christina of Sweden*. Stockholm: Svenska bokförlaget/Bonnier, 1966.
Weibull, Martin, and Höjer, Magnus. "Sveriges storhetstid, från år 1611 till år 1718." In *Sveriges historia fran äldsta tid till våra dagar*, vol. 4. Minneapolis: Svenska Amerikanska Postens förlag, 1900.

## Chapter IX

Andersson, P. Gunnar. *Svenska snillen*. Stockholm: Natur och kultur, 1964.
Barton, H. Arnold. "Gustav III of Sweden and the East Baltic, 1771–1792," *Journal of Baltic Studies* 7 (1976): 13–30.
Boberg, Stig. *Gustav III och tryckfriheten, 1774–1787*. Stockholm: Natur och kultur, 1951.
Boëthius, Bertil. *Gruvornas, hyttornas och hamrarnas folk*. In *DSAH*. Stockholm: Tiden, 1951.
Brolin, Per-Erik. *Hattar och mössor i borgarståndet, 1760–1766*. Uppsala: Lundquist, 1953.
Carlsson, Sten. *Bonde—präst—ämbetsman: svensk ståndscirkulation från 1680 till våra dagar*. Stockholm: Prisma, 1962.

————. *Byråkrati och borgarstånd under frihetstiden*. Uppsala: Svenska bokförlaget/Norstedt, 1963.

————. *Ståndssamhälle och ståndspersoner, 1700–1865: studier rörande det svenska ståndssamhällets upplösning*. 2nd rev. ed. Lund: Gleerup, 1973. On the replacement of the old estate society in Sweden by a class society. With good summary in English.

————. *Svensk historia*. vol. 2. Stockholm: Svenska bokförlaget/Bonnier, 1961.

Chydenius, Anders. *Politiska skrifter*. Helsinki: Edlund, 1880.

Hagberg, Knut. *Carl Linnaeus*. London: Jonathan Cape, 1952.

Hatton, Ragnhild. *Europe in the Age of Louis XIV*. London: Harcourt, Brace & World, 1969.

Hennings, Beth. *Gustav III som kronprins*. Stockholm: Geber, 1935.

Hildebrand, Ingegerd. *Den svenska kolonien S:t Barthélemy och Västindiska kompaniet fram till 1796*. Lund: Lindstedt, 1951.

Holst, Walfrid. "Frihetstiden." In *SHGT*, vol. 3.

Ingers, E. *Bonden i svensk historia*. vol. 2. Stockholm: Lantbruksförbundets tidskriftsaktiebolag, 1948.

Jägerskiöld, Olof. *DSUH*, vol. 2, part 2 (*1721–1792*).

Kalm, Per. *Resa till Norra Amerika*. 3 vols. Helsinki: Tidnings- och tryckeri-aktiebolaget, 1904–1915. For a good English edition see *The America of 1750. Peter Kalm's Travels in North America*. Revised and edited by Adolph B. Benson from the English version of 1770. 2 vols. New York: Wilson-Erickson, 1937.

Kent, H. S. K. *War and Trade in Northern Seas: Anglo-Scandinavian Economic Relations in the Mid-eighteenth Century*. Cambridge: Cambridge University Press, 1973.

Lagerroth, F. *Frihetstidens författning: en studie i den svenska konstitutionalismens historia*. Stockholm: Bonnier, 1915.

————. *Levande och dött i frihetstidens statsskick: en principutredning*. Stockholm: Geber, 1947.

Lindroth, Sten, ed. *Swedish Men of Science, 1650–1950*. Stockholm: Swedish Institute/Almqvist & Wiksell, 1952.

Montelius, Sigvard; Utterström, Gustaf; and Söderlund, E. *Fagerstabrukens historia: arbetare och arbetarförhållanden*. Uppsala: Almqvist & Wiksell, 1959.

Nordmann, Claude. *Grandeur et liberté de la Suède (1660–1792)*. Paris: Béatrice-Nauwelaerts, 1971.

Olán, Eskil. *Östindiska Compagniets saga: historien om Sveriges märkligaste handelsföretag*. 2nd ed. Gothenburg: Wettergren & Kerber, 1923.

Roberts, Michael. *Swedish and English Parliamentarianism in the Eighteenth Century*. Belfast: Queen's University of Belfast, 1973.

Samuelsson, Kurt. *From Great Power to Welfare State: 300 Years of Swedish Social Development*. London: Allen & Unwin, 1968.

Stavenow, Ludvig. *Frihetstiden: dess epoker och kulturliv*. 3rd ed. Gothenburg: Wettergren & Kerber, 1921.

Stearns, Raymond Phineas. *Science in the British Colonies of America*. Urbana: University of Illinois Press, 1970.

Thanner, Lennart. *Revolutionen i Sverige efter Karl XII:s död: den inrepolitiska maktkampen under tidigare delen av Ulrika Eleonora d.y:s regering*. Uppsala: Almqvist & Wiksell, 1953.

Troili, G. K. *Ur handelns och sjöfartens häfder: efter de bästa källor*. Gothenburg: Göteborgs handels-tidning, 1876.

Uggla, Arvid Hj. *Linnaeus*. Stockholm: Swedish Institute, 1957.

## Chapter X

Austin, Paul Britten. *The Life and Songs of Carl Michael Bellman, Genius of the Swedish Rococo*. Malmö: Allhem, 1967.

Bain, Robert Nisbet. *Gustavus III and His Contemporaries, 1746–1792: an Overlooked Chapter of Eighteenth Century History*. 2 vols. London: K. Paul, Trench, Trübner, 1894.

650    Selected Bibliography

Barton, H. Arnold. *Count Hans Axel von Fersen: Aristocrat in an Age of Revolution*. Boston: Twayne (G. K. Hall), 1975.

Benson, Adolph B., and Hedin, Naboth, eds. *Swedes in America, 1638–1938*. New Haven: Yale University Press, 1938.

Björklund, Stefan, ed. *Kring 1809: om regeringsformens tillkomst*. Stockholm: Walström & Widstrand, 1965.

Boberg, Stig. *Gustav III och tryckfriheten, 1774–1787*. Stockholm: Natur och kultur, 1951.

Carlsson, Sten. *Gustaf IV Adolf: en biografi*. Stockholm: Wahlström & Widstrand, 1946.

―――. *Svensk historia*. vol. 2. Stockholm: Svenska bokförlaget/Bonnier, 1961.

Clason, Sam. "Karl XIII och Karl XIV Johan." In *SHVD*, vol. 11.

Dalgren, Lars Ejnar. *Sverige och Pommern, 1792–1806: statskuppen 1806 och dess förhistoria*. Uppsala: Appelberg, 1914.

Elovson, Harald. *Amerika i svensk litteratur, 1750–1820: en studie i komparativ litteraturhistoria*. Lund: Gleerup, 1930.

Gustafson, Alrik. *A History of Swedish Literature*. Minneapolis: University of Minnesota Press for the American-Scandinavian Foundation, 1961.

Hennings, Beth. *Gustav III: En biografi*. Stockholm: Norstedt, 1957. A general biography by the leading Swedish authority on this enigmatic monarchy.

―――, ed. *Gustav III och Grevinnan de Boufflers: en brevväxling från vänskapskultens tidevarv*. Stockholm: Hökerberg, 1928.

Holmberg, Åke. *Sverige efter 1809: politisk historia under 150 år*. Stockholm. Svenska bokförlaget/Bonnier, 1959.

Ingers, E. *Bonden i svensk historia*. vol. 2. Stockholm: Lantbruksförbundets tidskriftsaktiebolag, 1948.

Landberg, Georg. *Gustaf III inför eftervärlden*. Stockholm: Proprius, 1968.

Svenson, Sven G. *Gattjinatraktaten 1799: studier i Gustaf IV Adolfs utrikespolitik, 1796–1800*. Stockholm: Almqvist & Wiksell, 1952.

van Loon, Hendrik Willem, and Castagnetta, Grace. *The Last of the Troubadors*. New York: Simon & Schuster, 1939. On Bellman.

Wahlström, Lydia. "Gustavianska tiden." In *SHGT*, vol. 3.

## Chapter XI

Alin, Oscar. *Carl Johan och Sveriges yttre politik, 1810–1815: historisk studie*. Stockholm: Norstedt, 1899.

―――. *Den svensk-norska unionen. Uppsatser och aktstycken*. Stockholm: Norstedt, 1889.

Barton, Dunbar Plunkett. *The Amazing Career of Bernadotte, 1763–1844*. Boston: Houghton Mifflin, 1929.

Clason, Sam. *Karl XIII och Karl XIV Johan*. *SHVD*, vol. xi.

Girod de l'Ain, Gabriel. *Bernadotte: chef de guerre et chef d'Etat*. Paris: Librairie académique Perrin, 1968.

Höjer, Torvald. *Carl XIV Johan*. 3 vols. Stockholm: Norstedt, 1939–1960. For a French condensed translation of this definitive biography see *Bernadotte—Maréchal de France, Roi de Suède*. 2 vols. Paris: Librarie Plon, 1971.

―――. "Karl XIV Johan." In *Sveriges historia genom tiderna*, vol. 4. Stockholm: Saxon & Lindström, 1948.

Koht, Halvdan. *1814: norsk dagbok hundre aar efterpaa*. Oslo: Aschehoug, 1914.

Scott, Franklin D. *Bernadotte and the Fall of Napoleon*. Cambridge: Harvard University Press, 1935.

Schinkel, Bernt von. *Minnen ur Sveriges nyare historia*. Edited and composed by C. W. Bergman. 12 vols. & 3 supplements. Stockholm: Norstedt, 1852–1883.

Weibull, Jörgen. *Carl Johan och Norge, 1810–1814: unionsplanerna och deras förverkligande*. Lund: Gleerup, 1957.

## Chapter XII

Anderson, Edgar. "The Crimean War in the Baltic Area," *Journal of Baltic Studies* 5 (1974): 339–361.

Carlsson, Sten. *Lantmannapolitiken och industrialismen: partigruppering och opinionsförskjutningar i svensk politik, 1890–1902.* Stockholm: Lantbruksförbundets tidskriftsaktiebolag, 1953.

Carr, W. *Schleswig-Holstein, 1815–1848: a Study in National Conflict.* Manchester: University Press, 1963.

Hadenius, Stig. *Fosterländsk unionspolitik. Majoritets partiet, regeringen och unionsfrågan, 1888–1899.* Uppsala: Almqvist & Wiksell, 1964.

————, ed. *Historia kring Oscar II.* Stockholm: Wahlström & Widstrand, 1963.

Hallendorff, Carl. *Oscar I, Napoleon och Nikolaus: ur diplomaternas privatbrev under Krimkriget.* Stockholm: Geber, 1918.

Hirschfeldt, Lennart, ed. *Svensk utrikespolitik under 1900-talet.* Stockholm: Kooperativa förbundets bokförlag, 1958.

Knaplund, Paul, ed. *British Views on Norwegian-Swedish problems, 1880–1895: Selections from Diplomatic Correspondence.* Oslo: I kommisjon hjå J. Dybwad, 1952.

Lindberg, Folke. *Kunglig utrikespolitik: studier i svensk utrikespolitik under Oscar II och fram till borggårdskrisen.* Rev. ed. Stockholm: Aldus/Bonnier, 1966.

Lindgren, Raymond E. *Norway-Sweden: Union, Disunion, and Scandinavian Integration.* Princeton: Princeton University Press, 1959.

Lundh, Hans Lennart. *Från Skandinavism till neutralitet: utrikespolitik och utrikesdebatt i Sverige under Carl XV:s sista år.* Trollhättan: Trollhättans tryckeri, 1950.

Mårald, Bert. *Den svenska freds- och neutralitätsrörelsens uppkomst.* Gothenburg: Akademi förlaget, 1974.

Møller, Erik. *Skandinavisk stræben og svensk politik omkring 1860.* Copenhagen: Gad, 1948.

Sars, Johan Ernst W. *Norges politiske historie, 1815–1885.* Kristiania: Andersen, 1904.

Söderhjelm, Alma, and Palmstierna, Carl-Fredrik. *Oscar I.* Stockholm: Bonnier, 1944.

Weibull, Jörgen. *Inför unionsupplösningen 1905: konsulatsfrågan.* Stockholm: Norstedt, 1962.

## Chapter XIII

Barton, H. Arnold, ed. *Letters from the Promised Land.* Minneapolis and Chicago: Swedish Pioneer Historical Society, 1975.

————, ed. *Scandinavians and America: Essays Presented to Franklin D. Scott.* Chicago: Swedish Pioneer Historical Society, 1974.

Bremer, Fredrika. *New Sketches of Every-day Life: a Diary together with Strife and Peace.* London: Longman, Brown, Green, and Longmans, 1844.

Carlsson, Sten. *Ståndssamhälle och ståndspersoner 1700–1865: studier rörande det svenska ståndssamhällets upplösning.* 2nd rev. ed. Lund: Gleerup, 1973.

————. *Svensk historia.* vol. 2. Stockholm: Svenska bokförlaget/Bonnier, 1961.

Danielson, Hilding. *Till Carl Rudenschölds biografi.* Lund: Gleerup, 1922.

Elmen, Paul. *Wheat Flour Messiah, Erik Jansson of Bishop Hill.* Carbondale: Southern Illinois University Press / Chicago: Swedish Pioneer Historical Society, 1976.

*Emigrationsutredningen: betänkande med bilagor.* 20 vols. Stockholm: Norstedt, 1908—1914.

Gustafsson, Berndt. *Socialdemokratien och kyrkan, 1881–1890.* Stockholm: Svenska kyrkans diakonistyrelses bokförlag, 1953.

Höjer, K. J. *Svensk socialpolitisk historia.* Stockholm: Norstedt, 1952.

Hovde, Brynjolf J. *The Scandinavian Countries, 1720–1865.* 2 vols. 1943. Reprint. Ithaca: Cornell University Press, 1948.

Johnson, Amandus. *The Swedish Settlements on the Delaware.* 2 vols. Philadelphia: University of Pennsylvania Press, 1911.

Kastrup, Allan. *The Swedish Heritage in America.* Minneapolis: Swedish Council of America, 1975.

Moberg, Vilhelm. *The Emigrants. Unto a Good Land. The Last Letter Home.* Stockholm: Bonnier, 1949–1959.

Molin, Adrian. *Vanhäfd, inlägg i emigrationsfrågan.* Stockholm: Norstedt, 1911.

Montgomery, Arthur. *The Rise of Modern Industry in Sweden.* Stockholm: Norstedt, 1939.

──────. *Svensk socialpolitik under 1800-talet.* 2nd rev. ed. Stockholm: Kooperativa Förbundet, 1951.

Murray, Robert, ed. *The Church of Sweden: Past and Present.* Malmö: Allhem, 1960.

Neveus, Torgny, ed. *Historia kring Stockholm: från frihetstiden till sekelskiftet.* Stockholm: Wahlström & Widstrand, 1967.

Olsson, Nils William. *Swedish Passenger Arrivals in New York, 1820–1850.* Chicago: Swedish Pioneer Historical Society, 1967.

Scott, Franklin D. *Wertmüller: Artist and Immigrant Farmer.* Chicago: Swedish Pioneer Historical Society, 1963.

──────, ed. *Baron Klinkowström's America, 1818–1820.* Evanston: Northwestern University Press, 1952.

Simon, Erica. *Réveil national et culture populaire en Scandinavie: La genèse de la højskole nordique, 1844–1878.* Paris: Presses universitaires de France, 1960. An excellent study of Nordic educational developments, broader than title indicates.

Sjöstrand, Wilhelm. *Pedagogikens historia.* 3 vols. Lund: Gleerup, 1954–1965.

Sundkler, Bengt G. M. *Svenska missionssällskapet, 1835–1876: missionstankens genombrott och tidigare historia i Sverige.* Dissertation. Uppsala, 1937.

Thomas, Dorothy Swaine. *Social and Economic Aspects of Swedish Population Movements, 1750–1933.* New York: Macmillan, 1941.

Unonius, Gustaf. *A Pioneer in Northwest America, 1841–1858.* 2 vols. Chicago: Swedish Pioneer Historical Society, 1950, 1960.

Westman, Erik G., and Johnson, E. Gustav. *The Swedish Element in America.* 4 vols. Chicago: Swedish American Biographical Society, 1931–1934.

Wordsworth, John. *The National Church of Sweden.* The Hale Lectures, 1910. London: Mowbray, 1911.

## Chapters XIV and XV

Ander, O. Fritiof. *The Building of Modern Sweden: the Reign of Gustav V, 1907–1950.* Rock Island, Ill.: Augustana Book Concern, 1958.

Anderson, Ivar. *Arvid Lindman och hans tid.* Stockholm: Norstedt, 1956.

Blake, Donald John. "The Trade Unions and the Social Democratic Party; the Early History of the Swedish Labor Movement, 1870–1914." Dissertation. Berkeley, 1956.

Borell, Berit. *De svenska liberalerna och representationsfrågan på 1840-talet.* Uppsala: Almqvist & Wiksell, 1948.

Carlsson, Sten. *Lantmannapolitiken och industrialismen. Partigruppering och opinionsförskjutningar i svensk politik 1890–1920.* Stockholm: Lantbruksförbundets tidskriftstaktiebolag, 1953.

De Geer, Louis. *Minnen.* 2 vols. in 1. Stockholm: Norstedt, 1892.

Edén, Nils. *Den svenska riksdagen under femhundra år.* Stockholm: Norstedt, 1935.

Fusilier, Raymond. *Le parti socialiste Suédois: son organisation.* Paris: Les éditions ouvrières, 1954.

Gjöres, Axel. *Co-operation in Sweden.* Manchester: The Co-operative Union, 1937. By one of the prime movers of the cooperative society.

Gustafsson, Berndt. *Socialdemokratien och kyrkan, 1881–1890.* Stockholm: Svenska kyrkans diakonistyrelses bokförlag, 1953.

Hadenius, Stig, ed. *Kring demokratins genombrott i Sverige.* Stockholm: Walström & Widstrand, 1966.

Hadenius, Stig; Molin, Björn; and Wieslander, Hans. *Sverige efter 1900: en modern politisk historia.* 5th ed. Stockholm: Aldus/Bonnier, 1972.

Hansson, Sigfrid. *Den svenska fackföreningsrörelsen.* Stockholm: Tiden, 1938.

Hedin, Adolf. *Tal och skrifter.* Edited by Valfrid Spångberg. Stockholm: Bonnier, 1904.
Hellner, Johannes. *Minnen och dagböcker.* Edited by W. Odelberg. Stockholm: Norstedt, 1960.
Höglund, Zeth. *Hjalmar Branting och hans livsgärning.* 2 vols. Stockholm: Tiden, 1928–1929.
Höjer, K. J. *Svensk socialpolitisk historia.* Stockholm: Norstedt, 1952.
Johansson, Hilding. *Folkrörelserna och det demokratiska statsskicket i Sverige.* Lund: Gleerup, 1952.
Karlbom, Torvald. *Den svenska fackföreningsrörelsen.* Stockholm: Tiden, 1955.
Kihlberg, Leif. *Karl Staaff.* 2 vols. Stockholm: Bonnier, 1962–1963.
Lindorm, Erik. *Carl XIV Johan—Carl XV och deras tid, 1810–1872: en bokfilm.* Stockholm: Wahlström & Widstrand, 1942.
Lundkvist, Sven. "Folkrörelser och reformer, 1900—1920." In *Från fattigdom till överflöd.* Edited by Steven Koblik. Stockholm: Wahlström & Widstrand, 1973. Also in English translation in Koblik, *Sweden's Development from Poverty to Affluence, 1750–1970.* Translated by Joanne Johnson in association with the University of Minnesota Press and Steven Koblik, Minneapolis: University of Minnesota Press, 1975.
Möller, Gustav. *När vi började.* Stockholm: Tiden, 1959.
Palme, Sven Ulric. *På Karl Staaffs tid.* Stockholm: Aldus, 1964.
Thermaenius, Edvard. *Lantmannapartiet. Dess uppkomst, organisation och tidigare utveckling.* Uppsala: Almqvist & Wiksell, 1928.
———. *Svensk bondepolitik.* Stockholm: Bonnier, 1931.
Thulstrup, Åke. *Nära demokratin bröt igenom: konturerna av Sveriges historia, 1905–1920.* Stockholm: Bonnier, 1937.
Tingsten, Herbert. *Den svenska socialdemokratiens idéutveckling.* 2 vols. *DSAH.* Stockholm: Tiden, 1941. Also in English translation, *The Swedish Social Democrats.* Totowa: Bedminster, 1973.
Verney, Douglas V. *Parliamentary Reform in Sweden, 1866–1921.* Oxford: Clarendon Press, 1957.
Zweigbergk, Otto von. *Svensk politik, 1905–1929: parlamentarismens första kvartssekel.* Stockholm: Bonnier, 1929.

## Chapter XVI

Adelswärd, Gösta. *En historia om forskraft.* Åtvidaberg, 1962.
———. *Varaktigare än kopparn. Åtvidaberg, 1413–1963.* Stockholm: Åtvidabergs Industrier, 1963.
Adelswärd, Theodor. *Beskrifning öfver Åtvidaberg med närmaste omgifningar 1911.* Linköping: Linköpings lithografiska aktiebolag, 1911.
*The Development and Present Scope of Industry in Sweden.* Stockholm: Sveriges industriförbund, 1953.
Gasslander, Olle. *History of Stockholm's Enskilda Bank to 1914.* Stockholm: Stockholms Enskilda banken, 1962. Industrial development as well as banking history.
Jörberg, Lennart. *Growth and Fluctuations of Swedish Industry, 1869–1912.* Stockholm: Almqvist & Wiksell, 1961.
Lindahl, Erik; Dahlgren, Einar; and Kock, Karin. *National Income of Sweden, 1861–1930.* 2 vols. London: King & Son, 1937.
Lundström, Ragnhild, ed. *Kring industrialismens genombrott i Sverige.* Stockholm: Wahlström & Widstrand, 1966.
Martinius, Sture. *Jordbruk och ekonomisk tillväxt i Sverige, 1830–1870.* Gothenburg: Ekonomiskhistoriska institutionen, 1970.
Modig, Hans. *Järnvägarnas efterfrågan och den svenska industrin, 1860–1914.* Stockholm: Läromedelsförlagen, 1971.
Myrdal, Alva. *Nation and Family: the Swedish Experiment in Democratic Family and Population Policy.* New York: Harpers, 1941. A translation of *Kris i befolkningsfrågran.* Stockholm: Bonnier, 1934.

Nilsson, Carl-Axel. *Järn och stål i svensk ekonomi, 1885–1912: en marknadsstudie.* Lund: Gleerup, 1972.

Samuelsson, Kurt. *From Great Power to Welfare State: 300 Years of Swedish Social Development.* London: Allen & Unwin, 1968.

Samuelsson, Kurt. *Hur vår moderna industri vuxit fram.* New rev. ed. Stockholm: Prisma, Seelig, 1967.

Schiller, Bernt. *Storstrejken 1909: förhistoria och orsaker.* Gothenburg: Akademiförlaget, 1967.

Söderberg, Tom. *Hantverkarna i genombrottsskedet, 1870–1920.* Utgiven av Sveriges hantverksoch industriorganisation, SHIO, vid 60-årsjubiléet 1965. Stockholm: Medén i distribution, 1965.

Söderlund, Ernst. *Swedish Timber Exports, 1850–1950.* Stockholm: Almqvist & Wiksell, 1952.

*Sveriges industri.* Stockholm: Sveriges industriförbund, 1967.

Tolf, Robert W. *The Russian Rockefellers. The Saga of the Nobel Family and the Russian Oil Industry.* Stanford, Cal.: Hoover Institution Press, 1976.

## Chapter XVII

Carlgren, W. M. *Ministären Hammarskjöld: tillkomst, söndring, fall; studier i svenska politik, 1914–1917.* Stockholm: Almqvist & Wiksell, 1967.

————. *Neutralität oder Allianz: Deutschlands Beziehungen zu Schweden in den Anfangsjahren des ersten Weltkrieges.* Stockholm: Almqvist & Wiksell, 1962.

Consett, Montagu William W. P. *The Triumph of Unarmed Forces (1914–1918).* London: Williams & Norgate, 1923.

Gihl, Torsten. *DSUH*, vol. 4 *(1914–1919).* Stockholm: Norstedt, 1951.

Grass, Martin. *Friedensaktivität und Neutralität. Die skandinavische Sozialdemokratie und die neutrale Zusammenarbeit im Krieg August 1914 bis Februar 1917.* Bonn-Bad Godesberg: Schriftenreihe des Forschungsinstituts der Friedrich-Ebert-Stiftung, vol. 117, 1975.

Håstad, Elis. *Sveriges historia under 1900-talet.* Stockholm: Bonnier, 1958.

Heckscher, Eli F. et al. *Sweden, Norway, Denmark, and Iceland in the World War.* New Haven: Yale University Press, 1930.

Hellner, Johan. *Minnen och dagböcker.* Edited by W. Odelberg. Stockholm: Norstedt, 1960.

Koblik, Steven. *Sweden: the Neutral Victor: Sweden and the Western Powers, 1917–1918.* Lund: Läromedelsförlagen, 1972. Sweden's relations with Great Britain and the United States during World War I.

*Neutrality: Its History, Economics and Law.* 4 vols. New York: Columbia University Press, 1935–1936.

United States Department of State. *Foreign Relations of the United States, 1914–1916.* Washington: Government Printing Office, 1914– .

United States Naval War College. *International Law Documents, 1917–1918.* Washington: Government Printing Office, 1917– .

## Chapter XVIII

Adler-Karlsson, Gunnar. *Functional Socialism: a Swedish Theory for Democratic Socialization.* Stockholm: Prisma, 1969.

Ames, J. W. *Without Boundaries; Co-operative Sweden Today — and Tomorrow.* Manchester: Co-operative Union, 1971.

Andrén, Nils. *Power Balance and Non-alignment.* Stockholm: Almqvist & Wiksell, 1967.

Andrén, Nils, and Landquist, Åke. *Svensk utrikespolitik efter 1945.* Stockholm: Almqvist & Wiksell, 1965. Valuable document collection.

Barros, James. *The Åland Islands Question: Its Settlement by the League of Nations.* New Haven: Yale University Press, 1968.

Bonow, Mauritz. *International Co-operation for Self-reliance: Some Swedish Experiences.* Stockholm: Swedish Co-operative Centre, 1975.

Branting, Hjalmar. *Tal och skrifter*. 11 vols. Stockholm: Tiden, 1926–1930.

Carlgren, Wilhelm M. *Svensk utrikespolitik, 1939–1945*. Aktstykken utgivna av utrikesdepartmentet. Ny serie. Stockholm: Allmänna förlaget, 1973. Important wartime documents issued by the Foreign Office.

Childs, Marquis. *Sweden the Middle Way*. Rev. ed. New Haven: Yale University Press, 1951.

Dahmén, Erik. *Entrepreneurial Activity and the Development of Swedish Industry, 1919–1939*. Translated by Axel Leijonhufvud. Homewood, Ill.: R. D. Irwin for the American Economic Association, 1970.

Danius, Lars. *Samhället och försvaret*. Stockholm: Medborgarskolan, 1956.

Elvander, Nils. *Intresseorganisationerna i dagens Sverige*. Lund: Gleerup, 1966. On the strong role played in government by special interest organizations.

Fritz, Martin. *German Steel and Swedish Iron Ore, 1939–1945*. Gothenburg: Institute of Economic History, 1974.

Furuland, Lars. *Statare. Statarklassens historia i ord och bild till 30-års minnet av sista statarlasset*. Stockholm: Nordiska Museet/ Sveriges Radio, 1975.

———. *Statarna i litteraturen*. Stockholm: Tiden, 1962.

Glete, Jan. *Kreugerkoncernen och Boliden*. Stockholm: LiberFörlag, 1975.

Graham, John. *Housing in Scandinavia*. Chapel Hill: University of North Carolina Press, 1940.

Hinshaw, David. *Sweden: Champion of Peace*. New York: Putnam's, 1949.

Höjer, K. J. *Svensk socialpolitisk historia*. Stockholm: Norstedt, 1952.

Johanson, Curt. *Lantarbetarna i Uppland, 1918–1930: en studie i facklig taktik och organisation*. Stockholm: Läromedelsförlagen, 1970.

Johansson, Östen. *The Gross Domestic Product of Sweden and Its Components, 1861–1955*. Stockholm: Almqvist & Wiksell, 1967.

Kastrup, Allan. *The Making of Sweden*. New York: American-Swedish News Exchange, 1953.

Kylebäck, Hugo. *Konsumentkooperationen och industrikarteller*. Stockholm: Rabén & Sjögren, 1974.

Lindman, Arvid. *Dagboksanteckningar*. Edited by Nils F. Holm. Stockholm: Kunglig Samfundet för utgivande av handskrifter rörande Skandinaviens historia, 1972.

Lo-Johansson, Ivar. *Statarna*. Stockholm: Bonnier, 1937.

———. *Stockholmaren*. Stockholm: Bonnier, 1954.

Lönnroth, Erik. "The Diplomacy of Östen Undén." In *The Diplomats*, Edited by Gordon Craig. Princeton: Princeton University Press, 1953.

Montgomery, Arthur. *How Sweden Overcame the Depression*. Stockholm: Bonnier, 1938.

———. *Svensk ekonomisk historia, 1913–1939*. Stockholm: KF, 1946.

Ruin, Olof. *Kooperative förbundet, 1899–1929: en organisationsstudie*. Stockholm: Rabén & Sjögren, 1960.

———. *Mellan samlingsregering och tvåpartisystem, 1945–1960*. Stockholm: Bonniers, 1968. A detailed study.

Rustow, Dankwart. *The Politics of Compromise: a Study of Parties and Cabinet Government in Sweden*. Princeton: Princeton University Press, 1955.

*Sveriges förhållande till Danmark och Norge under krigsåren*. Stockholm: Norstedt, 1945. Sweden's official white book.

Thulstrup, Åke. *Reformer och försvar*. Stockholm: Bonnier, 1938.

Tingsten, Herbert. *The Debate on the Foreign Policy of Sweden, 1918–1939*. London: Oxford University Press, 1949.

———. *Mitt liv*. 4 vols. Stockholm: Wahlström & Widstrand, 1961–1964.

———. *Den svenska socialdemokratiens idéutveckling*. 2 vols. *DSAH*. Stockholm: Tiden, 1941.

———. *The Swedish Social Democrats*. Totowa, N.J.: Bedminster, 1973. Abbreviated translation of work cited in previous entry; introduction by Richard Tomasson.

Undén, Östen. *Minnesanteckningar*. Stockholm: Bonnier, 1966.

———. *Tal från krigsåren*. Stockholm: Rabén & Sjögren, 1970.

Weibull, Jörgen. *Sweden, 1918–1968*. London: University College, 1968.

Wigforss, Ernst. *Minnen.* 3 vols. Stockholm: Tiden, 1951–1954.

Zetterberg, Kent. *Liberalism i kris.* Stockholm: LiberFörlag, 1975.

Zweigbergk, Otto von. *Svensk politik, 1905–1929: parlamentarismens första kvartssekel.* Stockholm: Bonnier, 1929.

## Chapter XIX

Åberg, Carl Johan. *Med sikte på 80-talet; en sammanfattning av långtidsutredningen 1975.* Stockholm: LiberFörlag, 1975.

af Trolle, Ulf. *Sweden in the 1980s: an Economic Assessment.* in *Current Sweden,* Viewpoint, October 1975.

Anderson, Stanley V. *The Nordic Council: a Study of Scandinavian Regionalism.* Seattle: University of Washington Press/American-Scandinavian Foundation, 1967.

Anton, Thomas J. *Governing Greater Stockholm; a Study of Policy Development and System Change.* Berkeley: University of California Press, 1975.

*Arbetsrättsreform: Demokrati på arbetsplatsen.* Regeringens proposition 1975/76: 105. With two supplements: *Lag om offentlig anställning* and *Lag om medbestämmande i arbetslivet.* Stockholm: Riksdagen, 1976. For a summary of experience from the experimental period see also the 45-page pamphlet, in English, "Board Representation of Employees in Sweden," issued by the National Swedish Industrial Board (Stockholm: LiberFörlag, 1976).

Arvidson, Stellan. "Education for Democracy." In *Scandinavian Democracy,* edited by J. A. Lawerys. Copenhagen: Danish Institute, 1958.

Benoit, Emile. *Europe at Sixes and Sevens: the Common Market, the Free Trade Association, and the United States.* New York: Columbia University Press, 1961.

Bergevin, Paul. *Adult Education in Sweden.* Indiana University Monograph Series in Adult Education, no. 1. Bloomington, Ind., 1961.

Bergquist, Mats. *Sverige och EEC.* Stockholm: Norstedt, 1970.

Bexelius, Alfred. *The Swedish Institution of the Justitie-ombudsman.* Stockholm: Swedish Institute, 1966. Brief account by the ombudsman himself.

*Blandekonomi på villovägar?* Stockholm: Studieförbundet Näringsliv och Samhälle, 1972.

Board, Joseph. *Government and Politics of Sweden.* Boston: Houghton Mifflin, 1970.

———. "A New Look at Swedish Politics: Compromise and Change." *Scandinavian Studies* 46 (1974): 1–19.

Burstedt, Åke et al. *Social Goals in National Planning: a Critique of Sweden's Long-term Economic Survey.* Stockholm: Prisma, 1972.

Collinder, Björn. *The Lapps.* Princeton: Princeton University Press/American-Scandinavian Foundation, 1949.

*Constitutional Documents of Sweden: the Instrument of Government, the Riksdag Act, the Act of Succession, the Freedom of the Press Act.* Stockholm: Swedish Riksdag, 1975.

*Documents on Swedish Foreign Policy.* Stockholm: Allmänna förlaget, 1950– . Annual translations of *Utrikesfrågor,* foreign policy documents.

Dörfer, Ingemar. *System 37 Viggen. Arms, Technology and the Domestication of Glory.* Oslo: Universitetsforlaget, 1973. On the relations of government and technology.

EFTA. *EFTA bygger ett frihandelsområde i Europa.* Rev. ed. Genève, 1968.

Enochsson, Jorma, and Petersson, Roland. *Gunnar Hedlund.* Stockholm: Norstedt, 1973.

Erlander, Tage. *1901–1954.* 3 vols. Stockholm: Tiden, 1973–1974.

*Expanded Nordic Economic Cooperation.* Report by Nordic Committee of Government Officials. Nordisk utredningsserie 1969:17. Stockholm, 1969.

Fleisher, Frederic. *Folk High Schools in Sweden.* Stockholm: Swedish Institute, 1968.

———. *The New Sweden. The Challenge of a Disciplined Democracy.* New York: McKay, 1967.

Gendell, Murray. *Swedish Working Wives: a Study of Determinants and Consequences.* Totowa: Bedminster, 1963.

Hammarskjöld, Dag. *Markings.* New York: Knopf, 1964.

Hancock, M. Donald. *Sweden: the Politics of Postindustrial Change*. Hinsdale, Ill.: Dryden Press, 1972.

Hancock, M. Donald, and Sjöberg, Gideon, eds. *Politics in the Post-Welfare State: Responses to New Individualism*. New York: Columbia University Press, 1972.

Heilborn, Adèle. *Travel, Study and Research in Sweden*. 7th ed. Stockholm: LT, 1975.

Hendin, Herbert. *Suicide and Scandinavia: a Psychoanalytic Study of Culture and Character*. New York: Grune & Stratton, 1964.

Hermansson, Carl-Henrik. *För socialismen*. Stockholm: Arbetarkultur, 1974.

Hewins, Ralph. *Count Folke Bernadotte, His Life and Work*. Minneapolis: Denison, 1950.

Huntford, Roland. *The New Totalitarians*. New York: Stein & Day, 1972.

Husén, Torsten. *Differentiation and Guidance in the Comprehensive School*. Stockholm: Almqvist & Wiksell, 1959.

Husén, Torsten, and Boalt, Gunnar. *Educational Research and Educational Change; the Case of Sweden*. Stockholm: Almqvist & Wiksell, 1968.

*Individen och skolan*. SOU 1975: 9. Stockholm: Utbildningsdepartementet, 1975.

*Jämlikhet*. Första rapport från SAP-LOs arbetsgrupp för jämlikhetsfrågor. [First report from the Socialist Workers Party and Labor Organization Working Group for Equality-questions.] Stockholm: SAP-LO, 1969.

Kleppe, Per. *EFTA-NORDEK-EEC: Analys av de nordiska ländernas integrationsproblem*. Studier och debatt, no. 4. Stockholm: Studieförbundet näringsliv och samhälle, Forum, 1970.

*Långtidsutredningen 1975, Huvudrapport*. SOU 1975: 89. Stockholm: Finansdepartementet, 1975.

Lewin, Leif. *Planhushållningsdebatten*. Stockholm: Almqvist & Wiksell, 1967.

Lewin, Leif; Jansson, Bo; and Sörbom, Dag. *The Swedish Electorate, 1887–1968*. Stockholm: Almqvist & Wiksell, 1972.

Lindbeck, Assar. *Swedish Economic Policy*. Berkeley: University of California Press, 1975. Translation of *Svensk ekonomisk politik. Problem och teorier under efterkrigstiden*. Stockholm: Aldus/Bonnier, 1968.

Lindmark, Sture. *Riksdagens årsbok 1974*; *Riksdagens årsbok 1975*; *Riksdagens årsbok 1976*. Stockholm: Riksdag, 1974–

Linnér, Birgitta. *Sex and Society in Sweden*. New York: Random House, 1967.

Myrdal, Alva. *Nation and Family; the Swedish Experiment in Democratic Family and Population Policy*. New York: Harpers, 1941. Translation of *Kris i befolkningsfrågan*. Stockholm: Bonnier, 1934.

Myrdal, Gunnar. *Beyond the Welfare State*. New Haven: Yale University Press, 1960.

———. *Population: a Problem for Democracy*. The Godkin Lectures, 1938. Gloucester, Mass.: Peter Smith, 1962.

Nabseth, Lars; Gustafsson, Siv; and Löfgren, Torsten. *Svensk industri under 70-talet med utblick mot 80-talet*. Stockholm: Industriens utredningsinstitut, 1971.

Navarro, V. *National and Regional Health Planning in Sweden*. Washington: Government Printing Office, 1974.

Ohlin, Bertil. *Memoarer: ung man blir politiker*. Stockholm: Bonnier, 1972.

———. *Memoarer, 1940–1951*. Stockholm: Bonnier, 1975.

Orring, Jonas. *Comprehensive Schools and Continuation Schools in Sweden: a Summary of the Principal Recommendations of the 1957 School Commission*. Stockholm: Kunglig Ecklesiastikdepartementet, 1962. Translation of *Grundskola och fackskolor*. Stockholm: Fritze, 1961.

———. *School in Sweden*. Stockholm: Board of Education, 1969.

Ortmark, Åke. *De okände makthavarna. De kungliga — militärerna — journalisterna*. Stockholm: Wahlström & Widstrand, 1969.

Paulston, Rolland. *Educational Change in Sweden: Planning and Accepting the Comprehensive School Reform*. New York: Teachers College Press, 1968.

Rosenthal, Albert H. *The Social Programs of Sweden: a Search for Security in a Free Society*. Minneapolis: University of Minnesota Press, 1967.

Ruong, Israel. *The Lapps in Sweden*. Stockholm: Swedish Institute, 1967.

*Samerna: Sverige.* SOU 1975: 99 (plus supplements).
*Samhället och distributionen.* Betänkande av distributionsutredningen. SOU 1975: 69; Bilagor, SOU 1975: 70. Stockholm: LiberFörlag/Allmänna förlaget, 1975.
*Scandinavian Review,* 3 (1975). Entire issue deals with the problem of health.
Schmidt, Folke. *The Law of Labour Relations in Sweden.* Uppsala: Almqvist & Wiksell, 1962. Laws on labor courts, collective bargaining, etc., translated into English, comprise 100 pages of the book.
Schwarz, David. *Svensk invandrar- och minoritets-politik, 1945–1968.* Stockholm: Prisma, 1971.
————, ed. *Svensk minoriteter.* Stockholm: Aldus/Bonnier, 1966.
Scott, Franklin D. *The American Experience of Swedish Students.* Minneapolis: University of Minnesota Press, 1956.
*Skolans inre arbete.* Regeringens proposition 1975/76: 39. Stockholm: Riksdagen, 1976.
*Social Benefits in Sweden, 1974–1975.* Stockholm: Trygg-Hansa, 1974.
Söderpalm, Sven Anders. *Direktörsklubben. Storindustrin i svensk politik under 1930- och 40-talen.* Tema Teori 12. Stockholm: Zenit/Rabén & Sjögren, 1976.
Stenholm, Britta. *Education in Sweden.* Stockholm: Swedish Institute, 1970.
*Svensk ekonomi, 1971–1975, med utblick mot 1990.* 1970 års långtidsutredning. Huvudrapport. SOU 1970:71. Stockholm: Finansdepartementet, 1970.
Swedenborg, Birgitta. *Swedish Direct Investment Abroad, 1965–1970.* Stockholm: Almqvist & Wiksell, 1974. Translation of *Den svenska industrins investeringar i utlandet 1965–1970.* Stockholm: Almqvist & Wiksell, 1973.
*The Swedish Budget, 1976/77.* Stockholm: Ministry of Finance, 1976. A summary.
Tegborg, Lennart. *Folkskolans sekularisering, 1895–1909; upplösning av det administrativa sambandet mellan folkskola och kyrka i Sverige.* Uppsala: Universitetet; Stockholm: Almqvist & Wiksell, 1969.
Tomasson, Richard F. *Sweden, Prototype of Modern Society.* New York: Random House, 1970.
Urquhart, Brian. *Hammarskjold.* New York: Knopf, 1972.
Verney, Douglas V. *Public Enterprise in Sweden.* Liverpool: Liverpool University Press, 1959.
Wallenberg, Marcus. *Ekonomisk politik, teknisk utveckling, framstegstakt.* Valda föredrag och artiklar. Stockholm: Bonnier, 1969.
Wendt, Frantz. *The Nordic Council and Co-operation in Scandinavia.* Copenhagen: Munksgaard, 1959.
Wheeler, Christopher. *White-Collar Power. Changing Patterns of Interest Group Behavior in Sweden.* Urbana: University of Illinois Press, 1975.

## Chapter XX

Ahlström, Gunnar. *Det moderna genombrottet i Nordens litteratur.* Stockholm: Kooperativa förbundet, 1947.
Austin, Paul Britten. *On Being Swedish; Reflections towards a Better Understanding of the Swedish Character.* Coral Gables: University of Miami Press, 1968. Insights of an Englishman who married a Swede and made Sweden his country.
Beer, Eileene Harrison. *Scandinavian Design. Objects of a Life Style.* New York: American-Scandinavian Foundation, 1975.
Bergsten, Staffan. *Osten Sjöstrand.* New York: Twayne, 1974.
*Boken. Litteraturutredningens huvudbetänkande.* SOU 1974: 5. Stockholm: Utbildningsdepartementet, 1974.
Carlson, Harry G., ed. "Seeking the Unknown Strindberg," Special section in *Scandinavian Review* 64, no. 3 (1976): 5–38.
*Design in Sweden.* Stockholm: Swedish Institute in collaboration with the Swedish Society for Industrial Design, 1972.
Eskeröd, Albert. *Swedish Folk Art.* Stockholm: Nordiska museet, 1964.
Gate, Bengt, et al., eds. *New Architecture in Sweden. A Decade of Swedish Building/Ny arkitek-*

*tur i Sverige, 1950-talets svenska byggnadskonst.* Stockholm: Svenska arkitekters riksförbund, 1961.

Granath, Olle. *Another Light: Swedish Art Since 1945.* Stockholm: Swedish Institute, 1975.

Gustafson, Alrik. *A History of Swedish Literature.* Minneapolis: University of Minnesota Press for the American-Scandinavian Foundation, 1961.

Gustafsson, Berndt. *Svensk kyrkohistoria.* 4th ed. Stockholm: Verbum, 1968.

Hald, Arthur, and Skawonius, Sven Erik. *Contemporary Swedish Design.* Stockholm: Nordisk rotogravyr, 1951.

Hård af Segerstad, Ulf. *Modern Scandinavian Furniture.* Stockholm: Nordisk rotogravyr, 1963.

Heilborn, Adèle. *Travel, Study and Research in Sweden.* Stockholm: Sweden-American Foundation, 1975. A guide to programs, institutions, and how to live in Sweden; kept up-to-date by successive revisions.

Hendin, Herbert. *Suicide and Scandinavia: a Psychoanalytic Study of Culture and Character.* New York: Grune & Stratton, 1964.

Idestam-Almqvist, Bengt. *När filmen kom till Sverige.* With captions and summary in English. Stockholm: Norstedt, 1959.

Klaf, Franklin S. *Strindberg: the Origin of Psychology in Modern Drama.* New York: Citadel, 1963.

Laurin, Carl G. "A Survey of Swedish Art." In *Scandinavian Art.* New York: American-Scandinavian Foundation, 1922.

Lindblom, Andreas A. F. *Sveriges konsthistoria från forntid till nutid.* Stockholm: Nordisk rotogravyr, 1947.

Lindroth, Sten, ed. *Swedish Men of Science, 1650–1950.* Stockholm: Swedish Institute/Almqvist & Wiksell, 1952.

Marker, Fred J. and Marker, Lise-Lone. *The Scandinavian Theatre: a Short History.* Totowa: Rowman & Littlefield, 1975.

Murray, Robert. *Brief History of the Church of Sweden: Origins and Modern Structure.* Stockholm: Verbum, 1969.

*New Cultural Policy in Sweden: a Proposal.* Stockholm: Swedish National Council for Cultural Affairs/Swedish Institute, 1973.

*Nutida svenskt måleri.* 3rd ed. 2 vols. Stockholm: Svensk litteratur, 1948–1950.

Odelberg, Wilhelm. *Swedish Scholars of the 20th Century.* Stockholm: Swedish Institute, 1972. Pamphlet.

Odén, Birgitta. *Lauritz Weibull och forskarsamhället.* Stockholm: LiberFörlag, 1976.

Plath, Iona. *The Decorative Arts of Sweden.* New York: Scribner's, 1948.

Pleijel, B. *Tradition and Progress in Swedish Music.* Stockholm: Musikrevy, 1973.

Rodhe, Edvard. "Kyrkans utveckling och de religiösa rörelserna." In *SFGT*, 10: 49–86.

*Science Policy and Organization of Research in Sweden.* Paris: UNESCO, 1974.

*Den statliga kultur-politiken.* Kunglig Majestäts proposition, 1974: 28. Stockholm: Riksdagen, 1974.

Sundgren, N. P. *New Swedish Cinema.* Stockholm: Swedish Institute, 1970.

Sundkler, Bengt G. M. *Nathan Söderblom, His Life and Work.* Lund: Gleerup, 1968.

Sundman, Per Olof. *The Flight of the Eagle.* New York: Pantheon, 1960.

Wizelius, Ingemar. *Sweden in the Sixties: a Symposium of Facts and Views in 17 Chapters.* Stockholm: Almqvist & Wiksell, 1967.

# Index

# INDEX

663

FRANKLIN D. SCOTT is Curator of Nordic Collections, Honnold Library of the Claremont Colleges, and Emeritus Professor of History at Northwestern University.

STEVEN KOBLIK is Professor of History at Pomona College, Claremont, California.